Macroeconomics

MACROECONOMICS

AN INTRODUCTION TO KEYNESIAN–NEOCLASSICAL CONTROVERSIES

Second Edition

Rosalind Levačić

and

Alexander Rebmann

MACMILLAN

Reprinted 2003, 2007

First edition 1976
Reprinted five times
Second edition 1982

Published by
MACMILLAN PRESS LTD
Houndmills, Basingstoke, Hampshire RG21 6XS
and London
Companies and representatives
throughout the world

International Edition ISBN 978-1-4039-3299-0

ISBN 0-333-34145-7

A catalogue record for this book is available from the British Library.

Printed and bound in India by Replika Press Pvt. Ltd.

For Sasha

WEST BEAST: EAST BEAST

Upon an island hard to reach,
the East Beast sits upon his beach.
Upon the west beach sits the West Beast.
Each beach beast thinks he's the best beast.

Which beast is best? . . . Well, I thought at first
that the East was best and the West was worst.
Then I looked again from the west to the east
and I liked the beast on the east beach least.

DR SEUSS (1979)

Contents

Preface

When I finally came to write a second edition of *Macroeconomics* I quickly realised two related facts. Over the last six years macroeconomics, like Topsy, had grown and the consensus in which I had been brought up had all too clearly broken down. To deal with these developments I did two things – recruited a co-author and completely restructured the book so that it uses the Keynesian–neoclassical conflict as an expositional device from beginning to end. This restructuring plus dealing with the new developments without overloading the book meant a complete rewrite. The second edition is really a new book, hence its new sub-title.

The 'new' *Macroeconomics*, to borrow a phrase much used by fellow economists of all persuasions, is divided into five sections. These are deliberately arranged in order of difficulty. The first section, which covers the Keynesian–neoclassical synthesis for a closed static economy and section II on money and the open economy, together with Chapter 20 on inflation and the last chapter, can on their own form the basis of an intermediate course on macroeconomic theory and policy. Sections IV and V are more advanced and deal with current theoretical controversies and the related policy issues.

We have found the Keynesian–neoclassical conflict a good framework for organising the whole book. However, we use the Keynesian–neoclassical distinction as a useful expositional device and not as two categories into which all economists can be neatly allocated. Individuals are often loath to put a label on themselves for fear that ideas which they do not hold will be attributed to them. Many individuals hold eclectic positions, taking ideas from the different schools of thought.

The Keynesian–neoclassical distinction gives a central and recurrent theme for the book. It enables us to emphasise that the differences in policy conclusions stem from different assumptions about how the economy works and that the crucial distinction between Keynesian and neoclassical macro theory centres on different conceptions about how the supply of output responds to changes in demand.

Since Keynesians believe that markets fail, whereas neoclassicists hold that markets work, the crucial difference in their specification of the aggregate supply function follows quite obviously. However, until supply-side economics became fashionable it was standard practice to emphasise the demand side and related local skirmishes. One of the fascinating aspects of studying a subject for many years is the dawning realisation that changes are not necessarily brought about by new theories but by different ways of looking at old theories. Nuances and emphases are crucial, especially for minds coming to a subject fresh and unformed.

Putting modesty aside there are several things we like about our textbook. We hope that within the framework of the Keynesian–neoclassical conflict we have developed an interesting exposition of current theory and policy so that they are closely and naturally related to each other and to their broad historical context. We feel pretty strongly that any macroeconomics textbook which relates to Britain or any non-US advanced mixed economy must deal with the theory of a small open economy. This we have done, in three chapters in section II, and in smaller sections in later chapters, including a discussion of the New Cambridge model in its proper context in Chapter 21.

Another strength of the book we feel is that it makes accessible to students recent important work on neo-Keynesian non-market-clearing models and on new classical market-clearing models with rational expectations.

Writing this book has been a challenging and enjoyable task but not one we have the stamina to repeat, at least not for a few years. We have been greatly assisted by friends and colleagues, in particular Jock Oliver and Laurence Harris, who spared us their time to comment on our efforts. Macmillan's anonymous reviewer also made an invaluable contribution to certain parts. We thank them and acknowledge the usual responsibilities for errors, omissions and lack of clarity. However, without Moira Hilder we doubt whether there would have been a typescript to read. If we had been forced to rely on the secretary who typed the first edition (Rosalind Levačić!) we could not have faced the task of rewriting the book. So we would like to express our heart-felt thanks to Moira for all her help. For once the author will not be thanking his wife and children for their forbearance while he neglected them in the furtherance of his academic output.

ROSALIND LEVAČIĆ
ALEXANDER REBMANN

The Open University
Middlesex Polytechnic
July 1982

List of Algebraic Symbols

This list is not exhaustive: a few symbols used only briefly within a single chapter are not listed here. Due to the limitations of the alphabet some letters have been used to symbolise more than one variable, though never in the same chapter. The chapters in which such a divergence from the most common use of the letter in question are indicated.

A = absorption
AE = autonomous expenditure (Ch. 14)
An = annual income on bond (Ch. 3); annuity (Ch. 12)
a = average cost of capital
B = number of government bonds issued, each paying £1 per year in income (market value of firm's debt: Ch. 13)
B^D = domestic bonds held by domestic residents
B^F = domestic bonds held by foreigners
B_p = price of bonds (Ch. 3)
BOF = balance for official financing on the balance of payments
b = marginal propensity to consume
C = consumption (currency holdings of non-bank public: Ch. 9)
CA = current account of balance of payments
CAP = capital account of balance of payments
c = desired currency–bank deposit ratio
D = bank deposits (dividends: Ch. 13)
D^S = sight deposits
D^T = time deposits
DC = domestic credit
E = aggregate demand
e = exchange rate defined as number of units of foreign currency exchanging for one unit of domestic currency
e = cost of equity capital (Ch. 13)
F = imports in terms of foreign currency (imports in terms of domestic currency: Ch. 21)
FR = foreign exchange reserves
f = marginal propensity to import

G = government expenditure
g = growth rate of some variable (growth rate of dividends: Ch. 13)
g^e = expected growth rate of some variable
H = high-powered money (hours of work available: Ch. 5)
I = investment
i = real interest rate
i_D = rate of interest paid on time deposits
i_f = foreign rate of interest
i_L = interest rate on bank loans
K = capital stock
k = inverse of velocity (long-run MPC: Ch. 12)
L = labour units
L^D = demand for labour
L^S = supply of labour
L_R = central bank lending rate
M = money stock
M^D = demand for money stock
M^S = supply of money
m = bank multiplier
N = firm's net cash flow (Ch. 13)
NW/P = real net wealth
P = price level
Pd = domestic price level
Pf = foreign price level
P^T = price of tradables
P^N = price of non-tradables
$\dot{P}/P$ = inflation = π in Ch. 20
$E(\dot{P})/P$ = expected rate of inflation = π^e in Ch. 20
pk = price of a unit of real capital
Q = labour productivity
$\dot{Q}/Q$ = rate of change of labour productivity

$$q = \text{Tobin's } q = \frac{\text{Real rate of return on investment}}{\text{Cost of capital}}$$

R = cash reserves of banking system (Ch. 9) (leisure hours: Ch. 5)
r = nominal rate of interest (banks' reserve ratio: Ch. 9)
S = savings (total market value of shares: Ch. 13; hours worked: Ch. 5)
s = marginal propensity to save
T = tax revenues or state of technology
t = tax rate
U = unemployment
U^N = natural rate of unemployment
V = velocity of circulation of money (net present value of firm's net cash flows: Ch. 13)
v = capital–output ratio
W = money wage rate (wealth: Ch. 12)
$w = W/P$ = real wage rate
X = exports in terms of domestic currency

Y = nominal national income
y = real income
y_d = disposable income
y_p = permanent income
η_F = elasticity of demand for imports
η_x = elasticity of demand for exports
π = profits (inflation: Ch. 20)
ρ = marginal efficiency of capital

1 Introduction to Macroeconomics

1.1 The development of macroeconomics

Macroeconomics is the study of the behaviour of the whole economy. It is concerned with the determination of the broad aggregates in the economy, in particular the national output, unemployment, inflation and the balance-of-payments position. The main body of macroeconomic theory applies to a developed, capitalist economy. A capitalist economy is one where productive assets are owned either directly by individuals or by individuals through the medium of firms. These employ others to work with the productive assets in order to produce output. In such an economy, economic decisions are taken by individuals and firms acting independently of one another and co-ordinated via the market mechanism. All these decisions then interact to determine the values of variables such as output and prices. Economies that are nowadays classified as 'capitalist' all have important state sectors which in various and differing ways intervene in the operation of market forces to redirect or suppress them.

The way in which we nowadays study macroeconomics largely owes its origins to John Maynard Keynes's *The General Theory of Employment, Interest and Money* [1]. Published in 1936 *The General Theory* was regarded by its author, and by many others since, as a revolutionary work. In it Keynes set out to challenge the mainstream neoclassical economic thought of his day, which he castigated as unable to explain or offer policy solutions for the high level of unemployment which, in Britain between 1921 and 1939, was just under 10 per cent at its lowest level and rose to 22 per cent at the depth of the depression in 1932.

The main premise of neoclassical economics is that markets do work and that price signals will bring about the necessary adjustments in the economy in response to economic change. Neoclassical economics grew out of the marginalist school of the latter part of the nineteenth century which developed economic theory on the basis of maximising behaviour. These ideas were elaborated by Alfred Marshall, Leon Walras and others and provide the theoretical underpinning to modern economic theory. Keynes himself used neoclassical theory to develop investment and labour demand functions. A main policy conclusion of the neoclassical economists of that period was that government intervention to regulate the economy was unnecessary and brought about distortions.

In *The General Theory* Keynes argued that once an economy had moved into a situation of high unemployment, the price mechanism would not work to adjust the economy back to a high level of employment. Instead, the government needed to raise the demand for output by increasing public expenditure. Once demand had increased firms would supply more output and employ more people, which in turn would increase demand still further.

The General Theory is a complex book and not particularly easy to understand. As befits a classic work it is capable of several interpretations. In order to simplify and disseminate its ideas, a number of Keynes's disciples developed a relatively simple theoretical framework within which to present the main arguments. It is this body of theory which became known as 'Keynesian economics' and which will be outlined here and in subsequent chapters.

The Keynesian model of the economy, which shows it capable of coming to rest at a high level of unemployment, has important policy implications. By managing the level of aggregate demand, raising it when unemployment is high, or reducing it if excess demand is causing inflation (defined as a situation of continually rising prices), the government can stabilise the economy, which otherwise would fluctuate between booms and long periods of depression. Many early Keynesians in fact believed that depression was a chronic state for a capitalist economy which would persistently exhibit too low a level of demand to employ all the work-force. The policy conclusions of Keynesian economics also have important political implications. It concludes that the government can improve the performance of a capitalist economy by managing the level of aggregate demand. This is done by fiscal policy, which involves changing the levels of taxation or of government expenditure, or by monetary policy, which affects interest rates and the supply of money and credit. These policies only require a modest amount of government intervention at a very general and aggregate level. They do not require detailed intervention at the micro level of individual markets and firms. Thus the policy recommendations of Keynesian economics are appealing to those with social-democratic persuasions. The capitalist economy can be modified and tamed by government intervention without the loss of individual freedom inherent in very detailed state supervision of economic life. For Marxists, Keynesian economics is less attractive. Although Keynesian analysis can be viewed as a critique of the capitalist market-orientated economic systems, its policy conclusions, if correct, enable the capitalist economy to survive because its performance has been improved.

The success and failure of Keynesian economics

Keynesian demand-management policies were not actually practised in Britain until the late 1940s, though government commitment to maintaining a high and stable level of employment was first pronounced in the 1944 White Paper on *Employment Policy*. During the war and immediately after the economy was tightly controlled: individual markets were governed by quotas rather than prices. It was not until 1948 that the Labour government abandoned attempts to continue planning the economy and took up Keynesian demand management. A characteristic feature of Keynesian demand management has always been a reliance on fiscal policy and a disregard for the efficacy of monetary policy. This policy attitude was the natural outcome of early Keynesian theoretical work, which tended to ignore the influence of money on other macro variables.

The advent of Keynesian economics inspired economists with great confidence in the ability of their discipline to enhance human well-being. At last we had the solution to mass unemployment. The economy could be depicted as a vehicle with controls. Wise policy-makers armed with the insights of Keynesian economics could now manipulate the levers and steer the economy along its desired path. (This was the tenor of what one was taught as an undergraduate in the 1950s and up to the mid-1960s.)

In post-war Britain up to the mid-1960s this optimism seemed quite well founded. Unemployment in Britain was low. Between 1948 and 1966 the measured rate of unemployment averaged 1.7 per cent and never went above 2.6 per cent. This was well below the rate Keynes and Beveridge, author of the influential report *Full Employment in a Free Society* (1944) [2], had envisaged. (Keynes thought that Beveridge's estimate of the irreducible minimum rate of unemployment as 3 per cent was optimistic.) Inflation, although regarded with some concern, was very modest by today's standards. Real GNP also grew steadily, though at a low rate relative to most other developed economies. Unlike the pre-war period GNP never fell in absolute terms during recessions, which instead were characterised by a slowing down in the rate of growth of real GNP. With the benefit of hindsight the 1950s appear to have been an economic golden age. However, during this period considerable dissatisfaction was expressed at Britain's relatively slow growth rate and tendency to incur balance-of-payments deficits whenever the economy was run at a peak level of demand.

Since the mid-1960s the performance of the UK economy has steadily worsened. Between 1967 and 1980 the unemployment rate averaged 3.9 per cent. Each cycle in economic activity has been accompanied by a higher unemployment rate than the previous one. In 1981 unemployment, at 10 per cent, had attained pre-war levels. Real GNP now falls absolutely in a recession, the first dip occurring in 1975, the next one in 1980. At the same time the average annual rate of inflation has tended to increase over the post-war period. It was 2.9 per cent from 1953 to 1963, 4.4 per cent from 1964 to 1970, and 13.9 per cent from 1971 to 1980. This experience is in marked contrast to the inter-war period when prices either fell or remained stable during the depression.

Britain's experience has not been unique. The increasingly intractable problems of rising unemployment, a slower growth rate and higher inflation have been experienced by most other developed economies, though to varying degrees. Figure 1.1 shows the post-war behaviour of these indicators for the United Kingdom, the USA and Australia.

The increasing difficulties that individual economies have faced in meeting

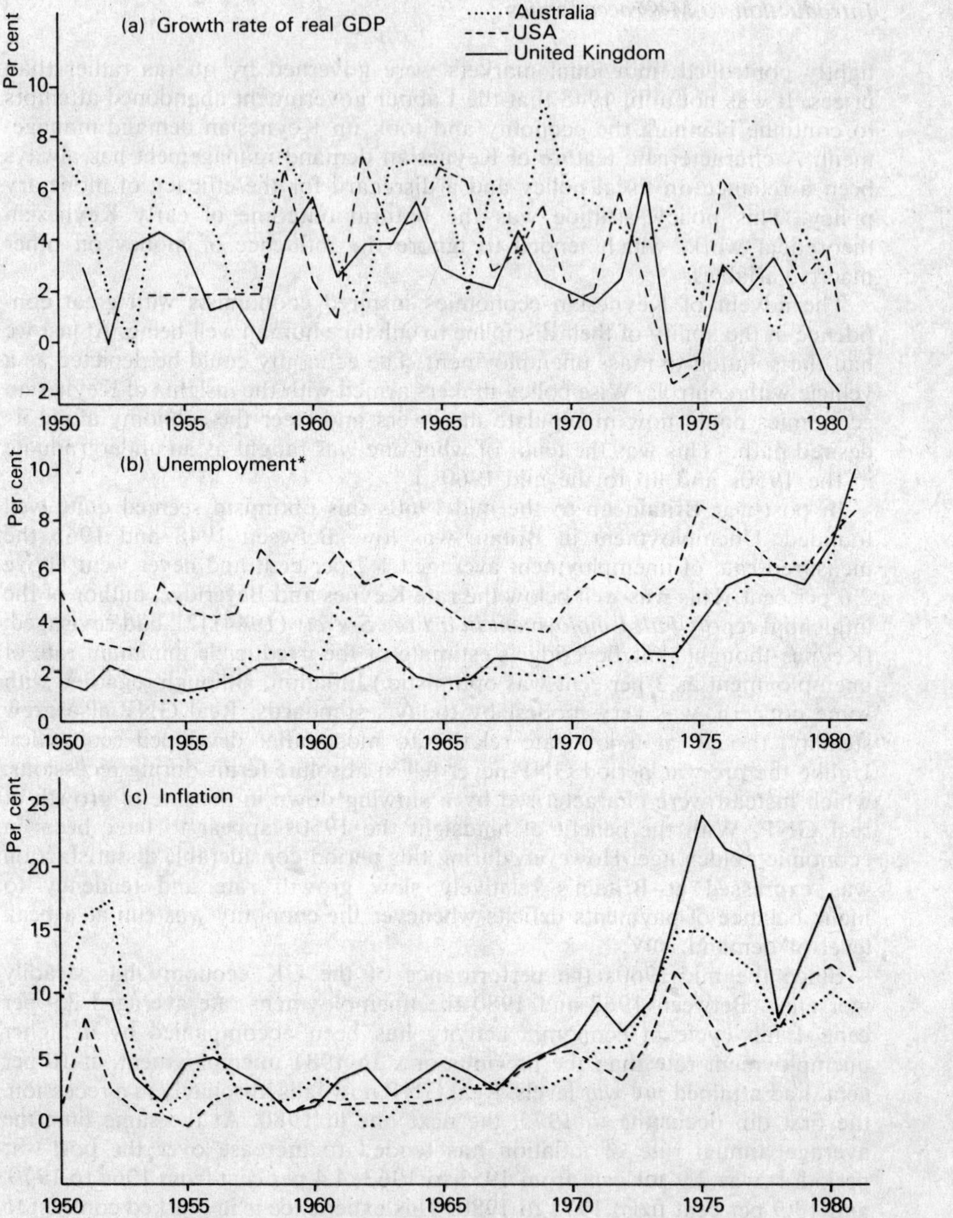

FIGURE 1.1 *Indicators of economic performance for the United Kingdom, the USA and Australia, 1950–81*

*Since unemployment is measured differently in different countries direct comparisons of unemployment levels are not possible from this graph. There is a break in the Australian series in 1966.

Sources: *Australian Year Book*; *Australian Seasonally Adjusted Indicators*; *UN Statistical Year Book*; *OECD Main Economic Indicators*; *Economic Trends.*

the post-war aspirations for good economic performance have been mirrored by developments in the international economic order. From 1944 to 1971 international economic relations were conducted within a stable, fixed exchange rate system under the auspices of the International Monetary Fund. This system finally broke down in 1971 as it could no longer cope with the adjustments required when countries started inflating at quite different rates. The USA's balance-of-payments problems finally precipitated the demise of the fixed exchange rate system when it could no longer maintain the price of dollars in terms of gold. This had been maintained at $35 per ounce of gold since 1934. Since 1971 the world has operated a flexible exchange rate system, though not one in which market forces are allowed full reign. Central banks do intervene to influence at least short-run movements in the exchange rate. Flexible exchange rates have presented policy-makers with new problems which have taken some time to be perceived.

Further significant developments in the post-war period have been the growth in international trade and the entry into this trade of newly industrialised countries such as South Korea, Taiwan and Brazil. Since about 1960 Britain has steadily become a more open economy. Imports and exports are now both over one-third the size of net national income, proportions not attained since the early decades of this century. Britain, in common with other older developed economies, has faced increasing competition in more mature industries from the newly industrialising nations. Such developments imply a need for more rapid structural adaptation in order to shift resources away from uncompetitive industries into more competitive goods and services.

In the light of these economic developments, the apparent inability of Keynesian demand-management policies to produce the hoped-for economic performance has led to an increasing questioning of Keynesian economics and to a resurgence of neoclassical thinking in macroeconomics. This had never completely died out. Even at the high tide of Keynesian dominance, a few outposts in the USA held out and remained sceptical of governments' ability to stabilise the economy using Keynesian techniques.

This critique of Keynesian theorising had several important aspects. One was to show that the money supply had a much more pervasive influence on economic behaviour than Keynesians had allowed for. Associated with the stress on money was also an emphasis on inflation as a policy problem in contrast to the Keynesians' traditional focus on unemployment. The resurgence of neoclassical thinking in the field of monetary economics has become known as *monetarism*.

Another important feature of post-war neoclassical theorising has been its concern with tracing out the long-run implications of changes in economic variables. This contrasts with the Keynesian preoccupation with the short run, as justified by Keynes's famous dictum that 'in the long run we are all dead'. Keynesian short-run models analysed the economy as coming to rest in equilibrium, while there were still imbalances in the economy which were bound to cause further adjustments, yet these were not considered. A further significant critique of Keynesian policy models is that they fail to take proper account of the private sector's expectations, in particular their expectations of what government policy will be. As a result of this critique, macroeconomic models, even of a Keynesian persuasion, nowadays incorporate fuller monetary sectors and make greater allowance for the role of expectations and long-run adjustment than did the Keynesian models of the 1950s.

Over the last five years or so a greater polarisation between Keynesian and neoclassical macroeconomics has taken place. This is in contrast to the debates of the 1940s and 1950s which established a common framework of analysis, known as the Keynesian–neoclassical synthesis. As this framework still dominates expositions of macroeconomic theory and policy, one cannot get very far in studying macroeconomics without it. It is the task of the first few chapters of this book to explain this framework and to pinpoint the different underlying assumptions made by Keynesian and neoclassical economists when they work within this common expositional device.

The greater polarisation that now exists is evident from the completely conflicting economic advice being offered to governments. For instance, in early 1981 the London Business School recommended that the Chancellor of the Exchequer should cut the government's budget deficit and reduce the rate of growth of the money supply, while the National Institute for Economic and Social Research advocated orthodox Keynesian reflation. Contrasting policy recommendations stem from some combination of differences in objectives and differences in opinions as to how the economy works. Most people would agree that lower unemployment and a reduction in inflation are desirable, though they would differ over the priority accorded them. Far greater differences arise in advocating the means to achieve given objectives. These disagreements stem from both the different political implications of particular policy instruments as well as from contrasting views as to how these instruments would actually work.

The most fundamental difference between Keynesians and neoclassicists concerns the effectiveness of markets as an adjustment mechanism relative to government intervention. Keynesians hold that markets work very imperfectly, a major reason for this failure lying with the inflexibility of prices due to institutional arrangements. As prices fail to do the job properly, the government must intervene to bring about the required adjustment. Keynesian models are therefore characterised by the assumption that prices are fixed or extremely sticky. In contrast, neoclassical economists believe that prices are reasonably flexible and that a lot of policy mistakes have arisen from failing to take account of the inexorable impact of market forces. In neoclassical models prices are flexible and adjust demand and supply in individual markets. Whereas in Keynesian thinking government is depicted as a benign, well-informed guardian of the public interest, critics of intervention see it as no better informed about economic events than the private sector and, like it, composed of self-seeking individuals who aim to maximise their own utility. So although markets do not work perfectly, governments may do even worse.

In this book Keynesian and neoclassical economics are treated as basic and contrasting approaches to macroeconomics. This is an expositional device. One will not find that all economists and politicians can be neatly placed in either a Keynesian or a monetarist-cum-neoclassical pigeonhole, and that all those in one of the pigeonholes have identical views. There is a spectrum of views and any individual may hold some opinions which could be labelled as

Keynesian and some others which are neoclassical. Labels are useful devices which enable us to distinguish between objects or ideas in general terms but they can be misleading if applied too rigidly or too specifically.

Bearing this in mind we shall proceed in Chapter 2 to outline a simple Keynesian model of the economy and a simple neoclassical model. As we progress, these models are extended in two ways: more variables are considered, and the behaviour over time of the modelled economy is analysed in greater depth. As you study these models and the fundamental debate about economic policy to which they are addressed, keep asking yourself three questions.

1. What assumptions are made?
2. What conclusions are reached?
3. How do these conclusions depend on the assumptions made?

A further crucial question then arises: 'How does one choose between competing theories?' It would be heartening if one could answer: 'On the basis of objective evidence', as would be possible were economics a natural science. Although most empirical research in economics does seek to gather factual evidence, mainly in the form of econometric testing of variables for which statistical data have been collected, the results are not sufficiently conclusive to rule out most hypotheses. One reason for this is that the theories being tested are not precise enough to be refutable. Another is that the data are inadequate given the statistical methods that have to be employed. Considerable leeway is therefore afforded to subjective judgement in evaluating a whole body of econometric evidence on any given economic relationship. This leaves ample scope for intuition and the casual empiricism of personal observation, intermingled with the influence of political preferences in choosing between rival hypotheses. It is not too difficult to start out with an *a priori* belief about economic relationships and find evidence to back it rather than the opposite method of starting out with no preconceptions and basing one's final conclusions on the objective facts of the case. (The cynical would say that this is how economists get themselves appointed as advisers!)

A quite different methodological approach to selecting economic theories is to look for logical inconsistencies, rejecting those that are not consistent. But this still leaves an important role for subjective judgement in deciding which logically consistent theory seems most applicable to the actual world it is trying to model and hence explain. For instance, many man-hours have been expended to prove mathematically that the conditions required for markets to allocate resources optimally are so special as to be most unlikely to exist in practice. Therefore, it has been argued that government intervention is necessary. But without a demonstration that the reality of government intervention, as opposed to an idealised form of it, will achieve a given objective better than imperfect market forces, one still has to make the choice on the basis of a necessarily subjective evaluation of the available evidence. Because we have not got much in the way of undisputably objective evidence on whether or not markets work effectively, the debate between the advocates of government intervention and the proponents of market forces will continue to flourish.

1.2 Some preliminaries

Before examining basic versions of Keynesian and neoclassical models of the economy, it is useful to consider the analytical procedures that are common to both classes of model.

Aggregation

Most macroeconomic models are highly aggregated in order to make them simpler. Although the economy does consist of millions of individual economic agents, such as households and firms, who are all buying and selling vast quantities of different goods and services each with its own price, it is useful to suppress most of this information in order to concentrate on those relationships which seem most important in explaining the functioning of the economy as a whole. For instance, the multitude of different goods and services produced in the economy over a given period of time are usually aggregated into a single variable, national output, which thus has a single price, the aggregate price level. Similarly labour is treated as homogeneous, with each unit selling for the same wage rate. The ratio of the money wage rate to the price level is the real wage rate, i.e. the quantity of goods earned by, say, one hour's work. The real wage rate is a key variable; whether and in what sense it may be too high to bring about the employment of all those willing to work has been, and still is, hotly debated. Hence aggregation has suppressed the existence of differing relative real wage rates between different types of labour and focused attention on the exchange rate between hours of labour and (wage) goods.

One basic difficulty with aggregation is to ensure that the measure of the aggregate accurately reflects the relative quantities of the constituents of the aggregate. One aspect of this problem involves obtaining an appropriate unit of measurement for the aggregate.

Aggregation: real and nominal quantities

An example of the difficulties attached to using a single unit of measurement is provided by the measurement of national output. Millions of heterogeneous goods and services cannot be measured using a common physical unit. A common unit in which they can be measured is money. National output is therefore measured by the sum of the quantity of each good or service times its price in terms of money. The problem with this measurement is that we are interested in the physical or real quantity of national output, as this gives us some indication of the standard of living of the members of the economy. The real quantity of national output is inaccurately measured by national output in money terms because this measure of national output may increase in value, not because of an increase in the physical quantity of goods and services produced, but because of a general rise in the level of prices. To isolate changes in the physical quantity of output from changes in the price level, output has to be measured at constant money prices. This is done by comparing over time real output levels obtained by measuring national output in all the years in the prices that ruled in only one of those years. This is equivalent to deflating national output at current prices by an index of the price level. We thus get the following definitions:

1. *Money or nominal value* of a variable is its value in current prices.
2. *Real value* of a variable is its value in constant prices: that is, the nominal value deflated by an index of the price level.

In this book the following notation is used in order to distinguish between nominal and real values:

$Y =$ nominal national output (that is, measured in current prices) per period of time, such as one year
$y =$ real national output (that is, measured in constant prices) per period of time
$P =$ index of the aggregate price level over a given period of time
$y = Y/P$

A price index is the weighted average of the prices of a limited number (in relation to total output) of goods and services. The price of each commodity is weighted by the proportion of total expenditure devoted to that commodity. Because the pattern of supply and demand changes, the proportion of expenditure allocated to various goods changes with time. This introduces bias into a price index. Therefore, the weights used in constructing a price index are intermittently revised to correct this bias.

Aggregration: fixed relative quantities

Aggregate analysis cannot allow for changes in the composition of the individual items that constitute the aggregate. When we aggregate over all commodities to obtain the aggregate national output, its composition in terms of relative quantities of goods and services is assumed fixed. This means that in this type of macro analysis we take relative prices as fixed and treat the sum of all goods and services as if it were a single good. Most macro models which contain aggregate functions are constructed in terms of a single aggregate output.

This makes for a particular problem because of the need to include consumption goods, which are used up for current enjoyment, and capital goods, which are used to produce future consumption, in the same model. If one is assuming a single aggregate output, then one is assuming that the price of consumption goods relative to capital goods is fixed and therefore determined outside the model. All the models dealt with formally in this book are of this type.

Capital is an aggregate which is particularly difficult to measure since it consists of heterogeneous goods, differing in age and in the kind of technology that they embody. It is difficult to derive even a monetary measure of the value of the capital stock. The prices at which the existing capital goods were acquired in the past do not reflect their current value. Allowance has to be made for depreciation, which is difficult to calculate accurately, and for the current replacement cost of the capital goods. There is the further problem of deflating the monetary value of the capital stock by an appropriate price index to obtain its real value.

Problems arise in deriving aggregate relationships between variables by summing over the individual components. For instance, one can postulate a particular functional relationship between household consumption and household disposable income for each of N households, but one may not be able to derive the form of the aggregate relationship between total consumption and total income without making further assumptions. In the simple case of linearity

$$C_i = a_i + b_i y_{di}$$

where C_i is the consumption of the ith household and y_{di} is the disposable income of the ith household. The aggregate relationship is

$$C = \sum_{i=1}^{N} C_i = \sum_{i=1}^{N} a_i + \sum_{i=1}^{N} \frac{y_{di}}{y} b_i y$$

The aggregate marginal propensity to consume (MPC) is $(\sum_{i=1}^{N} b_i y_{di}/y)$ and is the weighted average of the individual MPCs. The weights are each household's income as a proportion of total income. An additional variable, namely the distribution of income, explains aggregate consumption but it is not a determinant of individual household consumption.

It needs to be borne in mind that aggregation does present problems but if we are to do any analysis that goes beyond the level of the individual decision-maker we have to aggregate. Imperfect knowledge of the composition of the aggregates one is working with does not necessarily mean that one cannot produce useful results. Natural science made great progress without knowing the composition of the atom.

Equilibrium analysis

Equilibrium is a fundamental concept in economic analysis and is defined as a state of rest (or balance) when there are no forces making for further change in the system. It is extremely important, as the post-war debates have shown, to distinguish clearly between *short-run equilibrium* and *long-run equilibrium.* Long-run equilibrium is a true equilibrium in that the system has come fully to rest and no further changes can occur, unless they come from outside the system. A short-run equilibrium is only temporary and is a simplifying analytical device that means one either ignores changes in certain variables altogether or allows for their impact in the subsequent time period. For instance, it is normal to assume in short-run macro models that firms invest but that the capital stock is constant even though investment means adding to the capital stock. A single-period model totally ignores the effect of an increased capital stock, whereas a multi-period analysis would have a succession of short-period equilibria where in each time period firms revised their investment plans as they adjusted the actual stock of capital to its desired level.

It is also necessary to distinguish between *stationary equilibrium*, where all variables remain at a constant level, from *dynamic equilibrium*, where some variables grow at a steady rate so that constant ratios are maintained between variables. For example, in a steady-state growth model, national income and saving would grow steadily but the savings/income ratio would remain constant. So a model in dynamic equilibrium has its variables moving through time along an equilibrium time path. A static or stationary equilibrium is timeless, in the sense that one period is just like the next.

Much of economic analysis is concerned with comparing positions of equilibrium. A variable such as the level of government spending, or a coefficient such as the marginal propensity to consume, is changed and the initial equilibrium values of the variables are then compared with their values in the new equilibrium. This enables the direction of change to be predicted, but by itself does not guarantee that this change will in fact occur. For this to happen the new equilibrium must exist and the system must be stable. In other words, it must be capable of returning to equilibrium once disturbed. An unstable system would remain permanently in disequilibrium. The analysis of disequilibrium states is still a relatively uncharted sea. In recent years it has become more evident that the analysis of economic systems out of long-run equilibrium is really being conducted in terms of a succession of short-period equilibria which will, if the system is stable, eventually converge to a long-run equilibrium.

Market-clearing

Traditional Keynesian national income models are now being interpreted as short-run equilibrium models in which markets do not clear. A market clears when trade occurs at a price at which demand equals supply. In traditional neoclassical economic analysis market-clearing, with its balancing of demand and supply, is a necessary condition for equilibrium. If markets do not clear, prices and quantities will change, and this is incompatible with equilibrium. In contrast to this, Keynesian models are characterised by an ability to attain an equilibrium without all markets being cleared. In particular, the labour market and the goods market exhibit excess supply, but nevertheless the system is in equilibrium, albeit a short-run one, because prices do not change despite the absence of market-clearing.

Microeconomic foundations

The post-war work of both Keynesian and neoclassical economists has been increasingly influenced by the desire to build aggregate macroeconomic relationships upon microeconomic foundations. Microeconomic theory investigates individual behaviour, taking as fixed those variables that the individual cannot alter by him or herself. The behaviour of individuals is depicted as rational in that they attempt to maximise their own utility subject to constraints.

By proceeding in this way, microeconomic models, which determine a limited number of variables, such as the price and output of a particular product, are constructed. This method of analysis is known as *partial-equilibrium analysis* since all other variables in the economy are assumed to be unaffected by changes in the few variables being analysed. Micro theory is thus concerned with a single market or a set of closely related markets which are assumed not to influence the rest of the economy.

Macroeconomics considers the interaction of all the individual decision units in the economy and must therefore involve *general-equilibrium analysis*. In micro theory we examine the consumption and saving behaviour of a household in relation to the rate of interest which is externally given to that household. At the macro level we look at how households' savings plans and their demands for financial assets interact with the investment and financing plans of firms to determine the level of interest rates in the economy. The essential feature of macroeconomics is that it analyses the interdependencies between variables and the repercussions of a change in one variable upon other variables together with the feedback effects on that variable. A macro model solves for *general equilibrium* when all its interrelated markets are in equilibrium.

One approach to macroeconomic analysis is to work with all the micro equations of the economy and to determine the prices of commodities and factors of production and the quantities of commodities produced by solving the model for general equilibrium. As each commodity, factor of production and household is represented by its own behavioural equations, such models are difficult to handle.

The alternative and more widely used approach in macro analysis is to suppress the individual behavioural relationships and to work with broad aggregates. A common procedure is to derive behavioural relationships at the individual, micro level and to generalise to the aggregate level. For instance, one hypothesises that a household's consumption will vary directly with its disposable income and then one extends this hypothesis to a relationship between aggregate consumption and national disposable income.

In this book the micro foundations of macroeconomic analysis is dealt with mainly in sections II to IV. Section I, which follows this chapter, is largely concerned with constructing basic macroeconomic models using the main aggregate macroeconomic relationships whose micro foundations at this stage are only sketchily indicated.

References

[1] J. M. Keynes, *The General Theory of Employment, Interest and Money* (London: Macmillan, 1936).

[2] W. Beveridge, *Full Employment in a Free Society* (London: HMSO, 1944).

I COMPARATIVE STATICS IN THE CLOSED ECONOMY

The five chapters which make up section I are concerned with building models of a closed economy. One basic model is developed which, by changing a few crucial assumptions, becomes either a Keynesian model or a neoclassical one. This basic model forms what is known as the Keynesian–neoclassical synthesis. We start in Chapter 2 with a one-sector model: the neoclassical model has only a monetary sector, whereas the Keynesian model has just a goods market. In Chapters 3 and 4 the simple Keynesian and neoclassical models are combined to form the *ISLM* model, which has both a monetary sector and a real sector. Chapter 5 discusses the third sector – the supply side of the economy. This is added in Chapter 6 to the *ISLM* model to give a three-sector macro model.

The models developed in section I can be used to conduct comparative-static equilibrium analysis. One starts from a position of static equilibrium, changes something in the model, derives a new equilibrium and compares it with the old one.

2 One-Sector Neoclassical and Keynesian Models

This chapter outlines the simplest one-sector versions of the neoclassical and Keynesian models. Even in their rudimentary form they exhibit the essential difference in the two schools of thought, which centres on the role of the price mechanism.

2.1 The quantity theory of money

The neoclassical approach to macroeconomics is closely derived in large part from the quantity theory of money, which was particularly well developed in the writings of David Hume (1711–76). A key factor in understanding how a decentralised market economy operates is the role of money. All macro models distinguish between the *real sector* of the economy, which is made up of markets for physical goods and services, including labour, and the *monetary sector*, which embraces the money market and any other financial assets which may be included in the model. A crucial question in macroeconomics and one to which we will keep returning is: 'Do changes in the supply of money have any effect on the real variables in the economy, i.e. on the quantity of national output produced, on the level of employment and on the composition of the national output?' The answer given by the quantity theory of money is that changes in the money supply may have real effects in the short run but will not have in the long run.

To see how this conclusion is reached imagine a simple economy in which the only financial asset is money. Money is held in order to facilitate transactions in a non-barter economy. If all goods and services were exchanged only for other goods and services, as in a pure barter economy, there would be no role for money to function as a generally accepted medium of exchange. The existence of money means that time can elapse between the moment an economic agent supplies goods or services in one market and the moment it demands other goods and services in some other market using the income obtained from selling goods or labour. The amount of money which an economic agent wishes to hold on average over a given period of time is called the *demand for money.* This is a demand to hold a *stock* of money. The quantity of money demanded depends upon the value of transactions being financed over a period and upon various factors affecting payments habits such as the time between income receipts, the number of shopping trips per income period, and so on. If payments habits are assumed constant, then the demand to hold money is some constant fraction of the value of transactions. The value of transactions is identical to the number of transactions per period multiplied by the average price per transactions. The money value of transactions exceeds the money value of national output since transactions include the exchange of intermediate goods and of second-hand goods. Since data on the value of transactions are less readily available than those for national output and it is the latter variable that is of primary interest anyway, it is more useful to express the demand for money in terms of national output. The demand for money equation can thus be written as

$$M^D = kY = kyP \tag{2.1}$$

where

M^D = demand for nominal money balances
k = constant
Y = nominal national output over a time period (see p. 9)
y = real national output ($Y/P = y$) (see p. 9)
P = index of the aggregate price level over that time period

Retaining the assumption of a constant k coefficient presupposes some fixed relationship between the volume of transactions and the level of real national output over a period such as a year. Since money changes hands several times in a given period we can expect the value of k to be less than 1.0 but positive. An alternative way of viewing the k coefficient is to multiply both sides of equation 2.1 by $1/k = V$. We get

$$MV = yP \tag{2.2}$$

V is now the income velocity of circulation of money, which is the average number of times a unit of money turns over in the course of financing the nominal national output. V is measured by dividing the value of national output in current prices by the stock of money in existence, or

$$V \equiv \frac{yP}{M} \tag{2.3}$$

where $\equiv$ indicates an identity or definitional relationship. By assuming V to be constant we move away from a purely definitional relationship to the demand for money function we started with in equation 2.1.

To obtain the quantity theory prediction that changes in the money supply have no long-run real effects, we need to add an equilibrium condition for the money market. The demand for money must in equilibrium be equal to the actual stock of money in existence, M^S. The condition for money market equilibrium is

$$M^D = M^S \tag{2.4}$$

where M^S = nominal money supply. Substituting 2.4 into equation 2.1 we get

$$M^S = kyP = \left(\frac{1}{V}\right) yP \tag{2.5}$$

To derive the quantity theory result two further assumptions are required:

1. Real national output is fixed at an equilibrium level which is determined by the interaction of demand and supply for products and for factors of production.
2. The money stock is not affected by changes in nominal income.

If the money supply is then increased, the only way a new equilibrium can be achieved is if the demand for money increases to match the enlarged money supply. Given that the equilibrium values of y and k are fixed, the only way equilibrium can be restored is for the price level to rise. This sort of analytical exercise is known as *comparative-static equilibrium analysis*, since all it involves is comparing positions of equilibrium following some change in the *parameters* (i.e. constants) of the model. There are two kinds of parameters that can be changed.

Exogenous or *independent* variables are those assumed to be determined outside the system or model, such as y and M^S in the above analysis. Coefficients are constants, such as k, which may in turn be based on some underlying assumptions about economic behaviour, as is the case with velocity $(1/k)$. If a parameter is changed, then the equilibrium values of the variables whose values are determined within the model, the dependent variables, must also change, as does P in this model.

Dependent variables, whose values are determined within the model, are also known as *endogenous variables*.

Comparative-static equilibrium analysis of the type we have just conducted is somewhat incomplete as it says nothing explicitly about what economic behaviour causes the system to move from one equilibrium to another. In other words, economic analysis also has to specify the transmission mechanism or type of dynamic behaviour that will adjust the economy from one equilibrium position to another. In the quantity theory model this is done by specifying that the demand for goods and services will be affected by any disequilibrium in the money market. If the stock of money exceeds the demand for money balances, the excess cash will be spent on output. Conversely, if the demand for money exceeds the stock of money in the economy, people will build up their money balances by cutting back spending and saving more. It is here that the crucial and distinctive feature of the quantity theory model comes into play. Prices are assumed flexible. If the demand for goods exceeds the quantity producers wish to supply, prices are raised until demand is reduced and again equal to supply. If demand is less than supply, producers reduce prices until the market is cleared. In the simple, static version of the quantity theory, equilibrium output is fixed so that any excess demand created by expanding the money supply must cause higher prices. When prices have risen sufficiently to increase the demand for money balances by the full amount of the increase in the money supply, equilibrium is restored. In the opposite case of a reduction in the money supply, and a consequent decrease in the demand for goods, producers lower prices in order to induce their customers to purchase the same quantity as before. So underlying the assumption of fixed equilibrium national output is the premise that prices, including wages, are flexible and adjust to preserve market-clearing. More explicitly, dynamic versions of this model, which we shall study in later chapters, allow for output also to adjust as the economy moves between positions of equilibrium.

The policy implications of the basic quantity theory model are:

1. Changes in the money supply will disturb the economy. In particular increases in the money supply will raise the price level but in the long run leave the real variables unaffected. Continual increases in the money supply cause inflation.
2. The price mechanism enables a decentralised economy to adjust itself back to equilibrium.

2.2 The simple Keynesian model[1]

This is a one-sector model which includes only the goods market. There is no monetary sector. In stark contrast to the quantity theory model it assumes an exogenously fixed price level. The major conclusion of the model is that it can solve for an equilibrium value of national output which is less than the maximum amount firms would wish to supply at the existing price level. In this situation firms would produce more at current prices if only aggregate demand were higher.

Apart from an exogenous price level, the model makes a number of simplifying assumptions. It assumes that both the stock of capital and the labour force, which when fully utilised determine the maximum level of real output the economy can produce, are constant, An underlying behavioural assumption of the model is that firms act as profit maximisers. If demand for their output exceeds supply, firms increase production, providing there are spare resources to put to work. Conversely, if supply exceeds demand, firms reduce output.

The model is a short-run model and determines the value of real national output for a particular period of time, such as a year. The model solves for the static equilibrium level of real output, this being the value of real output (or any other variable) that has no tendency to change once it has been established. Static equilibrium in this model requires that firms in aggregate neither expand nor contract the quantity of output which they are currently producing. This

[1] It is assumed that students are already acquainted with the simple Keynesian model and with basic national income accounting to the level achieved in such books as Black [1].

requires that the supply of real national output, y, equals the quantity of national output which people wish to buy, E. The condition for static equilibrium in this model is therefore

$$y = E \tag{2.6}$$

where E is the desired aggregate demand or, alternatively, desired aggregate expenditure.

We then define aggregate demand as being composed of real consumption expenditure, C, and real investment expenditure, I. This is another example of a definitional relationship and is written

$$E \equiv C + I \tag{2.7}$$

A further behavioural assumption is made, namely that real consumption varies directly with real national income. This behavioural relationship is written

$$C = a + by \tag{2.8}$$

where $b = dC/dy$ and is known as the marginal propensity to consume. The MPC is the change in consumption that results from a change in income. Another simplifying assumption is that investment is exogenous or autonomous. This is indicated by writing $I = I_0$. The values of the parameters and the form of the relationships which make up the model are referred to as the model's structure. Equations 2.6, 2.7 and 2.8 are the *structural equations* of the model.

Consumption and income are endogenous variables as they are determined in the model. To solve the model in order to find the static equilibrium values for consumption and real income we substitute equation 2.8 into 2.7 and the result into 2.6 to obtain

$$y = a + by + I_0 \tag{2.9}$$

and solving this for y gives

$$y = \frac{a + I_0}{1 - b} = \frac{AE}{1 - b} \tag{2.10}$$

where AE is the autonomous expenditure and $1/(1-b)$ is known as a *multiplier*. By substituting equation 2.10 into 2.8 we obtain

$$C = a + bAE/(1 - b) \tag{2.11}$$

Equations 2.10 and 2.11 are called the *reduced-form equations* of the model as they express each endogenous variable in terms of the exogenous variables only.

An alternative to the algebraic exposition is the Keynesian cross diagram shown in Figure 2.1. The equilibrium condition is given by the 45° line along which $y = E$. Aggregate demand is given by the $E_0 \equiv C_0 + I_0$ schedule, the slope of which depends on the marginal propensity to consume. The two lines cross at the equilibrium level of national output, y_0^E. Because prices are assumed fixed there is nothing in the model to ensure that the equilibrium level

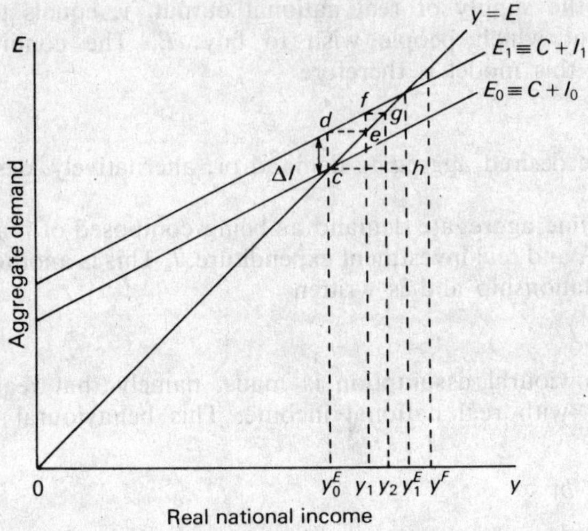

FIGURE 2.1 *The Keynesian one-sector model: comparative static and dynamic analysis*

of output is the same as the maximum amount of output firms would be willing to produce at these prices. The latter level of output is known in Keynesian analysis as the full-employment level of national output, shown as y^F in Figure 2.1.

The crucial, distinctive characteristic of a Keynesian model is that it can solve for an *equilibrium* level of output at which the capital stock and labour force are not fully employed. The goods market does not clear because firms are willing to sell more output at current prices but cannot find customers. Similarly the labour market does not clear as workers are willing to supply more labour at the current wage rate than firms wish to employ.

If the level of aggregate demand is increased, as shown in Figure 2.1 by the shift from E_0 to E_1, the equilibrium level of output will rise from y_0^E to y_1^E because output is in perfectly elastic supply at current, fixed prices. From equation 2.10, the increase in output as a result of a permanent increase in autonomous expenditure is given by

$$\Delta y = \frac{1}{1-b}\Delta AE \tag{2.10a}$$

where $1/(1-b)$ is the Keynesian multiplier.

If the level of aggregate demand exceeds the full-employment level of national output, then the amount produced is limited to the full-employment level, y^F, by the quantity of capital and labour available in the short run. At this point there is a discontinuity in the model. When aggregate demand exceeds the full-employment level of output, the assumption of fixed prices is no longer tenable. But the one-sector Keynesian model has no means of determining the price level or its rate of change. All it can say is that once aggregate demand exceeds the full-employment output level, prices rise. Inflation will only be brought to an end if aggregate demand is reduced to the level of full-employment output. In a Keynesian model in which prices as well as money wages are assumed fixed, the quantity of national product supplied depends entirely on the level of aggregate demand, up to the full-employment level of output.

The capital stock is assumed to be sufficiently large to employ all the workers who wish to supply their labour at the current money wage. This means that any unemployment above the level which would exist at full employment is attributed to insufficient aggregate demand. It is important to realise that in both Keynesian and neoclassical models full employment does not mean a zero amount of unemployment. Even at full employment there will be some people out of work because they are in the process of changing jobs. The concepts of unemployment and full employment are examined further in Chapter 5.

Dynamic analysis

The Keynesian model we have worked with so far is a static model which can be used for comparative-static analysis in order to predict the direction in which a variable will move following a change in its determinants, as well as the final magnitude of the change if the system came to rest at equilibrium again.

A static model cannot be used to predict what values a variable takes on as it moves from one position of equilibrium to another. It will tell us, as shown in Figure 2.1, that an increase in investment of $\Delta I = cd$ will, when equilibrium is regained, have caused an increase in real output of ch from y_0^E to y_1^E.

If we wish to trace out a time path of output as we move from one equilibrium position to another, we must construct a dynamic model. Such a model postulates lags in the adjustment of variables in which the current value of a variable depends upon the past values of either itself or of other variables. Dynamic models containing separate time periods of analysis, say intervals of a quarter of a year, are couched in terms of discrete time periods. A dynamic model may alternatively relate the rate of change of a variable to the rates of change of other variables (i.e. first- or higher-order derivatives). Such a model is constructed in terms of continuous time. For example, growth models relate the rate of change of real output to those of the capital stock and the labour force.

The one-sector model of income determination can be made dynamic simply by postulating a lag in the adjustment of consumption to income. Let us assume that if incomes change, people do not respond immediately but change their consumption in the next quarter. The consumption function is therefore lagged one period and written

$$C_t = a + by_{t-1} \tag{2.12}$$

where the subscript t refers to the time period to which the variable relates, C is consumption in the current period (quarter in this example), and y_{t-1} is income in the previous period. Since static equilibrium requires that income remains unchanged over time, this condition is written as

$$y_t = y_{t-1} = y^E$$

If investment increases, we can trace out a time path of income – which we could not do in the static model. After one period income rises by the increase in investment, ΔI, which is assumed to be a permanent increase. Consumption in the first quarter does not rise at all as there was no change in output in the previous quarter when the system was in equilibrium. In Figure 2.2 output rises in the first quarter by ΔI, which equals *cd* in Figure 2.1, which in turn equals *de*. In the second quarter income rises because consumption increases by b times the first quarter's rise in income. The second quarter's increase in income is $b\Delta I$, which equals *ef* in Figure 2.1, which in turn equals *fg*. Thus after two quarters income has risen by *de* + *fg* to y_2. This sequence of income increases is shown in Table 2.1. Each time output increases, a fraction, b, of this is injected back into aggregate expenditure via an increase in consumption and becomes next period's increase in output. This analysis shows how a given increase in autonomous or exogenously determined expenditure generates over time a greater increase in income. This process is the expenditure multiplier at work.

The final increase in income is obtained by summing the increase for each period, i.e.

$$\Delta y = \Delta I(1 + b + b^2 + \ldots + b^{N-1}) \tag{2.13}$$

Multiply both sides of equation 2.13 by b and subtract the result from equation 2.13 so that

$$(1 - b)\Delta y = (1 - b^N)\Delta I$$

$$\Delta y = \lim_{N \to \infty} \frac{(1 - b^N)\Delta I}{(1 - b)} = \frac{\Delta I}{(1 - b)}$$

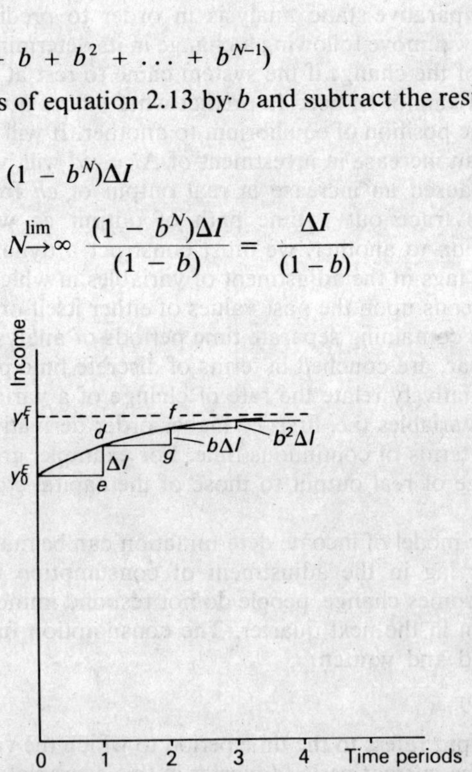

FIGURE 2.2 *The adjustment path of income in a one-sector Keynesian model*

TABLE 2.1 *The dynamic sequences of the expenditure multiplier*

	Change in I	Change in C	Change in y
After 1 period	ΔI	0	ΔI
After 2 periods	0	$b\,\Delta I$	$b\Delta I$
After 3 periods	0	$b^2\Delta I$	$b^2\Delta I$
⋮	⋮	⋮	⋮
After N periods	0	$b^{N-1}\Delta I$	$b^{N-1}\Delta I$

since if $0 < b < 1$, b^N tends to 0 as N tends to infinity. In the dynamic model income approaches equilibrium gradually, never quite attaining it since some small change, $b^N\Delta I$, is still going on but becomes negligibly small with time. In this case income is said to converge towards equilibrium. The time path for the above model is shown by the stepped adjustment path in Figure 2.2.

A continuous time model would give a smooth adjustment path, as indicated in Figure 2.2. If b were equal to or greater than 1.0, equilibrium would be unstable since any change in income would be respectively equal to or greater than the previous period's change in income. Over time output would steadily diverge from its static equilibrium value. As long as b lies between plus and minus 1.0, the model has a stable equilibrium, so that when disturbed from equilibrium it returns towards it.

The quantity theory model could be similarly dynamised by postulating a lag in the adjustment of excess money balances so that only part of the discrepancy between the amount of money demanded and the amount actually held is spent on goods and services in any one period. The construction of models which specify lags in the adjustment of variables is particularly important for policy purposes. Policy-makers need to know not only the direction of change and its final magnitude but also how long it takes to institute a change of a given magnitude. We can therefore distinguish *impact multipliers*, which give the short-run variation in income consequent upon a change in one of its determinants, from the *long-run multiplier*, which gives the final change in income when all readjustments have worked themselves out.

2.3 Conclusions

The distinctive features that separate the simple Keynesian model from the neoclassical model, and which also divide the more complex models of each type, relate to the following issues:

1. *Price flexibility*. In neoclassical models prices are flexible, while in Keynesian models they are fixed or only flexible upwards. Keynesians often interpret the fixed-price assumption as a simplified way of dealing with their view that prices are sticky downwards.

2. *Market-clearing*. This is synonymous with equilibrium in neoclassical models but not in Keynesian ones.
3. *Analysis with stock or flow variables*. A *stock variable* is one that is measured at a moment in time, like the stock of money or the stock of capital goods. A *flow variable*, such as national income, is one that can only be measured as a rate of flow per period of time. To say that national output is £1,000 billion is meaningless unless one specifies the time period, such as a year, over which it is measured. The quantity theory model emphasises the role of stock adjustment, whereby changes in the demand for goods is the outcome of adjusting the actual stock of money held to the desired stock. The Keynesian model, on the other hand, concentrates on flow variables. Aggregate demand depends on another flow variable, national income. The two forms of analysis are mutually consistent, since adjusting a stock variable, such as the quantity of money held, gives rise to a flow variable, in this case a flow of spending or saving.

In the next chapter the real and monetary sectors are combined to build up a single model, the *ISLM* model, which, on making different assumptions about price flexibility and the behaviour of aggregate supply gives rise to Keynesian or neoclassical versions of a common analytical framework.

Reference

[1] J. Black, *The Economics of Modern Britain: An Introduction to Macroeconomics*, 2nd edn (London: Martin Robertson, 1980).

3 The *ISLM* Model

The one-sector Keynesian model of the economy, which was reviewed in Chapter 2, deals only with the demand for output in the real sector or, as it is alternatively named, the goods market. This sector is concerned with the receipts of the national product by factors of production and the expenditure of this income by households and firms. The model can easily be extended to include a government sector and a foreign trade sector, but it does not concern itself with how expenditure is financed. In other words, there is no explicit consideration of the role of money. The one-sector model was developed by Keynes's disciples as a simple exposition of the distinctive Keynesian view that the supply of national output is demand determined. *The General Theory of Employment, Interest and Money*, as its title indicates, did include an explicit consideration of the monetary sector.

The *ISLM* model is a two-sector model, containing both a real sector, the goods market, and a monetary sector or market for financial assets. It was originally developed by J. R. Hicks [1] as an interpretation of *The General Theory* and has since been incorporated into the body of theory which makes up the neoclassical–Keynesian synthesis. Depending on whether prices are assumed fixed or flexible, the *ISLM* model comes in Keynesian and neoclassical versions. It is a useful expositional device because it analyses the interrelationships between real and monetary variables. Today's large scale, multi-variable econometric models of the economy are just extensions of the *ISLM* model. They include more variables and have a greater degree of disaggregation.

3.1 The interaction of the real and monetary sectors of the economy

The role of money as a medium of exchange was initially examined in Chapter 2's account of the quantity theory of money. The existence of a generally accepted medium of exchange dramatically lowers the costs of exchange as compared with a barter economy. As well as being a medium of exchange, money acts as a *numéraire* or unit of account in which the prices of all commodities are expressed. The third function of money is that it serves as a store of wealth, i.e. as an asset. When performing this function money links past and future time periods.

In any one time period a decision-unit's expenditure may differ from its income. If expenditure is less than income, the unit is saving and is said to be a surplus unit (terminology popularised by Gurley and Shaw [2]). The general rationale for saving is the postponement of consumption from the present to the future. Surplus units require a means by which they can carry forward into the future their claim to purchasing power which they decide not to exercise in the present but which they wish to enjoy in the future. Such a means is known as a store of value or an asset. Any commodity which lasts for some considerable time can act as a store of value. This would be the only type of asset in a barter economy. In a monetary economy the store of value function is also performed by money and by paper claims upon other people's income.

Such paper claims, known as financial assets, arise from financing the expenditure of deficit units who currently spend in excess of their income. In order to spend more on resources than they are entitled to by their current income, deficit units take up those resources that surplus units do not wish to consume in the present. In return, the deficit units issue paper claims upon themselves, which commit them to repay at some future date the resources that they have borrowed from the surplus units, together with a rate of return. These claims are liabilities to the deficit units who issue them, but are assets to those who own them.

Financial assets take many forms in the real world. One of these is a bond or debenture, which is a promise to repay a nominally fixed sum of money at some future date (infinity in the case of perpetuities) and to pay at stated intervals a nominally fixed income which is calculated as a constant rate of interest on the original sum lent. (For example, £100 originally lent for twenty years at an original, or coupon rate, of 5 per cent pays £5 a year for twenty years plus £100 at the end of the twentieth year.) Marketable financial assets, such as bonds, can be exchanged at a price so that the original lender can obtain cash without waiting twenty years for the bond to be redeemed. Non-marketable claims, such as building society shares and post office savings accounts, have to be repaid by the borrower before the lender can exchange his store of value for goods and services.

The distinction between expenditure and portfolio allocation decisions

In a monetary economy the process of lending and borrowing results in a stock of financial assets being built up over time. This means that in any one period trading takes place both in newly issued and in existing financial assets. An economic unit has two distinct decisions to make:

1. It must decide what proportion of its current income to spend. For a household this is its consumption decision and necessarily its saving decision also. For a firm it is a decision about its real investment, which is its demand for real capital goods.

2. A financing or portfolio decision must also be made. A deficit unit needs to decide what types of liabilities to issue, and a surplus unit what kinds of assets to hold. In any one period of time the unit's portfolio decision involves not only the financing of its current consumption or real investment plans but also the rearranging of its existing portfolio of assets and liabilities. A portfolio decision is concerned with a change in the composition of one's stock of assets and liabilities.

Flow equilibrium and stock equilibrium

The consumption and real investment decisions directly involve decisions about the values of the flow variables in the economy. Flow equilibrium requires that the amount of output produced must be taken up by willing purchasers. This means that the volume of resources to which surplus units receive a claim that they decide not to exercise in the current period must be transferred, via the operation of the financial system, to deficit units for consumption or real investment. Some of the resources saved by surplus units are transferred to deficit households to be consumed by them. After taking account of this transfer, we are left with the net aggregate saving of the economy.

It must be noted that an individual act of saving does not automatically lead to a corresponding act of planned investment. The resources released by the saver must be lent to another household to finance its consumption, in which case the resources are used. If savers store their savings in already existing assets, such as money or bonds issued in the past, they do not directly transfer the reserves they did not wish to use in the current period to a firm wishing to finance real investment.

If aggregate desired saving exceeds planned investment, aggregate demand will be less than the supply of output, whereas there will be inflationary pressures if the planned demand for real investment exceeds aggregate desired saving at a given level of real income. For the real sector to be in equilibrium we therefore require the flow equilibrium condition that investment equals saving.

Stock equilibrium in the financial sector requires that people are willing to hold the existing stock of both real and financial assets at their current prices. If the demand for assets does not equal the supply, the prices of assets will be changing and this will have repercussions on consumption and real investment decisions. Similarly, if flow equilibrium does not exist, say investment exceeds saving and firms lower asset prices to borrow more funds, stock equilibrium cannot exist either. Therefore, for overall equilibrium of the economy we require both flow and stock equilibrium.

3.2 The *ISLM* model: the Keynesian version

The goods-market equations

We start with a closed economy in which there is no government. When there are idle resources the price level is assumed to be constant and exogenously determined, so that the price index, P, can be set equal to 1.0. All the variables in the model are in real terms. Since $P = 1$ we do not need explicitly to deflate each variable by the price level.

The following symbols are defined:

y = real national output
Y = nominal national output
$y = Y/P = Y$ when there are idle resources and $P = 1$
E = desired aggregate demand = national expenditure
C = planned consumption
I = planned investment
S = planned saving
i = the market rate of interest

There are two definitions:

$$E \equiv C + I \quad (3.1)$$

and

$$Y \equiv C + S \quad (3.2)$$

Equation 3.1 states that aggregate demand consists of consumption and investment, and equation 3.2 shows that households can dispose of their income either by consuming or saving. For static flow equilibrium we must have real output equal to the aggregate demand for it. The flow equilibrium condition is given by equation 3.3 or by the alternative version in equation 3.4:

$$y = E \quad (3.3)$$

and substituting 3.1 and 3.2 into 3.3 we obtain

$$C + S = C + I \quad (3.4)$$

$$\therefore \quad S = I \quad (3.4a)$$

As previously discussed, flow equilibrium necessarily requires that desired saving and investment are equal.

'Ex ante' and 'ex post' values of variables

Although planned saving and investment are only equal in equilibrium, actual saving is always identical to the actual amount of investment done by firms, whether or not the economy is in equilibrium. If saving exceeds planned investment (that is, real output exceeds aggregate demand), firms will find unsold stocks of goods on their hands which they have to add to their inventories. In such an event firms engage in unplanned inventory investment so that the actual amount of investment done equals the actual amount of saving. Of course, with actual investment exceeding planned investment, firms will not be in equilibrium and will therefore alter their production plans in the next period, so that static equilibrium cannot prevail. The values that variables actually take on after the effects of economic decisions have worked themselves out are referred to as being *ex post* values. The planned values of variables are known as their *ex ante* values. The *ex post* value of a variable will differ from its *ex ante* value in disequilibrium. When saving exceeds planned investment, then *ex ante* or planned, investment is smaller than *ex post* investment. It is the planned or desired values of variables that directly influence the actual values that variables take on. It is firms' planned investment, not their *ex post* investment, that determines their demand for capital goods. Equilibrium requires equality between the *ex ante* and *ex post* quantities of each variable.

The investment function

The *ISLM* model brings in the connection between the real and financial sectors by postulating that investment is inversely dependent on the rate of interest. Investment is the demand for capital goods that are wanted because they will produce additional goods and services in the future. Thus expectations about the future are a crucial determinant of investment demand. When a firm buys a capital good the costs are incurred in the present but the revenues the firm expects to obtain from the sale of commodities produced using the capital good will accrue in the future. The firms must therefore compare costs and revenues which occur at different time periods. The way of doing this is to bring all future costs and revenues to their value in the current period. This is known as their *present value.*

If there is a positive market rate of interest, say 10 per cent, then £100 received next year is worth less than £100 received today. This is because £100 received now can be lent at 10 per cent and becomes £100 (1 + 0.1) = £110 next year. The present value of £110 received in one year's time is £110/(1 + 0.1) = £100, since an individual would be indifferent between the prospect of receiving £100 now and lending it at 10 per cent and receiving £110 in a year's time. Similarly, £100 lent for two years at 10 per cent would be worth £100 $(1 + 0.1)^2$ = £121 in two years' time. Thus the present value of £121 received in two years' time is £121/$(1 + 0.1)^2$ = £100. From this it can be seen that a present-value calculation is the reverse of a compound-interest calculation. In general the present value of £x received in n years' time when the rate of interest is i per cent and is paid at annual intervals is £$x/(1 + i)^n$.

The net present value (NPV) of an investment project is the discounted value of all revenues minus the discounted value of all costs, and is given by the following expression, where the market rate of interest is called the discount rate:

$$\text{NPV} = -S_0 + \frac{R_1}{(1+i)} + \frac{R_2}{(1+i)^2} + \frac{R_3}{(1+i)^3} + \ldots + \frac{R_n}{(1+i)^n}.$$

The initial cost of the capital equipment is given by S_0 and the net revenue expected in the tth year by R_t. The net revenue is calculated as the revenue from selling the output produced by the capital equipment minus operating costs. These include maintenance and the costs of other factors of production used in the process but do not include depreciation or financing costs. Any scrap value that the capital has at the end of its life is included in the net revenue for the final year.

Given that firms have the objective of maximising their overall net present value, which is equivalent to maximising the present value of their future expected profits, they will adopt all investment projects which have a non-negative net present value. If expectations improve so that the estimated net revenue stream increases, or the price of capital goods declines, or the market rate of interest falls, the net present value of any particular investment project will rise. This means that there will be more investment projects with a positive net present value and hence a greater demand for investment goods. In the *ISLM* model expectations and the price of capital goods are taken to be constant, whereas the rate of interest is endogenous.[1] The investment function which enters the *ISLM* model is

$$I = I(i) \qquad (dI/di < 0) \tag{3.5}$$

It must be remembered that each investment schedule exists for a particular value of the state of expectations and the price of capital goods.

Savings are assumed to depend directly on the level of income. The savings function, equation 3.6, is the counterpart to the consumption function given by equation 2.2:

$$S = -a + sy \tag{3.6}$$

where s is the marginal propensity to save.

There are now two endogenous variables to solve in the model, namely the real level of national output and the rate of interest. For the goods market to be in equilibrium, planned investment must equal planned saving. Substituting equations 3.5 and 3.6 into equation 3.4a we obtain

$$-a + sy = I(i) \tag{3.7}$$

$$y = \frac{a + I(i)}{s} \tag{3.7a}$$

Equation 3.7a shows that there are various combinations of the level of real output and of the rate of interest that will make investment and saving equal. A higher interest rate which reduces investment has to be balanced by a lower y which reduces saving. The locus of good-market equilibrium values of real output and the interest rate is called the *IS* schedule. This is now derived geometrically in Figure 3.1.

Turning to quadrant 1 we see that when income is y_0 the desired amount of saving is S_0, which is transferred on to the vertical axis in quadrant 2. The 45° line in quadrant 2 converts any distance along the vertical axis (the ordinate) into an equal distance on the horizontal axis (the abscissa). Investment must

[1] Many expositions of the *ISLM* model assume the supply curve of capital goods fixed, rather than the price, in order to derive, in a somewhat unsatisfactory way, a determinate investment schedule. If the price of investment goods is allowed to vary, this conflicts with the assumption of an exogenous price level. The derivation of an investment schedule is discussed further in Chapter 13.

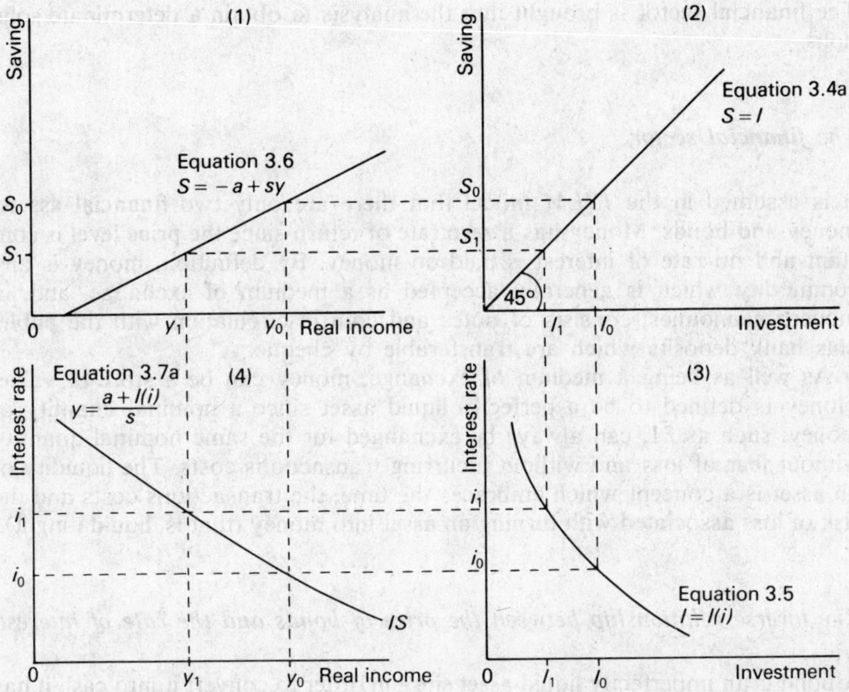

FIGURE 3.1 *Derivation of the IS function*

equal I_0 for it to equal saving when income is y_0. The investment schedule in quadrant 3 shows that given a particular state of expectations and price of capital goods the rate of interest must be i_0 to result in a level of investment of I_0.

The co-ordinate of i_0 and y_0 is then plotted in quadrant 4. We then have one combination of income y_0 and interest rate i_0 for which saving equals investment. The same process is repeated for income level y_1 to obtain an interest rate of i_1 which makes saving, when income is y_1 equal to the level of investment. In this way we can obtain a large number of interest rates and output levels for which investment equals saving, and by joining them obtain the locus of all such points which is the *IS* schedule. This geometric derivation of the *IS* schedule is identical to the process we went through to obtain the *IS* function algebraically What we have done here geometrically is to substitute equations 3.5 and 3.6 into 3.4 so as to derive equation 3.7a.

The *IS* schedule alone is insufficient to determine both the level of real income and the interest rate since we have a single equation (3.7a), which is the equation of the *IS* schedule, in two unknown variables, real income and the rate of interest. To solve a model we must obtain determinate and hence equilibrium values for all the endogenous variables. This requires that we have as many independent equations as there are endogenous variables. To solve the *ISLM* model we therefore need another function in addition to the *IS* function.

The financial sector is brought into the analysis to obtain a determinate solution.

The financial sector

It is assumed in the *ISLM* model that there are only two financial assets: money and bonds. Money has a zero rate of return since the price level is constant and no rate of interest is paid on money. By definition, money is any commodity which is generally accepted as a medium of exchange, and, in modern economies, consists of notes and coin in circulation with the public plus bank deposits which are transferable by cheque.

As well as being a medium of exchange, money can be a store of value. Money is defined to be a perfectly liquid asset since a nominal quantity of money, such as £1, can always be exchanged for the same nominal quantity without fear of loss and without incurring transactions costs. The liquidity of an asset is a concept which embraces the time, the transactions costs and the risk of loss associated with turning an asset into money (that is, liquidating it).

The inverse relationship between the price of bonds and the rate of interest

A bond is an imperfectly liquid asset since in order to convert it into cash it has to be sold on a market at the risk of making a capital loss if the selling price is less than the price at which the bond was originally bought. The alternative of waiting till the bond matures and the principal is repaid involves time, which is included in the concept of *illiquidity*. Hence a financial asset is regarded as more illiquid, the longer its time to maturity. The price of a bond on a market is the present value of the income stream to which the bond is a claim. This can be expressed as

$$\text{bond price} = B_p = \frac{A_n}{(1+i)} + \frac{A_n}{(1+i)^2} + \ldots + \frac{A_n + R}{(1+i)^n} \tag{3.8}$$

where A_n is the nominally fixed annual income and R is the principal which is repaid after n years. If the bond is a perpetuity, such as the UK government's consolidated fund (consols), the price is

$$B_p = \frac{A_n}{(1+i)} \sum_{t=0}^{\infty} \left(\frac{1}{1+i} \right)^t \tag{3.8}$$

Applying the formula for summing a geometric progression with an infinite number of terms we obtain (see p. 22):

$$B_p = \frac{A_n}{1+i} \left(\frac{1}{1 - 1/(1+i)} \right) = \frac{A_n}{1+i} \left(\frac{1+i}{i} \right) = \frac{A_n}{i} \tag{3.9}$$

From equation 3.9 we see that if the current interest rate rises, the price of existing bonds must fall. This happens in order to equalise the rate of return on bonds issued at different dates at different coupon rates. Take the example of a consol issued at £100 with a coupon rate of 2.5 per cent in the 1930s. This bond pays an annual income of £2.50. If currently new bonds worth £100 have a coupon rate of 10 per cent, they give an annual income of £10. To make people willing to hold the 1930s consol its price will fall to £25 to give a rate of return of £2.50/25, which gives us 10 per cent.

This example illustrates the inverse relationship between the price of bonds and the current rate of interest. The current interest rate is the yield on bonds, which is defined to be that rate of interest which, used as a discount rate, makes the present value of the future income from a bond equal to its market price. In the case of a perpetuity the yield is obtained by rearranging equation 3.9:

$$\text{yield} = \frac{\text{annual income}}{\text{current bond price}} = \frac{A_n}{B_p} \tag{3.10}$$

Thus, if bond prices rise, the yield or current interest rate falls. As the *ISLM* model contains only one interest-bearing financial asset, there is only a single rate of interest to be considered. In an economy with a number of financial assets, differing in marketability, riskiness and date to maturity, there exists a whole range of interest rates which is known as the interest-rate structure. There is a tendency for interest rates to move in line with one another so that reducing the number of interest rates to one is a simplification which still allows us to conduct a useful analysis.

The demand for money

The demand for money is the demand to hold a stock of money balances. It can be expressed either in nominal or in real terms. The nominal value of money, M, is the actual number of currency units, such as pounds, in existence. The real value of money, M/P, is its nominal value deflated by an index of the price level. This gives the purchasing power of a particular stock of money in terms of goods and services it can buy. The desire to hold money derives from its functions as a medium of exchange and as a store of value. The rationale for the demand to hold money as a medium of exchange was outlined in Chapter 2 as part of the exposition of the quantity theory of money. The quantity of nominal money required to finance transactions is presumed to depend on the nominal value of national income and can be generally expressed as

$$M^D = f(y) = f(Y) \tag{3.11}$$

Note that the functional notation f replaces the constant coefficient k, or constant velocity assumption, used in Chapter 2.

Alternatively, the demand for money function can be expressed in real terms. If the price level doubles, while real output remains unchanged, and the demand for nominal money balances also doubles, the demand for real money balances has stayed the same.[1] Written in real terms equation 3.11 becomes

$$\frac{M}{P} = f(y) \tag{3.11a}$$

The relationship between the quantity of real transactions balances demanded and real national income depends on various features of the payments mechanism. The more frequently people are paid per year, the smaller is the average value of transactions balances they need to hold. The use of credit cards, and arrangements whereby depositors pay banks annual bills at monthly intervals, reduce the average bank balances people need to keep. All such factors are assumed exogenous to the *ISLM* model and any change in them would alter the relationship given by equation 3.11 or 3.11a.

Money is also demanded as an asset. There are substitutes in the form of other financial assets and real assets for the store of value function of money. In the *ISLM* model there is only one financial asset substitute, namely bonds. The advantage of holding a bond is that it bears a rate of interest; the disadvantage is that a bond is imperfectly liquid since a capital loss may be incurred when it is sold. The higher is the rate of interest, the larger is the return on bonds and the greater the opportunity cost of holding money rather than an interest-bearing asset. The demand for money is therefore hypothesised to vary inversely with the rate of interest. Expectations about the future returns likely to be yielded by the various types of assets will also affect the demand for them, including money. For instance, if asset holders change their expectations and think that bond prices will fall in the future, there will be an incentive to sell bonds and move into money. An additional determinant of the demand to hold money is the total stock of wealth to be allocated between money and bonds. The demand for money will rise with increased wealth.

In the *ISLM* model the state of expectations and the stock of wealth are assumed to be exogenous. The total demand for real money balances both as a medium of exchange and as a store of value is therefore written as

$$\left(\frac{M}{P}\right)^D = \frac{M}{P}(y, i) \tag{3.12}$$

Stock equilibrium in the financial sector: Derivation of the LM function

Equilibrium in the financial sector requires that the demand for money equals the stock of money and that the demand to hold bonds also equals the stock of bonds supplied. Since we have only two financial assets, it must be the case

[1] The demand for real money balances is said to be homogenous of degree zero in money prices. To ascertain the degree of homogeneity of $y = f(x)$ the dependent and all independent variables are multiplied by a constant, λ, so that $\lambda^n y = f(\lambda x)$. The degree of homogeneity is given by n. In $n = 0$, y is unaffected by multiplying the x variables by λ.

that if the bond market is in equilibrium so is the money market.[1] If people were holding excess money balances, they would be running these down to buy bonds and bond prices would be rising. This means that it is sufficient to work with money-market equilibrium without giving specific consideration to the bond market. The money supply is assumed to be exogenously determined.

The condition for stock equilibrium in the *ISLM* model is therefore that the demand for money should equal the exogenously determined money supply, M_0^S:

$$\left(\frac{M}{P}\right)^D = \left(\frac{M}{P}\right)(y, i) = \frac{M_0^S}{P} \tag{3.13}$$

If we wish to depict the demand function for money on a two-dimensional diagram, we need to hold all except one determinant constant. Figure 3.2 shows the demand for money as a function of the rate of interest. Each demand for money schedule holds income, as well as the exogenous variables which determine it, constant. Demand schedule D_0D_0 is plotted for a level of real national income which is constant at y_0. The supply of money, (M_0^S/P), is given by the vertical line, as it is assumed exogenous and hence unaffected by the interest rate. If the level of output is y_0, the interest rate must be i_0 for the demand and supply of money to be equal. At a higher level of output, y_1, the transactions demand for money is greater, and hence a higher interest rate, i_1, is required to make the asset demand for money lower so as to still equate the money stock with the demand for money. In Figure 3.3 we plot the various combinations of the level of real income and the rate of interest which, given a

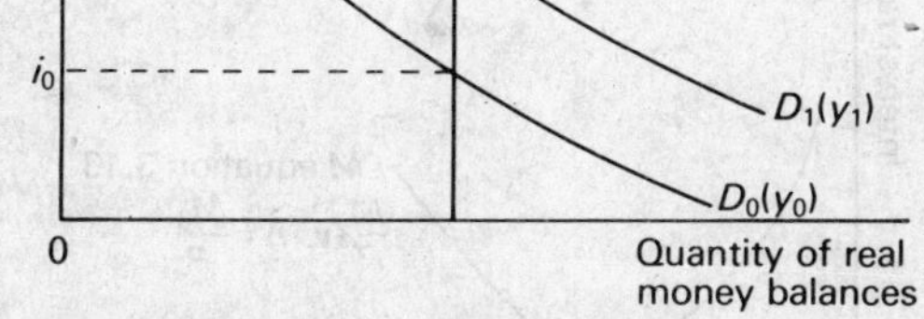

FIGURE 3.2 *The demand for money as a function of the rate of interest, all other variables remaining constant*

[1] The proposition that a model with n market-clearing equations solves for $n-1$ independent equations and hence $n-1$ variables, allowing the nth variable to be dropped from explicit consideration, is known derived from Walras's law. This explained in Chapter 16, pp. 292–4.

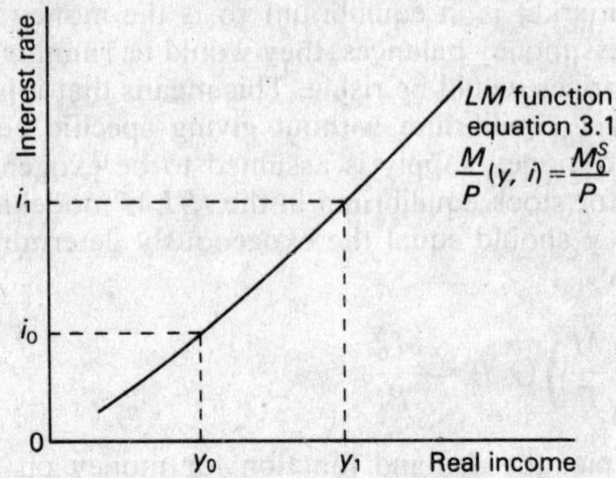

FIGURE 3.3 *Derivation of the LM function*

particular demand function for money and a certain stock of money, (M_0^S/P), make the demand for money equal to the supply. The locus of such real-income and interest-rate combinations is known as the *LM* function, whose equation is given by equation 3.13.

Goods- and money-market equilibrium

Now that we have derived the *IS* and *LM* functions it becomes possible to solve the model. It is very important to bear in mind that we are talking in terms of real magnitudes. When both the goods and money market are in equilibrium, as indicated by the intersection of the *IS* and *LM* functions in Figure 3.4, we have determined the interest rate and the real level of output for which the aggregate demand for real output equals the aggregate supply of real

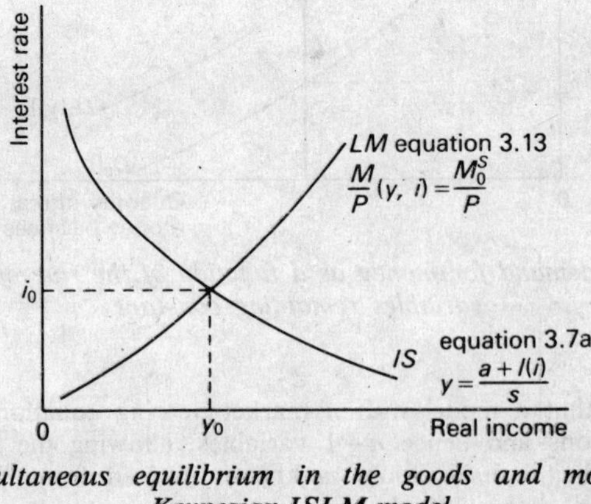

FIGURE 3.4 *Simultaneous equilibrium in the goods and money markets: the Keynesian ISLM model*

output and for which the demand for real money balances equals the real quantity of money in existence.

Since the model is concerned with real values, we must not forget the role of the price level in determining real values. At the outset we made a simplifying assumption that the price level is fixed at 1.0. An exogenous price level characterises the Keynesian version of the *ISLM* model. The assumption of a constant price level can be made if we assume that there exists a considerable degree of unemployed labour and underutilised capacity in the economy. One justification for the fixed price assumption is that the existence of idle resources means that firms' short-run average costs are constant. They can expand or contract output at unchanged average costs and hence the price level remains constant as the volume of output changes. The aggregate supply function is therefore assumed to be perfectly elastic up to the full-employment level of output.

It is very important to understand that the Keynesian *ISLM* model of national income determination is an entirely demand-orientated theory. It applies to the short-run determination of output when the economy is less than fully employed. In these circumstances the amount of output that is produced is determined by the quantity that is demanded. The quantity demanded in equilibrium is determined by the joint equilibrium of the goods and money markets and is y_0 in Figure 3.4. It is important to appreciate that the level of output consistent with *ISLM* equilibrium is the *aggregate demand* for output. This only becomes equal to the *aggregate supply* of output when a perfectly elastic aggregate supply curve for output is postulated.

The aggregate supply of output function which underlies the Keynesian *ISLM* model is depicted in Figure 3.5. It is perfectly elastic at the fixed price level $P = 1$ until the full-employment level of output, y_f, is reached. At this point it becomes completely inelastic and the fixed price assumption breaks down. If we transpose the equilibrium aggregate demand for output, y_0, from Figure 3.4 to Figure 3.5, the actual quantity supplied will be determined. If aggregate demand is less than the full-employment level, y_f, the actual quantity

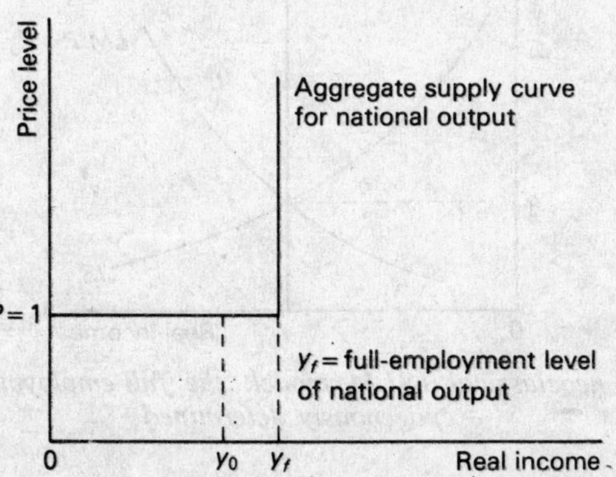

FIGURE 3.5 *The Keynesian ISLM model: demand for output determines the supply of output up to full employment*

supplied is demand-determined and identical to y_0. In the case of y_0 exceeding y_f, the real quantity of output is restricted to y_f, and the price level must be higher than $P = 1$. As yet we have no means of determining the price level as an endogenous variable in a Keynesian model. To do this we need to add the labour market, and this is done in Chapter 6. As this model has only two independent markets,[1] those for goods and money, and hence has only two independent equations, the *IS* function and the *LM* function, it can only solve for just two endogenous variables. These are the interest rate and the level of output in the Keynesian version of the model.

3.3 The neoclassical version of the *ISLM* model

In the neoclassical version of the *ISLM* model prices and costs are assumed to be endogenous and the equilibrium level of real output is determined exogenously at y_f when all resources are fully employed. In the Keynesian *ISLM* model real income and the interest rate are the two endogenous variables determined in the model. The major difference between the neoclassical and Keynesian versions of the *ISLM* model is not in their specification of aggregate demand (that is, the *IS* and *LM* functions) but in the assumptions made about the supply side of the economy. The aggregate demand functions could be identical but this specification of different supply-side responses results in different conclusions regarding the outcome of given policy actions.

Specifying flexible prices in the neoclassical *ISLM* model means that goods-market equilibrium determines the interest rate quite independently of the money market. This can be seen from Figure 3.6. Given that the equilibrium level of employment is y_f, the equilibrium rate of interest, which equates investment to the level of savings forthcoming at income level y_f, is i_f. This leaves

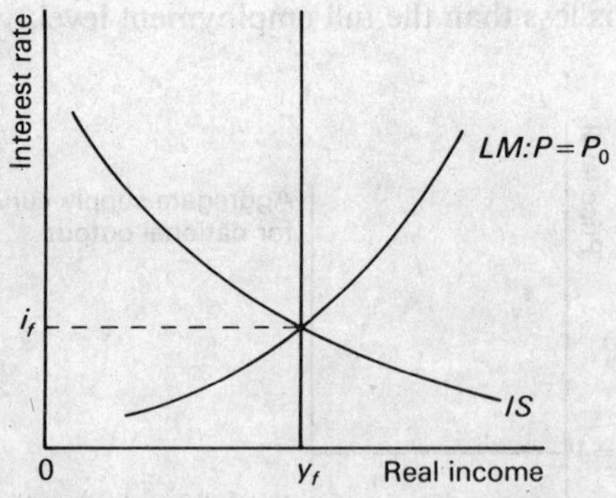

FIGURE 3.6 *The neoclassical ISLM model: the full-employment level of output exogenously determined*

[1] The third market, for bonds, is not independent, for when the money markets are in equilibrium so must the bond market.

money-market equilibrium to establish the equilibrium price level. The demand for real balances which is consistent with goods-market equilibrium is determined, once the equilibrium output level and interest rate are established, and is $(M/P)(y_f, i_f)$. For money-market equilibrium this must equal the supply of real money balances. The nominal stock is given as M_0^S, which means that the equilibrium price level is that which makes the real value of M_0^S equal to the equilibrium demand for real money balances. Looking at Figure 3.6, the equilibrium price level of P_0 establishes a real value of the money supply such that the *LM* function intersects the *IS* function at the point with co-ordinates i_f and y_f. If the *LM* curve were in any other position, it would be inconsistent with equilibrium in the goods market.

3.4 Changing the exogenous variables

Shifts in the IS function

If any of the parameters in the *IS* equation changes, there will be a shift of the *IS* schedule. This illustrated in Figure 3.7 for an increase in desired investment caused by improved expectations about the future returns from investment. Initially the investment schedule is I_0I_0 and the *IS* schedule is given by IS_0. Due to improved expectations of future earnings desired investment at every rate of interest increases, so that we have a new investment schedule I_1I_1. This means that the rate of interest which equates investment to saving at each level of output must rise. At output y_0 we now require an interest rate of i_0' for equilibrium in the goods market. Thus an increased desire to invest shifts the

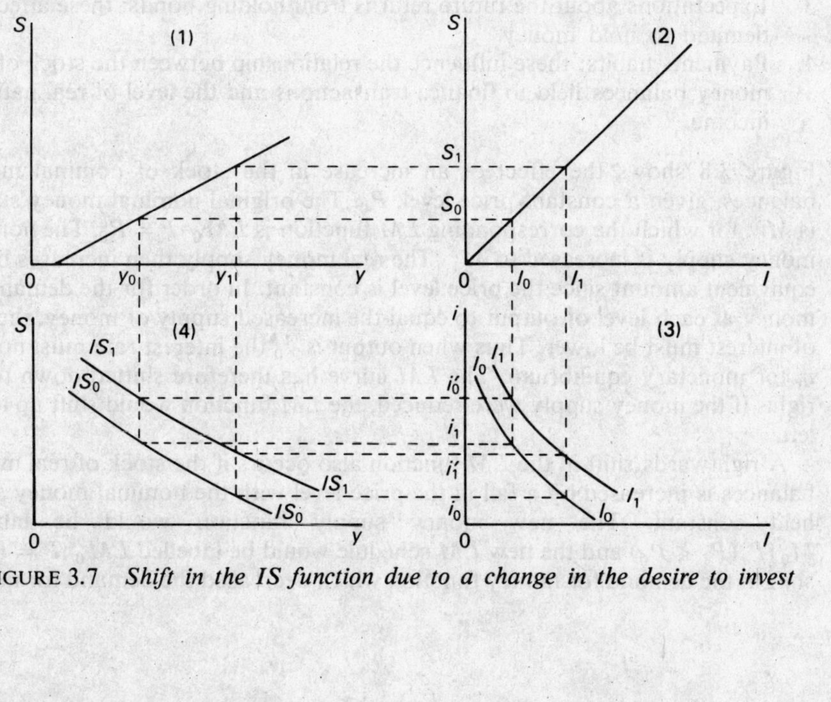

FIGURE 3.7 *Shift in the IS function due to a change in the desire to invest*

IS schedule upwards to the right. The reverse movement in the *IS* curve will result from a decline in investment due to a fall in expectations about future returns.

A change in any of the exogenous variables which determine either investment or saving will shift the *IS* function. These are:

1. Factors affecting the expected profits from investment.
2. The marginal propensity to save. A fall shifts the *IS* curve up to the right and also alters its slope. The new *IS* function will be further away from the old one, the higher the level of income. A rise in the MPS (fall in the MPC) has the opposite effect.
3. A shift in the total savings function caused by a change in the constant a. An increase in a shifts the *IS* function up and to the right. One factor that could cause such a shift is a change in wealth if it is assumed that consumption is positively related to the amount of wealth people own. At present we are assuming wealth to be constant and hence have not included it as a separate variable in the consumption and savings functions. This assumption will be revised in later chapters.

Shifts in the LM function

Similarly a change in the parameters of the demand for money or supply of money functions will shift the *LM* schedule. The exogenous variables which can cause such shifts are:

1. The nominal stock of money.
2. The price level, as this affects the real value of the money stock.
3. Expectations about the future returns from holding bonds; these affect the demand to hold money.
4. Payments habits; these influence the relationship between the stock of real money balances held to finance transactions and the level of real national income.

Figure 3.8 shows the effect of an increase in the stock of nominal money balances, given a constant price level, P_0. The original nominal money supply is M_0^S, for which the corresponding *LM* function is $LM_0{:}P = P_0$. The nominal money supply is increased to M_1^S. The real money supply then increases by an equivalent amount since the price level is constant. In order for the demand for money at each level of output to equal the increased supply of money, the rate of interest must be lower. Thus when output is y_0 the interest rate must now be i_0' for monetary equilibrium. The *LM* curve has therefore shifted down to the right. If the money supply were reduced, the *LM* function would shift up to the left.

A rightwards shift in the *LM* function also occurs if the stock of real money balances is increased by a fall in the price level with the nominal money stock held constant. The new money supply function would be labelled $M_0^S/P_1(P_1 < P_0)$ and the new *LM* schedule would be labelled $LM_0{:}P = P_1$. A shift in the demand for money function which decreased the demand for money

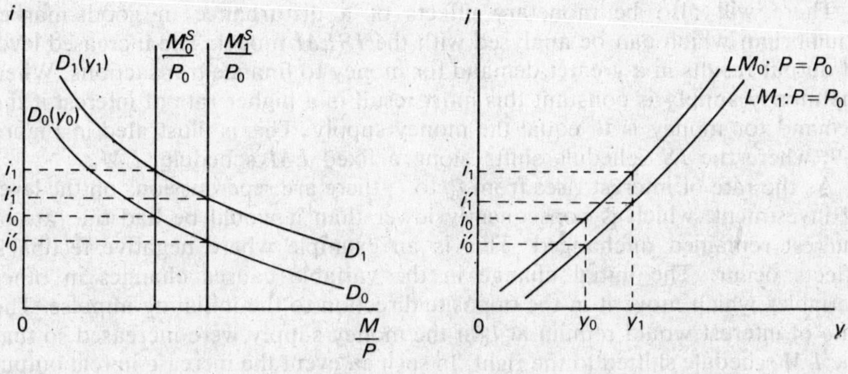

FIGURE 3.8 *Shift in the LM function due to a change in the supply of money*

would also cause a rightwards shift in the *LM* function since at any given level of output, say y_0, the rate of interest required to equate the demand for money with the money supply would be lower.

3.5 Comparative-static analysis: the Keynesian model

Shifts in the IS schedule

An increase in either investment or consumption will shift the *IS* function upwards to the right, as is shown in Figure 3.9, where the *IS* schedule shifts from IS_0 to IS_1. A new equilibrium is established at i_1, y_1. As in the one-sector Keynesian model, an increase in aggregate demand gives rise to an increase in national output. This is the familiar multiplier effect and is an example of positive feedback: the initial impulse, an increase in aggregate demand, causes changes which move the initiating variable in the same direction.

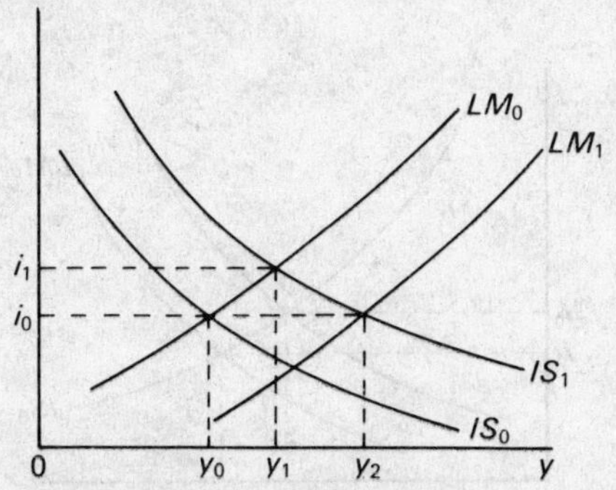

FIGURE 3.9 *The impact of negative feedback from the monetary sector on the size of the expenditure multiplier*

There will also be monetary effects of a disturbance in goods-market equilibrium which can be analysed with the *ISLM* model. The increased level of output results in a greater demand for money to finance transactions. When the money supply is constant this must result in a higher rate of interest if the demand for money is to equal the money supply. This is illustrated in Figure 3.9, where the *IS* schedule shifts along a fixed *LM* schedule, LM_0.

As the rate of interest rises from i_0 to i_1 there are repercussions on the level of investment, which is consequently lower than it would be had the rate of interest remained unchanged. This is an example where negative feedback effects occur. The initial change in the variable causes changes in other variables which move it in the opposite direction to the initiating impulse. The rate of interest would remain at i_0 if the money supply were increased so that the *LM* schedule shifted to the right. In such an event the increase in real output would be greater, rising to y_2 since there are no disincentive effects of a higher interest rate on investment. If the rate of interest remains unchanged, the expenditure multiplier is the same size as it is in the simple one-sector Keynesian model. The multiplier is smaller, the more the interest rate changes as a result of the larger transactions demand for money consequent upon the increase in output.

The interest rate will rise further, the steeper the slope of the *LM* schedule, i.e. the more interest-inelastic is the demand for money. If the demand for money were perfectly elastic with respect to the rate of interest, the *LM* schedule would be horizontal and the upwards shift in the *IS* function would increase output to y_2. Provided that the *LM* schedule does slope upwards, the size of the expenditure multiplier is smaller than in the one-sector Keynesian model.

A decrease in investment or consumption will shift the *IS* function downwards to the left and decrease output and the interest rate.

Shifts in the LM function

An increase in the nominal supply of money will shift the *LM* schedule downwards and to the right, from LM_0 to LM_1, as shown in Figure 3.10.

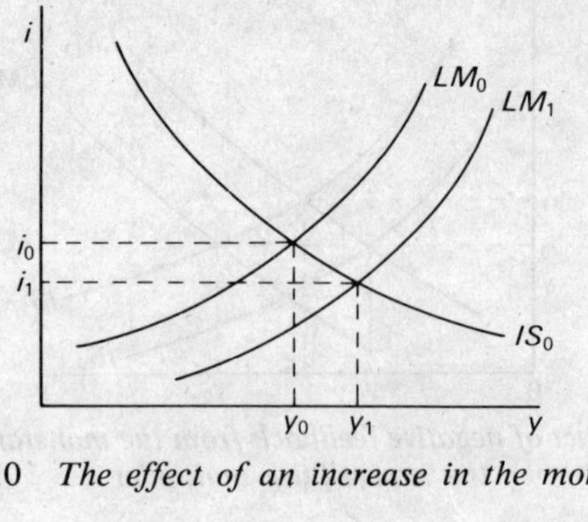

FIGURE 3.10 *The effect of an increase in the money supply*

The increase in the money stock means that at interest rate i_0 the demand for money is less than the amount actually held. Consequently the demand for bonds increases, driving up the price of bonds and hence lowering the interest rate. (The bond price and the interest rate always move in opposite directions.) A lower interest rate stimulates investment, so that if other exogenous variables stay unchanged then output rises. Conversely, an upwards shift to the left of the *LM* function will increase the interest rate and lower output.

3.6 Comparative-static analysis: the neoclassical model

The analysis just undertaken with the Keynesian model assumed that output was in the range where it could be expanded at a fixed price level. Once full employment of resources is reached the Keynesian and neoclassical models converge.

Shifts in the IS function

Suppose that investment or consumption increases but the level of output is in equilibrium at its full-employment level, y_f, where IS_0 and $LM:P = P_0$ intersect in Figure 3.11. The *IS* schedule now shifts up to IS_1. At the initial interest-rate and price level there is now excess aggregate demand. Consequently the price level rises. As it does so the quantity of real money balances falls and the *LM* function shifts to the left, eventually reaching its new equilibrium position at $LM:P = P_1$. Once the price level has risen to P_1 and the interest rate to i_1, the demand for money has fallen sufficiently to now equal the reduced stock of real money balances. There is no change in real output. The rise in the interest rate has a disincentive effect on investment that exactly offsets the initial increase in aggregate demand which set off the process.

A reduction in aggregate demand which shifted the *IS* function to the left would cause prices to fall. Here the analysis of the neoclassical model is quite

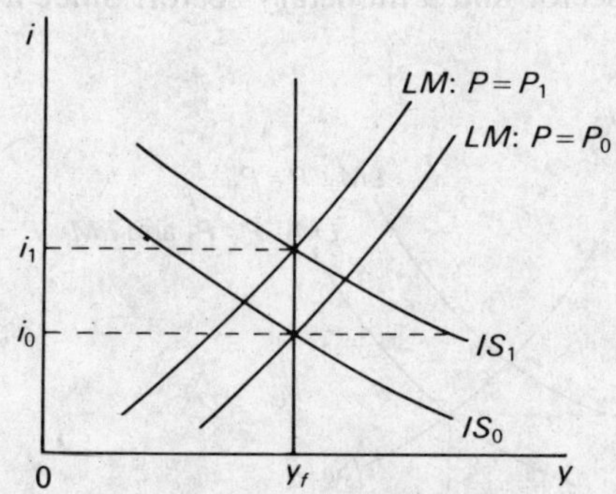

FIGURE 3.11 *The effect of an increase in investment demand when the economy is fully employed*

different from the Keynesian model, in which the price level is fixed. To see the contrasting conclusions of the two models, look again at Figure 3.11. Assume the initial equilibrium is at i_1, y_f, where $LM:P = P_1$ and IS_1 intersect. When the IS_1 schedule shifts down to IS_0 there is deficient aggregate demand. Consequently the price level falls and the real value of the money supply rises. The *LM* schedule shifts down to the right. As the real money stock increases the interest falls in order to preserve monetary equilibrium. The fall in the rate of interest stimulates investment, output rises and so does consumption. Aggregate demand rises until it is again equal to y_f. Equilibrium at full employment has been restored by means of price flexibility. This is in contrast to the Keynesian model, in which the price level remains fixed and a decrease in aggregate demand leaves the economy stuck in an equilibrium in which both labour and capital resources are underutilised. The reasons underlying the Keynesian assumption of price rigidity and the issue of whether this is the only factor giving rise to Keynesian under full-employment equilibrium will be explored in later chapters.

Shifts in the LM function

A decrease in the nominal stock of money is shown to shift the *LM* function upwards from $LM_1:P = P_1$ to $LM_0:P = P_1$ in Figure 3.12. Initially with the lower money stock there is deficient aggregate demand because the rise in the interest rate reduces investment. Consequently the price level falls until the real value of the money supply has returned to its original level. The *LM* function therefore shifts back to its original position but is now labelled $LM_0:P = P_0$. The nominal money stock and the price level have fallen by the same proportion. Again price flexibility guarantees the restoration of output at an equilibrium, full-employment level.

3.7 Conclusion

In this chapter we have introduced the *ISLM* model, which is characterised by having both a goods sector and a monetary sector. Since it has only two inde-

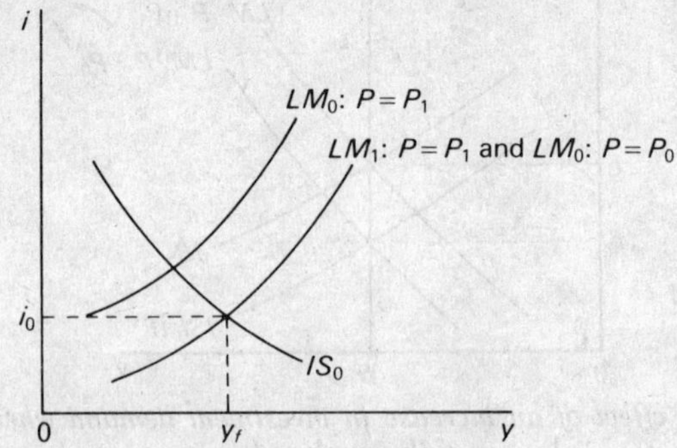

FIGURE 3.12 *The effect of a reduction in the money supply in a neoclassical model*

pendent markets it can only solve for two endogenous variables. The Keynesian version of the model treats output and the interest rate as endogenous, assuming the price level fixed until full employment is reached. At this point the Keynesian and neoclassical *ISLM* models converge. The neoclassical version of the model treats the price level and the interest rate as endogenous variables. The differences between the two models are only really apparent when aggregate demand falls below the full-employment level of output. When different supply-side responses are assumed, price flexibility in the neoclassical model allows the real quantity of money to adjust and so restore the equilibrium level of aggregate demand to the full-employment level. Behind the scenes price flexibility in individual product markets enables supply and demand to be brought into equilibrium.

The *ISLM* model so far constructed has a number of limitations:

1. It has no government or foreign trade sectors. These are introduced in Chapters 4 and 7 respectively.
2. It cannot solve for output, the interest rate and the price level simultaneously. This is achieved by adding the labour market (see Chapter 6).
3. It is entirely concerned with positions of static equilibrium.

This last point is very important. Although we have sketched out some of the adjustment mechanisms by which the model moves from one position of static equilibrium to another, we have not got a dynamic specification which allows us to trace the time path of the endogenous variables. As the economy is constantly experiencing random shocks, analysed as changes in the exogenous variables in an economic model, we know that it is almost always out of comparative-static equilibrium. It is extremely important for policy-makers to know the adjustment path followed by the economy. A knowledge of its comparative-static equilibrium properties, although essential, is not sufficient for the successful implementation of macroeconomic policies.

If the aggregate demand functions were continually shifting, in particular if the marginal propensity to consume and the relationship between the demand to hold money and the level of income and the interest rate were frequently changing, this degree of instability would make it extremely difficult for policy-makers to know what to do. A certain amount of stability in these functions is required in order to know how to implement macroeconomic policies successfully. On the other hand, complete stability in the form of no changes in the exogenous variables would remove the need for such policy actions.

References

[1] J. R. Hicks, 'Mr Keynes and the "Classics": A Suggested Interpretation', *Econometrica*, 5 (April 1937) 147–59.

[2] J. Gurley and E. Shaw, *Money in a Theory of Finance* (Washington, D.C.: Brookings Institution, 1960).

4 Fiscal and Monetary Policy Analysis in an *ISLM* Model

By adding the government sector to the *ISLM* model we can use it to start analysing the role and effectiveness of fiscal and monetary policies. The advocacy of deliberate government action to regulate the level of aggregate demand is the hallmark of Keynesian economics. In orthodox Keynesian analysis the economy can get stuck at an equilibrium level of output which is below the full-employment level. Here the government is able to restore full employment by raising the level of aggregate demand. It can do this by either increasing government expenditure, reducing taxation which raises consumers' demand or by increasing the money supply. Inflation caused by excess aggregate demand can be controlled by the converse set of policies which reduce the level of aggregate demand.

Government action to stabilise economic activity by stimulating it in a recession and reducing it in an inflationary boom is known as 'fine-tuning'. It is further characterised as discretionary policy because the government makes deliberate policy changes in response to particular economic circumstances.

4.1 The *ISLM* model with the government sector

The analysis of the effect of the government sector on the economy can be readily incorporated into the *ISLM* model. Consumption and saving now become functions of disposable income, *yd* (that is, income after tax). Government expenditure, G_0, is assumed exogenous, while for simplicity the government's tax revenues, *T*, are assumed to be proportional to national income, the factor of proportionality being the tax rate, *t*. The savings function is given by equation 4.1:

$$S = -a + syd \tag{4.1}$$

And

$$yd = y - T \tag{4.2}$$

$$T = ty \tag{4.3}$$

Substituting 4.2 and 4.3 into 4.1 we obtain

$$S = -a + s(1 - t)y \tag{4.4}$$

Aggregate demand now includes government expenditure as well as investment and consumption, so that goods-market equilibrium requires

$$y = E = C + I + G_0 \tag{4.5}$$

Disposable income is divided between saving and consumption:

$$yd = y - T = C + S \tag{4.6}$$

Therefore

$$y = C + S + T \tag{4.7}$$

Substituting 4.7 into 4.5 and removing C from both sides of the equation shows that goods-market equilibrium requires

$$S + T = I + G_0 \tag{4.8}$$

Substituting 4.4 and 4.3 into 4.8 we obtain the equation for the *IS* function:

$$I(i) + G_0 = -a + s(1 - t)y + ty \tag{4.9}$$

The geometrical derivation of the *IS* function (4.9) is shown in Figure 4.1.

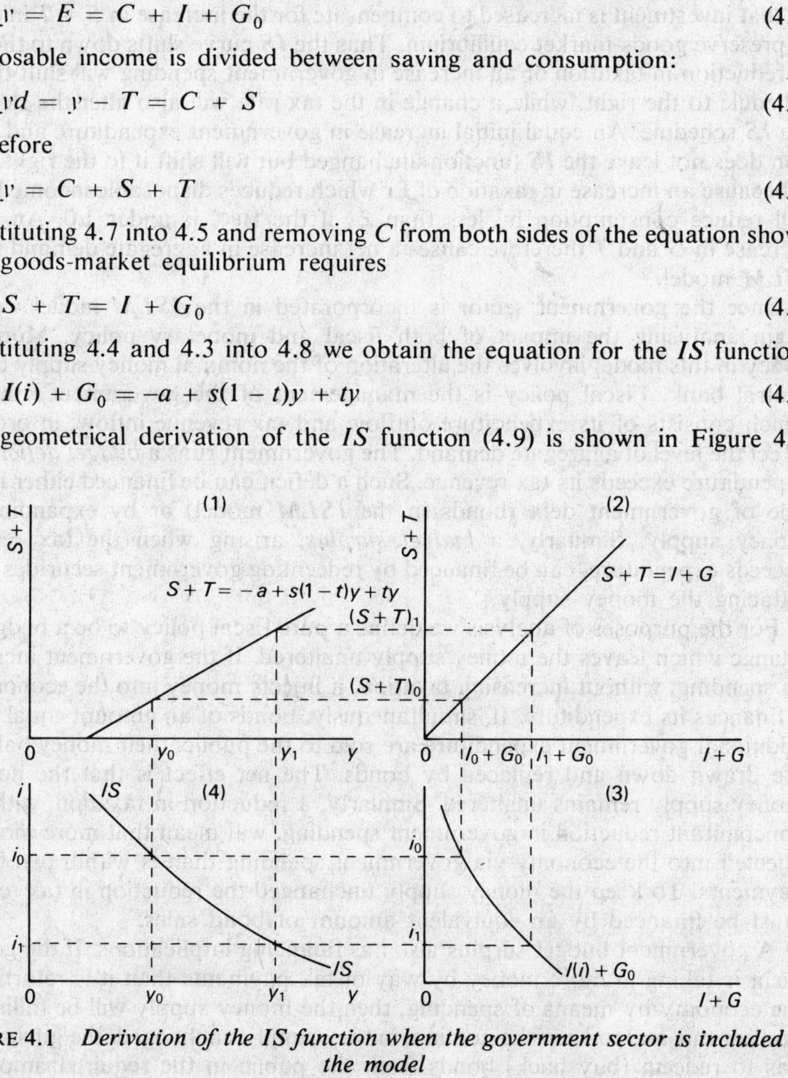

FIGURE 4.1 *Derivation of the IS function when the government sector is included in the model*

Quadrant 1 indicates the level of savings plus tax that is associated with various real income levels. If the level of real output is y_0, the level of savings plus tax would be $(S + T)_0$. Quadrant 2 shows that, to equal $(S + T)_0$, investment plus government expenditure must be $I_0 + G_0$. The rate of interest required to bring this about is i_0. Thus we get one particular combination of the interest rate and output level which gives goods-market equilibrium. If we repeat the procedure for another level of income, y_1, we get another point on the *IS* schedule.

An increase in the tax rate will cause the $S + T$ function to swing towards the left. This means that for each output level a lower interest rate is required, so that investment is increased to compensate for the increase in $S + T$ in order to preserve goods-market equilibrium. Thus the *IS* curve shifts down to the left. A reduction in taxation or an increase in government spending will shift the *IS* schedule to the right, while a change in the tax rate will also alter the slope of the *IS* schedule. An equal initial increase in government expenditure and taxation does not leave the *IS* function unchanged but will shift it to the right. This is because an increase in taxation of £*x* which reduces disposable income by £*x* will reduce consumption by less than £*x* if the MPC. is under 1.0. An equal increase in *G* and *T* therefore causes a net increase in aggregate demand in the *ISLM* model.

Once the government sector is incorporated in the *ISLM* model we can begin analysing the impact of both fiscal and monetary policy. Monetary policy in this model involves the alteration of the nominal money supply by the central bank. Fiscal policy is the management of the government's budget, which consists of its expenditure outflow and tax revenue inflow, in order to affect the level of aggregate demand. The government runs a *budget deficit* if its expenditure exceeds its tax revenue. Such a deficit can be financed either by the sale of government debt (bonds in the *ISLM* model) or by expanding the money supply. Similarly, a *budget surplus*, arising when the tax revenue exceeds expenditure, can be financed by redeeming government securities or by reducing the money supply.

For the purposes of analysis we define a pure fiscal policy to be a budgetary change which leaves the money supply unaltered. If the government increases its spending, without increasing taxation, it injects money into the economy as it finances its expenditure. If, simultaneously, bonds of an amount equal to the additional government expenditure are sold to the public, their money balances are drawn down and replaced by bonds. The net effect is that the nominal money supply remains unaltered. Similarly, a reduction in taxation, without a concomitant reduction in government spending, will mean that more money is injected into the economy via government spending than is withdrawn by tax payments. To keep the money supply unchanged the reduction in tax revenue must be financed by an equivalent amount of bond sales.

A government budget surplus also has financing implications. If the government is taking in more money by way of tax payments than it is returning to the economy by means of spending, then the money supply will be falling. To prevent this and to keep the nominal money supply unchanged, the government has to redeem (buy back) bonds from the public in the required amount.

The assumption of a pure fiscal policy measure is an analytical device that enables us to separate out the effects of changes in government spending and taxation from the effects of changes in the money supply. In practice, a change in fiscal policy is likely to have implications for the supply of money.

4.2 Policy analysis in a Keynesian model

Fiscal and monetary policy will be examined in the context of a Keynesian model with idle resources. This means that an expansion of aggregate demand will cause an increase in real output.

Fiscal policy

An expansionary pure fiscal policy caused by either an increase in government expenditure or by a reduction in taxation will shift the *IS* schedule upwards to the right, as shown in Figure 4.2. Because we have assumed a pure fiscal policy, the resulting government budget deficit is financed by bond sales to the public. The assumption of an unchanged money supply allows us to assume that the *LM* curve does not shift as it would if the money supply were increased in order to finance the fiscal deficit. The increased government spending, or increased private spending due to a tax cut, stimulates output, which increases from y_0 to y_1. The interest rate also rises for the same reasons previously discussed when analysing an upwards shift in *IS*. At a higher level of income the demand for money would exceed the unchanged money supply if the rate of interest remained unaltered. At a rate of interest of i_1 and an income level of y_1 the demand for money is once more equal to the supply of money.

The increase in the interest rate following a fiscal expansion will be greater, the more interest-inelastic is the demand for money, since a larger change in the interest rate is required to persuade people to hold a given money stock at a higher level of income. This is shown in Figure 4.3.

D_0^E and D_0^I are alternative demand for money functions with respect to the rate of interest when output is held constant at y_0. D_0^E is more elastic than D_0^I. The demand and supply of money are initially in equilibrium when output is y_0

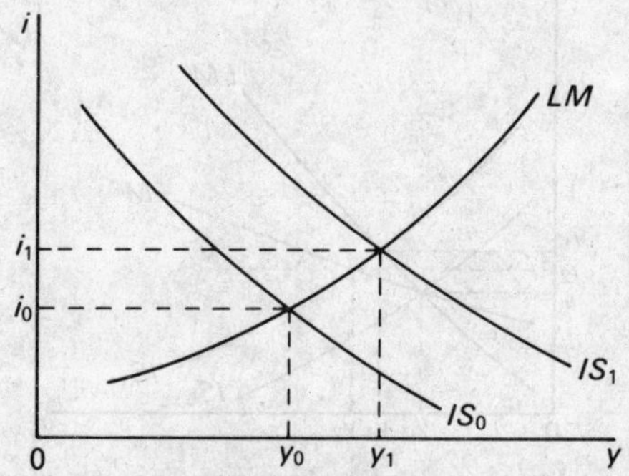

FIGURE 4.2 *An expansionary, pure fiscal policy*

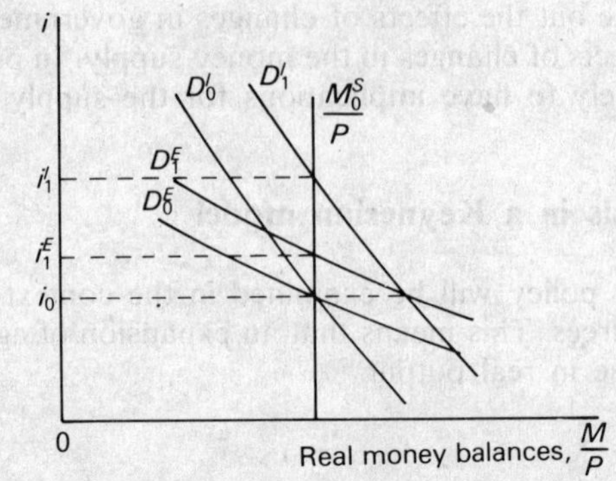

FIGURE 4.3 *The size of the change in the rate of interest consequent upon a change in the demand for money increases as the demand for money becomes more interest-inelastic*

and the interest rate is i_0. Output then increases to y_1 due to expansionary fiscal policy. D_0^E shifts up to D_1^E, and D_0^I. Each demand schedule shifts by the same horizontal distance. In the case of the more elastic function the rate of interest rises only to i_1^E to equate the increased demand for money with the constant money stock. If the demand for money is less interest-elastic, the rate of interest will rise further to i_1^I.

We have thus seen from Figure 4.3 that the change in the rate of interest required to maintain monetary equilibrium when output changes is greater, the more interest-inelastic is the demand for money. This means that the slope of the *LM* function is steeper, the more interest-inelastic is the demand for money.

Since the increase in the rate of interest following a given expansionary fiscal policy is greater, the more interest-inelastic is the demand for money, the resulting increase in real output is smaller. This is due to the larger contractionary impact of the interest rate on private investment. This point is illustrated by Figure 4.4. Expansionary fiscal policy shifts the *IS* schedule from IS_0 to IS_1.

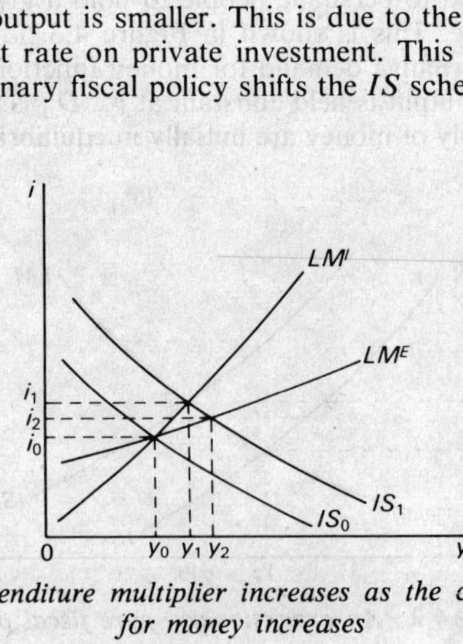

FIGURE 4.4 *The expenditure multiplier increases as the elasticity of the demand for money increases*

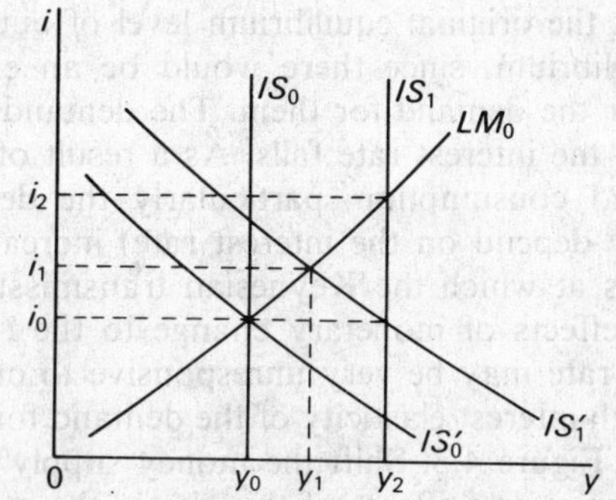

FIGURE 4.5 *Fiscal policy is more effective, the less interest-elastic is investment*

In the case of a relatively elastic money demand function the *LM* schedule is LM^E. The rate of interest rises only to i_2, and hence real output increases as far as y_2. The fiscal policy multiplier is larger than if the money demand function is more interest-inelastic. The relevant *LM* schedule is then LM^I, the interest rate rises further to i_1 and consequently the rise in output to y_1 is smaller.

The effectiveness of fiscal policy would not be impaired at all by an increase in the interest rate if investment were perfectly unresponsive to interest-rate changes. If investment is autonomous (unrelated to income or the rate of interest), the *IS* schedule would be vertical. Only one level of income would produce the level of saving equal to the volume of autonomous investment. Figure 4.5 illustrates the case when investment is perfectly interest-inelastic; the fiscal policy multiplier is the same size as in the one-sector Keynesian model (output rises by y_0y_2). The multiplier diminishes as the interest elasticity of investment increases.

With the same fiscal expansion, output only increases by y_0y_1 when investment is interest-responsive and the *IS* function is downward-sloping. We have therefore deduced that the fiscal policy multiplier is larger

(a) the more interest-elastic is the demand for money,
(b) the less interest-elastic is the demand for investment goods.

Monetary policy

A standard method of changing the money supply is for the central bank to engage in open-market operations in government securities. To increase the money supply the central bank buys bonds from the public. In order to persuade the public to hold fewer bonds and more money, the government has to raise the price of bonds, i.e. to lower the rate of interest. This means that the interest rate falls in the process of monetary expansion and rises if there is monetary contraction.

The *ISLM* model presented here features the usual Keynesian transmission mechanism whereby monetary policy affects aggregate output. An increase in the money supply at the original equilibrium level of output and interest rate would cause disequilibrium, since there would be an excess supply of real money balances over the demand for them. The demand for bonds increases, bond prices rise and the interest rate falls. As a result of the reduced interest rate, investment (and consumption, particularly the demand for consumer durables, which may depend on the interest rate) increases and output rises. There are two points at which the Keynesian transmisstion mechanism may fail to transmit the effects of monetary change to the real sector.

First, the interest rate may be very unresponsive to changes in the money supply due to the high interest elasticity of the demand for money. This can be seen by reference to Figure 4.3. Shift the money supply function to the right and compare the interest-rate effects of this rise in the money stock along D_0^E and D_0^I. If the demand for money function is interest-elastic (D_0^E), the interest rate will not fall as much as if the demand for money function is more interest-inelastic (D_0^I). The more interest-elastic is the demand for money, the less the interest rate falls for a given increase in the money supply and the less stimulus there consequently is to investment. This means a smaller increase in national output.

A second factor which would render monetary policy ineffective would be the unresponsiveness of investment and consumption to interest-rate changes. Even if an increase in the money supply caused a fall in the interest rate, this would have little effect on aggregate demand or, consequently, on output.

In conclusion, then, the size of the money multiplier (that is, the increase in national income due to an increase in the money supply) is larger

(a) the less interest-elastic is the demand for money, and
(b) the more interest-elastic is the demand for investment goods.

These conclusions emerge from specifying a Keynesian transmission mechanism which has two distinctive features. It is restricted to a limited number of financial assets (a single one, bonds, in the *ISLM* model) and is indirect because monetary changes only affect demand via a prior change in interest rates.

Monetarists who work within the neoclassical framework stress a more direct and widely diffused transmission mechanism. If the demand and supply of money are out of equilibrium, then adjustment occurs across a wide range of assets, including goods. Hence the demand for goods and services is a direct function of any discrepancy between demand for money and the actual stock of money.

4.3 Policy analysis in a neoclassical model

The justification for discretionary fiscal and monetary policies to regulate the level of aggregate demand is either much weaker in the neoclassical view or even non-existent. As the economy is capable of self-adjustment, the only justification is that a change in the government's fiscal stance or in its monetary policy would speed up and/or smooth out the process of adjustment. This rationale for macroeconomic policies applies also in a Keynesian world, but there the possibility of an under-full-employment equilibrium provides an additional and stronger reason.

This chapter is restricted to comparative-static analysis so it does not develop the dynamic analysis required to explore the role of fiscal and monetary policies in speeding up adjustment.

Fiscal policy and 'crowding out'

In the neoclassical *ISLM* model fiscal policy cannot alter the level of real national output; it only affects the price level and the interest rate. This result is shown in Figure 4.6. The *IS* schedule is moved up from IS_0 to IS_1, by increased government expenditure or by reduced taxation. This is financed by bond sales, so the nominal money supply remains unchanged at M_0. Excess aggregate demand results, the price level rises, reducing the real value of the money stock and shifting the *LM* function up to the left. In order to equate the now smaller stock of real balances with the demand for real balances the interest rate must rise to i_1. The higher interest rate chokes off some private-sector investment. If the expansionary fiscal policy involves reduced taxation, the rise in the interest rate would serve to channel resources away from investment and into additional consumption. If increased government expenditure is the cause of the shift in the *IS* schedule, then the rise in the interest rate chokes off some private-sector investment in order to make room for additional public-sector expenditure. This effect is known as *crowding out* because resources are taken away from the private sector in order to meet the requirements of public-sector expenditure. The rise in the interest rate is the mechanism by which this occurs.

A reduction in government spending or an increase in taxation would have exactly the opposite effects. The *IS* function in Figure 4.6 would shift from IS_1 to IS_0, the price level would fall, shifting the *LM* schedule down from $LM'_0 : P = P_1$ to $LM_0 : P = P_0$ and the interest rate would fall. In a neoclassical *ISLM* model fiscal policy therefore has no effect on the equilibrium level of

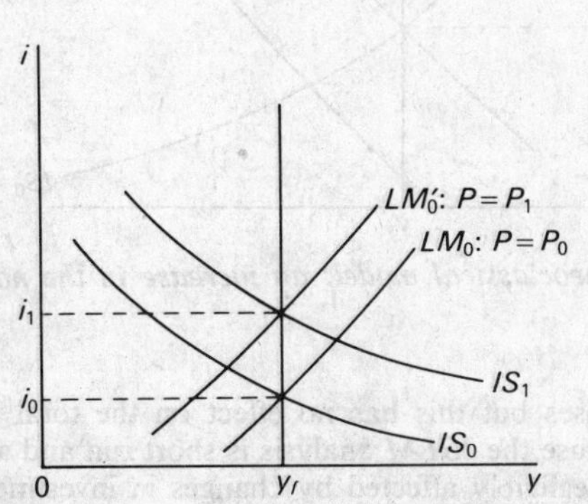

FIGURE 4.6 *Fiscal policy and 'crowding out'*

real output but effects the division of that output between the public and private sectors and between consumption and investment.[1]

Monetary policy

In the neoclassical *ISLM* model changes in the money supply only affect the equilibrium price level and have no impact on the equilibrium values of the real variables, the interest rate and the level of income. Figure 4.7 shows the effect of an increase in the nominal stock of money which shifts the *LM* schedule down to the right from $LM_0 : P = P_0$ to $LM_1 : P = P_0$. The increase in the nominal money supply disturbs monetary equilibrium; money balances are in excess supply. The consequent movement into bonds reduces the interest rate, aggregate demand is stimulated and the price level rises. The price level reaches a new equilibrium value of P_1, once it has risen sufficiently to reduce the real money stock back to the level at which it once more equals the quantity of real balances demanded at the equilibrium interest rate and output level, i_0 and y_f. Equilibrium is regained once the *LM* schedule has returned to its original position. During the adjustment from one equilibrium position to another real income and employment will be affected, but these will return to their former values once the price level has attained its new equilibrium.

If the monetary authorities kept on increasing the nominal stock of money, the process just outlined would be repeated with the price level continuously rising. A distinctive feature of neoclassical analysis is that inflation is caused by excessive monetary expansion and that controlling the money supply is the key to reducing inflation. As was pointed out in the earlier discussion of government budget deficit financing, one way to finance the budget is by expanding

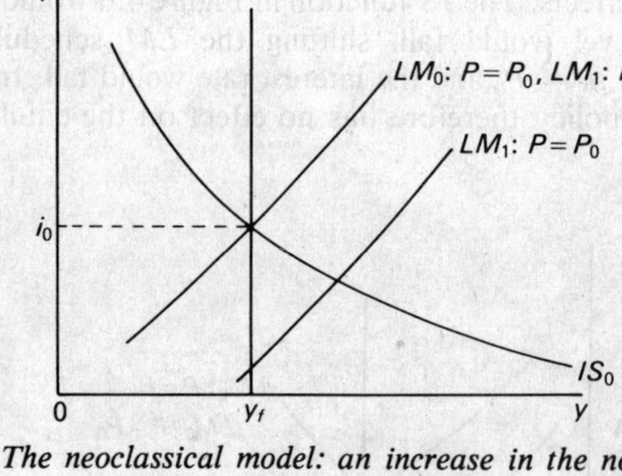

FIGURE 4.7 *The neoclassical model: an increase in the nominal money supply*

[1] The interest rate rises but this has no effect on the total amount of real output supplied. This is because the *ISLM* analysis is short run and assumes that the size of the capital stock is negligibly affected by changes in investment. This assumption is removed in Chapters 15 and 21.

the money supply. Government budget deficit financing is a major source of monetary expansion. This is why the desire to control the money supply in order to reduce inflation translates into the need to reduce the budget deficit, or public sector borrowing requirement as it is alternatively called. Even if the budget deficit is financed by bond sales, the neoclassical *ISLM* model developed here shows that to be inflationary as well, though less so than a money-financed budget deficit.

4.4 The role and relative effectiveness of fiscal and monetary policy

Part of the debate between Keynesians and monetarists has centred on the relative effectiveness of fiscal and monetary policy as deduced from comparative-static analysis. In section 4.2 we made the following deductions:

1. The size of the fiscal policy multiplier is larger (i) the more interest-elastic is the demand for money, and (ii) the less interest-elastic is the demand for investment goods.
2. The size of the money multiplier is larger (i) the less interest-elastic is the demand for money, and (ii) the more interest-elastic is the demand for investment goods.

So it can be seen that the factors which make for effective fiscal policy are the same as those which render monetary policy less effective and vice versa.

Keynesian views

Typically Keynesians have held that fiscal policy is a much more effective policy tool, and this view was particularly strong in the early years of Keynesianism. At its most extreme the demand for money was depicted as perfectly interest-elastic, a condition known as the *liquidity trap* which gives rise to a horizontal *LM* schedule. In addition, investment (and consumption) were regarded as more or less invariant with respect to the interest rate.

A less extreme position is the Keynesian–neoclassical synthesis found in many textbook expositions, which holds that these interest elasticities vary with the state of economic activity. In a deep recession the demand for money will be pretty interest-elastic (the *LM* schedule is therefore horizontal or nearly so). As the economy moves towards full employment, the interest elasticity of the demand for money falls toward zero when the *LM* schedule becomes vertical or nearly so at full employment.

The Keynesian attitude towards fiscal policy was particularly strong in Britain in the 1940s and, although the Conservative administration of the early 1950s paid greater attention to monetary policy, its importance waned. It was really not until the mid-1970s that monetary policy was taken more seriously in Britain. This can be attributed to the combined effects of the influence of the neoclassical revival in academic economics in the form of monetarism and the consequences of the ill-fated 1970–3 Barber boom. The then Conservative Chancellor of the Exchequer tried to boost economic growth by means of an orthodox Keynesian fiscal expansion during which the money supply was allowed to grow extremely rapidly (by normal British standards). In 1972 and 1973 the money supply grew at an annual rate of 26 and 28 per cent (as measured by the broad definition of the money supply, M_3). Subsequently from 1974 to 1977 the rate of inflation rose to its highest levels since the First World War. By that time the boom had already burst as a result of internal supply bottlenecks, balance-of-payments problems, and concern at the rising inflation rate, which was exacerbated by the first OPEC oil price hike of 1973. The subsequent Labour government felt constrained by the need to keep the public sector borrowing requirement under some kind of control in order to prevent excessively rapid monetary growth. The move away from post-war Keynesian-style demand management was finally completed when the Conservative government under Mrs Thatcher adopted as the chief plank of its economic policy a steady reduction in the rate of monetary growth.

The USA has a similar history of adoption and discarding of Keynesian ideas, though Keynesian policies were not espoused until Kennedy became President in 1960. At first the Keynesian prescription seemed to work and the level of unemployment, which by British standards had been moderately high in the 1950s, fell. The impact of financing the Vietnam war in addition to the earlier fiscal stimulus led to higher inflation and balance-of-payments deficits, ultimately accompanied by even higher unemployment levels than those experienced in the 1950s. An explicitly non-Keynesian economic policy programme found favour with the electors in 1980.

Neoclassical views

The growing body of post-war academic work in the neoclassical tradition gradually influenced politicians and broke the earlier consensus regarding demand-management policies. There was a decisive swing away from Keynesian macroeconomic policies by a number of Western governments in the late 1970s and early 1980s. This period of Keynesian decline has also seen an extension in the use of private monopoly power accompanied by an increase in micro-level government intervention. Neither of these interrelated developments appeals to those of neoclassical persuasions who see the growth of rigidities in the market mechanism and of extra-market power as major sources of our current macroeconomic problems. So the neoclassical revival in economic policy is far from complete, but the alternative that is gaining ground is not so much Keynesianism but variants of corporatism in which the major economic decision-makers are the state and other powerful interest groups.

The neoclassical resurgence in macroeconomics has, over the years, evolved a number of facets. One has been to emphasise the importance of monetary policy and to downgrade that of fiscal policy.

The crowding-out issue has been one focus of this debate. Crowding out is a revival of the pre-war 'notorious' Treasury view which refuted Keynes's argument that public works could reduce unemployment. Keynesians had regarded this issue as dead and buried. The fact that crowding out will occur at full employment is not a matter for dispute. But the extent to which it will diminish the effectiveness of fiscal policy when resources are not fully employed has been a source of disagreement. If the analysis is restricted to the comparative-static *ISLM* analysis we have conducted so far, then the degree of crowding out increases as the size of the fiscal policy multiplier falls. So crowding out is greater the less interest-elastic is the demand for money and the more interest-elastic is investment.

Trying to establish the size of these elasticities is an empirical matter. In the post-war period hundreds, if not thousands of econometric studies have been made, spawned by ever-expanding computer facilities. The impact of these is reviewed in later chapters. For now we can note that the extreme Keynesian views regarding the interest elasticities of the demand for money and of investment have not been upheld.

The debate between Keynesians and neoclassicists has now moved on from the relative effectiveness of fiscal and monetary policy to the question of whether Keynesian macroeconomic policies are even feasible.

One aspect of the neoclassical critique is that the lags between changes in one variable which result in changes in another are both long and very imperfectly known. Given the complexities and uncertainties surrounding our knowledge of how the economy works, the government is most unlikely to be able to fine-tune the economy. Its knowledge of when to act, with what variables and by how much is totally inadequate to enable discretionary macro policies to have the desired effect.

A further critique of Keynesian economic policy models is that they assume that the existence of government policy does not modify the behaviour of individual agents so as to alter the coefficients (parameters) of the structural equations constituting the model. According to this critique, macroeconomic models should incorporate *rationally formed expectations* of economic agents about the future values of variables. Expectations are rational when they are formed by using the model of the economy which is thought to explain its workings. The application of the *rational expectations hypothesis* to macroeconomics has been an important development in the last few years. Models incorporating fully rational expectations have been developed to show that both fiscal and monetary policy will have no impact at all on the real variables if the government's policy reaction to economic events has been forecast by the private sector. Rational expectations models are examined in greater detail in Chapters 18, 19 and 22.

We can thus distinguish three facets of the neoclassical critique of Keynesian economic policy:

1. Monetary policy is more important than fiscal policy. This is demonstrated by an appeal to empirical evidence on the relevant interest elasticities which are interpreted by means of comparative-static equilibrium analysis in an *ISLM* model.
2. Discretionary fiscal and monetary policy cannot be successfully implemented because of insufficient knowledge of the dynamics of the economy.
3. Fiscal and monetary policy can have very little impact on the real variables because of the formation of rational expectations by private-sector decision-makers.

4.5 Extensions to the basic *ISLM* model

It cannot be emphasised too much that in economic analysis the conclusions depend crucially upon the assumptions made. We start out with some assumptions about what are the important variables to concentrate upon and what sort of behaviour motivates economic agents. The next process is that of making valid deductions on the basis of these assumptions. These deductions can only be faulted if they are logically incorrect. Whether or not these deductions can be applied and valid policy recommendations based on them depends on whether the necessarily simplifying assumptions upon which they rest capture sufficiently well the features of the real economy we are trying to model. There is no easy or direct test of this. Whether one thinks that the assumptions are adequate depends partly on a subjective interpretation of one's own observations of how the economy appears to work. A further test is to confront the deductions with the empirical evidence. In the methodology of positive economics this is regarded as the only scientifically valid approach. Unfortunately, econometric testing does not in practice eliminate enough hypotheses and there still remain contending theories to choose between.

Given the limitations of empirical testing pure theorising has a vital role to play in helping us to choose between rival explanations or policy recommendations. This is to see how robust the conclusions are when the assumptions are changed. If conclusions do change when alternative assumptions are specified, then it becomes more difficult not to remain agnostic.

The conclusions regarding the impact of fiscal and monetary policy which have been reached in this chapter are based upon particular assumptions which make up the 'basic' *ISLM* model in its Keynesian and neoclassical variants. At this point we would like to alert you to three types of assumption which, when altered, may affect the conclusions reached about monetary and fiscal policy.

(i) Instantaneous adjustment

The basic *ISLM* model contains no time lags. Each dependent variable in time t depends on the values of its determining variables in time t only. There is no role for the influence of past values. This means that adjustment from one equilibrium to another is instantaneous and we can only conduct comparative-static equilibrium analysis.

To undertake dynamic analysis we have to specify adjustment lags, for instance that it takes time for the demand for money to alter in response to interest-rate changes, and further time for investment plans to be revised. In dynamic analysis we also need to consider the repercussions of a change in one variable upon another and the feedback effects on the original variable. Take the example of an increase in the money supply which initially lowers the interest rate. The fall in the interest rate stimulates aggregate demand. Real output increases, the demand for transactions balances increases and the interest rate rises. This has a depressing impact on investment and output, which feeds back to the interest rate. Comparative-static analysis has nothing to say about the pattern of repercussions among variables; it only predicts the final outcome when equilibrium is re-established.

Comparative-static analysis is helpful in allowing us to make predictions about the long-run direction and size of a change in a variable, but any assessment of the methods of demand management must include knowledge of the ways in which the economy adjusts to fiscal and monetary measures. We have sketched out some adjustment mechanisms and indicated some possible policy conclusions that may stem from the existence of long and uncertain adjustment lags, but much more remains to be done by way of formal specification of adjustment lags and time paths.

(ii) Constant wealth

The basic *ISLM* model has assumed that wealth is constant. The problem with this assumption is that if the government runs a budget deficit (or surplus), and even if it finances this by selling (or buying) bonds to keep the money supply unchanged, the stock of bonds in private-sector hands rises (or falls) and therefore total private-sector wealth increases (or decreases).[1] The ratio of bonds to money also changes. This presupposes that some form of portfolio adjustment (that is, altering the ratio of bonds to money and moving from financial assets into real goods or vice versa) must occur. In other words, a government fiscal deficit or surplus cannot be consistent with long-run equilibrium. The effect of allowing for the requirement of government budget balance in long-run or full equilibrium is examined in Chapter 21.

Because we have assumed wealth constant in the 'basic' *ISLM* model we have not included wealth as a determinant of consumption. The only transmission mechanism linking changes in the money supply with changes in consumption and investment is the indirect Keynesian one in which people adjust to any excess demand or supply of money by respectively moving out of or into bonds. This affects the interest rate, which in turn influences investment and possibly the demand for consumer durables.

The monetarist transmission mechanism is both more direct and involves a wider range of assets, including real-goods assets as well as financial ones. In this view a change in the money supply will cause people to adjust directly via their expenditure on goods as well as via financial assets. This means that consumption depends upon wealth and is particularly affected by any discrepancy between the stock of real money balances consumers wish to hold and the amount they actually hold. The introduction of a wealth effect into the consumption function means that changes in the money supply have a more direct and diffuse impact on aggregate demand than that allowed for in the Keynesian transmission mechanism.

(iii) A closed economy

The basic *ISLM* model is a closed economy (that is, one with no foreign sector). This is in the spirit of Keynes's 'General Theory', which was developed

[1]If the private sector takes into account the present value of the future tax payments needed to service the additional government debt, then there is no increase in private-sector net wealth.

in the context of a closed economy, as was much early Keynesian theorising. Although the early post-war Keynesians extended the approach to international trade, they only took account of a limited range of adjustments, and the Keynesian message for domestic demand management continued for a long time to be taught to most students in the context of a closed-economy model. When the foreign sector was included only a limited range of impacts was allowed for, so that only incomplete adjustments had occurred in a state which purported to be an equilibrium one.

In the immediate post-war world this bias in theorising was not so misleading for policy purposes as it subsequently became because foreign trade and capital transactions were highly regulated by tariffs, quotas and exchange controls. These only gradually disappeared as the world emerged from the war. For most of the 1950s British trade was subject to exchange controls, which were not removed for trade in goods and services until 1958 (and not lifted on capital transactions until 1979). As these controls were dismantled and countries reconstructed their economies or became newly industrialised, foreign trade expanded so that individual economies became more and more interdependent.

It has therefore become increasingly necessary to analyse macroeconomic policies for Britain in terms of models of a relatively small open economy. Such models are introduced in the next section of the book.

In the remainder of this section we continue with the closed-economy assumption in order to focus attention on the labour market and on the analysis of unemployment. The addition of a third market to the *ISLM* model's goods and money markets enables us to remove one of that model's limitations. We can now solve for three endogenous variables: the interest rate, the level of real income, and the price level.

5 Unemployment and the Labour Market

Unemployment is an emotive issue and this is reflected in the terminology adopted in the economic analysis of unemployment. The Keynesian concept of *full employment* has already been used in the previous chapters but without any careful consideration of what it means. The social objective of achieving 'full employment' has had a powerful appeal in this century and, following the adoption of Keynesian economics, its maintenance has been treated as a prime responsibility of government. Only in the last decade has it become increasingly apparent that government policies are unable to produce the low rates of unemployment experienced in the 1950s and early 1960s. Consequently more attention is now being given to analysing the supply side of the economy. It is to this topic that we now turn, this chapter outlining Keynesian and neoclassical ideas on the determination of the level of unemployment. In doing so we consider whether full employment has a satisfactory theoretical definition and, if given such a definition, it is possible in practice to measure its appropriate level.

Keynes based his own analysis of unemployment on the neoclassical theory of the labour market. In the past Keynesians and neoclassicists have adopted the same approach to the demand side of the labour market but have differed over specifying the supply side of that market.

5.1 The demand for labour

The macro models we consider in section I are short run. They solve for a static equilibrium and hence abstract from growth. The short-run nature of these models is evident from their assumptions. The stock of capital, the labour force and the level of technical change are all assumed constant. In a long-run (growth) model all these are allowed to vary. A brief consideration of the long run is needed in order to derive the short-run demand for labour.

The long-run demand for labour

In the long run the level of output that can be produced depends on the quantities of labour and capital and on the state of technical knowledge. This relationship is expressed in terms of an aggregate production function:

$$y = f(L, K, T) \qquad (5.1)$$

where y is the real output per period of time, L is the *flow* of labour services used per period of time, K is the capital *stock* which yields a proportionate flow of capital services per period of time, and T is the state of technical knowledge.

This is a highly aggregated production function. National output is in effect treated as if it were made up of a single type of good. Labour and capital are each assumed to be homogeneous factors of production. Other factors of production do not enter the analysis at this level of aggregation since net national product is defined to be final output. Intermediate stages of production are netted out in the aggregation procedure and in an open economy imports of raw materials and intermediate goods are subtracted from the value of firms' production. Thus net national output is calculated as the value added by the application of labour and capital to raw materials.

In neoclassical theory labour and capital are assumed to be substitutable *ex ante*. This means that there is a whole range of possible production techniques, each representing a particular combination of labour and capital, available to produce a given level of output. Once a particular technique is chosen as being the least-cost technique at that time, capital becomes embodied in specific types of goods. This means that there is a smaller degree of substitutability between labour and capital *ex post* than *ex ante*.

In a growing economy equilibrium in the labour market can only be maintained at the current real wage if the stock of capital equipment grows in line with the expansion of the labour force. Unemployment will result if the labour force grows more rapidly than the stock of capital and if factor price adjustments fail to increase the demand for labour so that it matches the supply of labour. This kind of unemployment will not respond to increases in aggregate demand unless these are accompanied by a more rapid increase in the capital stock.

The short-run demand for labour

Since the stock of capital and the state of technology are regarded as fixed in the short run, output will vary only with the quantity of labour employed. The short-run aggregate production function is therefore written as

$$y = f(L, \bar{K}, \bar{T}) \qquad (5.2)$$

where $\bar{K}$ and $\bar{T}$ are constants.

The short-run demand for labour is derived from the short-run aggregate production function. In short-run macro models it is normally assumed that a certain degree of substitutability between capital and labour does exist in the short run so that the proportions in which the two factors are used may be varied. The marginal product of labour is positive but declines as employment increases. An additional assumption in the models of the type developed in section I is that the level of employment is not constrained by an insufficient stock of capital. Given that firms operate in perfectly competitive goods and labour markets, the price of goods and the wage rate will be unaffected by the amount of output produced by any single firm. The addition to marginal revenue from employing an extra unit of labour – the marginal revenue product of labour – is thus the marginal physical product of labour *times* the product price:

$$MPL \times P$$

At the aggregate level product price is replaced by a price index covering all goods and services. A profit-maximising firm will hire labour until the marginal revenue product of labour is just equal to the marginal cost of that labour unit which is its money wage rate, W. In symbols this statement is

$$MPL \times P = W$$

Dividing both sides by P we get

$$MPL = \frac{W}{P} = w = \text{the real wage rate}$$

The *real wage rate* per unit of labour is the money wage rate divided by the price of the product labour makes. It therefore measures the cost of labour in real terms since it is the number of physical units of output that can be exchanged for one time unit of work. When the additional units of output produced by hiring an extra unit of labour (MPL) exceed the marginal cost of labour in real terms (w) then a firm will make a positive profit on the marginal labour unit. Thus a profit-maximising firm will hire labour until the marginal product of labour equals the real wage rate. Given the assumption that the marginal product of labour is positive but declining as output increases in the short run, then the lower is the real wage, the greater will be firms' demand for labour. The demand for labour therefore varies inversely with the real wage rate, as shown in Figure 5.1 (p. 67) and is aggregated over all firms in the economy.

Mathematical derivation of short-run demand for labour

A firm's short-run profit function is

$$\pi = P\,y(L) - WL - TFC \tag{5.3}$$

where π is profits, P is the price of output or, on aggregation the price index, W is the money wage rate, $y(L)$ is the short-run production function, and TFC is total fixed costs.

Differentiating equation 5.3 with respect to the quantity of labour employed, L, we obtain the first-order condition for a profit maximum:

$$\frac{d\pi}{dL} = P\frac{dy}{dL} - W = 0 \tag{5.4}$$

Therefore

$$\frac{dy}{dL} = \frac{W}{P} \tag{5.5}$$

Equation 5.5 shows that profit-maximising firms in perfectly competitive product and labour markets will hire that quantity of labour for which the marginal product of labour, dy/dL, equals the real wage, W/P.

If the product market is imperfectly competitive, a firm's demand function being $P = P(y)$, a profit-maximising firm will equate the marginal product of labour with the ratio of the money wage to the marginal revenue, i.e.

$$\pi = P(y)y(L) - WL - TFC$$

$$\frac{d\pi}{dL} = P\frac{dy}{dL} + y\frac{dP}{dy}\frac{dy}{dL} - W = 0$$

$$P\frac{dy}{dL}\left[1 + \frac{y}{P}\frac{dP}{dy}\right] = W$$

$$\frac{dy}{dL} = \frac{W}{P\left(1 + \frac{dP}{dy}\frac{y}{p}\right)} = \frac{W}{P(1 + 1/e)}$$

where e is the price elasticity of demand for the firm's product. Therefore,

$$\frac{W}{P} = (1 + 1/e)\frac{dy}{dL} = (1 - k)\frac{dy}{dL}$$

where k is the degree of monopoly in the Lerner sense, i.e.[1]

$$k = \frac{P - \text{marginal cost}}{P}$$

If the factor market is also imperfectly competitive so that the wage rate the firm pays is $W = W(L)$, the result of profit maximisation will be

$$\frac{dy}{dL} = \frac{W}{P}\left[1 + 1\Big/\frac{dL}{dW}\frac{W}{L}\right]\Big/(1 - k)$$

where $(dL/dW)W/L$ is the elasticity of the supply of labour. Therefore, the

[1] Since marginal cost = marginal revenue = $P + y\,dP/dy$

$$k = \frac{P - P - y\,dP/dy}{P} = -\frac{y}{P}\frac{dP}{dy} = \frac{-1}{e}$$

assumption of imperfect competition does not alter the deduction that if firms are profit maximisers the demand for labour depends on the real wage rate.

If we assume the law of variable proportions (that is, diminishing marginal returns), the marginal product of labour declines with the amount of labour employed. Profit-maximising firms will only be induced to hire additional labour and produce more output if the real wage falls. The demand for labour is assumed to be a decreasing function of the real wage rate, as expressed in equation 5.6, given that the technical conditions of production and the degree of market competitiveness are held constant:

$$L^d = g\left(\frac{W}{P}\right); \quad \left(\frac{dL^d}{d(W/P)} < 0\right) \tag{5.6}$$

5.2 The supply of labour

In the long run the supply of labour is determined by such factors as population growth and the rate of participation of the population in the work-force. The latter has increased over the post-war period due to the greater proportion of married women seeking work. The supply of labour is not the total potential labour force; it is the amount of labour willing to work at a particular real wage rate. Like the demand for labour, the labour-supply function has a choice-theoretic basis. Each worker is assumed to obtain utility from leisure time and from real income which can only be increased by forgoing leisure. The labour-supply decision for each individual involves maximising the utility over some time horizon from leisure and work given a maximum number of possible working hours and the real wage rate per hour that can be earned. The crucial question here is what will be the effect on labour supply of a rise in the real wage rate. A rise in the real wage rate increases the opportunity cost of leisure. Leisure becomes more expensive. The substitution effect of this relative price change is to reduce leisure time and increase work time. But an increased real wage rate raises the real income for a given work time. This income effect raises the demand for leisure.

Thus an increase in the real wage will increase the supply of labour hours per worker only if the substitution effect outweighs the income effect. Over the long run it is apparent that the income effect has been stronger. As real wages have risen over time so people's working hours per week have fallen. The evidence for the short run is much less clear cut. A rise in real wages is likely to increase the labour supply by increasing the number of people who wish to participate in the labour force. Workers already in employment are induced to supply more labour by the payment of overtime rates. Some empirical studies have shown that women and teenagers have a more elastic supply of labour than adult males so that the proportion of the population participating in the labour force tends to increase when real wages rise, though the hours supplied by workers already employed tend to fall. Empirical work suggests that while the long-run labour-supply function is inelastic with respect to the real wage rate, over the short run the supply of labour does respond positively to increases in the real wage rate. (For one such study and a summary of these see Lucas and Rapping [1].) It is usual to assume in short-run macro models an aggregate supply function of labour which depends positively on the real wage rate, as shown in Figure 5.1.

Mathematical derivation of the supply of labour function

The utility function of the *i*th household which obtains its income from selling labour services is

$$U_i = f(y_i, R_i) \tag{5.7}$$

where y_i is real income and R_i is the number of 'hours' of leisure. In this type of utility function real income is an aggregate variable that embraces both current consumption and future consumption in the form of current saving. Utility is maximised subject to the constraint on the total number of 'hours' available:

$$R_i = H_i - S_i \tag{5.8}$$

where H_i is the total number of 'hours' available and S_i is the total number of 'hours' worked. A further constraint is

$$y_i = S_i w \tag{5.9}$$

where w is the real wage rate per 'hour'. Real income may also include income from non-human wealth but this will be unaffected by the number of hours currently worked, though it will influence how many hours the household decides to work. It is assumed that real income and leisure have positive marginal utility:

$$\frac{\partial U_i}{\partial y_i} \left(\frac{\partial U_i}{\partial R_i} > 0 \right) \tag{5.10}$$

The household maximises the utility it obtains from real income and leisure, subject to the constraints 5.8 and 5.9. The first-order condition for this maximum is obtained by differentiating the utility function 5.7 with respect to the number of 'hours' worked and setting the first derivative equal to zero, i.e.

$$\frac{dU_i}{dS_i} = \frac{\partial U_i}{\partial y_i}\frac{dy_i}{dS_i} + \frac{\partial U_i}{\partial R_i}\frac{dR_i}{dS_i} = 0 \tag{5.11}$$

From equation 5.9 $dy_i/dS_i = w$, and from equation 5.8 $dR_i/dS_i = -1$. Therefore

$$\frac{\partial U_i}{\partial y_i} w = \frac{\partial U_i}{\partial R_i} \tag{5.12}$$

Equation 5.12 expresses the equilibrium condition for a household. It will choose to work that number of 'hours' per period of time which equates the marginal utility of real income from an 'hour's' work to the marginal disutility of that 'hour's' work. (This is the marginal utility forgone by not devoting that 'hour' to leisure.) An alternative statement of this is that the real wage rate equals the marginal rate of substitution of utility from leisure for utility from real income, $(\partial U_i/\partial R_i)/(\partial U_i/\partial y_i)$. This marginal rate of substitution is assumed to increase as work is substituted for leisure in the short run so that the real wage will have to rise if leisure time is to decrease through voluntary choice. Therefore, the aggregate supply function for labour is expressed as an increasing function of the real wage rate:

$$L^s = h\left(\frac{w}{P}\right); \quad \left(\frac{dL^s}{d(W/P)} > 0\right) \tag{5.13}$$

The specification of labour supply as a function of the real wage is an important feature of neoclassical analysis and one on which Keynes focused his criticism in *The General Theory*.

5.3 Neoclassical labour-market equilibrium

In a neoclassical model the labour market is in equilibrium at that real wage rate which equates the demand for labour with the supply of labour, so that the labour market is *cleared*. This is depicted in Figure 5.1 at an equilibrium real wage rate of w_e and an equilibrium employment level of L_e. Once L_e is established the amount of output produced is read off from the short-run production function. This gives the equilibrium level of output that lies behind the neoclassical version of the *ISLM* model in which y_e was assumed to be fixed exogenously. The equilibrium level of employment established at the market-clearing real wage rate is consistent with full employment. Nobody who is willing to work at the equilibrium real wage rate is unemployed, except while searching for a job.

Frictional unemployment and job search

An equilibrium or full-employment level of employment does not imply a zero level of unemployment. Some positive amount of unemployment always exists.

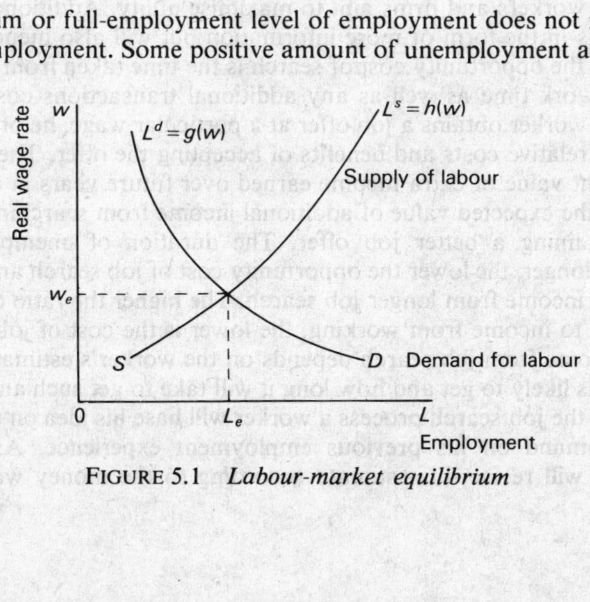

FIGURE 5.1 *Labour-market equilibrium*

Even in the 1950s unemployment never fell below 1 per cent (see Figure 1.1, p. 4). Despite there being some unemployment there are also job vacancies. We therefore need to show that equilibrium in the labour market is consistent with the existence of some unemployment and vacancies. The essence of this reconciliation is that because it takes time for workers to search for jobs and for employers to hire new workers there will always exist some *frictional* unemployment and some unfilled vacancies.

The existence of frictional unemployment is explained in terms of the special characteristics of the labour market which distinguish it from most product or service markets. Transactions are conducted on a highly personal basis and involve individual contracts between worker and employer. This contrasts with ordinary product markets where retailers, who act as middlemen between buyer and seller, hold stocks of the product. Alternatively there are waiting-lists, which are a typical feature of purchasing services. Vacancies and unemployment serve the same functions as inventories and waiting-lists in other markets.

In any market buyers and sellers need to get information on the prices at which exchanges are likely to occur. The information is obtained by a process of search. Job-search theories of unemployment have burgeoned in recent years (see references [2]–[6]). These theories seek to explain unemployment as the outcome of job search by both workers and employers in markets characterised by imperfect information which is costly to acquire. Because of their characteristics labour markets require a more extensive search than many other markets where prices are posted daily (as on stock or commodity markets) or are displayed by retailers. To obtain information about the going wage rate for one's labour services it is often not sufficient to examine posted prices as indicated in job advertisements. Personal applications are required to discover if the individual would in fact receive a job offer. Similarly, a firm needs to advertise vacancies and hold interviews in order to discover what quantity and quality of job acceptances it will get at the wage rates it offers.

Job-search theories have an explicit choice-theoretic foundation: they assume that workers and firms aim to maximise utility. Additional search will bring benefits in the form of more information but will also incur extra costs. For workers the opportunity cost of search is the time taken from either leisure pursuits or work time as well as any additional transactions costs. When an unemployed worker obtains a job offer at a particular wage, he or she needs to estimate the relative costs and benefits of accepting the offer. The benefits will be the present value of extra income earned over future years in that job. The cost will be the expected value of additional income from searching longer and possibly obtaining a better job offer. The duration of unemployment will therefore be longer, the lower the opportunity cost of job search and the greater the expected income from longer job search. The higher the ratio of unemployment benefit to income from working, the lower is the cost of job search. The expected income from job search depends on the worker's estimate of the best job offer he is likely to get and how long it will take to get such an offer. At the beginning of the job-search process a worker will base his idea on the real wage he can command on his previous employment experience. As job search proceeds he will revise this estimate according to the money wage offers he receives. Thus an unemployed worker has a reservation real wage and will not accept a job below this wage and is likely to revise the reservation wage downwards as the duration of unemployment lengthens.

Job-search theory predicts that unemployed workers may reject job offers because of incorrect information. They may think they can obtain better wage offers and fail for some time to realise that market conditions have changed and that the equilibrium wage rate has changed. In a neoclassical model a decline in aggregate demand would be reversed by downward movements in the money wage rate and the price level. If unemployed workers fail to realise that the equilibrium *money* wage has fallen because they have to search to find out this piece of information, then they will extend their duration of unemployment. The rate of unemployment, which depends both on the numbers unemployed and their duration of unemployment, will rise.

Job-search theory in the context of a macro model helps to explain

(a) the existence of an equilibrium level of unemployment and vacancies, together with an equilibrium full-employment level of employment, and
(b) the deviation of unemployment and vacancies from their equilibrium values as a result of random shocks to the economy giving rise to incorrect perceptions about appropriate wages and prices.

So far we have not given explicit recognition to the fact that the aggregate labour market is not a single market for homogeneous labour time but a complex of interrelated labour markets for different skills in different locations. Even within a micro labour market for a particular skill, labour is not homogeneous; some workers are more efficient with their time than others. The heterogeneous nature of labour markets is an important element in job-search theories because it makes information more difficult and hence more costly to obtain. Some job-search theories (Phelps [5]) have focused on the spatial distribution of jobs as the key to why information on wages rates and job offers require extensive search.

Structural unemployment

Job-search theory can explain frictional unemployment in individual labour markets which are in basic equilibrium. However, as structural changes occur in the economy some industries, some labour-skill categories and some regions of the country decline while others expand. This results in disequilibrium with excess labour supply in contracting sectors while there is excess demand for labour in growing sectors.

Labour resources will move from declining sectors into expanding ones in response to wage differentials, but the adjustment takes time and may remain incomplete. The displaced workers have different skills and live in different locations to the new job opportunities. Retraining takes time and some displaced workers may not be capable of being retrained. The mobility of workers will be restricted by difficulties with rehousing or strong preferences for their current location. This type of unemployment is known as *structural* unemployment. Technical change also contributes to structural unemployment by altering the balance of demand and supply in specific product markets and more generally by improving labour productivity. The acquisition of labour-saving capital equipment will reduce firms' demand for specific types of labour and for labour in general unless demand growth keeps pace with the increase in labour productivity.

The distribution of unemployment and vacancies among individual industries and regions will determine their aggregate level for the economy as a whole. So long as some sectors experience an excess supply of labour, even if the majority of sectors have excess labour demand, there will be a positive level of unemployment.

In addition to the frictional and structural factors causing unemployment there is a proportion of the unemployed who for reasons of health or work attitudes find it difficult to remain in steady employment. This category is usually subsumed under frictional unemployment.

Thus in neoclassical analysis the existence of unemployment and vacancies does not imply that labour markets remain permanently uncleared. Aggregate labour-market equilibrium is consistent with frictional unemployment and vacancies, while at the micro level individual labour markets will be continually adjusting to the changes in demand and supply which characterise dynamic economies.

5.4 Keynesian unemployment

The distinguishing feature of Keynesian unemployment is that it is attributed to an insufficient level of aggregate demand. The condition results from a different specification of the labour-supply function from that in neoclassical analysis. In *The General Theory* Keynes assumed that workers are unwilling to accept a cut in money wages in order to secure more employment, even though they would accept an equivalent reduction in the real wage rate brought about by an increase in the price level while the money wage rate remained unchanged. Keynes did not attribute this to irrationality on the part of workers but to a desire to preserve their wage relativities. Workers are concerned with the real wage they receive and not just its money value. Because the price level is not determined in any single labour market, workers can only bargain directly for money wages and not real wages. Therefore, workers are willing to accept a cut in real wages that stems from a rising price level but not one caused by a cut in money wages, because the former affects all workers more or less equally and does not alter relative real wages. In contrast a cut in money wages is seen as affecting only that particular group of workers and adversely affecting their real wage relative to other income groups. In the static interpretation of the Keynesian model the money wage is assumed to be fixed. It is exogenous to the model and explained by institutional factors and past history.

Therefore, in a Keynesian model the supply of labour is, within limits, perfectly elastic with respect to the current money wage rate. An example of a

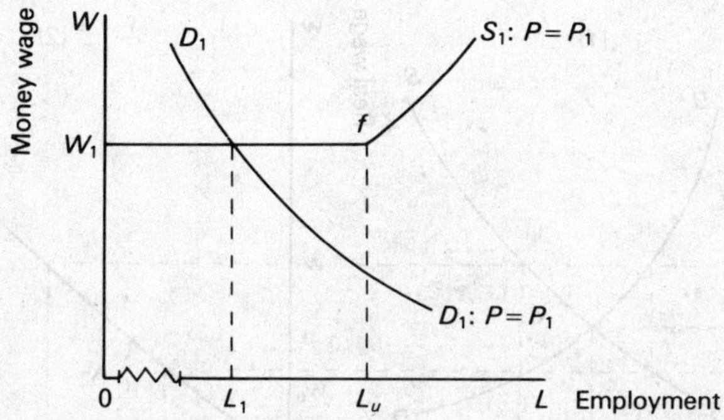

FIGURE 5.2 *Keynesian labour supply function*

Keynesian labour-supply function is drawn in Figure 5.2 as schedule W_1fS_1. Its position depends on the fixed money wage rate, W_1, and upon a given price level, which we take to be P_1. Schedule W_1fS_1 shows that given a money wage of W_1 and a price level of P_1, up to OL_u units of labour are supplied. However, to induce more than OL_u labour units to supply themselves when the price level is P_1 the money wage has to rise above W_1, so ensuring a higher real wage.

In Figure 5.2 the demand for labour is also plotted with respect to the money wage, holding the price level fixed at P_1. As the money wage rises the real wage rate also rises along D_1D_1 since the price level is assumed fixed at P_1. Given a money wage of W_1 and a price level of P_1, only OL_1 labour units are demanded while OL_u are supplied. There is an excess supply of labour equal to L_1L_u units. The labour market is uncleared and there is unemployment.

The Keynesian labour market

The relationship between the neoclassical and Keynesian specifications of the labour market and the derivation of the demand and supply of labour schedules with respect to the money wage depicted in Figure 5.2 are shown in Figure 5.3.

Quadrant 1 in Figure 5.3 shows the neoclassical demand for and supply of labour schedules with respect to the real wage rate. The equilibrium real wage which clears the labour market is w_e. We start by assuming that the money wage rate is fixed at W_1 and the price level at P_1. Quadrant 2 shows what the resulting real wage rate will be. Schedule OP_1 is drawn for a particular price level, P_1, and all along it $w = W/P_1$. When the money wage is W_1 and the price level is P_1 we read off from schedule OP_1 that the real wage is w_1. In quadrant 3 the 45° line enables us to transfer the money wage rate from the horizontal axis of quadrant 2 to the vertical axis of quadrant 3. From the vertical axis in quadrant 3 the money wage rate can then be transferred to the vertical axis in quadrant 4. Looking at quadrants 1 and 4 together we can see that when the money wage rate is W_1 in 4 the real wage rate, given a price level of P_1, is w_1. Quadrant 1 shows that when the real wage is w_1 the demand for

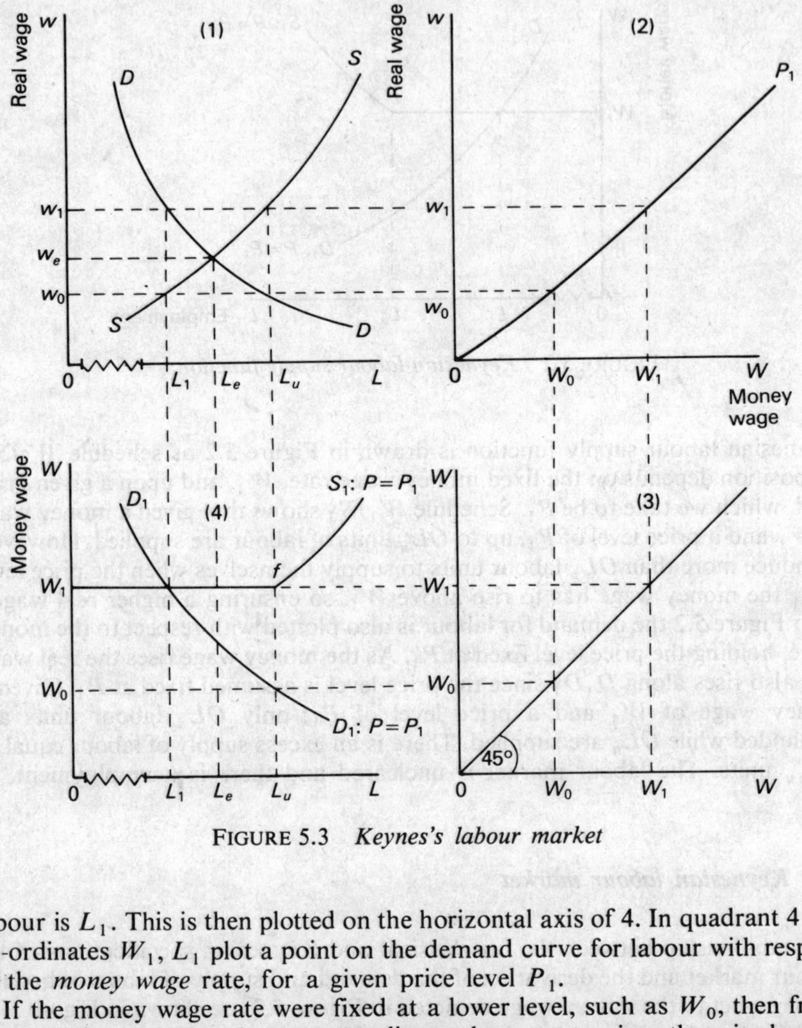

FIGURE 5.3 *Keynes's labour market*

labour is L_1. This is then plotted on the horizontal axis of 4. In quadrant 4 the co-ordinates W_1, L_1 plot a point on the demand curve for labour with respect to the *money wage* rate, for a given price level P_1.

If the money wage rate were fixed at a lower level, such as W_0, then from quadrant 2 we get that the corresponding real wage rate, given the price level is still fixed at P_1, is w_0. From quadrant 1 the demand for labour when the real wage is w_0 is L_u. In quadrant 4 the co-ordinates W_0 and L_u provide another point relating the demand for labour and the money wage rate when the price level is fixed at P_1. Joining all such points in quadrant 4 we get the demand for labour schedule D_1D_1 with respect to the money wage rate when the price level is constant at P_1.

Given Keynes's hypothesis about the supply of labour, then, the amount of labour supplied when the money wage is fixed at W_1 and the price level at P_1 is given by schedule W_1fS_1 in quadrant 4. The Keynesian labour-supply schedule for a current money wage, W_1, and $P=P_1$ is horizontal until point f and then slopes upwards. This shape is due to Keynes's assumption that workers are willing to accept a cut in real wages that comes from a rise in the price level but are unwilling to accept a cut in the money wage rate when there is unemployment. Given W_1 and P_1, the real wage is w_1 and at this real wage quadrant 1 shows that OL_u labour will be supplied. Therefore, if the price level remains at P_1, the only way to induce more than OL_u units of labour to supply themselves is to raise the real wage rate by raising the money wage above W_1. Therefore, the Keynesian aggregate labour-supply schedule corresponds to the neoclassical one at employment levels above OL_u.

In quadrant 4 the positions of the demand for and supply of labour schedules with respect to the money wage rate are fixed in relation to a particular price level. Along schedules D_1D_1 and W_1fS_1 the price level is held constant at P_1. If the price level changes, then both the demand for and supply of labour schedules in quadrant 4 shift. These shifts are shown in Figure 5.4.

Let us assume that the price level rises from P_1 to P_2. In quadrant 2 the $w = W/P$ identity pivots down to OP_2. At each money wage rate the corresponding real wage is now lower. For instance, from quadrant 2 we see that at a money wage of W_1 and a price level of P_2 the corresponding real wage is now w_1'. Quadrant 1 shows that at a real wage of w_1', OL_1' labour is

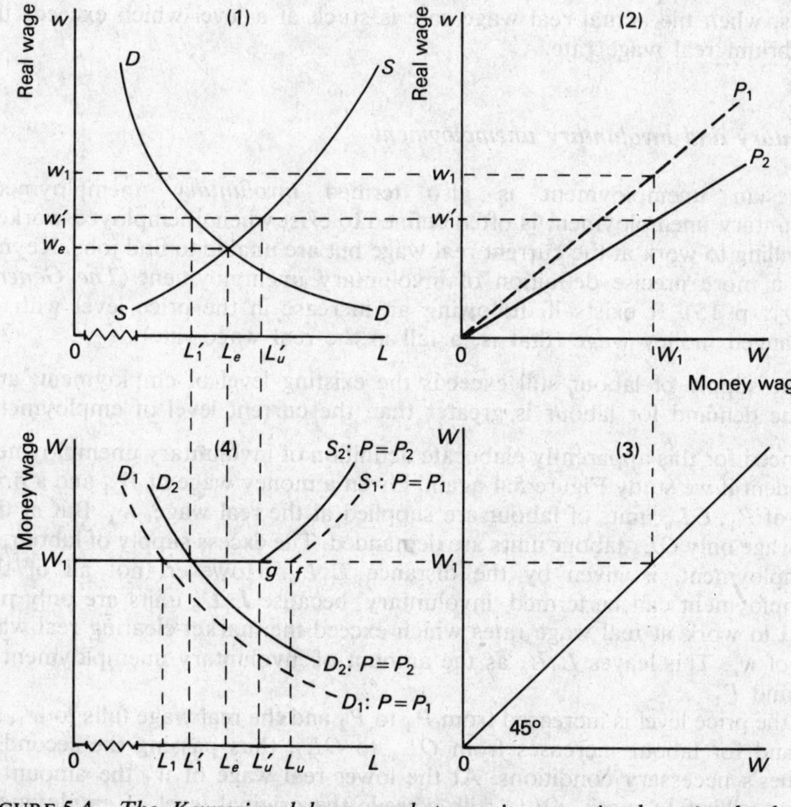

FIGURE 5.4 *The Keynesian labour market: an increase in the price level raises employment*

demanded. So in quadrant 4 the co-ordinates W_1, L'_1 give a point on a new demand for labour schedule D_2D_2 with respect to the money wage rate when the price level is P_2. Because the real wage has fallen from w_1 to w'_1 some marginal labour units are no longer willing to work and the labour supply contracts along the neoclassical labour supply function to L'_u. However, OL'_u units of labour are still willing to work at or below the existing real wage of w'_1. Thus the Keynesian labour-supply function at price level P_2 is W_1gS_2.

So in Keynes's analysis, when the amount of labour willing to work at the existing money wage and price level exceeds the demand for labour, employment can be increased by policies which raise the demand for labour. This is done by raising the price level relative to the money wage rate. For instance, in Figure 5.4 an increase in the price level from P_1 to P_2 shifts up the demand function for labour with respect to the money wage rate. Although the real wage falls because the money wage is fixed at W_1 while the price level rises, the amount of labour supplied still exceeds the demand for it. Therefore, total employment rises from OL_1 to OL'_1.

When the Keynesian labour-supply function is operative, labour is said to be *off* the neoclassical labour-supply function. In Keynes's analysis this will occur at levels of employment below the market-clearing amount of employment: that is, when the actual real wage rate is stuck at a level which exceeds the equilibrium real wage rate.

Voluntary and involuntary unemployment

Keynesian unemployment is also termed *involuntary* unemployment. Involuntary unemployment is often defined to exist when unemployed workers are willing to work at the current real wage but are unable to find jobs. Keynes gave a more precise definition of involuntary unemployment (*The General Theory*, p. 15). It exists if, following an increase in the price level with an unchanged money wage (that is, a fall in the real wage rate)

(a) the supply of labour still exceeds the existing level of employment, and
(b) the demand for labour is greater than the current level of employment.

The need for this apparently elaborate definition of involuntary unemployment is evident if we study Figure 5.4 again. Given a money wage of W_1 and a price level of P_1, OL_u units of labour are supplied at the real wage, w_1. But at this real wage only OL_1 labour units are demanded. The excess supply of labour, or unemployment, is given by the distance L_1L_u. However, not all of this unemployment can be termed 'involuntary' because L_eL_u units are only prepared to work at real wage rates which exceed the market-clearing real wage rate of w_e. This leaves L_1L_e as the amount of involuntary unemployment at W_1 and P_1.

If the price level is increased from P_1 to P_2 and the real wage falls to w'_1, the demand for labour increases from OL_1 to OL'_1, thus passing the second of Keynes's necessary conditions. At the lower real wage of w'_1 the amount of labour willing to work, OL'_u, still exceeds the original level of employment, OL_1, and so the first necessary condition for involuntary unemployment is met. Real wage rates w_1 and w'_1 are above the equilibrium real wage. Once the real wage has fallen to the market-clearing level, w_e, and employment is L_e, the conditions for involuntary unemployment no longer exist. As before, the demand for labour can only be increased by lowering the real wage. However, if the real wage falls below w_e, then the supply of labour will fall below L_e, the current employment level, as shown in quadrant 1. The first condition for involuntary unemployment no longer holds. Therefore, if the money wage is W_1, the price level is P_1 and the total excess supply of labour is L_1L_u, only L_1L_e of that is involuntary unemployment and the amount L_eL_u is not involuntary. This is why in Keynes's model labour is only *off* the neoclassical labour-supply function at real wage rates which exceed the market-clearing real wage rate. The algebraic expression for Keynes's labour-supply function is thus

$$W = W_1 \text{ for } W_1/P > w_e \text{ (\textit{off} the neoclassical supply function)}$$

$$L^s = h(W_1/P) \text{ for } W_1/P \leqslant w_e \text{ (\textit{on} the neoclassical supply function)}$$

In the neoclassical model labour is always on the labour-supply function, as workers respond in the same way to a given change in the real wage whether it is due to a price-level change or to a change in the money wage. If the actual real wage exceeds the equilibrium real wage, then in neoclassical analysis the ensuing unemployment is voluntary. A sufficiently large cut in the real wage due either to a fall in the money wage or a rise in the price level, or perhaps to some combination of both, would reduce the supply of labour until it equalled the demand for it.

As should by now be apparent, the distinction between voluntary and involuntary unemployment is not a particularly easy one to make, especially when the heterogeneity of the labour market is taken into account. For instance, is a doctor who cannot find a medical job involuntarily unemployed because he declines to work as a refuse collector? Hahn [7] classifies this case as one of involuntary unemployment, but one can also argue that the refusal to work at a lower real wage implies voluntary unemployment. When we move from purely theoretical defintions of unemployment to empirical work, the distinction between involuntary and voluntary unemployment becomes even harder to make, as can be seen below.

What, then, is the point in making such a distinction in the first place? It is partly political, in that presenting unemployment as involuntary stresses the need for some alleviating government remedy. More important for economic analysis is that involuntary unemployment, unlike voluntary unemployment, could be reduced by government measures to increase aggregate demand. Completely different policies are required to reduce voluntary unemployment, such as decreasing unemployment benefit. This measure aims to increase the cost of job search and so reduce the amount of frictional unemployment.

Full employment

The difficulty of distinguishing between voluntary and involuntary unemployment means that full employment, defined as existing when the aggregate labour market clears, is not easily measured in practice when we are dealing with the thousands of interrelated labour markets rather than a single homogeneous labour market. What aggregate amount of frictional and structural unemployment is consistent with overall labour-market equilibrium cannot be readily determined and it will change over time.

The operational problems associated with defining full employment as existing when the level of unemployment is consistent with overall labour-market equilibrium have led to other definitions of full employment. Some have defined it in terms of an arbitrary percentage of unemployment which obtained in the past, while others have described it in terms of a level of unemployment which is deemed to be desirable if not feasible. In this book we shall stick to equating full employment with equality between the demand for and supply of labour, allowing for frictional unemployment and vacancies.

5.5. Why did unemployment increase in the 1970s?

The behaviour of the percentage rate of unemployment in post-war Britain was outlined in Chapter 1 (see p. 3 and is summarised in Table 5.2, p. 79, and Figure 1.1, p. 4). Since 1967 the annual average rate of unemployment has not fallen below 2.5 per cent of the work-force, a rate only approached in recessions in the earlier post-war period. In the boom years of 1973–4 unemployment fell to an annual average of 2.6 per cent and then rose steadily. In the subsequent upturn of 1978–9 unemployment only fell slightly to 5.4 per cent and in the following recession attained a pre-war level of 10 per cent.

The factors which could explain the rise in unemployment are:

1. An increase in the amount of structural and frictional unemployment.
2. An upwards shift to the left in the labour-supply function.
3. A growth in Keynesian involuntary unemployment.

It is very difficult in practice to separate the influence on total unemployment of these different factors. The problem with interpreting unemployment statistics is that they do not measure any of the theoretical concepts of unemployment. In the United Kingdom the rate of unemployment is measured as the number of registered unemployed taken as a proportion of the labour force (employed plus registered unemployed). Hence a change in the incentive to register will alter measured unemployment even if there is no change in the real underlying rate of unemployment. The numbers of registered unemployed give no indication of the reservation real wage rates of the unemployed. There is no direct test of whether an individual is involuntarily unemployed or voluntarily unemployed while searching for a job at or above his reservation real wage.

Structural factors

Although the number of jobs has risen over the last thirty years (from 23.3 million in 1950 to 25 million in 1979) it has failed to increase as fast as the working population. (This has risen from 23.5 million to 26.3 million in the period 1950–79.) A closer look at the working population reveals three broad groups that have experienced a relative increase in unemployment. These are the young, the unskilled and, since the mid-1970s, women.

Classifying the unemployed by age groups reveals that the percentage rate of unemployment falls steadily with age until about 55, when it rises. However, duration of unemployment rises continuously with age. Unemployment rates tend to be higher and have risen more rapidly over time among the unskilled than among skilled workers. When unemployment is differentiated by sex, it is apparent that male unemployment rose relative to vacancies from 1966 onwards but that the female unemployment–vacancy relationship only shifted outwards after 1974 following equal-pay legislation.

All the three groups which have experienced a relative deterioration in their employment prospects have had a steady rise in their relative wages. The average hourly earnings of youths under 21 calculated as a percentage of adult male earnings rose during the post-war period from 45 per cent to over 60 per cent. Similarly, the ratio of wages of skilled workers as a percentage of unskilled workers wages fell during the 1970s. For example, in the engineering industries this fell from 145 per cent to 130 per cent. The ratio of male to female earnings fell from 186 per cent in 1970 to 154 per cent by 1977. Similar trends have been observed in other Western economies (Haveman [8]).

Unemployment in some sectors and regions has risen more rapidly than in others. The manufacturing sector in particular has experienced a decline in employment since 1971. Within that sector some industries, such as the motor industry, have declined with particular rapidity. (From 1972 to 1979 the output of passenger-cars produced in the United Kingdom fell from 1.9 million to 1 million, while demand in 1979 at 1.7 million registrations was slightly higher than in 1972.) Manufacturing industry was particularly severely affected in the 1980–1 recession, which mirrored a number of structural features of the inter-war depression when very heavy unemployment occurred in staple export industries hit by foreign competition.

Frictional unemployment

Up until the mid-1960s the relationship between the number of vacancies and unemployment was pretty stable but then it began to change, first for men in 1966–7 and in 1974 for women.

A given level of vacancies became associated with higher unemployment rates. One explanation for this is that frictional unemployment increased because the opportunity cost of unemployment fell. The ratio of income when out of work to post-tax income when in work (the replacement ratio) has risen since the 1950s – see Table 5.1. A significant increase occurred in 1966 when earnings-related supplement to unemployment benefits was introduced. This contribution towards frictional unemployment has declined with the phasing out of earnings-related supplement in 1981–2. The replacement ratio is higher for lower-income workers and for those with large families, both being categories which have higher-than-average unemployment rates (Nickell [9]).

TABLE 5.1 *Average replacement ratio**

1950–9	38.8 per cent
1960–5	44.7 per cent
1966–76	71.4 per cent

$$* \left[\frac{\text{Standard rate of unemployment benefit} + \text{ERS} + \text{Family allowances}}{\text{Average weekly earnings} + \text{Family allowances} - \text{Tax} - \text{National insurance contributions for a married man with two children}} \right]$$

Source: Scott and Laslett [10].

A number of studies (references [10]–[14]) have reported that higher replacement ratios can explain up to 70 per cent of the increase in unemployment recorded in 1967–72 (for a contrary result see [15]). The fact that the increased duration of unemployment can explain most of the increase in the stock of unemployed in the period 1967–77 is also consistent with an increase in frictional unemployment.

There is considerable agreement that the rate of unemployment consistent with labour-market equilibrium has increased over the 1970s but its precise value at any particular time cannot be at all accurately estimated. Two studies, [10] and [15] using quite different methods have estimated the equilibrium or full-employment rate of unemployment as respectively 3.4 per cent in 1976 (when the total unemployment rate was 5.3 per cent) and as 4 per cent in 1977 (compared with the total rate of 5.7 per cent).

Upward shift in the labour-supply function

An upward and leftward shift in the labour-supply function (see Figure 5.1, p. 67) would raise real wages and reduce employment. If this occurred, there would still be no excess supply of labour in equilibrium but it is likely that the numbers registered as unemployed would rise.

One explanation of such a shift in the labour-supply function is derived from job-search theory and emphasises the role of incorrect information. Workers maintain higher money and hence higher real reservation wages because they do not know what the equilibrium wage rate is. One would expect this type of shift to be only temporary since incorrect information results from cyclical changes in the economy. As workers revise downwards their estimate of the going wage rate, the labour-supply schedule shifts back towards the right and employment rises again.

A quite different explanation of upwards shifts in the labour-supply function attributes it to the power of trade unions to obtain real wage increases which exceed the increase in the value of output per worker. Unit labour costs rise, causing the demand for labour to contract. (See Scott and Laslett [10] for a

TABLE 5.2 *Real wages, productivity and unemployment*

Annual average	Rate of change of real wage rate (per cent) (1)	Rate of change of output per person employed (per cent) (2)	Difference between columns 1 and 2 (3)	Percentage rate of unemployment (4)
1950–4	0.30	1.91	−1.61	1.68
1955–9	1.76	1.62	+0.14	1.72
1960–4	0.98	2.38	−1.40	1.94
1965–9	0.62	2.62	−2.00	2.1
1970–4	3.85	1.89	+1.96	2.98
1975–9	2.79	1.64	+1.15	5.2

development of this hypothesis.) Table 5.2 shows that significantly higher rates of increase in real wages were obtained in the 1970s compared with the earlier periods and that these exceeded the rate of increase of labour productivity (column 2). The resulting increase in unit costs will not only affect the short-run demand for labour, as can be analysed in Figure 5.1, it will also affect the long-run demand. Firms will have an incentive to substitute capital for labour by investing in labour-saving capital equipment. This would not by itself cause higher unemployment if a sufficiently large amount of investment occurred, so that the rise in investment offset the effect of labour substitution on the demand for labour. This has not happened, as there has been insufficient incentive for firms to invest. The rate of return on capital has tended to fall over the post-war period; for instance, the real rate of return from equity fell from 6.8 per cent p.a. in the period 1954–64 to −2.7 per cent in the period 1965–76 (Lawson [16]).

Keynesian unemployment

A further possibility is that labour is off the neoclassical supply function and that an increase in the level of aggregate demand would permanently reduce the amount of unemployment. Keynesian unemployment is essentially cyclical unless there is an insufficient stock of capital to employ the work-force. In order to explain the trend for unemployment to rise over time there would need to be a growing amount of slack in aggregate demand reflected in an increasing volume of excess capacity.

Conclusion

Neoclassical and Keynesian analysis provide different perspectives on the factors which can explain the rising trend in unemployment. Different analyses of the underlying causes of unemployment imply different policy responses.

The remedy of increased aggregate demand as a means of permanently reducing unemployment will only work if the Keynesian analysis of a substantial part of unemployment being involuntary is correct. In the next chapter we examine Keynesian policy to combat unemployment in the context of a three-sector model of the economy in which the labour market is added to the goods and money markets of the *ISLM* model.

References

[1] R. E. Lucas and L. A. Rapping, 'Real Wages, Employment and Inflation', *Journal of Political Economy*, 77 (1969).

[2] D. T. Mortensen, 'A Theory of Wage and Employment Dynamics', in *Microeconomic Foundations of Employment and Inflation Theory*, ed. E. Phelps (London: Macmillan, 1970).

[3] C. C. Holt, 'How Can the Phillips Curve be Moved to Reduce Both Inflation and Unemployment?', in *Microeconomic Foundations*, ed. Phelps.

[4] C. C. Holt, 'Job Search, Phillips Wage Relation and Union Influence: Theory and Evidence', in *Microeconomic Foundations*, ed. Phelps.

[5] E. Phelps, 'Money Wage Dynamics and Labour Market Equilibrium', in *Microeconomic Foundations*, ed. Phelps.

[6] M. N. Baily, 'On the Theory of Lay-offs and Unemployment', *Econometrica*, 45, 5 (1977) 1043–63.

[7] F. Hahn, 'Unemployment from a Theoretical Viewpoint', *Economica*, 47 (1980).

[8] R. E. Haveman, 'Unemployment in W. Europe and the US: A Problem of Demand, Structure and Measurement', *American Economic Review* (1978).

[9] S. Nickell, 'A Picture of Male Unemployment in Britain', *Economic Journal*, 90 (December 1980).

[10] M. Scott and R. Laslett, *Can We Get Back to Full Employment?* (London: Macmillan, 1978).

[11] D. MacKay and G. Reid, 'Redundancy, Unemployment and Manpower Policy', *Economic Journal*, 82 (1972).

[12] D. Gujerati, 'The Behaviour of Unemployment and Unfilled Vacancies', *Economic Journal* (March 1972).

[13] D. Maki and Z. A. Spindler, 'The Effect of Unemployment Compensation on the Rate of Unemployment in Great Britain', *Oxford Economic Papers*, 27 (November 1975).

[14] J. S. Cubbin and K. Foley, 'The Extent of Benefit Induced Unemployment in Great Britain: Some New Evidence', *Oxford Economic Papers* (March 1977).

[15] R. A. Batchelor and T. D. Sheriff, 'Unemployment and Unanticipated Inflation in Post War Britain', *Economica*, 47, 186 (May 1980).

[16] G. Lawson, 'Comparing Profits: The Grand Illusion', *The Sunday Times* (30 January 1978).

6 The Three-Sector Macro Model

The *ISLM* model reduces to only two independent markets or equations and can therefore solve for just two endogenous variables: the level of real output and the interest rate in the Keynesian version; the price level and the interest rate in the neoclassical version. The introduction of the labour market provides a third independent equation and enables one to solve for all three variables: the interest rate, the price level and the quantity of real national output. This chapter outlines the three-sector macro model in which the goods, money and labour markets interact. The behavioural equations which make up the three markets can be reduced in number and summarised in the form of aggregate demand and aggregate supply functions. The aggregate demand function which is derived from the *IS* and *LM* equations takes the same basic form in both the neoclassical and Keynesian versions of the model. The fundamental difference between the two approaches lies in their specification of the supply side of the economy, as we have just seen in Chapter 5.

6.1 The aggregate demand function

The aggregate demand function indicates how the volume of real aggregate demand rises as the price level falls. The derivation of the aggregate demand schedule from the *IS* and *LM* functions is shown in Figure 6.1. Part A of Figure 6.1 shows intersections of the *IS* and *LM* schedules. The *LM* schedule is shown for different price levels. As the price level rises, the real value of the money stock falls, so the *LM* schedule shifts up to the left. All the exogenous variables are held constant. When the price level is P_0 the goods and money markets are both in equilibrium at interest rate i_0 and at an aggregate demand for output of y_0. Part B of Figure 6.1 plots the price level, P_0, and the corresponding level of aggregate demand, y_0, which are consistent with simultaneous equilibrium in the goods and money markets, and so give another point on the aggregate demand schedule. The pairs of price and output combinations at which both the goods and money markets are in equilibrium trace out the aggregate demand schedule *AD*.

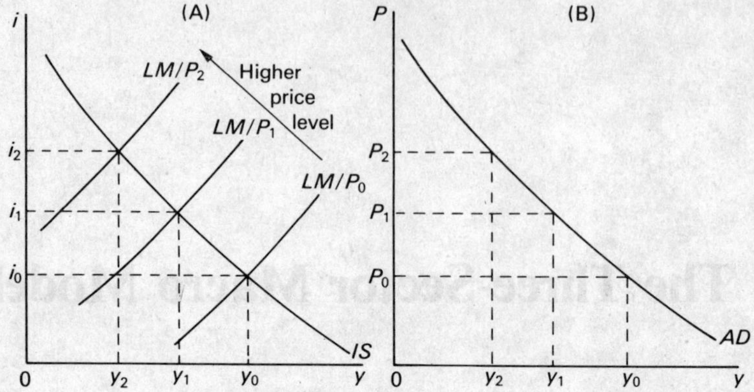

FIGURE 6.1 *Derivation of the aggregate demand schedule*

Any change in the exogenous variables which affects behaviour in the goods and money markets will cause a shift in the aggregate demand schedule. For instance, an increase in government spending which shifts the *IS* function upwards to the right will move the *AD* schedule outwards to the right. Similarly, an increase in the nominal money stock which shifts each *LM* schedule for a given price level to the right will also shift the *AD* schedule outwards.

To complete the model it is only necessary to derive a relationship between aggregate supply and the price level which, together with the aggregate demand relationship, determines the equilibrium price and real output level. The aggregate-supply/price-level relationship is obtained from the conditions required for equilibrium in the labour market and the aggregate production function. The neoclassical and Keynesian versions of the model are distinguished by their different assumptions about the supply side of the labour market which were outlined in the previous chapter.

6.2 The neoclassical three-sector model

The basic specification of the goods and money market and hence the aggregate demand schedule are the same in the neoclassical and Keynesian versions of the model.

For completeness, the specification of the equations which make up the model are set out below:

The goods market

Savings function:

$$S/P = s(1 - t)y \tag{6.1}$$

Investment function:

$$I/P = I(i)/P \tag{6.2}$$

Government expenditure:

$$G/P = G_0/P \tag{6.3}$$

Tax function:

$$T/P = t(y) \tag{6.4}$$

Goods-market equilibrium:

$$\frac{S}{P} + \frac{T}{P} = \frac{I}{P} + \frac{G}{P} \tag{6.5}$$

Therefore, the equation of the *IS* function is

$$|s(1 - t) + t|y = I(i)/P + G_0/P \tag{6.6}$$

The money market

Demand for money function:

$$\left(\frac{M}{P}\right)^D = \frac{M}{P}(y, i) \tag{6.7}$$

Exogenous supply of money:

$$M^S = M_0^S \tag{6.8}$$

Money-market equilibrium:

$$\left(\frac{M}{P}\right)^D = \frac{M^S}{P} \tag{6.9}$$

Equation of *LM* function

$$\frac{M_0^S}{P} = \frac{M}{P}(y, i) \tag{6.10}$$

Equations 6.1–6.10 specify the *ISLM* model as developed in Chapters 3 and 4. Finally, the labour market or production sector outlined in Chapter 5 is added. The distinguishing neoclassical characteristic is that the supply of labour equation (6.13) is a positive function of the real wage rate throughout its range.

Production sector

Short-run production function:

$$y = f(L, \bar{K}, \bar{T}) \tag{6.11}$$

Demand for labour function:

$$L^D = g(W/P) \tag{6.12}$$

Supply of labour function:

$$L^S = h(W/P) \tag{6.13}$$

Labour-market equilibrium:

$$L^S = L^D = L_e \tag{6.14}$$

Substituting equation 6.14 into equation 6.11 gives

$$y_f = f(L_e) \tag{6.15}$$

(where y_f and L_e indicate market-clearing levels of real output and employment; K and T are omitted as they remain constant).

The model has twelve endogenous variables, namely real output, real saving, real government expenditure, real tax revenue, real investment, the real wage rate, the demand for real money balances, the supply of real money balances, the demand for labour, the supply of labour, the real rate of interest and the price level. There are twelve independent equations ([6.1, 6.2, 6.3, 6.4 and 6.5] [6.7, 6.8 and 6.9] [6.11, 6.12, 6.13 and 6.14]). These twelve equations collapse into three independent equations in three variables: real output, the interest rate and the price level. Equations 6.1–6.5 give the *IS* function (6.6). Equations 6.7–6.9 give the *LM* function (6.10). Equations 6.11–6.14 give the aggregate supply function (6.15), which is now derived.

The neoclassical aggregate supply function

The aggregate supply function is derived from the demand for labour and supply of labour functions together with the short-run aggregate production function. This derivation is shown in Figure 6.2.

The assumption of market-clearing in the labour market (part a) means that

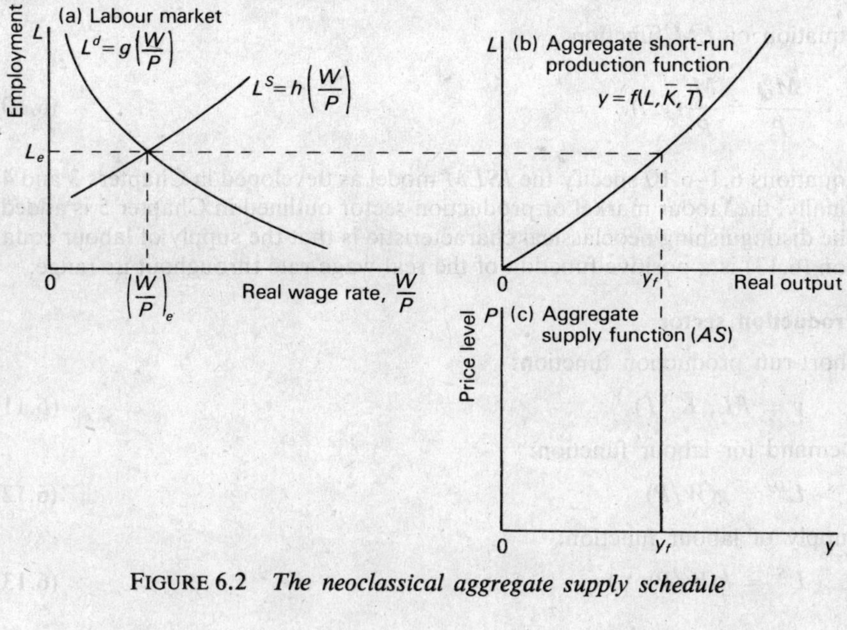

FIGURE 6.2 *The neoclassical aggregate supply schedule*

the equilibrium real wage rate (W/P_e) is established, at which the level of employment is L_e. There is no excess supply of labour at this real wage rate. Given the equilibrium level of employment, L_e, we can read off the corresponding amount of real output supplied from the short-run aggregate production function (part b). This level of real output is labelled y_f to indicate that it is consistent with full employment as defined in Chapter 5 (p. 75). The aggregate supply function is depicted in part c of Figure 6.2 as a vertical line since it is invariant with respect to the price level. Were the price level to fall, the equilibrium real wage $(W/P)_e$ would be restored by a proportionate fall in the money wage rate. The adjustment mechanism postulated is that a rise in the real wage rate above its equilibrium level caused by a fall in the price level would reduce the demand for labour. In order to secure employment unemployed workers would be willing to accept lower money wage rates than had previously ruled. Thus the money wage rate would fall until the real wage was once more at its market-clearing equilibrium level and the excess supply of labour had been eliminated. Real output would once more be equal to y_f, Hence the equilibrium real output level, y_f, can prevail at any price level because money wages are flexible.

The complete neoclassical model

The model is solved by requiring that overall equilibrium is simultaneously achieved in all three sectors. In other words, the aggregate demand for and aggregate supply of real output are equal. This general equilibrium is illustrated in Figure 6.3. As can be seen from this diagram, shifts in the aggregate demand schedule have no effect on the equilibrium level of real output. They only affect the price level and the money wage rate, leaving the market-clearing equilibrium real wage rate unchanged. Thus in a stationary neoclassical model (that is, one that abstracts from growth) the equilibrium level of output is determined in the production sector only.

If the nominal stock of money is increased, the locus of *IS* and *LM* equilibria, depicted in Figure 6.1, will change, causing the *AD* schedule to shift

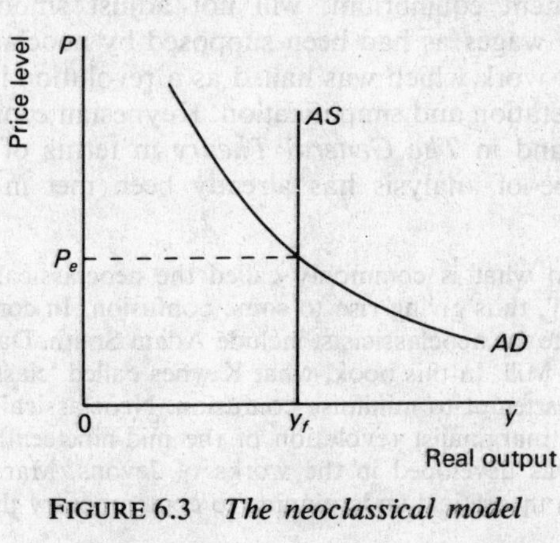

FIGURE 6.3 *The neoclassical model*

up to the right. The price level will be proportionately higher. This is the standard neoclassical result that a change in the nominal money stock, *ceteris paribus*, will leave the static equilibrium values of the real variables unchanged. This property of money is referred to as the *neutrality* of money. Thus we get the conclusion that, given the constancy of the institutional factors which influence the demand for money, which is a stable function of its determinants, the nominal quantity of money determines the price level and has no long-run effect on the real variables. This leaves the goods market to determine the rate of interest and hence the division of real output between consumption and investment. The equilibrium interest rate is thus independent of the price level in static equilibrium. The static equilibrium analysis of the role of money in a neoclassical model is identical to the notion of money as a veil which could be lifted to reveal the workings of the real forces in the economic system, unaffected in any significant way by monetary factors. This concept has caused considerable confusion in economic thinking which is avoided if we keep reminding ourselves that comparative-static analysis is only a simplifying mode of thought which guides our predictions about directions and magnitudes of change in a stable economy. The nominal quantity of money may not affect static equilibrium states but the story is quite different when we analyse the economy out of static long-run equilibrium. Then the quantity of money does affect real values in both Keynesian and neoclassical analysis as the economy adjusts from one long-run equilibrium point to the other, as will be shown in later chapters, in particular Chapters 18, 19 and 20.

6.3 The Keynesian three-sector model

Keynes criticised the neoclassical[1] economic thinking of his day for its failure to see that the predictions of static, certainty models cannot be applied directly to short-run analysis of a world in which the future is uncertain and in which equilibrium is a state towards which an economy, if stable, is gradually adjusting.

The General Theory attempts to explain why a capitalist economy, disturbed from full-employment equilibrium, will not adjust smoothly by means of flexible prices and wages as had been supposed by neoclassical analysis. The book is a complex work which was hailed as a revolution in economic theory. It required interpretation and simplification. Keynesian economists propagated the ideas they found in *The General Theory* in terms of comparative-static analysis. This type of analysis has already been met in the *ISLM* model.

[1] Keynes referred to what is commonly called the neoclassical school of economic thought as 'classical', thus giving rise to some confusion. In common usage classical thinkers, who predate the neoclassicists, include Adam Smith, David Ricardo, Thomas Malthus and James Mill. In this book, what Keynes called 'classical' is referred to as 'neoclassical' in an attempt to minimise confusion. Neoclassical economic thought is associated with the marginalist revolution of the mid-nineteenth century, and in the United Kingdom was developed in the works of Jevons, Marshall and Pigou, and it provides the main theoretical underpinning to contemporary theory.

Neoclassical ideas have also been reformulated within the same analytical framework to give the neoclassical–Keynesian synthesis which is being developed in this section of the book. Such precisely formulated models are not to be found in *The General Theory* itself but were developed subsequently.

We shall now develop the standard version of the Keynesian three-sector model which has evolved out of the work of Hicks [1], Hansen [2] and Modigliani [3], keeping as closely as possible to Keynes's exposition. The Keynesian three-sector model differs from the neo-classical model in its specification of the supply side of the economy. As explained in Chapter 5, Keynes held that the money wage rate was inflexible downwards and that workers were willing to accept a cut in their real wage rate due to a rise in the general price level but would resist a real wage rate reduction brought about by a lower money wage. Keynes's specification of labour-supply behaviour results in a different aggregate supply function from that in the neoclassical model.

The Keynesian aggregate supply function

The derivation of the Keynesian aggregate supply function is shown in Figure 6.4. Part a of Figure 6.4 depicts the demand for labour as the real wage rate varies, together with a neoclassical labour-supply schedule which is needed to determine that the market-clearing equilibrium real wage rate is $(W/P)_e$. Part b

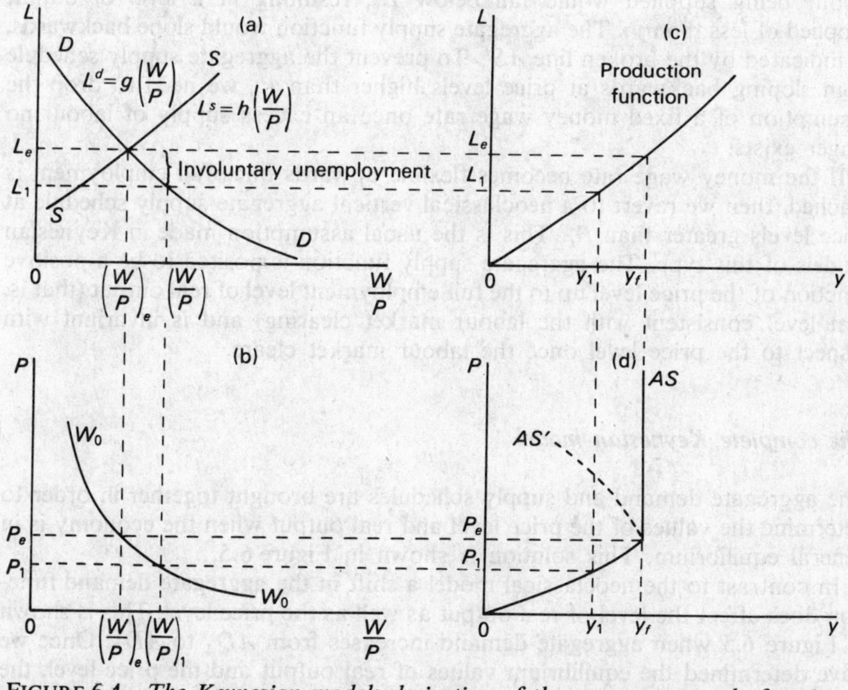

FIGURE 6.4 *The Keynesian model: derivation of the aggregate supply function*

of the diagram shows what the real wage rate is for various price levels given that the money wage rate is fixed at W_0. For example, if the price level is P_1, then the real wage rate is $(W/P)_1$ and is above the market-clearing real wage rate. If the real wage rate is $(W/P)_1$, the demand for labour in part a is L_1. Turning to part c of the diagram we can read off from the short-run production function that the amount of real output supplied will be y_1. So we now know that for a given money wage rate W_0, if the price level is P_1, the amount of real output supplied will be y_1. The co-ordinates P_1, y_1 are plotted in part d of Figure 6.4 to give one point on the aggregate supply schedule. Another point on the aggregate supply schedule can be found by trying another price level, finding the corresponding real wage rate when the money wage rate is W_0 and seeing what amount of labour will be demanded and hence output supplied at this real wage rate. The Keynesian aggregate supply function is upward-sloping since as the price level rises with the money wage rate fixed the real wage rate falls, thus stimulating employment and increasing the supply of output so long as an excess supply of labour persists.

The Keynesian aggregate supply function ceases to slope upwards once the economy is back on the neoclassical labour-supply function. Given a money wage rate of W_0 this happens once the price level has risen to P_e. The real wage rate is now at its market-clearing level and the corresponding supply of real output is y_f. If the price level were to rise above P_e while the money wage remained at W_0, the real wage rate would fall below its market-clearing level of $(W/P)_e$. There would now be excess demand for labour and the amount of labour being supplied would fall below L_e, resulting in a level of output supplied of less than y_f. The aggregate supply function would slope backwards, as indicated by the broken line AS'. To prevent the aggregate supply schedule from sloping backwards at price levels higher than P_e we need to drop the assumption of a fixed money wage rate once an excess supply of labour no longer exists.

If the money wage rate becomes flexible upwards once full employment is reached, then we revert to a neoclassical vertical aggregate supply schedule at price levels greater than P_e. This is the usual assumption made in Keynesian models of this type. The aggregate supply function is posited to be a positive function of the price level up to the full-employment level of real output (that is, that level consistent with the labour market clearing) and is invariant with respect to the price level once the labour market clears.

The complete Keynesian model

The aggregate demand and supply schedules are brought together in order to determine the values of the price level and real output when the economy is in general equilibrium. This solution is shown in Figure 6.5.

In contrast to the neoclassical model a shift in the aggregate demand function does affect the level of real output as well as the price level. This is shown in Figure 6.5 when aggregate demand increases from AD_1 to AD_2. Once we have determined the equilibrium values of real output and the price level, the equilibrium level of employment is determined via the short-run production

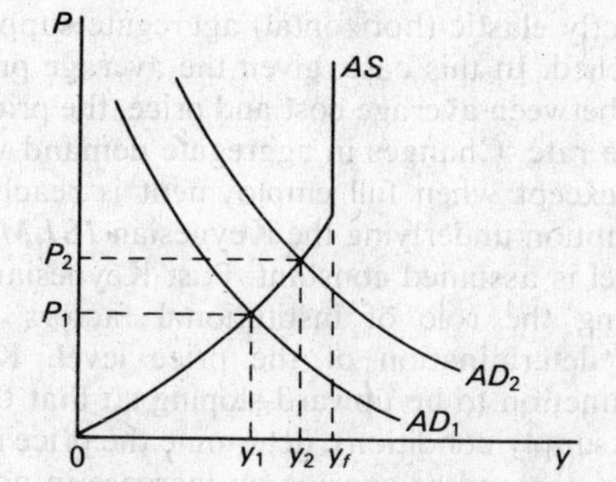

FIGURE 6.5 *Equilibrium in the Keynesian three-sector model*

function and the labour market in Figure 6.4. The equilibrium interest rate can be determined by the intersection of the *IS* and *LM* functions which is established once we know *y* and *P*.

The crucial characteristic of the Keynesian model is that equilibrium is consistent with involuntary unemployment: that is, with the absence of market-clearing in the labour market. This result is in complete contrast to the neoclassical model, in which equilibrium only occurs when all markets clear. If markets fail to clear in the neoclassical model, goods prices and/or money wages will adjust until market-clearing relative prices are attained. In the Keynesian model price adjustment is deemed not to occur in a downwards direction as the money wage rate is treated as fixed.

Determinants of the price level in a Keynesian model

In the Keynesian model real output and the price level are determined by the interaction of the aggregate demand for output with the aggregate supply of output. This is shown in Figure 6.5, the price level and the volume of real output being determined by the intersection of the aggregate demand and supply schedules. The price level in the short run is determined by two sets of factors. The price at which firms are willing to supply real output depends on the productivity of labour and the money wage rate. The upward-sloping aggregate supply curve is derived on the assumption that the marginal product of labour declines with output in the short run. Also there may exist costs of using capital which rise with the level of production. Both factors cause firms' marginal-cost curves to slope upwards so that profit-maximising firms will only produce additional output if price rises. An increase in aggregate demand enables firms to charge higher prices for their products and this induces an increase in the supply of real output.

If there were constant short-run marginal and average costs due to labour and capital being used in fixed proportions up to full employment, the aggregate short-run demand schedule for labour would be perfectly elastic with respect to the equilibrium real wage rate up to full employment. To this would correspond a perfectly elastic (horizontal) aggregate supply schedule until full employment is reached. In this case, given the average product of labour and the profit mark-up between average cost and price, the price level is determined by the money wage rate. Changes in aggregate demand would have no effect on the price level except when full employment is reached.

This is the assumption underlying the Keynesian *ISLM* model of Chapter 3, where the price level is assumed constant. Post-Keynesians echo this assumption by emphasising the role of institutional factors which govern wage bargaining in the determination of the price level. Keynes assumed the aggregate supply function to be upward-sloping so that the level of aggregate demand, as well as supply conditions, determine the price level. He analysed an increase in effective demand as causing an increase in nominal income which may be divided between a rise in real output and a rise in the price level.

We can thus distinguish three approaches to price-level determination in a macro model:

(1) *The neoclassical view*. The long-run equilibrium price level is determined by the stock of nominal money balances in the economy. An increase (decrease) in the stock of nominal money balances will not affect the equilibrium real variables in the economy, but will lead to an equivalent increase (decrease) in the equilibrium price level. However, given some interest elasticity in the demand for money, then in the neoclassical macro model outline in section 6.2, an increase (decrease) in either the equilibrium level of government expenditure, or investment expenditure, will lead to an increase (decrease) in the price level, while the real level of income stays unchanged. (This was analysed in Chapter 4, pp. 53–5.)

(2) *Keynes's approach*. The equilibrium price level is determined by both aggregate demand (that is, by the nominal money supply, the level of government spending, the marginal propensity to consume, etc.) and by aggregate supply factors (the money wage rate and its underlying institutional determinants and the productivity of labour).

(3) *The post-Keynesian approach*, in which the price level is not affected by aggregate demand except at full employment and above. Prices are institutionally determined: bargaining processes set money wage rates and these together with labour productivity determine average costs. Prices are then set by firms as some mark-up on average costs. This approach virtually makes the price level an exogenous variable as its institutional determinants are not economic variables which can be made endogenous in a macro model. Treating the price level as well as the money wage rate as an exogenous variable has been a characteristic of post-Keynesian economics.

The significance of the fixed money wage assumption

The Keynesian assumption of money wage rigidity is crucial to the conclusion in this model that increases in aggregate demand can raise the equilibrium level of real output. The level at which the money wage rate is fixed determines the position of the Keynesian aggregate supply function in the P, y plane. The money wage remains constant up to full employment along any given aggregate supply schedule. If the money wage rate increases to a new higher fixed level, then the real wage rate at every price level is also higher. (You can verify this by shifting the W_0W_0 schedule in Figure 6.4(b) to the right and tracing out the consequent shift in aggregate supply.) The demand for labour at each price level would be less, shifting the aggregate supply schedule up to the left. Given a higher money wage rate, the aggregate supply of output is lower at each price level. As can be seen from Figure 6.5, if the aggregate supply schedule shifts to the left as a result of an increase in the money wage rate the equilibrium quantity of real output will fall. A decrease in the marginal product of labour would also shift the aggregate supply function to the left. Conversely, the aggregate supply function would move to the right if the money wage rate fell or if the marginal productivity of labour rose.

One can deduce that an increase in aggregate demand (that is, an upward shift in the *AD* schedule in Figure 6.5) increases real output when it is below its full-employment equilibrium level provided that the money wage rate is inflexible. If it is, then as the price level rises due to the increase in aggregate demand, the real wage rate falls and induces an increase in the supply of real output. In terms of the diagrammatic presentation, the fixed money wage rate assumption allows the aggregate demand schedule to shift up an unchanged aggregate supply schedule. If the money wage rate increased following an increase in aggregate demand which raised the price level, then the aggregate supply schedule would also shift. If it shifted leftwards sufficiently far because money wages rose in line with goods prices, the real wage rate would return to its original level and equilibrium real output would remain at the previous level of y_1.

Keynesian analysis of wage and price flexibility as an adjustment mechanism

In addition to maintaining that prices are inflexible downwards because of the downwards rigidity of the money wage rate, Keynes also argued that even if prices and money wages did move downwards the economy would not return to full-employment equilibrium as in neoclassical analysis. In the neoclassical approach (as in the Keynesian model outlined here) unemployment occurs when the real wage rate exceeds its market-clearing level. The neoclassical adjustment mechanism is that unemployed workers bid down the money wage rate in order to secure employment. Provided that prices fall less rapidly than the money wage rate, the real wage rate falls, causing an increase in the demand for labour and consequently in the supply of real output. Keynes pointed out that this adjustment process does not occur in such a simple fashion if prices fall as rapidly as money wages leaving real wages unchanged. He reasoned that this would occur because of a lack of sufficient aggregate demand to take up the additional output produced. When money wages and hence real wages fall, inducing firms to produce more output, the income equivalent to the increased production is paid out to factors of production. If the marginal propensity to spend out of this additional income is less than 1.0, the resulting increase in aggregate demand will be less than the increase in output. The excess supply of output will cause prices to fall further and real wages will again rise unless money wages continue to fall. Furthermore, Keynes conjectured that there might be no floor to the downward spiral of prices and money wages. He suggested that the actual downward rigidity of the money wage rate was a stabilising factor preventing such a destabilising fall in prices and money wages and should not be blamed for the failure of the market adjustment mechanism to work.

Keynes thought that the only way falling money wages could bring about an increase in real output was through their effect on the real quantity of money. As prices fell so the real value of a fixed nominal money supply would rise, causing the interest rate to fall. Investment would therefore increase and, via the multiplier effect, cause a further rise in real output. This process of adjustment, summarised in Figure 6.6, is known as the *Keynes effect*.

Keynes suggested that the Keynes effect was likely to break down in two possible places. First, the interest rate might not fall as the real money supply increased. This would occur if the demand for money were perfectly interest-elastic, i.e. if there were a liquidity trap. Because people are prepared to hold unlimited real money balances at the existing rate of interest, the interest rate does not fall when real balances expand. Given a Keynesian transmission mechanism, the absence of any decline in the interest rate means that monetary expansion has no effect on aggregate demand and hence on output.

The second possible break in the Keynes effect link between a fall in the price level and a rise in real output is the failure of investment to respond to a fall in the interest rate. One strand in this argument was Keynes's belief that the expected return from investment had become so low in the 1930s' depression that a very low interest rate would be needed to establish the full-employment level of investment. As already mentioned, Keynes doubted if the interest rate could be pushed this low. In addition, Keynes thought that even if the interest rate did fall, investment would be slow to react and the total response would be small: 'moderate changes in the prospective yield of capital or in the rate of interest will not be associated with very great changes in the rate of investment' (*The General Theory*, p. 250). Keynesian economists interpreted this argument for static analysis in terms of totally interest-inelastic investment.

Either of the two breakdowns in the Keynes effect, the failure of the interest

FIGURE 6.6 *The Keynes effect*

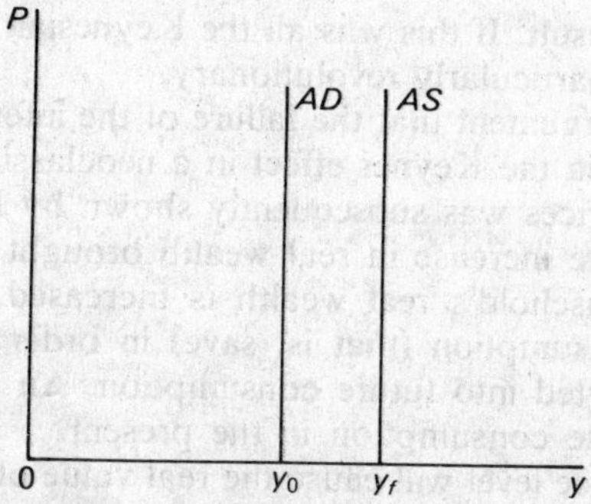

FIGURE 6.7 ***The extreme Keynesian case: the impossibility of full-employment output at any price level***

rate to fall when the real money supply increases or a very interest-inelastic investment function, would be sufficient on its own to prevent an adjustment towards neoclassical equilibrium via the Keynes effect, even if money wages were flexible downwards. Keynesians argued that either of these conditions would prevent aggregate demand increasing as the price level fell and would thus give rise to a vertical aggregate demand schedule, as shown in Figure 6.7. This means that even with a neoclassical aggregate supply function, the labour market will fail to clear unless the aggregate demand and supply schedules just happen to coincide. The model contains no adjustment mechanism to ensure such a coincidence. Real output is constrained to equal the smaller of either aggregate demand or aggregate supply. If the two schedules were as depicted in Figure 6.7, real output would be below its full-employment level. If the aggregate demand schedule has these extreme Keynesian characteristics, then the price level is indeterminate and is set exogenously by institutional factors.

6.4 The net wealth effect of changes in the price level

The Keynesians attempted to show that the neoclassical model with flexible money wages and prices would not adjust towards a static equilibrium solution. The adjustment process will fail if the interest-rate mechanism does not equate investment with the full-employment level of saving, either because investment is perfectly interest-inelastic or because wealth-holders' demand for money is such that it prevents the interest rate from falling to a sufficiently low level. At that stage in the debate (the 1940s and 1950s) it was necessary to show the absence of the neoclassical market adjustment mechanism in the presence of flexible wages in order to substantiate Keynes's claim that his theory was the generally applicable one, whereas the neoclassical model was only a special case. If all Keynes's theory amounted to was that market-clearing will not occur if money wages are rigid and therefore the return to full-employment equilibrium is blocked, then there would be little disagreement. Neoclassical economists would be quite happy to accept that if money wages are rigid and cause the real wage rate to exceed its equilibrium market-clearing level, then unemployment will result. If this was all the Keynesian revolution was about, it would not appear particularly revolutionary.

The Keynesians' argument that the failure of the interest-rate mechanism to restore equilibrium via the Keynes effect in a neoclassical model with flexible money wages and prices was subsequently shown by Pigou [4] to be flawed because it ignored the increase in real wealth brought about by a fall in the price level. If a household's real wealth is increased, there is less need to sacrifice present consumption (that is, save) in order to accumulate wealth which can be converted into future consumption. An increase in real wealth will therefore increase consumption in the present.

Changes in the price level will cause the real value of assets which are fixed in nominal terms to vary in the opposite direction. When the price level falls the real value of money and of fixed interest assets rises, since they are worth more in terms of goods and services. The owners of such assets consequently have an increased claim to goods and services. On the other hand, the issuers of nominally fixed debt feel worse off as the real value of their debt has risen. It is a standard practice in macro analysis to set the real value of private-sector liabilities against the real value of private-sector assets so that they are netted out one against the other. This is known as 'consolidating balance-sheets'. Thus if holders of private-sector bonds feel better off when the price level falls and consequently save less, this is assumed to be exactly offset by the issuers of these liabilities feeling worse off and reducing their consumption. The *net wealth* or *net worth* of the economy is the real value of all assets held *less* the real value of all liabilities. We are concerned here with analysing the effect of changes in the price level on the *real net wealth* of the economy. The effect of a decline in the price level, which increases real net wealth and thus causes an increase in consumption, is known as the *Pigou effect*. An increase in net wealth due only to a net increase in the real value of the money supply is known as the *real balance effect*.

If a fall in the price level is to increase real net wealth and thereby stimulate consumption, there must be some financial assets held by the private sector which are not matched by corresponding private-sector liabilities. One financial asset held by the private sector is money, which in a modern economy consists of currency and commercial bank deposits. Currency (that is, notes and coins) is issued by the government and can be regarded as a form of government debt. Because the government has no need to redeem its past issues of currency for goods, it will feel no worse off when the price level falls and the real value of the stock of currency rises. On the other hand, private-sector currency-holders will feel better off so there is a positive real net wealth effect when the real value of currency rises. Because currency is net wealth it has been given the term 'outside' money. (The terms 'outside' and 'inside' money were introduced by Gurley and Shaw [5].)

Bank deposits, in contrast to currency, are not entirely net wealth. Although they are wealth to their private-sector holders, commercial bank deposits are matched on the other side of banks' balance-sheets by bank loans to the private sector and by bank reserves in the form of currency and deposits at the central bank. Private-sector bank loans, being liabilities to bank borrowers, offset a good proportion of the positive wealth effect of private-sector bank deposits. As some bank reserves in the form of cash and deposits at the central bank are not private-sector liabilities, then that portion of the commercial bank deposits backed by such bank reserves is net wealth and thus is also 'outside' money. (The part backed by bank loans is termed 'inside' money because it is not part of net wealth.) Outside money therefore consists of currency held by banks and the private sector plus commercial banks' deposits at the central bank. (An equivalent definition is that outside money equals currency held by the non-bank private sector plus bank reserves.) A fall in the price level will increase the real value of outside money and hence it will have a positive real net wealth effect.

Whether real net wealth should include the real value of government interest-bearing debt is a debatable question. One argument is that since the government can always finance its expenditure by taxing or issuing debt or money, it feels no worse off when the real value of its debt is increased by a fall in the price level (see Metzler [6] and Smith [7]). The real value of government interest-bearing debt held by the private sector is therefore included in net wealth. Alternatively, it may be assumed that the public discounts the real value of the future tax payments they must make in order to service the government debt (Mundell [8]). In this case an increase in the real wealth of government debt-holders will be exactly offset by the increased present value of taxpayers' liabilities. (This assumes that the same rate of interest is used to discount income from human and non-human sources of wealth.)

The net wealth of the economy also consists of the stock of real capital goods but its real value will not vary with the equilibrium price level. This is because capital is measured in terms of physical units and the analysis assumes that the relative price of capital goods in terms of consumption goods forgone to produce them is fixed.

By not counting government interest-bearing debt as net wealth and only including outside money as net wealth which could be varied by price-level changes, Keynesians sought to show that the net wealth effect of a fall in the price level is quantitatively unimportant. The size of the Pigou effect is somewhat enhanced if it is argued that inside money can also have positive net wealth effects when the price level declines. Pesek and Saving [9] have argued that inside money does give rise to positive net wealth effects if the banking system is not perfectly competitive.[1]

[1] An imperfectly competitive banking system, which is restricted by government policy from producing the real stock of deposits which maximises its profits, may be able to increase its real stock of deposits when the price level falls. This will increase its profits and thus the real net wealth (capitalised profits) of its equity-holders. This net wealth effect is independent of the increase in real assets experienced by the banks' deposit-holders which is offset by the increased real value of the liabilities of its borrowers. The effect is likely to be small and only reinforces any net wealth effect due to the increase in the real value of outside money brought about by a lower price level. Patinkin [10] shows that net wealth effects due to a fall in the price level arise from money whose real value rises proportionately more than the costs of maintaining that stock when the price level falls. In a banking system producing the profit-maximising level of real deposits for which marginal revenue and cost are equalised, this can only occur for 'outside money' (that is, high-powered money). This is because the real value of outside money, which is government fiat money, rises when the price level falls by more than the costs of maintaining the increased real stock of money. There is therefore an increase in net wealth.

The theoretical significance of the Pigou effect is that it ensures that a model in which both the price level and money wage rate are flexible (that is, endogenous) will have a static equilibrium market-clearing solution. This is achieved by explicitly making consumption depend on real net wealth as well as on income and the interest rate. The Pigou effect would be incorporated into the neoclassical model outlined on page 82 by including real net wealth in the savings function:

$$\frac{S}{P}=f\left(y, i, \frac{NW}{P}\right) \tag{6.1a}$$

where NW/P is real net wealth, which is inversely related to the level of real saving.

The Pigou effect is designed to show that static full-employment equilibrium exists if money wages are flexible. It states little about the dynamics of wage flexibility as a mechanism for attaining full employment. For this mechanism to work we require that the process of a falling price level does not set off other reactions which nullify the effect of increased net wealth on the level of aggregate demand.

The dynamics of the Pigou effect require that a falling price level continually increases aggregate consumption by increasing real net wealth. In terms of the *ISLM* model this would be shown by a rightward shift in the *IS* function as the price level falls, until it intersects the *LM* schedule at the full-employment level of real output. The outward shift in the *IS* function would consequently shift the aggregate demand schedule up to the right. Even if the Keynes effect were nullified by the failure of the interest-rate equilibrating mechanism so that the aggregate demand schedule is vertical as depicted in Figure 6.7, the Pigou effect would ensure a full-employment equilibrium solution. The falling price level would shift the aggregate demand schedule rightwards until it coincided with the aggregate supply function.

Although not denying that a static market-clearing equilibrium would exist in a model with flexible money wages and prices, once the Pigou effect was taken account of, Keynesians question the stability of such an equilibrium. They argue that once the economy is out of market-clearing equilibrium the Pigou effect is unlikely to restore this equilibrium because of the destabilising effects of a falling price level (see Patinkin [11] and Tobin [12]). The Pigou effect, by assumption, ignores the change in the distribution of wealth that is likely to result from the decline in the price level. Such a redistribution has unpredictable effects on aggregate demand. One likely outcome of a falling price level is that, since it increases the real value of nominally fixed debt, firms become insolvent and go out of business. This disruption reduces aggregate production and employment. A declining price level generates expectations of further falls. Such expectations will cause people to postpone purchases until prices have fallen further. Thus consumption and investment are further reduced. Keynes thought it likely that a high degree of wage flexibility would be destabilising. If this is the case, the downward rigidity of money wages is not a barrier to equilibrium, as in a world of stable equilibrium, but a check to destabilising price and output movements.

> The chief result of this policy [flexible money wages] would be to cause a great instability of prices, so violent perhaps as to make business calculations futile in an economic society functioning after the manner of that in which we live. To suppose that flexible wage policy is a right and proper adjunct to a system which on the whole is one of *laissez-faire*, is the opposite of the truth. It is only in a highly authoritarian society, where sudden, substantial, all-round changes could be decreed, that a flexible wage policy could function with success. (*The General Theory*, p. 269)

In the neoclassical–Keynesian synthesis the Pigou effect was accepted as an equilibrating device which ensures the existence of market-clearing equilibrium when money wages and prices are flexible. But it was regarded as too small, too slow in working and possibly dynamically unstable to be relied upon. Therefore, it did not do any damage to the policy conclusions of Keynesian economics.

6.5 Policy implications of the neoclassical–Keynesian synthesis

The neoclassical–Keynesian synthesis that developed out of *The General Theory* and the ensuing debate of the 1940s and 1950s can be summarised in terms of a downward-sloping aggregate demand schedule and an upward-sloping aggregate supply function which becomes vertical at the full-employment level of output. This is shown again in Figure 6.8.

The consensus accepted that Keynesian analysis applied when the economy was in a depression and neoclassical analysis was more appropriate for inflation in boom conditions, though the dividing-line between the two states was somewhat hazy. Applying this analysis to policy issues led to the conclusion that the level of aggregate demand could be managed by the government in order to bring about planned changes in the price level and in the real quantity of output if that were below the full-employment level.

The policy message of *The General Theory* was almost entirely concentrated on increasing real output and employment in an economy diagnosed to be in

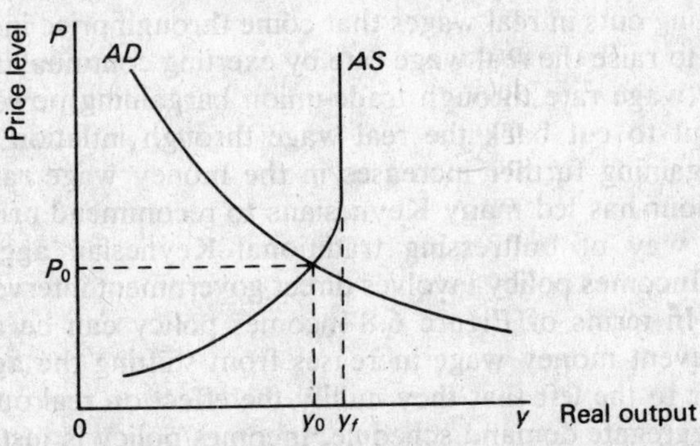

FIGURE 6.8 *The neoclassical–Keynesian synthesis*

underfull-employment equilibrium. Keynes argued that the neoclassical adjustment mechanism of downward movements in prices and money wages could only restore full employment if it stimulated aggregate demand via increasing the real quantity of money. Given that the Pigou effect works, this would eventually happen. However, Keynesians have held that this mechanism is slow and unreliable and that the same effect on aggregate demand could be achieved by a direct government stimulus to demand. The most effective stimulus, in Keynesian thinking, would come from increased government expenditure or reduced taxation rather than from monetary expansion.

If government policy shifts the aggregate demand curve upwards, firms can charge higher prices and still sell more output. Provided that the real wage rate falls because output prices rise, firms will wish to supply more output. Given the fixed money wage rate of the Keynesian model, the effect of government policy is that the higher price level achieves a reduction in the real wage rate that workers would not have accepted had it come in the form of a cut in money wages at an unchanged price level. The effectiveness of government policy, given Keynes's analysis of the labour market, depends entirely on workers' willingness to accept a cut in real wages. Only if the aggregate supply schedule is perfectly elastic (horizontal) with respect to the price level will an increase in aggregate demand bring about an increase in the supply of real output without the real wage falling. In this case firms have constant marginal costs and are willing to expand output without any increase in product prices, so long as there is demand for their output. This is a position that has been adopted by many post-Keynesians, particularly in Britain.

However, in *The General Theory* Keynes assumed that firms face rising marginal costs, so that the aggregate supply schedule is upward-sloping. In this case an upwards shift in the aggregate demand schedule would fail to increase equilibrium real output if workers were not prepared to accept a cut in their real wages. If the rising price level causes money wages to rise, the aggregate supply curve will shift to the left. The equilibrium real wage rate will not fall and the supply of output in equilibrium will remain at its original level of y_0 (in Figure 6.8). Keynes's assumption that workers are prepared to accept a cut in real wages which occurs due to a rise in the general price level has been difficult to sustain in the post-war period. Indeed, many post-Keynesian economists subscribe to a belief in 'real wage resistance' (Hicks [13]). Workers are seen as not only resisting cuts in real wages that come through price increases but also as attempting to raise the real wage rate by exerting continual upward pressure on the money wage rate through trade-union bargaining power. Attempts by the government to cut back the real wage through inflation are resisted by trade unions gaining further increases in the money wage rate.

This behaviour has led many Keynesians to recommend prices and income policies as a way of buttressing traditional Keynesian aggregate demand management. Incomes policy involves direct government intervention in money wage setting. In terms of Figure 6.8 incomes policy can be analysed as the attempt to prevent money wage increases from shifting the aggregate supply function so far to the left that they nullify the effect on real output of upward shifts in the aggregate demand schedule. Incomes policy is just another means of trying to induce workers to accept real wage cuts.

References

[1] J. R. Hicks, 'Mr Keynes and the Classics: A Suggested Interpretation', *Econometrica* 5, 2 (1937).
[2] A. Hansen, *A Guide to Keynes* (New York: McGraw-Hill, 1953).
[3] F. Modigliani, 'Liquidity Preference and the Theory of Interest and Money', *Econometrica*, 12 (1944).
[4] A. C. Pigou, 'The Classical Stationary State', *Economic Journal*, 53 (December 1943).
[5] J. G. Gurley and E. S. Shaw, *Money in a Theory of Finance* (Washington, D.C.: Brookings Institution, 1966).
[6] L. A. Metzler, 'Wealth, Saving and the Rate of Interest', *Journal of Political Economy*, 59 (April 1951).
[7] W. Smith, 'Current Issues in Monetary Economics', *Journal of Economic Literature*, 8, 3 (September 1970).
[8] R. A. Mundell, 'The Public Debt, Corporate Income Taxes and the Rate of Interest', *Journal of Political Economy*, 60 (1960).
[9] B. P. Pesek and T. R. Saving, *Money, Wealth and Economic Theory* (New York: Macmillan, 1967).
[10] D. Patinkin, 'Money and Wealth: A Review Article', *Journal of Economic Literature*, 7 (1969).
[11] D. Patinkin, 'Price Flexibility and Full Employment', originally published in *American Economic Review*, 38 (1948), revised version in *Readings in Monetary Theory*, ed. American Economic Association (New York: Blakiston, 1962).
[12] J. Tobin, *Asset Accumulation and Economic Activity* (Oxford: Blackwell, 1980) 9–11.
[13] J. Hicks, 'What is Wrong with Monetarism?', *Lloyds Bank Review*, 118 (October 1975).

II MONEY AND THE OPEN ECONOMY

Section II deals with two crucial and interrelated aspects of an economy such as Britain's. First of all it is an open economy since its residents engage in foreign trade and borrow and lend abroad. Second, it is a monetary economy. The vast majority of transactions between domestic residents and between residents and foreigners involve the exchange of money for goods, services and financial assets. These two aspects are closely related because the balance of payments is a monetary phenomenon. As will be explained, a balance-of-payments deficit (surplus) implies an outflow (inflow) of foreign currency reserves and this has effects on the domestic money supply. Alternatively, looking at it from the monetary angle, disequilibrium between the demand for and supply of money results in portfolio adjustment which affects the demand for domestic goods, services and financial assets as well as their foreign equivalents. Thus the balance of payments cannot be in equilibrium unless the demand and supply of money is also in equilibrium.

Chapter 7 outlines the relationship between the balance of payments and the exchange rate and then discusses the Keynesian analysis of the current account of the balance of payments. Chapters 8 and 9 examine the demand for and the supply of money and show how the determination of the money supply is affected by the openness of the economy. Chapters 10 and 11 are concerned with open-economy models with international capital flows. Chapter 10 presents the Keynesian Mundell–Fleming model from which the modern monetary approach to the balance of payments, examined in Chapter 11, took off.

7 The Balance of Payments and Keynesian Analysis

The analysis of macroeconomic behaviour in section I was conducted in the context of a closed economy. The introduction of trade with other economies widens the choices available to consumers, producers and investors. In an open economy consumers are no longer restricted to domestically produced goods, while producers are no longer confined to the domestic market. Therefore, a change in total domestic expenditure on final goods and services no longer implies an equal change in the expenditure on domestic output, as part of domestic expenditure falls on foreign-produced goods and services, while part of the expenditure on domestic production is due to foreign purchases of domestic output.

Over the last thirty years economies have become increasingly open. International trade has grown at a faster rate than the real output of most countries. During this period there has been a decline in tariffs and controls on trade in goods and services between developed economies. This trade liberalisation and the growth of new centres of production have resulted in a greater degree of substitutability between domestic and foreign goods than existed in the first post-war decade. Domestic producers now face greater competitive pressures to become more efficient.

A related post-war development has been the weakening of exchange controls in the advanced economies and the growth of international capital markets such as the Euro-dollar market, accompanied by a closer integration of national financial markets. Foreign securities and real assets have consequently become closer substitutes for their domestic equivalents. These developments have made it more difficult for national monetary authorities to influence their domestic interest rates. In the light of these considerations both the monetary and goods sectors of the close-economy models require substantial modification when analysing an open economy.

7.1 The exchange rate

The exchange rate is the price of domestic currency in terms of foreign currency. It is the number of units of foreign exchange, *e*, that one unit of domestic currency will buy. The exchange rate for a given currency, such as sterling, is determined by the demand and supply of it on the world's foreign exchange markets. When UK residents buy foreign goods and services or lend abroad by purchasing foreign assets, they supply sterling to the foreign exchange market in order to secure the required foreign currencies. Similarly, a demand for sterling is created when foreigners wish to buy UK goods, services and assets and need to exchange their currencies into sterling. The exchange rate for sterling is in equilibrium when the demand for and supply of sterling are equal at the current rate.

A rise in the price of sterling in terms of foreign exchange (a rise in *e*) is termed an *appreciation* of sterling, while a fall in the price of sterling in terms of foreign exchange is termed a *depreciation*. The demand and supply of sterling on the foreign exchange market will bear the usual relation to the price of sterling. Where UK exports are imperfect substitutes for foreign goods, depreciation will lower the foreign exchange price of UK exports, provided that it does not induce an exactly offsetting rise in UK production costs. Assuming that the demand for exports is negatively related to their price and that this falls in terms of foreign exchange, then depreciation will increase export demand and thus increase the demand for sterling. Where domestic and foreign goods are perfect substitutes, the price of the goods will be determined on world markets, as the United Kingdom is a relatively small economy. In this case a depreciation of sterling will not change the foreign exchange price of these internationally tradable goods but it will increase their sterling price. Provided that domestic costs rise less than the sterling price of exports, then exporters' profits increase and will increase even further if they produce more for sale abroad. This, too, will increase the demand for sterling. The sterling price of imports is increased by a depreciation, as the United Kingdom is not a dominant buyer in world markets. Given a normal demand function, this will reduce the demand for imports as long as all domestic prices do not rise in proportion to the depreciation. Provided that import demand is price-elastic, this will reduce the supply of sterling.

If, at the current exchange rate, the supply of sterling exceeds the demand for sterling in the foreign exchange market, then there will be a tendency for sterling to depreciate given normal short-run supply and demand functions for sterling. In the absence of intervention by either the Bank of England, or other countries' central banks, the exchange rate for sterling will fall. Similarly, when the demand for sterling exceeds the supply of sterling in the foreign exchange market, there will be a tendency for sterling to appreciate.

Flexible exchange rates

A flexible or floating exchange rate is one which is allowed to find its own level as determined by the forces of supply and demand. In the absence of intervention in the foreign exchange market by central banks and other government agencies (often called 'official intervention'), the exchange rate will settle at the point at which the market clears. This equilibrium rate is illustrated in Figure 7.1 by the exchange rate e_e which equates the demand for, and supply of sterling by traders and investors. A 'clean float' is a flexible exchange-rate system in which no official intervention occurs. A 'managed float' (also known as a 'dirty float') is a flexible exchange-rate system in which central banks intervene in the foreign exchange market in order to modify movements in exchange rates. Currently (1982) the major trading nations are on a managed float.

Fixed exchange rates

A fixed exchange-rate system is one where each country has its currency's exchange rate fixed at a given parity rate in terms of some international money or vehicle currency. Under the gold standard system the international money was gold, while under the Bretton Woods agreement on fixed exchange parities which lasted from 1944 to 1971, the US dollar was the vehicle currency in which other countries fixed their exchange rates. Under a fixed exchange-rate system the domestic currency is *devalued* when it is moved from one parity in terms of the vehicle currency to a lower parity. This is illustrated in Figure 7.1 by a move from e_d to e_s. If the domestic currency is moved to a higher parity in terms of the vehicle currency, then it is *revalued.*

Under a fixed exchange-rate system the short-run equilibrium rate will often depart from the fixed exchange rate following some real or monetary change which shifts the demand or supply curves for foreign exchange. In order to maintain the fixed exchange rate, the central banks concerned will have to eliminate the excess demands or the excess supplies of their currency. They do this by either purchasing or selling foreign currency in exchange for their own currency.

Consider the case in Figure 7.1 where the exchange rate for sterling has been fixed in terms of the US dollar at the parity rate e_d. In a fixed exchange-rate system where the US dollar is the vehicle currency, this also fixes it against all other currencies. This rate is above the equilibrium exchange rate, e_e.

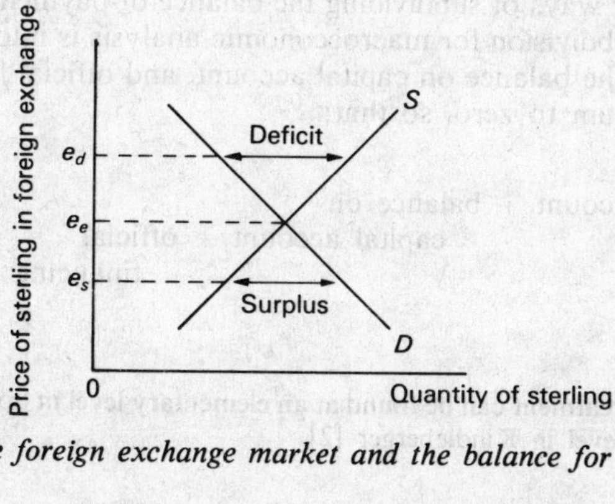

FIGURE 7.1 *The foreign exchange market and the balance for official financing*

Therefore, the supply of sterling on the foreign exchange market by international traders and investors is greater than their demand for it. In this case sterling would depreciate unless the Bank of England purchases the excess supply of sterling with foreign currency. The Bank obtains this foreign currency by either running down its foreign currency reserves or by borrowing from foreign central banks and financial institutions. Alternatively, if the rate is fixed at e_s in Figure 7.1, then it will be below the equilibrium rate, e_e. An excess demand for sterling would develop and the rate will only stay at e_s if the Bank of England purchases foreign exchange with sterling. This leads to an increase in the Bank's foreign currency reserves.

If over a period of time the Bank of England is a net purchaser of sterling in the foreign exchange market, then the cumulative purchase of sterling over the period is measured by a deficit in the balance for official financing (BOF) in the balance-of-payments accounts for the period. When the Bank of England is a net seller of sterling in the foreign exchange market then the BOF will show a surplus. A deficit on the BOF measures the excess supply of sterling, while a surplus on the BOF measures the excess demand for sterling in the foreign exchange market over the time period.

7.2 The balance of payments

The money flows arising from transactions in goods, services and assets between the United Kingdom and foreign residents over a given period of time are summarised in the balance-of-payments accounts.[1] In these accounts all items which lead to a purchase of sterling in the foreign exchange market are given a positive sign, while all items which lead to a sale of sterling in the foreign exchange market are given a negative sign. In the foreign exchange market, as in any market, *ex post* purchases must equal *ex post* sales. As the UK balance-of-payments accounts include all the *ex post* transactions in sterling over a given time period, the total of all the items in the balance-of-payments accounts must sum to zero. Therefore, when one refers to a surplus or a deficit on the balance of payments, one is referring to the sum of the items in a sub-account of the balance-of-payments accounts, rather than to the balance-of-payments accounts as a whole.

There are many ways of subdividing the balance-of-payments accounts, but the most useful subdivision for macroeconomic analysis is into the balance on current account, the balance on capital account, and official financing. These must identically sum to zero, so that:

$$\text{balance on current account} + \text{balance on capital account} + \text{official financing} = 0$$

[1] A more detailed treatment can be found at an elementary level in Södersten [1] and at a more advanced level in Kindleberger [2].

or

$$\text{balance on current account} + \text{balance on capital account} = -\text{official financing}$$

The sum of the current and capital account is called the balance for official financing (BOF) which is often called the total currency flow or overall balance of payments. In some other countries a similar balance is called the balance for official settlement. Table 7.1 sets out the balance-of-payments accounts for the United Kingdom in 1980.

The balance on current account is equal to the value of exported goods and services, *plus* the value of net current transfers, *minus* the value of imported goods and services. The export of services includes the receipt of interest and dividends from foreign financial and real assets owned by UK residents and companies, while the import of services includes the payment of interest and dividends to foreign owners of UK financial and real assets. The balance of trade is a subdivision of the balance on current account. It is equal to the difference between the value of exported goods and the value of imported goods and refers exclusively to the trade in so-called 'visibles'.

Kindleberger [2] calls the balance on current account the *net worth balance*, as it shows the net acquisition of foreign assets by the economy as a whole. Any country with a surplus on current account must be either increasing its ownership of foreign assets or decreasing its indebtedness to foreigners. Conversely, a deficit on current account means that a country is either increasing its foreign indebtedness, or is selling its foreign assets. A persistent deficit on the balance on current account leads to increased foreign ownership of domestic assets.

The capital account records both the borrowing and lending of funds abroad by domestic residents and companies. It records the sale by domestic residents to foreigners of financial and real assets, as well as the purchase by domestic residents of financial and real assets from foreigners. The sum of the balance on current and capital accounts is equal to the balance for official settlements or total currency flow.

The balance for official financing (BOF) or total currency flow is a record of the difference between the demand and supply of sterling by traders and investors in the foreign exchange market over some time period, usually one year. It is equal to the cumulative sum of the Bank of England's intervention in the foreign exchange market through purchases and sales of sterling over that time period. A deficit on the BOF measures the excess supply of sterling on the foreign exchange market by traders and investors over the period in question. It shows the amount of sterling that the Bank of England purchased over the time period in order to offset the excess supply of sterling by traders and investors in the foreign exchange market. Such purchases of sterling by the Bank of England would lead to a decline in the money stock unless this is prevented by an equal open-market purchase of bonds by the Bank of England. Similarly a surplus on the BOF measures both the excess demand for sterling by non-official sources on the foreign exchange market and the resulting sale of

TABLE 7.1 *The UK balance of payments account in 1980*

	£ million
Export of goods	+47,389
Import of goods	−46,211
Export of services	+15,809
Import of services	−11,621
Receipt of interest, profits and dividends from overseas	+ 8,204
Payment of interest, profits and dividends overseas	− 8,242
Net current transfers	− 2,112
Balance on current account	**+ 3,206**
Non-official borrowing abroad plus sale of assets to foreigners	+10,488
Non-official lending abroad plus purchase of assets from foreigners	−11,963
Balance on capital account	**− 1,475**
Change in Bank of England foreign currency reserves (increase −, decrease +)	− 291
Change in borrowing by Bank of England from foreign banks (increase +, decrease −)	−1,081
Allocation of new reserve created by the IMF (special deposit receipts)	+ 180
Official financing	**− 1,192**
SUMMARY OF BALANCE OF PAYMENTS	
Balance on current account	+ 3,206
Balance on capital account	− 1,475
Balancing item due to errors and omissions in the above balances	− 539
Balance for official financing	+ 1,192
Official financing	− 1,192
	0

Note: Average estimate of 1980 G.D.P. = £191,666 million.

Source: *The Balance of Payments* (Pink Book), (London: HMSO, 1981), tables 1.2, 1.3. (The only difference between the classification above and that in tables 1.2 and 1.3 is that the allocation of special deposit receipts has been moved from a position of its own to the official financing account.)

sterling on that market by the Bank of England. This would lead to an increase in the UK money stock unless offset by equal open-market sales of bonds by the Bank of England. Open-market sales and purchases of bonds designed to offset the impact on the domestic money supply of a surplus or deficit on the BOF is called *sterilisation*. Therefore, the balance for official financing has repercussions on the UK money stock and UK financial markets whenever it is not equal to zero. This makes it an important factor in the macroeconomic analysis of an open economy. Only when the balance for official financing or total currency flow is zero is the foreign exchange market in equilibrium and there are no external repercussions on the domestic money supply and financial markets.

7.3 Absorption and the balance of payments

In an open economy part of domestic aggregate expenditure falls on foreign goods and services, while part of domestic production is bought by foreigners. In order to measure national income by means of expenditure on the national product, one has to subtract from the total expenditure by domestic residents on final goods and services that portion which is spent on imported goods and services and add to the result foreign expenditure on domestically produced goods and services. The *ex post* national income accounting identity is now

$$Y \equiv C + I + G + \text{exports} - \text{imports} \tag{7.1}$$

where Y is national income, C is consumption, I is investment, G is direct government expenditure on goods and services, and all the variables in identity 7.1 are measured in domestic prices. We need to be careful to measure all these expenditures in the same currency. Let the imports of goods and services amount to F units of foreign currency. They can be valued in terms of the domestic currency by dividing F by the exchange rate, e, which is measured in terms of the number of units of foreign currency which exchange for one unit of domestic currency. Therefore

$$Y \equiv C + I + G + X - \frac{1}{e}F \tag{7.2}$$

where X is the value of exports in domestic currency.

If we divide through both sides of identity 7.2 by a price index, P, which measures the current price level, we get a similar identity in real terms:

$$y \equiv \frac{C}{P} + \frac{I}{P} + \frac{G}{P} + \frac{X}{P} - \frac{\frac{1}{e}F}{P} \tag{7.3}$$

By rearranging identities 7.2 and 7.3 we get

$$Y - (C + I + G) \equiv X - \frac{1}{e}F \tag{7.2a}$$

and

$$y - \left(\frac{C + I + G}{P}\right) \equiv \frac{X}{P} - \frac{\frac{1}{e}F}{P} \tag{7.3a}$$

The term on the right-hand side of both identities is the balance of payments on current account. In equation 7.2a this is measured in domestic currency at current prices, while in 7.3a this is measured in real terms. On the left-hand side of both identities the term in brackets is equal to total domestic expenditure on final goods and services, or *domestic absorption.* It is in current-price terms in 7.2a and in real terms in 7.3a. Therefore, setting $C + I + G = A$, we get

$$Y - A \equiv X - \frac{1}{e}F \tag{7.2b}$$

$\equiv$ balance of payments on current account in domestic currency

$\equiv$ net acquisition of foreign assets by domestic residents and the central bank

and

$$y - \frac{A}{P} \equiv \frac{X}{P} - \frac{\frac{1}{e}F}{P} \tag{7.3b}$$

$\equiv$ balance of payments on current account in real terms

These identities always hold. They show that the balance of payments on current account is a macroeconomic phenomenon and that it must *always* be equal to the difference between national income and domestic absorption.

A deficit on the current account implies that current domestic absorption (or domestic aggregate expenditure on goods and services) is greater than national income and that excess of expenditure over income is financed by borrowing abroad, selling existing assets to foreigners or by running down foreign exchange reserves. The identities 7.2b and 7.3b show that *any* policy which will successfully eliminate a balance-of-payments deficit on current account must either increase national income more than it increases domestic absorption, or else decrease domestic absorption more than it decreases national income. In a fully employed economy no increase in real income is possible. Here, identity 7.2b shows that only those policies which reduce real domestic absorption (that is, lower real domestic expenditure) will improve the balance of payments on current account. In a fully employed economy neither import controls nor exchange devaluation can improve the balance on current account if there is no decrease in domestic absorption. Given full employment, any switch of domestic demand from foreign goods to domestically produced goods brought about by such policies must result in a decline in the volume of goods available for export. The net effect of this is a decline in the volume of trade, while the balance on current account stays unchanged (this was first pointed out by Alexander [3]).

The identities also show that a surplus on current account necessarily requires domestic absorption to be smaller than domestic national income. This implies that domestic savings and taxes are larger than domestic investment and government expenditure and that the difference is spent on the net acquisition of foreign assets. This can be seen if we remember that by definition real income can be classified into its component uses, so that

$$y \equiv \frac{C}{P} + \frac{S}{P} + \frac{T}{P} \tag{7.4}$$

where C/P is real consumption, S/P is real savings by the private sector and T/P is the real value of government tax receipts. Equating the right-hand side of identity 7.4 with the right-hand side of identity 7.3 and then rearranging terms gives

$$\left(\frac{S}{P} - \frac{I}{P}\right) + \left(\frac{T}{P} - \frac{G}{P}\right) \equiv \frac{X}{P} - \frac{\frac{1}{e}F}{P} \tag{7.5}$$

Identity 7.5 shows that the balance of payments on current account must be equal to the difference between private-sector saving and investment, plus the government budget surplus or deficit. The first term in brackets on the left-hand side of the identity is equal to the sum of the net acquisitions by the private sector of government bonds, money and foreign assets. This is sometimes called the *net acquisition of financial assets by the private sector.*

According to the 'New Cambridge' school of economists, the net acquisition of assets by the private sector $(S - I)$ is a stable linear function of disposable income (see Fetherston and Godley [4] esp. pp. 34, 58). Therefore, they conclude that fluctuations in income and in the balance on current account are often induced by changes in the government's fiscal stance. If $S - I$ is not greatly changed by an increase in income, then identity 7.5 implies that any change in the government budget deficit or surplus will be mirrored in the balance on current account. Hence any increase in the government budget deficit (that is, fall in budget surplus) will result in a deterioration in the balance on current account. This line of analysis seemed to explain the fluctuations in the UK current account of the late 1960s and early 1970s. Unfortunately by the late 1970s the net acquisition of financial assets by the private sector seems to have become more unstable and this 'New Cambridge' approach no longer gave accurate predictions of the variations in the balance on current account. However, one must remember that any increase in the public-sector deficit not offset by an equal fall in investment must lead to some deterioration in the current account, as absorption will increase relative to income.

7.4 Keynesian approaches to the current account

The early Keynesian approach to the balance of payments was concerned with the determination of the current account in situations with involuntary unemployment, excess domestic productive capacity, price rigidity and constant production costs in both domestic and foreign economies. This approach also assumed that the central bank could sterilise any surpluses or deficits on the balance for official financing and thus prevent the balance of payments from having any effect on the domestic money supply. Later extensions dealt with the impact of economic growth on the balance of payments and extended the model in an *ad hoc* way to deal with the capital account. However, Keynesian and neo-Keynesian analyses of the balance of payments have primarily focused on the current account.

Let us assume that we are dealing with a small open economy in the sense that changes in its domestic income, imports and exports have an insignificant effect on the rest of the world's income. This is a crucial simplifying assumption and one that applies reasonably well to the United Kingdom. Not all the results derived from the small open economy case will hold for a large open economy. However, the results we stress are robust enough to hold in a large open economy when realistic parameter values are assumed for the consumption and import demand functions in both the domestic and foreign economies.

Our small open economy is assumed to have involuntary unemployment, excess capacity and a horizontal supply curve for current domestic output. The same assumptions hold for foreign economies. An additional simplifying assumption, commonly found in Keynesian open-economy models, is that imported goods are distinct from domestic production and the country is specialised in the production of its export goods, so that it has some market power in its export market. Given these assumptions, we can think of the demand for the country's exports, X, as being a function of foreign incomes y^* and the relative prices of domestic and foreign goods, where exports increase with an increase in y^* and decrease with a currency appreciation (i.e. a rise in e). Therefore, we can write

$$X = X\left(y^*, \frac{Pf}{ePd}\right) \tag{7.6}$$

such that $\partial X/\partial y^* > 0$, and $\partial X/\partial e < 0$.

Here X is the value of exports in domestic currency, e is the foreign exchange rate in terms of units of foreign currency per unit of domestic currency, Pd is the price level for domestic goods in domestic currency and Pf is the price level of foreign goods in foreign currency. As we are dealing with a small-economy model, foreign income, y^*, is exogenous. Also, Pd and Pf are constant due to the assumption of constant production costs and horizontal aggregate supply functions both at home and abroad. Therefore, we can rewrite equation 7.6 as

$$X = X(e) \tag{7.7}$$

where $\partial X/\partial e < 0$.

If we measure imports, F, in foreign prices, then the demand for imports is a function of domestic income, y, and relative prices. F increases as domestic income, y, increases, as part of any increase in domestic income is spent on imported goods. F will also increase as the exchange rate, e, rises, as with unchanged foreign price levels for import goods an exchange appreciation of the domestic currency will lower the domestic price of imports and increase the quantity of imports demanded. Therefore, we can write

$$F = F\left(y, \frac{Pf}{ePd}\right) \tag{7.8}$$

where $\partial F/\partial y > 0$, and $\partial F/\partial e > 0$. As Pd and Pf are constant in terms of their respective currencies we can also rewrite this in the simplified functional form:

$$F = F(y, e) \tag{7.9}$$

We can simplify this expression further if we assume that, with unchanged relative prices, total domestic expenditure on imports is a simple linear function of domestic income. Then, measuring imports in terms of domestic currency, we get

$$\frac{1}{e}F = \frac{1}{e}\phi(e)y \tag{7.10}$$

If we set $(1/e)\phi(e) = f$, where f is the marginal propensity of the domestic economy to import foreign goods at the constant exchange rate e, then

$$\frac{1}{e}F = fy \tag{7.11}$$

We can now extend the Keynesian goods-market equations of Chapter 4 to include the foreign sector, by adding equations 7.7 and 7.11 to the equation system described in equations 4.1 to 4.6 on page 47 of Chapter 4. In addition, we have to replace the equilibrium condition in equation 4.5 by the new equilibrium condition:

$$y = C + I + G + X - \frac{1}{e}F \tag{7.12}$$

Solving the extended system composed of equations 4.1 to 4.4 together with equation 4.6 and equations 7.7, 7.11 and 7.12 we get the *IS* function:

$$y = \frac{a + I(i) + G_0 + X(e)}{s(1-t) + t + f} \tag{7.13}$$

In this expression f is a function of e and will only be constant if e stays unchanged. This *IS* function has the normal negative relationship between the values of y and i due to the effect of the level of interest rate, i, on the volume of investment.

If we assume that under a fixed exchange rate, e^*, the government can control the money supply, then we can set out our *ISLM* model. The *IS* function is equation 7.13, while the *LM* function is equation 3.13 of Chapter 3. These are set out below:

$$y = \frac{a + I(i) + G_0 + X(e^*)}{s(1-t) + t + f} \quad (IS \text{ function}) \tag{7.13}$$

$$\frac{M_0^S}{P} = f(y, i) \quad (LM \text{ function}) \tag{7.14}$$

These are illustrated in Figure 7.2, given that P is fixed by assumption.

From equation 7.13 we can see that the IS function will shift to the right if there is either an autonomous increase in any of I, G and X or a decrease in the marginal propensity to import, f. Any of these changes will shift the IS function to the right, from IS_1 to IS_2 in Figure 7.2, and will lead to an expansion of income from y_1 to y_2 given the supply-side assumptions. The only difference between this result and the closed-economy model discussed earlier is that there is an impact on the level of domestic income from exports and the marginal propensity to import. Given the assumption of a perfectly elastic supply of domestic output, income rises when either exports increase or the marginal propensity to import decreases; and income falls when either exports decrease or the marginal propensity to import rises, other things being equal.

Given a central bank policy that stabilises the rate of interest at i^* and a fixed exchange rate e^*, we can find the multiplier for an autonomous change in any of the variables in the numerator of the IS function. This is obtained by differentiating y in equation 7.13 with respect to these terms. This gives

$$\frac{dy}{dI} = \frac{dy}{dG} = \frac{dy}{dX} = \frac{1}{s(1-t)+t+f} \tag{7.15}$$

This is the multiplier in the open-economy Keynesian model under a fixed exchange-rate system, where the government allows the money supply to adjust to the demand for money at the constant rate of interest, i^*. The multiplier is illustrated in Figure 7.2. Any change in I, G or X which shifts the IS function from IS_1 to IS_2 will lead to an increase in income from y_1 to y_3 if i stays unchanged at i^*. This requires an increase in money supply in order to shift the LM_1 function to LM_2 so as to keep i at i^*. Here the increase in income is larger than in the case where the money supply is constant.

The three multipliers given above are identical due to the small-economy assumption. In the large-economy case the three multipliers will not be identical, as an autonomous increase in exports will initially depress the level of

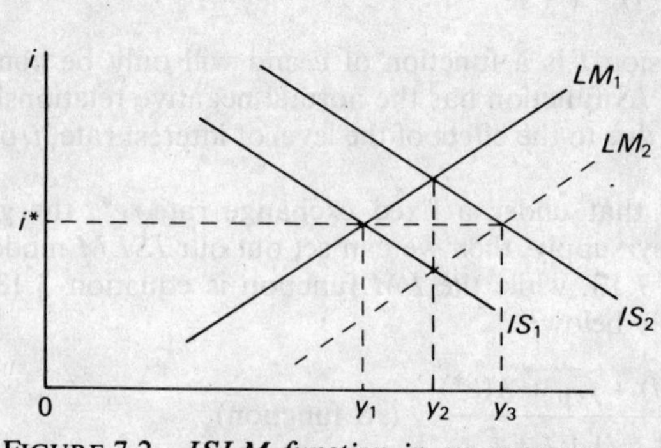

FIGURE 7.2 *ISLM function in an open economy*

foreign income and this will have negative feedback effects on the level of domestic exports and income. In this large-economy case

$$\frac{dy}{dI} = \frac{dy}{dG} > \frac{dy}{dX} > 0$$

In the small-economy model with a fixed exchange rate, e^*, the balance of payments on current account can be written as

$$CA = X - fy \tag{7.16}$$

The current account, CA, is expressed in terms of the domestic currency. X is a function of the level of foreign real income and is therefore exogenous. Here, given the fixed exchange rate e^* and constant domestic and foreign price levels, there is only one level of income, $y = X/f$, at which $CA = 0$. Any expansion in domestic expenditure will worsen the balance on current account, as part of the resulting change in income will lead to a rise in imports. In this case domestic absorption will rise faster than income. This is illustrated by the vertical line $CA = 0$ in Figure 7.3. Any income that is greater than X/f involves a deficit on the current account, while any income smaller than X/f involves a surplus on the current account.

For the $CA = 0$ line to shift, it is necessary that either X changes or the marginal propensity to import, f, changes. An autonomous increase in exports, from X to $X + \Delta X$ will improve the balance on current account by shifting the $CA = 0$ line to the right, to $CA' = 0$ in Figure 7.3. However, as this increase in exports will shift the IS_1 function to the right, to IS_2 in Figure 7.3, the induced increase in domestic income from X/f to y, will lead to a rise in domestic absorption and imports. Hence the improvement in the current-account balance will be smaller than the increase in exports. The results stated in this paragraph and in the previous one hold in the large-economy case, but they depend on the specific Keynesian assumptions of the model.

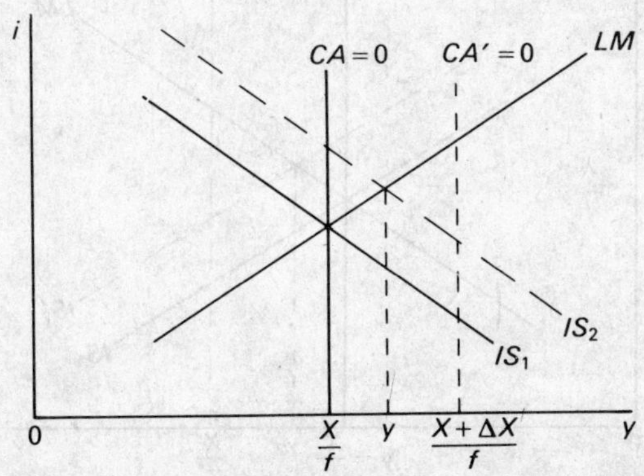

FIGURE 7.3 *The current account in a fixed exchange-rate ISLM model*

Effect of exchange-rate changes on aggregate demand

We have seen that a change in either exports, X, or the marginal propensity to import, f, will affect both the IS function and the balance on current account, thereby shifting the IS function and the $CA = 0$ line. One factor that affects both X and f is a change in the exchange rate, e. Let us first of all consider what effect a depreciation in the exchange rate, e, is likely to have on the current account of the balance of payments, assuming that we start from an initial position where $CA = 0$. A depreciation in the sterling exchange rate lowers the foreign currency price of exports but, given constant production costs, leaves the sterling price unaltered. Therefore, the total sterling earnings from export sales will rise provided that foreigners buy a greater volume of UK exports. This they will do, if their price elasticity of demand for UK exports exceeds zero.

However, whether the current account measured in sterling goes into surplus following a devaluation also depends on what happens to UK residents' expenditure on imports. The sterling price of imports rises following a depreciation so that for total expenditure on imports to fall it is not sufficient just for the volume of imports to decline. For the import bill in terms of sterling to fall, the absolute percentage decrease in the volume of imports must exceed the percentage increase in the sterling price of imports. For this to occur the price elasticity of the demand for imports must exceed 1.0. Whether the current account moves into surplus following a devaluation depends on the sum of its impact on export earnings and its effect on the import bill. If devaluation is to have a favourable impact on the current account, then the sum of the price elasticity of the demand for exports plus the price elasticity of the demand for imports must exceed 1.0. This is known as the *Marshall–Lerner condition* for a devaluation to improve the current account of the balance of payments. A proof of the Marshall–Lerner condition is set out in the Appendix to this chapter. If the Marshall–Lerner condition holds, then a devaluation shifts the CA line in Figure 7.4 to the right so that the current account balances at a

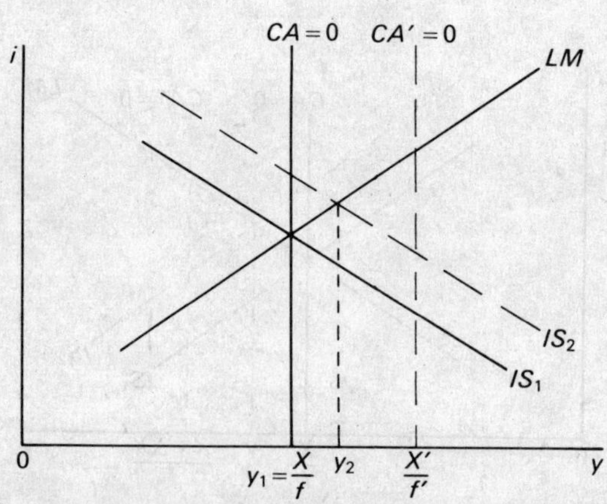

FIGURE 7.4 *The effect of a devaluation*

higher level of national income. A revaluation has the opposite effect and shifts the CA line in Figure 7.4 to the left.

If the Marshall–Lerner condition holds, then a devaluation leads to a net increase in exports minus imports ($X - F/e$) and this results in an increase in the aggregate demand for domestic output. In these circumstances a devaluation shifts the IS function up to the right, from IS_1 to IS_2 in Figure 7.4. Then, given the assumption of a perfectly elastic aggregate supply function with unchanged unit production costs, the effect of a devaluation is to increase real national output from y_1 to y_2 in Figure 7.4. If output were already at its full-employment level in a Keynesian model, then a devaluation could not increase output. Furthermore, it could only improve the current account if the government simultaneously cut domestic absorption so that resources could be switched to producing exports and/or import substitutes. Given an absence of excess demand a revaluation of the currency would shift the CA_0 line and the IS function to the left and so cause a reduction in national output.

In the early post-war era many economists were pessimistic about the possibility that the sum of the elasticities of demand was greater than 1.0. This was due to two factors, the first being the low estimates of the elasticities of demand produced by the early econometric studies. This evidence was later discounted due to the faulty methodology of the studies, and later studies, such as that by Houthakker and Magee [5], have found substantially higher elasticities. The other factor leading to elasticity pessimism in the early post-war years was that many devaluations did not have the desired effect. This was due to the fact that most economies were operating at full capacity during this period and there was little chance of increasing output. In such circumstances our earlier discussion of the absorption approach would lead one to predict that, no matter what the elasticities of demand were, switching both domestic and foreign demand towards domestic output by devaluing the currency will have no effect on the current account unless domestic absorption is cut. If domestic absorption is not allowed to fall when output is at full capacity, then the balance on current account will not improve. In recent years professional opinion has switched to the belief that the elasticities of demand are always large enough to satisfy the Marshall–Lerner condition.

7.5 Devaluation and real wage resistance

The discussion of Keynesian open-economy models assumed that the price of domestically produced goods did not change with either changes in output or changes in the exchange rate. This is an extreme simplifying assumption, and the results will still hold in an attenuated form provided that domestic prices and costs have a smaller response to exchange-rate changes than do the prices of foreign imports in domestic currency. Once prices respond to changes in the exchange rate the model becomes more complicated, as a change in the exchange rate no longer results in an equivalent change in either the relative prices of home- and foreign-produced goods or in the relative costs of home versus foreign production. In the case of a devaluation, as long as home-produced goods become relatively cheaper compared with foreign-produced goods and the home economy has some relevant spare capacity, the earlier Keynesian results predicting an increase in domestic output and an improvement in the current account still stand. However, these results depend *crucially* on the assumption that the aggregate supply function shifts up by a smaller proportion than the rise in the price of imports in domestic currency following a devaluation.

We can illustrate this in terms of the aggregate demand and supply apparatus developed in Chapter 6. At any given price level, *Pd*, for domestic goods, aggregate demand for these goods will be higher, the lower the exchange rate, *e*. Therefore, a devaluation will shift the aggregate demand function in Figure 7.5 from AD_1 to AD_2. If domestic wages and costs remain unchanged, then the aggregate supply function will stay unchanged at AS_1 and output will increase from y_1 to y_2. Here the results developed in the appendix (pp. 121–4) predict an improvement in the current account.

Since domestic goods are in perfectly elastic supply a devaluation leaves their price, *Pd*, unchanged. If workers consume only domestic goods, then their real wage will not change as a result of devaluation. However in most countries and particularly in the United Kingdom, workers spend some proportion of their wages on imported goods. Here the rise in the domestic price of imported goods results in a fall in workers' real wages. Unless there is a great deal of involuntary unemployment, as defined by Keynes (see Chapter 5, p. 74), this will result in market pressure for an increase in money wages, particularly as output and employment have increased following the devaluation. This results in the aggregate supply curve shifting up. Provided the aggregate supply curve shifts up by quite a bit less than the domestic price of imports, output will still increase and the balance on current account will improve.

If workers consume imported goods and they have 'real wage resistance' in the sense that employed workers wish to maintain the purchasing power of their wages, then workers will demand money wages that will completely compensate them for the effects of higher import prices. As the devaluation has switched some demand to domestic goods, employers are not totally unwilling to increase money wages by the required amount. The rise in money wages increases the marginal costs of all domestic producers and leads to a shift up in

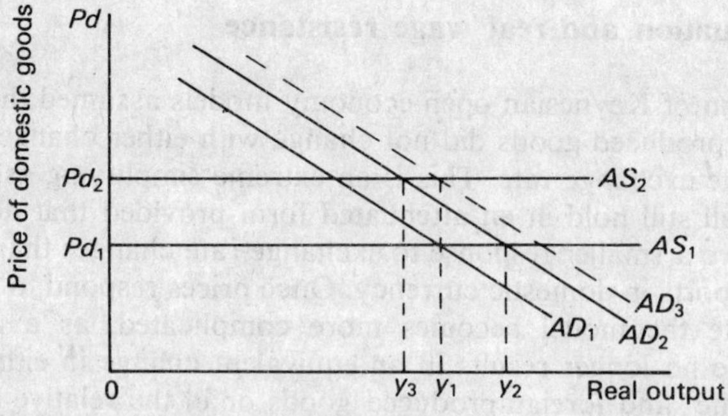

FIGURE 7.5 *Shifts in aggregate demand and supply following a currency depreciation*

the aggregate supply function for domestic goods. This leads to an increase in the price of domestic goods, *Pd*. As a result there is further pressure for money wage increases in order to fully compensate for the rise in domestic prices and this in turn leads to a further shift up in the aggregate supply function.

Let us assume that following a devaluation the government does not allow an increase in the nominal money supply and keeps constant the level of real government expenditure on final goods and services. In this case, if workers' real wage resistance is not affected by the level of unemployment, then the process described in the previous paragraph will end when the aggregate supply function has shifted up by the same proportion as the rise in import prices. This is shown by the shift from AS_1 to AS_2 in Figure 7.5. Here output and employment will be slightly lower than before the devaluation, at the point y_3. Domestic absorption will be lower than it was originally and the balance on current account will improve. This fall in absorption is brought about by higher rates of interest and the real balance effect on expenditure resulting from the decline in real money balances due to the rise in domestic prices. If real wage resistance is affected by unemployment, then the scenario is similar, as real wages will only fall if unemployment increases and output falls. Here the final position will once again involve a lower level of output and employment compared with the situation before devaluation. Once again absorption will fall and the current account will improve due to the real balance effect of the devaluation. However, in this case there will be a slight fall in real wages and in the relative price of domestic goods.

On the other hand, if the government does not allow domestic absorption to fall, then it will have to increase the money supply to keep real money balances constant. This will result in a further shift of the aggregate demand function following its initial shift to AD_2 in Figure 7.5. The aggregate demand function will finally come to rest at AD_3 and, in the final equilibrium following the devaluation, the prices of domestic goods, *Pd*, nominal money balances and money wages will all have increased by the same proportion as the increase in the domestic price of imports. Real output will return to its pre-devaluation level, y_1, as will real absorption, so that in real terms the balance on current account will be unchanged. At this point the price of domestic exports in foreign currency will have returned to its pre-devaluation level, as will the relative price of imports and domestic goods. The trade-switching effects of a devaluation are therefore short-lived[1] when workers have real wage resistance and the government prevents real output from falling by allowing nominal money balances to increase.

The long-run results in the two preceding paragraphs are consistent with the monetary approach to the balance of payments, which will be discussed in Chapter 11. Although we started with a Keynesian open-economy model, the introduction of real wage resistance by workers leads to an adjustment of wages and prices to the devaluation. In the cases where either nominal money stocks were allowed to increase to keep interest rates constant or where real wage resistance is not affected by unemployment, then the full adjustment of

[1] See Ball, Burns and Laury [6] for a rigorous analysis of this.

wages and salaries to devaluation leads the aggregate supply function to shift up by the same proportion as the domestic price of imports. Here relative prices return to their pre-devaluation level and any trade-switching effects will only occur due to lags in the adjustment in domestic output prices and wages to the change in exchange rates. Such trade-switching will disappear once full adjustment takes place. Where nominal money balances are kept constant and real wage resistance is sensitive to unemployment, there will be some trade-switching brought about by the fall in absorption and output resulting from the decline in real balances. This long-run result is also consistent with the monetary approach.

Real wage resistance by workers implies a neoclassical aggregate supply in the medium to long run and is inconsistent with the existence of involuntary unemployment as defined by Keynes. In the involuntary unemployment case workers are willing to take a cut in real wages at a higher level of output and employment, if this is brought about by a rise of the price level. This would imply a proportionally smaller upward shift in the aggregate supply function than the proportionate rise in the domestic price of imports following a devaluation. This is why the assumption of involuntary unemployment is a *crucial assumption* in the Keynesian open-economy model. This is recognised by Keynesian writers such as Meade [7] and Fetherston and Godley [4].

There is some evidence that real wage resistance operated in UK labour markets in the late 1960s and in the 1970s. For an example of this evidence see Horne [8]. Ball, Burns and Laury [6] carried out a simulation study of the impact of devaluation on UK macroeconomic activity and the current account. They used the 1976 version of the London Business School forecasting model, which was then a Keynesian open-economy econometric model. Their study showed that any impact of a devaluation on either output or the balance on current account was due to lags in the adjustment of domestic wages and prices and that these adjustments were completed within four to six years. They concluded that, in the United Kingdom, 'with free collective bargaining wages and prices are likely to rise by the full extent of the devaluation in the long run' ([6] p. 1). In their simulations, following a devaluation the UK aggregate supply function had a lagged upward adjustment so that it eventually rose by the same proportion as the rise in the sterling price of UK imports. This is some supporting evidence for a belief that the United Kingdom has a neoclassical aggregate supply function over the medium to long run, though not in the short run.

Other supporting evidence comes from the 1979 version of the Treasury macroeconomic model [9]. Here there is eventually a complete response of wages to prices. On a European level Thygessen [10] reports that the OPTICA[1] study for the European Commission concluded that exchange-rate changes in the late 1970s have become unsuitable for any purpose except that of permitting different national rates of inflation. The OPTICA group also carried out a simulation of the Italian economy on the University of Bologna's macroeconomic model. This showed that wages eventually adjusted completely to any price changes brought about by a change in exchange rates.

In conclusion, Keynesian analysis of the open economy seems only relevant

[1] Optimum Currency Area report, or OPTICA.

to the very short run in the United Kingdom. The analysis assumes that the government can control either the money stock or the rate of interest and it relies on price rigidities and lagged adjustments in domestic wages and prices. Policies based on such short-run analysis can be very misleading if they either take time to implement or if their repeated application encourages behavioural responses by individuals that are inimical to long-run stability.

Mathematical appendix: derivation of the Marshall–Lerner condition and of the effect of a devaluation on the level of income

The balance of payments on current account can be expressed in terms of domestic currency by the equation

$$CA = X - \frac{1}{e}F \tag{7.17}$$

Here X is a decreasing function of the exchange rate, e, while F is an increasing function of both e and the level of domestic income, y. Totally differentiating the expression in 7.17 with respect to e gives

$$\frac{d(CA)}{de} = \frac{dX}{de} - \frac{1}{e}\frac{dF}{de} - \frac{\partial\left(\frac{1}{e}F\right)}{\partial y}\frac{dy}{de} + \frac{1}{e^2}F$$

$$= -\frac{X}{e}\left\{-\frac{e}{X}\frac{dX}{de}\right\} - \frac{F}{e^2}\left\{\frac{e}{F}\frac{dF}{de}\right\} + \frac{F}{e^2} - \frac{\partial\left(\frac{1}{e}F\right)}{\partial y}\frac{dy}{de} \tag{7.18}$$

Now the two items in brace brackets in 7.18 are, respectively, the elasticity of foreign demand for exports, η_X, and the home elasticity of demand for imports, η_F. In deriving these elasticities we assumed that a change in the exchange rate, e, results in an equal proportionate change in relative prices and that a given change in aggregate demand translates into an equal change in supply. This will occur when there is excess capacity, involuntary unemployment and constant average costs of production in each country. If these assumptions do not hold, then a change in aggregate demand would not call forth an increased supply at unchanged domestic prices. We would then either have to abandon this approach or else develop a much more complex equation involving supply elasticities in order to predict the effect of a change in e on the current-account balance.

If we partially differentiate equation 7.11 with respect to y, we see that the term:

$$\frac{\partial\left(\frac{1}{e}F\right)}{\partial y}$$

is equal to f, which is the marginal propensity to import of the domestic economy. Therefore, substituting into equation 7.18 for the terms in the brace brackets and for $\partial(1/e\,F)/\partial y$ we get

$$\frac{d(CA)}{de} = -\frac{F}{e^2}\left\{\frac{eX}{F}\eta_X + \eta_F - 1\right\} - f\frac{dy}{de} \tag{7.19}$$

where η_X is the elasticity of foreign demand for exports and η_F is the elasticity of domestic demand for imports.

If the government stabilises the level of income in the economy through the use of monetary and fiscal policy, then $dy/de = 0$. Substituting this value into equation 7.19 gives us an expression for the rate of change in the current account resulting from a change in the exchange rate, e. This is

$$\frac{d(CA)}{de} = -\frac{F}{e^2}\left\{\frac{eX}{F}\eta_X + \eta_F - 1\right\} \tag{7.20}$$

This will be negative if

$$\frac{eX}{F}\eta_X + \eta_F > 1$$

If this inequality holds, then both an appreciation or revaluation of the currency will worsen the balance on current account, while a depreciation or devaluation of the currency will improve the balance on current account. If trade is approximately balanced to start with, then $eX = F$ and the condition for an improvement on the current account following a devaluation which is coupled with income stabilisation becomes

$$\eta_X + \eta_F > 1 \tag{7.21}$$

This is the *Marshall–Lerner condition* required for a devaluation to improve the balance on current account. If this condition holds for our small-economy model so that the sum of the elasticities of demand for imports and exports is greater than 1.0, then a devaluation will shift the $CA = 0$ line in Figure 7.4 to the right to $CA' = 0$, while a revaluation will shift the $CA = 0$ line to the left. This result is consistent with the absorption approach, as the satisfaction of the Marshall–Lerner condition implies that a devaluation switches both foreign and domestic demand towards domestic output. To keep income constant in this case, the government would have to cut domestic absorption.

We now have to look at the change in real income that results from a change in the exchange rate, e, in our small open economy, in order to determine the conditions in which a depreciation or devaluation will shift the *IS* function to the right. In the open-economy extended *ISLM* model the goods-market equilibrium condition

$$y = C + I + G + X - \frac{1}{e}F \tag{7.12}$$

can be written as

$$y = C + I + G + CA \tag{7.12a}$$

Totally differentiating equation 7.12a with respect to the exchange rate, *e*, and assuming that *G* and *I* are not affected by the short-run induced changes in *y* gives

$$\frac{dy}{de} = \frac{\partial C}{\partial y}\frac{dy}{de} + \frac{d(CA)}{de} \tag{7.22}$$

Here there is an implicit assumption that the interest rate is stabilised. In equation 7.22 $d(CA)/de$ can be found by using the result in equation 7.19 on page 122. The term $\partial C/\partial y$ is the marginal propensity to consume out of total income, and using equations 4.3, 4.4 and 4.7 in Chapter 4 (p. 47) this is found to be equal to $(1 - s)(1 - t)$ in the open-economy *ISLM* model. Here *s* is the marginal propensity to save out of disposable income and *t* is the tax rate. Substituting these results into equation 7.22 gives

$$\frac{dy}{de} = (1 - s)(1 - t)\frac{dy}{de} - \frac{F}{e^2}\left\{\frac{eX}{F}\eta_X + \eta_F - 1\right\} - f\frac{dy}{de} \tag{7.23}$$

Collecting all the terms for dy/de in equation 7.23 and then simplifying gives

$$\frac{dy}{de} = -\frac{\frac{F}{e^2}\left\{\frac{eX}{F}\eta_X + \eta_y - 1\right\}}{s(1 - t) + t + f} \tag{7.24}$$

Here dy/de will be negative if the Marshall–Lerner condition holds. In this case provided that our assumptions of excess capacity and involuntary unemployment are satisfied, a devaluation or currency depreciation (a fall in *e*) will shift the *IS* curve to the right. This is illustrated in Figure 7.4 by a shift in the *IS* function from IS_1 to IS_2.

Given the assumptions of the small open-economy model and a stabilised rate of interest, i^*, the rate of change of income with respect to a change in the exchange rate is equal to the rate of change in the current account that would occur if income were held constant (see equation 7.20) *times* the open-economy multiplier from equation 7.15. Therefore, given normal expectations about the size of the elasticities of demand, the *IS* function will shift to the right with a devaluation and to the left with a revaluation provided that the aggregate supply function does not shift.

When income is not stabilised we can find the effect of a devaluation on the current account by substituting for dy/de in equation 7.19, using the result in 7.24. After simplification this gives us

$$\frac{d(CA)}{de} = -\frac{s(1 - t) + t}{s(1 - t) + t + f}\left(\frac{F}{e^2}\right)\left\{\frac{eX}{F}\eta_X + \eta_F - 1\right\} \tag{7.25}$$

This must always be negative if the Marshall–Lerner condition is satisfied.

Therefore, a devaluation must always improve the balance on current account provided our small open-economy and perfectly elastic aggregate supply assumptions are satisfied. This implies that a devaluation or depreciation of the domestic currency will shift both the $CA = 0$ and IS functions to the right, with the $CA = 0$ function moving further to the right than the IS function. This is illustrated in Figure 7.4, where a devaluation moves the IS function from IS_1 to IS_2 and moves the $CA = 0$ line from $CA = 0$ to $CA' = 0$. In the diagram the current account goes into surplus following the devaluation, having originally been in balance.

References

[1] Bo Södersten, *International Economics*, 2nd edn (London: Macmillan, 1980) ch. 23.
[2] C. P. Kindleberger, 'Measuring Equilibrium in the Balance of Payments', *Journal of Political Economy*, 77 (1969).
[3] S. S. Alexander, 'Effects of a Devaluation on a Trade Balance', *IMF Staff Papers*, 1 (1952).
[4] M. J. Fetherston and W. H. Godley, 'New Cambridge Macroeconomics and Global Monetarism: Some Issues in the Conduct of UK Economic Policy', in *Public Policies in Open Economies*, vol. 9 of the Carnegie–Rochester Conference Series on Public Policy, ed. K. Brunner and A. Meltzer (Amsterdam: North-Holland, 1978).
[5] H. S. Houthakker and S. P. Magee, 'Income and Price Elasticities in World Trade', *Review of Economics and Statistics* (1969).
[6] R. J. Ball, T. Burns and J. S. E. Laury, 'The Role of Exchange Rate Changes in Balance of Payments Adjustment: The United Kingdom Case', *Economic Journal* (1977).
[7] J. E. Meade, *The Balance of Payments* (London: Oxford University Press, 1951) p. 202.
[8] J. Horne, 'The Effect of Devaluation on the Balance of Payments and the Labour Market: The United Kingdom, 1967', *Economica* (1979).
[9] HM Treasury, *Treasury Macroeconomic Model* (London: HMSO, 1979).
[10] N. Thygessen, 'Inflation and Exchange Rates: Evidence and Policy Guidelines for the European Community', *Journal of International Economics* (1978).

8 The Demand for Money

The choice of how much money to hold is an example of a portfolio decision as it concerns allocating one's wealth over a number of different assets. Money is a unique type of asset: not only does it perform the store of value function common to all assets but it also serves as a medium of exchange. A preliminary account of the theory of the demand for money was given in Chapter 2 (p. 15) and Chapter 3 (pp. 25, 32), where it was deduced that the demand for real money balances depends positively on income and inversely on the rate of interest. In this chapter we shall examine the microeconomic basis of the demand for money function a little more thoroughly and review some of the empirical work in this field. (For a detailed and more rigorous review of the literature, students can consult any one of references [1]–[4] or read some of the classic articles such as [5]–[8].)

8.1 The transactions demand for money

To focus attention on the rationale for holding money which stems from its function as a medium of exchange we shall assume that an individual's or household's income in a given period exactly equals its expenditure. Since there is no saving, there is no need to hold assets or incur liabilities over from one period to another. In the zero-saving case the only portfolio decision concerns how the household or firm finances its spending during the period of time which elapses between income payments. In order to see why money is held as a medium of exchange it is useful to envisage situations in which no money would be held at all.

One such situation would be a barter economy in which goods are exchanged directly for goods. At the other extreme we can imagine an economy in which money is never actually held by individuals but nevertheless acts as a common unit of account or *numéraire* in which the prices of all goods and services are expressed. Each household receives its income for the period as a book-entry credit and undertakes zero saving. Instantaneously upon receiving income it registers on the debit side of the account book its consumption demands for the period and immediately obtains the required goods and services. At no point in time is the book entry either positive or negative. Thus no money, even of the book-entry type such as bank deposits, is actually held, though it serves as a unit of account. It is the perfect synchronisation of income receipts and expenditure outlays that accounts for there being no need to hold money in this example. Therefore, the demand to hold money to finance transactions exists because barter is a very costly way of conducting exchange and because the timing of income and expenditure is not coincidental. A typical household receives income in the form of money at regular, discrete intervals of time and makes payments throughout the period of time between income payments.

If we simplify the analysis by assuming certainty, then the exact timing and size of payments and receipts is known. Given zero saving, the individual's stock of money balances at the beginning of the income period equals the period's income and dwindles to nothing by the next payday. The average amount of money held on each 'day' of the income period is said to be the individual's demand for money.

If there exists an asset other than money, which earns a higher pecuniary rate of return than money, households will forgo that rate of return if they hold their temporary reserve of purchasing power in the form of money. For simplicty we assume that there are two assets, money, which has no rate of interest paid on it, and bonds, which have a rate of return which is known with certainty. If there are no transactions costs involved in the buying and selling of bonds, no rational household or firm would hold money. The money received at the beginning of the income period would be put into bonds straight away. As the household or firm needs money to finance expenditure it would sell bonds and immediately purchase goods and services. Therefore, in the absence of uncertainty and given the existence of bonds, the holding of money is explained by the transactions costs of moving from money into bonds and vice versa. These transactions costs include the brokerage fees paid when assets are bought and sold, telephone and other communication costs, the wages firms pay to employees administering their liquid assets and the time spent by private individuals in trying to economise on their money balances in this way.

The inventory approach to the demand for transactions balances

Money held by firms is analogous to any other type of working capital. The holding of an inventory of money balances reduces costs, but also ties up capital that could alternatively be invested at the market rate of interest. This concept can be extended to the demand for money balances by households. Such an inventory-theoretic approach to the demand for money was developed separately by Baumol [5] and Tobin [6]. In both Tobin's and Baumol's models the size and timing of the household's expenditure plans are given and known with certainty. To simplify the analysis it is assumed that payments are spread evenly throughout the income period. In this case, if there are T days in the income period, then the household's expenditure per day will be $1/T$ of its income per period. If the household keeps all its transactions balances in the form of money, then it starts the period with y money balances (where y = income), halfway through it is holding $y/2$ money balances, which fall to zero by the end of the period. The average amount of money held per day throughout the income period is $y/2$ when expenditures occur evenly over time.

Once interest-bearing bonds are brought into the picture then holding money incurs an opportunity cost. This gives the individual an incentive to buy bonds at the beginning of the period, which are then sold off at discrete intervals to obtain money for financing transactions. Each time bonds are purchased or sold, transactions costs are incurred. Suppose that the income period of T days is subdivided into K equal intervals of time, each lasting T/K days. At the beginning of the income period $1/K$ of income is retained in the form of money to finance transactions during the first interval. The rest, $[(K-1)/K]y$, is used to purchase bonds. The bonds are sold in equal-sized batches at the beginning of the second and subsequent intervals. If fixed transactions costs of b are incurred each time bonds are purchased or sold, then the cost of all such transactions undertaken during the income period is bK. The smaller the average cash balance held for a given level of expenditure, the larger are the transactions costs because bonds are sold off more frequently. This relationship is shown in Figure 8.1. The income received per period is Oy. The brokerage costs of purchasing and selling bonds rises along schedule AB as the size of the average money holdings per day is reduced by engaging in more bond transactions. The advantage of holding on average less money and more bonds is the interest earned. The cost of forgone interest is the average amount of money held times the rate of interest, i. As the individual holds y/K money balances at the beginning of each interval within the income period and expenditures occur continuously at an even rate, then the average money holding is $y/2K$. The opportunity cost of these money balances is $(y/2K)i$ and is given by line OR in Figure 8.1. Combining the brokerage and interest costs

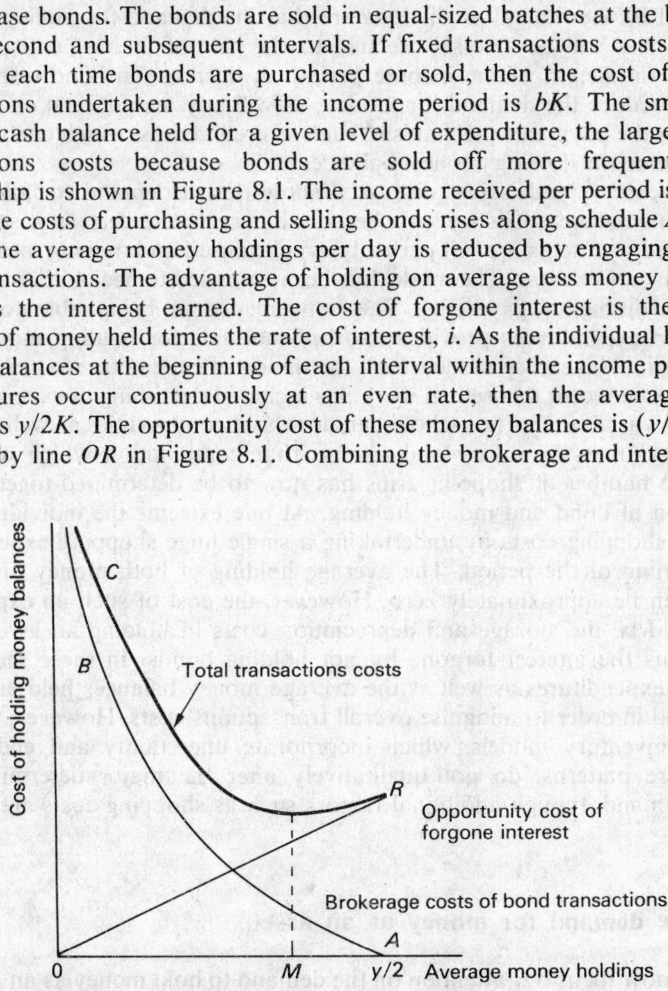

FIGURE 8.1 *Minimising the cost of transactions balances*

gives the U-shaped cost function *CR*, which is minimised when *OM* money balances are held.

In the inventory approach the quantity of money balances held to finance transactions is determined by cost-minimisation considerations. When an individual's income is not sizeable or is paid at frequent intervals it is not worth while to incur the brokerage charges of moving into and out of bonds. Hence the approach is more relevant to explaining firms' demand for transactions balances. Once income is sufficiently large to justify bond transactions economies of scale begin to apply. As income rises it becomes worth while to engage in more bond transactions per income period because each bond sale incurs a fixed cost regardless of its value. The inventory approach therefore predicts that the demand for money balances will rise with income but less than proportionately (that is, the income elasticity of money demand is positive but less than 1.0). Additional predictions are that the demand for money transactions balances will be inversely related to the rate of interest and positively related to the length of the income period. A decrease in bond transactions costs will reduce the demand for money, as will any institutional or technical changes to the payments mechanism, such as credit cards, which enable people to economise on holding money balances.

The inventory models just discussed show that a demand to hold money transactions balances exists even when there is complete certainty, so long as receipts and payments are not perfectly synchronised and moving into and out of bonds is not costless. The model has been extended to deal with uncertainty about the timing of payments. The convenience of being able to finance unexpected expenditures provides another rationale for holding money.

The original inventory models took the timing of expenditures as exogenous, whereas more recent theoretical work has included the timing of expenditure as a decision variable. The household can now hold commodities as well as bonds and money in its inventory and choose that combination which minimises costs. The number of shopping trips has now to be determined together with the pattern of bond and money holding. At one extreme the individual could minimise shopping costs by undertaking a single huge shopping expedition at the beginning of the period. The average holding of both money and bonds would then be approximately zero. However, the cost of such an expenditure plan would be the storage and depreciation costs of holding an inventory of goods, plus the interest forgone by not holding bonds. In these models the timing of expenditures as well as the average money balances held are jointly determined in order to minimise overall transactions costs. However, the more complex inventory models, which incorporate uncertainty and endogenous expenditure patterns, do not qualitatively alter the major determinants of money demand, though additional factors such as shopping costs are brought in.

8.2 The demand for money as an asset

We shall now focus our attention on the demand to hold money as an asset, i.e. as a way of storing up purchasing power in a form that is held for more than one income period. In order to do this we remove the assumption that the decision-unit spends all of its current income in the current period. This means that assets are held over for more than one time period. A household's consumption plans can be thought of as extending over its lifetime and to be constrained by the household's wealth. Such consumption plans will involve saving in some years and dissaving in others.

A household stores up its claim to future consumption in various types of assets. The only asset which can directly produce future goods and services is real capital. In a capitalist economy households can own indirect, marketable claims to real capital in the form of equity, bonds and other financial assets.

The portfolio decision of the household concerns the allocation of its wealth among the various types of assets, including money. We initially simplify the analysis by assuming that there are two types of financial assets: non-interest-bearing money and default-free bonds. The future interest rate on bonds is not known with certainty. Therefore, a wealth-owner may make a capital gain or loss by holding bonds, depending upon whether the interest rate falls or rises respectively. If the individual knows definitely that he wants to make a purchase of £*x* in three years' time and can buy bonds which mature three years hence at a terminal value of £*x*, there would be no risk involved in bond-holding as the future sum of money is certain.

Holding bonds is risky when the holder is uncertain when he wants to undertake future consumption and does not know for certain what the future bond price will be. Money is riskless in the sense that it is perfectly liquid because its price in terms of nominal money units does not change. If the price level changes, the value of money (and of bonds) will alter in real terms. So long as any change in the price level is fully anticipated the real value of money in the future is known with certainty. In this section we assume that the price level is not expected to change, so that money is expected with certainty to maintain its real value.

Keynes's speculative demand for money

In Chapter 13 of *The General Theory* Keynes viewed the transactions and asset demands for money as quite distinct and attributed the latter to the speculative motive for holding money. He assumed that there are only two financial assets that people could hold: money and bonds. Money is non-interest-bearing but riskless because the price level is assumed constant. Bonds earn interest but are risky because the interest rate may change. If the future rate of interest rises (falls), bond prices will fall (rise). The rate of return from holding a bond consists of the interest payment plus the capital gain or loss. A sufficiently large capital loss will mean a negative rate of return from bond-holding. If an individual expects the interest rate to rise sufficiently in the future to give a negative rate of return on bonds, then that individual will speculate by holding his entire portfolio in money until such time as he expects a positive return from bond-holding.

Thus expectations are crucial in determining Keynes's speculative demand for money. Interest-rate expectations are formed by comparing the current rate of interest with what is regarded as the 'normal' rate of interest, which is based largely on past values of the interest rate. The lower the current rate of interest compared with the normal rate, the larger the number of financial investors who expect the interest rate to rise and who therefore want to hold money. Thus the demand for speculative money balances varies inversely with the rate of interest. A liquidity trap would occur when all investors expected a non-positive rate of return from bonds and were therefore willing to hold unlimited money balances at the going rate of interest.

Because of the role accorded to expectations, Keynesians have typically regarded the demand for money function as being unstable. If the demand for money is strongly dependent on expectations and these fluctuate continually, then one cannot predict the demand for money from a knowledge of its other determinants, namely income and the rate of interest.

One particularly unsatisfactory aspect of Keynes's speculative theory is that each financial investor is assumed to assign to the future rate of interest only one value which he holds with certainty, rather than a range of possible values. This rather peculiar characterisation of uncertainty means that each investor holds an undiversified portfolio of all bonds or all money, and does not hold both. In order to overcome this problem Tobin [7] applied what has become known as *portfolio theory* to the analysis of the asset demand for money.

The portfolio theory of asset-holding[1]

Tobin's portfolio model of asset choice shows that wealth-owners will hold a diversified portfolio of assets, one of which is money. Holding a number of different assets reduces the overall risk of a portfolio by the well-known principle of not putting all one's eggs into the same basket. An asset is generally thought to be riskier, the greater the likelihood of its actual return diverging from its expected return. Asset *A*, which has an expected return of 10 per cent that may turn out to be anywhere between –10 per cent and +20 per cent, is riskier than asset *B* with an expected return of 5 per cent but which may lie between –1 per cent and +11 per cent. So long as the returns of assets *A* and *B* are not perfectly and positively correlated (that is, they do not move directly together so that when the rate of return on *A* is 20 per cent, that on *B* is 11 per cent, or when the rate of return on *A* is –10 per cent that on *B* is –1 per cent) a financial investor can reduce the overall risk of his portfolio by holding both assets. If events turn out badly for asset *A*, so that its actual return is below its expected return, this is partially offset by the return obtained from asset *B*.

Thus a wealth-owner will have less risk if he holds both assets *A* and *B* than if he holds only one of these assets. The higher the amount of asset *A* held, the greater the expected return, but increasing the share of asset *A* in the portfolio above the risk-minimising level increases the overall risk. A risk-averter is a person who will only accept additional risk if compensated by a higher expected rate of return and who therefore has a trade-off between expected return and risk.

[1] For a simple but useful account of this topic see Baumol [9].

In the simplified version of Tobin's portfolio model the portfolio-holder's planning horizon is one period long. There are just two assets: money, which is riskless because it has a certain return – of zero; – and perpetual bonds, which are risky. Unlike Keynes's speculative model, each investor has a range of interest rates within which he thinks the future interest rate will lie. Some values of the future interest rate seem more likely than others. So each financial investor can be characterised as assigning a probability distribution to the future interest rate. The mean of this probability distribution determines the expected rate of return on bonds. The risk of holding a bond is measured by the dispersion of the possible future rate about the expected future interest rate (which is the mean of the probability distribution over the future rate of interest). This measure of risk is the standard deviation of the interest-rate probability distribution. The larger the standard deviation, the greater the riskiness of bond-holding.

Each investor is assumed to be risk-averse. This means that the expected return from a portfolio of assets yields positive utility but that risk gives negative utility. The individual can make up an asset portfolio which consists of various combinations of the riskless asset, money, and the risky asset, bonds. The greater the proportion of wealth held in bonds, the higher the expected return from the portfolio, but the higher also is its riskiness. The individual chooses that combination of money and bonds which maximises his utility given his preferences regarding return and risk.

The rationale for holding money is that doing so reduces the riskiness of an asset portfolio. The opportunity cost of risk reduction is the expected return forgone by not holding bonds. If the rate of return on bonds rises (either because the current interest rate increases or because the future price of bonds is expected to rise), then the opportunity cost of holding money increases. The substitution effect will cause portfolio-holders to increase their bond-holdings and reduce their demand for money. However, there is also an income effect. An increase in the expected return from bonds means that fewer bonds need to be held in order to maintain the same level of expected income from the portfolio at the cost of less risk. The income effect will cause risk-averse financial investors to hold more money and fewer bonds. Thus the portfolio model does not yield unambiguous predictions about the effect of an increase in the interest rate on the demand for money. So long as the substitution effect outweighs the income effect in aggregate, then a rise in the rate of interest will reduce the demand for money in the economy as a whole.[1]

[1] This analysis assumes that the individual starts the period with a constant value of wealth which he or she has to allocate between money and bonds. Therefore, a change in the interest rate has no effect on the amount of wealth the individual starts out with. If we considered people already holding their wealth in bonds, the present value or price of their bonds would move in the opposite direction to any change in the interest rate. We have that the wealth in bonds equals B/i, where B is the number of bonds in existence, each of which entitles the owner to receive £1 of nominal income in perpetuity. Thus a rise in the interest rate would reduce bond-holders' wealth and cause a reduction in the demand for money. This effect would reinforce the substitution effect of an increase in the rate of interest.

The portfolio model also deduces that wealth and expectations affect the demand for money. Since the model is concerned with the allocation of wealth among different kinds of assets, the greater the level of wealth, the larger is the demand to hold money. Expectations about future interest rates affect the riskiness of bonds. The lower the risk of holding bonds, the smaller one would expect the demand for money to be.

Tobin's analysis can be extended to the selection of a large number of risky assets. Wealth-owners first decide in which proportions the risky assets should be held. Each wealth-owner then decides what proportion of his portfolio to hold in money, the remaining fraction being held in the optimal combination of risky assets.

The above analysis rationalises the demand to hold money in a world in which money is the only riskless asset and there are no transactions costs involved in buying and selling the risky assets. However, there are short-term assets, such as trustee savings bank deposits and building society accounts, which share with money the characteristic of having a nominally fixed capital value but which also earn a rate of interest. If owners of such assets are certain of being able to withdraw from the financial intermediaries the amount of money that they deposited, and there are no transactions costs involved in holding such assets, there is no rational motive for holding currency and current-account bank deposits since these earn no rate of interest. In this event other riskless assets would completely replace currency and current-account bank deposits as money. In the absence of transactions costs the portfolio approach would explain the demand to hold riskless interest-bearing assets with a lower rate of return than that expected from risky assets.

The rationale for holding non-interest-bearing money

It is therefore apparent that uncertainty by itself is insufficient to explain the holding of currency and current-account bank deposits when other riskless interest-earning assets are available. The demand to hold money is ultimately attributable to money's function as a medium of exchange. This characteristic is possessed by those commodities which minimise the transactions costs of financing expenditures.

If a household were certain about the timing of its future flow of expenditure, it could buy bonds the maturity of which was timed to coincide with future consumption expenditure. Thus capital uncertainty in nominal terms would be avoided, while a higher rate of return would be obtained than if money were held. This rate of return would have to exceed the transactions cost of moving in and out of bonds to make such bond-holding an attractive proposition. Uncertainty about the timing of future expenditures, combined with no fear of capital loss from bond-holding, would also result in no rational person holding money as an asset unless this was warranted by the saving in asset transactions costs. The combined uncertainty about the future capital value of marketable assets and the timing of future expenditure explains the holding of lower-return financial assets which have nominally fixed capital values. Only fear of default by financial intermediaries and the transactions costs of moving from money into close money substitutes, which are not themselves generally acceptable as a medium of exchange, explain the holding of money by a rational person.

The demand for non-interest-bearing money therefore arises when there exists both uncertainty (about the timing of expenditure and about the rate of return from non-money assets) and transactions costs of moving between money and other assets.

8.3 The effect of inflation on the demand for assets

The analysis so far has not dealt with changes in the general price level. Real assets, including equities, have their income denominated in real terms. As the general level of prices rises, so do the prices of houses, paintings and capital goods used in production. Since the nominal value of dividends rises with secular increases in the price level, shares are claims to uncertain real-income streams. Price index-linked national savings bonds have also been introduced in Britain.

Other types of financial assets have their income, price, or both, fixed in nominal terms. The income yielded by all types of fixed-interest securities, such as bonds, bills of exchange, building society shares, is fixed in money terms. The market price or capital value of marketable assets is variable, whereas the capital value of non-marketable assets, such as premium bonds, building society shares or money is fixed in nominal terms. Variations in the price level cause movements in the opposite direction in the real value of a given nominal return from a nominally fixed asset.

If lenders consider equities and bonds to be equally risky, then in a world with a constant expected general price level market forces will equalise the rates of return on both assets. (If equities are considered more risky, there will be a risk premium established so that the equity rate of return exceeds the bond yield. This in no way alters the analysis with respect to inflation.) The rate of return on equities is then the real rate of return on capital, which for capital-market equilibrium must equal the rate of interest on bonds.

If instead of expecting the price level to remain stable asset-holders anticipate a positive rate of inflation, then the real rate of return on bonds will be the market rate of interest on bonds *minus* the expected rate of inflation. For example, if the market rate of interest on bonds is 7 per cent and the anticipated rate of inflation is 3 per cent, the real rate of return from holding bonds is 4 per cent. If the real rate of return on capital is 7 per cent, no asset-holder will wish to hold bonds and will hold equity instead. This means that the price of bonds will fall until bonds offer a money or nominal interest rate of 10 per cent, making the real rate of return on bonds equal to 7 per cent. We thus obtain in equilibrium, when full adjustments have been made for expected inflation, that[1]

[1] There is an additional term on the right-hand side of the equation which is $i[(1/P)(dP/dt)]^e$. This term decreases as the discounting period diminishes and tends to zero when discounting becomes continuous. See references [10]–[12] for more detailed expositions of the theory.

$$r = i + \left[\frac{1}{P}\frac{dP}{dt}\right]^e \tag{8.1}$$

where r is the nominal rate of interest, i is the real rate of interest, and $(1/P)(dP/dt)^e$ is the expected rate of inflation.

Thus the real rate of return on assets with a nominally fixed income can be kept independent of the rate of inflation by market adjustments which reduce bond prices and thus raise the nominal interest rate to account for expected inflation.

If money pays no rate of interest, the opportunity cost of holding money is the rate of return forgone by not holding alternative assets such as bonds or real capital. In a period of stable prices this opportunity cost is the real rate of interest. If inflation is expected, there will be an additional element in the anticipated opportunity cost of holding money. This is the loss in the real value of money due to the expected increase in the price level. Thus the *opportunity cost of holding money consists of the real rate of interest forgone plus the expected loss in the purchasing power of money due to the rate of inflation.* This opportunity cost equals the nominal rate of interest. Of course, in the case of expected deflation, the nominal rate of interest will lie below the real rate of interest since nominally fixed assets enjoy an increase in their real value.

8.4 The quantity theory approach to the demand for money

Money competes for a place in the portfolios of firms and households with all other assets. Thus the demand for money is determined by the attractiveness of holding money relative to that of other assets. Money balances can be thought of as giving their holders utility and hence entering as an argument in the utility function. This utility stems from the convenience of holding money to finance transactions and from the reduction in portfolio risk. Assuming that the marginal utility of money declines with the quantity of money balances held, one deduces that a utility-maximising economic unit will hold that quantity of money which equates the marginal utility of money balances to the marginal utility forgone by not holding some alternative asset. This way of analysing money considers money to be analogous to a consumer-durable good.

An alternative approach is to regard money balances as leading to a saving on transactions costs by providing convenience and liquidity. We then analyse money as a producer good, i.e. as an input into the process by which goods and services are produced. Money is then analogous to working capital. Each household or firm uses money in such a way as to minimise costs. The optimal amount of money to hold is the quantity for which the marginal saving in transactions costs equals the expected rate of return forgone by not holding some alternative asset.

Viewing money as either a consumer's good or as a producer's good, we can obtain a general form of the demand for money function. This approach subsumes both the transactions and the asset demands for money discussed earlier. In this the demand for real money balances depends on the level of real income, the real interest rates obtainable on other assets and the expected rate of change of the price level.

We can thus write the demand for real money balances as[1]

$$\left(\frac{M}{P}\right)^D = v\left[y, i^B, i^E, \left(\frac{dP}{dt}\frac{1}{P}\right)^e\right] \tag{8.2}$$

where i^B and i^E are the real rates of interest on bonds and equities respectively.

Equation 8.2 can be expressed alternatively as the demand for nominal money balances. In this case the nominal value of national income is a determinant of the volume of nominal money balances demanded. The price level will also enter as an argument in this form of the demand for money function since the volume of services provided by £1 depends on the purchasing power of a nominal unit of money. The demand for nominal money balances is therefore

$$M^D = v\left[Y, P, i^B, i^E, \left(\frac{dP}{dt}\frac{1}{P}\right)^e\right] \tag{8.3}$$

Velocity

The ratio of the nominal value of income to the nominal money stock is known as the income velocity of the circulation of money. (It is the same as the ratio of real income to the stock of real money balances.) Thus

$$V = Y/M \tag{8.4}$$

Velocity of the broader money measures lies between 2 and 4 in the United Kingdom. If velocity equals 3, this means that the stock of money required to finance all the transactions that are incurred in producing and distributing the annual national produce is one-third of the value of national income. The money stock is a fraction of the value of national income because a unit of money passes from person to person several times in the course of a year and can therefore finance several income-generating transactions.

The velocity of circulation is related to the demand to hold money. The higher is velocity, the more rapidly are people passing on money, and therefore the lower is the average stock of money balances, relative to income, which households and firms wish to hold. We need to distinguish the actual velocity of circulation, which is an *ex post* concept, from the *ex ante*, desired velocity. Actual velocity, V^A, is the ratio of income to the money stock, M^S, in existence:

$$V^A = Y/M^S \tag{8.4a}$$

It can readily be calculated from income and money supply data. The desired

[1] For a fuller discussion of this formulation of the demand for money function see Friedman [8].

velocity of circulation, V^D, is the ratio of income to the stock of money people wish to hold:

$$V^D = Y/M^D \tag{8.4b}$$

Thus actual and desired velocity are only equal in monetary equilibrium when the demand and supply of money are equal.

Desired velocity can be derived from equation 8.3. It is necessary to assume that the demand for money is a demand couched in real terms. If nominal income and the price level rise by the same proportion, the other variables remaining constant, the demand for nominal money balances rises by the same proportion. This means that the ratio between real income and real money balances stays the same.[1] Therefore, we can divide all the nominal variables in equation 8.3 by nominal income and leave the form of the relationship unchanged:

$$\frac{M^D}{Y} = \frac{1}{V^D} = v\left[1, \frac{P}{Y}, i^B, i^E, \left(\frac{dP}{dt}\frac{1}{P}\right)^e\right] \tag{8.5}$$

where

$$V^D = \phi\left[y, i^B, i^E, \left(\frac{dP}{dt}\frac{1}{P}\right)^e\right] \tag{8.6}$$

Equation 8.6 states that desired velocity depends on real income, real interest rates and the expected rate of price change.

If equation 8.5 is rearranged, it again becomes a demand for money equation:

$$M^D = \frac{1}{V^D}Y = \frac{1}{V^D}yP \tag{8.7}$$

In this form it stresses the relationship between the demand for money and national income, suppressing the other determinants of the demand for money. It now closely resembles the simply quantity theory approach to the demand for money which was introduced in Chapter 2, (pp. 15–18). Equation 2.1 on page 16 is very similar in appearance to 8.7 in which k is replaced by $1/V$. The crucial difference is that in the modern restatement of the quantity theory (due to Friedman [8]) velocity is not a constant but is explicitly made dependent on the determinants of the demand for money.[2]

[1] The technical expression for this is that the demand for real money balances is assumed to be homogeneous of degree zero in money income and prices (i.e. the nominal demand for money is homogeneous of degree one).

[2] The quantity theory of money can be found in the writings of David Hume. It was developed in this century by Irving Fisher [13], who, by concentrating on the institutional factors determining velocity, interpreted it as subject only to slow changes. Equation 8.7, written as $MV = Py$, is known as the Fisher equation. Written as $M^D = Y/V = kY$ it is known as the Cambridge equation, which was developed by Marshall and Pigou, for whom k depended on the interest rate. Keynes, by emphasising the rate of interest as a determinant of money demand, stressed the variability of velocity.

The stability of velocity

The modern restatement of the quantity theory by Friedman [8] contains the same type of variables as a Keynesian formulation of the demand for money function. The difference revolves around the question of whether velocity is a stable or unstable function of its determinants. In Keynesian theory, asset-holder expectations are thought to be volatile, causing the demand for money schedule with respect to the level of interest rates to shift. Thus velocity cannot be predicted from a knowledge of the values of the arguments of equation 8.6. In contrast, the monetarist approach emphasises the stability of velocity and maintains that the demand for money can be predicted from the values of the arguments in equation 8.6.

The quantity theory, according to Friedman, is a theory of the demand to hold money. As such it does not differ in its specification of variables from a Keynesian demand for money function. The quantity theory gains its distinctive characteristics when combined with other assumptions. The most important of these is that the money supply is not endogenous and purely demand-determined, by the banking system always supplying the amount of money that the economy wishes to hold. (This will be explained more fully in Chapter 9.) If a change in the money supply is exogenous, it will cause a discrepancy between the demand to hold money and the existing money stock. Thus an increase in the money supply causes portfolio imbalance. The marginal utility of a pound held in money balances falls below the marginal utility of a pound allocated to other uses, such as buying commodities or other financial assets. People therefore adjust their portfolios by spending the excess money balances on goods and financial assets. In the quantity theory view such portfolio adjustment occurs over a wider range of variables and is much more diffuse than a Keynesian analysis, where it is restricted to financial markets. In an open economy excess money balances are spent on foreign goods and assets as well as domestic ones.

In a closed economy or in an open economy under flexible exchange rates (see Chapter 11), the quantity theory is interpreted by monetarists as a theory of the determination of the nominal value of national income. Rewriting equation 8.7 as

$$Y = V^D M^D \tag{8.8}$$

and substituting into equation 8.8 the condition for monetary equilibrium that $M^D = M^S$ we obtain a relationship between nominal income and the stock of nominal money:

$$Y = V^D M^S \tag{8.9}$$

Looking at equation 8.9 we can see that *the vital link between nominal national income and the money stock is velocity.* If velocity is highly variable, then the link will break down and one will not be able to predict changes in nominal income that are caused by changes in the money stock. Monetarists therefore stress the stability of velocity and the ability to predict it from a knowledge of the values of its determinants. If the level of interest rates changes when the money stock is altered, velocity also changes. One would therefore need to specify the structural relationships in the economy, particularly the demand for money function, in order to know how changes in the money supply affect velocity and hence nominal income. On the basis of taking desired velocity to be relatively constant monetarists explain changes in nominal income as arising from changes in the money stock. Critics of this approach consider velocity to be subject to short-run fluctuations which make it impossible to predict accurately changes in nominal income arising from changes in the money stock.

All schools of thought agree that any increase in nominal income due to an increase in the nominal money stock is, in the short run, divided between a rise in real income and a rise in the price level. How the change in nominal income is divided between real and nominal changes is not yet satisfactorily explained and is the subject of current analytical work. In the long run real income is seen as determined by real forces, such as the productivity of factors of production, the rate of technical progress and the propensity to save. This means that in the long run increases in the nominal money stock only cause increases in the price level without affecting real output. If additional nominal money balances are provided, each individual thinks he can obtain more goods and services, now or in the future, by spending excess money balances on current consumption or the acquisition of financial assets. But it is impossible in aggregate for individuals to do this if the aggregate supply of output cannot be increased. The ensuing excess aggregate demand causes the price level to rise in the long run.

8.5 Empirical work on the demand for money

Theoretical work on the demand for money has given rise to a number of questions that have been subject to considerable empirical testing. The most important of these are as follows:

1. Is the demand for money correctly specified in real terms? If it is, one would expect the price elasticity of the demand for nominal money balances to be 1.0.
2. Is the demand for money better expressed as a function of income or of wealth? Transactions demand for money suggests income, whereas in the asset demand for money approach it is wealth that places a constraint upon the size of the individual's portfolio. What is the size of the income or wealth elasticity of the demand for money?
3. Are interest rates a significant determinant of the demand for money, and, if so, what is the size of the interest-rate elasticity?
4. Are the coefficients which relate the demand for money to its determining variables stable over time or do they vary so erratically that it is not possible to predict what the demand for money will be on the basis of given values of its determinants?

The definition of money

A further question facing empirical researchers concerns the most satisfactory definition of money in a modern economy with a complex financial system.

The crucial distinguishing feature of any object which is to be called 'money' is that it must be generally accepted as a medium of exchange. Two types of money can be distinguished: commodity money and fiat money. Commodity money is a good which has an intrinsic value of its own, independent of its function as a medium of exchange, gold being the best-known example. Fiat money, which may be issued by the government or by private-sector banks, has a value greatly in excess of its worth as a non-monetary commodity. This excess value is due entirely to the commodity being accepted as a means of payment. Nowadays coins have a metallic content which, if melted down, is worth less than the face-value of the coin. Paper notes have a value stemming from their acceptability as a medium of exchange which is much greater than their production costs. A UK £1 bank-note declaims its promise to pay the bearer on demand the sum of one pound. This promise relates to the days before the First World War, when gold coins circulated internally, and a paper pound note could be exchanged at a bank for a gold sovereign. Nowadays all this promise indicates is that notes, as well as coins, are legal tender and regarded by law as an acceptable means of payment. General public confidence in sterling as an acceptable medium of exchange for domestic transactions makes a £1 note equal to £1's worth of goods and services.

Notes and coin, known as cash or currency, which are in circulation with the non-bank public are obviously a medium of exchange and so are part of the money supply. In modern economies current-account bank deposits (or sight deposits) are payable in cash on demand and can be transferred by cheque. As they are generally acceptable as a means of payment, sight deposits are defined to be money.

Unlike current or sight deposits, deposit accounts (time deposits) do earn a rate of interest. Whether deposit accounts are rightfully part of the money supply is debatable. Deposit accounts are not repayable on demand since the interest paid on them by the bank is forfeit if insufficient notice of intended withdrawal is given. Furthermore, deposit accounts cannot be directly transferred by cheque as a general means of payment. These characteristics imply that deposit accounts are not a medium of exchange and hence not part of the money supply. However, time deposits can very easily be converted into sight deposits or cash and so are extremely close substitutes for those assets which are used as a direct means of payment. On these grounds it would be misleading to exclude deposit accounts from the definition of the money supply.

UK official statistics present several definitions of the money supply. The narrow definition of money is M_1. It consists of notes and coin in circulation with the non-bank public plus sterling current-account bank deposits. A broader definition of money is sterling M_3 (£M_3). This includes notes and coin in circulation together with the domestic sector's total sterling current and deposit accounts with banking institutions. An even broader definition is M_3, which is £M_3 plus foreign currency bank accounts held by domestic residents.[1]

[1] M_2 is M_1 plus sterling deposit accounts of the London clearing banks. It has been discontinued in official UK statistics.

Given these alternative measures of the money supply, an important question for empirical work has been whether a narrow definition of money which excludes time deposits is a better specification of what is money than a broad measure which includes them.

The identification problem

Any researcher in this area is faced with the identification problem that the available data are for the supply of money and not for the demand for money. Most econometric studies, particularly the earlier ones, assumed, often implicitly, that the demand for money was always equal to the supply of money. Figure 8.2 illustrates two kinds of rationale for this assumption.

Along the demand for money function, *DD*, all variables which determine the demand for money, other than the interest rate, are kept constant. If the monetary authorities operate a target for the interest rate, which may vary over time, then they need to supply that quantity of money which people wish to hold at the target rate of interest. The money supply is thus demand-determined and, depending on the interest-rate target, is a horizontal schedule such as M_0^S or M_1^S. Alternatively the money supply is exogenous so that the supply schedule is vertical. When the money supply increases from $M_0'^S$ to $M_1'^S$ the interest rate adjusts instantaneously from i_0 to i_1 so that the new quantity of money, *OB*, is willingly held. So if the money supply schedule shifts along an unchanged demand schedule, the demand function is identified. Let us now suppose that the demand for money fails to adjust instantaneously to an exogenous change in the money supply. When the money supply increases from *OA* to *OB* the interest rate remains stuck at i_0. The demand for money would be *OA* but the amount actually held would be *OB*. The demand for money would be incorrectly measured if money stock data are used.

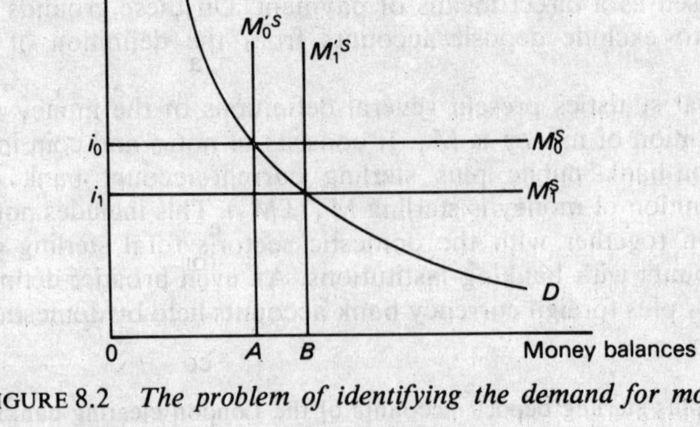

FIGURE 8.2 *The problem of identifying the demand for money*

Empirical work

Many studies have tried to solve this problem by allowing for non-instantaneous adjustment and distinguishing between the short-run and long-run demand for money. The long-run desired level of real money balances is assumed linearly, or more commonly, log-linearly related to its determinants:

$$\left(\frac{M}{P}\right)^* = a_0 + a_1 y_t + a_2 i_t \tag{8.10}$$

where $(M/P)^*$ is the long-run level of desired real money balances.

The independent variables in equation 8.10 are usually some combination of income, wealth and long- or short-term interest rates. When individuals are holding their long-run desired volume of money balances no further adjustments take place. If long-run equilibrium is disturbed by a change in income or interest rates, then adjustment costs cause individuals to adjust slowly towards the new long-run equilibrium level of desired money balances. In each short-run period the amount of money held is the quantity actually demanded for that period, given that to adjust more quickly is too costly to make it worth while. This behaviour is captured, as in equation 8.11 below, by specifying a partial stock adjustment process whereby only a fraction, θ, of the difference between the desired and actual stock of real money balances is adjusted in each period. The lower the value of θ, the slower the adjustment. The equation is

$$\left(\frac{M}{P}\right)_t - \left(\frac{M}{P}\right)_{t-1} = \theta\left[\left(\frac{M}{P}\right)^*_t - \left(\frac{M}{P}\right)_{t-1}\right] \tag{8.11}$$

where $0 < \theta < 1$. Adding $(M/P)_{t-1}$ to both sides we obtain

$$\left(\frac{M}{P}\right)_t = \theta\left(\frac{M}{P}\right)^*_t + (1-\theta)\left(\frac{M}{P}\right)_{t-1} \tag{8.12}$$

Substituting equation 8.10 into equation 8.12 we obtain

$$\left(\frac{M}{P}\right)_t = \theta a_0 + \theta a_1 y_t + \theta a_2 i_t + (1-\theta)\left(\frac{M}{P}\right)_{t-1} \tag{8.13}$$

The reduced-form equation 8.13 can be written as

$$\left(\frac{M}{P}\right)_t = b_0 + b_1 y_t + b_2 i_t + b_3\left(\frac{M}{P}\right)_{t-1} \tag{8.13a}$$

where the *b*'s are the coefficients which are estimated. The structural coefficients can be calculated from the reduced-form coefficients as follows:

$$b_0 = \theta a_0 \quad b_1 = \theta a_1 \quad b_2 = \theta a_2 \quad b_3 = 1 - \theta$$

Using 8.13 as a regression equation imposes the constraint that the lag on all the independent variables is the same.

Econometric studies of the demand for money undertaken in the 1950s and 1960s by and large tested some variation of either equation 8.10 or 8.13. Most economists were satisfied that the results for the United Kingdom, and especially for the USA, showed the demand for money to be a stable function of income or wealth and the rate of interest. These results held for different definitions of money, income, wealth and the rate of interest.

In the turbulent 1970s the estimated demand for money function appeared to break down. Estimates of the demand for money in the 1970s derived on the basis of estimated coefficients in demand for money regression equations differed widely from the actual money stock. (In the United Kingdom the demand for money was underestimated and, to a lesser extent, overestimated in the USA.) Attempts to re-estimate regression equations based on 8.10 and 8.13 failed to give coefficients which remained stable over time, or else produced unsatisfactory lag estimates (very small or negative values for θ).

Two conclusions can be drawn from this. One is that the demand for money is not stable after all. The other is that the demand for money function is stable but that the pre-1970 studies failed to identify it because of faulty specification and lack of data (particularly in the United Kingdom as compared with the USA). There is not much to say about the first possible conclusion so we shall concentrate on examining the second one.

Several lines of investigation have been pursued in order to explain why the earlier studies failed to identify a stable demand for money function given that one does exist. The explanations can be grouped in two categories depending on whether or not they accept that both the short-run and long-run demand for money can be assumed to equal the existing money stock.

A plausible case can be made that M_1 is demand-determined. If people do not want to hold currency or current-account deposits, then they move into time deposits or close substitutes. If people want more cash then up until now it has been the UK authorities' policy to supply it. Coghlan [14] and Hendry [15] have re-specified equation 8.13 so that the dependent variable is nominal M_1 balances. The independent variables, income, the interest rate and the price level, are allowed to have different lags and not the same lag structure as in the earlier studies. They report estimates of the demand for M_1 which are reasonably stable and produce acceptable forecasts of M_1 demand when projected beyond the sample period. The failure of the earlier studies is thus attributed to mis-specifying the dynamics of money demand adjustment.

Explaining the behaviour of the demand for M_3 in terms of a re-specification of the conventional equation (that is, one which treats the demand for money as equal to the money supply) has been less successful. One explantion is that the demand function for M_3 should include its own rate of interest since portfolio-holders shift between time deposits and near monies in response to the interest differential between them. However, when Haache [16] and Artis and Lewis [17] included a measure of the own rate of interest on money they failed to obtain sufficient improvement in M_3 demand estimates to reject the hypothesis of instability. Another explanation is that the various institutional changes which have beset the money supply process make it difficult to identify an underlying stable demand for money function.

The alternative approach to the problem is to reject the assumption that the money supply always equals the amount of money demanded. This is the approach taken by Artis and Lewis [17], who argue that because there was a sharp increase in the money supply in the mid-1970s[1] it remained for several years in excess of the demand for money. This explanation is supported by evidence on the long-run behaviour of velocity, shown in Figure 8.3. This graphs the regression of the increase of velocity, M/Y, on the interest rate using data for 1920–57:[2]

$$\log M/Y = 4.718 - 0.584 \log r \tag{8.14}$$

The values of M/Y for 1958–79 are then plotted in relation to the curve estimated from 1920–57 data. The fact that most of the later observations of M/Y lie close to the estimated curve gives some indication of a stable demand schedule. The years 1973–6 lie well above the line, indicating a considerable fall in velocity (rise in M/Y) during and following the period of rapid monetary expansion. By 1977 velocity had adjusted back to its normal value, given the level of interest rates.

If the money supply is better characterised as exogenous rather than as demand-determined, then the interest rate is determined by the interaction of the demand and supply of money (and in turn by all the other functional relationships in an interdependent system). If one then treats the interest rate as

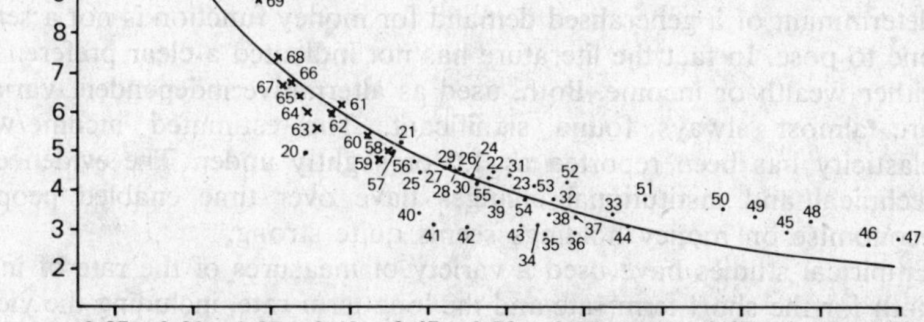

FIGURE 8.3 *Interest rates and the demand for money, 1920–79*
Source: Artis and Lewis [18].

[1] This was due to the introduction of 'Competition and Credit Control' in 1971 and to government policies which expanded the money base.

[2] M = currency + sterling deposits of London clearing banks
Y = GNP at factor cost
r = yield on $2\frac{1}{2}$% Consols

an independent variable in a demand for money study, as do single-equation demand for money estimations, one mis-specifies the function. This also applies to the other 'independent' variables, such as real income and the price level. Ideally the demand for money should be estimated as part of a complete model of the economy. Since this is a difficult thing to do, various simplified approaches have been tried (for example, by Artis and Lewis [17] and Laidler [19]). Artis and Lewis [17] treat the interest rate as the variable which bears the main brunt of adjustment when the demand and supply of money are in disequilibrium. They therefore obtain estimates of the demand for money coefficients by regressing the rate of interest, the dependent variable, on to the money supply, treated as an independent variable. Reasonable results, indicative of stability, are obtained for M_3. They also try an alternative version of specifying money as the independent variable. The inverse of velocity, M/Y, is related to real income, the interest rate, lagged M/Y and a variable designed to capture exogenous changes in the money supply (for example, changes in currency and bank reserves and in the domestic borrowing requirement). Improved results and evidence of stability are reported, particularly for M_1. Laumas [20], using a variable parameters estimation method, also finds in favour of a stable demand for money function.

Given that we can accept that a stable demand for money function exists, we can proceed to summarise the answers given in the empirical literature to the questions posed on page 138. (For a table of quantitative results see [1] or [14].)

1. Money is correctly specified in real terms. Some studies (for example, Coghlan [14]), using nominal money demand, have produced price coefficients of under 1.0, indicating an adjustment lag.
2. If one thinks (as does Coghlan [14]) that the demands for different types of money are quite distinct, with income determining one type and, perhaps, wealth another, then the question of whether income or wealth is the better determinant of a generalised demand for money function is not a sensible one to pose. In fact the literature has not indicated a clear preference for either wealth or income. Both, used as alternative independent variables, are almost always found significant. The estimated income/wealth elasticity has been reported as 1.0 or slightly under. The evidence that technical and institutional changes have over time enabled people to economise on money holdings seems quite strong.
3. Empirical studies have used a variety of measures of the rate of interest both for the short-term rate and the long-term rate, including the yield on equities. Some researchers (e.g. Hamburger [21]) favour including at least two rates of return in order to reflect the monetarist view that portfolio adjustment occurs over a wide range of assets. The common use of a single interest rate, on Treasury bills or on government bonds, is more within the Keynesian tradition. There is general agreement that the demand for money is negatively interest elastic, though there is much less agreement as to whether the interest elasticity remains stable over time. Estimates of the interest elasticity range from about –0.7 to –0.1, with –0.5 as a rough average. There is little evidence that the demand for money is highly interest-elastic.

There is still no consensus on whether a narrow or a broad definition of money results in a better specification. This state of affairs is not surprising if one thinks that the demand for money has to be disaggregated into its different components.

Another important aspect of the quantitative evidence concerns adjustment lags. Recent work suggests that money demand adjusts with a different speed depending on which determinant it is responding to, though it has not been fully established whether the adjustment is faster in response to interest changes rather than to income changes. The adjustment appears to be quite fast, most of the adjustment occurring within two to four quarters and being completed within eighteen months.

8.6 Conclusion on the stability of the demand for money

The stability of the demand for money is seen as a crucial theoretical and empirical issue, particularly for the monetarist camp. This is because the main transmission mechanism in monetary analysis is portfolio adjustment, which occurs when asset demands and supplies differ. Changes in the money supply are important because they cause portfolio disequilibrium and this in turn affects prices, output or the balance of payments. A known, stable demand for money function enables one to predict the outcome of monetary changes. However, an unstable demand for money function does not necessarily imply that portfolio adjustment fails to occur or does not have important effects, merely that one cannot make quantitative predictions about monetary adjustment with acceptable accuracy. This state of affairs means that deliberate policy interventions would have random and unpredictable effects.

This applies to both monetarist and Keynesian policy prescriptions. The demand for money function is not an isolated relationship. As the general macro model shows, it interacts with the other functional relationships to determine nominal income, employment and the balance of payments or exchange rate. If the demand for money, or any other relationship, is unstable, then it is difficult to make useful predictions about the behaviour of macroeconomic variables. This type of economy would not be amenable to any form of government economic policy, Keynesian or otherwise, which tried to attain particular values for certain key objective economic variables by manipulating other variables. Unstable economic functions put a spoke in the wheel of any form of economic policy which depends on regulating the behaviour of private-sector economic agents.

References

[1] R. Coghlan, *The Theory of Money and Finance* (London: Macmillan, 1980) ch. 4.

[2] D. Fisher, *Monetary Theory and the Demand for Money* (London: Martin Robertson, 1978) chs 3, 5.

[3] L. Harris, *Monetary Theory* (New York: McGraw-Hill, 1981) chs 9–11.

[4] D. Laidler, *The Demand for Money: Theories and Evidence*, 2nd edn (New York: Dunn-Donnelly, 1977).
[5] W. Baumol, 'The Transactions Demand for Cash: An Inventory Theoretic Approach', *Quarterly Journal of Economics*, 66 (November 1952).
[6] J. Tobin, 'The Interest Elasticity of the Transactions Demand for Cash', *Review of Economics and Statistics*, 38 (August 1956).
[7] J. Tobin, 'Liquidity Preference as Behavior Toward Risk', *Review of Economic Studies*, 25 (February 1958).
[8] M. Friedman, 'The Quantity Theory of Money: A Restatement', in M. Friedman (ed.), *Studies in the Quantity Theory of Money* (University of Chicago Press, 1956).
[9] W. J. Baumol, *Portfolio Theory: the Selection of Asset Combinations* (New York: McCaleb-Seiber Publishing Co., 1970).
[10] Irving Fisher, *The Rate of Interest* (London: Macmillan, 1907).
[11] Irving Fisher, *The Theory of Interest* (London: Macmillan, 1930).
[12] M. Friedman, *The Optimum Quantity of Money* (London: Macmillan, 1969).
[13] I. Fisher, *The Purchasing Power of Money*, 2nd edn (London: Macmillan, 1913).
[14] R. Coghlan, 'A Transactions Demand for Money', *Bank of England Quarterly Bulletin*, 18, 1 (March 1978).
[15] D. Hendry, 'Predictive Failure and Modelling in Macroeconomics: the Transactions Demand for Money', in P. Ormerod (ed.), *Economic Modelling* (London: Heinemann, 1979).
[16] G. Haache, 'The Demand for Money in the UK: Experience since 1971', *Bank of England Quarterly Bulletin* (September 1974).
[17] M. J. Artis and M. K. Lewis, 'The Demand for Money in the UK 1963–73', *Manchester School*, 44, 2 (1976).
[18] M. J. Artis and M. K. Lewis, *Monetary Control in the UK* (Philip Allan, 1981).
[19] D. Laidler, 'The Demand for Money in the US – Yet Again', in K. Brunner and A. Meltzer (eds), *On The State of Macroeconomics*, Carnegie–Rochester Conference Series on Public Policy (1980).
[20] G. Laumas, 'A Test of the Stability of the Demand for Money', *Scottish Journal of Political Economy*, 25, 3 (November 1978).
[21] M. Hamburger, 'The Behaviour of the Money Stock', *Journal of Monetary Economics* (1977).

Further reading

Coghlan [1], Fisher [2], Harris [3] and Laidler [4] are texts on money. Tobin [7] and Friedman [8] are classic articles that should be read by students.

9 The Money Supply

In the first two post-war decades when Keynesianism dominated official thinking monetary policy was concerned with interest rates and the availability of credit rather than with the supply of money as such. It is only in the last decade that, under the influence of monetarism, governments have gradually turned more attention to the supply of money. Whether the authorities can control the stock of money and, if so, what are the best methods to use have now become crucial policy issues.

This chapter examines the determination of the money supply in an economy. Although each economy has different financial institutions and practices which influence the determination of the stock of money, there is a common theoretical framework for analysing money supply determination, and this we examine in this chapter. Institutional detail is kept to a minimum in the interests of brevity. (Readers who want more on this should consult Gowland [1], Congdon [2] or Zawadzki [3].

9.1 Financial intermediation

Bank deposits make up over 80 per cent of the £M_3 measure of the money stock in the United Kingdom. Thus a theory of money supply determination must include a theory of bank behaviour. A bank borrows from people willing to deposit cash with it in return for a claim on the bank in the form of a bank deposit. Cash is an asset to the bank, while deposits are a liability since the bank must repay them on demand (current accounts) or on short notice (deposit accounts). The bank, knowing that at any one time only a small proportion of its deposit-holders will demand to convert their deposits into cash, can make a profit by acquiring interest-earning assets in the form of bank loans. A simplified balance-sheet showing a bank's assets and liabilities is shown in Table 9.1. As in all balance-sheets, the total of assets equals the total of liabilities. Note that on the asset side the bank does not hold all of its assets as loans. A proportion is held as cash in order to be always able to repay deposits on demand and thus avoid insolvency.

TABLE 9.1 *A simple bank balance-sheet*

Liabilities		Assets	
Current-account (sight) deposits	£50,000	Cash	£10,000
Deposit accounts or time deposits	£50,000	Loans	£90,000
Total	£100,000		£100,000

A bank is a financial intermediary. It borrows from one set of economic agents by issuing liabilities on itself. These are financial assets to the bank's creditors. The bank then lends to another set of agents, who issue claims on themselves which the bank holds as assets. In the absence of a financial intermediary an agent who wished to spend in excess of its income and borrow money would have to do so directly from some other agents who wished to save and acquire financial assets. Financial intermediaries provide asset-holders with assets which are more liquid than those issued by ultimate borrowers. *Liquidity* refers to the ease with which an asset can be exchanged for cash. The concept of liquidity embraces the transactions costs of changing an asset into cash, the time that has to elapse before the asset is due to be repaid in cash (that is, the maturity of the asset) and the risk of capital loss when encashing the asset. The less liquid an asset, the higher in general is the rate of return in order to compensate its holder for illiquidity. Since a bank deposit is more liquid than a bank loan a bank can pay its deposit-holders less in interest than it charges its borrowers. The margin between interest payments on deposits and the interest received on loans is sufficient to cover operating expenses over and above those directly charged for on current accounts and so provides banks with a profit.

The financial sector of a developed economy consists of a whole range of financial intermediaries, such as various types of banks, building societies, pension funds and unit trusts. The principle of financial intermediation is basic to them all. The financial intermediary borrows by issuing claims on itself, known as 'secondary claims', which are more liquid than the assets the financial intermediary acquires. As a result of financial intermediation, a whole stock of financial assets and liabilities is built up over time and offers lenders and borrowers a range of financial instruments which differ in marketability, risk and rate of return.

9.2 A mechanistic model of bank deposit determination

As just mentioned, a bank only needs to hold a relatively small proportion of its total assets in the form of non-earning cash. This cash is known as *reserve assets* because it is held in reserve to ensure that the bank remains solvent by always being able to repay its current-account depositors on demand. The ratio of reserve assets to total assets is called the *reserve ratio*. Here we assume that the reserve ratio is fixed at r either by the bank's own practices or by government dictat. The currency part of the money supply is held either by banks as reserve assets or as currency in circulation with the non-bank sector. We assume that the non-bank public have a desired ratio in which they hold currency and bank deposits and that this remains fixed at c.

We now have three relationships which can be manipulated to obtain an expression for the supply of money. These relationships are stated in equations 9.1 to 9.3 and hold for the entire banking system.

(i) *A definition of the money supply*

$$M = C + D \tag{9.1}$$

where

M = money supply
C = currency in circulation with non-bank public
D = bank deposits.

(ii) *A bank reserve ratio*

$$r = \frac{R}{D} \quad (0 < r < 1) \tag{9.2}$$

where R = cash reserves held by banks and it is assumed that all the banks in the economy maintain a fixed reserve ratio of r.

(iii) *A desired currency–deposit ratio*

$$c = \frac{C}{D} \quad (0 < c < 1) \tag{9.3}$$

Substituting $C = cD$ from equation 9.3 into equation 9.1 we get

$$M = (1 + c)D \tag{9.4}$$

Adding equations 9.2 and 9.3 gives

$$r + c = \frac{R + C}{D} \tag{9.5}$$

Rearranging equation 9.5 we get

$$D = \frac{R + C}{r + c} \tag{9.6}$$

Substituting 9.6 into 9.4 gives

$$M = \left\{\frac{1 + c}{r + c}\right\}(R + C)$$

$$= m(R + C) \tag{9.7}$$

The term $m = (1 + c)/(r + c)$ is known as a *bank multiplier* since the money supply, M, is some positive multiple, m, of $R + C$. The bank multiplier is considerably larger than 1.0 since r and c are quite small numbers. For the United Kingdom given a c of roughly 0.2 and a cash reserve ratio operated by banks of about 0.04, we get a bank multiplier of around 5. The total amount of currency held in circulation with the public and as bank cash reserves, $R + C$, is known as *high-powered money*, or as the *monetary base*, since one extra unit of high-powered money, H, gives rise to a multiple increase in the total money supply. Thus money supply equation can be summarised as

$$M = mH \tag{9.8}$$

It is important to appreciate that equation 9.8 only provides a *theory* of money supply determination if the bank reserve equation 9.2 and the currency ratio equation 9.3 are *behavioural* equations. They are necessarily identities since one can always measure r as actual bank reserves divided by actual bank deposits and c as currency actually held as a ratio of actual bank deposits. So equation 9.8 will always hold as an identity. Equations 9.1 to 9.8 provide a basic *model* of money supply determination if banks' *demand* for reserves is a constant proportion of their deposits and if the public's demand for currency is a constant proportion of their holdings of bank deposits. The model as it stands is rightly criticised as mechanistic because it treats r and c as fixed parameters and does not take account of the behaviour of banks and the public which determines r and c. We therefore extend the basic model to take account of some aspects of such behaviour.

9.3 A behavioural model of money supply determination

Behavioural models of the money supply process treat banks as firms. A bank produces an output of banking services which can for simplicity be regarded as varying directly with the volume of bank deposits created by the bank. Attention is then focused on bank deposits as a proxy for bank output. The production of bank deposits incurs costs and these are of two kinds. First, there are the real resource costs of employing capital and labour to manage and operate bank accounts and bank loans. Second, there are the interest payments banks need to pay in order to attract deposits and hence gain reserves against which bank loans can be extended. Therefore, we can express a bank's cost function as

$$Z = Z(D) + D^T i_D \tag{9.9}$$

where

Z = bank costs
$Z(D)$ = real resource costs, which depend on the total volume of deposits, and we assume $dZ/dD > 0$
i_D = rate of interest paid on time deposits
D^T = volume of time deposits
D = volume of time plus sight deposits

A bank's revenue depends on the level of bank charges, a, it levies per unit of sight deposits, and on the interest rate obtained on bank loans, i_L. For simplicity we assume just one type of bank loan. (In practice banks hold a range of assets of varying liquidity which include government debt instruments as well as loans to individuals and firms.) The volume of bank loans is the amount of total deposits minus the amount held as cash reserves, as can be seen in Table 9.1. That is, Loans $= D - R$. Equation 9.2 gives $R = rD$. Substituting for R in the expression for loans gives Loans $= (1 - r)D$. Therefore, the bank's interest income is $D(1 - r)i_L$ and total bank revenues are

$$\text{REV} = aD^S + D(1 - r)i_L \tag{9.10}$$

where $D^S =$ sight deposits. Bank profits, π^B, are therefore

$$\pi^B = aD^S + D(1 - r)i_L - Z(D) - D^T i_D \tag{9.11}$$

If the banking industry is competitive, then the interest rates on deposits and on bank loans will remain unchanged when an individual bank changes its quantity of deposits. Differentiating 9.11 with respect to D we get the usual profit-maximising conditions for a perfectly competitive firm:

$$\frac{d\pi^B}{dD} = \left\{a\frac{dD^S}{dD} + (1 - r)i_L\right\} - \left\{\frac{dZ}{dD} + \frac{dD^T}{dD}i_D\right\} = 0 \tag{9.12}$$

The term in the first set of brackets is marginal revenue, which for a competitive bank is constant given a fixed ratio of sight to time deposits; the term in the second set of brackets is marginal cost, which rises with the volume of deposits because of the assumption of an increasing marginal-cost function for the real resource costs of bank asset and liability management.

For a competitive banking industry as a whole i_D and i_L will not remain constant, as the volume of deposits and loans made by all the banks changes. To know how these interest rates alter with the volume of deposits produced by the whole banking industry we need to introduce behavioural functions for the banks' depositors and borrowers. Let us assume that the non-bank public can hold four types of assets. These are currency, sight deposits, time deposits and loans to the ultimate borrowers in the economy who can either borrow directly from the non-bank public or from banks. We now need to specify the non-bank sector's demand functions for these four assets.

The non-bank public's demand to hold currency is related to such long-term trends as the size, coverage and sophistication of the banking system. The movement from rural to urban centres has decreased the demand for currency, as has the development of bank and credit cards. The desire to evade tax and the extent of the black economy increase the demand for currency. A decline in confidence in the solvency of the banking system, as occurred in the USA in the 1930s, also increases the proportion of the money supply held as currency. In the short run one would expect the demand for currency to vary inversely with the rate of return on bank deposits. The currency–deposit ratio, c, is no longer constant as in the mechanistic model but falls as the rate of interest on deposits, i_D, rises. Similarly the ratio of sight to time deposits will fall as i_D rises. Finally, as asset-holders can either hold money or bonds (loans), the demand for all types of money can be expected to fall as the bond rate and bank loan rate, which we assume are both equal to i_L, rise relative to the deposit rate.

Therefore, given a constant volume of high-powered money, the banking system as a whole can only increase its volume of deposits by putting up the interest rate on time deposits and so attracting more cash reserves by persuading the public to hold less currency. The banking industry's marginal-cost curve for deposit production, given by the term in the second set of brackets in equation 9.12, is shown in Figure 9.1. Marginal costs rise both because of increasing marginal management costs and because of the higher interest rate needed to attract more deposits by lowering the non-bank public's currency–deposit ratio.

To derive the banking industry's average revenue function we need to introduce the demand by borrowers for bank loans. The demand for bank loans depends directly on the demand for consumer credit and for investment funds. This will increase if the interest rate on bank loans falls or if an increase in expected future income and profits raises the demand for credit. Thus we can write

$$L^D = f(i_L, X) \qquad (dL^D/di_L < 0) \tag{9.13}$$

where X stands for all other factors influencing the demand for bank loans. So if X is constant, the banking system can only expand loans and hence deposits by lowering the bank lending rate. The average revenue from bank deposit creation therefore declines for the industry as a whole as deposits are expanded. A competitive banking industry will expand deposits up to the level at which average revenue equals marginal cost. This occurs at OD_c deposits in Figure 9.1.

If the banking industry is a monopoly or collusive oligopoly, then the industry's marginal revenue will lie below its average revenue function. Unlike the competitive case each bank will find that when it expands loans it will have to lower its lending rate. The profit-maximising monopoly or joint profit-maximising oligopoly will equate marginal revenue with marginal cost and

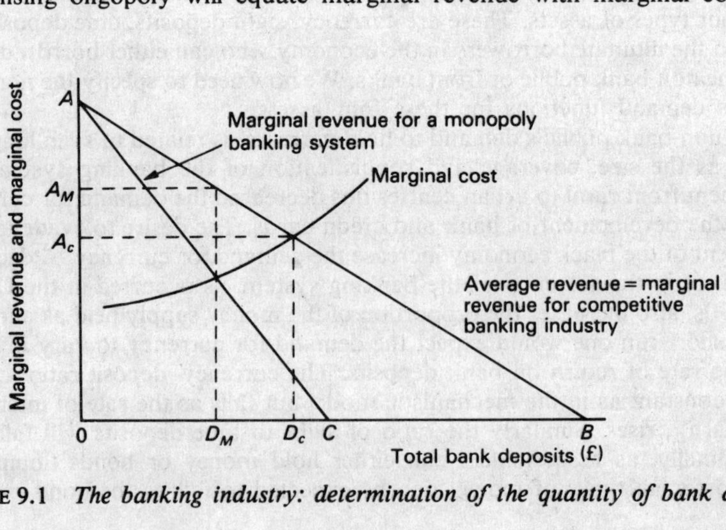

FIGURE 9.1 *The banking industry: determination of the quantity of bank deposits*

produce only OD_M deposits. The monopoly industry will charge a higher loan rate and provide a lower deposit rate than would a competitive banking industry.

Factors influencing the supply of money

If investment in real capital goods becomes more profitable and the demand for bank loans rises, then the banking industry's average and marginal revenue curves will shift out to the right in Figure 9.1. Banks can only extend more credit by attracting more cash reserves. Given that all other factors remain unchanged, in particular the amount of high-powered money, bank reserves can only be increased by putting up the rate on time deposits. The non-bank sector is induced to hold a smaller currency–deposit ratio so that a higher proportion of high-powered money is held by the banks. The banks therefore move up the marginal-cost curve, deposits expand and both deposit and loan rates rise. In terms of the basic bank multiplier approach given by equation 9.8 on p. 150, the currency–deposit ratio has fallen because i_D and i_L have risen, causing the bank multiplier to become larger. So introducing behavioural relationships transforms the bank multiplier from a fixed parameter to a behaviour variable and makes the money supply vary directly with the demand for bank loans.

If the currency ratio rose because of a change in the public's taste for currency, then the banks would face an upward shift in their marginal costs. At each level of deposits banks would have to pay a higher deposit rate to attract deposits. The loan rate would rise along an unchanged bank average revenue function and fewer bank loans would be demanded. The total amount of deposits outstanding would contract.

If there were an exogenous expansion in the amount of high-powered money, due, say, to the actions of the monetary authorities, then banks would need to pay less to depositors to attract a given volume of time deposits. This means that the marginal-cost function would shift down to the right in Figure 9.1. Banks would lower their lending rate, more bank loans would be demanded and deposits would thus expand.

The reserve ratio and prudential banking

So far we have assumed that the reserve ratio is constant and that the only way that banks can initiate an increase in their reserves is by raising the time deposit rate and so persuading the non-bank public to hold a lower ratio of currency to deposits. The problem of such a system is the danger of banks becoming insolvent. The fact that a bank might not be able to pay its depositors cash on demand can set off a run on the bank. If more depositors than the bank bargained for demand repayment in cash, they cannot be paid immediately, as cash reserves become exhausted and loans cannot be liquidated straightaway. If the bank then collapses, the depositors lose their money and the panic can spread to other banks and financial institutions.

To prevent such occurrences an economy establishes a central bank, or one evolves. One of the chief functions of a central bank is to provide the banking system with cash reserves when needed and so remove the fear of bank insolvency. In principle the central bank supplies additional reserves by extending loans to the banks and can choose the interest rate at which it lends. Banks now have two ways of increasing their cash reserves, either by borrowing from the non-bank public or from the central bank. If banks are able to choose their reserve ratio, then r also becomes a behavioural variable and not a fixed parameter as in the mechanistic model. The advantage of a high reserve ratio from the banks' point of view is that it lowers the risk of running short of reserves and having to borrow them at a penal rate of interest, i_R, from the central bank. However, the disadvantage is that interest income is forgone by holding reserves rather than loans. A variable reserve ratio introduces a further element of variability into the bank multiplier of equation 9.8. For instance, if the demand for bank loans shifts up so that the bank loan rate rises and banks choose to expand loans by operating with a lower reserve ratio, then the bank multiplier rises just as it does if the currency–deposit ratio falls. Thus we need to modify the mechanistic bank multiplier approach of

$$M = \frac{1 + c}{r + c} H \tag{9.8}$$

by specifying that

$$c = f_1(i_D) \qquad (dc/di_D < 0) \tag{9.14}$$

$$i_d = f_2(i_L) \qquad (di_D/di_L > 0) \tag{9.15}$$

$$r = f_3(i_L, i_R) \quad (dr/di_L < 0;\ dr/di_R > 0) \tag{9.16}$$

In the last expression (9.16) the reserve ratio falls when the bank loan rate rises, but increases if the central bank lending rate, i_R, rises because it is now more expensive for banks to run out of reserves.

In Britain the central bank lending rate was known as Bank Rate prior to 1971, and then as Minimum Lending Rate (MLR). However, the theoretical description here in which the central bank lends directly to the banks is more in accord with US practice than with British. The Bank of England provides the banking system with additional reserves by buying back from the banks short-term government debt (Treasury bills). This puts cash into the hands of the banks. The price at which the Bank of England buys back (or rediscounts) Treasury bills determines the rate of interest the banks have to pay for the additional reserves. The lower the price the banks get for their Treasury bills relative to the price they bought them at, the more penal is the rate of interest they in effect pay.

The money supply as an exogenous variable

In the mechanistic model of section 9.2 the money supply is completely exogenous. Provided that high-powered money, H, is exogenously given, the money supply is also exogenous because the money multiplier, m, is fixed. In the behavioural model, however, the money supply is partly endogenous because the reserve ratio and the currency ratio vary with interest rates and hence with the demand for the various assets and liabilities created by the financial system. However, provided that H is still exogenous and that r and c are related to interest rates in a stable manner, the money supply still exhibits a strong element of exogeneity. The less c and r vary, the greater the degree of exogeneity. The typical monetarist view of the money supply accords with the behavioural model. The money multiplier is not a fixed parameter: it does vary but in a stable manner and without large and sudden changes. If H rises (falls), the money supply rises (falls) independently of the state of the demand for money, and so portfolio disequilibrium between the demand and supply of money is created. If the money supply exceeds the amount people wish to hold, portfolio adjustment occurs as the excess money balances are spent on goods, services and other financial assets. This portfolio adjustment affects prices, wages and interest rates. Thus the view that the money supply can be changed independently of the demand for money lies at the heart of monetarist analysis.

9.4 A demand-determined view of the money supply process

An alternative view, held by anti-monetarists, is that the supply of money is determined by the demand for money and so cannot be changed independently of the demand for money. There are a number of facets to the demand-determined view of the money supply process. One critique of the multiplier model is that the reserve and currency ratios are highly variable and so make the multiplier unstable. Another critique relates to the way the banking system, particularly in the United Kingdom, actually operates. The Bank of England does not and cannot restrict banks' access to reserves because the banking system must be kept liquid to maintain confidence in its solvency. Hence an increase in the demand for bank credit would be always met by banks because they know they will always obtain extra reserves from the Bank of England.

A more extreme critique, such as that provided by Kaldor [4], maintains that the view of the money supply process presented in sections 9.2 and 9.3 is totally inapplicable in a credit economy. In such an economy it is liquidity and the availability of credit which influence spending decisions rather than the money supply as such. This is because money cannot be properly distinguished from the liabilities of non-bank financial intermediaries as these are very close substitutes to bank deposits. The view that this intangible variable, liquidity, is the crucial monetary variable was at its most influential in the early 1960s following the publication of the Radcliffe Report [5].

A further development of this view is the argument that the amount of financial intermediary deposits is determined by the demand for them. If the private sector wants more credit, this will be created for it by the financial system. One way of depicting this is in terms of Figure 9.1. If the short-run marginal-cost function for deposit production is gently sloped, then an increase in the demand for bank loans will shift the average and marginal revenues out to the right and give rise to a considerable expansion in the money supply. The longer the time horizon, the flatter the marginal-cost function as banks and other financial institutions devise new ways of meeting the demand for credit. If the long-run marginal-cost function is horizontal, then the output of deposits is completely demand-determined. In this model the supply of money can only be contracted if the demand for credit is reduced.

The Kaldor-type view of the money supply process is criticised on the grounds that it confuses the demand for credit with the demand for money (e.g. Brunner and Meltzer [6]). Bank borrowers want credit in order to finance expenditure: they do not want to hold their bank loans as money. The bank deposits spent by bank borrowers end up in the asset portfolios of other economic agents who may not want to hold money. So although the extra money comes into existence because of a demand for credit there can still be an excess supply of money over and above the amount people want to *hold*.

9.5 Methods of monetary control

The idea that government should seek to control the stock of money in existence stems primarily from the monetarist analysis that inflation is due to expanding the money supply too rapidly so that it exceeds the demand to hold money at the existing price level. Excess money balances are spent and, given a neoclassical supply function, prices must eventually rise (see Chapter 2, pp. 17–18, Chapter 4, p. 54, and Chapter 6, p. 86, for a simple exposition and Chapter 19 for a more sophisticated one). In this context controlling the money supply refers to the *nominal* stock of money. The real quantity of money is determined by all those forces within the private and public sectors which determine the price level. The real quantity of money is only very indirectly under government control. All models of the monetary sector are concerned with the nominal quantity of money. The real quantity of money can only be determined when the monetary sector is combined with all the other sectors to form a model of the whole economy.

In Britain the advent in 1979 of a Conservative government committed to monetarist policies brought the issue of monetary control, its rationale and its implementation to the forefront of economic policy debate. The monetary authorities have three basic ways of influencing the money supply. Which of these is advocated is highly dependent on how one thinks the money supply process operates.

1. Money base control

The multiplier approach to money supply determination provides the rationale for the use of the monetary base as the fulcrum for controlling the supply of money. In a closed economy which has no commodity money the only source of high-powered money is the government and the monetary authorities.[1] If

[1] If gold or silver is mined in the country and used as money, then the private sector is also a source of *H*.

government expenditure exceeds its tax revenue, then any part of the budget deficit or public sector borrowing requirement (PSBR) not financed by selling government debt to the non-bank sector must be financed by means of high-powered money. In Britain any government bills or bonds required to finance the PSBR and not funded, i.e. not sold, to the non-bank sector are taken up by the private banking sector or the Bank of England. If banks thereby run short of reserves, these are then provided by the Bank of England, so increasing H.

The monetary authorities can also influence the stock of H independently of whether the PSBR is in deficit or surplus by engaging in open-market operations. (These have already been mentioned in Chapter 4.) Let us assume that the PSBR is zero and the authorities sell additional government bonds. To persuade individuals to hold more bonds and less money the rate of interest on government bonds rises. The non-bank public buy the bonds with bank deposits. The private-sector banks experience a contraction in their cash reserves. To prevent their reserve ratios from falling too low, they need to do one or more of the following: raise the deposit rate to attract more reserves by lowering the currency–deposit ratio, c; acquire reserves from the central bank at a penal rate; cut back on loans and hence deposits. The bank loan rate must rise and so fewer bank loans are demanded. A multiple contraction of bank deposits then ensues.

The working of money base control is illustrated in Figure 9.2. The demand for money is given by schedule DD and the supply by schedule SS, which slopes upward because the money multiplier, m, rises when c and r fall due to higher interest rates. If the authorities reduce the volume of H, banks marginal-cost curves shift up to the left, as does the money supply function in Figure 9.2 from S_0 to S_1. The quantity of money contracts from M_0 to M_1 and the level of interest rates rises from i_0 to i_1. If the authorities engage in open-market purchases of government bonds or bills, H is increased, interest rates fall and a multiple expansion of deposits occurs.

Monetary base control can be reinforced by the central bank requiring the individual banks to keep a minimum reserve ratio rather than one of their own choosing. If the required minimum r is above the one banks would choose to maintain, then r becomes a fixed parameter giving the authorities greater control over the money multiplier, $(1 + c)/(r + c)$. The multiplier can be lowered by increasing the minimum required r.

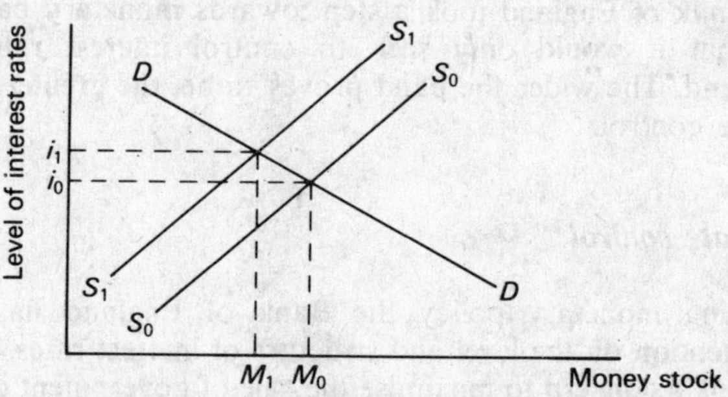

FIGURE 9.2 *Monetary base control*

Under monetary base control the quantity of money is regulated by operating on the quantity of high-powered money. There is no direct link between the size of the public sector borrowing requirement and the change in the volume of high-powered money, since what matters is the amount of government expenditure not financed either by tax revenues or sales of government debt to the non-bank public. The following identity holds in a closed economy over any given time period:

$$\Delta H = \text{PSBR} - \text{net sales of government debt to non-bank public} \quad (9.17)$$

The change in high-powered money equals the PSBR (treated as positive when the budget is in deficit) minus the difference between total sales of government debt and total purchases plus redemptions. If purchases of government debt plus redemptions exceed sales, then ΔH will be larger than the PSBR. Therefore, one way of controlling H is to keep a tight reign on the PSBR. This is not the only method, as H can be controlled even though the PSBR is large provided that the PSBR is adequately funded. However, the larger the PSBR that requires funding, the higher will interest rates be driven, *ceteris paribus*, in order to persuade the non-bank sector to hold the extra government debt. This may crowd out private-sector expenditure and so be considered undesirable.

Criticisms of monetary base control take several forms. One argument is that interest rates would become volatile, thus destabilising financial markets and increasing uncertainty. It is held to conflict with the central banks' overriding concern with the liquidity and solvency of the banking system, since monetary contraction implies keeping banks short of cash. The central bank cannot prudently do this, so therefore the monetary base control is inoperative. Imposing a minimum required reserve ratio on banks penalises banks as against other financial intermediaries, which will expand at the banks' expense. So although bank deposits appear to be controlled, the supply of credit in general, which is what really matters according to these critics, is not controlled in the long run. This argument rests on the supposition that bank deposits and the deposits of other types of financial intermediary are very close substitutes and, in its extreme form, merges into Kaldor's contention that the money supply cannot be controlled via the money base because the money supply is always demand-determined.

From 1920 until 1981 Britain did not operate monetary policy by means of monetary base control. It relied instead on two other methods outlined below. In 1981 the Bank of England took a step towards monetary base control by announcing that it would only seek to control interest rates within an undisclosed band. The wider the band proves to be, the greater the degree of monetary base control.

2. *Interest-rate control*

When operating monetary policy the Bank of England has traditionally focused its attention on the level and structure of interest rates. This has been due to the Bank's concern to maximise the sale of government debt combined with the belief that financial markets have Keynesian-type expectations. If the Bank tries to press sales of government debt and interest rates rise, then speculators will expect interest rates to rise further and thus expect bond prices to fall in the future. Therefore, they hold back from purchasing government debt.

If monetary policy is conducted with an interest-rate target in view, then the money supply cannot be controlled independently of that target. This is illustrated in Figure 9.3. If the monetary authorities want the level of interest rates to be i_2, they must allow the supply of money to be the quantity that is demanded at i_2, given the values of the other determinants of the demand to hold money. Any value other than M_2 for the money supply is inconsistent with this interest-rate target.

Institutional structures and practices in the United Kingdom are not geared to monetary base control. Since the 1920s it has been the practice of the Bank of England to supply as much currency as the banks and non-bank public require. During this period the Bank has never sought to keep the banks short of reserves, but has always stood ready to buy back Treasury bills held by the banking system. The only control the Bank has operated is the choice of whether or not the rate at which Treasury bills are rediscounted is a penal one. If it is a penal rate, then an upward pressure is exerted on the interest-rate structure.

Given the increasing emphasis in recent years on controlling the supply of money, the Bank of England and other commentators have begun to interpret interest-rate targets as a form of monetary control (see the Green Paper on *Monetary Control* [7]). This interpretation is linked to the idea that the money supply is demand-determined. The way to reduce the supply of money is therefore to reduce the demand for it by raising the level of interest rates. So if in Figure 9.3 interest rates were raised to i_3 by raising MLR (the central bank lending rate) and simultaneously engaging in open-market sales of government debt, the demand for money will fall to M_3 and so the money supply will contract. Kaldor [4] goes so far as to argue that the national output must first be contracted in order to reduce the demand for money, which will then give rise to a smaller money stock.

To a monetarist the idea of reducing the stock of money by operating on the demand for money seems very odd when more direct methods are available (see Friedman [8]). Furthermore, any attempt to control the stock of money

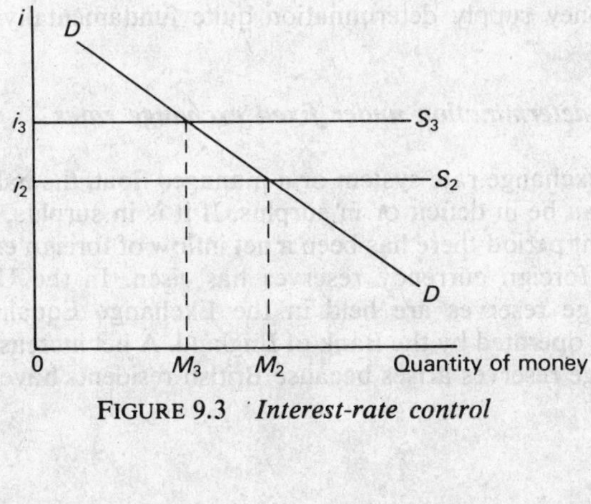

FIGURE 9.3 *Interest-rate control*

without regulating the supply of high-powered money is doomed to failure. So long as the banks can obtain adequate reserves they can expand deposits. A further problem with the interest-rate method is that a rise in interest rates stimulates the supply of money if it reduces the currency ratio and fails to stem the demand for bank credit. Up to mid-1981 the Bank of England had not tried monetary base control and had found interest-rate control inadequate to the task. It therefore used various forms of credit rationing via direct controls on bank lending.

3. *Direct controls on bank lending*

In the 1960s direct controls on bank lending took the form of Bank of England directives to banks to restrict their total amount of lending and to discriminate in favour of certain types of borrower (for example, loans for industrial investment rather than personal consumption). Rather than allowing the available quantity of loans to go to those borrowers who were prepared to pay the most for it, credit was rationed via non-price means. In the 1970s a form of direct control called 'the Corset' was tried, whereby banks were only allowed to expand their deposits by a given percentage amount. If this rate was exceeded, penalties were imposed in the form of having to place non-interest-earning special supplementary deposits with the Bank of England.

Direct controls on bank lending are criticised for being inefficient because they interfere with the allocation of credit by means of market criteria. They discriminate against domestic banks by impeding their ability to compete with other financial intermediaries. These have in fact grown much faster than the clearing banks. This problem, referred to as *disintermediation*, is considerably greater in an open economy, particularly one which has abolished exchange controls (as did Britain in 1979). Because of these criticisms direct controls were abandoned in 1980.

9.6 Money supply determination in an open economy

So far we have discussed money supply determination in the context of a closed economy. Extending the discussion to an open economy alters the analysis of money supply determination quite fundamentally.

Money supply determination under fixed exchange rates

Under a fixed exchange-rate system or a managed float, the balance for official finance, BOF, can be in deficit or in surplus. If it is in surplus, this means that over the relevant period there has been a net inflow of foreign exchange and the total stock of foreign currency reserves has risen. In the United Kingdom foreign exchange reserves are held in the Exchange Equalisation Account (EEA) which is operated by the Bank of England. A net increase in the stock of foreign exchange reserves arises because British residents have been net sellers of goods, services and assets to foreigners. In return British residents receive foreign exchange which they convert into sterling by selling it to the EEA. British residents' holdings of sterling money balances have thus increased, and since this sterling has been supplied via the Bank of England, it is high-powered money. We have therefore arrived at the important fact that in an open economy high-powered money increases as a result of a surplus on BOF. The BOF source of H is not under the direct control of the central bank, unlike the closed-economy case.

If the BOF is in deficit, then foreign exchange reserves decline over the relevant period. The Exchange Equalisation Account (EEA) is a net seller of foreign exchange to British residents who have to run down their sterling balances in order to acquire the foreign exchange needed to finance their net purchases of goods, services and assets from foreigners. The high-powered money stock therefore declines when the BOF is in deficit.

The increase (decrease) in H that results from a surplus (deficit) on the BOF gives rise to a multiple expansion (contraction) of the money supply. The central bank can try to prevent an imbalance on the BOF from affecting the domestic money supply by engaging in offsetting open-market operations in government debt. This activity is known as *sterilisation.* If, for instance, the BOF is in surplus so that H would otherwise increase, the EEA sells government debt to the value of the BOF surplus to the non-bank domestic sector. The open-market sales reduce H and so offset the increase in H that would otherwise occur when there is an inflow of foreign exchange reserves. Similarly, when the BOF is in deficit and H would otherwise decline, the EEA sterilises by engaging in open-market purchases of government debt from the non-bank domestic sector. The debt purchases put H into the hands of the non-government sector and so offset the decline that would otherwise occur because of the deficit on BOF.

In an open economy with a fixed exchange rate or with a managed float, the following identity holds for the sources of high-powered money:

$$\Delta H = \boxed{\begin{array}{l}\text{PSBR}\\ \text{(+ when}\\ \text{government}\\ \text{budget is}\\ \text{in deficit)}\end{array}} - \boxed{\begin{array}{l}\text{Net sales of}\\ \text{government debt}\\ \text{to non-bank}\\ \text{domestic sector}\\ \text{and to foreigners}\end{array}} + \boxed{\begin{array}{l}\text{BOF surplus (+)}\\ \text{or}\\ \text{deficit (}-\text{)}\end{array}} \quad (9.18)$$

From this identity we can see that there need be no direct relationship between ΔH and the PSBR or BOF because the monetary authorities can engage in offsetting open-market operations. This is particularly so in the short run. However, over the longer run, it is difficult for the authorities to continue sterilising the monetary effects of an imbalance on the BOF. This is because sterilisation involves persuading wealth-holders to alter continually their portfolio balance between money and bonds. For example, sterilising the effects of a surplus on BOF involves increasing the proportion of bonds to money that the non-bank private sector holds and so means raising the rate of interest. This attracts more funds from foreign financial investors, so reinforcing the balance-of-payments surplus. A similar argument follows for attempts to sterilise a deficit on BOF. Now the interest rate has to fall as the ratio of money to bonds increases. Foreign capital flows out, so perpetuating the BOF deficit. These problems will be discussed more fully in the next chapter.

An important conclusion which emerges from the analysis of how the BOF affects the domestic money supply is that a country which operates a fixed exchange rate or a managed float cannot have an exogenously determined money supply unless it can sterilise successfully. Monetarists are more dubious than Keynesians about the ability of the monetary authorities to sterilise the effects of BOF imbalances on the domestic money stock. Therefore, monetarists regard the domestic money supply as being *endogenous* under a fixed exchange rate or managed float. The money supply cannot be controlled by the monetary authorities because it is affected by the BOF, which in turn depends on the decisions of private-sector economic agents, given the exchange rate the authorities decide to maintain.

If foreign currency flows cannot be sterilised, then the government cannot choose *both* the *exchange rate and the money supply as independent policy targets*. If the government chooses a particular exchange rate, then the money supply has to adjust to be consistent with it.

The money supply under perfectly flexible exchange rates

Under perfectly flexible exchange rates the BOF remains at zero because the exchange rate adjusts to achieve overall balance of payments equilibrium. Since BOF is zero it has no effect on the domestic money supply. The domestic supply of money is therefore exogenous because H is exogenous in the same way as in a closed economy. The government can now select the stock of money as a policy target, but has to accept whatever rate of exchange is consistent with the money supply target.

9.7 Conclusions: controlling the money supply

The monetarist position is that the money supply in a closed economy or in open economy with flexible exchange rates has a large element of exogeneity. Although the bank multiplier, m, does vary to some extent in the short run with interest-rate changes, these variations are not large and erratic. The money base, H, is ultimately under the government's control and this gives it control over the money supply. However, if the exchange rate is managed, then the resulting imbalances in BOF affect H so that the domestic money supply is endogenous. Anti-monetarists argue that the money supply is not exogenous under any circumstances because the multiplier m varies substantially and erratically and because H is not under the monetary authorities' control. Instead they have to vary H in response to the private sector's demand for credit and money, hence the money supply always adjusts to whatever the demand for it is.

Since 1976 British governments have announced target rates of growth for

TABLE 9.2 *£M₃ target and out-turn*

Financial year (April–April)	Target rate of growth for $£M_3$ (per cent)	Actual rate of growth of $£M_3$ (per cent)
1976–7	9–13	8.2
1977–8	9–13	16.1
1978–9	8–12	11.0
1979–80	7–11	11.3
1980–1	7–11	21.0
1981–2	6–10	11.5 (first six months at an equivalent annual rate)

the $£M_3$ definition of the money supply. Table 9.2 shows the $£M_3$ annual targets and the subsequent outcomes. It is evident that the authorities do not always succeed in keeping within the targetted band for the rate of growth of the money supply. Why these difficulties have arisen has been hotly debated. For anti-monetarists the reason is that the money supply is not amenable to control because it is demand-determined. To monetarists it appears that the authorities have not used appropriate means to control the money supply. By mid-1981 the Bank of England had still not adopted money base control and still stood willing to supply reserves to the banks. In addition the PSBR had not been kept under control and the BOF had been in surplus. The observation that it is more difficult to control the supply of money in an open economy which has no foreign exchange controls would probably command quite wide agreement. However, this does not imply that a siege economy battened down by import quotas, tariffs and exchange controls would be desirable.

References

[1] D. Gowland, *Controlling the Money Supply* (London: Croom Helm, 1982).

[2] T. Congdon, *Monetary Control in Britain* (London: Macmillan, 1982).

[3] K. Zawadzki, *Competition and Credit Control* (Oxford: Blackwell, 1981).

[4] N. Kaldor, *Evidence to the Select Committee on Monetary Policy*, vol. 1, HC 720, Session 1979–80 (London: HMSO).

[5] Radcliffe Committee on the Working of the Monetary System, *Report*, Cmnd 827 (London: HMSO, 1959).

[6] K. Brunner and A. Meltzer, 'An Aggregative Theory for a Closed Economy', in J. Stein (ed.), *Monetarism* (Amsterdam: North-Holland, 1976).

[7] HM Treasury, *Monetary Control*, Green Paper, Cmnd 7858 (London: HMSO, 1980).

[8] M. Friedman, *Evidence to the Select Committee on Monetary Policy*, vol. 1, HC 720, Session 1979–80 (London: HMSO).

10 Money, Capital Flows and the Open Economy

In an open economy high-powered money issued by the central bank must be backed by either foreign exchange reserves, FR, or government debt, DC. Therefore

$$H \equiv FR + DC \tag{10.1}$$

where H is high-powered money. That portion of H which is backed by government debt represents the central bank's creation of domestic credit, DC. Any increase, ΔH, in the stock of high-powered money must be matched by an increase in foreign reserves, FR, or an increase in central bank domestic credit, DC, or both. Therefore

$$\Delta H \equiv \Delta FR + \Delta DC \tag{10.2}$$

When the central bank purchases (sells) domestic currency in the foreign exchange market, foreign exchange reserves fall (rise) by an equivalent amount. Thus the change in foreign reserves, ΔFR, for any period must equal the balance for official financing (BOF). Therefore

$$\Delta FR = \text{BOF} \tag{10.3}$$

and

$$\Delta H = \text{BOF} + \Delta DC \tag{10.4}$$

Chapter 9 showed that the domestic money supply tends to move directly with H. The money supply, M^S, can be modelled by

$$M^S = mH = m\,(FR + DC) \tag{10.5}$$

where m is the bank multiplier. Therefore

$$\Delta M^S = m\,\Delta H = m\,(\Delta FR + \Delta DC) \tag{10.6}$$

Equations 10.4 and 10.6 show that for the money supply to stay constant we must have

$$\Delta DC = -\Delta FR = -\Delta \text{BOF} \tag{10.7}$$

ΔDC in equation 10.7 represents the open-market operations in government debt that are necessary to sterilise the BOF.

One of the crucial differences between Keynesian and monetary models of the open economy is that the former assume that the central bank can sterilise the effects of the BOF on the money stock,[1] while the latter are models in which sterilisation does not occur. Given the difficulty, discussed in Chapter 9 (p. 161) of sterilising a persistent surplus or deficit over an extended time period, Keynesian models are necessarily short run.

10.1 The Mundell–Fleming Keynesian model

The fixed-price Keynesian open-economy model set out in Chapter 7 was developed in the 1940s and early 1950s. This was a period of miniscule private capital flows (or international trade in securities) due to the comprehensive battery of exchange controls which each country had erected during the Second World War. The neglect of capital flows in this model was therefore a product of its time. As trade developed in the post-war years, exchange controls began to be seen as a hindrance to the continued growth and integration of the capitalist world economy. During the 1950s this led to a weakening of exchange controls in developed capitalist economies. In this climate of growing trade and weakening exchange controls, international trade in securities also grew. By the end of the 1950s it was apparent that capital flows had to be included in any open-economy macro model.

At the start of the 1960s Mundell[2] and Fleming, who had been colleagues at the International Monetary Fund, extended the Keynesian open-economy model to include capital flows (see [1], [2] and [3]). They postulated that net capital flows between countries occurred in response to differences between domestic and foreign interest rates when expectations about exchange-rate changes were static. They modelled the balance of payments on capital account (CAP) by a function of the form

$$\text{CAP} = \psi(i - i_f) \tag{10.8}$$

Here i is the domestic rate of interest, while i_f is the foreign rate of interest, which is exogenous if one makes the small-country assumption. CAP increases as the positive difference between i and i_f increases, so that

$$\frac{\partial(\text{CAP})}{\partial i} = \psi_i > 0$$

[1] Keynesian open-economy models are not consistent with the anti-monetarist views set out in Chapter 9, p. 147.

[2] In the late 1960s and early 1970s Mundell played an important role in developing the monetary approach to the balance of payments.

From the definition of the balance for official financing we have

$$\text{BOF} = \text{current account and capital account}$$

Substituting from equation 10.8 for the capital account and from equation 7.16 (p. 115), for the current account in this definition gives

$$\text{BOF} \equiv X(e) - f(e)y + \psi(i - i_f) \tag{10.9}$$

Here e is the exchange rate expressed in terms of foreign currency per unit of domestic currency, y is domestic income in constant domestic prices, while $X(e)$ and $f(e)$ are exports and the marginal propensity to import, both expressed as functions of the exchange rate, e.

Equation 10.9 is the equation for the foreign exchange market in the Mundell–Fleming model. The rest of the Mundell–Fleming model is identical to the open-economy *ISLM* model in Chapter 7, except that the money supply equation becomes equation 10.5. Remembering that BOF $= \Delta FR$, where ΔFR is the change in foreign reserves of the central bank, we can rewrite 10.9 as

$$\Delta FR = X(e) - f(e)y + \psi(i - i_f) \tag{10.10}$$

This indicates the amount of sterilisation that the central bank has to carry out in order to keep the stock of domestic money balances constant at the current rate of exchange. Under a fixed exchange rate it is possible in the short run to sterilise the effects of ΔFR on the money supply through open-market operations provided that ΔFR is not too large. However, due to the difficulty in sterilising a persistent deficit or surplus over the long run, the BOF will have to be zero for a long-run equilibrium solution. Hence given a fixed exchange rate, e, the equilibrium solution for the foreign exchange market becomes

$$0 = X(e) - f(e)y + \psi(i - i_f) \tag{10.11}$$

Given the exchange rate, e, the BOF $= 0$ equation becomes a function relating i and y. This must show a positive (or non-negative) relationship between i and y, as an increase in domestic income at the given exchange rate will lead to a deterioration in the current account (see Chapter 7, p. 115). For the BOF to stay equal to zero, the current-account deterioration must be offset by a capital-account improvement. This will only occur if the domestic rate of interest, i, rises relative to the foreign rate of interest, i_f. Therefore, the BOF $= 0$ function will have one of the forms shown in Figure 10.1. These alternative forms are labelled 1, 2 and 3.

The BOF_1 function represents an imperfect international capital market, so that capital flows are not very responsive to the differential between domestic and foreign interest rates. The BOF_3 function represents perfect international capital mobility where any differential in interest rates sets up very large capital flows. Here foreign securities are perfect substitutes for domestic securities. With perfect capital mobility, sterilisation of the effects of ΔFR on the money stock becomes impossible due to the large size of ΔFR. BOF_2 is an intermediate case between very imperfect and perfect capital mobility.

All points below and to the right of a BOF $= 0$ function in Figure 10.1 represent a deficit on the BOF, while all points above and to the left of the function represent a BOF surplus. Given that the Marshall–Lerner conditions hold

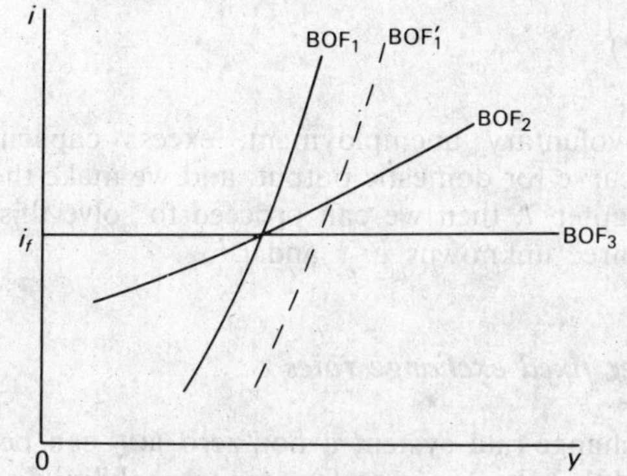

FIGURE 10.1 *Alternative possible shapes of the BOF = 0 function*

and that domestic prices do not adjust completely to a change in the exchange rate (see Chapter 7, sections 7.4 and 7.5), then a depreciation or devaluation of the domestic currency will shift the BOF = 0 function to the right from BOF_1 to BOF'_1 in Figure 10.1. An appreciation or revaluation has the opposite effect, with the BOF = 0 function shifting to the left from BOF'_1 to BOF_1. An increase in the level of foreign interest rates also leads to an upward shift in the BOF = 0 function from BOF'_1 to BOF_1 since an increase in the foreign rate of interest, i_f, requires a higher domestic level of interest, i, to keep BOF = 0. The other forms of the BOF = 0 function that are illustrated in Figure 10.1 will have identical upward shifts. Similarly, a fall in i_f will lead to a downward shift in all the forms of the BOF = 0 function illustrated in Figure 10.1. The shifts in the BOF = 0 function that occur in response to changes in foreign interest rates imply that domestic interest rates cannot depart too far from the level of foreign interest rates, as such a departure will cause problems with the balance of payments.

Under flexible exchange rates the foreign exchange market equilibrium condition is identical to equation 10.11. In this case, unlike the fixed exchange-rate case, the exchange rate adjusts to bring into equality the demand and supply of domestic currency in the foreign exchange market. Under a clean float ΔFR must always be equal to zero and the exchange rate must continually adjust in order to clear the foreign exchange market.

We can now set out the complete Mundell–Fleming model. It is composed of equation 10.11, which represents equilibrium in the foreign exchange market, the *IS* function in equation 7.13 representing goods-market equilibrium and the *LM* function in equation 7.14 representing money-market equilibrium, assuming that the central bank can sterilise the effects of any foreign reserve changes on the money stock. We re-label the *IS* function 10.12 and the *LM* function 10.13:

$$0 = X(e) - f(e)y + \psi(i - i_f) \tag{10.11}$$

$$y = \frac{a + I(i) + G_0 + X(e)}{s(1-t) + t + f(e)} \tag{10.12}$$

$$\frac{M^S}{P} = f(y, i) \tag{10.13}$$

If we assume involuntary unemployment, excess capacity, a horizontal aggregate supply curve for domestic output, and we make the small-economy assumption of Chapter 7, then we can proceed to solve this system of three equations in the three unknowns e, y and i.[1]

Fiscal policy under fixed exchange rates

Under a fixed exchange-rate system a non-zero BOF can be sterilised in the short run, provided that there is imperfect capital mobility. In this case the BOF = 0 function for the fixed exchange rate, e^*, is not a binding constraint in the short run. Short-run quasi-equilibrium solutions in which the goods and money markets are cleared, but the foreign exchange market is uncleared (i.e. BOF $\neq 0$), are possible.

An expansionary fiscal policy involving an increase in government expenditure, or a decrease in taxes, or both, will shift the IS curve to the right from IS_0 to IS_1 in Figure 10.2. The BOF = 0 function does not shift as a result of the fiscal policy as neither the exchange rate e^* nor the foreign rate of interest is affected by it. Given sterilisation of the BOF surpluses or deficits resulting from the fiscal policy, the LM curve also does not shift in the short run. However, both the size and direction of the BOF and the resulting sterilisation problem depend on how responsive are international capital flows to the differential between the domestic and foreign rates of interest.

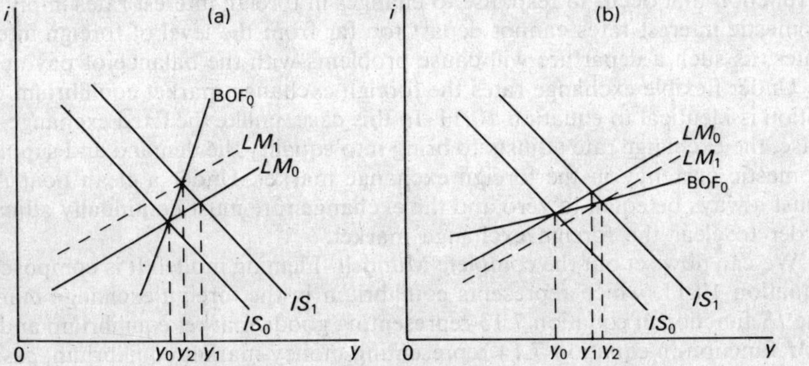

FIGURE 10.2 *Fiscal policy under fixed exchange rates*

[1] Notice that this equation system involves a simplifying approximation that P is not related to the domestic price of imports. This does not crucially affect the results deduced in *this chapter.* For a Mundell–Fleming model in which P is a weighted average of the prices of domestic goods and imports, see chapter 10 in Stern [4].

Figure 10.2(a) illustrates imperfect capital mobility where the BOF = 0 function is less interest-elastic than the LM function. The fiscal expansion which shifted the IS function from IS_0 to IS_1 has led to a new short-run quasi-equilibrium at y_1, where real income has increased above its original level of y_0. At this point the domestic interest rate, given by the intersection of the LM_0 function and IS_1 is below that rate necessary for equilibrium on the foreign exchange market and there is a deficit on the BOF. This is due to the current-account deterioration brought about by the increase in real income which has not been completely offset by a sufficient improvement on the capital account. Here the increase in income can be maintained at y_1 as long as the central bank is able to finance the resulting BOF deficit and sterilise its impact on the domestic money supply. In the long run this becomes impossible and as the central bank's foreign exchange reserves run out, the money supply will have to shrink until it reaches a point where the BOF is zero once again. This is illustrated by the shift of the LM function from LM_0 to LM_1 in Figure 10.2(a). The long-run equilibrium level of income, y_2, will be lower than the short-run solution, y_1, but higher than the original level, y_0, provided that the higher domestic interest rate induces a larger capital inflow to offset the increase in imports so that BOF = 0.

Figure 10.2(b) illustrates the case where the BOF = 0 function for the fixed rate, e^*, is more interest-elastic than the LM function. Here the fiscal expansion shifts the IS function from IS_0 to IS_1. The intersection of IS_1 with the LM_0 function leads to a configuration of income and interest rate which results in a BOF surplus. In the short run income rises to y_1. In the long run, when sterilisation of the surplus becomes difficult, the money supply increases until the interest rate falls to the point where the BOF is zero once again. This induced monetary expansion reinforces the original fiscal expansion and makes it more effective. The induced shift of the LM function from LM_0 to LM_1 in Figure 10.2(b) leads to an even higher equilibrium level for income at y_2. Therefore, we see that given the Keynesian aggregate supply assumption and a fixed exchange rate, fiscal policy is effective, and it becomes more effective, the more responsive capital flows are to interest-rate differentials. A similar analysis to the one above can be carried out for a contractionary fiscal policy.

Monetary policy under fixed exchange rates

An expansion in the domestic money stock through central bank open-market purchases of debt initially shifts the LM function to the right from LM_0 to LM_1 in Figure 10.3. In this figure the economy was initially in equilibrium with a zero BOF. The monetary expansion lowers the domestic rate of interest and this leads to an increase in the short-run equilibrium level of income from y_0 to y_1. The lower rate of interest and higher level of income lead to a BOF deficit. This deficit is larger, the more responsive are capital flows to interest-rate differentials.

Here the monetary expansion leads to a problem of sterilising the resulting deficit. As exchange reserves are depleted, either the money stock must adjust back to its old level, or there must be a devaluation in order to shift the BOF = 0

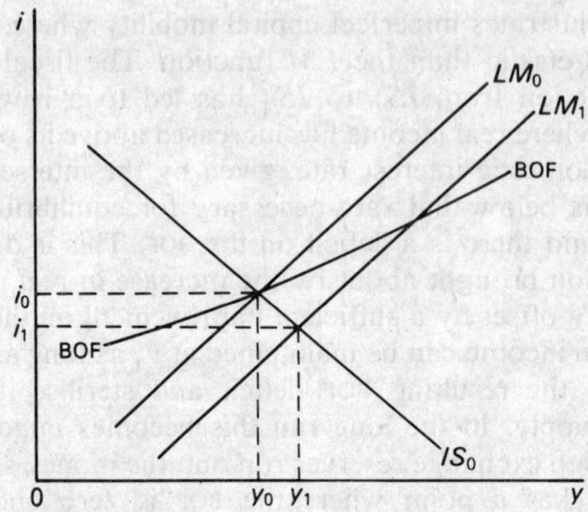

FIGURE 10.3 *Monetary policy under fixed exchange rates*

function so that it passes through the point (i_1, y_1). If the exchange rate is maintained at its original level, then the net long-run result of the original increase in the money stock is that the central bank holds more government debt and less foreign exchange reserves. Income, employment, the rate of interest and the money stock will return to their original equilibrium level.

Similarly, for an economy originally in equilibrium with a zero BOF, a decline in the domestic money stock will lead to an increase in interest rates, a fall in income and a BOF surplus. Continual sterilisation of this BOF surplus will be required in order to keep the domestic money stock at this lower level. Once sterilisation ceases, the growing foreign reserves will increase H to its previous level. At this point the money stock, interest rate and income return to their original levels and the BOF becomes zero. As before, when monetary policy starts from an equilibrium position with a zero BOF, its effects are nullified in the long run under a fixed exchange rate. Here the money stock must be largely endogenous.

Under fixed exchange rates an expansionary monetary policy must always lead to a deterioration in the BOF, while a contractionary monetary policy will always lead to an improvement in the BOF. This is a robust conclusion from the Mundell–Fleming model that also holds for other open-economy models with international capital flows. If a monetary expansion occurs when the BOF is in surplus, then this would merely speed up the increase in the money stock that would have eventually occurred as a result of the surplus. The surplus will diminish and there will be a smaller accumulation of foreign reserves as a result of the monetary expansion. Here the effects of the policy on the domestic money stock will not be nullified. Similarly, when the BOF is in deficit under a fixed exchange rate, a monetary contraction will accelerate the adjustment in the domestic money stock that would eventually occur as a result of foreign exchange reserve losses. This will limit the extent of reserve loss and in this case the monetary contraction is not nullified in the long run.

Monetary policy under flexible exchange rates

Under a clean float the exchange rate adjusts so that the BOF is always zero and there is no change in the central bank's foreign reserves. As $\Delta FR = 0$, the domestic stock of money can be completely controlled by the monetary authorities both in the short run and the long run. This allows domestic autonomy for monetary policy under a flexible exchange-rate system which is not available under a fixed exchange-rate system.

An expansion in the money supply under a clean float will shift the LM function to the right from LM_0 to LM_1 in Figure 10.4. The resulting fall in the domestic rate of interest will lead to a deterioration in the capital account. Assuming the Marshall–Lerner condition is satisfied, the exchange rate will have to fall sufficiently to create an offsetting increase in the current account so as to maintain foreign exchange market equilibrium. The fall in the exchange rate causes a net shift in domestic and foreign demand towards domestic output and results in a shift to the right in both the BOF $= 0$ and the IS functions. This is illustrated in Figure 10.4 by the shift from IS_0 to IS_1 and from BOF_0 to BOF_1; as a result real income increases from y_0 to y_1.

A contraction of the domestic money supply will lead to a rise in the domestic rate of interest and to a fall in the level of income. The resulting improvement in both the current and capital accounts of the balance of payments will lead to an appreciation of the domestic currency under a flexible exchange rate. The higher exchange rate will reinforce the negative effect of the higher interest rate on the level of expenditure on domestic output and will lead to a lower level of income and employment.

Under flexible exchange rates an important channel through which monetary policy acts on the economy is through the changes in real wages and in the relative price of domestic to foreign goods that result from a change in the exchange rate. We have seen that an expansionary monetary policy leads to a depreciation, while a contractionary monetary policy leads to an appreciation of the currency. With a Keynesian aggregate supply function, an appreciation of the currency will raise the price of domestic goods relative to the price

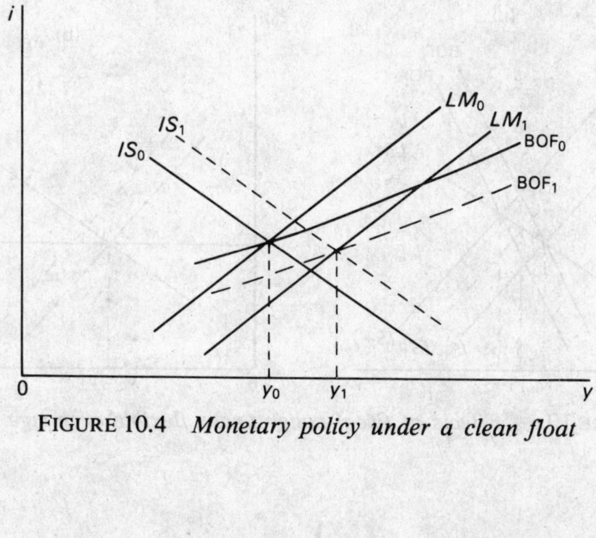

FIGURE 10.4 *Monetary policy under a clean float*

of foreign goods when both prices are expressed in the same currency. This will result in a shift in demand from domestic to foreign goods and have a depressing effect on domestic income and employment. A depreciation will have the opposite effect. Therefore, under Keynesian supply assumptions, a flexible exchange rate increases the impact of monetary policy on domestic income as the induced change in the exchange rate affects output in the same direction as the other channels of monetary influence. This impact is larger, the greater is capital mobility. However, under a neoclassical supply function, output cannot change in response to monetary changes, other than in the short run. Here a change in the exchange rate brought about by monetary policy will only have a short-run effect on the relative price of domestic to foreign goods and real wages (see Chapter 7, pp. 117–21).

Fiscal policy under flexible exchange rates

Given the Keynesian aggregate supply function and flexible exchange rates, the effectiveness of fiscal policy in affecting output and employment depends on whether the BOF = 0 function is more or less interest-elastic than the *LM* function. Where the BOF = 0 function is less interest-elastic than the *LM* function, fiscal policy is extremely efficient in affecting aggregate demand, as the change in exchange rates induced by the fiscal policy reinforces its impact on aggregate demand. This is illustrated in Figure 10.5(a). Here an expansionary fiscal policy shifts the *IS* function from IS_0 to IS_1. This leads to a deficit on the BOF at the current exchange rate, as the equilibrium position in the goods and money markets would be below the BOF_0 curve. Therefore, the exchange rate falls and, assuming the Marshall–Lerner conditions holds, this has a further stimulating effect on the economy as the fall in the exchange rate shifts the *IS* function further to the right to IS_2. The BOF = 0 function also shifts to the right, the process coming to an end where the BOF and *IS* curves intersect on the *LM* curve. The money supply did not change throughout this process

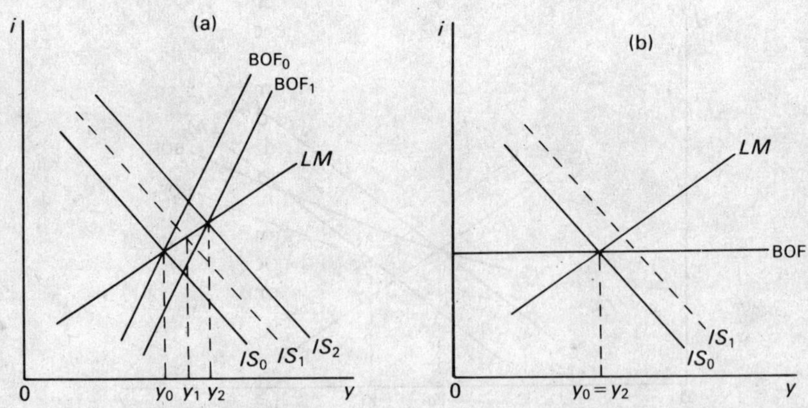

FIGURE 10.5 *Effects of fiscal policy under flexible exchange rates*

and there was no sterilisation problem as the exchange rate adjusted to keep $\Delta FR = 0$ at all times.

Fiscal policy is less effective under flexible exchange rates when the BOF = 0 function is more interest-elastic than the *LM* function. Here the rise in interest rates resulting from an expansionary fiscal policy will result in a BOF surplus if the exchange rate did not change. The excess demand for domestic currency in the foreign exchange market will cause it to appreciate. Given that the Marshall–Lerner condition holds, the effects of this appreciation will offset part of the expansionary impact of the fiscal policy. In the case of perfect capital mobility, fiscal policy becomes completely ineffective. This is illustrated in Figure 10.5(b). Here an increase in government expenditure on goods and services with an unchanged tax rate will shift the *IS* function to the right from IS_0 to IS_1. The resulting rise in the interest rate will bring about a capital inflow and create an excess demand for the domestic currency in the foreign exchange market, which will lead to its appreciation. This will lower exports and increase imports and will shift the *IS* function back to the left. In the case of the perfect capital mobility illustrated in Figure 10.5(b), the capital inflows are large enough to depreciate the exchange rate sufficiently to shift the *IS* function back to IS_0. Here the current-account deficit at income y_0 will have increased by exactly the same amount as the budget deficit at that level of income and there will be no increase in the equilibrium level of income even under Keynesian supply assumptions.

The neoclassical version of the Mundell–Fleming model

The original models by Mundell and Fleming assumed a Keynesian aggregate supply function and investigated the effectiveness of monetary and fiscal policy under different exchange-rate regimes. We can now modify this model by assuming a neoclassical aggregate supply function while keeping all the other assumptions of the model. Here deviations from the equilibrium level of output can only occur in the short run due to either the impact of unanticipated events or to lags in the adjustment of prices and wages to either changes in the money supply or the level of nominal expenditure in the economy.

In such a neoclassical economy, monetary and fiscal policy can have no effect on output and employment over the medium to long run. What they affect under fixed exchange rates is the BOF and the domestic price level. Under flexible exchange rates it is the exchange rate and the price level which are affected. Fiscal policy will also affect the proportion of output consumed or allocated by the state.

Under a fixed exchange rate, an expansionary monetary policy will lead to a deterioration in the BOF, and where domestic goods are differentiated from foreign goods it will lead to a rise in the price of domestic goods as a result of the increase in domestic expenditure. A monetary contraction will have to opposite effect on both the BOF and the price of domestic goods. Because of its effect on the BOF, monetary policy is not feasible over the long run under fixed exchange rates.

Under flexible exchange rates a monetary expansion will lower interest rates, and this will cause a capital outflow and a rise in domestic expenditure. This will result in a fall in the exchange rate and a rise in the price level. Once the price level and the exchange rate have fully adjusted to the money stock, interest rates will return to their previous levels and the economy will return to equilibrium at the original level of income and the previous level of real absorption. The relative price of domestic to foreign goods will return to its previous level. A monetary contraction will have the opposite effect, lowering the price level and raising the exchange rate.

10.2 Asset markets, expectations and exchange rates

By focusing on international capital flows, the Mundell–Fleming model was the first to stress the major role that asset market equilibrium and asset market adjustment play in determining exchange rates and the balance of payments. Prior to this, work on the determinants of exchange rates had stressed the effects of relative prices on the flow of goods and services and concentrated on the current account. Following the Mundell–Fleming model, most modern work has stressed the dominant role that asset market equilibrium plays in determining exchange rates and the balance of payments. This is particularly true of the monetary (Frenkel and Johnson [5]) and portfolio (Frenkel and Rodrigues [6]) approaches to the balance of payments and exchange-rate determination.

The Mundell–Fleming model has several weaknesses that have stimulated further theoretical work. It assumes a constant capital flow in response to an interest-rate differential, rather than a portfolio shift that has a large impact in the short run and then dies away in a stationary economy. In a growing economy there may be a long-run capital flow, but this will be much smaller than the short-run portfolio shift brought about by a change in interest rates. This may be a useful simplification for short-run analysis, but is very misleading if applied to medium-term economic policy-making extending over several years. This simplification allows the model to run a continuous current-account deficit and a capital-account surplus over an indefinite period with an expansionary fiscal policy under flexible exchange rates or with a fixed exchange rate when the BOF = 0 function is more interest-elastic than the *LM* function. This, together with the assumption of static expectations, prevents the current account from affecting the exchange rate.

Recent work by Dornbusch and Fischer [7] on asset market determination of exchange rates brings back the current account as a determinant of the exchange rate. From Chapter 7 (pp. 106–11) we can deduce that in a stationary economy a current-account surplus will lead to an increase, while a deficit will lead to a decrease, in domestically held wealth. In line with modern consumption theory (discussed in Chapter 12), an increase in domestically held wealth leads to an increase in domestic absorption, while a decrease in domestically held wealth leads to a fall in absorption. Therefore, a current-account surplus must lead to an increase, while a deficit leads to a decrease, in domestic absorption.

The model set out by Dornbusch and Fischer has a neoclassical supply function for domestic goods and flexible prices. Domestic goods are differentiated from foreign goods, and to induce foreigners to buy more of them they have to fall in price relative to the price of foreign goods. The exchange rate is flexible and adjusts to maintain foreign exchange market equilibrium. Therefore, BOF = 0 at all times and the capital account exactly offsets any current-account deficits or surpluses. Here a surplus on the current account implies a capital-account deficit. Domestic absorption is below domestic income and the excess of income over absorption is spent on the net acquisition of foreign assets. This leads to an increase in domestically held wealth and therefore to a rise in domestic absorption. Eventually domestically held wealth reaches a point where it is so large in relation to domestic income that no further accumulation is called for, so that domestic absorption rises to match income. Equilibrium is then restored to the current account.

The rise in absorption leads to an equal absolute fall in the net purchase of foreign securities. Part of the increase in absorption will be spent on domestic goods as they are differentiated from foreign goods, so that only part of the increase in absorption leads to a demand for foreign currency on the foreign exchange market. The fall in net purchase of foreign securities leads to an equal fall in demand for foreign currency on the foreign exchange market. Therefore, the net increase in domestic wealth brought about by a current-account surplus eventually leads to an excess supply of foreign currency on the foreign exchange market and the domestic currency will therefore appreciate. A similar analysis shows that a current-account deficit will lead to a depreciation of the domestic currency.

Given the effect that the current account has on the exchange rate in this model, expectations of economic decision-makers about exchange-rate changes must be consistent with the model's predictions, otherwise their expectations will be consistently wrong. Therefore, expectations of future exchange rates will be affected by the state of the current account, and people will act in line with those expectations. These actions will also affect the current exchange rate.

If the assumption of static expectations is removed, as in the Dornbusch and Fischer model, then a differential can exist between domestic and foreign interest rates without provoking large capital flows. Funds will be moved from one country to another as long as a higher return can be obtained for them with the same risk. A firm located in one country will move funds to another country as long as it can make more money in terms of domestic currency than it can make by buying domestic securities. The amount that it will make on its purchase of foreign securities will depend on both the foreign interest rate and the percentage change in the exchange rate between the time that it bought the foreign securities and the time that it sold them in order to repatriate the funds. There will be no advantage to moving funds from one country to another if

$$i = i_f - g_e^e \tag{10.14}$$

Here i is the domestic rate of interest, i_f is the foreign rate of interest and g_e^e is the expected proportional rate of appreciation in the exchange rate, e, where e is the number of units of foreign currency per unit of domestic currency.

Expression 10.14 is called *the interest-parity theorem* and it forms an important part of many current open-economy macro models. We shall meet it again when discussing the monetary approach to the balance of payments in the next chapter and it is a particularly important part of this approach when discussing exchange-rate determination under flexible exchange rates. The interest-parity theorem has the important implication that one can no longer predict the direction of capital flows from interest-rate differentials alone. If the domestic rate of interest, i, is lower than the foreign rate of interest, i_f, minus the expected growth in the exchange rate, g_e^e ($i < i_f - g_e^e$), then there will be a capital outflow from the domestic economy. However, i could be greater than i_f but still less than $i_f - g_e^e$ if g_e^e is negative because a depreciation of the domestic currency is expected in the near future. Thus a positive interest differential need not mean a positive capital flow once one abandons the unrealistic assumption of static expectations. Thus capital flows are affected by expectations of exchange-rate changes as well as by interest-rate differentials.

Another implication of the interest-parity theorem is that an analysis of how expectations are formed, particularly exchange-rate expectations, is an important part of any open-economy macro model. Currently it is recognised that expectations will always turn out to be incorrect if the expectations-generating mechanism used in a model produces expectations for any particular point in time that are inconsistent with the model's predictions. The *rational-expectations* approach specifies the expected value of a variable, such as the exchange rate, so that it is equal to the value predicted by the model, given the expected values of its determinants. The rational expectations approach is now commonly used to generate exchange rate expectations in open-economy models (see Frenkel and Johnson [8] for several examples and Chapter 18 for a detailed discussion of rational expectations).

10.3 Fixed versus flexible exchange rates

The advantage of a fixed exchange-rate system which is free of exchange controls is that it lowers international traders' risk and simplifies their profit-maximising calculations. Competition between producers located in different countries is facilitated and so is the integration of the world economy into a connected system of markets. This has beneficial effects on economic efficiency and growth in the same way as a common national currency promotes economic efficiency within the nation. The argument for fixed exchange rates is weakened if there are frequent changes in the fixed rates, as this increases uncertainty in foreign trade. The benefit of fixed exchange rates in promoting international trade and competition are lost if the fixed rates are kept in existence by trade and exchange controls.

The advantages of a fixed exchange system in promoting trade and efficiency led to the adoption of fixed exchange rates by the major trading nations over long periods since the last quarter of the nineteenth century. These fixed exchange systems broke down in periods of war or crisis due to inconsistent monetary and fiscal policies being pursued by different countries. A fixed exchange-rate system cannot survive when some countries run persistent BOF surpluses while others run persistent BOF deficits. We have seen in the Mundell–Fleming model (and this is reinforced by the monetary approach in the next chapter) that a BOF deficit is often the result of excessive domestic credit expansion, while a BOF surplus is often the result of a credit contraction. Fiscal policy also has an effect on the BOF. Therefore, the maintenance of a fixed exchange-rate system requires that individual countries adjust their monetary and fiscal policies to be consistent with the avoidance of persistent deficits and surpluses.

The last fixed exchange-rate system in existence was the Bretton Woods or IMF system.[1] This was set up in 1944, together with the International Monetary Fund, whose role was to supervise the system and provide temporary help in the form of foreign exchange loans to countries running BOF deficits. The Bretton Woods agreement required each member country of the IMF to define a par exchange rate for its currency in terms of either gold or the US dollar. Member countries were required to intervene in the foreign exchange market to prevent the exchange rate for their currency from deviating by more than 1 per cent from its par value with the US dollar. This par value was only supposed to be changed in the case of a 'fundamental disequilibrium' in a country's balance of payments. Fundamental disequilibrium was not defined, but exchange-rate changes were supposed to be infrequent. (For example, the pound sterling was devalued twice in the twenty-seven years of the Bretton Woods system, once in 1949 and then again in 1967.) In addition, member countries were to promote multilateral trade in goods and services by dismantling exchange controls on current transactions.

The Bretton Woods system lasted until 1972, when it collapsed into a system of managed flexible rates. This was due to the strains placed on the system by inconsistent monetary and fiscal policies run by the major member countries of the IMF. The final end of the Bretton Woods system was signalled by the floating of the pound sterling in February 1972. This occurred as a result of the deficits on the current and capital accounts of the United Kingdom that were caused by the monetary and fiscal expansion initiated by the Conservative government lead by Edward Heath.

In the 1960s academic and journalistic opinion moved against fixed exchange rates. In the Mundell–Fleming model it was seen that, under a fixed exchange rate, the BOF = 0 function must constrain any feasible solutions for income and interest rates. If international capital is relatively immobile (as in Figure 10.2(a), p. 168), then the balance-of-payments constraint may restrict the output and employment levels which can be attained through the use of monetary and fiscal policy. At that time most UK commentators thought that a Keynesian aggregate supply function was relevant for policy purposes, so that this balance-of-payments constraint upset them. Many of them advocated either exchange-rate changes or a flexible exchange rate in order to avoid this constraint on policy (see Johnson [10] for an example).

Given flexible exchange rates and the extreme Keynesian supply function, the Mundell–Fleming model gives us three equations (10.11, 10.12 and 10.13)

[1] For a historical description see Argy [9] chs 2–7.

which can be solved for the three unknowns, y, i and e. Here the policy instruments of monetary and fiscal policy can be set to achieve the desired target levels of y and i, while the exchange rate adjusts under the impact of market forces to maintain a zero BOF. Correct handling of the policy instruments, given a knowledge of the economy's structure, would allow the attainment of any output level within the economy's capacity. This particular form also holds with a less extreme form of the Keynesian aggregate supply function, but as shown in Chapter 7 (pp. 117–21) the existence of a Keynesian aggregate supply function over the medium term depends on workers lacking real wage resistance. Where this is the case, an exchange-rate change will change the relative price of domestic goods in terms of foreign goods, or the real exchange rate (Pf/ePd), in the same direction as the change in the exchange rate, e. These results, together with the demonstration that in the long run an independent monetary policy is only possible under flexible exchange rates, helped to change the climate of opinion in the 1960s in favour of flexible exchange rates.

Since then there have been two developments that have cast doubt on the policy advantages of flexible rates. The first is the growing evidence that the aggregate supply function has neoclassical characteristics over the medium to long run (see the end of Chapter 7 and Chapters 18–20 for some of this evidence). With such a supply function, the major constraint on macroeconomic policy is from the supply side. In this case the removal of the balance-of-payments constraint through flexible exchange rates does not significantly increase the range of output and employment levels that can be attained by macroeconomic policy, other than in the short run.

The second development not expected in the 1950s and 1960s is the great variability of flexible exchange rates. Since then we have come to realise that exchange rates are determined in asset markets, and so flexible exchange rates should display similar price variability to other asset prices. Their variability is smaller than the variability of prices on stock exchanges, but it is greater than the variability one would have predicted from the variability of the determinants of exchange rates.

The variability of exchange rates has led to dynamic versions of the asset market approach (in Dornbusch [11] and and Buiter and Miller [12]). In these models asset markets, such as the money market, adjust much more rapidly to monetary changes than either goods markets or prices. If we assume that there is an increase in the money stock, then in order for the money market to clear interest rates will have to fall. Due to the lag in the adjustment of prices and output, interest rates will fall below their new equilibrium level. Domestic interest rates will fall below interest parity (see equation 10.14), which will lead to a capital outflow and cause a fall in the exchange rate. The capital outflow will stop once the exchange rate falls sufficiently below its new long-run equilibrium level so that the expected appreciation of the domestic currency is equal to the difference between domestic and foreign rates of interest.

A similar analysis holds for a contraction in the money stock. Buiter and Miller [12] use a model of this sort to analyse the impact of the Conservative government's financial strategy in 1979 and 1980 on the UK economy and the competitiveness of UK tradables. There, the dynamics of adjustment lead the exchange rate to overshoot its long-run equilibrium level, and this may have unwanted real effects during the adjustment to the new equilibrium. The advent of flexible exchange rates appears therefore to have increased the difficulty of short- to medium-term economic forecasting, and has thus made the implementation of discretionary monetary and fiscal policy more hazardous.

References

[1] R. A. Mundell, 'The Monetary Dynamics of Adjustment under Fixed and Flexible Exchange Rates', *Quarterly Journal of Economics* (1960).

[2] R. A. Mundell, 'Capital Mobility and Stabilization Policy under Fixed and under Flexible Exchange Rates', *Canadian Journal of Economics and Political Science* (1963).

[3] J. Marcus Fleming, 'Domestic Financial Policies under Fixed and under Floating Exchange Rates', *International Monetary Fund Staff Papers* (1962).

[4] R. M. Stern, *The Balance of Payments* (London: Macmillan, 1973).

[5] J. A. Frenkel and H. G. Johnson (eds), *The Monetary Approach to the Balance of Payments* (London: Allen & Unwin, 1976).

[6] J. A. Frenkel and C. A. Rodrigues, 'Portfolio Equilibrium and the Balance of Payments: a Monetary Approach', *American Economic Review* (1975).

[7] R. Dornbusch and S. Fischer, 'Exchange Rates and the Current Account', *American Economic Review* (1980).

[8] J. A. Frenkel and H. G. Johnson (eds), *The Economics of Exchange Rates* (Reading, Mass.: Addison-Wesley, 1978).

[9] V. Argy, *The Postwar International Money Crisis: an Analysis* (London: Allen & Unwin, 1981).

[10] H. G. Johnson, 'The Case for Flexible Exchange Rates 1969', in H. G. Johnson, *Further Essays in Monetary Economics* (London: Allen & Unwin, 1972).

[11] R. Dornbusch, 'Expectations and Exchange Rate Dynamics', *Journal of Political Economy* (1976).

[12] W. H. Buiter and M. Miller, 'Monetary Policy and International Competitiveness: the Problems of Adjustment', *Oxford Economic Papers* (1981).

11 The Monetary Approach to the Balance of Payments

The monetary approach to the balance of payments and exchange-rate determination is a currently popular version of the asset market approach. This analyses changes in the exchange rate and the BOF in terms of stock adjustment in the money market in which the supply and demand for money adjust so that all domestic money balances are eventually willingly held. In this approach changes in economic variables will affect the BOF and the exchange rate through their impact on the demand for and supply of money balances. This stock-adjustment approach springs from the fact that a *necessary condition* for a non-zero BOF is some initial difference between the public's *actual* money stock and the public's *desired* money stock.

This necessary condition for a non-zero BOF can be derived from the definition of the BOF and the absorption approach discussed in Chapter 7.[1] By definition the BOF is equal to the current account plus the capital account. From the absorption approach, the current account is identically equal to national income, Y, minus domestic absorption, A. The capital account is identically equal to non-official borrowing abroad and sale of real assets abroad minus non-official lending abroad and purchase of real assets abroad. Now borrowing abroad involves the sale of a financial asset abroad, while lending abroad is the purchase of a financial asset abroad. Therefore, the capital account is identically equal to the sale of real and financial assets abroad, S_F, minus the purchase of real and financial assets abroad, P_F. Therefore, we can write

$$\text{BOF} \equiv (Y - A) + (S_F - P_F) \tag{11.1}$$

In the domestic economy we can look at all domestic transactions between non-central bank residents in real and financial assets. Here asset purchases (P_D) by domestic residents from domestic residents must necessarily equal

[1] For the original derivation, see H. G. Johnson (1958) 'Towards a General Theory of the Balance of Payments', reprinted in Frenkel and Johnson [1].

asset sales (S_D) by domestic residents to domestic residents, as they are opposite sides of the same transactions. Therefore, $S_D = P_D$. We exclude transactions between domestic residents and the central bank, as the purchase of assets by the central bank involves it in the expansion of the domestic credit component of high-powered money, H, while a sale of assets by the central bank involves a contraction in domestic credit and H. Using our identity $S_D = P_D$ we can write

$$\begin{aligned} \text{BOF} &\equiv (Y - A) + (S_F + S_D - P_F - P_D) \\ &\equiv (Y - A) + (S - P) \end{aligned} \tag{11.2}$$

Here P is the total purchases of assets by domestic residents from all sources excluding the domestic central bank, while S is the total sale of assets by domestic residents to everyone except the central bank. Now national income, Y, is equal to the sale of final goods and services by domestic residents, while absorption, A, is equal to the purchases of final goods and services by domestic residents. Therefore, we must have

BOF ≡	Total sales of goods, services and assets by domestic residents excluding the central bank
minus	Total purchases of goods, services and assets by domestic residents excluding the central bank.

(11.3)

From the identity derived above we see that a necessary condition for a deficit on the BOF is that current purchases by non-central bank domestic residents of goods, services and assets must be larger than their total sales of goods, services and assets. This difference can only be financed by domestic residents either running down their cash balances (this is called 'dishoarding'), or by their sale of assets to the central bank in exchange for funds to finance the difference between total purchases and sales. (All other sales of assets have already been included in S.) Now this purchase of assets by the central bank involves an increase in the central bank's creation of domestic credit. Therefore, a deficit on the BOF *necessarily* involves either dishoarding by domestic residents or an increase in the central bank's creation of domestic credit. In a similar way we can show that a BOF surplus *necessarily* involves either an increase in hoarding by domestic residents or a decline in domestic credit created by the central bank.[1]

In the absence of changes in domestic credit created by the central bank,[2] a

[1] Note that the Mundell–Fleming model is consistent with this, since a non-zero BOF involves either changes in central bank domestic credit as a result of sterilising the BOF, or it involves adjustments in money supply and demand that shift the *LM* function.

[2] At the beginning of Chapter 10 we showed that this implies the absence of sterilisation by the central bank.

BOF deficit can only persist while domestic residents are continuing to run down their cash balances (dishoarding). In this case the money stock would shrink automatically as the central bank purchased the excess supply of its currency on the foreign exchange market with some of its foreign exchange reserves. Here $\Delta H = \Delta FR$ and these are both negative. Now from equation 10.6 $\Delta M^S = m\Delta H$, so the money supply must contract. The resulting decline in money balances must eventually bring dishoarding to an end as domestic residents reach their desired level of money holdings. As this occurs, domestic absorption, or net asset purchases by domestic residents, or both, will fall as domestic residents reach their desired holding of wealth in relation to current income and their desired portfolio mix. Therefore, given a sufficiently stable demand for money function, dishoarding will come to an end within a reasonably short time span, provided that the central bank does not indulge in continuous credit creation. In this case, given adequate foreign exchange reserves, the BOF deficit will cure itself.

Similarly, in the absence of changes in central bank domestic credit, a surplus on the BOF will lead to an increase in H and in the domestic money supply. The surplus requires continual hoarding by domestic residents and it will come to an end as they achieve their desired holding of money balances and wealth and their desired portfolio mix. Once this has been achieved, absorption and net asset purchases adjust to keep wealth and the portfolio mix at their desired levels and this results in a zero BOF as purchases and sales by domestic residents become equal to each other. Therefore, in the absence of continuous central bank destruction of domestic credit, a BOF surplus must come to an end within a reasonably finite time horizon.

The above analysis implies that a persistent deficit on the BOF must be the result of continuous domestic credit creation by the central bank. This will occur either in the process of sterilising the deficit or through the central bank's direct financing of a government's budget deficit together with sterilisation of the BOF deficit. As a deficit on the BOF can only occur under a fixed or managed exchange rate, this implies that domestic prices and interest rates cannot adjust sufficiently to equalise the demand and supply for real money balances, as the substitutability of foreign goods and assets for domestic goods and assets limits the possible movement in domestic prices and interest rates. The continuous sterilisation of the deficit through the creation of additional domestic credit by the central bank (where $\Delta DC = -\text{BOF}$, from equation 10.8) keeps the domestic money stock at a higher level than that which domestic residents wish to hold at current interest rates and prices. However, domestic residents do have the option of exchanging excess cash balances for foreign goods and assets, thus creating a deficit on the BOF.

Similarly, a persistent surplus on the BOF implies that domestic residents wish to hold larger money balances than those currently in existence in the domestic economy, as their current purchases of goods and assets are smaller than their current sales of goods and assets. The difference is added to their cash balances through conversion into domestic money through the foreign exchanges. Here foreign reserves held by the central bank must increase, so that $\Delta FR > 0$. This process can only be kept going if the central bank prevents H and the domestic money stock from rising by destruction of some of its domestic credit, so that

$\Delta H = 0$ and $-\Delta DC = \Delta FR$ (see equations 10.6 and 10.7 at the start of Chapter 10).

The monetary factors underlying BOF deficits and surpluses led to the development of the monetary approach to the balance of payments, but this approach would not be a particularly useful way of predicting the BOF if the demand for money were very unstable. Therefore, exponents of the monetary approach assume a stable demand for money function. In addition, they usually assume that aggregate domestic expenditure is positively affected by the stock of wealth held by domestic residents and by the excess supply of domestic money balances. These latter assumptions are not consistent with the simple Keynesian consumption function used up to this point in the book, but they are consistent with some of the modern work on consumption theory discussed in the next chapter.

11.1 Monetary analysis under a fixed exchange rate

The simplest monetary model of the balance of payments assumes a stable demand for money function, a money supply function as set out in equation 10.5, the interest-parity theorem in equation 10.14, the *law of one price* and a neoclassical supply function. Such a model is developed by H. G. Johnson in 'The Monetary Approach to the Balance of Payments' (reprinted in Frenkel and Johnson [1]). In addition, we assume that we are dealing with a small open economy in the sense that it cannot significantly affect the world money stock, price level or interest rate. This small-economy assumption is not a necessary one for the monetary approach (see Frenkel and Johnson [1]).

The *law of one price* states that the price in terms of a common currency of any tradable commodity in any two markets will differ at most by the cost of transport, tariffs and difference in retail costs involved in moving goods from one market to the other. If the price difference is larger than this, then the profit-making opportunity will result in traders arbitraging goods from one market to the other. Competition between profit-making traders will lead towards equalisation of prices. However, over the short run prices in different markets may depart from the law of one price if there are lags in the reaction of traders to profitable opportunities. If the country concerned has competitors in all its product lines, then we can write the law of one price as

$$P = \frac{1}{e} Pf \tag{11.4}$$

Here P is the domestic price level, Pf is the foreign price level and e is the exchange rate expressed as units of foreign currency per unit of domestic currency. In this case we are assuming that all domestic and foreign production is composed of tradable goods. This latter assumption is abandoned in more complex two-sector monetary models, where production is divided into tradables and non-tradables (see Dornbusch in Frenkel and Johnson [2]). Non-tradables are goods and services whose transport costs are too high for them to enter into international trade.

The neoclassical aggregate supply function implies that, other than in the very short run, real income, y, is not affected by the level of aggregate demand in money terms, but is determined by the underlying real factors in the economy. Here $y = \bar{y}$, where $\bar{y}$ is fixed exogenously, but may be growing over time. This is a simplifying assumption which is useful for longer-run analysis. However, neither this assumption nor the law of one price is necessary for monetary models. (See Rodriguez in Frenkel and Johnson [1] for a model where neither assumption is used and Dornbusch and Fischer [3], where the law of one prices does not hold.)

We can now set out the complete small-economy model:

$M^D = P\,f(y, i)$	Demand for money	(11.5)
$M^S = m(FR + DC)$	Supply of money	(11.6)
$i = i_f - g_e^e$	Interest-parity theorem	(11.7)
$P = \frac{1}{e}Pf$	Law of one price	(11.4)
$y = \bar{y}$	Neoclassical supply function	(11.8)
$M^S = M^D = M$	Equilibrium condition	(11.9)

By substituting for the demand and supply of money in equation 11.9 from equations 11.5 and 11.6 we get

$$m(FR + DC) = P\,f(y, i) \tag{11.10}$$

and rearranging the terms in equation 11.10 gives

$$FR = \frac{P}{m}f(y, i) - DC \tag{11.11}$$

If we assume that the bank multiplier, m, is a constant, and if we totally differentiate equation 11.11 with respect to time, t, we get

$$\frac{d(FR)}{dt} = \frac{1}{m}\left\{f(y, i)\frac{dP}{dt} + P\frac{\partial f(y, i)}{\partial y}\frac{dy}{dt} + P\frac{\partial f(y, i)}{\partial i}\frac{di}{dt}\right\} - \frac{d(DC)}{dt} \tag{11.12}$$

Here the term on the left-hand side is the rate of change of foreign reserves at the central bank. If we compare this with equation 10.3, we see that this is equal to the BOF written as a rate of change over time, or BOF(t). Now, if we divide both sides of equation 11.12 by the stock of money, M, and manipulate each term in the right-hand side of the equation, we get

$$\frac{\text{BOF}(t)}{M} = \frac{1}{m}\left\{g_P + \eta_y g_y + \eta_i g_i\right\} - \frac{DC}{M}g_{DC} \tag{11.13}$$

Here g_P refers to the growth rate in the domestic price level, $(1/P)(dP/dt)$, g_y refers to the growth rate in real income; g_i refers to the growth rate in the rate of interest and g_{DC} refers to the growth rate in central bank domestic credit, the central bank-created component of H. Now η_y is the income elasticity of the demand for money and η_i is the interest elasticity of the demand for money. The term in brace brackets is the growth in the demand for money, and when multiplied by $1/m$ it shows the growth rate in the demand for high-powered money, H.

Given a fixed exchange rate, which is expected to stay fixed, there is a zero expected growth in the exchange rate, so that $g^e_e = 0$. From our small-economy assumption, i_f is exogenous, and we can assume it is fixed. Substituting these results into equation 11.7 transforms the interest-parity theorem into

$$i = i_f \tag{11.14}$$

Hence we can deduce that there is no growth in the interest rate and $g_i = 0$. Taking natural logarithms of both sides of the law of one price equation (11.4), and then differentiating through with respect to time, we get

$$g_P = g_{Pf} - g_e \tag{11.15}$$

Under fixed exchange rates, the exchange rate, e, does not change so that $g_e = 0$. Therefore, the growth in the domestic price level, g_P, must be equal to the growth in the foreign price level, g_{Pf}, under a fixed exchange rate. Using these results to substitute into equation 11.13 we get

$$\frac{\text{BOF}(t)}{M} = \frac{1}{m}\left\{g_{Pf} + \eta_y g_y\right\} - \frac{DC}{M} g_{DC} \tag{11.16}$$

Now, as $\text{BOF}(t) = d(FR)/dt$ and $g_{DC} = (1/DC)(d(DC)/dt)$, this can also be written as

$$\frac{d(FR)}{dt} = \frac{M}{m}\left\{g_{Pf} + \eta_y g_y\right\} - \frac{d(DC)}{dt}$$

$$= H\left\{g_{Pf} + \eta_y g_y\right\} - \frac{d(DC)}{dt} \tag{11.17}$$

where H is high-powered money (see equations 10.1 and 10.6 of Chapter 10).

If we assume for the moment that the foreign price, Pf, is constant and that the economy is stationary, then $g_{Pf} = 0$ and $g_y = 0$; substituting these values into equation 11.17 reduces it to

$$\frac{d(FR)}{dt} = -\frac{d(DC)}{dt} \tag{11.18}$$

Under these circumstances any attempt by the central bank to increase the money stock by expanding high-powered money, H, through increased domestic credit creation will be nullified by an exactly offsetting shrinkage in the foreign reserve component of H. This is shown by equation 11.18. In this fixed exchange-rate case the domestic money stock is completely endogenous and adjusts completely to the demand for money. Here the demand for money is fixed, as the determinants of the demand for money are not affected by the central bank's open-market operations. All that the central bank eventually alters by its open-market operations is the composition of the reserves backing H. Other than in the very short run monetary policy has no effect unless pushed to the point where loss of foreign reserves compels the abandonment of the fixed exchange rate. In this case, as in the Mundell–Fleming model, a monetary expansion leads to a BOF deficit and loss of foreign reserves, while a monetary contraction leads to a BOF surplus and accumulation of foreign reserves.

In the case where the foreign price level and domestic real income are growing, then $g_{Pf} > 0$ and $g_y > 0$, so that the demand for money is also growing. From equation 11.17 we can see that the BOF will be zero provided that domestic credit increases at the same rate as the demand for high-powered money. If the central bank exceeds this rate of increase in its expansion of domestic credit, then there will be a deficit on the BOF and a loss in foreign reserves. If the central bank's rate of expansion in domestic credit falls short of this, then there will be a BOF surplus and an increase in foreign exchange reserves. In either case, as there is no sterilisation, the money stock will grow at the rate set by the growth in the demand for money.

Therefore, *under fixed exchange rates the money stock is endogenous*. This result does not hold in such a simple form in the large-country case, as changes in domestic credit expansion by its central bank can lead to a change in its money stock in the same proportion as the proportionate change in the *world money stock* resulting from its operations. (For a demonstration of this see the articles by Swoboda and Rodriguez in Frenkel and Johnson [1].)

The impact of devaluation on the BOF

The law of one price in our all-tradables economy is

$$P = \frac{1}{e} Pf \tag{11.4}$$

Since a devaluation means a fall in e, P must also increase if the law of one price holds. If the money market were in equilibrium prior to devaluation, then equation 11.11 would be satisfied, so that

$$FR = \frac{P}{m} f(y,i) - DC \tag{11.11}$$

The rise in P increases the nominal demand for money and for high-powered money. As domestic interest rates are constrained by foreign rates through the interest-parity theorem in equation 11.7, the demand for nominal money balances must increase. If domestic credit, DC, is not allowed to expand, the demand for nominal money balances exceeds the money stock, so that

$$FR < \frac{P}{m} f(\bar{y}, i_f) - DC \tag{11.19}$$

Under the new fixed exchange rate the money demand cannot adjust to match the supply, as i is constrained. People will strive to achieve their desired stock of balances by making their total purchases of goods and assets smaller than their total sales of goods and assets. By identity 11.3 (p. 181) this must result in a BOF surplus and an inflow of foreign reserves so that $dFR/dt > 0$. This BOF surplus continues until the domestic money stock has reached the amount demanded. Once this occurs, total purchases become equal to total sales and the BOF returns to zero. In this case devaluation would lead to a *temporary* BOF *surplus* and an increase in the stock of foreign reserves. This contrasts with the Keynesian analysis of Chapter 7, where a devaluation from an equilibrium position would lead to a *permanent* current-account surplus, provided that workers did not have real wage resistance. The Keynesian result stems from the neglect of the impact of BOF imbalances on asset stocks.

If the devaluation occurred when the BOF was in deficit, then we start from a position where the demand for money is smaller, or growing at a slower rate, than the supply of money. The increase in the demand for money, caused by the rise in the price level following devaluation, will diminish or eliminate the excess stock of domestic money. As a result the BOF will improve, and this improvement will be permanent provided that the rate of growth of domestic credit moves to a rate which is consistent with the growth in the demand for money. A devaluation will not lead to an improvement in the BOF if it is accompanied by an increase in the rate of growth of domestic credit.

Fixed exchange rates and the rate of inflation

Under a fixed exchange rate the law of one price implies that over the medium to long run the rate of growth of prices in the domestic economy, g_P, must be equal to their rate of growth in the rest of the world, g_{Pf}. From equation 11.15, with e fixed, we get $g_P = g_{Pf}$. Let us suppose that there is a small economy on a fixed exchange rate whose government wants to maintain the fixed exchange rate but which also wants a lower rate of inflation than the world rate, g_{Pf}. They decide to curb the domestic rate of inflation by restricting the rate of domestic credit expansion by the central bank so that the domestic money supply grows at a rate below that required to support a growth in domestic prices equal to g_{Pf}. If, as a result of this, the domestic price level falls below $(1/e)Pf$, then commodity arbitrage will produce an increased foreign demand for domestic goods and a decreased domestic demand for foreign goods. The current account therefore improves and goes into surplus. Simultaneously, the lower rate of domestic credit expansion will cause domestic interest rates to rise above interest parity as domestic credit markets tighten and nothing has occurred to increase expectations of a devaluation. A surplus develops on the capital account and the BOF goes into surplus. This leads to an inflow of foreign reserves, which allows the domestic money supply to rise at the rate necessary to support a domestic rate of inflation equal to g_{Pf}. The domestic inflation rate becomes g_{Pf} in spite of the restriction on domestic credit. This analysis is summarised in equation 11.17.

If the law of one price does not hold because the country concerned is specialising in the production of specialised differentiated goods (as assumed in Chapters 7 and 10), then we can show that the same conclusion holds. From equations 7.6 and 7.8 (p. 112) we see that exports are positively related, while imports are negatively related to the relative price of foreign to domestic goods, Pf/eP. If $g_{Pf} > g_P$ and e is fixed, then the relative price of foreign goods to domestic goods will keep rising. If the Marshall–Lerner condition is satisfied, exports will increase, imports will decrease and a current-account surplus will develop and grow as long as $g_{Pf} > g_P$. This is a similar result to that derived from the law of one price, and so the rest of the analysis is identical to that in the previous paragraph. Therefore, once again, g_P is forced into equality with g_{Pf}, though in this case the relative price ratio (or real exchange rate), Pf/eP, can differ from its original ratio prior to the credit restriction.

Under fixed exchange rates a similar set of analyses apply if a government wants the domestic rate of inflation to be greater than g_{Pf}. Here the country will lose foreign exchange reserves as long as the central bank maintains its excessive rate of domestic credit creation. This reserve loss can only last as long as the country can finance it from its stock of foreign reserves and by borrowing. The domestic rate of inflation, g_P, cannot depart from the foreign rate, g_{Pf}, for any length of time, as the reserve losses will only allow the domestic money stock to grow at the rate necessary to satisfy the growth in the demand for money at the inflation rate, g_{Pf}, despite the faster growth in domestic credit.

Similar results also hold in the large-country case, except that here changes in the rate of growth of domestic credit lead to changes in the world rate of inflation, through their impact on the world money supply.

In the small-country case an increase in domestic credit by a single country does not significantly affect the world money supply and so has no effect on world inflation. The country involved will have a BOF deficit and foreign reserve losses to match its excessive credit expansion. However, in a world of small countries, if each country increased its rate of domestic credit expansion in order to increase its money stock by x per cent, then the world money stock would increase by x per cent and so would the world price level. As all countries have increased domestic money stock at an identical rate, there will be little change in the BOF of any country. (See Chapter 20, pp. 383–9, for a further discussion of world inflation.)

11.2 Monetary analysis under a flexible exchange rate

The monetary model which we will use to analyse the effects of monetary policy under a flexible exchange rate is identical to the one set out on page 184 and used to discuss the fixed exchange-rate case. It is composed of equations 11.4–11.9 inclusive. The only difference in the flexible exchange-rate case is that the exchange rate, e, adjusts in reponse to demand and supply in the foreign exchange market. Under a clean float e adjusts to clear the foreign exchange market. The BOF is zero and the stock of foreign exchange reserves remains constant, so that $d(FR)/dt = 0$. Under a clean float the central bank gains complete control over the nominal money stock, as there are no induced foreign reserve flows to alter the money stock from the level set by the central bank through its open-market operations.

A necessary condition for a zero BOF is that the demand for domestic money must always adjust to equal the domestic money stock. Under a clean float the domestic money stock is determined by the central bank. Therefore, in order to clear the foreign exchange market the adjustment in the exchange rate must alter the demand for money so that it equals the predetermined nominal money stock. It does this through its impact on the domestic price level and interest rate.

Since the domestic monetary authorities can control the domestic stock of money they can also determine the domestic rate of inflation. One can see this from the fact that equilibrium under a clean float requires BOF(t) in equation 11.13 to be zero. Thus we get

$$0 = \frac{1}{m}\{g_P + \eta_y g_y + \eta_i g_i\} - \frac{DC}{M} g_{DC} \tag{11.20}$$

If we multiply through by the bank multiplier, m, and remember that $M = mH$ from equation 10.5, we can write this as

$$0 = g_P + \eta_y g_y + \eta_i g_i - \frac{DC}{H} g_{DC} \tag{11.21}$$

Rearranging terms in equation 11.21 gives

$$g_P = \frac{DC}{H} g_{DC} - \{\eta_y g_y + \eta_i g_i\} \tag{11.22}$$

The term in brace brackets on the right-hand side of equation 11.22 is the rate of growth in the demand for money due to the rate of growth of real output and to any rate of change in the domestic interest rate. The rate of growth of the domestic money supply is given by $(DC/H)g_{DC}$ in equation 11.22. Thus domestic inflation accelerates (that is, $g_P > 0$) when the rate of growth in domestic credit exceeds the rate of growth in the demand for money due to real income and interest-rate changes. There is then said to be an excessive rate of growth in the domestic money supply. In contrast to the fixed exchange-rate case where the domestic rate of inflation is constrained to equal the world rate, under flexible exchange rates the domestic inflation rate *is affected* by the rate of domestic credit expansion. This result follows directly from the exogeneity of the money stock under a clean float.

However, the exchange rate only remains unchanged if the domestic rate of inflation is equal to the world inflation rate. We have already shown this when, using the law of one price, we derived equation 11.15:

$$g_e = g_{Pf} - g_P \tag{11.15}$$

Thus the exchange rate will appreciate when foreign countries inflate more rapidly than the domestic country and depreciate if the world inflation rate is lower than domestic inflation. We first simplify equation 11.22 by assuming a constant interest rate, so that $g_i = 0$.[1] We then substitute the resulting expression for g_P in equation 11.22 into equation 11.15. This gives

$$g_e = g_{Pf} - \frac{DC}{H} g_{DC} + \eta_y g_y \tag{11.23}$$

Equation 11.23 shows that an increase in the foreign rate of inflation or in the rate of growth of domestic real income will tend to appreciate the exchange rate. If $\eta_y g_y = (DC/H)g_{DC}$, so that domestic credit expands just sufficiently to meet the increased demand for money due to real income growth, then we must have

$$g_e = g_{Pf} \tag{11.24}$$

In this case a positive rate of foreign inflation causes an appreciation of the exchange rate. However, the domestic price level stays constant because there is no excess rate of growth in domestic credit. This, together with the law of one price, ensures that the exchange rate appreciates so as to prevent the rise in prices in terms of foreign currency affecting prices in terms of domestic currency. If $\eta_y g_y = (DC/H)g_{DC}$ and foreign prices are falling, then the exchange rate must be depreciating.

Thus under flexible exchange rates the behaviour of the exchange rate depends on the domestic country's inflation rate *vis-à-vis* other countries, and this in turn depends on domestic monetary policy. If there are no foreign reserves under a clean float so that $DC = H$ and $g_i = 0$, then equation 11.23 simplifies to

$$g_e = g_{Pf} - g_{DC} + \eta_y g_y \tag{11.25}$$

Now if $g_{Pf} = 0$ and $g_y = 0$, we have the simplest case of the monetary model where

$$g_e = -g_{DC} \tag{11.26}$$

Here the rate of growth of the exchange rate is equal in size, but opposite in

[1] From equation 8.1 (p. 134), the law of one price and the interest-parity theorem we can derive the result that

$$i = \text{foreign real interest rate} + g_P^e$$

If the foreign real interest rate is constant, then i will only change if the domestic rate of inflation is expected to change. Therefore, g_i is only non-zero when inflation is expected to either decelerate or accelerate. For a constant rate of inflation $g_i = 0$.

sign, to the growth of domestic credit. As in the flexible exchange-rate version of the Mundell–Fleming model in Chapter 10, an increase in domestic credit leads to a depreciation, while a decrease in domestic credit leads to an appreciation, of the domestic currency. In this case any increase in domestic credit expansion must lead to an increase in the price level, and the rate of domestic inflation will be exactly matched by the rate of currency depreciation given our assumption that $g_{Pf} = g_y = 0$. This is demonstrated from equation 11.15, which together with equation 11.26 and $g_{Pf} = 0$ gives

$$-g_e = g_P = g_{DC}$$

Keynesian criticism of the monetary approach

Some Keynesians like Currie [4] and Fetherston and Godley [5] have pointed out that the adjustment mechanisms of the monetary approach under a fixed exchange rate do not work when the BOF is sterilised. If the private sector is kept in portfolio equilibrium at interest parity, then sterilisation of the BOF should not result in large capital flows that make continued sterilisation difficult. Therefore, a non-zero sterilised BOF could be maintained for some time. Chapter 21 (pp. 415–18) deals with this argument in the context of a detailed exposition of the 'New Cambridge' Keynesian portfolio model of the open economy.

Empirical tests of the monetary approach

Like all new developments in economics, the monetary approach has spawned a vast empirical literature. This has subjected the data from a vast range of countries to econometric tests to see whether they are consistent with the predictions of the monetary approach. (A sample of this literature is contained in the empirical articles in references [1] and [2] together with references [6]–[10].)

The empirical studies of countries under a fixed exchange rate find that the data are consistent with the monetary approach. Reserve losses are related to domestic credit expansion, and under fixed exchange rates national inflation rates of OECD countries did not vary any more than the inflation rates among US cities, while devaluation had a temporary positive effect on the BOF which could be offset by excessive credit expansion.

Under flexible exchange rates the monetary approach has been used to predict the exchange rate. It has been relatively successful in predicting movements in bilateral exchange rates. For example, Bilson (in Frenkel and Johnson [2]) uses the monetary approach to model the sterling/deutsche mark exchange rate. In his model money markets in both countries have a partial-adjustment process in disequilibrium. His estimated model is consistent with the monetary approach and there are significant coefficients on the money variables in his estimating equation.

The results in modelling the UK effective exchange rate[1] are much more patchy. Haache and Townend [9] found no statistically significant coefficients on the monetary variables in their model of the effective exchange rate for the pound. On the other hand, Beenstock *et al.* [10] found statistically significant effects on the effective exchange rate from the money stock. They concluded that the monetary approach was not rejected by the data. However, they also found that a broader asset market approach which included bond stocks gave better results than the monetary approach, but the coefficient of the money stock on the exchange rate was four times as large as that on the stock of bonds. This last result implies that the monetary approach should be extended to include other asset stocks. This is the new direction for theoretical work in the monetary tradition. (See chapters 13 and 14 in Dornbusch [11] for an overview of this work.)

11.3 Policy implications of the law of one price

The law of one price was used as an important simplifying device in our monetary model of the balance of payments. The main policy implications of the monetary approach can be derived without the law of one price. These policy implications are that countries with excessive credit expansion will either have a BOF deficit or a currency depreciation, and that with a fixed exchange-rate system the rate of price inflation will tend to be equal in all countries. These deductions from the monetary approach can be obtained without the law of one price, provided the Marshall–Lerner condition holds, but the models used must necessarily be more complex.

The law of one price is based on the premise that international markets are competitive and that traders seek out profitable opportunities for exchange. If in any country the price of a good differs from the price in another country by an amount which exceeds transport costs, then traders will buy it in the low-cost country and sell it in the high-cost country. The price falls in the high-cost country and tends to rise in the low-cost country until the price, including transport costs, is equalised across countries. This process is known as *commodity arbitrage*. As the law of one price is the outcome of competition, it seems very plausible to those who believe that markets work. To deny the law of one price is to claim that major market imperfections prevent competition. This happens in markets affected by significant import quotas and non-tariff barriers to trade.

The law of one price in a Keynesian open-economy model

The law of one price has strong policy implications. We shall illustrate these by using a three-sector macro model of an open economy in which the law of one

[1] The effective exchange rate for the pound is a weighted index of the exchange rate for the pound against all other currencies. The weights used usually reflect each country's share in UK trade.

price holds. The model has a Keynesian aggregate supply function, and the standard consumption, investment, government spending, tax and money demand functions found in the *ISLM* and three-sector models of Chapters 3, 4 and 6. The money supply equation in our model is equation 10.5 of Chapter 10. We write this as $M^S = mH$, where H is high-powered money. In the absence of sterilisation, H increases with a BOF surplus and decreases with a BOF deficit, as $\Delta H =$ BOF. To simplify our model we assume that payments for current transactions can be made freely, while capital flows are subject to the effective exchange controls and are prohibited. Here the current account, CA is equal to the BOF and we assume that it is not sterilised. The complete model is set out in the Appendix (p. 199).

In this model, consumption, investment and government expenditure determine domestic absorption, A, so that

$$\frac{A}{P} = \frac{C}{P} + \frac{I}{P} + \frac{G}{P}$$

$$= a + c(1-t)y + I(i) + G_0 \tag{11.27}$$

Here P is the price level, C is consumption, I is investment, G_0 is direct government expenditure on goods and services, c is the MPC, t is the tax rate, y is real income and i is the rate of interest. A rise in the rate of interest has a negative effect on real domestic absorption through its negative effect on real investment. An increase in government expenditure or an autonomous increase in investment will have a positive initial effect on domestic absorption.

Under a fixed exchange rate, the law of one price will constrain the domestic price level, P, so that

$$P = \frac{1}{e} Pf \tag{11.4}$$

where Pf is the foreign price level. In the small-country case the foreign price level is exogenous and we can take it to be fixed. The law of one price determines aggregate demand in the economy, as any output not sold at home can be sold abroad at the world price, $P = (1/e)Pf$. Therefore, in Figure 11.1, we can draw the aggregate demand function, AD, as a horizontal line, where $P = (1/e)Pf$, e and Pf both being fixed. In the very short run aggregate demand may depart from this, as there may be lags in the adjustment of trade flows to changes in domestic absorption.

The Keynesian aggregate supply function is identical to that in Chapter 6 (pp. 87–91). Given a money wage fixed at W_0, then as the price level rises real output increases up to its full-employment level. This is illustrated in Figure 11.1 by the upward-sloping function $AS(W_0)$. An increase in the money wage rate, W, will shift the aggregate supply function vertically upwards, while a decrease in W shifts it vertically downwards.

In this model the level of domestic production is not constrained by lack of effective demand. Because of the small open economy and law of one price assumptions domestic firms face a perfectly elastic demand function. They can therefore sell as much as they wish to produce at the world price given their

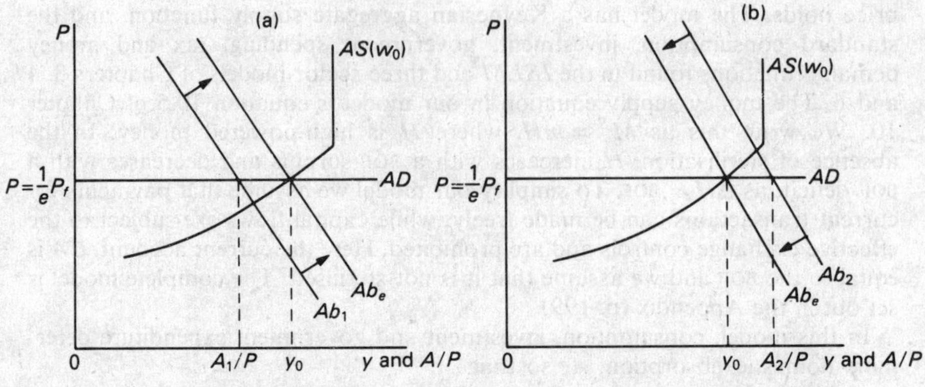

FIGURE 11.1 *Monetary and fiscal policy under a fixed exchange rate*

costs of production. Profit-maximising firms will produce that level of output for which the marginal product of labour equals the real wage rate. The lower the domestic real wage, the greater the amount of output produced by domestic firms. The level of real output is therefore determined at y_0 in Figures 11.1(a) and 11.1(b) by the intersection of the *AD* and *AS* schedules.

Given a fixed exchange rate and a constant foreign price level, the domestic price level is fixed. Thus the position of the *AD* schedule is fixed. Real domestic output can only change if the aggregate supply schedule shifts, and this only occurs if the money wage rate changes, given that current production techniques remain unaltered. Under a fixed exchange rate the level of domestic production can only increase in this model if the money wage falls and so brings down the real wage rate.

From equation 11.27 we can see that domestic absorption in our Keynesian model is determined by the level of the interest rate, *i*, and the politically determined level of real public expenditure, G_0. As there are no capital flows in the model, the domestic rate of interest can vary independently of the rate of interest in the rest of the world. Given the money wage, exchange rate and foreign price level, then real income and the price level are fixed in our model. The only variable that can adjust in order to equate the demand and supply for money in the short run is the rate of interest. Given money markets clear in the short run, changes in the stock of money can affect the rate of interest and so influence domestic absorption. If the domestic price level rises (due either to a fall in *e*, or a rise in *Pf*) while the money stock remains constant, then domestic interest rates have to rise in order to bring the demand for money into line with the existing stock. This rise in the interest rate reduces domestic investment and therefore domestic absorption. Thus, given the domestic money stock and the real level of government spending, the level of domestic absorption is negatively related to the price level. Therefore, we can draw a downward-sloping absorption function *Ab* for our economy in Figure 11.1. This absorption function is derived from equation 11.27 and the money-market equilibrium in the economy, given the level of *y* determined by the aggregate supply function, $AS(W_0)$, and the law of one price, *AD*.

Monetary and fiscal policy under a fixed exchange rate

If we start from an equilibrium condition where real absorption, A/P, is equal to y_0, then the balance of payments on current account, CA (and in this model the BOF) must be zero, as by the absorption approach in equation 7.2 of Chapter 7

$$CA = P\,y - A \tag{11.28}$$

As $P\,y$ is fixed, any decrease in absorption from this equilibrium must lead to a current-account surplus, with $Py > A$ as shown in Figure 11.1(a). An increase in taxes, a decrease in G_0, or a decrease in the money stock will lead to a decrease in absorption shown by a shift to the left in the Ab function from Ab_e to Ab_1 in Figure 11.1(a). This shift leads to a new level of absorption at A_1/P. This is not a final equilibrium position, as in the absence of capital flows the current account is equal to the BOF. An unsterilised BOF surplus will lead to an increase in high-powered money, which in turn increases the domestic money supply. This shifts the Ab curve to the right, the process continuing until the Ab curve has shifted back to Ab_e and the level of absorption is once more equal to the unchanged income level, y_0. At this point the BOF becomes zero and the money stock stops growing.

Similarly, a shift of the Ab function to the right through monetary or fiscal expansion results in a BOF and current-account deficit. This is illustrated in Figure 11.1(b), where $y_0 < A_2/P$ so that $CA = Py - A < 0$. There is a reserve loss and high-powered money falls. In the absence of sterilisation, the money supply falls and this shifts the Ab curve to the left. The money supply continues to decline until the Ab curve has shifted back to Ab_e in Figure 11.1(b). Absorption is then once more equal to the unchanged level of income, so that the BOF and current accounts become zero. In this model, as in the monetary model under fixed exchange rates, monetary policy is powerless to alter the money supply in the long run unless the central bank continuously sterilises the change in reserves. Here monetary policy has the same effect on the BOF as in our monetary model under fixed exchange rates.

Fiscal policy and crowding out under fixed exchange rates

In the very short run fiscal expansion increases absorption. If absorption and income had previously been equal, as in Figure 11.1(b), then the fiscal expansion leads to a current-account and BOF deficit as y is not affected by changes in domestic absorption, except over the time that it takes to trade flows to adjust to these changes. The money stock contracts as a result of the BOF deficit and interest rates rise as P and y are fixed. Consequently investment falls. As in the neoclassical *ISLM* model, fiscal expansion crowds out investment. In the case of an increase in government expenditure, G, not being financed by an increase in taxes, then in the very short run $\Delta G = -\Delta\text{BOF}$. The resulting decline in the money stock shifts absorption back to Ab_e in Figure 11.1(b), through the impact of higher interest rates on investment expenditure.

In the new final equilibrium investment spending decreases by an amount equal to the initial increase in government expenditure, ΔG, as interest rates and real money balances have no direct effect on consumption. Here an increase in government expenditure on goods and services leads to a *complete crowding out* of an equal amount of investment.

Money wages and employment

In the small-economy model the law of one price eliminates the possibility of unemployment being due to an inadequate level of aggregate demand since more output could be sold at the existing price level to the rest of the world. Unemployment is due to an inappropriate level of money (and therefore real wages) that makes it unprofitable for firms to expand output. This is illustrated in Figure 11.2. Here a fall in money wages from W_0 to W_1 leads to a shift in the aggregate supply function from $AS(W_0)$ to $AS(W_1)$. Output expands as additional output can now be sold at a profit due to the fall in costs. Income rises to y_1, increasing consumption and therefore absorption. This shifts the Ab function from Ab_0 to Ab_1. As the MPC is less than 1.0, absorption initially rises by less than income. A current-account surplus equal to BOF therefore develops, the surplus increases the money supply so there is a continued shift to the right in the Ab function until absorption becomes equal to the new level of income at y_1.

An increase in money wages, the exchange rate and foreign price level being fixed, has the opposite effect on income and employment, both of which must fall. Therefore, in a Keynesian open economy where the law of one price holds and involuntary unemployment exists, wage cuts will bring about an increase in output and employment. Unemployment is due to inappropriate money wages. The political unpalatability of this message has stimulated some empirical work aiming to provide evidence that markets are imperfect and the law of one price does not hold (see Kravis and Lipsey [12]).

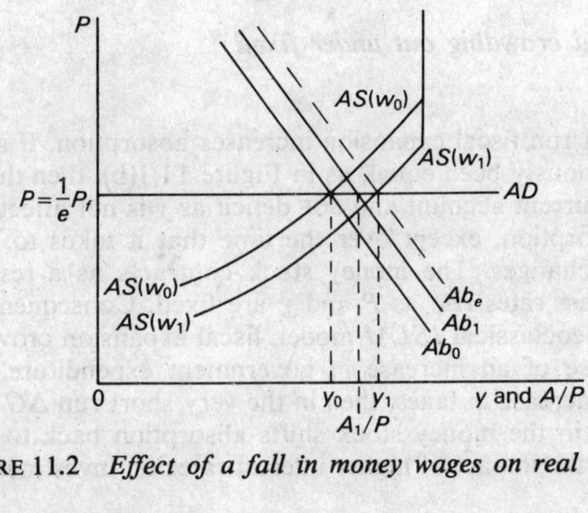

FIGURE 11.2 *Effect of a fall in money wages on real income*

Devaluation, the current account and employment

In this model a devaluation increases output and employment, provided that there is no real wage resistance. Here any involuntary unemployment (in the sense defined by Keynes) must be due to an inappropriately high money wage rate, W_0, in relation to the foreign price level, *Pf*, and the fixed exchange rate, *e*. Hence the real wage rate is too high for full employment. A devaluation raises the domestic price level, lowers the real wage and makes it profitable for employers to increase output and employment. This is illustrated in Figure 11.3, where a fall in the exchange rate shifts the aggregate demand schedule upwards from AD_0 to AD_1. The rise in the domestic price level causes a movement along the aggregate supply function from y_0 to y_1. However, because of adjustment lags, the movement from the old to the new equilibrium may not be monotonic (that is, always in the same direction).

The absorption function initially shifts to the right to Ab_1 in Figure 11.3 due to a higher level of consumption brought about by the rise in income due to devaluation. As the MPC is less than 1.0, the rise in absorption must be less than the increase in income and so a current-account and BOF surplus develops. This increases the domestic money supply (due to the impact of increased foreign reserves on *H*) and the *Ab* function shifts further to the right to Ab_e in Figure 11.3. In this final equilibrium position domestic absorption is equal once more to domestic income and the current account and BOF are again zero. The level of income is higher as a lower real wage rate makes it profitable to employ more workers. Real wage resistance would prevent the income expansion, but would not prevent a temporary balance-of-payments surplus as real money balances will fall because of the devaluation and the resulting rise in interest rates will cut absorption.

A rise in the foreign price level will raise the domestic price level and have exactly the same effect on domestic output, the balance of payments and ultimately on the money stock as a devaluation. The 'law of one price' Keynesian economy under a fixed exchange rate has the same predictions with

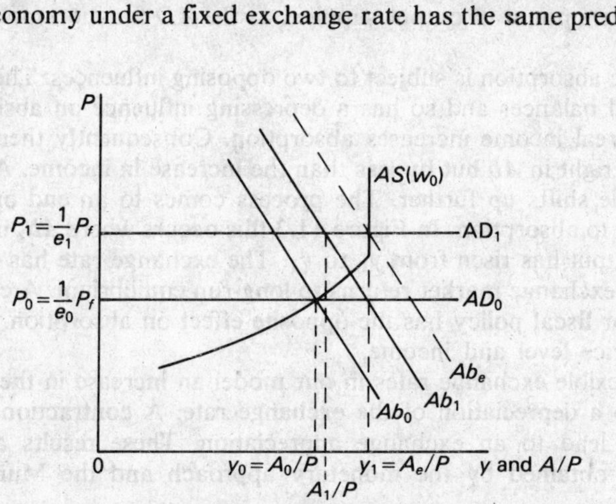

FIGURE 11.3 *Devaluation and real income where $e_0 > e_1$*

respect to the effects of monetary policy, devaluation and foreign price changes as our earlier monetary model. Monetary models which do not include the law of one price have similar predictions (see Rodriguez in Frenkel and Johnson [1]). In our Keynesian model devaluation improves the balance of payments, but if it starts from a position of equality between domestic absorption and income the improvement in the current account and BOF is only temporary. The balance-of-payments surplus disappears as money stocks increase. The difference between the results of this model and the Keynesian model of Chapter 7 is that the latter neglects changes in asset stocks brought about by a balance-of-payments surplus. Therefore, there is no further increase in domestic expenditure in relation to income due either to increases in wealth or to increases in the money stock.

Flexible exchange rates and the 'law of one price' Keynesian model

In our model a clean float implies a zero current account and BOF and hence continuous equality between domestic absorption and domestic income. Monetary and fiscal policy now regain some influence on real income because they affect the exchange rate. This in turn alters the domestic price level and so changes the real wage and the profitability of production.

The impact of an expansionary fiscal or monetary policy under flexible exchange rates is illustrated in Figure 11.3. The expansionary policy increases domestic absorption and so shifts the AB function from Ab_0 to Ab_1. Consequently Py is less than A and the resulting incipient current-account and BOF deficits lower the exchange rate. The domestic price level therefore rises and the aggregate demand curve, AD_0, starts shifting upwards. The rise in price, accompanied by a constant money wage level, lowers the real wage rate and so increases the amount of output supplied as the AD function moves up the AS schedule.

Domestic absorption is subject to two opposing influences. The rise in prices reduces real balances and so has a depressing influence on absorption, while the rise in real income increases absorption. Consequently there is a further shift to the right in Ab but by less than the increase in income. As a result the AD schedule shifts up further. The process comes to an end once income is again equal to absorption. In Figure 11.3 this occurs where Ab_e intersects AD_1 and real output has risen from y_0 to y_1. The exchange rate has stabilised and the foreign exchange market returns to long-run equilibrium. A contractionary monetary or fiscal policy has the opposite effect on absorption, the exchange rate, the price level and income.

Under flexible exchange rates in our model an increase in the money stock will lead to a depreciation of the exchange rate. A contractionary monetary policy will lead to an exchange appreciation. These results are consistent with those obtained by the monetary approach and the Mundell–Fleming model.

11.4 Policy implications of a small open economy model

After studying section II it is evident that the Keynesian policy conclusions derived in section I for a closed economy need to be modified when applied to an open economy. A fixed exchange rate imposes a further constraint on demand-management policies because any ensuing BOF deficit cannot be financed indefinitely. An additional constraint exists if the monetary effects of BOF imbalances cannot be sterilised, for then government policy cannot affect the level of aggregate demand except in the short run. Hence the ability to sterilise BOF imbalances is vital to the success of Keynesian policies. Under flexible exchange rates expansionary monetary and fiscal policy in a Keynesian–neoclassical synthesis model can only expand real output if the exchange rate depreciates, and this is consistent with a reduction in the real wage. The same is true of a devaluation.

Thus in an open economy with a freely floating exchange rate, a Keynesian aggregate supply function is sufficient to ensure the efficacy of expansionary demand-management policies. Under a fixed exchange rate the ability to sterilise the monetary effects of BOF imbalances is an additional requirement, otherwise the level of effective demand cannot be affected by government action except in the short run.

Appendix: general Keynesian model under the law of one price

Goods market

$$\frac{A}{P}=\frac{C}{P}+\frac{I}{P}+\frac{G}{P} \qquad \text{domestic absorption} \qquad (11A.1)$$

$$\frac{C}{P}=a+c\left(y-\frac{T}{P}\right) \quad (0<c<1) \qquad \text{consumption function} \qquad (11A.2)$$

$$\frac{I}{P}=I(i) \quad \left(\frac{dI(i)}{di}<0\right) \qquad \text{investment function} \qquad (11A.3)$$

$$\frac{G}{P}=G_0 \qquad \text{government expenditure} \qquad (11A.4)$$

$$\frac{T}{P}=ty \qquad \text{tax function} \qquad (11A.5)$$

$$yP = A + CA \qquad \text{income equals expenditure} \qquad (11A.6)$$

$$P = \frac{1}{e} Pf \qquad \text{law of one price} \qquad (11A.7)$$

Money market

$$M^D = Pf(y, i) \quad (f_i < 0; f_y > 0) \qquad \text{demand for money} \qquad (11A.8)$$

$$M^S = mH \qquad \text{supply of money} \qquad (11A.9)$$

$$M^D = M^S = M \qquad \text{equilibrium condition} \qquad (11A.10)$$

$$\frac{dH}{dt} = CA \qquad \text{change in high-powered money} \qquad (11A.11)$$

$$\frac{dM^S}{dt} = mCA \qquad \text{change in money supply} \qquad (11A.12)$$

Production function

$$y = \theta(L, \bar{K}, \bar{T}_e) \quad (\theta_L > 0) \qquad \text{production function} \qquad (11A.13)$$

$$L^d = g\left(\frac{W}{P}\right) \quad (g_{W/P} < 0) \qquad \text{demand for labour} \qquad (11A.14)$$

$$W = W_0 \qquad \text{fixed money wage assumption} \qquad (11A.15)$$

$$L^d = L \qquad \text{involuntary unemployment} \qquad (11A.16)$$

In the above model A is absorption, C is consumption, I is investment, G is direct government expenditure on goods and services, T is taxation, CA is the balance on current account, P is the price level, M^D is the demand for money, M^S is the supply of money, M is money and W is the domestic wage rate. All of these are in nominal terms in domestic currency. The domestic rate of interest is i and y is domestic real income. In terms of foreign currency we have Pf, the foreign price level, and e, the fixed exchange rate, giving the price of one unit of domestic currency in terms of foreign currency.

G_0 and W_0 are exogenously determined, while over the short run the domestic capital stock, $\bar{K}$, and technical change, $\bar{T}_e$, are also fixed. We are assuming that payments for current international transactions can be made freely, but capital flows are subject to control and are prohibited. Therefore, the BOF is equal to the current account and it is not sterilised.

All the results in section 11.3 are derived from this model. The model can be given a more monetarist flavour by assuming that real balances have a direct positive effect on consumption and investment expenditures.

References

[1] J. A. Frenkel and H. G. Johnson (eds), *The Monetary Approach to the Balance of Payments* (London: Allen & Unwin, 1976).

[2] J. A. Frenkel and H. G. Johnson (eds), *The Economics of Exchange Rates* (Reading, Mass.: Addison-Wesley, 1978).

[3] R. Dornbusch and S. Fischer, 'Exchange Rates and the Current Account', *American Economic Review* (1980).

[4] D. A. Currie, 'Some Criticisms of the Monetary Analysis of the Balance of Payments', *Economic Journal* (1976).

[5] M. Fetherston and W. A. H. Godley, 'New Cambridge Macroeconomics and Global Monetarism: Some Issues in the Conduct of UK Policy', in K. Brunner and A. H. Meltzer (eds), *Public Policies in Open Economies*, Carnegie–Rochester Series in Public Policy (Amsterdam: North-Holland, 1978).

[6] M. Connolly and D. Taylor, 'Testing the Monetary Approach to the Balance of Payments in Developing Countries', *Journal of Political Economy* (1976).

[7] M. Connolly and D. Taylor, 'A Test of the Monetary Approach Applied to Developing and Developed Countries', *Economica* (1979).

[8] P. Johnson, 'Money and the Open Economy: the United Kingdom 1880–1970', *Journal of Political Economy* (1976).

[9] G. Haache and J. Townend, 'Exchange Rates and Monetary Policy: Modelling Sterling's Effective Exchange Rate', *Oxford Economic Papers* (1981).

[10] M. Beenstock, A. Budd and P. Warburton, 'Monetary Policy, Expectations and Real Exchange Dynamics', *Oxford Economic Papers* (1981).

[11] R. Dornbusch, *Open Economy Macroeconomics* (New York: Basic Books, 1980).

[12] I. B. Kravis and R. E. Lipsey, 'Price Behaviour in the Light of Balance of Payments Theories', *Journal of International Economics* (1978).

III TRADITIONAL DYNAMICS OF THE REAL SECTOR

Section III contains a chapter on each of the two major components of aggregate demand: consumption and investment. The micro foundations of the two expenditure functions are examined. By considering the time horizon over which consumption and investment are planned, both forms of expenditure are shown to depend on expectations about the future values of their determinants. These expectations are in turn influenced by the past values of these variables. Dynamic analysis is required when consumption and investment depend on lagged values of their determinants. Chapter 14 shows how models made up of lagged consumption and investment functions can generate cycles in national output. Chapter 15 considers how the long-run analysis of saving and investment provides models of long-run growth in national output.

12 Consumption

Aggregate consumption is the largest component of aggregate demand. It is therefore important for the implementation of Keynesian economic policy to be able to predict consumption reasonably well. So it is not surprising that aggregate consumption theory is a major area of macroeconomic research.

12.1 The definition of consumption

To start with we need to be clear as to what the term 'consumption' means. Expenditure on a certain quantity of a commodity per period of time is distinct from actually using that commodity and so enjoying a flow of services from it. The term 'consumption' should be reserved for the using up of the services yielded by a good, while the act of purchasing it is 'consumer expenditure'. Goods vary in the length of time over which they yield services. For some, such as a restaurant meal or a bus journey, the length of time over which the commodity is enjoyed is quite short and occurs around the same instant of time as the purchase. Other goods such as motor-cars, refrigerators and the like yield services over a number of years. Goods which yield their services over a relatively short period are referred to as *non-durables* whereas goods which yield services to households over a number of years are known as *consumer durables*. The distinction between the two cannot be made precise: it depends on the definition of what is a 'short' period of time and on how long a good yields services to a particular consumer. For a fashion-conscious wearer, clothes are a non-durable, for others they can last longer than a car. Nevertheless, clothes are defined in official statistics as non-durables. Over a period of time, such as a year, consumption, in the sense of the derivation of utility from goods and services, is made up of the purchase of non-durable goods and services plus the depreciation of the existing stock of consumer durable goods. Consumer expenditure is the purchase of consumer non-durables and services and of new consumer durables. Expenditure on consumer durables forms part of aggregate demand for currently produced output, whereas the services yielded by the existing stock of durables do not. The expectation of obtaining such services is, however, a determinant of expenditure on consumer durables. The distinction between consumption and consumer expenditure is an extremely important one. Their actual numerical values will be different in a non-stationary economy and the determinants of expenditure on durables will be differentiated from those which determine the rate of using up durable goods.

A consumer durable is really an investment good since it is purchased in order to obtain a flow of future services. The usual distinction between purchasing consumer durables and investment relates to the types of economic agent involved. In the national income accounts a car owned by a company and a washing-machine owned by a launderette are capital goods, but are consumer goods if owned by a household, which is taken to be a non-productive unit, in the sense that it does not use these goods to produce services which are sold on a market. The same is true of goods which yield up their services quickly. Ice-cream in a shop's freezer is a capital good as it is part of the shop's inventory, but once purchased by a customer it becomes a consumer good, even if it remains in her freezer. In principle, the purchase of any good which is expected to yield services at some future date is an act of investment. In official statistics the term 'investment' is reserved for the purchase of a capital good (that is, one that will be used in the future) when it is done by a 'firm' with the intention of selling future services or goods produced by the capital good on a market. We have no distinct word to describe household investment in goods which will yield future services to the household and which are not traded on a market. Such purchases are normally classified as consumer expenditure on durables and so are included as part of total consumer expenditure even though they are essentially acts of investment.

When examining the determinants of the desire to purchase both capital and consumer goods, one must necessarily analyse the relevant decision-unit's behaviour over time. The present value of the expected future services of the good has to be compared with the purchase price of the good, both in deciding whether the good is worth buying in the first place, or, if already possessed, whether it is worth replacing. Thus the existing stock of goods and the type and time profile of the services they are expected to yield will affect current purchase of the good. The size of the existing stock of a consumer durable exerts a disincentive effect on the desire to purchase additional units of that good. Thus past decisions to purchase influence current decisions. This will also be the case for habit-forming goods such as drink and tobacco: past enjoyment of the commodity exerts a positive effect on current purchasing plans.

Households may allocate their current period's income to current or to future consumer purchases, the latter decision being known as *saving*. The act of saving is simply the act of not consuming current income. The most important motive for saving is the postponement of consumption in order to enjoy it at some future date, either directly oneself or through one's heirs.

The decision to spend current income on current consumer purchases necessarily involves some consideration of one's future consumption plans. Thus Keynes's dictum that 'consumption – to repeat the obvious – is the sole end object of all economic activity' (*The General Theory*, p. 104) is the central theme of the interrelationships among economic decision-units at the macro level. Consumption plans, saving plans and investment plans all involve economic decision-units in activities which are intended to obtain as much satisfaction as is possible from consuming the services of commodities over some time horizon.

12.2 The absolute income hypothesis

The aggregate consumption function is a core element in the Keynesian theory of income determination. In *The General Theory* Keynes gave primary importance to disposable national income as the chief determinant of aggregate consumption. He also made *a priori* assumptions about the form of the relationship between consumption and income. For a household, and hence for the economy as a whole, consumption as a proportion of income (the average propensity to consume) was assumed to decline as income rises. The basic form of the early Keynesians' consumption function is that current consumption depends on current income:

$$C_t = a + bY_t \tag{12.1}$$

The hypothesis that consumption is a function of current income, whether the relationship is linear or non-linear, is known as the *absolute income hypothesis*. Equation 12.1 is a linear consumption function since *b*, the marginal propensity to consume (MPC) is constant. A further feature of this consumption function is that it is non-proportional: the average propensity to consume (APC) $= C/Y = a/Y + b$ declines as Y increases (since the a/Y term falls). A linear non-proportional consumption function, $C = a + bY$, is graphed in Figure 12.1(a). If the MPC falls as income rises, then the consumption function is non-linear, as shown by the graph of $C = f(y)$ in Figure 12.1(b).

Confronting the empirical evidence

The consumption function was one of the first economic relationships to be estimated in the 1940s by the then recently developed techniques of

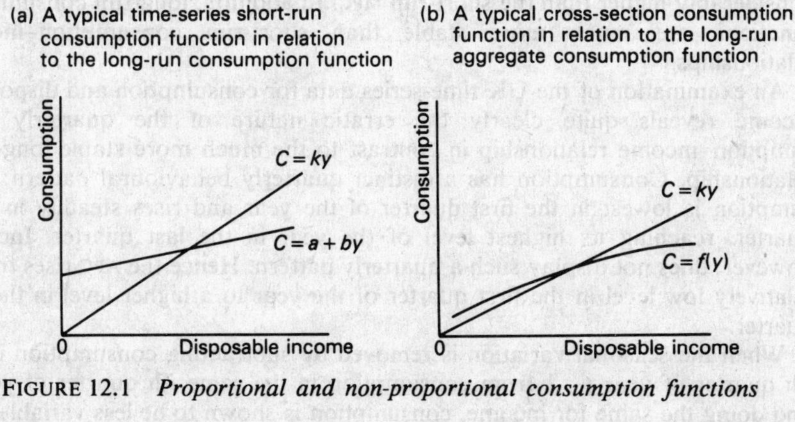

FIGURE 12.1 *Proportional and non-proportional consumption functions*

econometrics. As with most economic relationships two types of data, cross-section and time-series data, are available for testing the consumption function. Cross-section data are provided by sampling households to obtain information for a particular time period on their consumption expenditure, disposable income and other relevant explanatory variables such as family composition by age and sex, and social class. Such budget studies have shown that the average propensity to consume does decline with income and typically that low-income households dissave. There is also evidence that consumption functions fitted to budget-study data tend to be non-linear, as depicted by the curved consumption function in Figure 12.1(b).

The first time-series data to become available were those for the USA for the years 1929–41. These short-run time-series data produced linear non-proportional consumption functions. On the basis of such regression equations, American economists at the end of the Second World War attempted to forecast post-war consumption, and concluded that unless a high level of government expenditure continued aggregate demand would be insufficient to maintain full employment. In the event American post-war consumption was considerably greater than had been predicted by many economists and it appeared that the whole pre-war consumption function must have shifted upwards.

In 1946 Kuznets [1] published long-run time-series data for the USA which showed that the long-run APC had not fallen as national income had increased, but was on the whole quite stable, and maintained a long-run average of around 0.84–0.89, only rising to above 0.89 when national income fell in the decade 1929–38. From Kuznets's data is obtained a long-run consumption function such that the long-run APC and MPC are both constant and equal to k. This type of consumption function is known as a proportional one and is written

$$C = kY \tag{12.2}$$

So although the early empirical work showed that budget study data and short-run time-series data supported the absolute income hypothesis and Keynes's presumption that the APC falls as income rises, the long-run data conflicted with these conclusions. Empirical studies show that the long-run MPC is considerably higher than the short-run MPC. In addition, long-run consumption functions are much more stable than short-run consumption–income relationships.

An examination of the UK time-series data for consumption and disposable income reveals quite clearly the erratic nature of the quarterly consumption–income relationship in contrast to the much more stable long-term relationship. Consumption has a distinct quarterly behavioural pattern: consumption is lowest in the first quarter of the year and rises steadily in each quarter, reaching its highest level of the year in the last quarter. Income, however, does not display such a quarterly pattern. Hence the APC rises from a relatively low level in the first quarter of the year to a higher level in the last quarter.

When the seasonal variation is removed by subtracting consumption in the ith quarter of year $t-1$ from consumption in the same ith quarter of year t, and doing the same for income, consumption is shown to be less variable than

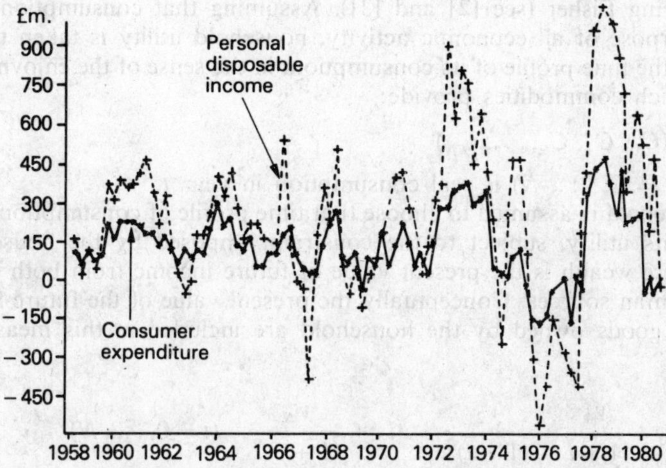

FIGURE 12.2 *Four-quarter changes in the consumption of non-durables and services and in disposable income, United Kingdom, 1958–80*
Source: various issues of *Economic Trends.*

income on a quarterly basis. This is shown in Figure 12.2, which reveals that quarterly changes in current income will be a poor explanatory variable for quarterly changes in consumption.

Although the APC displays a distinct quarterly pattern, its average value over the year does not vary much from year to year. There is, however, now evidence that the APC has declined secularly over the post-war period, from 0.99 in the late 1940s to 0.85 by 1979–80. This decline was not so evident in the 1960s, when the APC remained reasonably stable at around 0.92. Thus the belief that the long-run APC is constant, which first stemmed from Kuznets's US study, is no longer held generally. Later in this chapter we shall examine the various explanations put forward for the rising savings–income ratio.

The evidence on consumption reported so far reveals that, while there appears to be some stable relationship between consumption and income over the long run, in the short run current income alone offers a poor explanation of consumption behaviour. The inadequacy of the absolute income hypothesis was evident by the start of the 1950s and stimulated the search for alternative theories. Two closely related theories, the *permanent income hypothesis* (PIH) and the *life-cycle hypothesis* (LCH) have become generally accepted as the most useful line of approach. Both are concerned with analysing the household's choice of consumption and saving over a long time horizon. Since both hypotheses deal with intertemporal choice we shall now outline their common theoretical background.

12.3 Intertemporal choice

The intertemporal nature of consumption choice at the micro level of the household will be treated more formally, using analysis that originated in the work of Irving Fisher (see [2] and [3]). Assuming that consumption is the ultimate purpose of all economic activity, household utility is taken to be a function of the time profile of its consumption, in the sense of the enjoyment of services which commodities provide:

$$U = f(C_0, C_1, C_2, \ldots, C_N) \tag{12.3}$$

where C_t ($t = 0, \ldots, N$) is real consumption in year t.

The household is assumed to choose that time profile of consumption which maximises its utility, subject to the constraint imposed by the household's wealth, where wealth is the present value of future income from both human and non-human sources. Conceptually the present value of the future flow of services of goods owned by the household are included in this measure of wealth:

$$W = y_0 + \frac{y_1}{1+i} + \frac{y_2}{(1+i)^2} + \ldots + \frac{y_N}{(1+i)^N} \quad (t = 0, \ldots, N) \tag{12.4}$$

where

$$\left.\begin{array}{l} y_t = \text{disposable income in period } t \\ W = \text{wealth} \\ i = \text{market rate of interest} \end{array}\right\} \text{in real terms}$$

In this basic model of household consumption, decision-making conditions of certainty are assumed to prevail: that is, future income in each of the future years and the future market rate of interest are assumed to be known with a 100 per cent probability. The capital market is assumed to be perfectly competitive, so that the household can borrow or lend at the going market rate of interest as much as it wants, without affecting that rate. Transactions costs involved in borrowing and lending activities are taken to be zero.

Given the above assumptions we start by simplifying even further and consider the problem of intertemporal choice over two periods, the present and the next period, which can be called the future:

$$U = f(C_0, C_1) \quad \text{utility function}^1 \tag{12.3a}$$

$$W = y_0 + y_1/(1+i) \quad \text{wealth constraint} \tag{12.4a}$$

$$C_0 + C_1/(i+1) = W \tag{12.5}$$

Equation 12.5 gives the condition that the present value of consumption equals wealth on the assumption that all the income is spent over the two time periods. Rearranging equation 12.5 we get

$$C_1 = W(1+i) - C_0(1+i) \tag{12.6}$$

which is the equation of the budget line AB in Figure 12.3. This is the constraint subject to which utility is maximised. The slope of AB is $-(1+i)$ and its

[1]It is assumed that $\partial U/\partial C_0 > 0$, $\partial U/\partial C_1 > 0$ and that $\partial^2 U/\partial C_0^2 < 0$, $\partial^2 U/\partial^2 C_1 < 0$. This is required to fulfil the second-order conditions for a maximum.

position is determined by the size of W. For utility to remain constant it is necessary that the first-order total differential of equation 12.3a be set equal to zero, i.e.

$$dU = \frac{\partial U}{\partial C_0} dC_0 + \frac{\partial U}{\partial C_1} dC_1 = 0 \qquad (12.7)$$

Equation (12.7) is the equation of movements along a particular indifference curve, for instance U_1, which shows the various combinations of consumption in the present and consumption in the future which yield the same level of utility. In Figure 12.3 we see that U_1 is the highest indifference curve, or level of utility attainable given wealth constraint AB. Therefore, utility is maximised by choosing OC_0^1 consumption for the present and OC_1^1 consumption for the future period.

The slope of the indifference curve is given by rearranging 12.7:

$$\frac{dC_1}{dC_0} = -\frac{\delta U}{\delta C_0} \bigg/ \frac{\delta U}{\delta C_1} \qquad (12.7a)$$

This states that the marginal rate of substitution between present and future consumption equals the ratio of the marginal utility of present consumption to the marginal utility of future consumption, all along the indifference curve. Utility is maximised subject to the wealth constraint when the marginal rate of substitution of present for future consumption, which is determined by the household's preferences, equals the rate at which future consumption can be transformed into present consumption, which is given by the market rate of interest. This can be seen by differentiating the wealth constraint equation (12.6) so that

$$dC_1/dC_0 = -(1 + i) \qquad (12.6a)$$

When utility is maximised subject to the wealth constraint equation 12.6a is set

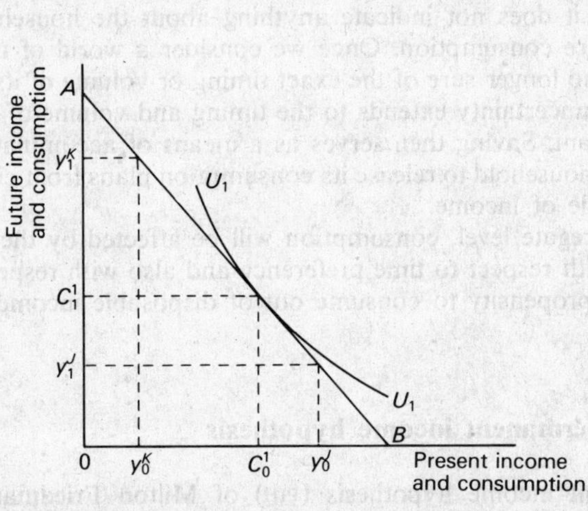

FIGURE 12.3 *Intertemporal consumption choice*

equal to equation 12.7a:

$$\frac{dC_1}{dC_0} = -(1 + i) = -\frac{\delta U}{\delta C_0}\Big/\frac{\delta U}{\delta C_1} \qquad (12.8)$$

There are many combinations of present and future income that will give the wealth constraint imposed by budget line AB. Two of the combinations, y_0^J, y_1^J and y_0^K, are shown in Figure 12.3. In the case of income stream y_0^J, y_1^J, utility is maximised by consuming less than current income in the present, and thus by consuming more than the next period's income in the future. This time profile of consumption and income is financed by saving out of current income an amount equal to the distance between C_0^1 and y_0^J, and investing it at the market rate of interest, which converts it into an amount equal to the distance $y_1^J C_1^1$, which is exactly equal to the amount by which the future period's consumption exceeds the period's initially given income of y_1^J. In the case of income stream y_0^K, y_1^K, utility is maximised by consuming more than current income in the present, and consuming less than the income which will accrue in the next period. This is financed by borrowing an amount equal to the distance $y_0^K C_0^1$, on which the market rate of interest, i, must be paid. The sum which must be repaid next period is $y_0^K C_0^1(1 + i)$, which equals the distance $C_1^1 y_1^K$, which is exactly equal to the extent to which next period's income, y_1^K, exceeds next period's planned consumption, C_1^1.

From this analysis one can deduce that, given this type of household behaviour, current household consumption plans depend not only on current income but also on the future expected income stream, the market rate of interest at which this income stream is discounted and the time preference of the consumer. A further important deduction is that the decision to save is inherently linked with the consumption decision, since the decision to save out of current income is a decision to postpone consumption, whereas dissaving involves consuming in the present at the expense of future consumption. The act of saving in the current period is the execution of a decision to postpone consumption; it does not indicate anything about the household's proposed timing of future consumption. Once we consider a world of uncertainty, the household is no longer sure of the exact timing or volume of its future income stream. Such uncertainty extends to the timing and volume of the future consumption stream. Saving then serves as a means of accumulating assets that will allow the household to release its consumption plans from closely following the time profile of income.

At the aggregate level, consumption will be affected by the distribution of households with respect to time preference and also with respect to income if the marginal propensity to consume out of disposable income differs among households.

12.4 The permanent income hypothesis

The permanent income hypothesis (PIH) of Milton Friedman [4] is based explicitly on the theory of intertemporal choice discussed in section 12.3. On the assumption that consumers take account of future income and future consumption possibilities when planning current consumption, changes in current income, which Friedman terms *measured income*, will only affect current consumption by way of resulting changes in wealth. In a world of certainty, permanent income is the return on the household's human and non-human wealth. The household's wealth is the present value of the future flow of income, which is expected by the household to be variable from year to year. The household's wealth is given by equation 12.4:

$$W = \sum_{t=1}^{N} \frac{Y_t}{(1+i)^t} \quad \text{wealth constraint} \tag{12.4}$$

where W is wealth, Y_t is income year t and i is the rate of interest.

The same level of wealth could be attained by receiving a constant annual annuity, A. Then

$$W = \sum_{t=1}^{N} \frac{Y_t}{(1+i)^t} = \sum_{t=1}^{N} \frac{A}{(1+i)^t} \tag{12.9}$$

The annuity A is that constant annual sum which, if paid out over each of the future years of the actual expected income stream, would have the same present value as that income stream. The annuity A is termed 'permanent income'. It is directly related to wealth, as can be shown by manipulating equation 12.9:

$$W = \frac{A}{i}\left[1 - \left(\frac{1}{1+i}\right)^N\right] \tag{12.9a}$$

Therefore

$$A = iW\left[1 - \left(\frac{1}{1+i}\right)^N\right]^{-1} \tag{12.10}$$

$$\lim_{N \to \infty} A = iW \tag{12.11}$$

Assuming an infinite time horizon, permanent income, A, is the stock of wealth multiplied by the interest rate, or annual return on wealth. Thus permanent income is the amount that can be consumed annually while leaving the stock of wealth intact.

Once uncertainty is introduced into the analysis, both the household future income stream and future interest rate depend on the household's expectations, and the concept of permanent income is less clearly defined. We think of it as that part of a household's measured income which is regarded as stable and as reflecting the household's income expectations. The difference between measured and permanent income, which may be positive or negative, is called by Friedman *transitory* income and occurs due to temporary and unanticipated changes in current income:

$$y_m = y_p + y_T \tag{12.12}$$

where y_m is measured income, y_p is permanent income, y_T is transitory income.

Friedman assumes that consumption, defined to mean the act of consuming the services of goods, is planned on the basis of permanent income and that the relationship between the two variables is proportional, i.e.

$$C = ky_p \tag{12.13}$$

The coefficient of proportionality, k, which is the 'true' underlying MPC and APC, is assumed to depend on those factors which affect the household's saving decision. These factors are household preferences, the nature of the uncertainties facing the household (an example of which is the extent of state welfare provisions), the rate of interest and the ratio of human to non-human wealth. Human wealth is the present value of future income that people expect to earn by using their personal skills and labour. Non-human wealth is the present value of income obtained from financial and capital assets. The particular uncertainties attached to labour income make it more difficult to borrow using human rather than non-human wealth as security. Thus the higher the ratio of human to non-human wealth, the greater is the incentive to save and acquire non-human wealth.

Since the permanent and transitory components of income are unobservable, the proportionality hypothesis cannot be refuted by an appeal to the facts unless the model is further specified. It is therefore assumed that zero correlations hold between y_p and y_T, and y_T and C. The last assumption means any positive transitory income is not spent on consumption but is saved. Saving is defined to include investment in consumer durables as well as in financial assets and capital goods. Thus, consumption refers purely to the using up of goods by enjoying their services. *These assumptions mean that any changes in measured income will only affect current consumption if they cause the household to alter its estimate of permanent income.*

Cross-section analysis

Friedman's proportionality hypothesis, $C = ky_p$, applies both to aggregate time-series and household consumption functions. We shall first discuss how the PIH reconciles the constancy of the long-run aggregate APC with the decline of the cross-section APC with household income. Cross-section studies regress measured household consumption on to measured household income using the following type of regression equation:

$$C = a + by_m \tag{12.14}$$

where b is an estimate of the cross-section MPC. According to the PIH, changes in consumption are due only to changes in permanent income, hence consumption will only change in response to changes in measured income to the extent that previously unanticipated changes in measured income are regarded as permanent and cause estimates of permanent income to be revised. Therefore, the measured MPC (that is, the change in current consumption due to a change in measured income) will be smaller than the 'true' MPC, k, which is the change in consumption due to a change in permanent income. This is because movements in measured income are greater than the corresponding movements in permanent income, while the changes in consumption are due to changes in permanent income. Since the measured MPC is $b = \Delta C/\Delta y_m$ while $k = \Delta C/\Delta y_p$ and $\Delta y_m > \Delta y_p$, b is biased downwards in relation to the 'true' MPC, k. (For a proof of this see Friedman [4] pp. 31–7.)

Time-series analysis

The PIH can also be used to reconcile the time-series observations on short- and long-run consumption functions over the trade cycle. Transitory income will be negative in the recession and positive at the peak, thus the higher APCs recorded in the depression years of the 1930s relative to the secular APC for the USA can be explained by relating consumption in that period to a level of permanent income which was larger than measured income. Similarly, the lower APCs of the Second World War years can be explained in terms of positive transitory income and negative transitory consumption then existing.

The shorter the time period over which data are taken, the greater one would expect to be the variability in aggregate measured income attributable to transitory income, and thus the greater the downward bias found in estimates of the MPC obtained by regressing measured consumption on measured income. The tendency for the estimated MPC to be smaller the shorter the time period of the regression is confirmed by an examination of the US data (Friedman [4] p. 16) and is consistent with the results obtained for post-war UK data (Friedman [4] p. 12).

One difficulty with testing the PIH is that permanent income is unobservable: it depends on people's expectations of their future income. Hence any testable form of the PIH has to contain some process whereby expectations are generated. Friedman [4] assumed that expectations of future income are formed on the basis of current and past levels of income. He used the *adaptive expectations hypothesis*, which assumes that estimates of the expected variable (permanent income in this case) are revised when differences are observed between the expectations that were held about the variable and the actual value that the variable takes. Hence

$$y_{pt} - y_{pt-1} = \lambda(y_t - y_{pt-1}) \tag{12.15}$$

Equation 12.15 shows that estimates of permanent income are changed when a discrepancy occurs between measured income, y_t, and the permanent income which was expected in the previous period to exist in the present period, y_{pt-1}. The coefficient of adjustment, λ, lies between 0 and 1, since the proportion of the difference between permanent and measured income which is due to transitory income will not cause ideas about permanent income to be adjusted.

Rearranging equation 12.15 we obtain

$$y_{pt} = (1 - \lambda)y_{pt-1} + \lambda y_t \tag{12.16}$$

If we iterate equation 12.16 backwards in time, we obtain current permanent income as a distributed function of past values of measured income. This type of equation is known as a *distributed lag function*:

$$y_{pt-1} = (1 - \lambda)y_{pt-2} + \lambda y_{t-1} \qquad (12.16\text{i})$$
$$y_{pt-2} = (1 - \lambda)y_{pt-3} + \lambda y_{t-2} \qquad (12.16\text{ii})$$
$$\vdots \qquad \vdots \qquad \vdots$$
$$y_{pt-N} = (1 - \lambda)y_{pt-N-1} + \lambda y_{t-N} \qquad (12.16n)$$

Substitute equation 12.16i into equation 12.16 to obtain

$$y_{pt} = (1 - \lambda)[(1 - \lambda)y_{pt-2} + \lambda y_{t-1}] + \lambda y_t \qquad (12.17)$$

Then substitute 12.16ii into 12.17 to obtain

$$y_{pt} = (1 - \lambda)^2[(1 - \lambda)y_{pt-3} + \lambda y_{t-2}] + \lambda(1 - \lambda)y_{t-1} + \lambda y_t \qquad (12.18)$$

The process is repeated by successively substituting equation $12.16n$ into $12.16n - 1$ and so on until we obtain

$$y_{pt} = (1 - \lambda)^{N+1}y_{pt-N-1} + \lambda \sum_{n=0}^{N} (1 - \lambda)^n y_{t-n} \qquad (12.19)$$

As $N \to \infty$, $(1 - \lambda)^N \to 0$, and the term $(1 - \lambda)^{N+1}y_{pt-N-1}$ approaches zero and drops out of equation 12.19.

Equation 12.19 is an example of a geometrically declining distributed lag function since the weight $(1 - \lambda)^n$ gets smaller with time as n gets larger. This means that past income has less influence on permanent income as time is extended backwards.

Using Friedman's proportionality hypothesis

$$C_t = ky_{pt}. \qquad (12.13)$$

Substituting equation 12.19 into equation 12.13 we obtain

$$C_t = k\lambda \sum_{n=0}^{\infty} (1 - \lambda)^n y_{t-n} \qquad (12.20)$$

A distributed lag function, such as equation 12.20, presents estimating problems because it contains many past values of the dependent variable which will be related to each other. The Koyck [5] transformation is a well-known method of simplifying geometrically declining distributed lag functions. This is done by first lagging equation 12.20 by one period, i.e.

$$C_{t-1} = k\lambda \sum_{n=0}^{\infty} (1 - \lambda)^n y_{t-n-1}. \qquad (12.21)$$

Equation 12.21 is then multiplied by $1 - \lambda$ to give

$$(1 - \lambda)C_{t-1} = k\lambda \sum_{n=0}^{\infty} (1 - \lambda)^{n+1} y_{t-n-1} \qquad (12.22)$$

Equation 12.22 is subtracted from equation 12.20:

$$C_t = k\lambda[y_t + (1 - \lambda)y_{t-1} + (1 - \lambda)^2 y_{t-2} + \ldots + (1 - \lambda)^N y_{t-N}] \qquad (12.20)$$

$$(1 - \lambda)C_{t-1} = k\lambda[(1 - \lambda)y_{t-1} + (1 - \lambda)^2 y_{t-2} + \ldots + (1 - \lambda)^N y_{t-N}] \quad (12.22)$$

$$C_t - (1 - \lambda)C_{t-1} = k\lambda y_t \quad (12.23)$$

$$C_t = k\lambda y_t + (1 - \lambda)C_{t-1} \quad (12.24)$$

The dependent variable, C_t, is a function of the independent variable and of itself lagged one period. The short-run marginal propensity to consume is obtained by differentiating consumption with respect to current income. Hence

$$\text{short-run MPC} = dC_t/dy_t = k\lambda$$

In the long run consumption will be fully adjusted to permanent income, and in static equilibrium will maintain the same value from one period to another. This condition gives

$$C_t = C_{t-1} = C \quad (12.25)$$

Substituting equation 12.25 into 12.24 we obtain the long-run consumption function with the long-run MPC equal to k, i.e.

$$C = ky_p \quad (12.13)$$

Since λ is less than 1.0, the short-run MPC is smaller than the long-run MPC. The size of the short-run MPC relative to the long-run MPC depends on the speed with which permanent income, and hence consumption, adjusts to a change in current income. The lower the value of λ, the longer it takes permanent income to adjust to a change in current income and hence the smaller is the short-run MPC.

Rational expectations

Although it has been extensively employed in empirical work, the adaptive expectations hypothesis has recently come under increasing attack because it assumes that economic agents do not use all the information available to them when forming expectations (e.g. Lucas [6]). Under adaptive expectations economic agents only consider the past values of the variable about which they are forming expectations. A rational economic agent would use information about the expected values of the determinants of the variable in question. Failure to use all the available information when forming expectations would result in errors between the actual outcome and the prediction which could have been avoided. If expectations are continually formed by looking only at past values of the variable, then a predictable or systematic error will be repeatedly made and this could be detected by looking at the behaviour of the determinants of the variable about which expectations are being formed. But if agents use all the available information in forming expectations, then the error between the expectations and the outcome will be unsystematic. It will have no detectable pattern and so will be a random, independent term. If expectations are based on all the available information, then they are said to be rational. In each time period the actual value of a variable, say income, will equal its expected value formed in the previous period plus an independent random error term. Hence

$$y_t = E_{t-1}(y_t) + u_t \tag{12.26}$$

where

y_t = actual income in period t
$E_{t-1}(y_t)$ = expectations of income in period t formed in period $t - 1$
u_t = random error term which is independent of y and of its own past values (that is, $E(u_t, y_t) = E(u_t, u_{t-i}) = 0$ for all $i \neq 0$)

The assumption of rational expectations will produce a different value for permanent income than will adaptive expectations if some future change in disposable income, such as that arising from a foreseeable tax change, is known. By assuming adaptive expectations that only look backwards, the known future change in disposable income is ignored in estimating permanent income. Given that current consumption depends on permanent income, then if adaptive expectations are assumed when expectations are in fact rational and some future change in income is known, consumption will be poorly predicted.

The use of rational expectations in determining permanent income implies that current consumption is fully explained in a regression equation by current income and consumption lagged one period:

$$C_t = b_1 y_t + b_2 C_{t-1} + u_t \tag{12.24a}$$

The addition of further lagged variables should not improve the fit of the estimated consumption function. This implication arises because, given rational expectations, consumption in the previous period was based on all the then available information. Additional lagged variables will contain no further information. New information, coming available in the current period, is contained in current income and the disturbance term.

Adaptive expectations and the Koyck transformation produce the same form of the regression equation (12.24) as that implied by rational expectations. However, the interpretation of the coefficients is different: b_2 ($1 - \lambda$ in equation 12.24) is not to be interpreted as an adjustment lag as under adaptive expectations.

12.5 The life-cycle hypothesis

The life-cycle hypothesis (LCH) developed by Ando, Brumberg and Modigliani (see [7]–[9] is, like the PIH, based on household utility maximising behaviour. Given that the household has a known life span and intends to leave no legacies, and also given certainty, the motive for saving is to rearrange lifetime consumption in relation to the expected future income stream. The LCH stresses the accumulation of non-human wealth as the means of achieving this aim. Uncertainty provides an additional, related motive of saving, that of protecting consumption plans from the effects of unexpected falls in real income.

The typical time profile of a lifetime income stream is one that rises in the early working years, reaches a plateau in middle years and is followed by a sudden decline upon retirement. To even out the time profile of lifetime consumption a typical household will dissave or save very little when young, save in the middle years and dissave upon retirement.

It is assumed that the household's current consumption (defined as non-durable consumption plus the rental value of consumer durables) is proportional to its total resources, the factor of proportionality depending on the interest rate used to discount future income, tastes and age of household. Total resources are subdivided into current income, y_t, the present value of future income from human sources, y^E, and accumulated assets, A_{t-1}, brought forward from the previous period. Total resources are the same as Friedman's present value of all future income expected from human and non-human sources, which forms the basis for estimating permanent income.

The difference between the LCH and PIH is one of emphasis, in that the LCH is concerned explicitly with the role of asset accumulation and the effect of age on household consumption. The LCH is similar to the PIH, in that it assumes that any change in total resources, due to any of the three components, will cause a proportional change in planned consumption in all future periods. The APC for a given age group is therefore deduced to be the same for all levels of income, to fall with middle age and rise again upon retirement. The middle years are a period when income is relatively high, consumer durables have been acquired and there is a need to accumulate assets with which to finance consumption upon retirement.

The result of a change in current income on consumption depends on the effect of that change upon the household's total resources. If the change is regarded as only temporary, it will have very little effect on current consumption. If the change is considered permanent it will cause expectations of income to be revised in the same direction. The younger is the household, the more its current consumption will be affected by a change in current income regarded as permanent, since there is a longer period over which the changed level of expected income will be discounted and hence a larger impact on total resources.

The consumption function for each age group is assumed to be

$$C_t^T = k^T(V_t^T) \tag{12.27}$$

where V_t is the total resources at time t and T indicates the age group to which the function applies. And

$$V_t^T = f(y_t^T, y^{TE}, A_{t-1}^T) \tag{12.28}$$

where y_t is the current income, y^E is the present value of future expected labour income, and A_{t-1} are assets. Making equation 12.28 linear and substituting into equation 12.27 we obtain

$$C_t^T = \alpha_1^T y_t^T + \alpha_2^T y^{TE} + \alpha_3^T A_{t-1}^T \tag{12.29}$$

Aggregate consumption will be a weighted average (the weight W^T attached to each C_0^T being the proportion of households in age group T) of the various age groups' consumption levels. If the economy were stationary (income and population constant over time) and certainty allowed people to fulfil their plans of consuming all their assets before death, the net saving of the working population would be exactly offset by the dissaving of the retired, given that the age structure of the population was constant. Goods and services not consumed in the current period by the savers would be transferred for consumption to the retired, who would finance this by selling their assets to the savers. Net saving would be zero, as would be net investment in a stationary economy. If national output is growing over time and the age structure of the population is constant, the savings of the working population would also be growing, since savings are a constant proportion of income. If the retired are living off fixed-interest securities, they are not sharing in the growth of national income and their dissaving is less than the saving of the working population. Net aggregate saving is positive and provides the resources needed for positive net investment, which is required to sustain growth.

The aggregate consumption function is a weighted average of equation 12.29 and is written

$$C_t = a_1 y_t + a_2 y^E + a_3 A_{t-1} \tag{12.30}$$

The aggregate APC is

$$\frac{C_t}{y_t} = a_1 + a_2 \frac{y^E}{y_t} + a_3 \frac{A_{t-1}}{y_t} \tag{12.31}$$

and is constant if, over time, future income is proportional to current income (steady growth or a stationary economy), and the net wealth–income ratio remains constant. Equation 12.31 can be simplified by assuming expected income is a function of current income, i.e.

$$y^E = \beta y_t$$

$$\begin{aligned} C_t &= (a_1 + \beta a_2) y_t + a_3 A_{t-1} \\ &= \alpha y_t + a_3 A_{t-1} \end{aligned} \tag{12.33}$$

where $\alpha = a_1 + \beta a_2$.

Cross-section analysis

The LCH reconciles the non-proportional consumption function produced by budget studies with the constancy of the long-run aggregate APC in a manner very similar to that of the PIH. Cross-section regression of current consumption on current income will produce non-proportional consumption functions because the higher-income households contain a larger proportion of people who have recently experienced an increase in income than do the lower-income households. To the extent that such increases are regarded as temporary there will be no corresponding increase in consumption and the household's observed APC will be lower than for a low-income household experiencing a temporary decrease in income.

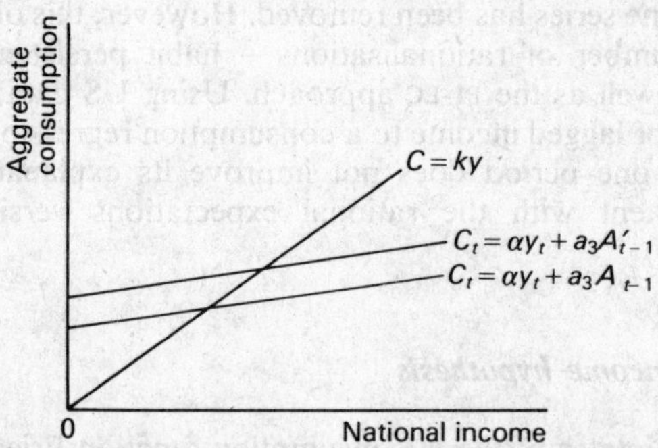

FIGURE 12.4 *The life-cycle hypothesis: the time-series consumption function*

Time-series analysis

The LCH also provides a reconciliation of the evidence on short-run and long-run consumption functions. The short-run consumption function, given by equation 12.33 is non-proportional, the intercept term being given by a_3A_{t-1}. As net wealth increases in a growing economy, so the short-run consumption function shifts up over time, as shown in Figure 12.4.

Cyclical variations in the APC are explained in the following way. In a recession, although current income falls, expected income is not much affected and assets can be used to sustain consumption; thus the APC rises. In the recovery the savings ratio rises as assets are built up to the level required to match the growth trend of income.

PIH and LCH: a summary

The PIH and LCH are closely related. Both are based explicitly on intertemporal utility-maximising behaviour by households. Although both hypotheses also assume that the underlying relationship between household consumption and permanent income is proportional, this particular assumption is not crucial to the validity of the basic approach. This basic approach treats the relationship between consumption, asset accumulation and income as the outcome of household planning over a long time horizon. This explains why current income is a poor predictor of current consumption and suggests that a measure of wealth or of long-term income will be a much better predictor. To the extent that past values of wealth or income determine current wealth or permanent income, then lagged values of wealth and/or income should be included in estimated consumption functions.

12.6 Empirical evidence on aggregate consumption

The most consistent result is that lagged consumption is a significant explanatory variable in consumption-function regression equations even when the trend in the time series has been removed. However, this observation is consistent with a number of rationalisations – habit persistence, emulation of social peers – as well as the PI–LC approach. Using US data, Hall [10] claims that the addition of lagged income to a consumption regression containing consumption lagged one period does not improve its explanatory power. This finding is consistent with the rational expectations version of the PI–LC hypotheses.

The permanent income hypothesis

In his original estimates of the PI consumption function Friedman [4] found a long-run MPC of about 0.9 for the USA. He estimated the adjustment coefficient, λ, for the impact of current income on permanent income to be 0.33, which, given a long-run MPC (k) of 0.9, gives a short-run MPC (λk) of around 0.3. According to the PIH, the greater the variability in a household's measured income, the less it will revise its estimate of its permanent income when its current income changes. If permanent income is not much affected by changes in current income, then the household's measured APC and MPC will be low. A test of the PIH is therefore to see whether households with variable incomes, such as farmers, have lower measured APCs and MPCs than households with stable incomes. Friedman [4] and others have reported that this is the case.

Many more studies on the PIH have been undertaken since Friedman's. On the whole they support the general approach, namely that consumption is determined by some stable long-term component of income. There is much less confirmation of Friedman's other assumptions: proportionality, and the absence of any effect of transitory income on consumption. Although the latter assumption, in its original form, has been frequently refuted, a good number of studies have confirmed a modified version of it. A typical result is that of Dolde [11]. The short-run MPC for consumer non-durable expenditure out of transitory income is positive but smaller than that out of permanent income. For consumer durable expenditure the short-run MPC for transitory income is higher than for permanent income. Quite a number of cross-section studies (for example, Bhalla [12]) have reported that the savings ratio rises with permanent income and recent time-series data also cast doubt on the long-run constancy of the APC.

The life-cycle hypothesis

Ando and Modigliani [8] estimated α in equation 12.33 to be in the region of 0.52–0.60. The estimated MPC rises to around 0.68–0.71 when another variable is added, which extends the expectations hypothesis to make y^E depend upon the proportion of the labour force employed. The coefficient on wealth, a_3, is estimated to be in the region 0.072–0.1. One would expect a LC consumption function to exhibit a smaller MPC than a PI version because the former also includes a wealth variable whereas in the latter the wealth effect is incorporated into permanent income. A good number of studies have supported the LCH by finding wealth, particularly liquid assets, to be a significant determinant of consumption. Cross-section data, such as those cited by Ando and Modigliani, also support the LC hypothesis regarding the behaviour of the savings–income ratio in relation to household age.

Recent UK evidence

In a thorough study of UK quarterly aggregate consumption from 1958 to 1976 Davidson *et al.* [3] report the following equation as providing the best functional form for a consumption regression (the variables are in natural logs and are in real terms):

$$\begin{aligned}\Delta_4 C_t = {} & \underset{(0.04)}{0.49}\,\Delta_4 \ln y_t - \underset{(0.05)}{0.17}\,\Delta_1\Delta_4 \ln y_t \\ & -\underset{(0.01)}{0.06}\ln(C/y)_{t-4} + \underset{(0.004)}{0.01}\ln \Delta_4 D_t^0 \qquad (12.34)\\ R^2 = {} & 0.71,\ \text{SE} = 0.0067\end{aligned}$$

where

$\Delta_4 C_t$ = difference between consumption[1] in *i*th quarter of year t and the *i*th quarter of year $t-1$

$\Delta_4 y_t$ = four-quarter difference in personal disposable income

$\Delta_1\Delta_4 y_t = \Delta_4 y_t - \Delta_4 y_{t-1}$

$\Delta_4 D_t^0$ = dummy variable for 1968(II) when future indirect tax increases were known

The interpretation of this equation is that consumers plan to spend in each quarter of the year the same as they spent in the equivalent quarter of the previous year, modified by a proportion of the annual change in income ($0.49\,\Delta_4 \ln y_t$) and by whether that change is a decrease or an increase in income ($-0.17\Delta_1\Delta_4 \ln y_t$). The negative sign on this last term means that households attempt to retain the previous consumption level and so temporarily increase their savings ratio when income rises. In addition, consumption is adjusted in line with a long-run proportional relationship between consumption and income, $C = ky$. This effect is captured in the $\ln(C/y)_{t-4}$ term. k, the long-run APC and MPC, will vary with the rate of growth of income. In a stationary economy there is no net investment and zero aggregate saving. k is thus 1.0. Hence in the long run the $\ln(C/y)$ term will be zero since $\ln 1 = 0$. However, if the economy is growing at an equilibrium growth rate, aggregate saving must be positive and k must be less than 1.0. In this case $\ln k$ will be negative as k is a positive fraction and the whole term $-\ln k$ exerts a positive influence on consumption. The behaviour of k in relation to the growth rate of the economy is consistent with the LCH.

[1] Consumption is defined to be expenditure on non-durables and services.

However, the short-run MPC is lower than the long-run one. The first-quarter impact of a 1 per cent increase in income is to raise consumption by 0.32 per cent (0.32 = 0.49 – 0.17) since the initial temporary impact of an increase in income is to lower the APC. This estimate of the short-run response of consumption to a change in current income is very similar to that of Friedman reported on page 215. After one quarter the temporary fall in the APC has been reversed so that the consumption response rises to 0.49 per cent. The model is constrained to have a proportional long-run income–consumption relationship so that there is ultimately a 1 per cent increase in consumption following a 1 per cent increase in income.[1]

The impact of inflation

The secular decline in the APC noted for the United Kingdom on page 209 has occurred in most Western countries. In the 1970s a number of aggregate economic relationships, including consumption, underwent marked parameter shifts. The APC fell from around 0.91 in the early 1970s to 0.88 in 1973 and continued to fall throughout the decade. This behaviour has been attributed to inflation. Several explanations of why inflation should increase the savings ratio have been put forward. The main ones are as follows:

1. Inflation increases uncertainty about future real incomes and hence induces people to accumulate more financial assets in order to protect future consumption levels.
2. Inflation erodes the real value of liquid assets. Households save more in order to rebuild their real liquid asset stocks. Townend [14] reports that real liquid assets are a significant, though minor, determinant of non-durables' consumption since 1965 and offer the best explanation of the rise in the savings ratio. Davidson *et al.* [13], however, reject the liquid assets explanation in favour of the next one.
3. Inflation causes individuals to misperceive relative prices. An individual only observes relatively few prices in, say, a week, and is unaware of what the current rate of inflation is, particularly when inflation is accelerating. Therefore consumers interpret a rise in the prices of the goods they purchase as an increase in relative prices when such an increase is in fact a general one. Since prices are regarded as having risen in relative terms, consumer expenditure is cut back and the savings ratio therefore rises.

Deaton [15] finds this last point a satisfactory explanation for the UK and US savings ratios using data from the mid-1950s up to 1974. Inflation is found to be a significant determinant of the savings ratio even in the first half of the period when inflation was quite low. Deaton's results are supported by Davidson *et al.* They find that a closer fit between actual and predicted consumption, for the twenty quarters beyond the period over which the data used to estimate the regression coefficients were sampled, is obtained if equation

[1]If $C = ky$, then $dC/dy = k$, $y/C = 1$.

12.34 is extended to include inflation. The best explanation for consumption is provided by equation 12.35 (again in logs):

$$\Delta_4 C_t = \underset{(0.04)}{0.47}\ \Delta_4 \ln y_t - \underset{(0.05)}{0.21}\ \Delta_1\Delta_4 \ln y_t - \underset{(0.02)}{0.10}\ \ln(C/y)_{t-4}$$

$$+ \underset{(0.003)}{0.01} \ln \Delta_4 D_t^0 - \underset{(0.07)}{0.13}\ \Delta_4 \ln P_t - \underset{(0.15)}{0.28}\ \Delta_1\Delta_4 \ln P_t \qquad (12.35)$$

$$R^2 = 0.77, \ \text{SE} = 0.0061$$

where

$\Delta_4 P_t$ = four-quarter measure of inflation

$\Delta_1\Delta_4 P_t$ = change in $\Delta_4 P_t$: that is, an acceleration-of-inflation term

The parameters of equation 12.35 are stable throughout the estimation period and it provides a good out-of-sample forecast of consumption. Inflation thus affects the long-run MPC. Davidson *et al.* estimated that k in $C = kY$ is 0.84, given a rate of growth of income of 0.02 and a rate of inflation of 0.05. If inflation rises to 0.15, the estimate of k falls to 0.74.

In general one can conclude that the empirical evidence reveals that consumption is based on a long-term view of income and that inflation seems to lower the APC. By itself a change in current income changes current consumption by about one-third of the income change. Variables other than current income are required in order to predict short-run changes in consumption.

While we may have a reasonably good idea of the long-run determinants of consumption, predicting consumption on a quarterly basis is far more problematic and still poses problems for short-run econometric forecasting models.

12.7 Consumption theory: policy implications

The application of Keynesian demand-management policies requires a reasonable knowledge of the determinants of short-run consumption. As we have seen, the short-run MPC is relatively small and the relationship between current consumption and current income, even on an annual basis, is quite erratic, while the quantitative effects of determinants other than income is still an unresolved issue.

There is still disagreement concerning the channels through which macroeconomic policy affects consumption expenditure. The traditional Keynesian view is that disposable income is the predominant channel in this transmission mechanism, while changes in the money supply and interest rates have very little influence. This leaves direct and indirect tax changes (including subsidies) as the principal means by which the government can regulate consumption. However, the PIH suggests a weaker influence for fiscal policy since tax changes can only affect consumption if they alter permanent income. Thus temporary tax changes will have no impact on consumption because they only affect transitory income. If expectations are formed rationally, then any tax changes which can be anticipated by households have already been taken account of in their estimates of permanent income. As these will not be revised when the anticipated tax changes occur, then only unanticipated tax changes, which are regarded as permanent, will affect consumption.

However, the PIH does predict that a change in transitory income will be entirely absorbed by household saving, which includes purchases of consumer durables. This enables tax changes to affect a sub-component of aggregate consumption expenditure. Opponents of the PIH maintain that households cannot borrow extensively on the expectation of uncertain future income. They therefore face a binding liquidity constraint which enforces a reasonably close correspondence between current consumption and current income.

The PI–LC hypotheses give monetary policy a greater role in determining aggregate consumption than does the traditional Keynesian approach with its emphasis on current disposable income. This difference arises because the PI–LC hypotheses treat consumption as determined by wealth or its permanent income equivalent. The monetarist view of the transmission mechanism is that monetary policy affects aggregate demand by causing portfolio adjustment. Any change in either total private-sector net wealth or in its composition will result in portfolio disequilibrium. Asset-holders will adjust back to equilibrium by shifting between the various types of financial and real assets (goods). The government can increase the total amount of private-sector wealth by increasing the stock of government bonds or money. Wealth will also increase if the ratio of money to bonds is increased, causing interest rates to fall. This, in turn, will increase the present value of future expected human income and raise the prices of financial assets, including equity. Therefore, total wealth will rise (see equations 12.9 and 12.10). In the monetarist transmission mechanism the effect of a change in the stock of money is thus both more direct, because consumption depends on wealth, and more pervasive because portfolio adjustment occurs across the whole range of financial assets and goods.

In contrast the traditional Keynesian transmission mechanism is indirect as it is restricted to interest-rate changes only. In addition, the consumption component of aggregate demand is regarded as unresponsive to interest-rate changes. Keynesians, especially in Britain, typically consider that monetary policy only affects consumption by changing the availability of credit, whereas its cost has little effect. However, these differences should not be exaggerated, particularly with respect to post-1960 developments. Keynesian economists such as Tobin [16] have been in the forefront of developing a general-equilibrium portfolio approach to financial analysis, and more recent Keynesian econometric models, particularly the US ones, do now incorporate a relatively comprehensive monetary transmission mechanism.

12.8 The consumption function in macro models

So far in this book when constructing a complete macroeconomic model we have assumed a simple, absolute income–consumption function. This can be a useful simplification if the main purpose of the model is to emphasise those features which are of fundamental importance to a particular theoretical approach. For instance, in a Keynesian model the absolute income–consumption function is an important ingredient because it is a simple way of obtaining a multiplier process.

Consumption functions in which the major determinant is the flow variable, income, are much favoured by Keynesians. Monetarists often prefer a stock-adjustment approach whereby consumption depends on wealth and the rates of return on different types of assets. However, the two approaches can be made equivalent, as the PI–LC hypotheses show.

In economic models with a more immediate policy application, a simple consumption function is inadeqaute since the effects of adjustment lags are an important consideration. A more complex function in which consumption depends in a specific way on the current and lagged values of its determinants is needed. This applies equally to the other functional relationships included in such models.

The inclusion of lagged relationships makes an economic model dynamic. The model can trace out a time path of adjustment for the endogenous variables. It is no longer restricted to comparative-static analysis alone, as is the *ISLM* model of Chapters 3 and 4 in which all variables are dated in current time. The quantitative size of the lags relating to each period of time will determine the adjustment path followed by the endogenous variables. For example, the lower the value of λ, which relates changes in current income to consequent changes in permanent income, the slower will be the speed of adjustment of national output following some disturbance to current output. Thus the lag structure of consumption (and the other functions) needs to be known with reasonable accuracy if the economy is to be regulated along Keynesian lines.

References

[1] S. Kuznets, *The National Product since 1869* (New York: National Bureau of Economic Research, 1946).

[2] I. Fisher, *The Rate of Interest* (London: Macmillan, 1907).

[3] I. Fisher, *The Theory of Interest* (London: Macmillan, 1930).

[4] M. Friedman, *A Theory of the Consumption Function* (Princeton University Press, 1957).

[5] K. M. Koyck, *Distributed Lags and Investment Analysis* (Amsterdam: North-Holland, 1954).

[6] R. E. Lucas, 'Econometric Policy Evaluation: a Critique', in K. Brunner and A. Meltzer (eds), *The Phillips Curve and Labour Markets*, Carnegie–Rochester Conference Series on Public Policy (1976).

[7] F. Modigliani and R. Brumberg, 'Utility Analysis and the Consumption Function: an Interpretation of Cross Section Data', in K. Kurihara (ed.), *Post-Keynesian Economics* (London: Allen & Unwin, 1955).

[8] A. Ando and F. Modigliani, 'Tests of the Life Cycle Hypothesis of Savings: Comments and Suggestions', *Bulletin of the Oxford University Institute of Statistics*, 19 (1957).

[9] A. Ando and F. Modigliani, 'The Life Cycle Hypothesis of Saving: Aggregate Implications and Taste', *American Economic Review*, 53, 1 (1963).

[10] R. E. Hall, 'Stochastic Implications of the Life Cycle–Permanent Income Hypothesis: Theory and Evidence', *Journal of Political Economy*, 86, 6 (December 1978).

[11] W. Dolde, 'Issues and Models in Empirical Research on Aggregate Consumer Expenditure', in K. Brunner and A. Meltzer (eds), *On the State of Macroeconomics*, Carnegie–Rochester Conference Series on Public Policy (Amsterdam: North-Holland, 1980).

[12] S. S. Bhalla, 'The Measurement of Permanent Income and its Application to Savings Behaviour', *Journal of Political Economy*, 88, 4 (August 1980).

[13] J. Davidson, D. Hendry, F. Srba and S. Yeo, 'Econometric Modelling of the Aggregate Time-Series Relationship between Consumers' Expenditure and Income in the United Kingdom', *Economic Journal*, 88 (December 1978).

[14] J. Townend, 'The Personal Saving Ratio', *Bank of England Quarterly Bulletin*, 16, 1 (March 1976).

[15] A. Deaton, 'Involuntary Saving through Unanticipated Inflation', *American Economic Review*, 67, 5 (December 1977).

[16] J. Tobin, 'A General Equilibrium Approach to Monetary Theory', *Journal of Money, Credit and Banking*, 1, 1 (1969).

13 Investment

Investment refers to the accumulation over time by firms of real capital goods (that is, those which will yield a future flow of services). Real capital goods can be subdivided into two types. *Fixed capital* is such items as plant, machinery, buildings and transport infrastructures which keep their particular physical form throughout their working life. *Working capital* consists of stocks of raw materials, manufactured inputs and final goods awaiting distribution. Each unit of working capital changes its form as it passes through the production process to the point of final consumption. In this chapter we shall be mainly concerned with the determinants of investment in fixed capital goods, alternatively referred to as *fixed capital formation*.

Although investment is a smaller component of aggregate demand than is consumption, it is more volatile and so is important in Keynesian analysis as a source of short-term changes in aggregate demand.

Investment is also a crucial variable on the supply side of the economy as it is the means by which changes in the real capital stock are brought about. The production function specifies how the services yielded by the capital stock are combined with labour to produce a flow of output. The essential feature of capital is that its creation requires the sacrifice of labour and other resources which could alternatively be used for present consumption. Hence the present consumption forgone in order to produce more capital goods is the opportunity cost of those capital goods. The incentive to incur this opportunity cost is the extra future consumption goods which can be produced from using the services of the additional capital goods. The choice of the size of the stock of capital is thus an intertemporal choice problem as it involves trading off present consumption for future consumption.

An economy can only produce additional output over time by acquiring greater quantities of factors of production, or (through technical progress) increasing the amount of output a given combination of factors can produce, or by a combination of both methods. The accumulation of capital is therefore a vital element in economic growth. This has two aspects: with a positive rate of return on capital and a given state of technical knowledge, the acquisition of capital enables the economy to produce more goods and services in the future;

when technical progress occurs, and is embodied in particular types of capital equipment, the acquisition of new capital is essential to the utilisation of such technical progress.

From the theoretical standpoint, a stationary economy is one in which technical progress is absent and the capital stock is constant. As capital is used up in the production of goods and services, it must be replaced by new equipment. Thus, in a stationary economy, the amount of replacement investment is identical to the amount by which the capital stock depreciates. In such an economy in long-run equilibrium all net national output will consist of consumption and net savings will be zero.

If the capital stock grows larger over time, the increase in capital stock per period of time is known as *net investment*. *Gross investment* is then made up of *replacement investment* and *net investment*. If the capital stock declines over time, disinvestment occurs since depreciation exceeds replacement. By saving, the community as a whole is releasing from present consumption resources which can be converted into capital goods, and hence into additional future consumption. Thus the process of capital accumulation, or net investment, involves net savings in aggregate by members of the community.[1] This can occur via the market mechanism through which individuals' saving and investment decisions interact or by government allocation of resources to capital accumulation.

13.1 Capital theory and the theory of the firm

In order to investigate the determinants of investment we need to study investment in the context of the firm's overall objectives, which are achieved by an interrelated set of decisions on how much output to produce, when to produce it and what factors of production to use. As in Chapter 5, where we derived a firm's demand for labour, we start by specifying a production function which relates net output to the quantity of inputs used and the state of technical knowledge:

$$y = f(L, K, T) \tag{13.1}$$

We still assume the state of technology, T, to be unchanged, but K, the capital stock, is now a choice variable. K appears as a *stock* variable and L, labour, as a *flow* variable because firms hire labour services, while to obtain capital services firms typically pay an initial lump sum for capital goods which will yield services over a number of time periods. Capital goods can also be leased, in which case the decision to invest in a stock of capital goods is made by the lessor. In this chapter we shall assume for ease of exposition that capital services are not hired but are acquired by purchasing a stock of capital goods. Since K in equation 13.1 represents a stock of capital, whereas it is the flow of capital services which is combined with labour to produce net output, we need

[1] An open economy can import capital goods, financing this by borrowing from abroad.

to assume that the flow of capital services per period of time is proportional to the size of the capital stock.

In each period a firm receives an inflow of cash, which is the total revenue from selling its net output, and experiences an outflow of cash due to paying for labour and for new capital goods. The net cash flow, N, for each time period is therefore

$$N_t = P_t y_t - W_t L_t - pk_t I_t \tag{13.2}$$

where

y_t = physical output
P_t = price of product
$W_t L_t$ = wage bill
pk_t = price of a unit of capital goods
I_t = investment: the number of capital goods purchased in period t

The objective of the firm in neoclassical analysis is taken to be that of maximising the value of its net cash flow. This ensures that the wealth of the firm's owners is maximised. If the firm is entirely financed by its shareholders and the shares are traded in a financial market, then the value of the firm is the total market value of the shares. The ultimate objective of economic agents is maximising utility from a time stream of consumption. If a firm is owned by a number of shareholders, they are likely to have different preferences regarding the timing of consumption. Nevertheless, the utility of all shareholders can be maximised by ensuring that the shareholders' wealth, in the form of their ownership claims on the firm, is maximised. So long as wealth is maximised, a shareholder who has a greater preference than the others for present-day consumption can still maximise her utility by selling shares in order to finance her consumption plans.[1]

In order to maximise the value of the firm it is not sufficient to consider only the current net cash flow. What matters is the whole time profile of expected future net cash flows from the present period until the time when the firm ceases to operate. The present value of the future expected net cash flows is obtained by discounting the net cash flows by the rate of interest, i, at which the firm can borrow or lend, as outlined in Chapter 3 (pp. 29–30). Thus the net present value of the firm's expected future net cash flows, assuming the firm has an infinite life span, is

$$V = \sum_{t=0}^{\infty} \frac{(P_t y_t - W_t L_t - pk_t I_t)}{(1+i)^t} \tag{13.3}$$

For the time being we are assuming a perfect capital market and a certain future cash flow. These assumptions imply that the firm is small and riskless,

[1] This assumes no transactions costs. But even if these are positive it is difficult to derive a better shareholder utility-maximising rule for the firm's management than that of wealth maximisation.

so that the interest rate is exogenous to the firm. It can borrow as much as it wants without increasing the rate of interest it has to pay.

From equation 13.3 we can see that V depends on total revenues and on labour and capital costs. Thus the decision regarding how much capital to hold in each period is arrived at jointly with the decisions concerning the volume of output to produce and the quantity of labour to employ in each period. The planned amount of capital for each period will depend on future as well as current output demand, wage rates and capital goods prices, once we make the explicit assumption that investment is irreversible. Once resources have been devoted to making a capital good, rather than a consumption good, then the capital good cannot be converted back into a consumption good. The only way a firm can undo its decision to acquire the capital good is by selling it. Given that markets in most capital goods are not well developed, a firm cannot easily switch between capital goods and consumption. In addition, capital goods take on a very specific physical form and cannot easily be converted into another type of capital good. This state of affairs can be represented by a production function in which substitutability between labour and capital is possible *ex ante* (that is, before the capital good is acquired) but is not possible *ex post*. Once the investment has been undertaken the capital goods have a specific form which includes the amount of labour required per unit of capital. Models incorporating *ex ante* substitutability with an *ex post* fixed capital–labour ratio are called *putty–clay models*. In a putty–clay world a firm's planned capital stock in each period depends on the current and *future* expected values of its determinants.[1]

A firm will undertake a given investment project if the resulting marginal addition to its capital stock has a positive net present value so that its adoption increases the present value of the whole firm. The change in the total value of the firm due to a marginal increase in the capital stock can be derived from equation 13.3:

$$\Delta V = \sum_{t=0}^{\infty} \frac{\Delta N_t}{(1 + i)^t} \tag{13.3a}$$

where

ΔV = net present value of investment project
ΔN_t = change in net cash flow due to the adoption of the investment project

Given that the marginal product of capital declines as the size of the capital stock increases, then the net present value of each marginal increment to the capital stock in any given time period will fall as the capital stock becomes larger. The firm achieves its optimal stock of capital when the net present value of any marginal addition to the capital stock has become zero.

[1] In a putty–putty model in which there is perfect substitutability *ex ante* and *ex post* so that investment is not irreversible, output, employment and capital-stock decisions in one period are independent of all other time periods.

Formally, the optimal capital stock is derived by differentiating the objective function given by equation 13.3 subject to the constraints faced by the firm. These constraints are:

1. The production function.
2. The demand function for the firm's product.
3. The wage rate (or the supply curve of labour if the firm faces an imperfectly competitive labour market).
4. The price of new capital goods.
5. The rate of depreciation of the capital stock. The firm has to allow for the fact that the capital stock depreciates over time. A convenient assumption is that the capital stock depreciates at a constant rate, δ, so that δK_t of the capital stock disappears in period t. Given this rate of depreciation, the actual addition to the capital stock over a period of time is

$$K_{t+1} - K_t = I_t - \delta K_t \qquad (13.4)$$

From maximising the objective function, V, subject to the constraints 1–5 one can derive an expression for c, the cost of employing the services of a unit of capital for one period:

$$c = pk(i + \delta) - \Delta pk \qquad (13.5)$$

The term $pk(i)$ is the interest charge on the price of one unit of the capital stock used for one period. The term $pk(\delta)$ is the depreciation charge, because a fraction of a unit of capital disappears over the period. The last term, Δpk, is the rise in the price of a unit of capital stock over the period. It is subtracted from the cost of capital services because a firm enjoys a capital gain if the price of the capital goods it owns rises.[1]

The cost of capital services, c, is the analogue of the wage rate. The optimal amount of capital services to use in any one period is the quantity for which the marginal-revenue product of capital services equals the marginal cost, c. The firm's desired capital stock in any period is the amount that will yield the optimal quantity of capital services.

From equation 13.3a we can see that a change in any variable which increases the net present value of the marginal addition to the capital stock will increase the size of the optimal capital stock. From equations 13.2 and 13.3a we can see that the net present value of any capital project will be greater the larger are the expected revenues from selling the net output, the lower is the price of capital goods and the lower is the rate of discount, i. A rise in the wage rate will increase investment by making the production process more capital-intensive, provided that this substitution effect is not completely offset by a reduction in planned output due to the higher cost of labour.

If we hold constant the current and future expected capital-goods prices, wage rates and product demand, then we can graph a relationship between the rate of discount and the current desired stock of capital. This is shown in Figure 13.1. Assuming that we can aggregate over all firms' demand for capital

[1] See Nickell [1] ch. 2, especially p. 10, for a derivation of equation 13.5.

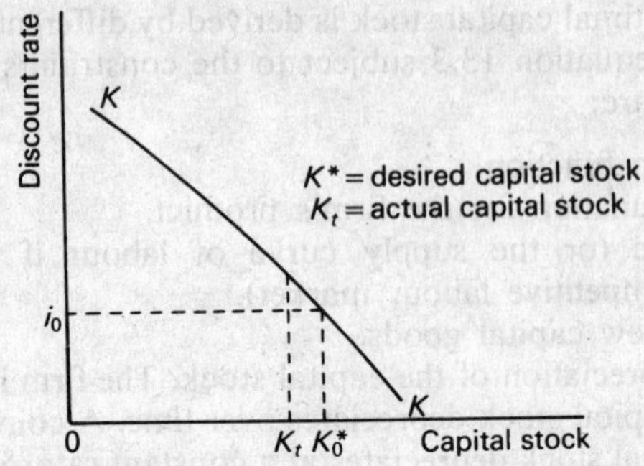

FIGURE 13.1 *The desired capital-stock schedule*

goods, Figure 13.1 depicts the aggregate desired capital-stock schedule. If the discount rate used by firms is i_0, then the desired capital stock will be K_0^*. A fall in the discount rate leads to a rise in the desired stock of capital. If any of the other determinants of the desired capital stock (factor prices and product demand) change, then the *KK* schedule will shift.

Investment and capital-stock adjustment

So far we have been considering the determinants of the desired stock of capital, not those of the rate of investment. Investment occurs when the stock of capital is adjusted. Since capital depreciates over time and with use replacement investment must take place if the size of the capital stock is to remain unchanged.

If the capital stock is to increase over time, then net investment must occur. The problem for economic theory is to relate the rate of investment to the discrepancy between the desired and the actual stock of capital. Such a discrepancy is depicted in Figure 13.1 by the gap between K_t and K_0^*, If there were no adjustment costs, then the capital stock would be adjusted instantaneously from K_t to K_0^*, so making the speed of adjustment infinitely fast.

Therefore, in order to derive a theory of investment we need to incorporate lags in the adjustment of the capital stock towards its optimal level. Lags are inherent in the investment process. It takes time for a firm to decide on its capital-stock requirements, orders have to be placed, there is then a delivery lag while the new capital goods are produced and finally there is a lag between delivery and installing the new capital goods. These lags can be generally attributed to costs in adjusting the capital stock. The faster the rate of adjustment, and hence the higher the rate of investment, the greater are likely to be the adjustment costs per unit of investment expenditure. These costs are due to factors internal to the firm, such as limited managerial and administrative capacity, as well as to external factors. In particular, upward-sloping supply curves in the capital-goods supplying industries will cause the price of capital goods to rise as their rate of production in the short run increases.

These considerations imply that a firm has some choice over the length of time it takes to adjust its capital stock. A firm concerned with maximising the present value of its net cash flow would balance the costs of faster adjustment against the benefits of bringing forward production by a more rapid increase in its capital stock. The optimal rate of investment would be that for which the marginal adjustment costs just equalled the resulting marginal net revenues.

Different firms and different kinds of capital goods can be expected to have different lags. This means that current aggregate net investment expenditures will be related to the discrepancies which have existed between the actual and optimal capital stock for a number of past time periods. Thus investment is specified to be a lagged function of past discrepancies between the desired and actual capital stock:

$$I = \omega(L(t))(K_t^* - K_{t-1}) \qquad (13.6)$$

where $\omega(L(t))$ is a distributed lag function specifying the time lags in the adjustment process.

The general expression for the desired capital stock can be written as

$$K_t^* = f(Z) \qquad (13.7)$$

where Z is the set of variables which determine K_t^*. As previously discussed, these are current and expected future product demand, wage rates, and the cost of capital services. The actual capital stock, K_{t-1}, which firms start out with at the beginning of period t is determined by past levels of gross investment and by the rate of depreciation.

The specification of investment demand given by equations 13.6 and 13.7 differs from that of the investment function used earlier in the *ISLM* model. In the *ISLM* formulation, investment depended directly on the rate of interest, whereas in this specification the interest rate affects investment by influencing the desired stock of capital. A determinate rate of net investment is then obtained by specifying it as some lagged function of the positive discrepancy between the desired and actual capital stock.

13.2 Finance and the cost of capital

The opportunity cost of accumulating capital is the present consumption thus forgone. This opportunity cost is referred to as the *cost of capital* and is not to be confused with the price (or cost) of new capital goods, *pk*, or with *c*, the cost of capital services, which depends in part on the cost of capital. The cost of capital is the appropriate discount rate to use in evaluating the present value of a future stream of net cash flows. Given certainty and a perfect capital market, the market rate of interest on debt correctly measures the opportunity cost of capital.

It becomes more difficult to establish what the appropriate discount rate is once we allow for uncertainty. This is because the different ways in which a firm can raise finance now need to be taken account of. There are three main methods by which investment finance can be obtained. First, there is the internal source of retained profits; the second is issuing new shares. Both these methods involve increasing the amount of equity. (Retentions give the existing shareholders an enlarged ownership claim on the firm's assets.) The third method is borrowing by issuing debt in the form of bonds or debentures. Both shares and debentures are external sources of finance. Given that a firm's future net cash flows are uncertain, equity finance is riskier than debt finance. A firm's debtors have first claim on its net income in the form of interest payments due on the firm's borrowings and on the firm's assets should it be wound up. Shareholders only have a residual claim on net income minus interest payments and on the firm's assets. The flow of dividends is uncertain, whereas interest payments are certain, barring default by the firm. Because shares are riskier financial assets than debt one would expect the real rate of return on shares to be generally higher than the real interest rate on debt, given that asset-holders are risk-averse.

Since different assumptions can be made of how the various ways of raising finance affect the riskiness of the returns from different financial instruments, the question of what is the appropriate rate of discount is a controversial one to which we cannot do justice here. All we can do is outline some of the factors which will affect the cost of capital and hence the demand for new capital goods.[1]

We can start by considering the cost of equity capital, i.e. the cost of finance obtained from share issues or retained profits. If shareholder wealth is to be maximised, then the return from new investment must at least equal the return shareholders are currently getting. Hence the current rate of return on shares is the appropriate measure of the opportunity cost of using equity finance. In order to calculate the rate of return on shares we need to know the future stream of dividends which the current shareholders are expected to receive. If the current divident stream is to be on average maintained into an indefinitely long future, then the firm must replace its real capital stock as it depreciates. Therefore, to arrive at the dividends the firm can pay out without diminishing the capital stock, we need to subtract from the firm's gross income (value of net output minus the wage bill) depreciation as well as interest payments to debtors. The remaining sum is called the firm's *earnings*. If the firm is expected to retain some of these earnings in order to finance future net investment, then the capital stock will grow and dividend payments will also be expected to grow. Assuming a constant growth rate of dividends, g, we get the sequential relationship:

$$D_t = (1 + g)D_{t-1} = (1 + g)^2 D_{t-2} = (1 + g)^n D_{t-n}$$

If dividends at the end of the current period are D, then the sum of future expected dividends is

$$\sum_{t=1}^{\infty} D(1 + g)^{t-1}$$

[1] Readers interested in a more rigorous and in-depth treatment of finance should refer to finance texts such as Franks and Broyles [2] or, at a more advanced level, Nickell [1].

The market price of a share will be the present value of the expected future flow of dividends per share. The market value, S, of the firm's total equity will be the share price *times* the number of shares outstanding. The present value of the firm's equity will be obtained by discounting the sum of expected future dividends by the rate of return on shares, e, which is the cost of equity capital:[1]

$$S = \sum_{t=1}^{\infty} \frac{D(1+g)^{t-1}}{(1+e)^t} = \frac{D}{e-g} \tag{13.8}$$

We cannot observe e directly but we can observe S and estimate D and g. So we can arrive at a value for e since it is that rate of discount which makes the present value of the expected future dividend stream equal to the market value of the firm's shares. Rearranging equation 13.8 we get

$$e = \frac{D}{S} + g \tag{13.9}$$

The cost of equity capital would be the same for retained earnings and for new issues of equity if there were no transactions costs to issuing new shares, and no tax distortions which make capital gains due to retentions preferable to dividend payments for shareholders. An additional consideration is the proposition that the firm's existing shareholders view the firm's prospects more

---

1

$$S = \sum_{t=1}^{\infty} \frac{D(1+g)^{t-1}}{(1+e)^t} = \frac{D}{1+e} \sum_{t=1}^{\infty} \left(\frac{1+g}{1+e} \right)^{t-1}$$

$$= \frac{D}{1+e} \left[\frac{1 - \left(\frac{1+g}{1+e} \right)^n}{1 - \frac{1+g}{1+e}} \right]; \text{ where } n \to \infty$$

If $g < e$ ($g, e > 0$), then

$$0 < \frac{1+g}{1+e} < 1$$

Therefore

$$\underset{\text{Lmt } n \to \infty}{S} = \frac{D}{1+e} \left(\frac{1}{1 - \frac{1+g}{1+e}} \right)$$

$$S = D\left(\frac{1}{e-g} \right)$$

optimistically than do outsiders and so are prepared to receive a lower immediate rate of return on retentions than new shareholders would expect (see Nickell [1]). All the above factors will make retained profits a cheaper form of finance than new equity. However, there is a limit to the proportion of earnings that firms can retain without raising the cost of capital if shareholders eventually prefer dividends to retentions.

Although the greater riskiness of shares compared with debt makes the cost of equity capital greater than the cost of debt, a firm cannot finance an unlimited proportion of its real assets by issuing debt without driving up its overall cost of capital. In one respect the existing shareholders gain if the firm finances new investment by issuing more debt rather than by equity, because the firm pays new debt-holders less per unit of borrowed funds than it would have to pay new shareholders. However, this benefit is to some extent offset by the greater variability in dividends that results when a larger proportion of earnings are committed to interest payments. To compensate for the greater financial risk of extra debt, potential shareholders demand a higher rate of return (which they can achieve through a fall in the share price: from equation 13.9 a fall in S causes e to rise). Thus the equity cost of capital rises with the firm's debt–equity ratio. In addition, there is an increased probability that as the debt–equity ratio rises the firm will fail to earn enough to pay its creditors and so becomes bankrupt. This fear will drive up both the cost of equity capital and of debt.

It is therefore not legitimate to use either the firm's cost of equity or the interest rate on its own as the appropriate discount rate because the two rates of return are interdependent. It is therefore appropriate to use as the discount rate the firm's average cost of capital, a. This is the weighted average of the firm's equity cost of capital and the interest rate on its debt and is given by equation 13.10:

$$a = \frac{eS}{V} + \frac{iB}{V} \tag{13.10}$$

where

S = market value of shares
B = market value of debt
$V = S + B$ = total market of the firm

There has been a lengthy debate over whether the firm's average cost of capital can be minimised by a judicious choice of its debt–equity ratio or whether a remains unchanged with respect to the firm's financial structure. The conclusion of this debate is that tax arrangements whereby interest on debt is tax-deductible cause the average cost of capital to fall as the debt–equity ratio rises. However, this effect is offset by the greater probability of bankruptcy as the proportion of debt rises and this fear eventually increases the cost of capital.

A further and continuing controversy surrounds the question of whether the firm's cost of capital rises as the amount raised to finance investment within any one period increases. This would occur if internal finance were cheaper than issuing new equity. In this case a firm would first finance investment from retained earnings and then it would move on to borrowing funds. Only when it had issued sufficient debt to raise the marginal cost of debt to that of the marginal cost of new equity would additional shares be issued, provided that the expected rate of return on investment still exceeded the cost of equity capital.

If the marginal cost of capital does increase with the amount of investment undertaken in any given period, then the cost of capital becomes a determinant of the rate of investment as well as of the desired stock of capital towards which the firm is adjusting. The endogeneity of the firm's cost of capital with respect to its own rate of investment implies that investment will depend on internal financial factors, such as earnings, cash flow, liquid asset holdings and the debt to total market value ratio. The alternative view, that the cost of capital is approximately exogenous to the firm, puts greater emphasis on external financial factors such as share prices, the yield on shares and the market rate of interest as determinants of the desired capital stock and hence of investment.

Tobin's q-ratio

Tobin [3] devised a way of relating investment demand to financial variables which is amenable to empirical treatment. Investment is hypothesised to depend positively on the *q* ratio, where

$$q = \frac{\text{rate of return on investment}}{\text{cost of capital}}$$

The rate of return on investment is that rate of discount, ρ, which makes the present value of the expected net cash flow from an investment project equal to the price paid for the capital equipment. In equation 13.3a the rate of return on investment is the value of ρ which will make the present value of the expected change in the firm's net cash flows, $\Sigma_{t=1}^{\infty}\Delta N_t$ equal to pkI, the initial cost of the capital equipment:

$$pk\,I = \sum_{t=1}^{\infty} \frac{\Delta N_t}{(1+\rho)^t} \tag{13.11}$$

(Alternative names for ρ are the internal rate of return or the marginal efficiency of capital.) If ΔN is the same in every year and t tends to infinity, then

$$\rho = \frac{\Delta N}{pk\,I} \tag{13.12}$$

In empirical work at an aggregate level ρ has to be measured as the average rate of return on the existing capital stock valued at its current replacement cost:

$$\text{average } \rho = \frac{N}{pk\,K} \tag{13.12a}$$

where

N = firms' current post-tax earnings, used as a proxy for expected future earnings

pkK = value of existing capital stock at its current replacement cost.

The cost of capital, a (see equation 13.10, p. 238), is measured in a similar way as

$$a = \frac{N}{V} \tag{13.13}$$

where

V = stock market value of equity plus debt and
$N = eS + iB$

Since

$$q = \frac{\text{Rate of return on investment}}{\text{Cost of capital}} = \frac{\rho}{a} \tag{13.14}$$

we get by substituting equation 13.12a for e and equation 13.13 for an empirical estimate for q:

$$q = \frac{V}{pk\,K} \tag{13.14a}$$

Hence q is alternatively called the 'valuation ratio' since it is the ratio of the market value of the firm to the replacement cost of its real assets.

A q in excess of 1.0 means that financial wealth-holders on the stock market are prepared to pay more for a claim to a unit of real capital than it costs the firm to buy and install it. Firms therefore have an incentive to invest and so investment is expected to be higher the larger is q.[1]

13.3 The accelerator theory of investment

The neoclassical theory of investment views it as being determined by the cost of investment relative to its expected return. Keynesians have traditionally

[1] Because of measurement and aggregation problems individual firms are likely to be undertaking positive net investment even when q is less than 1.0.

favoured the accelerator theory of investment, which emphasises the relationship between the capital stock and the flow of output, while disregarding the role of factor costs. The accelerator approach can be derived from neoclassical capital theory if we assume a constant returns to scale production function. Given constant returns to scale the optimal (that is, least-cost) capital–labour ratio is determined by the cost of capital relative to the cost of labour and is invariant with respect to changes in output. If, in addition, labour and capital costs are constant, then both factors are expanded proportionately when planned output rises. This means that the optimal capital–output ratio, v, remains unchanged as output expands.

The desired stock of capital, K^*, is therefore related to the volume of output firms plan to produce by means of v, the optimal capital–output ratio. This relationship is given by equation 13.15:

$$K^* = vy \tag{13.15}$$

The fixed relationship between the desired stock of capital and the planned level of output can be alternatively derived by making the non-neoclassical assumption that labour and capital cannot be substituted for each other, even *ex ante.* The labour–capital ratio and the capital–output ratio are then fixed parameters rather than decision variables.

The desired capital stock, K_t^*, which firms wish to have by the end of the current period in order to produce next period's output optimally is related to the expected volume of future output, y_t^e. Thus

$$K_t^* = vy_t^e \tag{13.16}$$

If the discrepancy between the actual capital stock, K_{t-1}, with which firms start the period, and the desired capital stock is entirely made up within the period, net investment is given by

$$I_t^n = K_t^* - K_{t-1} = v(y_t^e - y_{t-1}) \tag{13.17}$$

Equation 13.17 is the basic version of the accelerator theory which relates net investment to the expected increase in output *times* the optimal capital–output ratio, or *accelerator* coefficient, as it is known. For simplicity the *accelerator* relationship is assumed here to be linear. The incremental optimal capital–output ratio, dK/dy, which indicates how many additional units of capital are required by profit-maximising firms to produce an additional unit of output, is assumed to be constant and is therefore equal to the average capital–output ratio.

Expected output cannot be observed directly. The simplest expectations hypothesis is that which takes the current change in output to be the future expected change. This gives

$$I_t^n = v(y_t - y_{t-1}) \tag{13.18}$$

If the existing capital stock is not being fully utilised, net investment will be correspondingly smaller, and equation 13.18 is modified by subtracting that portion, γ, of the capital stock that is currently under-utilised:

$$I_t^n = v(y_t - y_{t-1}) - \gamma K_{t-1} \tag{13.19}$$

This simple version of the accelerator relationship failed to perform adequately when tested (e.g. Chenery [14]) and the value of v estimated in investment equations was considerably lower than the average capital–output ratio. This failure was probably due to neglecting the lags that occur in adjusting the capital stock. These are taken account of in *flexible accelerator* models of investment which assume that expected future output is a function of past output levels, with geometrically declining weights, μ, attached to previous output levels. The capital stock in existence in any time period then depends on past values of output:

$$K_t = v(1-\mu)\sum_{i=0}^{\infty} \mu^i y_{t-1} \quad (0 < \mu < 1) \tag{13.20}$$

Using the Koyck transformation we obtain[1]

$$K_t - \mu K_{t-1} = v(1-\mu)y_t. \tag{13.21}$$

Subtracting $(1-\mu)K_{t-1}$ from both sides

$$K_t - K_{t-1} = I_t^n = v(1-\mu)y_t - (1-\mu)K_{t-1}. \tag{13.22}$$

The expression for gross investment includes an item for replacement investment, which is usually assumed proportional to the existing capital stock:

$$I_t^G = I_t^n + \partial K_{t-1} = v(1-\mu)y_t - (1-\mu-\partial)K_{t-1}. \tag{13.23}$$

Thus we have the hypothesis that investment is related positively to the level of current output and negatively (providing $0 < \partial + \mu < 1$) to the existing capital stock. The flexible accelerator coefficient, $v(1-\mu)$, is lower than the average capital–output ratio, v.

13.4 The impact of inflation

The impact of inflation on the level of investment depends on whether the inflation is anticipated or unanticipated. If inflation is fully anticipated, then the nominal rate of interest on fixed-interest debt will rise by the rate of inflation (as discussed in Chapter 8, pp. 133–4). Net cash flows also increase by the rate of price change so the market value of the firm is unaffected. However, if money earns a zero rate of interest, a rise in the anticipated inflation rate will reduce the demand for real money balances and cause a movement into real assets. If real interest rates fall, the desired capital stock will be larger.

In practice, however, a significant proportion of inflation is unanticipated. If the variability of inflation increases with the rate of inflation, then more rapid inflation implies greater uncertainty, which in turn diminishes the incentive to invest. A further aspect of the impact of inflation is the higher nominal interest rate on debt which rises in order to compensate creditors for future price increases. This has the effect of bringing forward in time the firm's repayment of debt. This diminishes net cash flow in the early years of an investment

[1] See Chapter 12 (p. 216).

project, and this may cause the firm to invest less. A further disincentive effect of high fixed nominal rates occurs if firms entertain some probability that the inflation rate will fall in the future. If this occurred, then the firm would be saddled with a larger interest-payment commitment in real terms than if the current rate of inflation had continued, and this possibility will increase the firm's reluctance to borrow. Unanticipated inflation could have a favourable impact on investment if nominal interest rates rose less than the rate of inflation, resulting in a fall in the real rate of interest, which the firm correctly perceived.

Another way in which inflation can be detrimental to investment occurs when accounting practices are based on historic costs. When there is inflation historic-cost accounting conventions give rise to reported profits which are higher than the profits based on assessing depreciation and stock utilisation at replacement cost. Consequently firms have a lower level of real retentions since tax payments and dividends will be higher than they would be if profits were calculated on the basis of current rather than historic costs.

If the average propensity to save rises with inflation, as suggested in Chapter 12, then one could expect a favourable effect on investment via a fall in real interest rates, provided that private-sector savings are not channelled into foreign investment or into financing public-sector consumption.

All in all, no definite conclusions have been reached regarding the impact of inflation on investment, though on balance it would appear to be unfavourable.

13.5 Policy measures which affect investment

Fiscal policy

Fiscal policy can influence the level of private-sector investment through two distinct channels. On the demand side it may affect the level of future expected demand for output, while on the cost side tax changes can alter the cost of capital services. The latter has been the main instrument whereby governments have tried directly to influence the level and composition of investment.

UK governments have engaged in a variety of schemes to reduce the cost of investment to firms. Investment allowances enable firms to subtract in excess of the normal amount of depreciation from their taxable profits, thus reducing their tax liability. These were replaced from 1966 to 1970 by investment grants which reimbursed firms part of their expenditure on capital goods, regardless of whether they were liable to corporation tax. Both investment grants and allowances have discriminated in favour of manufacturing investment and particular regional locations. Corporation tax lowers the amount of post-tax earnings from which firms can finance investment and pay out dividends. It can be applied so as to favour retentions or debt. For instance, UK corporation tax is not payable on interest payments, and this reduces the cost of debt capital relative to equity. A higher rate of corporation tax reduces post-tax earnings and raises the pre-tax rate of return needed to pay shareholders a given post-tax dividend yield. However, the incentive to invest does receive an offsetting stimulus if investment allowances are paid so that a given amount of investment attracts a higher reduction in tax payments.

A temporarily higher rate of investment allowances or grants gives firms an incentive to accelerate their rate of capital-stock adjustment, though the long-run desired amount of capital stock is not altered. Empirical evidence suggests that governments can be more successful in altering the timing of private-sector investment than in increasing the rate of economic growth by raising the long-term rate of investment (see Nickell [1] and Sumner [4]).

Monetary policy

As with consumption, monetary policy affects investment by inducing a process of portfolio adjustment. An increase in the money supply relative to interest-bearing financial assets induces a switch into the latter type of assets, including equity. Asset prices rise and interest rates and dividend yields correspondingly fall. The cost of capital is thereby reduced, stimulating investment. Tobin's q-theory makes use of the same transmission mechanism, whereby changes in the relative quantities of financial assets induce changes in the stock of real capital. Portfolio adjustment following an expansion in the money stock increases q by raising firms' stock-market valuation and so stimulates investment.

However, a continuously lax monetary policy which leads to inflation and high nominal interest rates may well inhibit investment. Interest rates are also affected by fiscal policy. Government budget deficits financed by bond issues raise interest rates and so inhibit private-sector investment.

13.6 Empirical evidence

The econometric testing of investment functions has proved more difficult and more fraught with conflicting results than in the case of aggregate consumption. This is due to the strong dependence of investment on expectational variables which are not directly observable and to the complex lag structure between changes in the determining variables and the consequent change in investment.

The main questions for which empirical answers have been sought are as follows:

1. Is investment to be explained solely by output and capacity utilisation as in the accelerator approach?
2. Does the cost of capital services contribute to explaining investment as neoclassical theory suggests?
3. Are internal financial variables or external ones significant determinants of investment?
4. What is the lag structure of investment demand?

The most popular specification of investment demand and one which is common to all approaches is to express investment as a distributed lag function of differences between the desired and actual levels of the capital stock (that is, equations 13.6 and 13.7, as in Jorgenson [5] and [6]). Different hypotheses are distinguished by the choice of the determinants of the desired stock of capital.

Expected future product demand or output is the main determinant of investment in the accelerator approach. It is also a determinant of investment in neoclassical theory, but is not singled out for special emphasis. Expected future demand cannot be directly observed so it has to be proxied. Applying the adaptive expectations hypothesis yields a selection of proxies: past levels of output, sales, profits or cash flow.

Tests of the neoclassical approach seek to verify the role of relative factor prices in determining investment. Two major variants of this approach have appeared in the empirical literature. One is the Jorgenson model ([5], [6] and [7]) in which the desired stock of capital is deduced to depend on the price of output relative to the cost of capital services. The other is Tobin's q model [3] in which investment is positively related to q (see p. 239). The major contending theory is the accelerator hypothesis, which gives little or no explanatory power to relative factor prices.

There is broad agreement in both British and US studies that output or sales is an important determinant of investment. Estimates of the elasticity of demand for the capital stock with respect to output cluster around 1.0, as one would deduce from a constant returns to scale production function.

There is far less agreement about the role and importance of relative factor prices and financial variables. Since the 1960s a good number of US studies have reported interest rates to be a significant determinant of investment, so giving the neoclassical approach considerable support (see Jorgenson's work in particular.) Although the estimates of the price elasticity of the demand for capital differ quite widely, one can tentatively conclude from US work that external financial variables (interest rates, dividend yields, share prices and tax variables) seem to have performed better than internal financial variables (cash flow, retained earnings, profits, debt/market-value ratio). The first three internal financial variables are related to expectations about future product demand and so it is difficult to separate out this influence from that coming through a cost-of-capital effect.

Until recently UK studies have, with some exceptions, failed to show that the cost of capital is a significant determinant of investment. Savage [8] in a survey of British studies concluded that no satisfactory relationship had been found between investment in plant and machinery and cost-of-capital variables, though investment in housing was affected by interest rates. The Treasury model concurs with this view: manufacturing investment depends on lagged output and companies' cash flow. However, two UK studies (Oulton [9] and Jenkinson [10]), using Tobin's q ratio, have found q to be significantly related to investment and to offer a slightly better explanation of investment than a pure accelerator model. The cost of capital has also been found to be significant by Anderson [11].

Econometric investigations of investment differ quite considerably in their specification of lag structures. In the absence of any well worked out theoretical basis for investment lags, most specifications are *ad hoc.* The distributed-lag function may take various forms. The geometric distributed-lag function in which the weights decline steadily with time has already been mentioned (see pp. 215–16). A more likely distributed-lag function for investment is one where the weights at first rise with time, reach a peak and then decline. Of particular interest are the length of time it takes for a determinant to have its peak effect, the average lag (the time taken for 50 per cent of the effect of a change in a determinant to be felt) and the total length of time for such a change to work out its impact on investment.

It is useful to compare estimates produced by econometric studies of lags, which are of dubious reliability, with lag estimates obtained by questionnaire and interview studies. Mayer's study [12] of new industrial plant and plant additions started in the USA in 1954 and 1955 obtained an average lag from the investment decision to completion of seven quarters. Nobay [13] has calculated an average lag between ordering and delivery of engineering goods in the United Kingdom in 1965 of about four quarters. Addition of a planning period of one quarter gives an average five-quarter lag between appropriations and point of expenditure.

Although econometrically estimated lags differ quite considerably, both US and UK surveys (for example, Nickell [1] and Jorgenson [7]) conclude that the average lag between changes in the determinants of investment and in expenditure on investment is about $1\frac{1}{2}$–2 years. The evidence also suggests that the lag for output changes is shorter than that for cost-of-capital variables. This is consistent with the putty–clay characterisation of production functions.

13.7 Conclusion

Investment is a theoretically complex topic. In a textbook on macroeconomics we have only been able to indicate the basic theoretical framework. While simplified investment functions specify the determinants of investment as current and lagged values of output and interest rates, one must not forget that investment depends on expectations about the future. This factor, together with a complex lag structure, makes it particularly difficult to get reliable quantitative information about investment behaviour.

As the next two chapters show, investment, specified by a simple functional form, is a key variable in explanations of cyclical fluctuations and long-run growth in national output.

References

[1] S. J. Nickell, *The Investment Decision of Firms* (Cambridge University Press, 1978).

[2] J. R. Franks and J. E. Broyles, *Modern Managerial Finance* (New York: Wiley, 1979).

[3] J. Tobin, 'A General Equilibrium Approach to Monetary Theory', *Journal of Money, Credit and Banking*, 1 (February 1969).

[4] M. Sumner, 'Investment Grants', in D. Currie *et al.* (eds), *Macroeconomic Analysis* (London: Croom Helm, 1981).

[5] D. W. Jorgenson, 'Capital Theory and Investment Behavior', *American Economic Review*, 53 (May 1963).
[6] D. W. Jorgenson, 'The Theory of Investment Behavior', in R. Ferber (ed.), *Determinants of Investment Behavior* (New York: Columbia University Press, 1967).
[7] D. W. Jorgenson, 'Econometric Studies of Investment Behavior: A Survey', *Journal of Economic Literature*, 9 (1971); reprinted in P. G. Korliras and R. Thorn (eds), *Modern Macroeconomics* (New York: Harper & Row, 1979).
[8] D. Savage, 'The Channels of Monetary Influence: A Survey of the Empirical Evidence', *National Institute Economic Review* (February 1978).
[9] N. Oulton, 'Aggregate Investment and Tobin's q: the Evidence from Britain', *Oxford Economic Papers*, 33, 2 (July 1981).
[10] N. H. Jenkinson, *Investment, Profitability and the Valuation Ratio*, Bank of England Discussion Paper No. 17 (September 1981).
[11] G. J. Anderson, 'A New Approach to the Empirical Investigation of Investment Expenditures', *Economic Journal*, 91 (March 1981).
[12] T. Mayer, 'Plant and Equipment Lead Times', *Journal of Business*, 33 (1960).
[13] A. R. Nobay, 'Forecasting Manufacturing Investment 1959–67: Some Preliminary Results', *National Institute Economic Review*, 52 (May 1970).
[14] H. B. Chenery, 'Overcapacity and the Acceleration Principle', *Econometrica* (January 1952).

14 The Trade Cycle: Keynesian and Monetarist Interpretations

The long-run expansion of industrialised market economies has been accompanied by cyclical fluctuations in economic activity. This type of fluctuation is known as the business or trade cycle. The general feature of the cycle is that an expansion of economic activity is followed by a contraction, which is in turn succeeded by a further expansion. Explaining the occurrence of trade cycles has been a major preoccupation of macroeconomics for a long time.

Measuring cyclical fluctuations in economic activity is not particularly easy because a large number of variables, such as industrial production, total employment, fixed private investment, the price level and interest rates, are involved. Each one has its own specific cycle and does not move exactly in phase with the others. An aggregate measure of the trade cycle is obtained by recording a large number of specific cycles, comparing their respective phases and dating their turning-points. Those variables which then appear to cycle in a consistent way in relation to the others are then used to date the turning-points and phases of the general cycle in economic activity. This is termed the *reference cycle*. Figure 14.1 shows the UK reference cycle as dated by the Central Statistical Office. The top line gives the dates of troughs (T) and peaks (P) for the reference cycle.

In the nineteenth century and up to the Second World War trade cycles in the United Kingdom involved absolute increases and decreases in real GDP. The post-war cycles up to the mid-1970s involved no decline in absolute GDP during recessions, only a retardation in its rate of growth. This was in complete contrast to the inter-war cycles, which had been more severe than the nineteenth-century business cycles. In the post-war period cyclical fluctuations have been milder than the nineteenth-century ones. However, the two recessions since 1973 have been more severe and have involved absolute falls in GDP from one year to the next.

Another difference between pre-war and post-war trade cycles is that the price level fell during the pre-war recessions. In fact there was a downward trend in UK prices throughout the 1921–38 period. Since the Second World

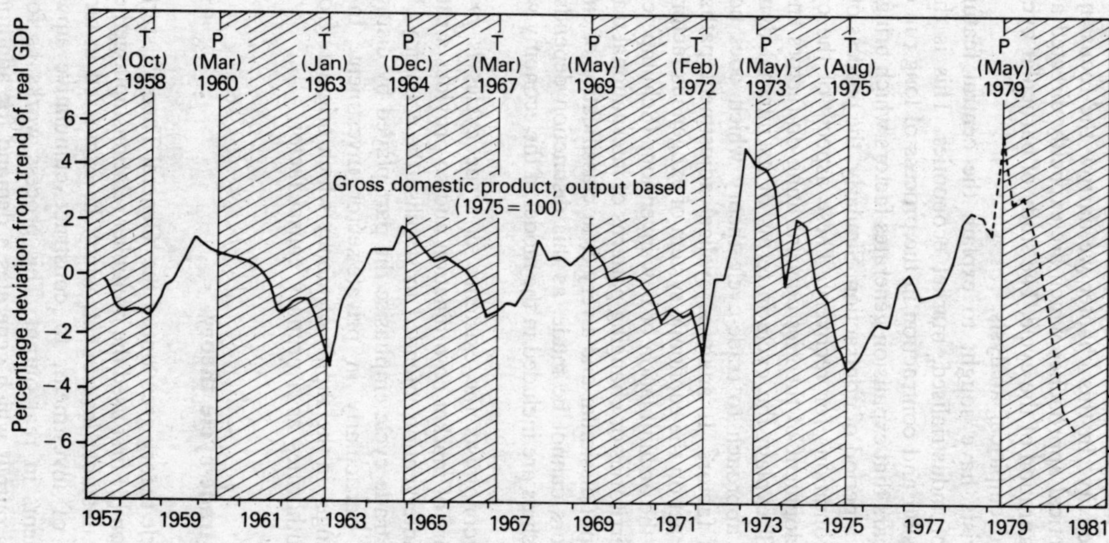

FIGURE 14.1 *The reference cycle and the cycle of GDP for the United Kingdom, 1957–81*

Sources: various issues of *Economic Trends.*

War prices have risen at all stages of the cycle, though there has been some tendency for inflation to slow down in the latter part of the recession phase (see Shapiro [1]).

A good deal of macroeconomic theory relates in one way or another to explaining trade-cycle behaviour. Theories of the determination of output, unemployment, investment, the price level, interest-rate levels and other relevant variables all play their part in explaining fluctuations in the general level of economic activity. In this chapter we narrow the focus in order to examine some theoretical approaches which are explicitly directed at explaining the general configuration of the cycle. The study of particular cycles would require more detailed empirical analysis.

Trade-cycle theorists have sought to explain the central feature of the cyclical behaviour of industrialised, market economies. This is the regular recurrence of expansion and contraction in the process of long-run economic growth. Thus it appears that expansion generates factors which bring about its own end and induce a period of contraction. Similarly, the process of contraction generates the conditions for recovery. These aspects of the cycle have encouraged the development of theories concentrating on factors endogenous to the cycle that will explain the cycle in terms of its internal dynamics.

There is another approach to trade-cycle theory which does not rely so strongly on internal factors. It analyses cyclical adjustment paths that are generated by the impact on the economic system of exogenous factors, such as population changes, the accumulation of new inventions (Schumpeter [2]), the opening up of new territories or changing patterns of international trade. These two approaches are not dissimilar and a very clear classification of endogenous and exogenous factors cannot be made, as this distinction depends on what behavioural relationships are included in the model of the economy with which one is working.

For Keynesian economists the existence of trade cycles is *prima facie* evidence of the failure of market co-ordination and so provides a rationale for active government intervention intended to stabilise the economy. Keynesian explanations of the trade cycle emphasise the part played by disturbances in the real variables, particularly in private-sector investment. In contrast, monetarists see changes in the supply of money which originate from actions by the monetary authorities as a primary causal factor.

14.1 Keynesian trade-cycle theory

Keynesian trade-cycle theory grew out of the 'General Theory', starting in the late 1930s. Samuelson [3] first used the multiplier relationship together with the key role played by unstable investment, which he expressed in terms of the accelerator theory of investment, to construct cumulative upwards and downwards movements in real output. This process works as follows. An expected increase in output which generates a demand for additional capital stock leads to an increase in investment. The increase in investment causes output to rise by an amount equal to the increase in investment *times* the income multiplier. The increase in income causes investment to rise further, and so the multiplier accelerator process continues. The money supply is implicitly assumed to adjust to the quantity of output. There is also no mention of price changes, as in the Keynesian tradition these are assumed fixed. Prices do not adjust: all adjustment is by quantities and hence gives rise to sizeable fluctuations in real output and investment. The supply of labour is assumed, in the typical Keynesian manner, to be perfectly elastic. As much labour as firms want to employ at existing prices is always forthcoming. The use of the multiplier–accelerator relationship to derive cyclical fluctuations is now examined in more detail.

The first-order multiplier–accelerator interaction

The simplest specification of the accelerator function for net investment, I^n_t, is the following first-order difference equation (see Chapter 13 for its derivation):

$$I^n_t = v(y_t - y_{t-1}) \tag{14.1}$$

In this version the capital stock is fully adjusted to its desired level at the end of each period. When firms enter the current period their capital stock is not optimally related to current output, as it was adjusted to last period's output. Investment (or disinvestment) therefore takes place but not until the end of the period. Consumption is assumed to depend proportionately on the current level of income:

$$C_t = (1 - s)y_t \tag{14.2}$$

where s is the marginal propensity to save. The model is solved by assuming short-run equilibrium is achieved in each period whereby aggregate demand equals national output:

$$y_t = C_t + I_t + AE_t \tag{14.3}$$

where AE is autonomous expenditure. Therefore, for short-run equilibrium we must have

$$y_t = (1 - s)y_t + v(y_t - y_{t-1}) + AE_t. \tag{14.4}$$

Output and demand vary from one period to another because aggregate demand depends on last period's income as well as on current income. When last period's income differs from this period's income aggregate demand changes from period to period. Solving equation 14.4 for y we obtain

$$y_t = \left(1 + \frac{s}{v - s}\right)y_{t-1} - \frac{AE_t}{v - s} \tag{14.5}$$

Equation 14.5 is an example of a first-order linear difference equation as it is lagged just one period. Using equation 14.5 we can derive the time path of income. We start from a static equilibrium level of income which equals AE/s. (This is derived from equation 14.4 by setting $y_t = y_{t-1}$ and solving for the static equilibrium level of income.) Income then diverges from its static equilibrium level. In the initial period 0 income is y_0: thus the initial divergence is $y_0 - AE/s$. From equation 14.5 we therefore obtain that income in period 1 is

$$y_1 = \left(1 + \frac{s}{v-s}\right) y_0 - \frac{AE}{v-s}$$

$$y_2 = \left(1 + \frac{s}{v-s}\right) y_1 - \frac{AE}{v-s}$$

$$= \left(1 + \frac{s}{v-s}\right) \left[\left(1 + \frac{s}{v-s}\right) y_0 - \frac{AE}{v-s} \right] - \frac{AE}{v-s}$$

$$= \left(1 + \frac{s}{v-s}\right)^2 y_0 - \frac{AE}{v-s} \left[1 + \left(1 + \frac{s}{v-s}\right) \right] \tag{14.6}$$

Therefore, continuing on for y_3, y_4, etc., by substituting into equation 14.5 we obtain

$$y_t = \left(1 + \frac{s}{v-s}\right)^t y_0 - \frac{AE}{v-s} \left[1 + \left(1 + \frac{s}{v-s}\right) + \left(1 + \frac{s}{v-s}\right)^2 + \cdots + \left(1 + \frac{s}{v-s}\right)^{t-1} \right]$$

$$= \left(1 + \frac{s}{v-s}\right)^t y_0 - \frac{AE}{s} \left[1 - \left(1 + \frac{s}{v-s}\right)^t \right]$$

$$= \left(1 + \frac{s}{v-s}\right)^t \left(y_0 - \frac{AE}{s}\right) + \frac{AE}{s} \tag{14.7}$$

$$= (1+g)^t \left(y_0 - \frac{AE}{s}\right) + \frac{AE}{s} \tag{14.7a}$$

where $g = s/(v - s)$.

Now g will be positive provided that v is greater than s. This is what one would expect given that s is less than 1.0, and v, the capital–output ratio is normally greater than 1.0. Since s is a fraction, $g = s/(v - s)$ will also be less than 1.0. We can interpret g as the growth of national output. Any initial divergence of output from its original level, y_0 is continually magnified at a rate of $1 + g$ each period.

In general there are four basic types of adjustment path that a variable can follow. The adjustment path can converge towards equilibrium, in which case the model is stable, or diverge from equilibrium, in which event the model is unstable or explosive. The adjustment path is further characterised as oscillating or monotonic. The latter path always moves in the same direction. The four kinds of adjustment path are shown in Figure 14.2 and illustrated using the general form of equation 14.7a in which $\alpha = 1 + g$:

$$y_t = \alpha^t \left(y_0 - \frac{AE}{s} \right) + \frac{AE}{s} \tag{14.7b}$$

The four types of adjustment path are:

1. *Stable and monotonic* when α lies between 0 and +1.0. α^t gets steadily smaller as t increases so that the divergence of income from equilibrium eventually becomes negligibly small.
2. *Stable and oscillating* when α lies between −1.0 and 0. As t tends to infinity α^t tends to zero but in doing so alternates between being positive when t is an even number and being negative when t is an odd number. The adjustment path oscillates around the equilibrium value of income, which is therefore overshot a number of times. As the oscillations gradually die away, the cyclical path is said to be damped.
3. *Explosive and monotonic* if α is greater than 1.0. As time progresses α^t gets larger. In the model discussed above the adjustment path is explosive because g lies between 0 and +1.0 so that $\alpha = 1 + g$ is greater than 1.0. Whether income is continually rising and falling is determined by whether the initiating movement was an increase or a decrease in output respectively.
4. *Explosive and oscillating.* If α is less than −1.0, α^t again tends to infinity as time passes. Since α is a negative number, α^t is alternatively positive and negative depending on whether t is an even or an odd number. Because α^t gets absolutely larger as time passes, equilibrium is overshot by ever-increasing amounts. Cycles of ever-increasing amplitude are said to be anti-damped.

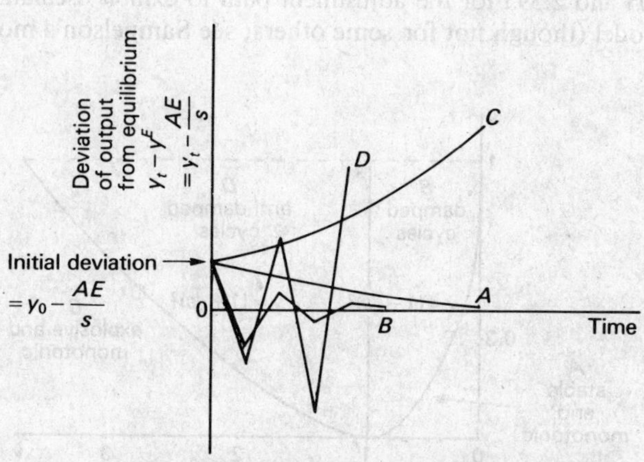

FIGURE 14.2 *The four types of adjustment path*

Since economically plausible values for s and v give a value of α in equation 14.7b which exceeds 1.0, a first-order multiplier–accelerator interaction cannot by itself generate cycles. It only produces continuous (that is, monotonic) upward or downward movements.

Second-order multiplier–accelerator interaction

Given the values of s and v that occur, we require income to be lagged by more than one time period if the multiplier–accelerator relationship is to generate cycles. A second-order multiplier–accelerator interaction contains both current income and income lagged by one and two periods. A number of models of this type, based on varying assumptions, can be set up. In the model outlined below consumption is assumed to be a function of income lagged one period. The accelerator equation assumes that, because of lags, net investment makes good last period's discrepancy between the desired and actual capital stock. This means that current investment is related to last period's change in output and not this period's. It is this factor that causes cyclical fluctuations:

$$C_t = (1 - s)y_{t-1} \tag{14.2a}$$

$$I^n_t = v(y_{t-1} - y_{t-2}) \tag{14.1a}$$

Substituting equations 14.2a and 14.1a into 14.3 we obtain

$$y_t = (1 - s + v)y_{t-1} - vy_{t-2} + AE \tag{14.8}$$

This of course has the same static-equilibrium solution as equation 14.7, namely that income equals AE/s. Equation 14.8 is a second-order difference equation because it has two lags.

The type of adjustment path followed by output in this model depends on the numerical values of v and s. Figure 14.3 shows the various combinations of values for v and s which will give the four types of adjustment path. Cycles will occur if v and s lie within the areas B or D. For example, if $s = 0.3$, v must lie between 0.205 and 2.395 for the adjustment path to exhibit oscillations. For this particular model (though not for some others; see Samuelson's model [3] for a

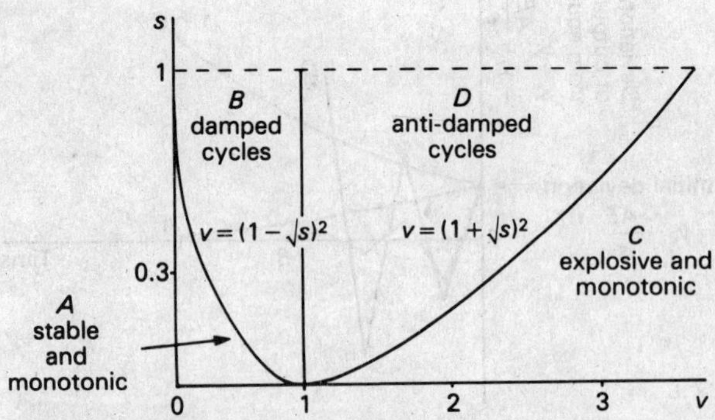

FIGURE 14.3 *The combinations of v and s which give the four types of adjustment path*

TABLE 14.1 *Adjustment path of national income following a one-period change in autonomous expenditure of 30*

Period	*A*: $s = 0.3, v = 0.2$			*B*: $s = 0.3, v = 0.8$			*C*: $s = 0.3, v = 3$			*D*: $s = 0.3, v = 1.5$		
	y_t	$y_{t-1} - y_{t-2}$	I_t^n	y_t	$y_{t-1} - y_{t-2}$	I_t^n	y_t	$y_{t-1} - y_{t-2}$	I_t^n	y_t	$y_{t-1} - y_{t-2}$	I_t^n
1	1,030	0	0	1,030	0	0	1,030	0	0	1,030	0	0
2	1,027	30	6	1,045	30	24.0	1,111	30	90	1,066	30	45
3	1,018.3	−3	−0.6	1,043.5	15	12.0	1,321	81	243	1,100.2	36	54
4	1,011.1	−8.7	−1.74	1,029.3	−1.5	−1.2	1,854	210	630	1,121.4	34.2	51.3
5	1,006.7	−6.8	−1.4	1,009.1	−14.3	−11.4	3,196	533	1,599	1,116.9	21.2	31
6	1,003.7	−4.4	−0.9	990.2	−20.2	−16.2	6,563	1,342	4,026	1,074.9	−4.6	−6.9
7	1,002	−2.9	−0.6	978.0	−18.9	−15.1				989.6	−41.9	−62.9
8	1,001.1	−0.9	−0.18	974.9	−12.5	−10.0				864.8	−85.4	−128.1
9	1,000.6	−0.5	−0.11	979.9	−3.1	−2.5				718.2	−124.8	−187.2
10	1,000.4	−0.2	−0.03	999.0	5.0	4.0				582.8	−146.6	−219.9
11				1,001.1	10.1	8.0				504.0	−135.4	−203.1
12				1,010.3	11.5	9.2				534.6	−78.8	−118.2
13				1,014.5	9.2	7.4				720.1	30.6	45.9
14				1,013.6	4.3	3.4				1082.3	185.5	278.3

different result) a capital–output ratio of less than 1.0 produces convergence, while a v greater than 1.0 causes divergence, irrespective of the size of the marginal propensity to save. In general a small capital–output ratio is required to produce anti-damped cycles.

Table 14.1 presents numerical examples which illustrate the four types of adjustment path by taking pairs of values for s and v from each of the areas A, B, C and D of Figure 14.3. The marginal propensity to save is taken to be 0.3 in all four cases and v is varied to give different adjustment paths. Autonomous expenditure is assumed to be equal to 300, which gives an equilibrium level of output of 1,000. The difference between 1,000 and income in period t gives the divergence from equilibrium.

The initial deviation from equilibrium is caused by an increase in period 1 of 30 in autonomous expenditure which returns to 300 in all subsequent periods. In the divergent monotonic case income moves steadily away from equilibrium. Cycles occur in cases B and D. After the initial shock, equilibrium is approached but is overshot. Income falls below equilibrium and returns, again overshooting. The cycles in case B diminish with time and there is convergence towards equilibrium, unlike case D.

The lagged capital-stock adjustment mechanism, linked with particular values of v and s is responsible for this cyclical behaviour. When income rises so does the desired capital stock, but the actual capital stock is not increased until the next period. Take case B. Income rises by 30 in period 1 but net investment does not rise (by 24) until the next period. This increase in investment demand stimulates an increase in income but, because autonomous expenditure falls back to 300, income rises less in period 2 than in period 1. Consequently net investment is lower in period 3 than in period 2. The fall in net investment causes income to descend from its peak level of 1,045. Since income has fallen, firms wish to hold less capital stock than actually exists. This is indicated by a desired disinvestment of –1.2. The fall in investment promotes a further fall in output which is carried below its equilibrium level. As income falls its rate of decline diminishes and disinvestment eventually reduces the actual capital stock below its desired level. Net investment becomes positive in period 10 and as a consequence output rises.

Modifications to the multiplier–accelerator interaction

There are several important features of actual trade-cycle experience which the multiplier–accelerator mechanism considered on its own fails to explain:

(1) While the accelerator theory could explain net fixed investment when it is positive it cannot explain *dis*investment. When the actual capital stock exceeds the desired stock, the rate of disinvestment is determined not just by the decline in output but also by the rate at which the capital stock depreciates. It is for this reason that the accelerator principle works better as an explanation of inventory investment than of fixed investment since the rate of both increases and decreases in stocks is directly linked to the behaviour of actual and anticipated sales. The accelerator principle therefore can quite plausibly be applied to the analysis of inventory cycles (as by Metzler [4]).

(2) Positive net investment, let alone gross investment, has not ceased entirely during depressions, as occurs in the multiplier–accelerator model outlined above. Even in the very severe depression of 1929–33, when US GNP fell by 30 per cent, real gross private investment fell by 90 and not by 100 per cent.

(3) The cycles generated by the multiplier–accelerator interaction are either damped or explosive. Only if v and s have particular values is a regular cycle of constant amplitude produced. To achieve this in the model developed here, v must equal 1.0 for all values of s. Such stringent requirements are unlikely to be fulfilled in practice, yet actual cycles have been fairly regular and have displayed no tendency to either die out or explode.

In order to provide a more satisfactory theory of the trade cycle the multiplier–accelerator relationship has been modified and supplemented in various ways. The relationship can be made non-linear by allowing s and v to vary over the cycle. The theory of permanent income rationalises pro-cyclical (that is, moving with output) movements in the MPS. The gap between the desired and actual capital stock can be expected to get smaller as the boom proceeds. Both factors reduce the rate at which aggregate demand grows and can thus rationalise an upper turning-point in the cycle.

An alternative but mutually compatible way of generating cycles is to limit the explosive path of the multiplier–accelerator interaction by imposing floors and ceilings to the level of real output. This is Hicks's [5] solution. The floor is set by autonomous investment and the ceiling is determined by limitations on the quantity of labour supplied and on the capacities of the capital-goods industries.

The role of money was not entirely rejected by Keynesian trade-cycle theorists. When included (as by Hicks [5]) it played a secondary role. In a boom the growth in the demand for money relative to its supply caused interest rates to rise and so helped to dampen investment. In the depression when the demand for money had fallen relative to income, low interest rates might help to stimulate investment once profit expectations had recovered somewhat.

14.2 The monetarist interpretation of trade cycles

The monetarist view, which stretches back to classical writings, holds that, while money has no long-run effect on real national output, in the short run monetary disturbances can exert powerful independent influences on real output. The relationship between money and income in the USA has been thoroughly documented by Friedman and Schwartz [6]. They single out four periods of economic stability, 1882–92, 1903–13, 1923–9 and 1948–60, during which real income grew at similar rates but the rate of change of the price level varied between minus 1 per cent and plus 2 per cent. The variation in the rate of change of the price level is explained by differences in the rate of growth of the money supply. They consider that the long-run rate of growth of real output and the money supply are largely independent.

Short-run monetary fluctuations are associated with similar fluctuations in real output. Friedman and Schwartz consider that the primary causal link goes from monetary changes to variations in real output. They believe this is particularly important in the explanation of severe contractions. Six of the contractions are classified as severe: 1873–9, 1892–4, 1907–8, 1921–2, 1929–33 and 1937–8. In the severe contractions the money supply decreased and four of them were accompanied by a banking crisis.

Since the money supply has generally continued to increase during less severe recessions. Friedman and Schwartz relate fluctuations in the rate of change of the money supply to variations in economic activity. One such exercise involves comparing the reference cycle with a step function in the rate of change of the money supply. Each step occurs when the rate of change of the money supply passes from a high to a low rate and vice versa. On average decreases in the rate of change of the money supply precede the reference peak by seven months, while increases in the rate of change of the money supply lead the reference-cycle trough by four months. The standard deviation of the lead in the money supply series is eight months at the peak and six months at the trough.

From this and other evidence Friedman and Schwartz conclude that changes in the rate of growth of the money supply cause changes in the same direction in real output which occur after quite a long and variable lag. It is this type of evidence which leads Friedman to eschew the use of discretionary monetary policy since it is likely in these conditions to be unsuccessful.

The arguments supporting the Friedman position have been the subject of controversy, particularly relating to whether changes in the money supply primarily depend on national income or occur independently. Another issue concerns the timing evidence. Friedman himself recognises that the timing of a relationship whereby variable X leads variable Y by no means justifies the conclusion that X causes Y. Tobin (see [8] and [9]) and others have devised models in which income is the causal factor but money leads income, or in which money is the prime-mover but income leads money. Although Friedman's theoretical underpinning of a causal and timing relationship that goes from money to income is not fully worked out, the alternative possibilities, such as an increase in output inducing a rise in the money supply several months before the increase in output actually occurs (Kalder [10]) seem less plausible.

In support of his contention that money supply changes occur independently of output and produce disturbances in output Friedman cites three occasions (January to June 1920, October 1931, and July 1936 to January 1937), when the Federal Reserve System[1] deliberately followed a restrictionary policy. This led to a sharp contraction in the money supply to be followed by a severe contraction in industrial output.

Cagan [11] provides further detailed evidence for the USA of the cyclical behaviour of the determinants of the money stock. He estimates that about one-half the variation of the money supply about its trend is accounted for by the currency–money supply ratio, one-quarter by the reserve ratio and one-fifth by 'high-powered' money. The latter variable has become more important in recent cycles. Since 'high-powered' money is subject to government control it can vary independently of income, unless the government chooses to allow it

[1] The central bank of the USA.

to vary with income. This leaves us with the currency and reserve ratios as variables which could depend on income and thus cause money to dance to the tune played by income.

As the demand for money grows more (less) rapidly in relation to its supply, the rate of interest is predicted to rise (fall). If a rise (fall) in the interest rate decreases (increases) the currency or reserve ratio, the money supply will expand (contract), given a constant 'high-powered' money base (see Chapter 9). In this event the direction of causality is from income to the money supply so that the latter is endogenous.

Cagan considers the evidence to support the interest-rate mechanism outlined above to be weak but finds other ways in which the state of business activity influences the currency and reserve ratios. As the expansion approaches the peak the currency ratio tends to rise. (The reasons for this are not clear.) The rate of growth of the money supply falls and checks the growth of output. Once the contraction sets in both ratios rise. Banks become more cautious about lending and wish to strengthen their liquid assets position. The public, experiencing similar uncertainties, raise their desired currency ratio. Both these factors lower the money supply (or alternatively its rate of growth) and strengthen the forces of contraction. This process may become self-generating, as the attempt by banks and the public to make their asset portfolios more liquid drains banks of cash reserves. Banks then need to liquidate more assets and the public, losing confidence in the banks, draw out more cash. A full-scale bank panic can be triggered off which exacerbates the contraction. Monetary factors can therefore contribute to cyclical disturbances in economic activity, both by occurring independently and by being related to changes in national income.

There are two aspects to the Keynesian argument that money is of little importance in influencing the level of economic activity in the short run. One, which we have just discussed, is that the money supply should be determined endogenously by national income. The other is that national income should be unresponsive to changes in the money supply. This necessitates velocity changing so that money supply changes are rendered ineffective. An increase in the money demand, accompanied by a reduction in the rate of growth of the money supply such as might occur at the peak, causes higher interest rates, which drive up velocity. This means people are financing each pound's worth of annual income with less money. If money is to have little influence, the changing demand for money with respect to output that occurs over the trade cycle must be accompanied by large pro-cyclical variations in velocity. Also, the change in interest rates which accompanies the change in velocity should have little effect on expenditure.

The observation that velocity rises in the upswing and falls in the downswing therefore weakens the case for the powerful influence of money. Friedman [12] distinguishes between measured velocity, the usual calculation of velocity, which is current income divided by the stock of money, and desired velocity, which is permanent income divided by the money stock. Since permanent income changes less over the cycle than measured income, desired velocity will vary less than it appears to do when measured inappropriately.

14.3 Conclusion

The Keynesian emphasis on the causal role of real variables, particularly investment, in generating trade cycles places the responsibility for cyclical fluctuations firmly with the private sector. This contrasts with the monetarist view that monetary disturbances are the major factor in causing cyclical fluctuations. The private sector is inherently stable but is subjected to monetary shocks brought about by the authorities. For instance, the 1929–33 depression is primarily attributed to the inappropriate policy of monetary contraction adopted by the Federal Reserve System following the Wall Street crash.

References

[1] E. Shapiro, 'Cyclical Fluctuations in Prices and Output in the UK 1921–71', *Economic Journal*, 86 (December 1976).

[2] J. Schumpeter, *Business Cycles* (New York: McGraw-Hill, 1939).

[3] P. Samuelson, 'Interactions between the Multiplier Analysis and the Principle of Acceleration', *Review of Economics and Statistics*, 21 (1939).

[4] L. A. Metzler, 'The Nature and Stability of Inventory Cycles', *Review of Economics and Statistics* (1941); reprinted in Gordon and Klein (eds), *Readings in Business Cycles* (London: Allen & Unwin, 1966).

[5] J. R. Hicks, *A Contribution to the Theory of the Trade Cycle* (Oxford University Press, 1950).

[6] M. Friedman and A. J. Schwartz, *A Monetary History of the United States 1867–1960* (Princeton University Press, 1963).

[7] M. Friedman and A. J., Schwartz, 'Money and Business Cycles', *Review of Economics and Statistics*, 45, 1, 2 Supplement (February 1963).

[8] J. Tobin, 'The Monetary Interpretation of History', *American Economic Review*, 55 (June 1965).

[9] J. Tobin, 'Money and Income: Post Hoc Ergo Propter Hoc', and M. Friedman, 'Comment on Tobin', *Quarterly Journal of Economics*, 84 (May 1970).

[10] N. Kaldor, 'The New Monetarism', *Lloyds Bank Review* (July 1970).

[11] P. Cagan, *Determinants and Effects of Changes in the Stock of Money, 1875–1960* (New York: National Bureau of Economic Research, 1965).

[12] M. Friedman, 'The Demand for Money: Some Theoretical and Empirical Results', *Journal of Political Economy*, 66 (1958).

15 Economic Growth

The short-run general macro model developed in section I was based on the following simplifying assumptions:

(1) The time period involved in the analysis was so short that the net investment taking place had no significant effect on the size of the economy's capital stock. This allowed us to concentrate on the effect which that net investment has on the size of aggregate demand while neglecting its effect in increasing the economy's productive capacity.

(2) A constant population. This allowed us to concentrate on the factors underlying the demand and supply of labour from a constant population. However, during the last century and a half the population of almost every country has been increasing at varying geometric rates. This has resulted in an increase in the labour force over time and has been another factor in increasing the productive capacity of the economy.

(3) An unchanging level of technical knowledge. This assumption also needs to be relaxed as increasing technical knowledge has resulted in a continual decrease in the real resources required per unit of output as well as in the introduction of new products. Technical change has been a major historical factor in increasing the economy's productive capacity. It has also stimulated the rate of growth of demand through its impact on the rate of investment.

It is now necessary to extend the earlier analysis in order to examine the effect that capital accumulation, population growth and technical progress have on the equilibrium solution for the economy. The reason for concentrating on equilibrium solutions are as follows:

(a) Equilibrium dynamic solutions are relatively easy to set up and solve, while disequilibrium dynamic systems are much more difficult to deal with as their behaviour depends on the error-adjusting mechanisms and lag structures specified.

(b) Neoclassical economists believe that the economy is inherently stable and that it tends to return to some full-employment growth path if it is displaced from this path. On the other hand, some Keynesians and neo-Keynesians believe that a capitalist economy is inherently unstable, with such stringent sufficient conditions for equilibrium full-employment growth that it is unlikely to be achieved. In order to throw some light on this difference of opinion it is necessary to examine the conditions necessary for the existence of full-employment equilibrium growth and the stability of this equilibrium growth path.

15.1 The impact of capital accumulation and population growth

We now consider what impact capital accumulation and population growth have on the economy. For the time being technical knowledge is assumed fixed. It must therefore be kept in mind that the conclusions of this section relate to an economy in which technical change is absent and some of them would be modified by the presence of technical progress. This is examined later in the chapter.

Capital accumulation and population growth mean that the quantity of available inputs in the aggregate production function increases over time. The concept of an aggregate production function was introduced in Chapter 5 when discussing the supply side of the economy. It is written as

$$y = f(L, K, T) \tag{15.1}$$

where y is the real output per period of time, L is the flow of labour services per period of time, K is the capital stock which yields a proportionate flow of capital services per period of time, and T is the state of technical knowledge which we assume fixed. The law of variable proportions is expected to hold in this economy, so that in the absence of technical change an increase in only one type of input, the other remaining fixed, will lead to a less than proportionate change in output and further increases in this input will lead to diminishing increases in output.

For simplicity we assume that the economy as a whole experiences constant returns to scale, so that a given proportionate increase in both capital and labour inputs per period of time will lead to the same proportionate increase in output per period. This implies that in the economy the size of the market for each industry's products is much larger than the capacity output of the plant with the lowest unit costs in the industry. Constant returns to scale for the economy as a whole implies that the aggregate production function is linearly homogeneous in capital and labour inputs. (See the mathematical appendix to this chapter, *note 1*, for the implications of linear homogeneity in the production function and for the proofs relating to the following discussion.) This means that in the absence of technical change the production function can be written as

$$\frac{y}{L} = F\left(\frac{K}{L}\right) \quad \text{or} \quad y = LF\left(\frac{K}{L}\right) \tag{15.2}$$

Thus the average product of labour in the economy, y/L, is an increasing function of the capital–labour ratio, given that factor proportions are variable.

However, the operation of the law of variable proportions allows us to deduce that y/L will increase at a diminishing rate as the capital–labour ratio increases. Therefore, a proportionate increase in both labour and capital inputs will keep average output per head constant, while a greater increase in labour inputs to capital inputs will decrease average product per head. This is illustrated in Figure 15.1.

The law of variable proportions implies that the marginal product of a factor decreases as relatively more of that factor is applied to the production of output. This leads to the deduction (see appendix, *note 1*) that the marginal product of capital decreases with increases in the capital–labour ratio, while the marginal product of labour decreases when the capital–labour ratio decreases. Therefore, in a competitive economy where profit-maximising entrepreneurs hire factors up to the point where their price is equal to their marginal value product, the equilibrium real wage and real interest rate will change with changes in the capital–labour ratio.

If the capital stock is growing faster than the labour force, real interest rates will fall and real wages will rise, while in the case where the labour force is growing faster than the capital stock, real interest rates will tend to rise and real wage rates fall. In both cases the increase in inputs into the production process results in a growth in output. However, output only grows at the same rate as any of the inputs if both inputs are growing at the same rate. In this case relative factor prices will remain constant as the capital–labour ratio stays unchanged.

The analysis in earlier chapters concentrated on the impact of net investment on aggregate demand and neglected its effect on the economy's productive capacity. In growth models explicit account is taken of the productive impact of positive net investment which equals the increase in the capital stock. Therefore

$$I = dK/dt \tag{15.3}$$

A constant labour force in the presence of net investment means that the rate of growth in output capacity will be below the rate of growth of the capital stock because of decreasing marginal returns. If incentives for entrepreneurs to

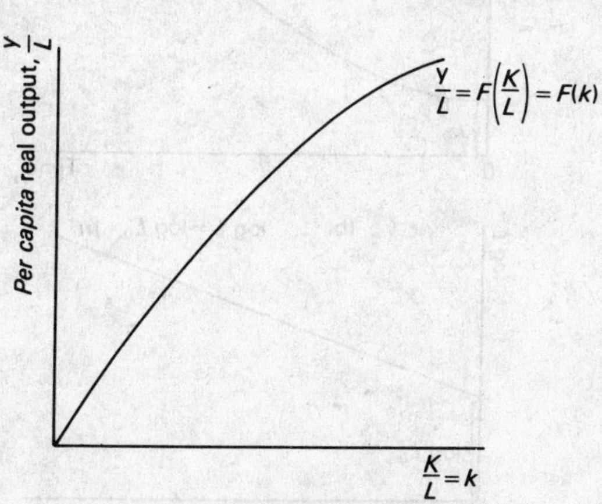

FIGURE 15.1 *Average output per unit of labour input as a function of the capital–labour ratio*

invest are to be maintained, the growth in the capacity to produce output must be matched by an increase in aggregate demand. Otherwise the growth of excess capacity will choke off any desire to invest. Therefore, as long as net investment is positive any solution for income over time in a macro model must involve some growth (or decay) path for income rather than a stationary long-run equilibrium value. A stationary long-run solution for income can only occur when there is no technical change, a constant labour force, no net investment and zero savings. Any other stationary situation will not persist in the long run.

If we introduce growth in the labour force so that the long-run supply of labour, L, grows at a steady exponential rate of μ, we have

$$L = L_0 e^{\mu t} \tag{15.4}$$

This growth path in the labour force is depicted in Figure 15.2a. We can also depict it in natural log form when equation 15.4 becomes

$$\log L = \log L_0 + \mu t \tag{15.4a}$$

This equation, plotted on semi-log graph paper, is shown in Figure 15.2b. Here the growth path is a straight line with positive intercept equal to $\log L_0$ and a positive slope equal to the exponential growth rate, μ.

The continual increase in the labour force will lead to an increase in the economy's productive capacity. Once again it requires an increase in the level of aggregate demand to maintain full employment and long-run equilibrium. If the capital stock increases less rapidly than the labour force, the capital–labour ratio falls. Because of diminishing returns output per head falls so that the rate

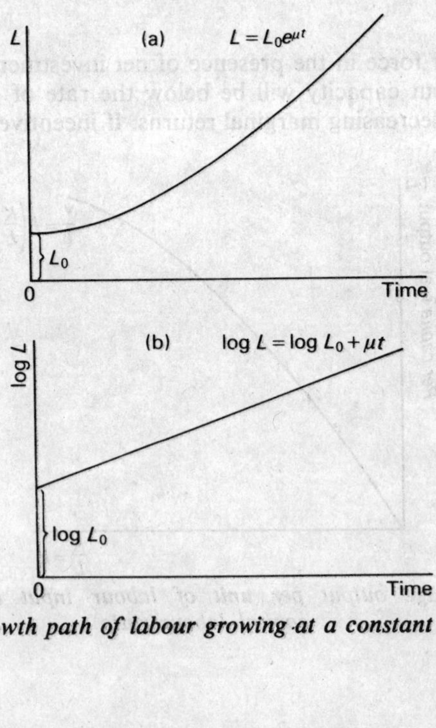

FIGURE 15.2 *The growth path of labour growing at a constant exponential rate, μ*

of growth of output is lower than the rate of growth of the labour force. In this event the real wage rate will have to fall if full employment is to be maintained. Once more equilibrium in the economy, other than in the very short run, will involve some growth path in real national income rather than a constant value of real national income.

When the labour force is growing at some exponential rate, μ, income per head, y/L, can only stay constant if the capital stock is also growing at μ and so is aggregate demand. In this situation all the flow variables in the economy must grow through time at the exponential rate, μ. The stock of money must also grow at this rate in order to keep the price level constant. Such a rate of growth in all the stock and flow variables would keep the real rate of interest and the real wage rate constant.

The above discussion has shown that any equilibrium solution in a macro model that includes capital accumulation and population growth must necessarily involve finding some growth path for the level of income. An equilibrium solution in a growth context of a closed economy macro model with a goods market, a money market and a production sector would involve a growth path in which

(a) at every moment in time desired investment and government spending are equal to desired saving plus taxes,
(b) the money market is in equilibrium so that $(M/P)^D = (M/P)^S$,
(c) full employment or a constant rate of unemployment exists, and
(d) there is equality between desired and actual capital stocks.

Growth models without a money market will have an equilibrium growth solution if conditions (a), (c), (d) are fulfilled, while the simplest growth model which concentrates on only the goods market will require (a) and (d) to be fulfilled. Steady-state equilibrium growth is an equilibrium growth rate which occurs at a steady exponential rate. Not all equilibrium growth paths are steady-state growth paths. However, most analyses of growth models have been of steady-state solutions.

For policy purposes it would be useful to analyse a macro growth model that includes a monetary sector, such as a growth version of the model developed in Chapter 6. The dynamic properties of such models are quite complicated (Tobin [1] and Johnson [2]. Therefore, it is easier to develop the conditions necessary for the existence of an equilibrium growth path and examine the stability properties of such a path in simpler models which exclude the monetary sector. In doing this we will be following the work of the pioneers of growth theory, such as Harrod, Joan Robinson, Solow and Swan.

15.2 The Harrod growth model

The simplest growth model is that formulated by Harrod (see [3], [4] and Domar [5]), which is made up of a goods market and a production sector. The model has the following features:

(1) It neglects the lag structure of the economy as this will have no effect on the steady-state equilibrium solution. This neglect of lag structures is common

to many simple growth models as lag structures only have an impact when the economy departs from the equilibrium growth path.

(2) A constant desired capital–output ratio, v. This occurs as Harrod assumes a constant long-run real rate of interest. In the absence of technical change, the assumption of constant relative factor prices will result in constant desired factor input ratios even though the aggregate production function allows factor substitution. It also results in a constant desired capital–output ratio, v, and a constant desired labour–output ratio, u.

(3) Savings are a constant proportion of real income in the economy. This is a simplifying assumption that is consistent with the permanent income hypothesis when measured income is growing at some constant exponential rate.

(4) The labour force is growing at some exogenously determined constant exponential rate, μ.

Goods-market equilibrium in the Harrod model

Goods-market equilibrium in this model requires that

(a) desired savings are equal to desired investment at each moment in time, and
(b) the capital equipment in the economy is fully utilised.

If desired investment is not equal to desired savings, then the usual multiplier response will occur and will shift the economy away from its current position until desired savings are once more equal to desired investment. If the existing capital stock is not fully utilised, there will be a decline in the entrepreneur's incentive to invest and investment will decline in the absence of some great burst of innovations. Given these two requirements for goods-market equilibrium, the equations specifying the goods market are

$$I = S \qquad \text{equilibrium in the goods market} \tag{15.5}$$

$$S = sy \qquad \text{desired savings function} \tag{15.6}$$

$$I = v(dy/dt) \qquad \text{investment function} \tag{15.7}$$

The investment function (15.7) is derived by assuming that on a growth path with continuous goods-market equilibrium expectations are always fulfilled in the aggregate. Therefore, entrepreneurs will carry out sufficient investment to achieve the capital stock which will give them the lowest total costs of production for the future expected level of output. This means that in each period entrepreneurs will invest just enough to keep the actual capital stock equal to the desired capital stock. In equation 15.7, v is the desired capital–output ratio given the existence of a fixed real rate of interest, while dy/dt is the expected rate of change in income. In equilibrium steady-state growth actual and expected rates of change in income are equal. Therefore, equation 15.7 omits specifying that the rate of change in income is the expected rate of change.

For the moment we assume that the economy's labour force is large enough and is growing sufficiently in order to supply any demand for labour from entrepreneurs. Then the economy's equilibrium growth path which maintains equilibrium in the goods market can be determined by simultaneous solution of equations 14.5, 14.6 and 14.7. Substituting for I and S in equation 15.5 gives a first-order differential equation in y and t:

$$v(dy/dt) = sy \tag{15.8}$$

Dividing through this equation by vy gives

$$\frac{1}{y}\frac{dy}{dt} = \frac{s}{v} \tag{15.9}$$

Now $(1/y)(dy/dt)$ is the proportional rate of growth of equilibrium real income over time. Therefore, equation 15.9 shows that the equilibrium growth rate of income in Harrod's model must be s/v. This equation can be integrated to give a solution for the time path of y in terms of s/v and t (see appendix, *note 2*). Therefore

$$y = y_0 \exp[(s/v)t] \tag{15.10}$$

where y_0 is the value of y at some arbitrary time 0.

The analysis above shows that the growth path of real income, y, which maintains equilibrium in the goods market requires the economy to grow at a steady exponential rate equal to s/v. This rate of growth is called the *warranted rate of growth*. The warranted rate of growth, G_w, is that rate of growth which allows desired savings to be equal to desired investment while maintaining full-capacity output at every point in time. It is determined by the parameters s and v so that $G_w = s/v$. This is the only rate of growth which will maintain goods-market equilibrium and allow expectations to be completely fulfilled. If at any time the growth rate expected by entrepreneurs is not equal to G_w, then the economy will not be on the warranted growth path.

Stability properties of the Harrod model

Let the rate of growth of real income expected in the near future by entrepreneurs be j. If the current level of real income is $\bar{y}$, then the level of real income at some time t in the near future that entrepreneurs will expect will be $\bar{y}e^{jt}$. The rate of change with respect to time of this expected real income will be

$$d/dt(\bar{y}e^{jt}) = j\bar{y}e^{jt} \tag{15.11}$$

Substituting this rate of change of expected real income for dy/dt in equation 15.7 gives the investment function for situations where expected growth in income is different from the actual growth in income. Therefore

$$I = v(d/dt)(\bar{y}e^{jt}) = vj\bar{y}^{jt} \tag{15.7a}$$

Substituting this value for I into the goods-market equilibrium condition $S = I$, and assuming that $S = sy$, gives

$$sy = vj\bar{y}e^{jt} \tag{15.12}$$

where y is the actual value of the real national income at any time t. Rewriting this gives

$$y = (v/s)j\bar{y}e^{jt} \tag{15.12a}$$

Therefore, actual income at time $t = (j/G_w)$ (expected income at time t).

This shows that the expected real income at time t can only equal the actual income at that time if the rate of income growth expected by entrepreneurs, j, is equal to the warranted rate of growth, G_w. When the warranted rate of growth equals the expected rate of growth then aggregate demand at every point in time will be just large enough to keep the economy's capital equipment working at its designed capacity.

If j is below the warranted rate, G_w, then actual income at any time t will be below the expected level of income for that period. This shortfall of actual income below expected income will lead to excess capacity in the economy as entrepreneurs had invested in sufficient capacity to meet the expected level of aggregate demand. If this excess capacity leads entrepreneurs to lower their expected rate of growth, this will lead to a further decline of the expected and actual growth rates below the warranted growth rate. The opposite situation will occur if j is above the warranted growth rate. This unstable property of the warranted growth path, where deviations off the growth path tend to lead to further movements away from it, is known as the 'knife-edge' property of the Harrod model.

Once the economy is off the warranted path in the Harrod model, whether it eventually moves to some warranted growth path depends on the error-adjustment mechanism adopted by the entrepreneurs to correct their mistaken expectations. Therefore, an analysis of the disequilibrium path of the model requires one to specify an error-adjustment mechanism and then carry out a dynamic analysis. Such analyses have been carried out by Jorgenson [6] and by Phillips [7] (see Ch. 10 of Allen). These analyses dropped the equilibrium requirement that the desired capital stock is always equal to the actual capital stock and set up error-adjustment functions for investment, so that any excess or shortfall in the desired capital stock over the actual capital stock was only corrected over a number of years, rather than in the immediately following year. These analyses found that unless the error-correcting period was longer than v/s years, once the economy was off the warranted growth path it tended to move further away from this path.

The natural rate of growth in the Harrod model

The analysis of the Harrod model up to this point has ignored the rate of growth of the labour force and technological change. Assuming that the labour force grows at an exogenous exponential rate, μ, the long-run labour supply equation is

$$L = L_0 e^{\mu t} \tag{15.4}$$

In the absence of technical change the desired labour–output ratio, u, is assumed to be constant and the maximum real output, y, that can be achieved by the economy at any time t is

$$y = (1/u)L_0e^{\mu t} \tag{15.13}$$

Therefore, the maximum sustainable rate of growth on the supply side of an economy without technical progress is

$$(1/y)(dy/dt) = \mu \tag{15.14}$$

This is called the *natural rate of growth* and in the absence of technical progress it is equal to the rate of growth of the labour force, μ.

Technical change can easily be introduced into this model if it is assumed to occur at a steady exponential rate, m, and is of a labour-augmenting type.[1] This form of technical progress occurs when the labour–income ratio, u, declines at a steady negative exponential rate through time so that

$$u = u_0e^{-mt}$$

This means that over time less labour input is required per unit of output and the capital–labour ratio increases. Therefore, the maximum real income attainable at any time t becomes

$$y = \frac{1}{u_0e^{-mt}} L_0e^{\mu t}$$

$$= \frac{1}{u_0} L_0e^{(m+\mu)t} \tag{15.15}$$

Thus with a growing labour force and steady labour-augmenting technical progress, the *maximum sustainable rate of growth on the supply side is the natural rate of growth which is equal to the sum of the rate of technical progress, m, and the rate of growth in the labour force.* Thus

$$(1/y)(dy/dt) = m + \mu \tag{15.16}$$

Conflicts between the warranted and natural growth rates

The earlier analysis of the warranted rate of growth demonstrated that, given s and v, this was the only rate of growth at which the economy could grow if desired savings were to equal desired investment and the actual capital stock were to equal the desired stock of capital. However, the ability of the economy to sustain a particular warranted growth path depends on the warranted growth rate either being equal to or less than the natural rate of growth.

If the warranted rate of growth is equal to the natural rate of growth, then it is possible to have a steady-state rate of growth with either full employment (the so-called 'golden age') or a constant rate of unemployment. In this steady-state condition income and capital stock per head will remain constant in the absence of technical change, while it will rise at the same exponential rate, m, as the rate of technical progress if labour-augmenting technical change occurs.

If the warranted rate is below the natural rate of growth, then it is possible to maintain steady-state growth at the warranted rate with continually increasing

[1] Unless technical progress is of this labour-augmenting or Harrod neutral type there will be no steady-state solution for the model.

unemployment. Here

$$G_w = s/v < m + \mu$$

In this situation the standard Keynesian monetary and fiscal policies used to deal with unemployment are totally inappropriate. If $G_w < m + \mu$ and the economy is growing at the warranted rate, G_w, then it is operating at full capacity. Unemployment is growing as investment and saving out of full-capacity output is too small to equip all the new arrivals in the labour force, plus those existing workers displaced by technological change, with the quantity of capital necessary for their employment.

Here unemployment is produced by inadequate capital accumulation and saving out of full-capacity output, given the desired constant capital–output ratio, v. It is not brought about by inadequate aggregate demand, as growth at the warranted rate involves the economy in full utilisation of its capital stock. The Keynesian monetary and fiscal policies to cope with unemployment were designed to deal with deficient aggregate demand. Therefore, applying them in this case will only make matters worse by diverting resources away from capital accumulation. This state of affairs makes standard short-run Keynesian analysis inappropriate for many developing countries.

The only sensible way to deal with growing unemployment when the economy is growing at the warranted rate is to increase the warranted rate. This requires either an increase in the rate of savings out of real income so as to increase the rate of capital accumulation out of full-capacity real income or a decrease in the desired capital–labour ratio. Both of these may eventually occur under the pressure of economic forces but the process does require a change in relative factor incomes and prices.

If political constraints prevent relative factor prices from changing sufficiently, or if the process of change is slow and difficult, the government could take action to increase the rate of savings. This can take the form of increasing the incentives for private saving, or directly increasing the rate of public-sector savings, or pursuing both policies simultaneously. Public-sector savings can be increased by raising the rate of taxation and by cutting non-productive government expenditure.

If the warranted rate of growth is above the natural rate of growth, the actual rate of growth will be periodically constrained below the warranted rate by a shortage of labour to man the newly produced capital equipment. The analysis in the previous section of the chapter showed that any decline in the expected or actual rates of growth below the warranted rate of growth will lead to excess capacity in the economy. The emergence of excess capacity will diminish the incentive to invest and thus reduce the rate of investment. This will lead to periods of declining aggregate demand and increasing unemployment due to deficient aggregate demand in relation to installed capacity. This is the situation for which traditional Keynesian monetary and fiscal remedies were developed. They have the desired impact on the level and rate of change of unemployment through their effects on aggregate demand. However, as long as the warranted rate of growth remains above the natural rate of growth, the economy will suffer from periodic depressions interspersed by periods of growth.

When the warranted rate of growth exceeds the natural rate of growth the government can reduce the warranted rate through fiscal policy. This is done by changing the proportion of real national income that the government spends on goods and services which do not add to the economy's productive capacity for marketable output and financing this change in expenditure by borrowing from the public.

In the following exposition we assume that the proportion of government expenditure in real national income is γ and that the government finances this expenditure entirely by selling bonds to the private sector. The modified Harrod model in this case is

$I + G = S$	goods-market equilibrium	(15.5a)
$S = sy$	savings function	(15.6)
$I = v(dy/dt)$	investment function	(15.7)
$G = \gamma y$	government expenditure function	(15.17)

Substituting for I, G and S in equation 15.5a gives

$$v(dy/dt) + \gamma y = sy \tag{15.18}$$

Manipulating this equation gives

$$\frac{1}{y}\frac{dy}{dt} = \frac{s-\gamma}{v} \tag{15.19}$$

This shows that the introduction of government expenditure has lowered the warranted rate of growth which is now $G_w = (s - \gamma)/v$. The warranted rate of growth can now be manipulated by changing the proportion of national income spent on public-sector consumption and financing this by an equal change in government borrowing from the public. Therefore, the government can lower the warranted rate of growth through changes in fiscal policy at the expense of increasing its fixed-interest debt. However, in an exponentially growing economy (unlike the case of a stationary economy) continual deficit financing will not create an insupportable burden of debt. While the government debt will increase absolutely through time, it will tend to some constant ratio with respect to the annual real income (Domar [8]).

In the absence of government expenditure and taxation the warranted rate of growth is equal to s/v, while the natural rate of growth is equal to $m + \mu$. In the Harrod model s, m and μ are all exogenously determined, while v is fixed due to the assumption of a constant real rate of interest. Therefore, in the likely event of the warranted rate of growth not being equal to the natural rate of growth (i.e. $s/v \neq m + \mu$) there are no economic forces changing these parameters and thus returning the economy to a long-run full-employment path. Any such path in the Harrod model is either fortuitous or attained through deliberate government policy.

This characteristic of the Harrod model does not seem to be particularly realistic for developed capitalist economies in a long-run growth context. Historically these economies have not experienced prolonged periods of rising unemployment as a result of either deficient demand or insufficient accumulation, though there have been short-run experiences of both phenomena. Therefore, much of the work on growth theory in the two decades following the Second World War was a respecification of Harrod's model so that s, or v, or both, became functions of other economic variables in the models.

Economists belonging to the Cambridge post-Keynesian school dealt with the problem of differing warranted and natural rates of growth by writing s as a function of income distribution. Due to the retention of profits by firms the marginal propensity to save out of profit income is specified as being higher than the marginal propensity to save out of non-profit incomes. This allows savings as a proportion of income to vary within a band, depending on the distribution of income between profits and non-profits. This allows the warranted rate of growth to take on a range of values. Provided that the natural rate of growth lies within this range, the economy will adjust to a steady-state growth path in the long run (see Kaldor [9]; Kaldor and Mirrlees [10]). The alternative approach to this problem is the neoclassical approach, which concentrates on changes in v, the desired capital–output ratio.

15.3 The Solow neoclassical model of economic growth

The neoclassical approach (Solow [11], [12], Swan [13] and Phelps [14]) assumes that factor prices are flexible in the long run and respond to excess demand. This allows factor substitution by firms in response to changes in relative factor prices. Aggregating this response by firms across the economy leads to changes in the factor proportions utilised in the aggregate production function, $y = f(L, K, T)$ and this alters the capital–output ratio, v.

The flexibility of factor prices means that in the long run the real rate of interest, ρ, changes to make investment equal to the rate of saving at full-capacity output. A fall in the real rate of interest increases the desired capital stock relative to any expected level of income, while a rise in the real rate of interest has the opposite effect. Therefore, the long-run neoclassical growth model does not possess an independent investment function. Investment is merely defined as the change in the capital stock, i.e.

$$I = dK/dt \tag{15.3}$$

The aggregate production function is assumed to be linearly homogeneous in labour and capital inputs and, in the absence of technical change, is written as

$$\frac{y}{L} = F\left(\frac{K}{L}\right) \tag{15.2}$$

This production function is graphed in Figures 15.1 and 15.3, which show a well-behaved production function. Defining $K/L = k$ and substituting for K/L into equation 15.2 this becomes

$$y/L = F(k) \tag{15.2a}$$

The savings function in the model is the proportional savings function used

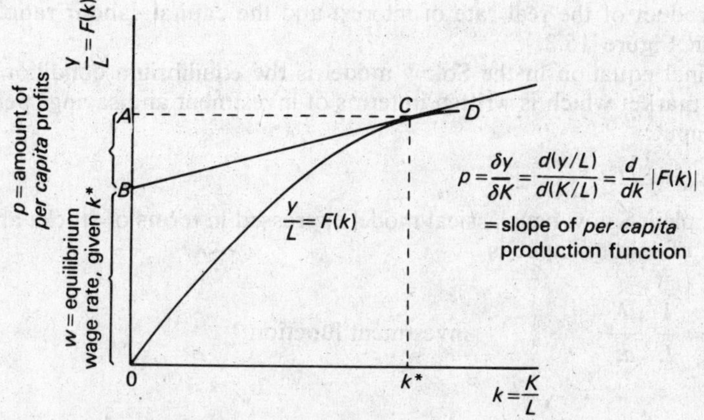

FIGURE 15.3 *The per capita production function: wage rate and interest rate in the Solow model*

in the Harrod model. This can be written in terms of saving per unit of labour input by dividing through both sides by L so that

$$S/L = s(y/L) \tag{15.6a}$$

The real wage rate in the neoclassical model is also assumed to be flexible in the long run. It adjusts to the level necessary to equate the demand for labour with the available labour force which is growing at an exogenous exponential rate of μ.

It is assumed that the economy is purely competitive[1] so that profit-maximising firms equate the value of the marginal product of a factor input to its price. Therefore, in equilibrium the real rate of interest, ρ, equals the marginal product of capital and the real wage rate, w, equals the marginal product of labour. This can be expressed as

$$\rho = \frac{\partial y}{\partial K} = \frac{d}{dk} F(k) \tag{15.20}$$

$$w = \frac{\partial y}{\partial L} = F(k) - k \frac{d}{dk} F(k) \tag{15.21}$$

where k is the capital–labour ratio. Equation 15.20 shows the rate of interest in equilibrium as being equal to the rate of change in output per unit of labour input with respect to changes in the capital–labour ratio. Equation 15.21 shows the equilibrium real wage as the difference between total output per unit of labour input and the amount of output per head paid out as profit, where profit

[1] The assumption of a purely competitive economy is a simplifying assumption. It is not crucial for the conclusions on the characteristics of the equilibrium steady-state growth path in the neoclassical model.

is the product of the real rate of interest and the capital–labour ratio. This is shown in Figure 15.3.

The final equation in the Solow model is the equilibrium condition for the product market which is written in terms of investment and savings per unit of labour input:

$$I/L = S/L \tag{15.5a}$$

The complete Solow neoclassical model expressed in terms of stocks and flows per unit of labour input is

$$\frac{I}{L} = \frac{1}{L}\frac{dK}{dt} \qquad \text{investment function} \tag{15.3a}$$

$$\frac{S}{L} = s\frac{y}{L} \qquad \text{savings function} \tag{15.6a}$$

$$\frac{I}{L} = \frac{S}{L} \qquad \text{equilibrium in goods market} \tag{15.5a}$$

$$\frac{y}{L} = F(k) \qquad \text{aggregate production function} \tag{15.2a}$$

$$L = L_0 e^{\mu t} \qquad \text{long-run labour supply function} \tag{15.4}$$

$$\rho = \frac{d}{dk}F(k) \qquad \text{demand for capital stock} \tag{15.20}$$

$$w = F(k) - k\frac{d}{dk}F(k) \qquad \text{demand for labour} \tag{15.21}$$

This gives a system of seven equations in the seven unknowns of *y*, *I*, *S*, *K*, *L*, ρ and *w* which solves for the values of each of these variables at each point in time. The solution of this model finds the warranted growth rate in income and the capital stock adjusting to the natural growth rate through changes in the desired capital–output ratio. Therefore, unless some limit to factor substitution is reached, there is no long-run conflict between the warranted and natural rates of growth. The equilibrium steady-state solution of the model is one where the warranted rate of growth has adjusted to the natural rate of growth. This change in the warranted growth rate requires a change in the rate of return to capital, ρ, and the capital–labour ratio, *k*. If the warranted rate were originally higher than the natural rate, the adjustment towards the steady-state growth path will require a drop in ρ and a rise in *k*. This will increase the desired capital–output ratio, *v*, which lowers the warranted growth rate, *s*/*v*. The opposite must happen if the warranted growth path were originally below the natural growth path.

Taking labour inputs as being measured in natural units (i.e. men) the model can be discussed in *per capita* terms such as savings per head, capital per head, etc. The increase in capital per head, dk/dt, can be looked at as the difference between the savings per head, $sF(k)$, and the capital accumulation per head, μk, necessary to equip new entrants to the labour force with the same amount of capital per head as existing workers currently enjoy. The first five equations of the Solow model (equations 15.2a, 15.3a, 15.4, 15.5a and 15.6a) can be solved in *per capita* terms to give such a relationship:

$$dk/dt = sF(k) - \mu k \tag{15.22}$$

This expression, in terms of the capital–labour ratio only, is the fundamental differential equation of the model (it is derived in the appendix, *note 3*). The equation is depicted in Figure 15.4.

If dk/dt is positive, the capital–labour ratio, k, must be growing through time. Income per head, y/L, must also be growing through time but at a slower rate than k due to the operation of diminishing returns. This can be seen in Figure 15.4(a), as a movement in k from k^* to k' causes a less than proportionate increase in y/L. Growth in k leads to an equal rate of growth in μk, the investment necessary to maintain the current level of k with the labour force growing at rate μ, but it leads to a slower rate of growth in savings per head, sy/L. This leads to a decline in dk/dt, and the process continues until dk/dt equals zero and $sF(k) = \mu k$. At this point desired savings per head is just

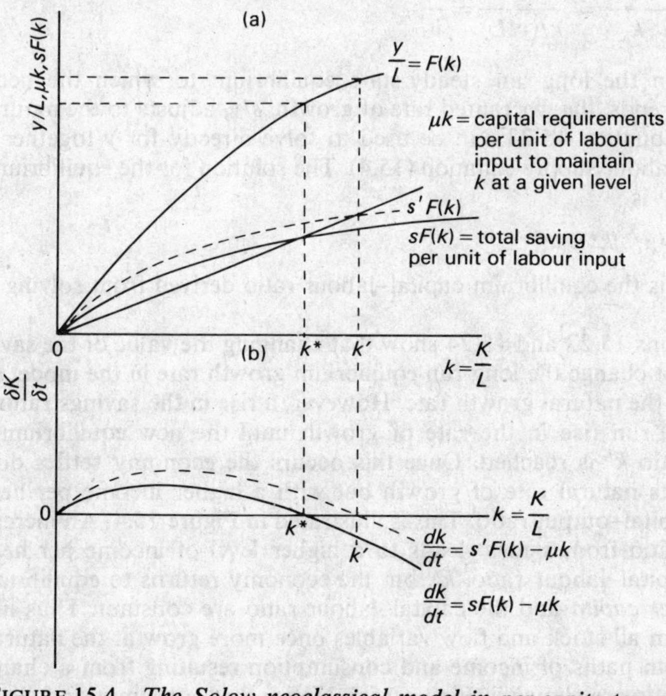

FIGURE 15.4 *The Solow neoclassical model in per capita terms*

equal to the investment per head necessary to maintain the capital–labour ratio at its current value, k^*. This can be seen in Figure 15.4 where $dk/dt = 0$ at k^* which is where $sF(k) = \mu k$. Any point to the left of k^* is one where $sF(k) > \mu k$ so that $dk/dt > 0$ and the capital–labour ratio, k, will be rising over time. Therefore, any chance shift to the left of k^* will set up a process of return to that value of the capital–labour ratio.

If dk/dt is negative then the capital–labour ratio, k, must be declining but at a slower rate. The decline in k will produce an equal proportional decline in μk, but a less than proportional decline in saving per head, $sF(k)$. Thus dk/dt moves towards zero, and the process continues until $dk/dt = 0$ and $sF(k) = \mu k$. This is illustrated in Figure 15.4. At any point to the right of k^*, $sF(k) < \mu k$, which means that $dk/dt < 0$ and k must be falling through time until k is once more equal to k^*.

The equilibrium solution for the differential equation (15.22) and therefore for the Solow growth model occurs when $dk/dt = 0$. The discussion above shows that this is a stable solution as any displacement from the point $k = k^*$ leads to a return to that value of k. At this point desired saving per head is just equal to the investment per head necessary to keep the capital–labour ratio constant given the rate of growth in the labour force. Therefore, in equilibrium

$$\mu k = sF(k) \tag{15.23}$$

or

$$\mu = \frac{s(y/L)}{k} = \frac{s}{k/(y/L)} = \frac{s}{v} \tag{15.23a}$$

Thus, in the long-run steady-state equilibrium to which the neoclassical economy tends, the warranted rate of growth, s/v, adjusts to the natural rate of growth. Equation 15.23 can be used to solve directly for y together with the long-run labour supply equation (15.4). The solution for the equilibrium growth value of y is

$$y = (\mu/s)k^* L_0 e^{\mu t} \tag{15.24}$$

where k^* is the equilibrium capital–labour ratio derived from solving equation 15.23.

Equations 15.23 and 15.24 show that changing the value of the saving ratio, s, does not change the long-run equilibrium growth rate in the model as it does not affect the natural growth rate. However, a rise in the savings ratio will lead to a short-run rise in the rate of growth until the new equilibrium capital–output ratio k' is reached. Once this occurs the economy settles down once more to its natural rate of growth but with a higher income per head and a higher capital–output ratio. This is illustrated in Figure 15.4. An increase in the savings ratio from s to s' leads to a higher level of income per head and a higher capital–labour ratio, k', but the economy returns to equilibrium where income *per capita* and the capital–labour ratio are constant. Thus in the new equilibrium all stock and flow variables once more grow at the natural rate, μ. The growth paths of income and consumption resulting from a change in the savings ratio are shown in Figure 15.5. Notice that consumption falls at first so

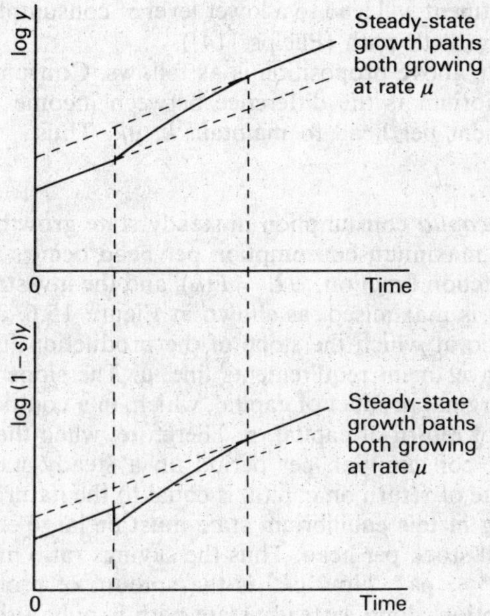

FIGURE 15.5 *Time paths of income and consumption following a rise in the savings ratio*

that any future rise in consumption is at the expense of forgone current consumption.

The neoclassical theorem: the golden rule of accumulation

The end of the last section showed that a rise in the savings ratio would increase incomes per head even though it would not affect the equilibrium long-run rate of growth. However, any such rise in saving means an immediate diminution of current consumption which need not be offset by a future increase in consumption. This is because the rise in capital per head increases the rate of investment per head, μk, necessary to keep the capital–output ratio constant. With the law of variable proportions the rise in μk may more than offset the rise in income per head, leaving no room for any rise in *per capita* consumption. Therefore, unless one knows of some way of raising the natural rate of growth through investment, an economy can invest far too large a proportion of its current income.

Given the natural rate of growth, the level of investment which will maximise consumption per head in each period along the steady-state growth path will be equal to the level of profits in the economy. This means that along such a steady-state maximal consumption path the rate of return on capital in a competitive economy will be equal to the natural rate of growth, μ (i.e. $\rho = \mu$). Any other rate of investment will lead to a lower level of consumption on the steady-state equilibrium growth path (Phelps [14]).

The proof of the above proposition is as follows. Consumption per head in steady-state equilibrium is the difference between income per head and the necessary investment per head to maintain k, μk. Thus

$$C/L = F(k) - \mu k$$

where C/L is *per capita* consumption in steady-state growth as in equilibrium $sF(k) = \mu k$. Now maximum consumption per head occurs when the distance between the production function, $y/L = F(k)$, and the investment requirements per head line, μk, is maximised, as shown in Figure 15.6. This occurs at the capital–labour ratio at which the slope of the production function is equal to the slope of the investment requirements line, μ. The slope of the production function is the marginal product of capital, which, in a competitive economy, is equal to the rate of return of capital, ρ. Therefore, when the capital stock per head is such that consumption per period on a steady-state growth path is maximised, the rate of return on capital is equal to the natural rate of growth.[1] The rate of saving in this equilibrium state must be large enough to maintain this level of capital stock per head. Thus the savings ratio must be adjusted so that $sF(k^*) = \mu k^* = \rho k^*$. Now ρk^* is the amount of profit per head. Thus maximal consumption along a steady-state path is only attained when saving per head is equal to profits per head. This implies that along such a growth path investment must equal the level of total profits.

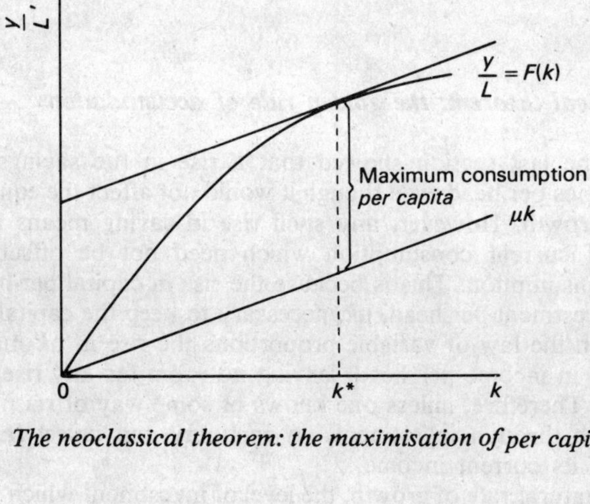

FIGURE 15.6 *The neoclassical theorem: the maximisation of per capita consumption*

[1] This result can be achieved by maximising $C/L = F(k) - \mu k$ with respect to k and interpreting the result.

Short-run stability in the neoclassical model

In the neoclassical model there is no problem of conflict between the warranted and natural rates of growth as factor price flexibility allows v to adjust so that the warranted rate coincides with the natural rate of growth. The key differences of this model from the Harrod model lie in the assumptions of

(a) factor price flexibility, and
(b) The absence of an independent investment function.

The absence of an independent investment function in the neoclassical model means that the model neglects the role of entrepreneurial expectations about the future in affecting the level of investment and income. This neglect of expectations simplifies the derivation of steady-state solutions which give some insight into the factors underlying the long-run trend growth rate. However, it is misleading to use models that neglect expectations to deal with short-run adjustment paths and fluctuations.

If one introduces an independent investment function, where investment depends on firms' expectations, into the neoclassical growth model, then the instability problem that exists in the Harrod model reappears in the short run. This is in spite of the possibility of factor substitution. This instability has nothing to do with the difference between the warranted and natural growth paths and will exist when these two paths are identical. The introduction of an independent investment equation over-determines the neoclassical growth model and an equilibrium solution can only be found if either one of the equations becomes dependent or if there is a chance consistency between the equations (i.e. chance dependency of one of the equations). Sen [15] demonstrates this problem using a neoclassical growth model with a Cobb–Douglas production function, $y = Ae^{mt}K^{\alpha}L^{1-\alpha}$, together with an independent investment function.

15.4 The impact of technical change on the neoclassical growth model

Technical change can be introduced into the neoclassical growth model in the form of labour-augmenting, or Harrod neutral technical change. In this form of technical change the capital–output ratio, v, does not alter so long as the real rate of interest, ρ, remains unchanged. Labour-augmenting technical progress occurs when machines are redesigned to produce the same output with a smaller labour force or if the labour force becomes more efficient so that fewer workers are needed to tend a given machine. This form of technical change has the same impact on the economy's capacity to produce output as an increase in the rate of growth of the labour force. It is the only form of technical progress that is consistent with steady-state equilibrium growth in both the Harrod and neoclassical models.

Labour-augmenting technical progress can be handled quite simply in the neoclassical model by dealing with labour in terms of efficiency units rather than in natural units. An efficiency unit can be defined as equal to the productive potential of a natural labour unit (worker) at some past date. With a constant capital–output ratio this productive potential can be measured by the output per worker at that past date. With labour-augmenting technical progress, which occurs at the rate m, output per unit of labour rises. Thus the number of efficiency units embodied in a natural unit of labour rises at the rate m over time. Therefore, the total number of labour efficiency units, L, at time t is

$$\bar{L} = Le^{mt} = L_0 \exp[(m + \mu)t]$$

We can now express each equation of the Solow model in terms of income per efficiency unit, capital per efficiency unit, etc. Solving the respecified model gives a differential equation in terms of capital stock per efficiency unit, i.e.

$$\frac{dk}{dt} = sF(k) - (m + \mu)k \tag{15.25}$$

This has an identical form to the fundamental differential equation (15.22), except that the coefficient of the last term is now $(m + \mu)$. This gives a stable equilibrium solution in which the warranted rate of growth is equal to the natural rate of growth, $m + \mu$. As the basic equation is identical, all the earlier conclusions relating to the impact of saving on the equilibrium growth rate, on instability and on the neoclassical theorem hold in the presence of labour-augmenting technical change.

The equilibrium state, with labour-augmenting technical change at the rate m, involves output, investment and the capital stock all growing at the rate $m + \mu$. Real wages will increase through time at the rate m, while the real rate of interest will remain at ρ^* because the capital stock grows faster than the labour force so that capital per labour efficiency unit stays constant despite the rise in real wages.

The Harrod and Solow models have been criticised for their treatment of technical change. In these models technical change affects the whole capital stock. Both new and old machines are treated alike. Such *disembodied* technical change is similar to a change in plant organisation that increases efficiency. However, in the real world most technical change is *embodied* in new machines while the old machines are not affected. To meet this criticism various neoclassical *vintage* growth models have been constructed (see Hamberg [16] and Solow [12] Ch. 3). These allow for differences in the efficiency of capital equipment acquired at different dates, each period of acquisition of capital involving a different 'vintage' of capital. All of these models are neoclassical in the sense that they assume factor price flexibility and do not have an independent investment function.

These vintage models differ in that some allow labour to be substituted for capital equipment that is already in existence, while others only allow factor substitution during the planning stage. Here once equipment is produced it has rigid factor proportions. There is also a vintage model which does not allow any factor substitution either in the planning stage or once the capital equipment has been installed. In all of these vintage growth models an increased rate of saving and investment raises the level of income per head but not the steady-state growth rate. This remains equal to the natural growth rate $m + \mu$ when technical change is labour-augmenting. This growth path is stable, though the adjustment to equilibrium is not smooth in models that do not allow factor substitution with existing equipment.

15.5 Cambridge criticisms of the aggregate production function

Cambridge post-Keynesians, Joan Robinson [17] in particular, have criticised the use of an aggregate production function in macroeconomic models. The basis of their criticism is that capital goods are produced means of production and that the value of any specific capital goods will be affected by changes in income distribution, particularly by changes in the rate of profit (real rate of interest, ρ), as well as by embodied technical change.

The criticism takes two forms. The first attacks the use of marginal productivity theory to determine the real rate of profit in a macro growth model. This, they claim, involves circular reasoning in a world with diverse capital goods. In such a world the aggregate capital stock can only be measured in money terms, by weighting each capital good by its current price, and then using this capital stock to determine the rate of profit via the marginal productivity of capital. If wages and profits enter into the prices of produced capital goods, this implies that the rate of profit must be known in order to determine the size of the capital stock so as to determine the rate of profit! This is why the post-Keynesians harp on about the need for an independent theory that determines the rate of profit (Kregel [18]), even though none of them has provided a consistent theory of the *rate of profit*, as distinct from the level of profit, that is independent of some measure of the capital stock.

To neoclassical economists this seems a mistaken criticism as they see the aggregate approach as just a simplification of a disaggregated general-equilibrium system that makes the system amenable to estimation, testing and useful for prediction and policy purposes. In a general-equilibrium approach one does not have an explanation based on prior cause and effect, of the rate of profit or of any other price. In a general-equilibrium system prices, profits and wages are all determined simultaneously. One does not have to deal with a unicausal determination of the rate of profit but with a system involving a mutual determination of all prices, including the rate of profit. This system operates in equilibrium and neoclassical economists believe that once out of equilibrium, the system eventually returns to it through some iterative process of adjustment. This adjustment need not be smooth, and even in disequilibrium there is a process of mutual interaction amongst the variables.

The Cambridge critique would be much more telling if it could show that there is no theoretical reason for the system, once in disequilibrium, to ever return to some equilibrium set of values. At present this critique seems to be directed against the construction of highly aggregated macro models which aim to give predictions in a disequilibrium situation.

The second form of the Cambridge criticism is theoretically more important, though its practical significance may prove to be small. This criticism is directed against the neoclassical concept of a smooth production function where low rates of interest are associated with high capital–labour ratios and vice versa.

Capital goods are themselves produced with the aid of capital and labour and their production takes time. This means that the interest component in the price of a capital good in a competitive system will vary, depending on the length of time it takes to produce it. The longer the time necessary to produce the capital good, the larger the impact of interest changes on its competitive long-run market price and the smaller the impact of changes in wages on this long-run price. Therefore, as different techniques differ in the length of time necessary to produce their associated capital equipment, changes in the level of interest rates may affect the total costs of using these techniques in different ways. One may find one technique being the lowest-cost technique at a very high rate of interest, becoming a high-cost technique at a lower rate of interest and reappearing as the lowest-cost technique at a very low interest rate.

This phenomenon is called 'reswitching'. The possibility of a lower capital–labour ratio being used when the rate of interest falls means that there is no *logical necessity* for the neoclassical assumption of an inverse correlation between the capital–labour ratio and the rate of interest to hold and there is a distinct possibility of discontinuities and reversals in the production function. However, there is no logical necessity for the correlation not to hold either.

The demonstration that there is no logical necessity for an assumption to hold does not mean that it is therefore useless and should be discarded. According to the approach of 'positive' economics, assumptions should not be judged on the basis of their logical necessity but rather on whether or not they give useful predictions that allow us to forecast events and thus, to some extent, control them. The Cambridge criticism, although logically impeccable, so far has been entirely negative and has given rise to a joke among some economists: 'there is positive economics and negative economics: the latter is what is taught at Cambridge'. The question of what is a useful theory or simplification cannot be decided on the basis of scholastic reasoning alone. The decision requires empirical testing to refute the theory and its replacement by a theory with a better predictive performance.

15.6 Conclusions

1. The long-run steady-state growth rate in the economy is determined by the rate of growth of the labour force and of technical change and not by the rate of investment. Therefore, an increase in the rate of investment will only lead to a short-run increase in the rate of growth, with the economy reverting to the natural rate of growth when it returns to a steady state. The only case where an increase in the rate of investment leads to an increase in the natural rate of growth is when this directly results in an increase in the underlying rate of technical change. This conclusion does not augur well for the comparative growth performance of the United Kingdom, where on both sides of industry there is a basic reluctance to accept change.

2. The neoclassical theorem shows that a country can invest too much from the point of view of maximising consumption per head on the steady-state growth path.
3. If either factor prices are rigid for political or institutional reasons, or factor substitutability is restricted, then a situation of full-capacity growth with unemployment can only be dealt with by increasing capital accumulation and savings and not by the traditional Keynesian remedies for unemployment.
4. There is a short-run problem of instability when investment is determined by entrepreneurial expectations.

The growth models considered in this chapter are very simple as they are highly aggregated and exclude a monetary sector. For policy-making purposes it is necessary to develop much more comprehensive disaggregated models which include both government and monetary sectors.

Mathematical appendix

Note 1

If $y = f(L, K, \bar{T})$ is a linearly homogeneous function in K and L, this implies that

$$\lambda y = f(\lambda L, \lambda K, \lambda \bar{T}) \tag{15.1a}$$

which is true for all values of λ. Substituting $\lambda = 1/L$ into the above equation gives

$$\frac{y}{L} = f\left(1, \frac{K}{L}, \bar{T}\right)$$

As $\bar{T}$ is assumed constant for the time being we can rewrite this as

$$\frac{y}{L} = F\left(\frac{K}{L}\right) \tag{15.2}$$

Here income per head is a function of only the capital–labour ratio and it is not a function of the absolute size of capital and labour inputs. Writing $K/L = k$, we obtain

$$y/L = F(k) \tag{15.2a}$$

Differentiating y/L with respect to the capital–labour ratio, k gives

$$\left.\begin{aligned} \frac{d}{dk}\left(\frac{y}{L}\right) &= \frac{d}{dk}[F(k)] \\ \frac{d^2}{dk^2}\left(\frac{y}{L}\right) &= \frac{d^2}{dk^2}[F(k)] \end{aligned}\right\} \tag{15.20}$$

We shall show in equations 15.20 and 15.27 that equilibrium in a competitive economy necessarily implies that

$$\frac{d}{dk}[F(k)] > 0 \quad \text{and} \quad \frac{d^2}{dk^2}[F(k)] < 0$$

Therefore, the two equations in 15.20 show us that increasing the capital–labour ratio, k, increases real income per head, but at a decreasing rate.

We can rewrite the production function for real income as

$$y = LF(k)$$

Therefore

$$\frac{y}{L} = F\left(\frac{K}{L}\right) \tag{15.2}$$

$$\frac{\partial y}{\partial K} = \frac{\partial}{\partial K}[LF(k)] = L\frac{d}{dk}[F(k)]\frac{\partial k}{\partial K}$$

$$= \frac{d}{dk}[F(k)] \tag{15.20a}$$

and

$$\frac{\partial y}{\partial L} = \frac{\partial}{\partial L}[LF(k)] = F(k) + L\frac{d}{dk}[F(k)]\frac{dk}{dL}$$

$$= F(k) - k\frac{d}{dk}[F(k)] \tag{15.21}$$

This shows us that both the marginal product of capital and the marginal product of labour are functions of the capital–labour ratio, k, only, and not of the absolute amounts of inputs of capital and labour. Making the usual assumptions that the law of variable proportions holds we know that

$$\frac{\partial^2 y}{\partial K^2} < 0 \quad \text{and} \quad \frac{\partial^2 y}{\partial^2 L} < 0 \tag{15.26}$$

Now

$$\frac{\partial^2 y}{\partial K^2} = \frac{\partial}{\partial K}\left[\frac{\partial y}{\partial K}\right] = \frac{\partial}{\partial K}\left\{\frac{d}{dK}[F(k)]\right\} = \frac{d^2}{dk^2}[F(k)]\frac{\partial k}{\partial K}$$

$$= \frac{1}{L}\frac{d^2}{dk^2}[F(k)] < 0 \tag{15.27}$$

As L is always positive this implies that

$$\frac{d^2}{dk^2}[F(k)] < 0 \qquad (15.27a)$$

In a competitive economy profit-maximising entrepreneurs hire inputs up to the point at which their marginal value product is equal to their price. Therefore, in a competitive economy in equilibrium

$$\rho = \frac{\partial y}{\partial K} = \frac{d}{dk}[F(k)] \geqslant 0 \qquad (15.20)$$

$$w = \frac{\partial y}{\partial L} = F(k) - k\frac{d}{dk}[F(k)] > 0 \qquad (15.21)$$

where ρ is the interest rate and w is the real wage rate. These must both be greater or equal to zero in any equilibrium solution in the real world. We may assume that $w > 0$ if wage-earners are to survive. Now

$$\frac{d\rho}{dk} = \frac{d}{dk}\left\{\frac{d}{dk}[F(k)]\right\} = \frac{d^2}{dk^2}[F(k)] < 0 \qquad (15.28)$$

This must be negative using the result in equation 15.27a. Now

$$\frac{dw}{dk} = \frac{d}{dk}\left\{F(k) - k\frac{d}{dk}[F(k)]\right\} = -k\frac{d^2}{dk^2}[F(k)] = -k\frac{\partial \rho}{\partial k} > 0$$

As $\rho > 0$ and from equation 15.28 we know that $d\rho/dk < 0$. Therefore an increase in the capital–labour ratio will lower the real rate of interest (the real return to capital) and raise the real wage rate. A decrease in the capital–labour ratio will lead to the opposite result.

From equation 15.20 we see that, in the absence of technical change, a constant real rate of interest requires a constant capital–labour ratio, k (and vice versa). Therefore, any policy of keeping the real rate of interest constant will lead profit-maximising firms to keep the capital–labour ratio constant (i.e. fixed factor proportions). Now

$$\frac{\partial w}{\partial L} = \frac{\partial}{\partial L}\left\{F(k) - k\frac{d}{dk}[F(k)]\right\}$$

$$= \frac{d}{dk}[F(k)]\frac{\partial k}{\partial L} - \frac{d}{dk}[F(k)]\frac{\partial k}{\partial L} - k\frac{d^2}{dk^2}[F(k)]\frac{\partial k}{\partial L}$$

$$= +\frac{k^2}{L}\frac{d^2}{dk^2}[F(k)] < 0$$

This is negative as $k^2/L > 0$ and $d^2/dk^2[F(k)] < 0$ from equation 15.27a. Therefore, the real wage rate decreases as employment increases, the capital stock remaining constant.

Note 2

Equation 15.9 can be rewritten as

$$\frac{1}{y}\, dy = \frac{s}{v}\, dt$$

Integrating both sides gives

$$\int \frac{1}{y}\, dy = \int \frac{s}{v}\, dt$$

or

$$\ln y = (s/v)t + C$$

Taking antilogarithms of both sides to the base e gives

$$y = A \exp[(s/v)t]$$

where $A = e^C$. If we are given that $y = y_0$ at $t = 0$, then substituting these values into the equation gives $A = y_0$, i.e.

$$y = y_0 \exp[(s/v)t] \tag{15.10}$$

Note 3

Substitute for investment per head and saving per head in equation 15.5 from equations 15.3a and 15.6a. This gives

$$\frac{1}{L}\frac{dK}{dt} = s\frac{y}{L} \tag{15.29}$$

Substituting for income per labour input from the aggregate production function, equation 15.2a gives

$$\frac{1}{L}\frac{dK}{dt} = sF(k) \tag{15.30}$$

Now differentiating both sides of the definition $k = K/L$ with respect to time gives

$$\frac{dk}{dt} = \frac{1}{L}\frac{dK}{dt} - \frac{K}{L}\frac{1}{L}\frac{dL}{dt} \tag{15.31}$$

The labour supply equation (15.4) gives the rate of growth of the labour force $(1/L)(dL/dt)$ as equal to μ. Substituting this into equation 15.31 and rearranging gives

$$\frac{1}{L}\frac{dK}{dt} = \frac{dk}{dt} + \mu k \tag{15.32}$$

Substituting for $(1/L)(dK/dt)$ in equation 15.30 gives us the fundamental differential equation of the model in terms of only the capital–labour ratio:

$$\frac{dk}{dt} + \mu k = sF(k) \tag{15.22a}$$

$$\frac{dk}{dt} = sF(k) - \mu k \tag{15.22}$$

References

[1] J. Tobin, 'A Dynamic Aggregative Model', *Journal of Political Economy*, 63 (1955); reprinted in A. K. Sen (ed.), *Growth Economics* (Harmondsworth: Penguin, 1970).

[2] H. G. Johnson, 'Money in a Growth Model', in his *Essays in Monetary Economics* (London: Allen & Unwin, 1967); reprinted in Sen, *Growth Economics*.

[3] R. F. Harrod, 'An Essay in Dynamic Theory', *Economic Journal*, 49 (1939); reprinted in Sen, *Growth Economics*.

[4] R. F. Harrod, *Towards a Dynamic Economics* (London: Macmillan, 1949).

[5] E. Domar, 'Capital Expansion, Rate of Growth and Unemployment', *Econometrica*, 14 (1946).

[6] D. Jorgenson, 'On Stability in the Sense of Harrod', *Economica*, new series, 27 (1960).

[7] R. G. D. Allen, *Macroeconomic Theory* (London: Macmillan, 1967) ch. 10.

[8] E. Domar, 'The Burden of Debt and National Income', *American Economic Review*, 34 (1964).

[9] N. Kaldor, 'A Model of Economic Growth', *Economic Journal*, 67 (December 1957).

[10] N. Kaldor and J. A. Mirrlees, 'Growth Model with Induced Technical Progress', *Review of Economic Studies*, 29 (1961–2).

[11] R. M. Solow, 'A Contribution to the Theory of Economic Growth', *Quarterly Journal of Economics*, 70 (1956).

[12] R. M. Solow, *Growth Theory: An Exposition* (Oxford University Press, 1970) chs 1–3.

[13] R. W. Swan, 'Economic Growth and Capital Accumulation', *Economic Record*, 32 (1956).

[14] E. S. Phelps, 'The Golden Rule of Accumulation: A Fable for Growthmen', *American Economic Review*, 51 (1961).

[15] A. K. Sen, 'The Stability of Neoclassical Growth with the Addition of an Investment Multiplier', in F. Hahn and F. Brechling (eds), *The Theory of Interest Rates* (London: Macmillan, 1965).

[16] D. Hamberg, *Models of Economic Growth* (New York: Harper & Row, 1971) ch. 5 and appendix.

[17] J. Robinson, 'Capital Theory Up To Date', *Canadian Journal of Economics*, 3 (1970).
[18] J. Kregel, *The Theory of Economic Growth* (London: Macmillan, 1972) pp. 23–9.

IV CURRENT CONTROVERSIES IN MACROECONOMICS

The current controversies in macroeconomics are essentially refinements of basic issues which have long preoccupied economists. The major issue which divides macroeconomists is whether or not the price mechanism performs adequately. In the Keynesian view prices fail to adjust so as to secure market-clearing general equilibrium, whereas in (neo-)classical models prices do perform this adjustment function. Chapter 16 on Walrasian and Keynesian adjustment mechanisms presents the theory underlying these two contrasting views on price adjustment. Chapter 17 deals with neo-Keynesian models in which the failure of prices to adjust and hence markets to clear means that quantities adjust instead. These models provide a rationale for Keynesian demand-management policies.

Chapters 16 and 17 focus attention on the aggregate supply function as the chief area of disagreement. The need for and efficacy of Keynesian demand-management policies are crucially dependent on the way the supply side of the economy functions. This theme is developed further in Chapter 18 on the Phillips relation, upon which much empirical and theoretical work has centred. The central issue here is whether or not an increase in inflation can secure a temporary or permanent increase in the supply of output. The answer depends on how prices and money wages adjust, and this in turn partly depends on the way expectations are formed.

Chapter 19 outlines the new classical macroeconomics. By building models in which markets clear, in which expectations are formed rationally and in which aggregate supply varies with agents' misperceptions of relative price movements, new classical economists conclude that Keynesian demand-management policies are not only ineffective but harmful.

Chapter 20 draws together a number of threads from this and earlier sections to review the controversy over the causes of inflation and policies to deal with it.

16 Walrasian and Keynesian Adjustment Mechanisms

Section I of this book outlined the analytical apparatus known as the neoclassical–Keynesian synthesis, which evolved through the debates conducted in the twenty years following *The General Theory*'s publication. Hahn ([1] p. 26) succinctly summarises the neoclassical–Keynesian synthesis:

> Keynes attempted to show that full-employment short-period equilibrium did not exist and in this he was, under plausible assumptions, wrong. His mistake was attributed to his neglect of real cash balances in influencing the demand for current goods.

The 'synthesis' reconciled Keynes's theory with that of the neoclassical school (or 'classics', in Keynesian terminology). In doing so it reduced Keynes's theoretical contribution to the unoriginal observation that markets could not adjust to full-employment equilibrium if prices, in particular money wages, were inflexible.

This conclusion is in stark contrast to Keynes's own assessment of his work as demonstrating the fundamental flaws of (neo-)classical economics and replacing it with a superior alternative. Keynes stated:

> I shall argue that the postulates of classical theory are applicable to a special case only and not to the general case, the situation which it assumes being a limiting point of the possible positions of equilibrium. Moreover the characteristics of the special case assumed by the classical theory happen not to be those of the economic society in which we actually live. (*The General Theory*, p. 3)

The neoclassical–Keynesian synthesis gives rise to the curious assessment that an economist whose work was treated as revolutionary and who founded a new and major branch of economics made only a trivial contribution to economic theory, though this had a great practical impact in the field of policy-making.

The synthesis has always been rejected by the group of post-Keynesian economists at Cambridge, whose older members (Joan Robinson, Richard Kahn) had participated in discussions about the 'General Theory' while it was being formulated. However, it was not until the mid-1960s that economists elsewhere, notably Clower [2] and Leijonhufvud [3], began to question the neoclassical–Keynesian synthesis as the correct interpretation of what Keynes had been trying to say. As a result of both this work and the neoclassical–Keynesian synthesis, we now have a much better idea of what are the essential features of the (neo-)classical theory which Keynes set out to attack. These features will be examined in the next section of this chapter. We also now have a recently developed analytical apparatus for examining the characteristic Keynesian contention that market adjustment fails to achieve market-clearing equilibrium. This analysis will be developed further in Chapter 17.

16.1 Walrasian equilibrium

The crucial feature of the neoclassical approach is that when market demands and supplies are in imbalance prices will adjust to bring about market-clearing equilibrium in all markets. The first major economist to expound this adjustment mechanism in a general-equilibrium context (that is, one that takes account of all interdependencies between all the markets) was Leon Walras [4], who gave his name to this branch of economic analysis. In the 1930s Walrasian economics was still a very undeveloped field. It was only by the very late 1930s that the mathematics required for Walrasian analysis was being developed and not until the 1950s that the Walrasian proposition that a perfectly competitive market-clearing equilibrium exists was proved mathematically. This means that nowadays we have a much clearer idea of the Walrasian micro foundations of (neo-)classical thinking than did Keynes and his contemporaries.

A pure exchange Walrasian model

The simplest kind of Walrasian economy is one in which there is no production of goods; only the exchange of already existing goods takes place. The economy consists of a large number of independent traders. Each starts with a given initial endowment of goods, of which there are a large number. Each trader's utility is a function of the quantities of the various goods he consumes and it is assumed that traders aim to maximise their utility. To do this they have to exchange goods. The basic Walrasian model is a barter economy. All exchange takes the form of swapping goods for goods, as there is no money in the model; there is no commodity which acts as a medium of exchange or as a store of value; and there is no role for a store of value or for assets, as the model is timeless. It is concerned with exchange in one period of time, divorced from any past or future time periods. These simplifications will be later modifed or commented upon.

Equilibrium can only be established once all possibilities for mutually advantageous exchange between the traders have been exhausted. Each trader's utility depends on the quantities of the various goods which he or she consumes in the period. We assume that there are m goods available. Formally the utility function is

$$U_i = f(q_{i1}, q_{i2}, \ldots, q_{ig}, \ldots, q_{im}) \tag{16.1}$$

where

U_i = utility of ith trader in goods
q_{ig} = quantity of gth good consumed by the ith individual, and there are m different goods

The individual trader's choice problem is to maximise his utility from consumption subject to the constraint on his desired purchases imposed by the value of his initial endowment. The budget constraint is that the total value of goods demanded by the trader must equal the value of his initial endowment and is written as

$$\sum_{g=1}^{m} p_g\, q_{ig}^d = \sum_{g=1}^{m} p_g\, \bar{q}_{ig}^s \tag{16.2}$$

where

p_g = the price of the gth good
q_{ig}^d = quantity of gth good demanded by trader i
q_{ig}^s = quantity of gth good in trader i's fixed initial endowment

Each trader is a perfect competitor: the prices of all the goods are given and cannot be altered by individual action. Maximising the utility function (16.1) subject to the budget constraint (16.2) we get the usual utility-maximising conditions that the ratio of the marginal utility of the gth good to the marginal utility of the hth good must equal the ratio of the price of g to the price of h. From this result we derive the individual's demand for each good as a function of the prices of all goods, his tastes (which determine the form of the utility function) and his income or initial endowment, all of which are treated as fixed parameters for the individual.

The individual's demand for a particular good consists of that portion of his initial endowment which each individual wishes to keep, plus the additional amount over and above the initial individual endowment that each trader wishes to buy. In order to acquire those goods which he wishes to consume in excess of the quantity in his initial endowment, the trader has to sell other goods from his endowment.

As the Walrasian model is a general-equilibrium model, it is concerned with the total market demand for each commodity. This is obtained by aggregating over the demand for the good by all the traders. Given there are n traders, the market demand function for the gth good is

$$\sum_{i=1}^{n} q_{ig}^{d} = q_{g}^{d} = f(p_1, p_2, \ldots, p_g, \ldots, p_m, I) \tag{16.3}$$

where

n = number of traders
q_g^d = market demand for good g
I = total value of initial endowments of all n traders (that is, aggregate income), and is fixed

Market demand also depends on the tastes of all the traders, but these, like the initial endowment of goods, are assumed fixed throughout our analysis of a pure exchange Walrasian economy.

The excess market demand for each good is the difference between the total quantity of the good in existence, the amount supplied ($\bar{q}_g^s$), and the amount demanded by the traders. The excess demand function for the gth good is

$$E_{qg}^{d} = q_g^d - \bar{q}_g^s = E(p_1, p_2, \ldots, p_g, \ldots, p_m, I) \tag{16.4}$$

As there are m goods, there are m such excess demand equations.

Walras's law

In a Walrasian economy particular importance attaches to the idea that each trader makes his demand and supply plans on the basis that he can buy and sell as much of any good as he wants to at the prevailing set of prices, given his budget constraint. This means that the sum of each trader's demands for all the goods must equal the value of his initial endowment as stated in the budget constraint (16.2) on page 293. No trader plans to spend more than his income or earn income in excess of his planned purchases. So although a trader's excess demand for a particular good may be positive or negative, when we sum over *all* his excess demands for all the goods, the sum must equal zero because of the budget constraint. If the trader has a positive excess demand over $m - 1$ of the goods, he must have an equal positive excess supply of the mth good in order to finance his planned net purchase of the $m - 1$ goods.

If the sum of excess demands over all m goods equals zero for one trader, then it must also equal zero for all traders and hence for the economy as a whole. This result, which is a consequence of the budget constraint, is known as *Walras's law. Walras's law states that the sum of excess demands over all the goods in the economy must equal zero and this applies whether or not the markets are in general equilibrium.* So if there is positive excess demand over $m - 1$ markets, there must be negative excess demand (that is, positive excess supply) in the mth market.

General equilibrium

The problem to which Walrasian analysis is addressed is as follows. Is there a set of prices (p_1 to p_m) such that in every market the demand for each good equals the quantity supplied, i.e. do we have competitive market-clearing general equilibrium? When general equilibrium is established no further possibilities for mutually advantageous exchange remain. If they did, so that it was possible for at least one trader to increase his utility without any other trader being made worse off (that is, a Pareto-efficient allocation of the goods had not yet been established), then further exchanges would take place. Because of the limitations of mathematical technique at that time Walras was unable to offer a rigorous proof that a competitive general-equilibrium set of prices exists.[1] Walras's demonstration that competitive equilibrium could be established was restricted to counting equations and dependent variables.

We have already established that there will be m excess demand equations of the form of 16.4. In general equilibrium each one must equal zero because each market is cleared. This would appear to give us m equations to determine m prices; however, because of Walras's law this is not the case. Walras's law states that the sum of excess demands over all m markets must always be zero. In general equilibrium the sum of excess demands over $m-1$ markets is zero; therefore, to obey Walras's law the excess demand in the mth market must also be zero. The mth equation is thus redundant because it yields no further information than that given by the $m-1$ equations. The mth equation is said to be dependent[2] on the other equations, so we are left with only $m-1$ independent excess demand equations.

It is therefore possible to determine only $m-1$ prices and these are *relative* prices. They state the rate at which one good will exchange for other goods. The number of relative prices (exchange rates) is always one less than the number of goods being traded. This can be readily seen by considering a model with only two goods, A and B. There is only one independent *relative* price, the price of A in terms of B, which gives the number of units of B which have to be exchanged in order to buy one unit of A. The relative price of B in terms of A is not independent because it is *just the reciprocal of A in terms of B*.

The key result of the analysis of a pure exchange Walrasian economy is that one can show that in an m-good economy there will be $m-1$ relative prices at which all markets will be cleared. The $m-1$ relative prices can be expressed in

[1] This has subsequently been proved by Arrow and Debreu (see [5] and [6]. A good, accessible exposition of the whole area is to be found in Weintraub [7].

[2] Mathematically an equation is linearly dependent if it can be formed from a linear combination of two or more equations in the system to which it belongs. For example, given the excess demands in a three-good model such that

$$Eq_1^d = E_1(p_1, p_2, p_3)$$
$$Eq_2^d = E_2(p_1, p_2, p_3)$$
$$Eq_3^d = E_3(p_1, p_2, p_3)$$

then if there exist any two numbers α and β such that

$$\alpha Eq_1^d + \beta Eq_2^d = Eq_3^d$$

for *all* values of p_1, p_2 and p_3, then the three excess demand functions are said to be linearly dependent.

terms of a common standard. One good (which one does not matter) is chosen as a *numéraire* and the relative prices of the other goods are expressed as the number of units of each good which exchange for one unit of the *numéraire*. If we choose good 1 as the *numéraire*, then the price of the *numéraire*, p_1, is fixed at 1 and the other $m-1$ prices are expressed in terms of units of good 1. Prices are not expressed in terms of money because we are dealing with a pure barter economy.

The Walrasian auctioneer

Although a set of relative prices consistent with Walrasian general equilibrium can be shown to exist, there is still the need to tell a story of how the competitive equilibrium set of relative prices is arrived at. The construction Walras used was to posit the existence of a fictional auctioneer who undertakes no trading. The auctioneer's job is to call out a set of relative prices and find the levels of excess demand on each market at this set of prices. If general equilibrium is not achieved, the auctioneer tries another set of prices. Prices are raised in markets with excess demand and are lowered in markets with excess supply. This is where Walras's law functions as an adjustment mechanism. According to Walras's law, excess demands in some markets must be matched by excess supplies in other markets so that prices rise and fall in each type of market in order to move it towards market-clearing equilibrium. The auctioneer keeps on trying different sets of relative prices in this way until he finds one set at which all markets are cleared. It is only then that trading actually occurs. The process by which the auctioneer gropes towards the equilibrium set of relative prices and quantities is known as *tâtonnement* (or groping).

In the Walrasian system trade only occurs when prices are at their market-clearing values. In other systems when trade does take place at non-market-clearing prices, it is called *false trading*. How to model the way economic agents actually adjust prices and quantities when false trading occurs is a fundamental problem which lies at the heart of much current theoretical research. Because this problem exists, the assumption of a Walrasian auctioneer or of similar black-box devices by which prices and quantities are established continues to underlie most macro models. Taken at face-value the Walrasian auctioneer seems a ridiculously unrealistic piece of fiction but alternative ways of modelling how prices and quantities get established are not, as yet, readily available.

Money and time in a Walrasian model[1]

In the pure barter Walrasian economy we have to concoct the auctioneer story so that there is no need for money. If trade only takes place after the auctioneer has discovered the market-clearing equilibrium set of relative prices and the traders exchange goods and services in their endowments for other goods and

[1] For a more complete survey of these models see Harris [8].

services via the auctioneer, there is no need for anyone to hold money. In order to create a transactions demand for money in a Walrasian economy it is necessary to impose the condition that goods and services exchange for money because barter exchange is prohibitively expensive. In order to activate the exchange process at the beginning of each transactions period, traders must hold money balances over from the previous trading period.

Once we admit money into the model we need to introduce some consideration of time. Traders will only have a demand for money balances to hold at the end of the trading period if it is to be followed by another period in which money will be required for transactions purposes. Individuals' utility now depends not only on the amount of the *m* goods consumed but also on the volume of money balances held at the end of the trading period. The budget constraint has also to be modified so that the demand for goods plus the demand for money balances, M_i^D, to hold at the end of the trading period is equal to the value of the initial endowment of goods plus the volume of money balances, M_i^S, held at the beginning of the trading period (that is, left over from the previous period). The budget constraint for each trader is now

$$\sum_{g=1}^{m} p_g q_{ig}^d + M_i^D = \sum_{g=1}^{m} p_g \bar{q}_{ig}^s + M_i^S \tag{16.5}$$

It is convenient to use money as the *numéraire* good, so the goods prices, p_g, are expressed in units of money. Walras's law now applies to the money market as well. If there is excess demand (supply) over all *m* goods markets, there must be an equivalent excess supply of (demand for) money. In other words, if traders want in aggregate to buy more goods than are in existence, they must be planning to finance their goods purchases by running down their money balances. This of course cannot be an equilibrium situation, so the auctioneer will proceed to call out another set of prices. In order to eliminate the excess demand for goods the auctioneer may well have to raise the prices of goods in terms of money as well as alter the relative prices between goods.

General equilibrium can only be established when all markets, including the money market, are cleared. We therefore need to add an aggregate excess demand for money function to the *m* excess demand for goods functions. The aggregate demand for money function is provided by the *quantity theory of money*, whereby the demand for money is a constant proportion, *k*, of the money value of transactions. Hence

$$M^D = k\sum_{g=1}^{m} p_g q_g \tag{16.6}$$

The total nominal stock of money is assumed fixed at M_0^S, so we can write the excess demand for money equation as

$$M^{ED} = k\sum_{g=1}^{m} p_g q_g - M_0^S \tag{16.7}$$

The excess demand for money equation plus the $m-1$ independent excess demand functions for goods (16.4) give a total of *m* independent equations to determine m goods prices in terms of money. So we now have $m - 1$ determinate relative goods prices and a determinate absolute price level since the prices of all m goods are fixed in terms of money units.

In the non-monetary Walrasian economy the relative prices of goods and services in terms of each other are determinate but the absolute value of the prices is indeterminate. For instance, if 2 units of good A trade for 1 unit of good B, then the price of B is $2A$. There is no determinate price of A and B in terms of money. A could cost £1 and B £2 or the goods could be priced at £100 and £200 respectively. The inclusion of an explicit monetary sector enables the model to determine a unique price level so that there is only one price in terms of the *numèraire* money for each good or service that is consistent with general equilibrium. This is because there is just one set of prices in terms of money which, given a particular nominal money stock, will make the excess demand equation for money equal zero.

Given k, the nominal quantity of money determines the absolute price level. To see this let us suppose that we start off from a position of general equilibrium. Then all traders have their nominal money balances doubled and the auctioneer calls out the previous equilibrium set of money prices. The money supply now exceeds traders' demand for money. Since Walras's law holds, the excess supply of money is matched by an equivalent excess demand for goods. To get back to general equilibrium the auctioneer has to double all money prices. The nominal demand for money now rises to equal the increased nominal money supply. Relative goods prices are the same as in the previous equilibrium. All that has changed is that absolute prices are twice as high as before. So we have the results that in a Walrasian economy the stock of nominal money has no effect on the competitive equilibrium set of relative goods prices: a change in the nominal quantity of money affects the absolute price level proportionately (that is, money is neutral).

In this scenario the demand for goods is affected by the quantity of real balances held when the money market is in disequilibrium. Traders are then undertaking portfolio adjustment. An excess supply of money balances exerts a positive impact on the demand for goods, whereas an excess demand for money balances depresses the demand for goods. In disequilibrium there is therefore a real balance or Pigou effect at work.

Production and exchange in a Walrasian economy

In principle the Walrasian pure exchange economy can easily be translated into one with production. Instead of traders receiving initial endowments of consumption goods, they now start out with endowments of factors of production. Traders can now be divided into two classes. Households own labour services which they sell to finance the purchase of consumer goods. Some households also have an ownership claim on firms' profits and the receipts from this are used to finance consumption. Firms own capital goods, hire labour and produce output which they plan to sell in order to maximise profit. Each household's utility depends positively on the quantities of the various goods it consumes, the amount of real balances it holds and the amount of leisure it can enjoy. The choice of how much labour to supply and what quantities of goods to consume is made in order to maximise utility subject to the constraint that the value of goods purchased plus money held at the end of the trading period must equal the value of factor services sold plus income derived from ownership rights in firms plus the initial volume of real balances. This decision problem is exactly the same one as that underlying the neoclassical supply of labour function which was explained in Chapter 5 (pp. 65–70). The only difference is that we have now disaggregated so that households' choices involve a whole range of goods and services, not just a single composite consumption good. Households and firms are price-takers in factor and product markets, and now that the model is extended to include p factors of production as well as m commodities and money it contains $p + m$ independent excess demand equations. When the excess demand equations are all set at zero, then the set of $p + m$ prices consistent with market-clearing equilibrium can be determined. If the set of prices is not the market-clearing set and if there consequently exists an overall excess supply of labour services, then Walras's law implies that this will be matched by an equivalent excess demand for goods, given that the money market is in equilibrium.

Uncertainty and time in Walrasian models[1]

Latter-day Walrasian models take full account of both time and uncertainty. Traders face an array of possible future states of the world. Hence the future has to be planned for and is uncertain. The choices made by traders are now more complex since they enter into exchange contracts for each possible state of the world. (For example, trade will take place at one set of prices if the quantity of oil available is halved and at another set of prices if it is doubled.) Such contracts are called *contingent contracts* since their actual execution is contingent on the state of the world that emerges. This type of Walrasian model contains many more markets than the timeless variety. If there are Z possible states of the world and g commodities to be traded over a time horizon of T periods, then there will be ZgT markets. In other words, markets exist not just for present-period exchange but there are also futures markets which establish prices for each contingency. There is now a proper role for asset markets as the uncertain future needs to be planned for in the present.

Walrasian economics and the neoclassical–Keynesian synthesis

Walrasian general-equilibrium analysis in the form we have it today was only developed from the late 1930s onwards, i.e. at the same time as the neoclassical–Keynesian synthesis was emerging from Keynes's work on unemployment. The interpretation of Keynes's *General Theory* was grafted on to Walrasian general-equilibrium analysis. A prime-mover in this development

[1] A further account of these models is provided by Weintraub [7].

was Hicks [9], whose *ISLM* apparatus became so widely used. In the 1930s Hicks was also working on value theory from a Walrasian perspective and in 1939 published *Value and Capital* [10], which has formed the basis of much microeconomic analysis, particularly in demand theory. The *ISLM* model makes use of Walras's law. The model contains three markets, goods, money and bonds, but determines only two variables, the interest rate and either the price level or real output. To prevent the model being over-determined one market must be discarded. This is done using Walras's law. If the goods and money markets are both in equilibrium, then, since excess demands must sum to zero, the bond market must also be in equilibrium and the excess demand function for bonds is a dependent equation.

The final stage in the creation of the neoclassical–Keynesian synthesis was Patinkin's *Money, Interest and Prices* [11], which included money in a Walrasian economy. This analysis obtained the standard (neo-)classical results discussed above (pp. 82–6), namely the neutrality of money and the impossibility of unemployment equilibrium when prices and wages are flexible.

16.2 Post-Keynesian economics

In the thirty years succeeding *The General Theory* mainstream economics concentrated on Walrasian microeconomics and the neoclassical–Keynesian synthesis in macroeconomics.

Meanwhile the group of post-Keynesian economists at Cambridge remained highly critical of the relevance of Walrasian general-equilibrium analysis. They have also been incensed at the way the neoclassical–Keynesian synthesis incorporated Keynesian economics into a Walrasian general-equilibrium framework. To post-Keynesians this development is a perversion of Keynesian economics as it is a total misrepresentation of what they think Keynes was really trying to say.

For true Keynesians the key to understanding the significance of the Keynesian revolution lies in its denial that Walrasian general equilibrium is a suitable framework for analysing macroeconomic problems. In Walrasian analysis the price mechanism works well as a co-ordinating device which makes the plans of economic agents consistent with one another and thus brings about general market-clearing. In contrast Keynesian economics is about the failure of the market-co-ordinating mechanism, a failure which is not to be attributed to price rigidity as such. The Keynesian message is that the price system fails because economic agents have to make decisions in the present which are contingent upon a future that is highly uncertain. The key features of the Keynesian economy in contrast to the Walrasian one are 'the dark forces of time and ignorance which envelop our future' (*The General Theory*, p. 155).

Time and uncertainty are inextricably linked in post-Keynesian thinking, as evident in the writings of Robinson [12] and Shackle [13]. They stress that economies must be analysed as a sequential process through time and not in an essentially timeless state. The present is seen as the link between a known past and a highly uncertain future. Money and financial assets play a key role in connecting the past, the present and the future. Because the future is so uncertain, the way expectations are formed, in particular the influence of the present upon such expectations, becomes extremely important.

It is in the light of these considerations that investment plays a key role in this interpretation of the 'General Theory'. For investment to occur the demand price of capital (that is, the present value of future expected net cash flows from the investment) must exceed the supply price (the cost of the capital goods). The demand price is determined by two sets of forces. The first set consists of those factors which determine the expected future net cash flow, and the second set consists of the determinants of the cost of financial capital which is used to discount the net cash flow stream. The first set of factors is subject to a lot of uncertainty and is not amenable to quantitative probabilistic calculation:

> [T]here is instability due to the characteristic of human nature that a large proportion of our positive activities depend on spontaneous optimism rather than on a mathematical expectation. (*The General Theory*, p. 161)

Thus entrepreneurs' expectations are attributed largely to inexplicable waves of optimism or pessimism called 'animal spirits':

> Most, probably, of our decisions to do something positive, the full consequences of which will be drawn out over many days to come, can only be taken as a result of animal spirits – of a spontaneous urge to action, rather than inaction. (*The General Theory*, p. 161)

In addition to the quicksilver nature of entrepreneurial expectations, the capital market, as colourfully described by Keynes, is a further source of investment instability which feeds through to the demand price of capital via its effect on the cost of capital. Entrepreneurs have to raise finance for investment by selling financial assets to wealth-holders. Asset-holders want a command over future purchasing power but, because the future is uncertain, they also desire liquidity or the ability to convert their assets into cash quickly and without much fear of loss. The desire for liquidity is greater in a period of stable or falling prices than it is when inflation, which reduces the real value of nominally fixed assets, is expected to continue. Keynes's stress on the role of liquidity preference was therefore more appropriate to conditions in the 1930s than today.

According to Keynes, the existence of capital markets on which financial assets are traded means that asset-holders are primarily concerned with the prices at which they can buy and sell financial assets and not with the present value of the real capital goods that were financed by issuing these financial assets. The expectations of operators on the capital market are dominated by anticipations regarding the likely movement of paper asset prices and not by expectations concerning business conditions. Capital-market operators 'are concerned not with what an investment is really worth to a man who buys it "for keeps", but with what the market will value it at under the influence of mass psychology, three months or a year hence' (*The General Theory*, p. 155). Keynes likens the stock market to a game of 'old maid' since the objective is to offload stocks and shares on to somebody else before prices fall. The formation of expectations in this way renders financial asset prices, and hence the cost of capital, unstable:

> A conventional valuation which is established as the outcome of the mass psychology of a large number of ignorant individuals is liable to change violently due to factors which do not really make 'much difference to the prospective yield' [on real capital]. (*The General Theory*, p. 134)

The foregoing views on investment behaviour pinpoint intertemporal markets (that is, those for capital goods and assets) as a crucial source of market failure. This is contrasted to neoclassical analysis, in which the rate of interest performs an equilibrating function. To see the difference between the adjustment mechanism in Walrasian and Keynesian analysis, consider an economy initially in market-clearing general equilibrium. There then occurs an exogenous increase in the desire to save. Households now want to defer more consumption from the present than previously in order to enjoy more consumption at some future date. To maintain market-clearing equilibrium the change in household's intertemporal consumption plans must be signalled to firms so that they can plan to produce the additional quantities of goods in the future. To fulfil such plans firms need to increase investment and so substitute additional investment demand for the reduction in consumers' demand to maintain full employment of resources in the present. There is no direct way that households can signal to firms their increased desire for future consumption. The intertemporal market mechanism is indirect, and in neoclassical analysis works via the fall in interest rates as the additional savings are channelled into non-money financial assets. Reduced interest rates then stimulate increased investment. Interest rates thus serve as an equilibrating mechanism which maintains the full-employment equilibrium level of aggregate demand in the face of fluctuations in either saving or investment and prevents them having an impact on the total volume of real output (although its composition is of course changed).

In Keynesian analysis the price-signalling system in intertemporal markets breaks down because of the way economic agents act in the presence of uncertainty. Unlike the latter-day Walrasian models with contingency markets there is in practice a total absence of a comprehensive array of futures markets in which contingent contracts can be made. The signals from households to firms about changes in their intertemporal consumption plans and the signals from firms to households about changes in the relative prices of consumption and investment goods (that is, in the relative price of consumption at different time periods) fail to get through. This failure stems from the preference for liquidity and the concern with short-run capital gains and losses that dominate financial asset markets. The movement in financial asset prices becomes divorced from movements in the relative price of consumption and investment goods. If profit expectations collapse, so that future consumption in terms of present forgone consumption becomes more expensive, this is not signalled to households via a sufficiently large fall in interest rates which is required to stimulate present consumption in order to prevent the emergence of idle resources. Interest rates are prevented from falling sufficiently by price-inelastic expecations: if the interest rate falls below its previous level, then the future interest rate is expected to be higher than its present level (that is, to move in the opposite direction to that in which it has just moved). Post-Keynesians therefore see Keynes's theory of liquidity preference as playing a vital part in explaining the failure of the market-signalling mechanism. In response to pessimistic business conditions there is a rush into liquid assets which impedes the transmission of intertemporal price signals. Post-Keynesians therefore see money as a crucial variable in the analysis of how a market economy evolves through time when the future is highly uncertain.

Policy implications of post-Keynesian views

The post-Keynesians' rejection of general-equilibrium analysis in favour of their own methodology of treating the economy as a historical process explains why their approach has had much less impact on policy formulation than the neoclassical–Keynesian synthesis. Models which stress uncertainty and indeterminate and volatile expectations hardly lend themselves to an analysis of fine-tuning the economy. Policy recommendations from this school are of the broad brush-stroke variety and would require major elements of government direction in the economy and the replacement of market price signals by bureaucratic decision-making. The spotlight placed on investment instability in Keynesian analysis has led to the advocacy of a greater socialisation of investment in the hope that it would then be more stable and allocated more in line with social preferences.

16.3 The reinterpretation of Keynes as non-Walrasian equilibrium economics

The post-Keynesian Cambridge economists have always maintained that they possessed the holy grail of a true understanding of Keynes's economics, but they remained an isolated band. It was not until the mid-1960s that economists elsewhere, notably in America, began to question the received version of Keynesian economics as propounded in the mainstream synthesis. This work, which was originated principally by Clower [2] and Leijonhufvud [3], has now brought forth a whole class of new or neo-Keynesian models. These models share with the Cambridge post-Keynesians the idea that the crucial feature of Keynesian economics is that it is non-Walrasian and hence non-market-clearing, but, unlike the post-Keynesians, the neo-Keynesians have developed their ideas in the context of a general-equilibrium framework.

Walras's law and its inconsistency with Keynesian economics

Clower [2] pointed out very clearly the inconsistency of Walras's law with Keynesian unemployment as analysed in the neoclassical–Keynesian synthesis. In the Keynesian three-sector model which enshrines the synthesis (and which was presented in Chapter 6) the bonds, money and goods markets are in

TABLE 16.1 *The inconsistency between Walrasian law and the Keynesian ISLM model*

Market	Keynesian *ISLM* model excess demand	Walrasian model excess demand
Bonds	0	0
Money	0	0
Goods	0	positive
Labour	negative	negative
Total	negative	zero

market-clearing equilibrium but the labour market is not. There is an excess supply of labour. This situation is summarised in the Keynesian *ISLM* column of Table 16.1.

Summing excess demands over all four sectors in the Keynesian *ISLM* model gives a total sum of excess demands which is negative. This result is in direct contradiction to Walras's law, which states that whatever the set of prices the sum of excess demands over all markets must be zero. Thus if there is negative excess demand in the labour market, while the bond and money markets are in equilibrium, then there must be an equivalent amount of positive excess demand in the goods market to give an overall sum of excess demands of zero, as indicated in the last column of Table 16.1. If households in a Walrasian model wish to sell more labour than firms wish to buy (that is, there is excess labour supply), then the corresponding position in the goods market is that households wish to buy more goods than firms desire to sell (that is, there is excess demand for goods). The households' demand for goods in a Walrasian model is based on the supposition that they can sell all the labour they wish to sell at the prevailing prices.

Walras's law is an important part of the Walrasian–neoclassical adjustment mechanism. If the goods market has positive excess demand, then goods prices (the price level) will rise, while in the labour market where there is a corresponding excess supply of labour, money wages will fall. The joint effect of a rising price level together with a falling money wage is that the real wage rate will drop. Market-clearing prices will be established as firms expand production, while households reduce the labour supply (and hence their demand for goods) in response to falling real wages.

The inconsistency of the Keynesian model with Walras's law leads to the conclusion that the key feature of Keynesian economics is its concern with economies in which Walras's law does not hold.

Notional and effective demand and supply

The crucial assumption behind Walras's law is that when trade takes place it occurs at market-clearing prices. This state of affairs is ensured by the existence of the Walrasian auctioneer. When trade is known to occur only at market-clearing prices, which the traders treat as given, then traders make choices on the assumption that they can buy and sell as much of any good or service as they please subject to their budget constraint. Clower [2] called demand and supply plans based on the assumption that trade takes place at market-clearing prices *notional* demands and supplies. Walras's law then holds for notional excess demand functions which are based upon traders' suppositions that they can buy and sell as much as they choose.

However, a trader's choice problem is quite different if he cannot either buy or sell as much as he wants to at prevailing prices. This is the situation which will arise once the Walrasian auctioneer is removed from the scene. With no auctioneer to find the market-clearing set of prices there will be *false trading* at non-market-clearing prices.

Once false trading takes place at non-market-clearing prices then it becomes unrealistic for traders to make plans based on the presumption that they can buy and sell as much as they would like to. If households find that there is an excess supply of labour, then not all households can sell as much labour as they would like to at prevailing prices. In other words, they are quantity-constrained (or rationed) on the labour market. Consequently some households' incomes are lower than they would have chosen them to be in the absence of quantity constraints on their sales of labour. This state of affairs in the labour market leads to repercussions in the goods market. With lower incomes than they would have had in market-clearing equilibrium, households cannot purchase as many goods as they would have chosen to by their notional demand functions. The *effective* demand for goods is the amount that households can actually purchase given the quantity constraint on their sales of labour. Given the distinction between notional and effective excess demands, Walrasian economics is characterised as considering only notional plans, whereas Keynesian economics is concerned with false trading in which effective excess demands are different from notional ones and it is the former that determine the level of output and employment.

The dual decision distinction

In the light of the distinction between notional and effective plans, Keynes's consumption function, by which effective demand depends on income, takes on considerable significance as it would not hold in a Walrasian non-quantity-constrained economy. In a Walrasian world a household would maximise utility, which is a positive function of the quantity of goods consumed and a negative function of the amount of time spent working. The value of consumption would be achieved so as to maximise

$$U = f(C, L) \quad \left[\frac{\partial U}{\partial C} > 0; \frac{\partial U}{\partial L} < 0\right] \tag{16.8}$$

where C = consumption and L = labour hours supplied, subject to the budget constraint that

$$C = wL + \text{non-wage income} \tag{16.9}$$

where w = real wage rate, and the time constraint that

$$L \leqslant \bar{L}$$

where $\bar{L}$ = total time available for work.

This decision problem can be depicted diagrammatically as in Figure 16.1. Each indifference curve shows the combinations of consumption and work time which yield equal utility. The budget constraint is given by AB. The distance $O\bar{L}$ gives the maximum amount of time available for work. The slope of budget line AB is determined by the real wage rate which gives the quantity of consumption goods which can be purchased by giving up one 'hour's' leisure and working instead. The household is assumed to have a non-wage income of OA. As usual utility is maximised where the budget line is tangential to the indifference curve. The household will choose OC_e consumption and supply labour time equal to OL_e hours per period. The optimal choice will occur at the consumption level and labour hours for which the ratio of the marginal utility of consumption to the marginal utility of leisure (the marginal rate of substitution of consumption for leisure) equals the real wage rate. The marginal rate of substitution of consumption for leisure equals the real wage rate where the slope of the highest obtainable indifference curve equals the slope of the budget line (the real wage rate). The real wage rate is the rate at which leisure can be transformed into consumption goods via the market. An important feature of this analysis is that the decision to supply labour (that is, give up leisure) and the decision of how much to consume are taken simultaneously. This has been termed the *dual decision hypothesis* by Clower [2]. Income is not exogenous, as in the Keynesian consumption function, it is an endogenous variable whose value is chosen by the household. The household's notional consumption function is therefore a function of the real wage rate (as well as tastes for goods and leisure), not income, which is a choice variable.

An increase in the real wage rate would pivot the budget line from A upwards to the left. Given that the substitution effect outweighs the income

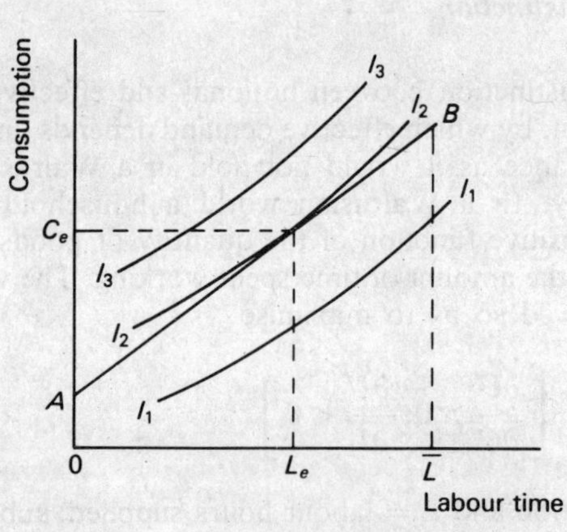

FIGURE 16.1 *The consumption–leisure choice*

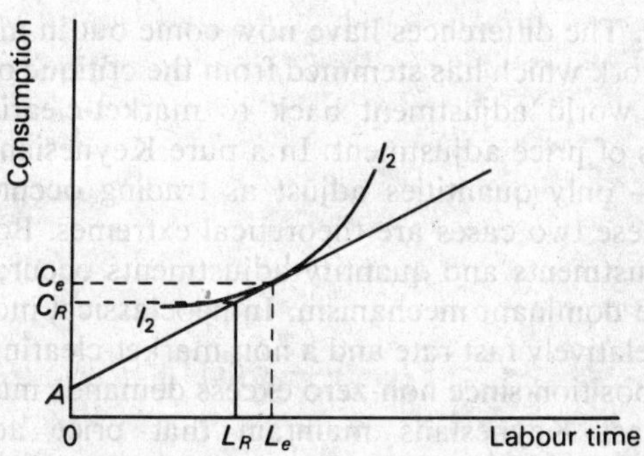

FIGURE 16.2 *The consumption–leisure choice under quantity rationing*

effect, then the demand for leisure will fall while more consumption also occurs. This supposition guarantees an upward-sloping neoclassical labour supply function with respect to the real wage rate.

The household's consumption–labour-supply choice problem has to be reformulated if the household trades at non-market-clearing prices. If the household is faced with a situation of excess supply in the labour market and cannot sell as much labour as it would like to, then it is rationed in the labour market. The fact that the household is rationed in the labour market affects its demand for consumption goods, as shown in Figure 16.2. If market-clearing prevailed so that the household was not quantity-constrained, the household would choose to have OC_e consumption and to supply OL_e labour, as in Figure 16.1. However, the household is now assumed to be rationed in the labour market and can only sell OL_R 'hours' of labour. Consequently the household can no longer attain its non-rationed utility level on indifference curve I_2I_2. Given it can only sell OL_R units of labour, the amount of consumption permitted by the budget constraint is OC_R. The Keynesian consumption function now holds. Income is not a choice variable. Instead it is determined by the rationed amount of labour the household can sell and by the real wage rate. Effective consumption depends directly on the quantity-constrained level of real income.

When households are rationed in the labour market so that effective consumption lies below its notional level, firms are also affected in the goods market. Because of the deficient level of effective demand firms can no longer sell the notional quantity of output they would wish to supply if they could sell all they would like to at prevailing prices. Firms are thus also rationed sellers – of goods. The demand for labour is now determined by the amount of output firms can sell and therefore by the level of effective demand, not by the real wage rate. We now come full circle. The labour supply exceeds firms' demand for labour and so households are rationed sellers in the labour market.

Conclusion: Walrasian and Keynesian adjustment mechanisms

The neoclassical–Keynesian synthesis failed to bring out clearly the crucial differences between Keynesian and neoclassical views on how market economies operate. The differences have now come out in much sharper relief as a result of the work which has stemmed from the critique of the synthesis. In a pure Walrasian world adjustment back to market-clearing equilibrium is achieved by means of price adjustment. In a pure Keynesian world there is no price adjustment – only quantities adjust as trading occurs at non-market-clearing prices. These two cases are theoretical extremes. Both schools recognise that price adjustments and quantity adjustments occur; the crucial question is which is the dominant mechanism. In neoclassical models price adjustment occurs at a relatively fast rate and a non-market-clearing situation cannot be an equilibrium position since non-zero excess demands must cause prices to change. In contrast Keynesians maintain that price adjustments occur relatively slowly and that the more important response is quantity changes. Unlike neoclassical models, neo-Keynesian models can produce equilibrium positions in which markets do not clear. This result has usually been obtained in models in which prices and money wages are fixed, but more recently it has been demonstrated in neo-Keynesian models which have some limited element of price flexibility. Fixed price neo-Keynesian models are discussed more fully in the next chapter.

References

[1] F. Hahn, 'Keynesian Economics and General Equilibrium Theory: Reflections on Some Current Debates', in G. Harcourt (ed.), *The Microeconomic Foundations of Macroeconomics* (London: Macmillan, 1977).

[2] R. W. Clower, 'The Keynesian Counter-Revolution: a Theoretical Appraisal', in F. H. Hahn and F. Brechling (eds), *The Theory of Interest Rates* (London: Macmillan, 1965); reprinted in P. G. Korliras and R. S. Thorn (eds), *Modern Macroeconomics* (New York: Harper & Row, 1979).

[3] A. Leijonhufvud, *On Keynesian Economics and the Economics of Keynes* (Oxford University Press, 1968).

[4] L. Walras, *Elements of Pure Economics*, trans. W. Jaffe (Homewood, Ill.: Irwin, 1954); original publication 1874.[1]

[5] K. J. Arrow and G. Debreu, 'Existence of an Equilibrium for a Competitive Economy', *Econometrica*, 22, 3 (July 1954).

[6] G. Debreu, *The Theory of Value* (New York: Wiley, 1959).

[7] E. R. Weintraub, *The Microfoundations of Macroeconomics* (Cambridge University Press, 1979).

[8] L. Harris, *Monetary Theory* (New York: McGraw-Hill, 1981) chs 4, 5, 14.

[9] J. R. Hicks, 'Mr. Keynes and the Classics: A Suggested Interpretation', *Econometrica*, 5 (1937).

[10] J. R. Hicks, *Value and Capital* (Oxford: Clarendon Press, 1939).

[1] A translation of the Edition Dèfinitive (1926) of the *Elements d'èconomie politique pure.*

[11] D. Patinkin, *Money, Interest and Prices*, 2nd edn (New York: Harper & Row, 1965).
[12] Joan Robinson, *Economic Heresies* (London: Macmillan, 1971).
[13] G. L. S. Shackle, *The Years of High Theory* (Cambridge University Press, 1967).

Further reading

Clower [2], Weintraub [7] and Harris [8].

17 Neo-Keynesian Quantity-Constrained Models

Neo-Keynesian quantity-constrained models[1] show the implications for output and employment of trading at non-market-clearing prices. They share with the post-Keynesian approach the rejection of Walrasian equilibrium, though unlike the latter they do not reject the other features of neoclassical methodology. Neo-Keynesians want to obtain Keynesian-type results in models which conform to the neoclassical view that economic agents must be treated as rational maximising decision-makers and that the interdependencies between variables must be studied within a general-equilibrium framework. Neo-Keynesian models contain an explicit choice-theoretic basis for modelling individual agents' behaviour which is then aggregated to yield macro behavioural relationships.

The crucial distinction between neo-Keynesian and neoclassical models is that the former do not presume that markets clear in equilibrium whereas the latter models do.

Neo-Keynesian models solve for temporary or short-run equilibrium in which markets are not necessarily cleared. The period of analysis is seen as relatively short, but within that period traders' plans are made consistent via quantity rather than price adjustment so there is no incentive for agents to change their plans within the time period of analysis. The economy is shown as moving from one short-run equilibrium to another since further adjustments do occur which prevent the short-period equilibrium from being a permanent resting-place. The short period is often characterised as one that is not long enough for price adjustment to occur, hence quantities have to do the adjusting. This characterisation reflects the Keynesian view that quantities adjust more rapidly than prices.

[1] These models are associated with the work of Barro and Grossman [1] and [2], Malinvaud [3] and [4] (and the group of French Keynesian mathematical economists), Hahn [5]–[7], and more derivatively in the United Kingdom by Muellbauer and Portes [8].

17.1 A taxonomy of non-market-clearing states

Neo-Keynesian models all take off from Clower's insight that trading at non-market-clearing prices requires economic agents to make different decisions from those that they would make if they could buy or sell as much of any commodity as they chose to at given market prices.

Walrasian equilibrium

Walrasian equilibrium provides the reference point with which non-market-clearing states of the world are compared. It is therefore useful to start by outlining Walrasian general equilibrium in the context of a highly aggregated macro model with a single goods market and a homogeneous labour market. This is done with the aid of Figure 17.1. It is built up from Figure 16.1 on p. 306 which showed households' labour–consumption choice.

We are assuming here that all national output is consumed so that households' choice of current income is identical to their choice of current consumption. Hence we are analysing one time period in isolation from any past or future time periods. As in Figure 16.1, the real wage line AB, whose slope is given by the real wage rate, shows the rate at which households can trade off leisure (sell labour time) in return for income and consumption. We assume that all households have the same utility function with respect to leisure and consumption. The family of indifference curves, I_0 to I_2, then applies to all households so that the diagram can be used for aggregate analysis. As in Figure 16.1, households will maximise utility at point W, where the indifference curve I_1 is tangential to the real wage line (i.e. where the real wage equals the marginal rate of substitution of income for leisure). Households supply OL_e labour units and demand Oy_e goods. Figure 17.1 also shows firms' choice with respect to the amount of labour they wish to employ and the amount of output they wish to supply. OF is the short-run aggregate production function. Perfectly competitive firms will maximise profits at the level of output for

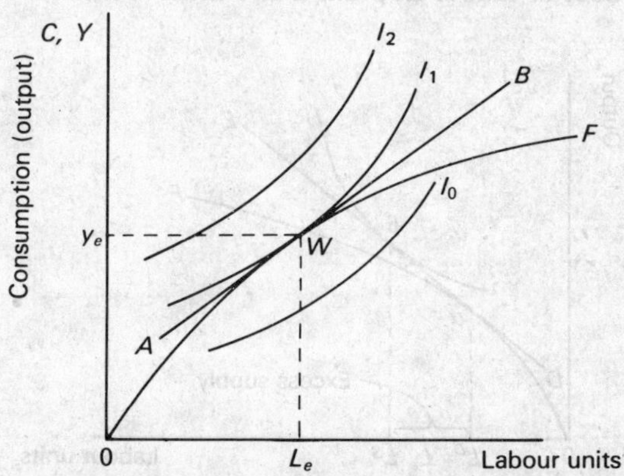

FIGURE 17.1 *Walrasian general equilibrium*

which the marginal product of labour equals the real wage rate. The real wage is the amount a firm has to pay in terms of goods to secure an additional unit of labour. Thus firms will maximise profits at point W, where the real wage line is tangential to the production function. Firms demand OL_e labour and wish to supply Oy_e output. So at a real wage of w_e households' and firms' choices are consistent. The demand for labour equals the supply of labour and the demand for goods equals the supply of goods. Both the labour market and the goods market are cleared and we have Walrasian general equilibrium.

As discussed in Chapter 16, the device of the Walrasian auctioneer ensures that trade does not occur unless the real wage is at a market-clearing level. The crucial difference between neoclassical and Keynesian thinking concerns the way prices and quantities actually adjust when false trading does occur (that is, trading at non-market-clearing prices). The extreme neoclassical assumption is that prices adjust quickly towards their equilibrium values and so ensure a return to equilibrium employment. The extreme neo-Keynesian assumption is that in the absence of the Walrasian auctioneer goods prices (and hence the price level) and money wages are fixed in the short run. False trading occurs at these prices. How the outcome now differs from that in Walrasian equilibrium depends on the values at which the money wage rate and the price level are fixed compared with the values consistent with Walrasian equilibrium in which markets clear. We now proceed to consider three kinds of non-market-clearing states which can arise when false trading occurs.

The classical unemployment case

We now assume that the money wage rate and the price level are fixed at values which yield a real wage in excess of the market-clearing real wage, w_e. The effect of this assumption on the demand for and supply of labour is illustrated in Figure 17.2.

A real wage higher than w_e pivots the real wage line from AB in Figure 17.1 to DE in Figure 17.2. The latter has a steeper slope. The real wage now equals the marginal product of labour at point α and firms' demand for labour is now

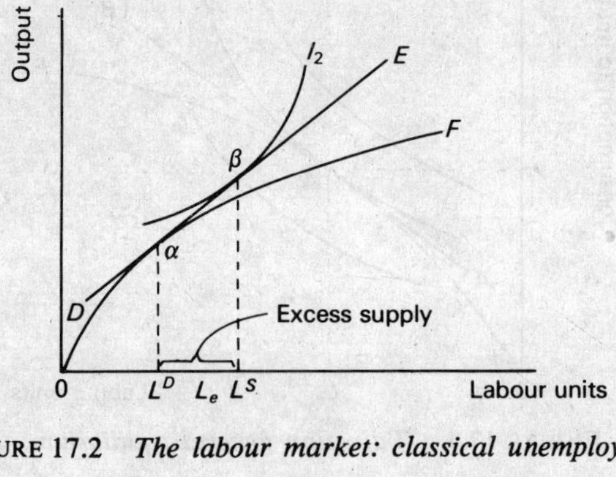

FIGURE 17.2 *The labour market: classical unemployment*

OL^D, compared with OL_e in Walrasian equilibrium. At the higher real wage households' indifference curve is tangential to the real wage line at β. Households supply OL^S labour, which is L_eL^S more than in Walrasian equilibrium. There is an excess supply of labour of L^DL^S units. The unemployment which arises when the real wage rate is greater than the market-clearing real wage is termed *classical unemployment* by neo-Keynesian writers.

Classical unemployment is the type of unemployment which Keynes analysed in *The General Theory* and which occurs in the Keynesian–neoclassical (K–N) synthesis model developed in section I of this book. Keynes states quite explicitly that unemployment is associated with a real wage rate which is too high in relation to the market-clearing real wage:

> Thus I am not disputing this vital fact which the classical economists have [rightly] asserted as indefeasible. In a given state of organisation, equipment and technique, the real wage earned by a unit of labour has a unique [inverse] correlation with the volume of employment. Thus *if* employment increases, then, in the short period, the reward per unit of labour in terms of wage-goods must, in general, decline and profits increase. (*The General Theory*, p. 17)

Later in this chapter we shall consider the position of Keynes's model *vis-à-vis* those of the neo-Keynesians.

The repressed inflation case

We now assume that the money wage rate and the price level are fixed at values which make the real wage less than that required for Walrasian equilibrium. The resulting situation in the labour market is illustrated in Figure 17.3.

With a real wage lower than w_e, the real wage line is now *GH* and has a less

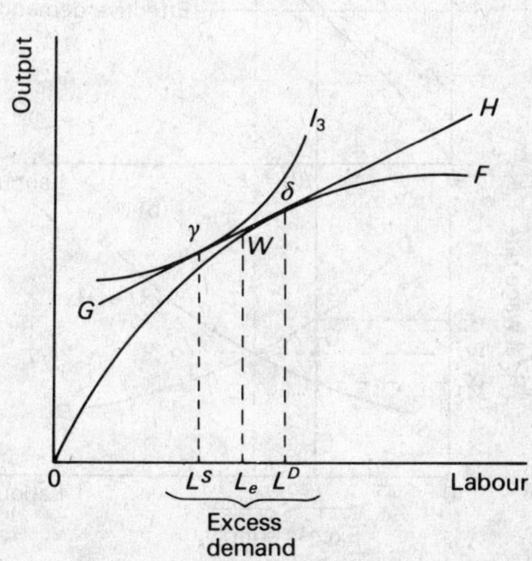

FIGURE 17.3 *The labour market: repressed inflation*

steep slope then the real wage line AB in Figure 17.1, for which $w = w_e$. Again households' indifference curve and the production function are tangential to the real wage line at different points (γ and δ respectively). Firms demand OL^D labour compared with OL_e units when $w = w_e$, whereas households are only willing to supply OL^S labour now that the real wage is below w_e. There is an excess demand for labour of $L^S L^D$ units. By assumption the money wage cannot rise even though there is excess labour demand; hence this case is termed repressed inflation.

The Keynesian unemployment case

Neo-Keynesians are anxious to show that unemployment can occur when the real wage rate is at or below its market-clearing level. The unemployment is due to an insufficient level of effective demand for goods. This situation is illustrated in Figure 17.4.

The money wage rate and the price level are again fixed, and they are consistent with the market-clearing real wage rate, w_e. The real wage line is therefore AB, as in the Walrasian equilibrium case. However, the effective demand for national output is assumed to be only Oy^{ED}. If firms produced the level of output, Oy_e, at which the marginal product of labour equalled the real wage rate, they could not sell all of it because of insufficient effective demand. Firms are therefore constrained to produce Oy^{ED} output. Hence their effective demand for labour is OL^{ED}, compared with a notional demand of OL_e. If firms

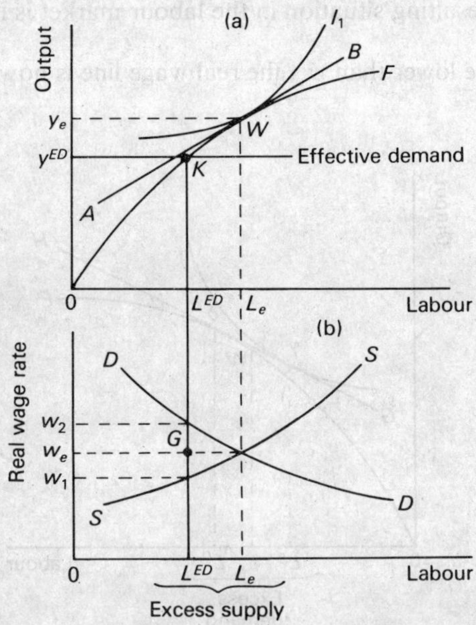

FIGURE 17.4 *The labour market: Keynesian unemployment*

were not quantity-constrained in the goods market, they would demand OL_e labour units and supply Oy_e output.

At the real wage of w_e we can see from part (b) of the diagram that households' notional supply of labour is OL_e units, but as they are rationed they can only sell OL^{ED} units. There is therefore an excess supply of labour of $L^{ED}L_e$ units. The labour market is operating at point G in Figure 17.4(b). Firms are off the notional demand for labour function and households are off the notional supply of labour function.

Unlike Keynes's own model (see the quotation on p. 313), there is no unique relationship between the real wage and employment. Given the effective demand constraint, Oy^{ED}, the level of employment of OL^{ED} is consistent with any real wage rate between w_2 and w_1. Above w_2 the demand for labour would be less than OL^{ED} and below w_1 the supply of labour would be less than OL^{ED}. When firms are quantity-constrained to produce Oy^{ED} but the real wage is w_e, the marginal product of labour is greater than the real wage. (At point K in Figure 17.4(a) the slope of the production function OF is steeper than the slope of the real wage line AB.) This means that firms would be willing to expand output and employ more labour at the existing real wage rate if the effective demand for output were higher.

Thus we get the important result for neo-Keynesian models that *involuntary unemployment can exist without the real wage being too high* (that is, above its market-clearing value). The real wage can be at or below the market-clearing one but a lack of effective demand gives rise to involuntary unemployment. This result is in complete contrast to Keynes's own statement that involuntary unemployment could only be reduced if there were a fall in the real wage.

17.2 A neo-Keynesian fixed-price quantity-constrained model

Having sketched out three possible non-market-clearing states that can exist once we allow false trading to occur, we shall now construct a simple macroeconomic model in which money wages and prices are fixed and agents can be quantity-constrained.

The model consists of three markets: the goods market, the labour market and the money market. We simplify by assuming that money is the only financial asset so that we can neglect bonds and the interest rate. We also assume that the money market adjusts quickly so that it is cleared in each short-run time period of analysis. This leaves us with two markets, the goods market and the labour market, which may remain uncleared. When a market experiences excess supply then sellers are rationed; when it has excess demand buyers are rationed. Households are sellers of labour and buyers of goods; firms are buyers of labour and sellers of goods. Hence we have the classification summarised in Table 17.1. For example, when there is excess supply in the labour market households are rationed sellers.

It is one of the axioms of quantity-constrained models that exchange is voluntary: no one is forced to buy more than he wants to or sell more than he wants to. A further axiom is that rationed sellers and rationed buyers cannot exist in the same market. These two postulates ensure that the actual quantity

TABLE 17.1

	Households	Firms
Rationed sellers	Excess supply in the labour market	Excess supply in the goods market
Rationed buyers	Excess demand in the goods market	Excess demand in the labour market

transacted in a market is always the lesser of the amount demanded or of the amount supplied.

For each market, when it is out of market-clearing equilibrium, there are two possible states of the world:

1. When there is excess supply, the actual quantity sold is equal to the amount demanded.
2. When there is excess demand, the actual quantity sold equals the amount sellers wish to supply.

Thus the short side of the market determines the quantity actually traded. Only in market-clearing equilibrium are demand and supply equal.

Quantity-constrained models place special emphasis on the dual decision hypothesis (see p. 305). Households' dual decision is that the amount of labour supplied and the amount of output demanded are interrelated. If unconstrained in either market, both decisions are taken simultaneously (see pp. 305–7). However, if households are rationed in the labour market, then the amount of output they effectively demand is constrained by the amount of labour they can sell. Alternatively, if households are rationed in the goods market, then this may affect their supply of labour decision. The amount of labour households would supply at the current real wage if they could spend as much as they want to on goods may exceed the amount supplied when households are rationed buyers in the goods market. This will occur when households prefer more leisure to earning income which cannot be currently spent.

Firms' dual decision involves the amount of labour to employ and the amount of output to supply. If unconstrained in both markets, these two decisions are determined together (as, for example, in the Walrasian equilibrium depicted in Figure 17.1). However, if firms are rationed sellers in the goods market, then the amount they sell is constrained to equal the level of effective demand for output. The effective demand for output constrains the amount of labour firms demand. If firms are rationed buyers in the labour market, then the amount of output they can supply is constrained by the quantity of labour which is supplied.

As just shown, the dual decision hypothesis means that a quantity constraint in one market affects demand or supply in another market. For instance, when households are rationed in the labour market, their demand for goods is affected and notional goods demand is no longer the effective demand for goods. This means that the specification of the effective functions for the supply of labour and output and for the demand for labour and output will vary according to whether or not firms and households are rationed sellers or buyers.

Given two non-clearing markets and two possible conditions, excess demand or supply for each market, there are four possible permutations of states of the world:

1. Excess supply in the labour market; excess supply in the goods market.
2. Excess supply in the labour market; excess demand in the goods market.
3. Excess demand in the labour market; excess demand in the goods market.
4. Excess demand in the labour market; excess supply in the goods market.

Each of the first three permutations corresponds to one of the non-market-clearing states outlined in section 17.1. The fourth is theoretically uninteresting and so will not be considered further. We shall now review the three types of non-market-clearing state and summarise the categories (see Table 17.2).

1. Keynesian unemployment

Keynesian unemployment exists when firms are rationed sellers in the goods market and households are rationed sellers in the labour market. Output is limited by effective demand so that at the existing level of output the real wage rate is less than the marginal product of labour. Because of the extent to which the supply of output is constrained by lack of effective demand households are rationed sellers of labour. As they would prefer less leisure, the marginal rate of substitution of leisure for income or marginal value of leisure, MVL is still below

TABLE 17.2 *A taxonomy of non-market-clearing states*

	Excess supply in goods market	Excess demand in goods market
Excess supply in labour market	*Keynesian unemployment* Households rationed in labour market. Firms rationed in goods market, $(w < MPL)$ $(w > MVL)$	*Classical unemployment* Households rationed in labour market. Households rationed in goods market, $(w = MPL)$ $(w > MVL)$
Excess demand in labour market	Unlikely	*Repressed inflation* Households rationed in goods market. Firms rationed in labour market. $(w < MPL)$ $(w = MVL)$

the real wage rate. Since household income is exogenous, the Keynesian consumption function applies. The level of effective demand thus determined falls short of the amount of output firms would be willing to supply at the current real wage. The sum of excess demands over the labour market, which is in excess supply, the goods market, also in excess supply, and the money market, which is cleared, is negative. Hence Walras's law must be rejected.

2. Classical unemployment

Households are still rationed sellers in the labour market but firms are not rationed in the goods market, which has excess demand. Firms are producing the level of output for which the marginal product of labour equals the real wage. Households' demand for goods exceeds the supply of goods but firms are only willing to expand output if the real wage falls. The excess demand persists because money wages do not fall, nor do goods prices rise as they are fixed by assumption. Since households are rationed sellers of labour, the marginal value of leisure remains below the real wage. As household income is exogenous, the Keynesian consumption function again applies. However, the level of effective demand exceeds the amount of output supplied, in contrast to the Keynesian unemployment case.

3. Repressed inflation

Repressed inflation is the label given to the situation of rationed buyers in both markets. Firms' output is restricted by their inability to hire more labour at the existing fixed real wage rate. Thus the marginal product of labour exceeds the real wage. The quantity of labour sold by households is the amount they choose to supply, given the real wage rate and given that they are rationed in the goods market. Hence the marginal value of leisure equals the real wage. Since income is a choice variable the Keynesian consumption function does not apply. The level of effective demand, given the amount of income households choose to earn, exceeds the amount of output firms can supply.

Household decision-making when they have time and money

As pointed out in Chapter 16, once money is admitted into a model there has to be some explicit consideration of time. In our simplified quantity-constrained model households can only hold goods and money as assets, there being no bonds. Hence households do not borrow or lend. Households' expenditure on goods and money balances is limited by their wage income, the dividends received from the ownership of firms and the money balances they begin the period with.[1] Dividend income and the stock of money balances at the start of

[1] In our quantity-constrained model the inability of households to borrow stems from the absence of any interest-bearing financial assets. In a model with such assets one could assume that households are completely credit-rationed and so cannot borrow to finance expenditure in excess of their current income and real money balances. This

the time period of analysis are assumed exogenous to the households whether or not they are quantity-constrained. Wage income is a choice variable unless households are rationed sellers in the labour market, when it becomes exogenous to the households. The households' budget constraint for each period is

$$\boxed{\text{Wages}} + \boxed{\text{Profits from ownership of firms}} + \boxed{\text{Money balances at beginning of period}}$$
$$= \boxed{\text{Expenditure on goods}} + \boxed{\text{Money balances held at the end of the period}}$$

We cope with time in the model in the simplest way possible by assuming households plan for just two periods, the present and the future. Household utility depends on current consumption and leisure and next period's consumption and leisure. Households' plans are now affected by their anticipations of market conditions in the next period. These anticipations concern the future real wage, the future price level, and the possibility of quantity constraints in the next period in either the goods or labour markets. For instance, if a household expects to be rationed in the labour market in the next period, it will wish to supply more labour in the current period in order to accumulate money balances to finance future consumption.

If unconstrained in the goods market, household decision-making now concerns how much wage income to earn (that is, how much labour to supply) and how much of its total resources to spend on goods and how much to keep in the form of money balances. Unlike the simple Walrasian equilibrium illustrated in Figure 17.1, aggregate household income in the form of wages and profits need not be equal to current consumption. This is because money balances are held and allow households to dissave (spend in excess of their income) or to save. Aggregate demand therefore depends on the stock of money balances held and on expectations about the future as well as on income (if households are rationed sellers of labour) or the real wage rate (if households are not rationed sellers).

Once we have introduced money into the model, so that the choice of current income is not necessarily the same as the amount of planned current consumption, it is no longer possible to use the diagrammatic exposition of Figure 17.1 to show the amount of output produced. To determine what the

---

would be an extreme assumption. However, some credit-rationing is a typical Keynesian assumption. It is justified by the view that households cannot borrow to any great extent because their only collateral is human wealth. This is a highly illiquid asset because there is no market in which it is traded. The assumption of credit-rationing brings in another uncleared market – the credit or bond market. It also implies the absolute income hypothesis of consumption and rejects the permanent income hypothesis because the latter requires households to be able to borrow as much as they want to at the current interest rate in order to obtain their preferred time profile of consumption.

actual level of production is we have to compare firms' supply plans with households' effective demand. To derive the level of effective demand we need to relate households' current income–labour-supply choice to households' current consumption–labour-supply choice. This is done by means of Figure 17.5.

Part (a) of Figure 17.5 shows households' current income–labour-supply choice. Given households are unconstrained in the labour market, then their choice of how much labour to supply in the current period will depend on their desire to consume and on their ability to finance this by other means than wage income (that is, with dividends and money balances). It will also be affected by their expectations about being rationed in the labour market in the future or in the goods market in either period.[1] If households are not rationed in the labour market, then they choose to supply OL_1 labour units and earn Jy_1 wage income.

Part (b) of Figure 17.5 shows how households choose to allocate their current period's resources between goods and real moneybalances. As stated in the budget constraint on page 319 households' current resources consist of wage income, dividends and the stock of real balances held at the start of the period. These resources can be spent on goods or on real balances. When households are not rationed in the labour market their wage income is Jy_1, and dividends are OJ, giving a total income of Oy_1. This is transferred to the vertical axis of part (b). We assume that households start out with real money balances equal to y_1M on the vertical axis of Figure 17.5(b). If households decided to spend all their resources on goods, they would demand OM goods. If they decided to put all their resources into money, then they would plan to end the period with OB real balances. Thus MB is the households' budget constraint stated on page 319. Households' preferences as between goods and real balances depend on their desire for present as compared with future consumption, their expectations about the income they will get in the future period and their expectations about being rationed in the goods market. These preferences determine the shape and position of the indifference curves in the goods–real balances plane. Given that the budget constraint is tangential to indifference curve U_1, households choose to demand OC_1 goods. Note that in this example households are saving.

Part (c) of Figure 17.5 shows the households' current consumption–labour-supply choice. When unconstrained in the labour market households demand OC_1 goods (from part (b)) and supply OL_1 labour (from part (a)). The co-ordinates OC_1, OL_1 give point Z in part (c) of the diagram.

Let us now consider what happens when households are rationed in the labour market. Turning to part (a) of Figure 17.5 we assume that households can only sell OL_0 labour. This means that their wage income falls to Jy_0 and their total income to Oy_0. In part (b) of the diagram the budget constraint shifts down to the left by the distance of y_0y_1 to ND. Effective demand falls to OC_0. In part (c) we plot the effective demand by households for output of OC_0 when the level of employment is constrained to be OL_0. The co-ordinates OC_0, OL_0

[1] We follow the example of Muellbauer and Portes [8] and subsume all these into the utility function.

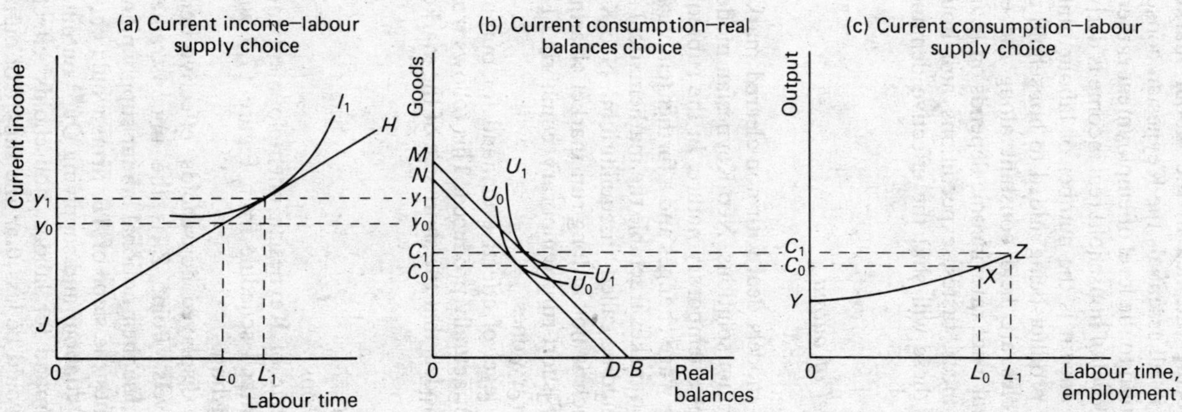

FIGURE 17.5 *Deriving the quantity-constrained effective demand relationship*

give point X. If we derived the effective demand at the levels of employment below OL_1, we would get a number of points such as X which lie on the YZ schedule.

The YZ schedule thus shows the effective demand by households for output at various levels of employment. Only at point Z is effective demand not constrained by households being rationed in the labour market. The effective demand schedule, YZ, is in all essentials the Keynesian consumption function except it relates consumption to the level of employment rather than to the level of income. However, the level of household real income is derived directly from the level of employment since it is the number of labour units sold *times* the fixed real wage rate, this product being added to household dividend income, OJ. A number of variables are held constant along the effective demand schedule. These are the real wage rate (income depends on w and employment), the quantity of real balances, tastes, expectations and household dividend income. Any changes in these will shift the effective demand schedule.

Determination of the level of output

Although neo-Keynesian models deal with non-cleared markets, they are designed to produce equilibrium solutions. Neo-Keynesian models envisage such an equilibrium as being of a temporary nature. In the subsequent time period there will be some price or wage changes and a further temporary equilibrium is established. This approach makes tractable the mathematical analysis of what, in a verbal exposition, would be called 'disequilibrium'. Neo-Keynesian models analyse an economy which is not in long-run market-clearing equilibrium in terms of a succession of short-run, temporary equilibria. The equilibria we discuss below are temporary ones.

In these equilibria the level of effective demand for output cannot be less than the amount of output actually produced. This follows from a basic axiom of quantity-constrained models that the short side of the market determines the actual quantity sold.

Keynesian unemployment

To illustrate the occurrence of Keynesian unemployment in Figure 17.6 we combine the effective demand schedule from Figure 17.5 with the short-run aggregate production function.

Along schedule YZ is displayed households' effective demand at various rationed employment levels. Point Z is the unconstrained choice when households are able to realise their notional labour supply plans. Given the real wage rate, which determines the slope of AB, firms would choose to maximise profits by employing OL^{ND} labour and supplying Oy^{NS} output. But if firms did employ their notional demand for labour, households' effective demand for consumption, at Oy^{ED^0}, would be less than the supply of output, Oy^{NS}. Firms could only sell Oy^{ED^0} output, so they would choose to employ only OL_0 labour. Effective demand would still be lower than the supply of output, so

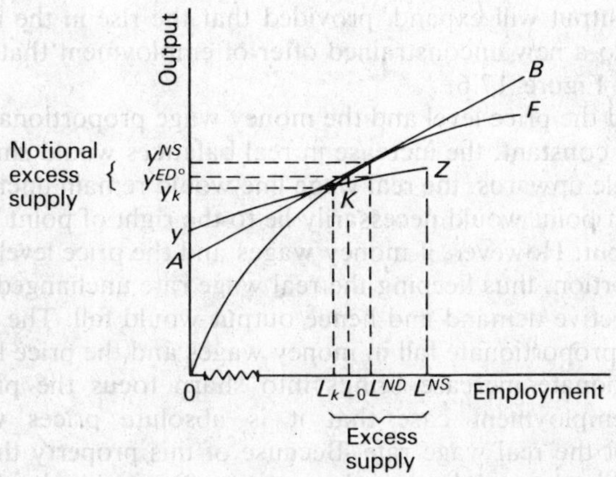

FIGURE 17.6 *Temporary equilibrium with Keynesian unemployment*

short-run equilibrium could not prevail. Output and employment will contract until we reach the levels Oy_k and OL_k at which the aggregate production function intersects the effective demand schedule at point *K*.

At this point effective demand is Oy_k, firms employ OL_k labour units to produce Oy_k output. The aggregate supply of output is thus determined by the level of effective demand and a temporary equilibrium is established at point *K*. Given the real wage rate, firms would like to supply Oy^{NS} output, but there is not sufficient effective demand to bring forth this level of production so there is excess notional supply in the goods market of $y_k y^{NS}$. The real wage is then lower than the marginal product of labour (the slope of *AB* is less than that of *OF* at y_k, L_k).

Households would like to supply OL^{NS} labour at the prevailing real wage so there is also excess supply in the labour market of $L_k L^{NS}$. The situation is thus one of Keynesian unemployment.

As we noted earlier in the chapter, Keynesian unemployment is consistent with the real wage being at or below its Walrasian equilibrium level. Unemployment is due to lack of sufficient effective demand. With the aid of Figures 17.5 and 17.6 we can see that at the root of the problem are wrong *absolute* prices, not the wrong relative price (that is, the real wage). If the price level were lower, real money balances would be larger. The budget constraint in Figure 17.5(b) would shift up to the right. Consequently effective demand would be higher and the effective demand schedule *YZ* in Figure 17.6 would shift up. If the money wage remained unchanged, then the real wage would rise. The real wage line *AB* in Figure 17.6 would pivot and slide down the production function. Firms' notional demand for labour would be less. Provided that the new real wage line is still tangential to the production function to the right of point *K*, then output would increase as a result of the increase in effective demand following the price fall. This shows that under conditions of Keynesian unemployment an expansion of output can be consistent with a rise in the real wage rate.

Exactly the same result can be achieved by a rise in the money wage with the price level constant. Because labour income increases, effective demand shifts upwards and output will expand, provided that the rise in the real wage does not lead firms to a new unconstrained offer of employment that is less than or equal to L_k in Figure 17.6.

If we lowered the price level and the money wage proportionately so the real wage remained constant, the increase in real balances would shift the effective demand schedule upwards, the real wage line would remain unchanged and the new equilibrium point would necessarily lie to the right of point K, ensuring an increase in output. However, if money wages and the price level were raised in the same proportion, thus keeping the real wage rate unchanged, real balances would fall. Effective demand and hence output would fall. The different effect on output of a proportionate fall in money wages and the price level compared with a proportionate increase brings into sharp focus the property of the Keynesian unemployment case that it is absolute prices which are inappropriate, not the real wage rate. Because of this property the real balance effect is crucial in determining whether or not effective demand is at the level required for a cleared goods market.

The quantity-constrained Keynesian unemployment model, when stripped of its mathematical formulation, reduces to the familiar Keynesian single-sector model which has been taught for years as part of elementary orthodox Keynesian economics. The diagram we have used (Figure 17.6) is in fact a reincarnation of the familiar 'Keynesian cross' diagram (see Chapter 2, p. 20) except that it uses employment rather than output along the horizontal axis. YZ is an aggregate demand function, and OF is an aggregate supply function up to the unconstrained level of output, Oy^{NS}, given the real wage. The crucial assumption which is responsible for unemployment equilibrium in both models is price and wage rigidity. The difference between a neo-Keynesian model and the 'Keynesian cross' one is that the former is based on an attempt to make price and wage rigidity consistent with treating economic agents as rational, utility-maximising decision-makers. This aspect of neoclassical methodology is incorporated in order to rebut the criticism that the Keynesian analysis of unemployment equilibrium rests on *ad hoc* assumptions about price rigidity which imply money illusion and other types of irrational behaviour.

Classical unemployment

Temporary equilibrium with classical unemployment is illustrated in Figure 17.7. Given the real wage rate, which determines the slope of real wage line DE, firms wish to employ OL^{ND} labour and supply Oy^{NS} output. When OL^{ND} labour is employed households' effective demand is Oy^{ED}. Firms are thus not rationed in the goods market but households are. The economy is at a temporary equilibrium position at point C. There is excess demand in the goods market of $y^{NS}y^{ED}$. Given the real wage rate households would like to supply OL^{NS} labour. (Point Z' shows households' unconstrained labour–consumption choice.) There is thus an excess supply of labour of $L^{ND}L^{NS}$. In this case output is not constrained by lack of effective demand but by the unwillingness of firms to expand production when that would involve marginal costs (the money wage rate) exceeding the marginal-revenue product of labour (MPL × price). In the case of classical unemployment a cut in the money wage

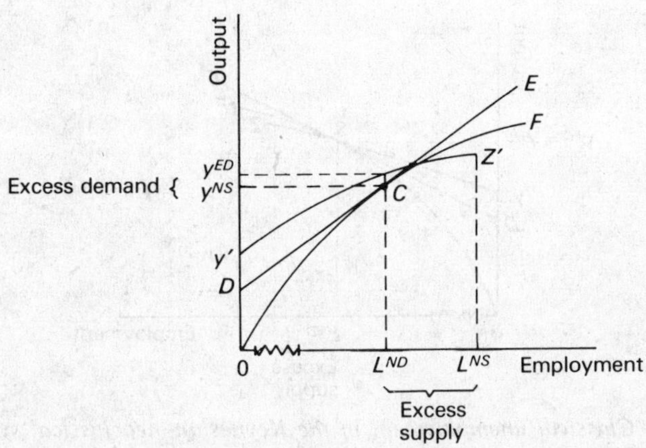

FIGURE 17.7 *Temporary equilibrium: classical unemployment*

or rise in the price level would increase output as firms would expand production in response to a fall in the real wage rate.

No classical or neoclassical economist would recognise this definition of classical unemployment, as in their view goods-market prices would rise absolutely in response to excess demand. This would lead to a fall in real balances until the goods market is cleared and output levels would be consistent with profit maximisation. This would be the case whether or not real wages stayed constant. A classical or neoclassical economist therefore sees unemployment created by an excess level of real wages as being accompanied by a cleared goods market.

The Keynesian–neoclassical synthesis model

The Keynesian–neoclassical (K–N) synthesis model can be made equivalent to a borderline case in a neo-Keynesian quantity-constrained model. The Keynesian version of the K–N synthesis model and Keynes's 'General Theory' model are consistent with a cleared goods market accompanied by excess supply in the labour market. Thus firms are not rationed in the goods market, but households are rationed in the labour market. The Keynesian consumption function therefore holds. The effective demand schedule intersects the production function at the point where it is tangential to the real wage line. This is shown in Figure 17.8.

Given the real wage rate and hence real wage line, *DE*, firms demand OL^{ND} labour and wish to supply Oy^{NS} output. Since the effective demand function, *Y'Z'*, intersects the production function at *S*, the effective demand for output when OL^{ND} labour is employed is equal to Oy^{NS}. The goods market clears but there is excess supply in the labour market, as households wish to sell OL^{NS} units of labour.

The Keynesian version of the K–N synthesis model differs however, from a neo-Keynesian model which happens to have a cleared goods market and an

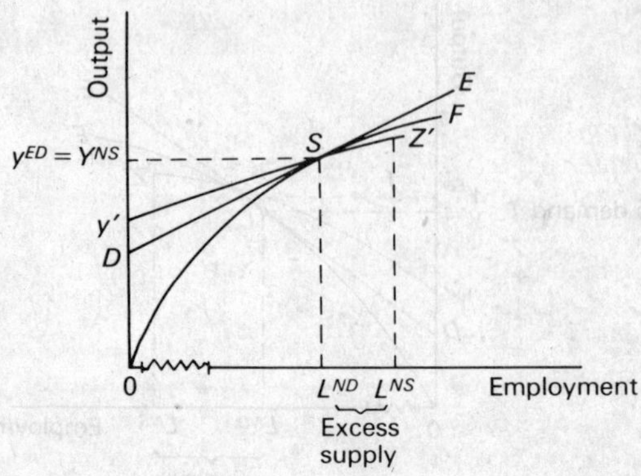

FIGURE 17.8 *Classical unemployment in the Keynesian–neoclassical synthesis case*

excess supply of labour. The Keynesian version of the K–N synthesis model has a flexible price level but a fixed money wage. Our neo-Keynesian model has both a fixed price level and a fixed money wage. The flexible price level assumption of the K–N synthesis model ensures that the goods market clears. As a consequence of this assumption unemployment in a K–N synthesis model is of the classical variety because a *fall* in the real wage rate is required in order to reduce unemployment and increase output. To see this let us suppose that the effective demand schedule, $Y'Z'$, in Figure 17.8 shifts up to the left but that the real wage remains unchanged. (This would happen if the money wage rate and the price level fell proportionately, thus increasing real balances.) Output would not increase because firms are unwilling to supply more than the existing amount of output unless the real wage falls.

The neoclassical case of the K–N synthesis model has both a flexible price level and a flexible money wage rate. In terms of Figure 17.8 this flexibility ensures that point Z' (households' unconstrained labour–consumption choice) coincides with point S to give both a cleared goods market and a cleared labour market.

Repressed inflation

Temporary equilibrium with repressed inflation is illustrated in Figure 17.9. Given the real wage rate which determines the slope of real wage line GH, firms demand OL^{ND} labour. However, the effective demand schedule is $Y''Z''$: households are only willing to supply OL^{NS} labour. Firms are therefore rationed in the labour market and are constrained to produce Oy^{ES} output. The temporary equilibrium position is therefore R. There is excess demand in the labour market of $L^{NS}L^{ND}$ and also excess demand in the goods market of $y^{ES}y^{ED}$, since households would like to purchase Oy^{ED} goods.

One interesting thing to note about the repressed-inflation case is that it involves a lower level of output and employment than would occur were the

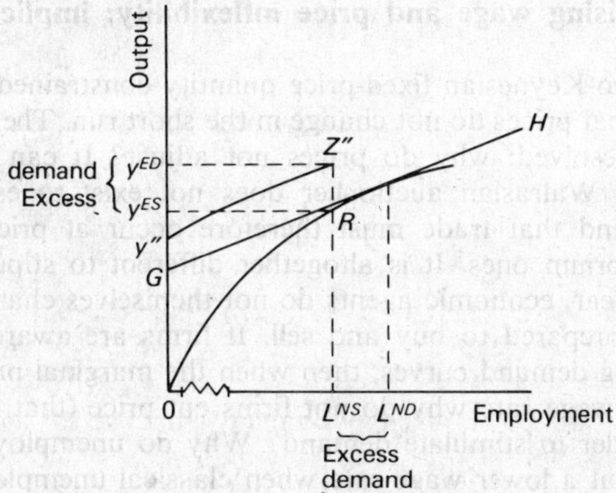

FIGURE 17.9 *Temporary equilibrium: repressed inflation*

real wage at its Walrasian equilibrium level. This is because the real wage lies below the Walrasian equilibrium level and households consequently supply less labour than in Walrasian equilibrium. Output is constrained by lack of labour. Thus any movement away from Walrasian equilibrium in a neo-Keynesian fixed-price model results in a lower output and employment level.

17.3 Quantity-constrained open-economy models

Most of the work on quantity-constrained models has only considered the closed-economy case. As Hahn ([6] p. 14) admits, 'considering international trade leads to a strengthening of the Walrasian case'. If the economy is a small open one, then it becomes much more difficult to maintain that firms producing tradable goods are rationed so that they cannot sell as much as they want to at the prevailing world price. Given that the price of tradables in a small open economy tends to the world price, either through internal price adjustment or exchange-rate adjustment, domestic firms cannot over the medium to long run affect the price of their product. They can sell as much as they want to at the prevailing world price. If this is so, then any unemployment of domestic resources must be attributed to the fact that any further increase in output would raise marginal costs above the world price level. Lack of export competitiveness implies classical rather than Keynesian unemployment. Quantity-rationing can then only apply to households in the labour market (as in Dixit's model [9]). Such a model is a Keynesian–neoclassical synthesis model since it has a cleared goods market with excess supply in the labour market.

Those who wish to argue for the existence of Keynesian unemployment in a small open economy need to restrict it to the non-tradables sector or have domestic firms producing specialist goods for export so that they face downward-sloping demand curves and therefore could possibly be quantity-rationed.

17.4 Rationalising wage and price inflexibility: implicit contracts

The results of neo-Keynesian fixed-price quantity-constrained models rest on the assumption that prices do not change in the short run. The crucial question still remains unresolved: why do prices not adjust? It can be very readily granted that the Walrasian auctioneer does not exist to establish market-clearing prices and that trade must therefore occur at prices that are not Walrasian equilibrium ones. It is altogether different to stipulate that, when markets fail to clear, economic agents do not themselves change the prices at which they are prepared to buy and sell. If firms are aware that they face downward-sloping demand curves, then when the marginal product of labour exceeds the real wage rate why do not firms cut price (that is, raise the real wage rate) in order to stimulate demand? Why do unemployed workers not offer themselves at a lower wage rate when classical unemployment occurs?

It seems generally accepted that these kinds of price adjustments have not readily occurred, especially in the post-war period. The usual response of firms when faced with a fall in demand is to lay off workers and to continue paying the remaining work-force the pre-recession hourly money wage. The alternative of lowering money wages and maintaining employment does not usually occur. Recent empirical work has drawn attention to the importance of temporary layoffs in total unemployment. Feldstein [10] reports that about three-quarters of adult male employees laid off in US manufacturing are subsequently rehired by their original employer. Hence workers must expect an intermittent pattern of employment even when they remain with the same firm. Since the alternative of steady employment but at fluctuating real wages does exist but is not frequently observed this implies that the prevailing pattern of intermittent unemployment must in some sense be chosen by both firms and workers, otherwise firms which offered unstable employment to their work-force would find it unacceptably difficult to recruit labour and would change their practices.

These considerations have led a number of economists to explain layoffs and sticky wages as the outcome of utility-maximising and hence rational behaviour by firms and workers. One motivation for this work is the desire to provide a firmer microeconomic basis for non-market-clearing macro models. Another motivation, coming from the opposite direction, is to give a neoclassical explanation for the existence of layoffs.

The basic idea underlying these rationalisations of layoffs and sticky wages is that workers and employers enter into long-term implicit contracts. If consistent behaviour by an economic agent can induce consistent reciprocal behaviour in another agent, so that each party acts more or less as it would do if legally constrained, then an implicit contract is said to exist. Thus a firm makes an implicit contract with its employees by paying a wage rate which does not vary with the state of demand and by operating certain rules for determining layoffs (such as least-senior workers being laid off first, and laid-off employees being recalled at their previous wage rather than being replaced by new workers at lower wages). Workers, in return, agree to be laid off and to wait for recall rather than seek permanent work with other firms.

Risk-shifting implicit contracts[1]

One rationalisation for sticky wages is the existence of implicit long-term contracts which shift the risk of unstable income from workers to firms. It is assumed that workers are risk-averse and dislike variable incomes, whereas firms are risk-neutral. This is ascribed to the inability of owners of human capital to diversify their portfolios, unlike non-human wealth-holders. (A worker would find it difficult to divide his time between numerous occupations.) Workers are treated as maximising their expected utility from income and leisure over different expected states of nature. The simplest way to model this is to have two possible states of nature, *G* (good) when demand is high, and *B* (bad) when demand is low. The sum of the probability of each occurring adds up to 1.0. If workers get no income and no utility from leisure when unemployed in state *B*, then they will maximise their utility by choosing the same wage rate in both state *G* and state *B* in return for employment in both states. The firm bears all the income variability but in return pays a lower expected wage rate.

We have not yet got an explanation for layoffs since they do not occur under this arrangement. However, if workers do get unemployment benefit or derive some utility from leisure when unemployed then they will wish to trade a higher constant wage rate in return for some risk of unemployment.

Some workers now get laid off in state *B*. As a result of the implicit contract between the firm and its workers, real wages are lower in state *G* and higher in state *B* than if wages were variable and set in the Walrasian manner to clear the market in both states of nature. The latter arrangement is referred to as a *spot auction market*.

The implicit contract puts an obligation on employers in slack times to keep more workers than they would choose to employ, given a rigid money wage, in the absence of any such contract. The other side of the bargain is that in a boom workers will supply more labour hours at the going real wage rate than they would choose at the time without the contract. The existence of such contracts implies that in equilibrium the current real wage is no longer equal to the current marginal productivity of labour. The real wage is related to the average expected productivity of labour over the various states of nature and it is reduced by the premium workers pay for the insurance against variable income.

This approach has been extended to explain why some workers can get risk insurance from their employers and generally avoid being laid off while others cannot. Grossman, for example, assumes more-senior workers are both more productive and less likely to default on their contracts by quitting the firm in good times. They get more or less full insurance against variable income as it is the latest recruits who bear the brunt of the layoffs. These workers prefer high wages in state *G* and unemployment in stage *B* to employment in state *B* at the low wage required to make them worth hiring when the firm has to honour its

[1] Such models have been developed by Azariadis [11] and Grossman ([12] and [13]).

commitments to the senior workers. Another variant is that it is the skilled workers who are spared layoffs because they are expensive to replace if they quit. Unskilled workers get laid off because to keep them on while still paying skilled workers the pre-recession wage would require such a low wage rate that these workers prefer unemployment.

Other rationalisations for sticky wages and prices

It is possible to explain implicit contracts, which also involve choosing non-variable wages together with a probability of layoff, without appealing to risk-averse behaviour. Feldstein [10] shows that when the unemployment benefit received by its laid-off workers is not paid for directly by the firm then both parties will benefit from choosing a variable pattern of employment. The parties agree to higher wages during recessions than would occur in a spot auction labour market, accompanied by layoffs for some workers. When demand is high workers contract to supply more labour at the contractually agreed wage. This means that workers choose to take more leisure when the value of their work is lower to the firm because of depressed demand and to then take advantage of the unemployment subsidy.

The notion of implicit contracts has also been extended to the firm and its customers. When there are costs to gathering price information it is argued that both parties gain by keeping prices constant in the face of temporary demand and supply fluctuations. Customers' search costs are reduced and in return the firm gains loyal customers. Analogous to the junior or unskilled workers who bear the brunt of layoffs there is a group of irregular customers who cannot get supplies when costs have risen but prices have not.

Implicit contracts and non-market-clearing

Ironically the development of implicit-contract theory has weakened rather than strengthened the non-market-clearing approach. Keynesians have interpreted layoffs as non-wage job-rationing and hence as *prima facie* evidence that markets do not clear. However, implicit contract theory rationalises layoffs and the associated wage stickiness as the outcome of utility-maximising choice by workers when the choice is exercised in the context of a lengthy time period and uncertainty. If workers actually choose inflexible wages together with the resulting periods of unemployment, then it becomes much more difficult to argue that markets do not clear and unemployment is involuntary. It is interesting to note that Grossman, whose work was important in developing the non-market-clearing approach, then proceeded to work on implicit-contract theory. This has led him to the following conclusion:

> Although these non-market-clearing models are superficially appealing they are also problematic . . . These risk-shifting models provide a rationale for observed stickiness of wage rates and explain alleged symptoms of employment rationing,

such as layoffs, while allowing markets to clear and private agents to realise all perceived gains from trade. (Grossman [14] p. 14)

It is difficult therefore to escape the conclusion that the microeconomic foundations of neo-Keynesian quantity-constrained models are still not on a sound footing.[1]

17.5 Policy implications in quantity-constrained models

Neo-Keynesian models are used to demonstrate the validity of orthodox Keynesian policies for reducing unemployment. An important result of these models is that such policies only work when unemployment is of the Keynesian rather than classical variety. To analyse policy we need to introduce a third type of economic agent – the government.

To keep the analysis as simple as possible we assume that there is no taxation. The government finances its expenditure by printing money. Fiscal policy thus consists of changing the level of government expenditure. The government can also conduct monetary policy by directly giving money to households or taking it away from them. Both monetary and fiscal policy changes shift the effective demand schedule, which now includes government demand as well as household consumption. The only difference between a monetary or fiscal expansion concerns the allocation of goods between households and the government. If the government increases the money supply, then households can spend more. If government expenditure increases, the government purchases more goods. Households end up with more money balances but this does not affect their demand for goods until the next time period. The government's third policy instrument is a prices and incomes policy, by which the government can arbitrarily change the price level and the money wage rate.

Keynesian unemployment

When the economy has Keynesian unemployment, output and employment can be increased by monetary or fiscal policies that raise the level of effective demand. This is illustrated in Figure 17.10 by a shift in the effective demand schedule from YZ to $Y'Z'$, which establishes a new equilibrium position at K'. Output rises from Oy_0 to Oy_1 and employment from OL_0 to OL_1.

A prices and incomes policy that reduced the price level and the money wage rate in the same proportion would increase real balances and would also shift the effective demand schedule up to the left. An increase in the money wage rate, with the price level kept constant, or a reduction in the price level with a fixed money wage would also increase effective demand. However, the

[1] This also applies to flexible-price neo-Keynesian models as they assume slow and incomplete wage and price adjustment. A few such models have been developed but are highly mathematical. The interested reader should refer to Hahn [7] and Malinvaud [4].

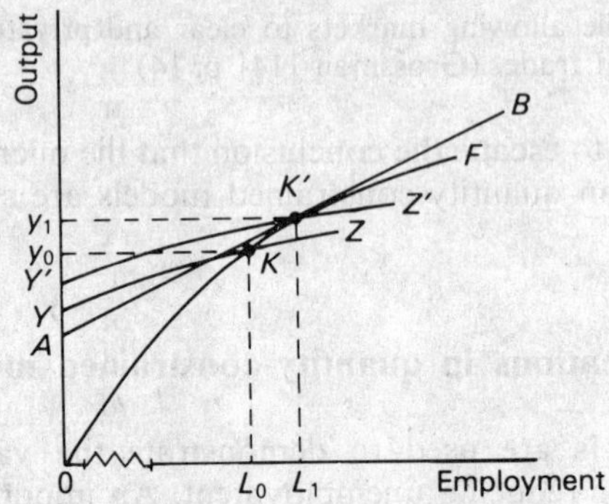

FIGURE 17.10 *Policies to increase output under Keynesian unemployment*

real wage rate would rise and output would only increase if the new real wage line is tangential to the production function to the right of the old equilibrium position, *K*.

A crucial feature of expansionary policy when there is Keynesian unemployment is that it does not require a reduction in the real wage. In fact, a rise in the price level would inhibit expansion because it reduces real balances. Furthermore, a rise in output is consistent with an increase in the real wage up to its Walrasian market-clearing level.

A quite inappropriate policy is one which raises prices and/or lowers money wages. This will reduce the level of effective demand and so reduce output and employment. Hence Keynes's criticism of money wage cuts as a cure for unemployment is correct if unemployment is of the Keynesian type. Similarly, the standard trade-union advocacy of higher money wages to increase output by stimulating demand would also be correct if firms are prepared to meet increased demand at a higher real wage rate.

Classical unemployment with excess demand in the goods market

If there is excess demand in the goods market but firms are unwilling to produce to that level, then further increases in effective demand can have no impact on employment. The traditional Keynesian remedy for unemployment is thus inappropriate. To increase the amount of output firms want to supply a cut in the real wage is needed. This is achieved by an increase in the price level, and/or a reduction in the money wage rate. However, both policies shift the effective demand schedule down to the right. This means that a cut in real wages will increase output provided that effective demand is not reduced too much and remains above the original level of output.

The required direction of price and money wage movements when there is classical unemployment is opposite to that needed to expand output when Keynesian unemployment exists. If the price level is reduced *vis-à-vis* the money wage under classical unemployment, then output falls because the real wage rate has risen.

Classical unemployment with a cleared goods market

In the K–N synthesis case of the neo-Keynesian model classical unemployment coexists with a cleared goods market. This is illustrated in Figure 17.11.

The economy is initially in equilibrium at point *C*, where real wage line *DE* is tangential to the production function. An increase in effective demand from *YZ* to *Y'Z'* will have no effect on the amount of output supplied because the real wage has not fallen. To increase employment there has to be a reduction in the real wage rate as well as an expansion of aggregate demand. In our fixed-price neo-Keynesian model an increase in effective demand accompanied by a prices and incomes policy that raised the price level *vis-à-vis* the money wage level would result in an expansion of output. If the real wage falls so that the real wage line shifts from *DE* to *AB*, then a new equilibrium with higher output and employment occurs at point *C'*.

In the K–N synthesis model, in contrast to the neo-Keynesian one, a deliberate prices and incomes policy is not required since goods prices are flexible. A policy which increases effective demand also causes firms to raise prices. Sufficient labour is willing to work at the existing money wage rate for firms to be able to expand production. Thus the real wage line shifts from *DE* to *AB* by means of private-sector price adjustment. This policy was analysed in Chapter 6 by means of aggregate demand and supply schedules in the *P–y* plane (see pp. 88–9).

In Keynes's 'General Theory' model a cut in real wages is also required to expand output. Keynes argued that a fall in real wages should occur via an increase in the price level and not via a cut in the money wage rate. This is because he supposed that a cut in money wages would result in falling prices and no change in real wages. A rise in effective demand due to the real balance effect would not raise output if the real wage failed to decline.

Repressed inflation

The case of repressed inflation requires an increase in the real wage rate to induce households to supply more labour and so enable firms to produce more

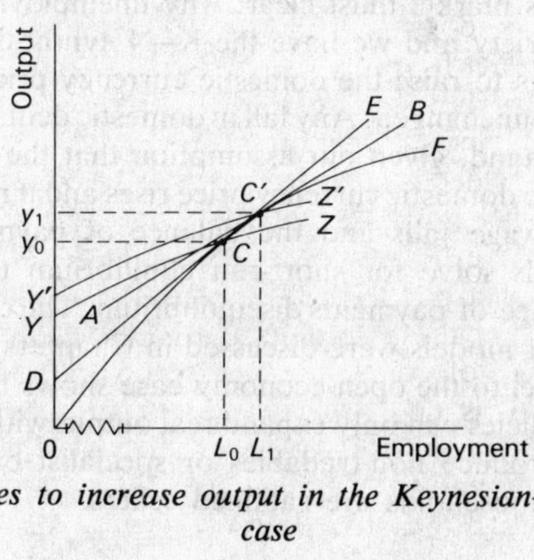

FIGURE 17.11 *Policies to increase output in the Keynesian–neoclassical synthesis case*

output. An easing of rationing in the goods market, which could be achieved by means of deflationary fiscal or monetary policy as well as by increasing the supply of output, is also likely to encourage households to supply more labour.

Policy in a small open economy

As we noted in section 17.3, the existence of Keynesian unemployment is less plausible in a small open economy than in a closed one. Firms can only be rationed sellers if they produce non-tradable goods or specialist tradable goods. To maintain the fixed price assumption we need to analyse the effects of monetary and fiscal policy under a fixed exchange-rate regime.

If firms are not rationed sellers because they produce tradable goods which are perfect substitutes for foreign producers' goods, then any unemployment must be of the classical variety. As in the closed-economy case, an increase in effective demand alone, without a fall in real wages, has no effect on output. Given a fixed exchange rate and the law of one price, the government cannot alter the price level. Hence real wages can only fall if there is a cut in money wages. This is why monetary and fiscal policy are impotent when the law of one price holds. The law of one price will not hold if domestic firms produce non-tradable goods or specialist export goods. If this is the case and, in addition, firms and households are rationed sellers, then Keynesian unemployment will exist and the usual fiscal and monetary remedies apply.

By manipulating the exchange rate the government can alter the price level in a neo-Keynesian open-economy model. This gives the government an additional policy instrument. If firms are rationed sellers and there is Keynesian unemployment, then a devaluation lowers the foreign currency price of domestic goods. Given the assumptions that firms and households are rationed sellers and that money wages and prices are fixed in terms of domestic currency, the real wage paid by firms remains unchanged while the effective demand by foreigners for domestic output increases. Consequently output expands.

If domestic firms produce tradables which are perfect substitutes for foreign goods, then the goods market must clear. Any unemployment must therefore be of the classical variety and we have the K–N synthesis case. Devaluation enables domestic firms to raise the domestic currency price while keeping the foreign currency price unchanged. Any fall in domestic demand is made up for by increased foreign demand, given our assumption that the goods market must remain cleared. As the domestic currency price rises and if money wages remain fixed then the real wage falls and the balance of payments improves. As neo-Keynesian models solve for short-run equilibrium they can ignore the repercussions of balance-of-payments disequilibrium. The consequences of such repercussions in other models were discussed in Chapters 10 and 11.

Extending the model to the open-economy case shows that monetary, fiscal and exchange-rate policies can only expand real output without a fall in the real wage rate if firms produce non-tradables or specialist export goods and, in addition, firms and households are rationed sellers.

Disaggregated markets

The policy conclusions of neo-Keynesian quantity-constrained models also need to be modified when the existence of many goods and labour markets is taken into account. In the aggregate model there is only one relative price, that of labour in terms of goods. With many markets there are many relative prices and there is much more scope for substitution. Excess demand in one market can be partially satisfied by purchasing alternative goods in other markets. Similarly, firms facing excess supply can switch production to markets which have excess demand. As Malinvaud ([4], p. 91) concludes, 'one may also guess that the added flexibility does stabilise the system and makes imbalance less serious'.

The existence of numerous markets also means that the economy can, at any one time, experience a variety of non-market-clearing states. Some markets may have repressed inflation while others suffer from Keynesian or classical unemployment. In this situation a set of policy measures designed to cure Keynesian unemployment would, if applied indiscriminately over the whole economy, produce undesired effects in markets experiencing repressed inflation or classical unemployment. Even if some markets are distinguished as having Keynesian unemployment, this may be due to long-term structural changes in the economy which have shifted demand away to other markets. In this case the benefits to producers of increasing the effective demand for their products have to be offset against the costs of resource misallocation, and this is, of course, a distributional issue.

One policy conclusion from neo-Keynesian models is clear cut: there has to be a correct diagnosis of the type of non-market-clearing state which applies to the economy or its particular sectors before even policy-makers of a Keynesian bent can decide what remedies are needed. It is particularly important to be able to distinguish whether the economy is experiencing Keynesian or classical unemployment since the remedies for one state are undesirable in the other. It seems that we have as yet no clear diagnosis of when and where these states exist. Keynesians such as Malinvaud [3] seem confident that casual observation is sufficient to establish that Keynesian unemployment is much more frequent than the classical type. On observing the world non-Keynesians see far more scope for the existence of classical unemployment. The appearance of classical unemployment requires the real wage to rise above its market-clearing value. This is equivalent to a decline in the productivity of labour. Malinvaud [3] and Dixit [9] analyse the increase in oil prices which oil-consuming countries have experienced in the 1970s in these terms, since an oil price rise increases production costs.

Keynesians, including Malinvaud, also argue that real wages can be pushed up independently of the state of demand by social tensions or by particular anticipations of the future. An additional factor in mature economies is the growth of competition from newly industrialising countries. This reduces the market-clearing real wage rate which domestic firms require to maintain sales in their existing markets. All such exogenous increases in the real wage compared with the market-clearing one are likely to increase the rate of economic obsolescence of machinery. This, combined with a relatively slow rate of investment, is likely to cause full-capacity constraints in goods markets to occur at correspondingly higher levels of labour unemployment than happened previously. All these occurrences would explain the emergence of classical unemployment.

An additional note of caution concerning policy conclusions, which applies to Keynesian and non-Keynesian models, is that dynamic considerations often lead to more ambiguous results than does comparative-static analysis by itself. In particular, the policy conclusions of neo-Keynesian models seem sensitive to the effects of expectations held regarding quantities. For instance, a falling excess supply of labour can make households more optimistic about future employment prospects and hence cause them to increase current consumption. The same conditions can cause firms to become more optimistic about sales and thus increase the demand for labour. Such behaviour could generate instability and gives quantity-constrained models more of a 'bootstraps' element than is present in models which only contain price expectations. (See Muellbauer and Portes [8] for an elaboration of this point.)

So while neo-Keynesian models have certainly helped to clarify our thinking on the microfoundations of macroeconomic analysis, any conclusions about policy applications must be tempered by due regard to the openness of the economy, its multi-market character and the role of expectations.

References

[1] R. J. Barro and H. I. Grossman, 'A General Disequilibrium Model of Unemployment', *American Economic Review*, 61 (1971).

[2] R. J. Barro and H. I. Grossman, *Money, Employment and Inflation* (Cambridge University Press, 1976).

[3] E. Malinvaud, *The Theory of Unemployment Reconsidered* (Oxford: Blackwell, 1977).

[4] E. Malinvaud, *Profitability and Unemployment* (Oxford: Blackwell, 1980).

[5] F. Hahn, 'Keynesian Economics and General Equilibrium Theory: Reflections on Some Current Debates', in G. Harcourt (ed.), *The Microeconomic Foundations of Macroeconomics* (London: Macmillan, 1977).

[6] F. Hahn, 'Monetarism and Economic Theory', *Economica*, 47 (February 1980).

[7] F. Hahn, 'Unemployment from a Theoretical Viewpoint', *Economica*, 47 (August 1980).

[8] J. Muellbauer and R. Portes, 'Macroeconomic Models with Quantity Rationing', *Economic Journal*, 88 (December 1978).

[9] A. Dixit, 'The Balance of Trade in a Model of Temporary Equilibrium with Rationing', *Review of Economic Studies*, 45 (1978).

[10] M. Feldstein, 'Temporary Layoffs in the Theory of Unemployment', *Journal of Political Economy*, 84, 5 (October 1976).

[11] C. Azariadis, 'Implicit Contracts and Underemployment Equilibria', *Journal of Political Economy*, 83 (December 1975).
[12] H. Grossman, 'Risk Shifting, Layoffs and Seniority', *Journal of Monetary Economics*, 4 (1978).
[13] H. Grossman, 'Employment Fluctuations and the Mitigation of Risk', *Economic Inquiry* (October 1979).
[14] H. Grossman, 'Rational Expectations, Business Cycles and Government Behaviour', in S. Fischer (ed.), *Rational Expectations and Economic Policy* (University of Chicago Press, 1981).

Further reading

Malinvaud [3], Hahn [7] and Grossman [14].

18 The Phillips Relation

The previous two chapters have considered two contrasting hypotheses about price adjustment. In neoclassical analysis prices adjust fully to bring about market-clearing equilibrium. A distinctive feature of the neoclassical model is that the equilibrium values of the real variables are invariant with respect to changes in the equilibrium value of the price level brought about by changes in stock of money. In Keynesian analysis prices either fail to adjust at all or only do so slowly so that markets remain uncleared. So from both perspectives interest focuses on how the price level varies over the trade cycle and how such variations relate, if at all, to fluctuations in real output and employment.

18.1 The early Phillips curve

Attention was drawn to a statistical relationship between unemployment and inflation by Phillips [1] in a now classic study published in 1958. The form of the relationship studied by Phillips was between the annual rate of change of money wages and the annual average percentage rate of unemployment using UK data for 1861–1957. Phillips concluded from the data that the rate of change of money wages seems to be inversely and non-linearly related to the percentage rate of unemployment. He displayed this relationship by fitting a curve to the data. The original Phillips curve is reproduced in Figure 18.1. Because the observations for 1948–57 lie quite close to the curve fitted for the years 1861–1913, it was thought that the relationship was a stable one that would persist over a long period of time.

One can move from a relationship between the rate of change of money wages and unemployment to one between the rate of change of the price level and unemployment by allowing for long-run changes in the productivity of labour. If the money wage rate increases at the same rate as labour productivity, then the average labour cost of producing goods remains unchanged. If goods prices are some stable mark-up on average costs, then prices will not change so long as the rate of increase of money wages equals that of labour productivity. One can therefore subtract the average rate of

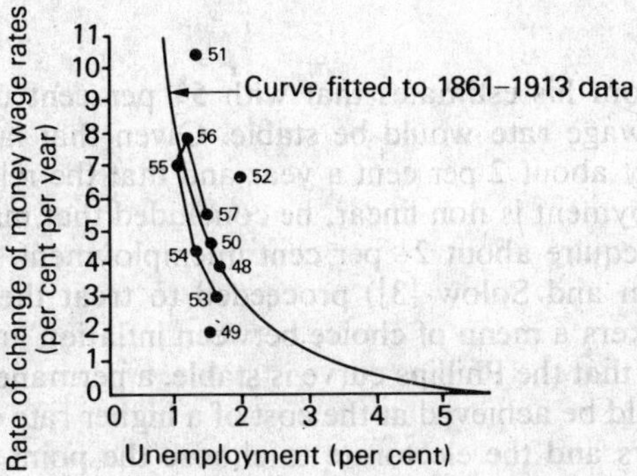

FIGURE 18.1 *The original Phillips curve*

increase of labour productivity, $\dot{Q}/Q$, from the rate of increase in money wages, $\dot{W}/W$, to obtain the resulting rate of increase in the price level, $\dot{P}/P$.[1] That is

$$\frac{\dot{P}}{P}=\frac{\dot{W}}{W}-\frac{\dot{Q}}{Q} \tag{18.1}$$

In the 1960s Phillips's work generated many more empirical studies of the relationship between the rate of change of money wages, inflation and unemployment. Other variables, not only unemployment, were tried as explanatory variables for wage or price inflation. Some studies found unemployment to be insignificant in explaining wage inflation, though these results tended to be for the post-war years using annual data. Studies using quarterly data were more successful in securing a significant effect for unemployment. On the whole the studies carried out in the 1960s tended to show a significant non-linear relation between wage inflation and unemployment. (A few of the early studies are summarised in Table 18.1, p. 354.) Not much attention was paid at the time to evidence which suggested that the Phillips curve was not stable over time. Two influential early studies (Phillips's own and Lipsey's [2]) did find that the relationship shifted over time as indicated by differences in the estimated coefficients for different periods.

1

$$\frac{\dot{Q}}{Q}=\frac{dQ}{dt}\frac{1}{Q}$$

$$\frac{\dot{W}}{W}=\frac{dW}{dt}\frac{1}{W}$$

And so on.

Policy inferences

Phillips inferred from his estimates that with $5\frac{1}{2}$ per cent unemployment the aggregate money wage rate would be stable. Given that labour productivity grew on average by about 2 per cent a year and that the relationship between $\dot{W}/W$ and unemployment is non-linear, he concluded that maintaining a stable price level would require about $2\frac{1}{2}$ per cent unemployment. Other economists (notably Samuelson and Solow [3]) proceeded to treat the Phillips curve as offering policy-makers a menu of choice between inflation and unemployment. On the assumption that the Phillips curve is stable, a permanently lower level of unemployment could be achieved at the cost of a higher rate of inflation. It was up to policy-makers and the electorate to choose the point along the Phillips curve which gave the preferred trade-off between unemployment and inflation.

The notion that a higher rate of inflation can give a permanently lower level of unemployment is at odds with the neoclassical macroeconomic model. In that model, as shown in Figure 6.3 (on p. 85), the level of real output and hence unemployment is invariant with respect to the price level. An increase in the price level, achieved by shifting the aggregate demand function up to the right, has no effect on long-run real output.

On the other hand, a stable Phillips curve does provide a dynamic analogue to the analysis of the effects of changes in aggregate demand in the Keynesian synthesis model. Here an increase in aggregate demand raises the price level relative to the money wage rate and this causes a permanent expansion in employment and output (see Figure 6.5, p.89). In the comparative-static world of this model output attains a higher equilibrium level with a lower real wage rate. At this new equilibrium the price level has moved up to a new constant level while money wage rates remain unchanged.

Theoretical underpinnings: excess demand

The Phillips curve started life as an empirical observation: its theoretical foundations were rather sketchy. Phillips's own explanation, which was elaborated by Lipsey, is that given a stable rate of change of labour productivity and the absence of sizeable import price fluctuations, money wages rise more rapidly the greater the amount of excess demand in the labour market. Formally, this is expressed as

$$\frac{\dot{W}}{W}=f\left(\frac{L^D-L^S}{L^S}\right) \tag{18.2}$$

where $\dot{W}/W=(1/W)(dW/dt)$ is the rate of change of the money wage rate, L^D is the demand for labour and L^S is the supply of labour. Now the demand for labour consists of those in employment, E, plus vacancies, V. The supply of labour is equal to employed workers plus the unemployed, U. Therefore

$$\frac{\dot{W}}{W}=f\left(\frac{V-U}{E+U}\right) \tag{18.3}$$

Since vacancies vary inversely with the unemployment rate and did so in a stable way up to the mid-1960s, unemployment by itself could be used as a measure of excess demand in the labour market. So we arrive at the Phillips relation

$$\frac{\dot{W}}{W}=f(U) \qquad \left(\frac{d(\dot{W}/W)}{dU}<0\right) \tag{18.4}$$

Equation 18.4 only specifies an adjustment mechanism. It tells us nothing about whether the disequilibrium which sets off the rate of change in money wages is caused by factors from the demand, or the supply side, or both sides of the labour market.

The coexistence of positive unemployment with rising money wage rates can be explained by the existence of frictional unemployment. Even when the labour market is in equilibrium, so that the demand and supply of labour are equal and there is no tendency for the money wage rate to rise, some frictional unemployment will exist. This would be the level of unemployment at which the Phillips curve cuts the horizontal axis. Any reduction in unemployment below this implies excess demand for labour and results in rising money wages even though unemployment is still positive.

An alternative but not mutually exclusive explanation for the Phillips curve cutting the horizontal axis at a positive unemployment rate is the aggregate nature of the statistical relationship. It is derived from aggregating over many individual labour markets. In each labour market the money wage rises when there is excess demand and falls when there is excess supply. In the Keynesian tradition it is supposed that the wage rate rises more rapidly for a given value of excess demand than it falls when there is equivalent amount of excess supply. The wage dynamics of each labour market would then be depicted as in Figure 18.2.

At any one time some markets will experience excess supply, others excess demand. When one averages over all markets then a positive average rate of unemployment due to the excess supply markets can be accompanied by a rising average money wage rate because wages in the excess demand markets rise more rapidly than they decline in the excess supply markets. The higher the

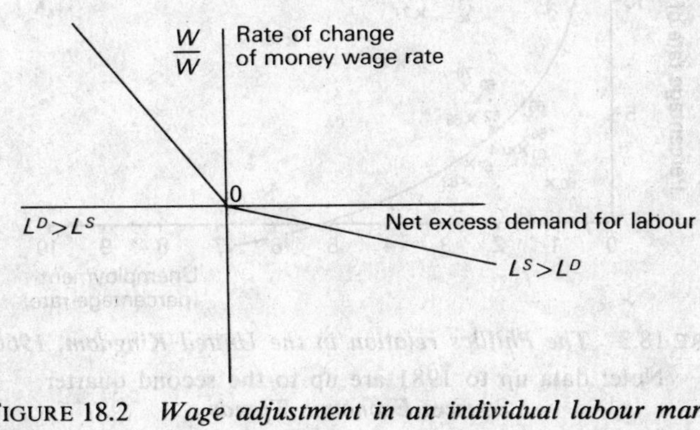

FIGURE 18.2 *Wage adjustment in an individual labour market*

general level of aggregate demand, the lower the average aggregate unemployment rate and consequently the faster is the increase in the average money wage rate. (A further exposition is given in Barro and Grossman [4].)

In the light of recent neo-Keynesian work one can see that this kind of theoretical rationalisation of the Phillips curve relies on the supposition that markets fail to clear. Money wages are changing because net excess demands in labour markets are not zero. A permanently lower level of unemployment can be achieved at the cost of higher inflation by maintaining a continual state of excess demand in the labour market. This can only occur if there is no adjustment to bring about a cleared labour market. The mechanism by which a more rapid rate of inflation could secure a permanently greater supply of real output was not at first properly investigated. Nevertheless, the belief that inflation could permanently lower the level of unemployment spread far beyond the economics profession in the 1960s and was generally regarded as a viable political option.

18.2 The natural rate of unemployment hypothesis

Cynics have observed that whenever an apparently stable economic relationship is discovered and then used for policy purposes, it promptly breaks down! The most famous example of this is probably the Phillips curve. The relationship between inflation and unemployment in the United Kingdom from 1960 to 1981 is shown in Figure 18.3. This shows pretty conclusively that the

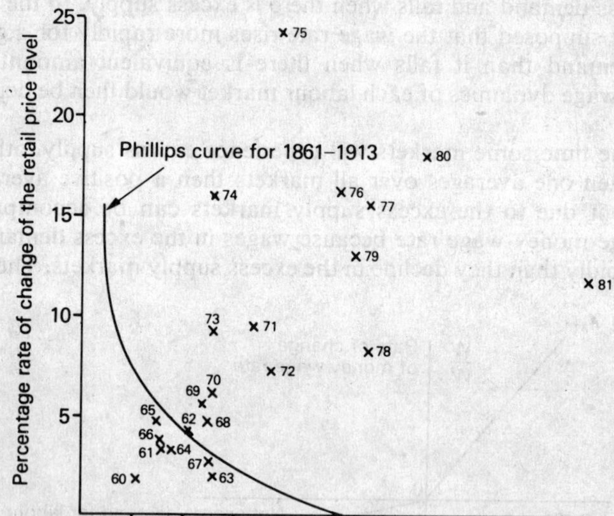

FIGURE 18.3 *The Phillips relation in the United Kingdom, 1960–81*

Note: data up to 1981 are up to the second quarter

Source: *Economic Trends.*

Phillips curve has not been a stable relationship; over the last fifteen years inflation and unemployment have both shown a marked secular increase. Other industrialised economies have displayed a similar tendency, though the levels of inflation and unemployment of some of these economies have remained below British rates. (See Figure 1.1 on page 4.)

The breakdown of the empirical Phillips relationship in the late 1960s coincided with new theoretical work, notably by Friedman [5] and Phelps [6], which denied the existence of a permanent trade-off between inflation and unemployment. The starting-point of this analysis is that microeconomic theory posits a relationship between the level of excess labour demand and the rate of change of *real* wages, not money wages as suggested by Phillips. Instead, the Phillips relation should be

$$\frac{\dot{w}}{w}=f(U) \tag{18.5}$$

where $\dot{w}/w=(1/w)(dw/dt)$ = rate of increase of the real wage rate. By definition, the actual rate of change of real wages equals the rate of change of money wages, $\dot{W}/W$, minus the rate of inflation, $\dot{P}/P$:

$$\frac{\dot{w}}{w}=\frac{\dot{W}}{W}-\frac{\dot{P}}{P} \tag{18.6}$$

When workers and employers set the money wage rate, each party is really concerned with the real wage rate at which labour will be hired. The perceived real wage rate implied by a particular money wage rate depends on what is the expected rate of inflation. Unless the economy is in long-run equilibrium so that expectations are always realised, there will be some divergence between the expected rate of inflation and the actual rate of inflation. This means that the appropriate relationship between the rate of change of the real wage rate anticipated by a worker and the rate of change in the money wage rate is

$$\frac{\dot{w}}{w}=\frac{\dot{W}}{W}-E\left(\frac{\dot{P}}{P}\right) \tag{18.7}$$

where $E(\dot{P}/P)$ = the expected rate of inflation.

If workers are rational, they fully adjust the increase in money wages for the expected increase in prices to obtain the resulting change in the real wage rate upon which they base their decision as to whether to remain in their present employment or to continue job search if unemployed, as the case may be. If workers do not fully take into account the inflation that they expect to occur when estimating their real income from their money income, they are said to have 'money illusion'. Behaviour due to money illusion is quite distinct from incorrect expectations. One can overestimate one's future real income because a higher rate of inflation occurs than one expected. This is distinct from money illusion, which would cause one not to act in response to one's future real income, even though one is correctly anticipating the rate of inflation that will occur. A coefficient, α, is subsequently attached to the price expectations variable. It will equal 1.0 if employees are both rational (that is, they do not suffer from money illusion) and can adjust fully their money wages to compensate for expected price increases.

If from equation 18.5 we substitute $f(U)$ for $\dot{w}/w$ in equation 18.7 and rearrange terms we get

$$\frac{\dot{W}}{W} = f(U) + \alpha E\left(\frac{\dot{P}}{P}\right) \tag{18.8}$$

where $\alpha = 1$ if, given the rate of unemployment, workers completely adjust their money wage to compensate for expected inflation, and $0 \leqslant \alpha < 1$ if they only partially adjust their money wage. Equation 18.8 is known as the *expectations-augmented Phillips curve*. The original Phillips relationship, shown in Figure 18.1, did not contain the $\alpha E(\dot{P}/P)$ term since it was based on the implicit assumption of a zero expected rate of inflation. When the rate of inflation was very low such an assumption was reasonably plausible. Once a positive rate of inflation becomes anticipated and given that $\alpha \neq 0$, then the rate of increase of money wage rates at all levels of employment will adjust to reflect anticipations about inflation. In terms of the Phillips-curve diagram, this means an upward shift in the entire relationship. There is therefore a whole family of short-run Phillips curves, each one corresponding to a given rate of expected inflation.

Friedman [5] proceeded to argue that the expectations-augmented Phillips curve would shift in such a way that in the long run a higher rate of inflation would result in no change in unemployment. This argument is explained in Figure 18.4 and it assumes that $\alpha = 1$ in equation 18.8. We start with an economy which has a stable price level and constant real and money wages. We are simplifying by assuming no growth in labour productivity. The short-run Phillips curve for a zero rate of expected inflation is PC_0. Since the price level is stable the unemployment level is U_N. This level of unemployment is termed the *natural rate of unemployment*. It is defined as that rate of unemployment which is consistent with labour-market equilibrium and at

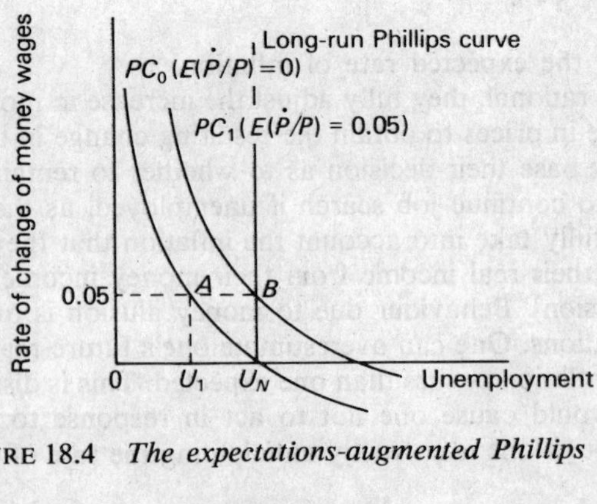

FIGURE 18.4 *The expectations-augmented Phillips curve*

which the price level could be stable. The natural rate of unemployment is determined by the real factors which affect the amount of frictional and structural unemployment in the economy.

The government has been told that there is a trade-off between unemployment and inflation. It therefore chooses to keep the economy at point A of the short-run Phillips curve PC_0 by expansionary policies which increase the money supply. The rate of inflation now rises to 5 per cent and the level of unemployment falls to U_1. We need an explanation of why unemployment falls and output rises when the rate of inflation increases. In the neoclassical interpretation of the Phillips relationship this occurs only because the inflation is *unanticipated.* Since demand has increased firms start raising prices and bidding up the money wage rate to attract more labour. Because workers' expectations of inflation are below the actual rate of inflation, they think that the higher money wages now being offered means that real wages have risen. The supply of labour therefore increases. This is shown in Figure 18.5 as a downward shift in the labour supply function from SS to $S'S'$. When actual and expected inflation are equal the labour supply schedule is SS. When inflation increases but expected inflation lags behind workers are deceived into offering to work for a lower real wage. The demand for labour increases as firms move down the demand for labour schedule. Unemployment falls and output rises as the economy moves up the short-run Phillips curve PC_0.

As expectations adjust towards the actual rate of inflation, workers realise that real wages are lower than they had anticipated and therefore require a more rapid increase in the money wage rate. The supply of labour schedule shifts back up until it regains its initial long-run position once expected and actual inflation are equal. As the supply of labour shifts back to its original position, the short-run Phillips curve also shifts outwards because the expected rate of inflation is rising. When expectations have fully adjusted to the new higher rate of inflation the short-run Phillips curve in Figure 18.4 has shifted up to PC_1, which is its position when the expected rate of inflation is 5 per cent. The economy is now at point B in Figure 18.4. Unemployment is back to its natural rate but there is now a 5 per cent rate of inflation. (This requires a permanently higher rate of increase in the money supply.) The idea that there is no

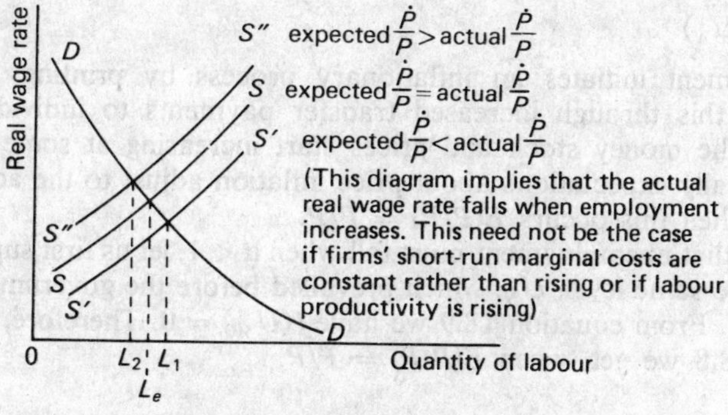

FIGURE 18.5 *The effect of differences between the actual and expected rates of inflation on the supply of labour*

way in which the rate of unemployment can be permanently held at a different level to the natural rate of unemployment is known as the natural-rate hypothesis (NRH). Another way of stating the same point is that the long-run Phillips curve is vertical.

The analysis also implies that if the government attempts to bring down the rate of inflation, unemployment will temporarily rise above the natural rate if expected inflation adjusts with a lag. For a while the expected rate of inflation based on past experience will lie above the actual inflation rate. Workers are offered a slower rate of increase in money wages by employers, given their increasing inability to raise prices in product markets at the previously experienced rate. As workers' expectations of inflation have not adjusted downward with this new development in the product market, they bargain for money wage rates in line with their unadjusted price expectations and their reservation money wage rate rises in line with these expectations. This leads to an upward shift in the supply of labour schedule in Figure 18.5. Real wages rise and employment falls. At first the economy moves down the current short-run Phillips curve (such as PC_1 in Figure 18.4) but as expected inflation falls the short-run Phillips curve shifts downwards and the natural rate of unemployment is restored once actual and expected rates of inflation are equal.

The Keynesian counter-argument

The natural-rate hypothesis, as we have just seen, depends on the expectations-adjustment coefficient, α, being equal to 1.0. Keynesian economists (see Tobin [7]), while accepting that a positive rate of expected inflation will reduce the size of the trade-off, have still maintained that because α is less than 1.0 some long-run trade-off occurs even when expected inflation has fully adjusted to actual inflation. To see why a long-run trade-off between inflation and unemployment will exist when $0 \leqslant \alpha < 1$ in equation 18.8, imagine an economy with no growth in either the labour force or labour productivity. The economy is in equilibrium with a constant price level, a constant cost–price mark-up and a rate of unemployment equal to U_N. In this equilibrium both $\dot{W}/W$ and $E(\dot{P}/P)$ are equal to zero, so that equation 18.8 becomes

$$0 = f(U_N) \tag{18.9}$$

The government initiates an inflationary process by printing money and distributing this through increased transfer payments to individuals in the economy. The money stock and prices start increasing at some predictable rate. Eventually expectations about price inflation adjust to the actual rate of inflation. When this occurs $E(\dot{P}/P) = \dot{P}/P$.

To show that unemployment must fall when $\alpha < 1$, let us first suppose that it stayed at the same level, U_N, which prevailed before the government initiated the inflation. From equation 18.9 we have $f(U_W) = 0$. Therefore, substituting 18.9 into 18.8 we get, when $E(\dot{P}/P) = \dot{P}/P$,

$$\frac{\dot{W}}{W} = \alpha\frac{\dot{P}}{P} \tag{18.10}$$

Subtracting $\dot{P}/P$ from both sides of the above equation and using equation 18.6 to rewrite the left-hand side of the resulting equation in terms of the rate of growth of real wages gives

$$\frac{\dot{w}}{w} = (\alpha - 1)\frac{\dot{P}}{P} < 0, \quad (\text{as } \alpha < 1) \tag{18.11}$$

In this case real wages will fall as a result of the induced inflation and it will be profitable for firms to hire more workers as their marginal-revenue product will be greater than the real wage. Hence employment must rise and therefore unemployment will fall below U_N. A long-run trade-off between inflation and unemployment must therefore exist. Notice that if $\alpha = 1$, then $\dot{w}/w = 0$ in equation 18.11, the real wage stays constant and the argument collapses. If $\alpha = 1$, there is *no* long-run trade-off.

When α is less than 1.0, the government can permanently reduce unemployment by inflation because the inflation decreases the real wage rate while not diminishing the supply of labour. A long-run trade-off depends on the existence of involuntary unemployment as defined by Keynes (see p. 74). The inflation-induced fall in the real wage increases the demand for labour and, since the additional labour supply is forthcoming, unemployment falls.

Keynesians have offered a number of explanations for why α should be less than 1.0. One reason is the traditional Keynesian one that workers are prepared to accept reductions in real wages that are brought about by inflation because markets fail to clear and so workers are off their notional labour supply function. Another reason profferred is that adjustment costs prevent money wages from adjusting fully for prices and workers are still prepared to supply more labour than before. Rees [8] has also suggested that the lower rate of unemployment brought about by inflation means that workers previously experiencing unemployment acquire skills which increase their productivity and hence the demand for their services, so that they remain in employment even when expected inflation has caught up with the actual rate. To neoclassical economists these reasons seem implausible and so fail to explain why α should not tend to 1.0 over time.

18.3 The 'new microeconomics' of the labour market

Since neoclassical theory predicts that the long-run equilibrium level of real output is invariant with respect to inflation, the apparent short-run trade-off between output and inflation needs to be rationalised. This has resulted in a reworking of neoclassical choice theory to include uncertainty and incomplete information. This approach has come to be known as the 'new microeconomics'. It first made its impact in a series of papers published in 1970 by Phelps *et al.* [9] under the title *The Microeconomic Foundations of Employment and Inflation Theory*. This analysis has already been applied in section 18.2 to explain the existence of a short-run trade-off.

The major innovation of the new microeconomics is that the assumption of complete information, which is guaranteed by the presence of the Walrasian auctioneer, is dropped. The other essentially neoclassical features are retained:

1. Economic agents maximise utility over time.
2. All exchanges which are perceived as mutually beneficial to economic agents are conducted.

In other words, markets clear, though the market-clearing equilibrium is only temporary if expectations turn out to be wrong.

The absence of the Walrasian auctioneer means that economic agents no longer get costless information about the values of equilibrium relative prices. Agents have to gather this information for themselves. One way of doing this for sellers is to experiment with price changes in order to find out what demand is. This situation implies that even if a market is perfectly competitive in the long run, individuals are not price-takers in the short run. Firms are therefore considered to be 'dynamic monopolistic competitors' because in the short run they can increase demand by lowering price or attract more labour by raising wages. Buyers and sellers also search for information by sampling price offers. Search theory, as it applies to labour markets, has already been reviewed in Chapter 5 (pp. 68–9) and it may be a good idea to have another look at those pages again.

The crucial idea for explaining the existence of a short-run negatively sloped Phillips curve is that workers search for jobs. It is presumed that job search is more effective when a person is unemployed since more time can be devoted to it. An unemployed worker has a reservation real wage in mind below which he will not accept employment. When a worker first starts searching for a job his reservation real wage is based on his previous money wage and his expectations about future changes in the price level. As he searches he gradually revises his reservation wage in the light of job offers received. The individual acts so as to maximise the present value of his (expected) utility, which depends on current and future consumption and leisure. The individual will only accept a job offer if the present value of the real income stream expected from the job exceeds the present value of expected income derived from continued search. The latter depends on how much income the worker expects to forgo by refusing the job offer and remaining unemployed and on how much income he expects to get by waiting for a better job offer.

If money wages are rising but actual inflation exceeds the expected rate, unemployed workers will take less time to find job offers which pay them more than their reservation wage. The duration of unemployment falls and so therefore does the total number of unemployed. While it is unanticipated, inflation results in a higher level of real output. As the actual inflation rate comes to be expected, workers revise their reservation money wage upwards, search takes longer and unemployment rises towards its natural rate. Search theory therefore provides a microeconomic foundation for the natural-rate hypothesis.

A crucial feature of this approach is that markets clear all the time. When expectations are being falsified by the outcome of events, only short-run temporary equilibria can exist.[1] Economic agents base their buying and selling

[1] Some economists refer to temporary equilibrium in this context as disequilibrium.

plans on their expectations about the future. Market prices adjust to reconcile the demands and supplies that are conditioned by these expectations. When expectations turn out to have been wrong, agents revise their plans and prices adjust accordingly. The 'new microeconomics' can therefore analyse dynamic changes in the economy by means of markets which are always in market-clearing equilibrium.

Critics of search theory

It is the market-clearing aspect of search theory that attracts most criticism. Search theory only provides an explanation of why workers choose to be unemployed when they either voluntarily quit their present job or are just entering the labour market. It does not explain why workers become unemployed through either layoffs or redundancy and it offers no explanation of job-rationing. This is regarded as a major weakness by the critics of search theory.

However, search theory provides an analysis of the factors affecting the duration of unemployment of all unemployed workers who are searching for jobs, no matter what was the initial cause of their unemployment. A crucial factor is that all unemployed workers have a reservation wage that is compared with the wage available from current job offers. If they reject current employment opportunities on the grounds that they pay less than their reservation wage, then they are choosing to prolong their unemployment.

A related criticism is that search theory models the labour market as a spot auction market, and this is claimed to be unrealistic. Implicit-contract theory (discussed on pp. 328–31) is specifically designed to rationalise the existence of sticky wages and job-rationing. The implication for the Phillips relation of implicit contracting is that those members of the unemployed who are temporarily laid off are not searching for jobs and are therefore not bidding down wage rates. One would therefore expect less downward wage adjustment during recessions than predicted by search theory. Similarly in a boom firms do not need to raise wages so much because the labour force has contracted to supply more hours without the inducement of higher wages. Implicit contract theory offers another reason for a positive rate of natural unemployment and suggests factors which determine the amount of natural unemployment. For instance, in Feldstein's layoff theory (see p. 330) more unemployment would be chosen the higher the unemployment-benefit subsidy. Implicit-contract theory and search theory are not necessarily inconsistent with one another. An eclectic view would see them as applying to different segments of the labour market.

Implicit-contract theory points to the existence of a group of favoured employees (the skilled, those with seniority) who can secure insurance against income variability. Since firms pay these workers higher wages in a recession than they would if a spot auction market operated, they would have to pay the others considerably lower wages which would be below these workers' reservation wages. These workers who move from job to job are searching for employment and will find the labour market to be more like a spot auction market. Whether or not the labour market is described as cleared if workers and firms agree to variable employment as part of an implicit contract is really a matter of semantics.

An alternative explanation of the Phillips relation to that given by search theory is the bargaining-power approach (see Kahn [10] for an example). This gives explicit recognition to the role of trade unions. The hypothesis is that trade unions' bargaining power increases with the degree of excess demand. Money wages therefore rise more rapidly when unemployment is low. Bargaining-power theory predicts that real wages will rise during the expansionary phase of the trade cycle and fall during recession, while search theory on the whole predicts the opposite.[1] To obtain this deduction the bargaining-power model requires imperfectly competitive markets in which monopoly power and hence profit margins decline during the expansion phase of the cycle.

18.4 Adaptive expectations

Given $\alpha = 1.0$, then the existence of a short-run trade-off between inflation and unemployment depends crucially on how expectations are formed. To derive a short-run trade-off we have so far assumed that expectations of inflation are based on past rates of inflation, so that whenever inflation accelerates expectations of inflation lag behind the actual rate. This assumption of how expectations are formed is termed the *adaptive-expectations hypothesis*. This has already been discussed in relation to consumption (p. 215) and investment (p. 242).

The adaptive-expectations hypothesis assumes that the expected rate of inflation is revised in the light of past errors in anticipating inflation. Expressed algebraically, it is

$$E\left(\frac{\dot{P}}{P}\right)_t - E\left(\frac{\dot{P}}{P}\right)_{t-1} = \lambda\left[\left(\frac{\dot{P}}{P}\right)_t - E\left(\frac{\dot{P}}{P}\right)_{t-1}\right] \tag{18.12}$$

where $E(\dot{P}/P)_t$ is that rate of inflation expected at time t to rule in the next period, $t + 1$, and λ is the adjustment parameter, which lies between 0 and 1. Therefore

$$E\left(\frac{\dot{P}}{P}\right)_t = E\left(\frac{\dot{P}}{P}\right)_{t-1} + \lambda\left[\left(\frac{\dot{P}}{P}\right)_t - E\left(\frac{\dot{P}}{P}\right)_{t-1}\right] \tag{18.12a}$$

Using the same method as in Chapter 11 (pp. 215–16) we get, by substituting for $E(\dot{P}/P)_{t-1}$, $E(\dot{P}/P)_{t-2}$, etc.,

$$E\left(\frac{\dot{P}}{P}\right)_t = \lambda \sum_{n=0}^{N} (1-\lambda)^n \left(\frac{\dot{P}}{P}\right)_{t-n} \tag{18.13}$$

[1] Although Phelps *et al.* [9] argue that dynamically oligopolistic firms are afraid to put up prices too much when demand expands because they fear their rivals will not follow. Therefore, for a time money wages rise more rapidly than prices.

Equation 18.13 states that the current expected rate of inflation depends on the past history of inflation. The closer is λ to 1.0, the more quickly expectations adjust.

When $\alpha = 1.0$, equation 18.8 can be written as

$$\frac{\dot{W}}{W} = f(U) + E\left(\frac{\dot{P}}{P}\right) \tag{18.8a}$$

It is often simpler to work with Phillips curves that are written in terms of the rate of change of prices as the dependent variable. One way to reach this result is to assume that prices are set in terms of a fixed mark-up over labour costs, so that

$$P = (1 + m)W \tag{18.14}$$

where m is the rate of mark-up over wage costs in the economy as a whole. Taking logarithms of both sides of equation 18.14 and then differentiating the result with respect to time one gets $\dot{P}/P = \dot{W}/W$. Substituting this into equation 18.8a gives

$$\left(\frac{\dot{P}}{P}\right)_t = f(U_t) + E\left(\frac{\dot{P}}{P}\right)_t \tag{18.15}$$

One can now substitute for $E(\dot{P}/P)_t$ from equation 18.13 into equation 18.15. By using the Koyck transformation (see p. 216), and by rearranging terms one then gets:

$$f(U_t) = (1-\lambda)\left(\frac{\dot{P}}{P}\right)_t - (1-\lambda)\left(\frac{\dot{P}}{P}\right)_{t-1} + (1-\lambda)f(U_{t-1}) \tag{18.16}$$

If $(\dot{P}/P)_t = (\dot{P}/P)_{t-1}$ then from 18.16 we have

$$f(U_t) = (1 - \lambda)f(U_{t-1}) \tag{18.17}$$

This implies that as long as inflation remains steady $f(U_t)$ will tend to zero as time passes, as from 18.17 one obtains

$$f(U_{t+1}) = (1 - \lambda)f(U_t) = (1 - \lambda)^2 f(U_{t-1})$$

and so on. As $(1 - \lambda)^t$ tends to zero as t becomes large, $f(U_t)$ will tend to zero in the limit. As the natural rate of unemployment is the rate which is a solution of the equation $f(U) = 0$, this rate will be re-established in the long run under adaptive expectations, given a prior increase in the rate of inflation. Therefore, no long-run trade-off exists under adaptive expectations. However, if we differentiate 18.16 totally with respect to t we get

$$f'(U_t)\frac{dU_t}{dt} = (1-\lambda)\frac{d}{dt}\left(\frac{\dot{P}}{P}\right)_t \tag{18.18}$$

The derivatives of the last two terms on the right-hand side of 18.16 are zero, as they are functions of values of variables that occurred in the past, and one cannot change the past by current action. The term $f(U_t)$ has a negative derivative with respect to U_t as the Phillips curve is a downward-sloping relationship between the rate of price change and unemployment. Therefore, $f'(U_t) < 0$. The term $d/dt(\dot{P}/P)$ refers to the rate of change of inflation, or the acceleration of inflation. Dividing both sides of 18.18 by $f'(U_t)$ gives

$$\frac{dU}{dt} = \frac{(1-\lambda)}{f'(U_t)} \frac{d}{dt} \left(\frac{\dot{P}}{P}\right)_t \tag{18.19}$$

The coefficient on $d/dt(\dot{P}/P)_t$ is negative, as $1-\lambda$ is positive given $0 < \lambda < 1$ and $f'(U_t)$ is negative. Therefore, unemployment must fall in the short run as inflation accelerates, as $dU/dt < 0$ when $d/dt(\dot{P}/P)_t > 0$.

In conclusion, it has been shown that under adaptive expectations:

(a) there is no long-run trade-off between unemployment and a steady rate of inflation; and
(b) a short-run trade-off exists as unemployment falls when inflation accelerates.

Point (b) offers the possibility of permanently lowering unemployment by continually accelerating inflation. This is known as the *acceleration hypothesis.*

18.5 Rational expectations

A powerful criticism of the adaptive-expectations hypothesis is that it assumes people keep basing their expectations on the values of lagged variables and fail to learn from their past errors. When inflation is rising the error between actual and predicted inflation is positive over successive periods, and so is serially correlated. This error is repeated and so is called systematic, yet no attention is paid to it if expectations are adaptive.

If economic agents are rational, they will make full use of all the available information when forming expectations and not just rely on past values of the relevant variable. Expectations which are conditioned on all the available information are called *rational* expectations. When expectations are formed rationally the errors between actual inflation and the expected rate are random and are serially uncorrelated or independent over time. There is no systematic error by definition because any systematic error would reveal that information had not been fully used when the expectations were formed. So the expected or mean error is zero. If expectations are rational, then

$$\left(\frac{\dot{P}}{P}\right)_t = E\left(\frac{\dot{P}}{P}\right)_t + \varepsilon_t \tag{18.20}$$

where ε_t is a serially uncorrelated error term with a zero mean.

When expectations are formed rationally then people use information derived from the model which they think explains how the economy behaves. This means that if inflation is due to monetary expansion, then information about the current movements in the money supply will be important in conditioning expectations. For instance, if the rate of inflation is determined by

$$\left(\frac{\dot{P}}{P}\right)_t = \rho\left(\frac{\dot{M}}{M}\right)_t + \varepsilon_t \tag{18.21}$$

where $(\dot{M}/M)$ is the rate of growth of the money stock, then

$$E\left(\frac{\dot{P}}{P}\right)_t = \rho\left(\frac{\dot{M}}{M}\right)_t \tag{18.22}$$

Substituting 18.21 and 18.22 into equation 18.15 (p. 351) gives

$$f(U_t) = \rho\left[\left(\frac{\dot{M}}{M}\right)_t - \left(\frac{\dot{M}}{M}\right)_t\right] + \varepsilon_t \tag{18.23}$$

The application of rational expectations therefore leads to the conclusion that there is not even a short-run trade-off between inflation and unemployment. The short-run Phillips curve in Figure 18.4 shifts up to PC_1 instantly. Equation 18.23 shows that unemployment is affected only by random errors, i.e. by unpredictable events. The government can only secure a short-run decrease in unemployment if it makes surprise increases in the money supply.

Although the instantaneous rate of adjustment derived from the full-information application of rational expectations may seem unrealistic, its basis, that people will make use of all the available information when forming expectations and not make correctable errors, is quite sound.

18.6 Empirical evidence

The numerous empirical studies of the Phillips relation have been concerned with finding out:

1. Whether there is a short-run trade-off between inflation and unemployment. This requires a negative and significant relationship between wage or price inflation and unemployment.
2. Whether there is a long-run trade-off. It has often been presumed that the absence of a long-run trade-off depends on α, the price expectations coefficient, being equal to 1.0.

1. A short-run trade-off?

The evidence for this is mixed. Of the studies summarised in Table 18.1, the following found unemployment or its proxies to be significant: Dicks-Mireaux [11], Klein and Ball [12], Batchelor and Sheriff [13]. Unemployment is reported as insignificant in Lipsey [2], Johnston and Timbrell [14], Henry *et al.* [15], Parkin ([16] and [17]), Coutts *et al.* [18]. Lucas and Rapping ([19] and [20]) explicitly test the hypothesis that the relationship between unemployment

TABLE 18.1 *A summary of some econometric studies of the unemployment–inflation trade-off*

Study	Data	Dependent variable	Regression equations	
Phillips [1] 1958	UK annual 1861–1957	W = rate of change of money wage rates (hourly)	$-0.900 + 9.638U^{-1.394}$ (fitted for average values 1861–1913)	
Klein and Ball [12] 1959	UK quarterly 1948–56	W = annual change in quarterly average weekly wage rates;	$-0.091U_t + 0.854P_t + 2.90F_t + 10.26$ (0.013)* (0.092)* (0.40)*	$R^2 = 0.93$
		P_t = quarterly rate of change of consumer price index	$35.65 + 0.421W_{ct}$(level) $+ 0.216M_{t-2} + 0.013T_x$ (13.01)*(0.013)* (0.03) (0.161)	$R^2 = 0.996$
Lipsey [2] 1960	UK annual 1862–1913	W	$-1.21 + 6.45U^{-1} + 2.26U^{-2} - 0.19\Delta U + 0.21P$	$R^2 = 0.85$
	[1923–39, 1948–57]		$0.74 + 0.43U^{-1} + 11.18U^{-4} + 0.34\Delta U + 0.69P$ (2.10)* (6.00)* (0.012)* (0.08)*	$R^2 = 0.91$ $R_{WU} = 0.38$ $R_{WP} = 0.75$
Dicks-Mireaux [11] 1961	UK annual 1946–59 (estimated by 2SLS)	W_e = rate of change of earnings, and salaries per person employed per year	$3.90 + 0.3P_t + 0.16P_{t-1} + 2.78E_{t-1/4}$ (0.63)* (0.13)* (0.10)* (0.82)*	$R^2 = 0.99$
		P = rate of change of final prices	$2.47 + 0.27W_{et} + 0.21M_{t-1/4} - 0.54\Delta X_t$ (1.39)* (0.04)* (0.04)* (0.16)*	
Solow [21] 1969	UK annual 1948–66	P = rate of change of price index for final product	$0.0618 + 0.575$ ulc $+ 0.093M - 0.0453CD - 0.1147LD + 0.2109P^e$ (0.72) (12.623) (13.307) (8.314) (2.062) (3.521) (adaptive expectations coefficients, θ, assumed = 0.7) $R^2 = 0.9808$	
	UK quarterly 1956–66		$-0.2325 + 0.0812$ ulc $+ 0.00243CU + 0.8085P^e$; $\theta = 0.7$, $R^2 = 0.8443$ (4.77) (1.63) (4.844) (8.113)	

Study	Data	Dependent variable	Estimated equations
Lucas and Rapping [19] 1969	US annual 1930–65 (W = money wage compensation per hour)	U_t = unemployment	$\underset{(0.01)^*}{0.042} + \underset{(0.08)^*}{0.59}\,\Delta \ln P_t - \underset{(0.24)^*}{0.41} W_t/W_{t-1} + \underset{(0.05)}{0.8} U_{t-1}$ $R^2 = 0.925$, $DW = 1.5$
Lucas and Rapping [20] 1969	US annual 1904–65 (W_t = hourly money wage compensation)	U_t	See below
Parkin [16] 1970	UK quarterly 1948(III)–69(I)	W	$\underset{(0.885)^*}{3.034} + \underset{(0.38)^*}{0.021}E + \underset{(0.203)^*}{0.436}P^e$ $\lambda = 0.440(0.204)^*$, $\rho_2 = 0.483(0.230)^*$ $S^2 = 0.701$
Johnston and Timbrell [14] 1974	UK annual 1959–71	W	$-3.19 + \underset{(0.47)}{1.171}\text{n} + \underset{(1.39)}{0.60}P^e + \underset{(1.96)}{2.699}U$ $R^2 = 0.684$, $D\text{–}W = 2.09$
Henry *et al.* [15] 1976	UK quarterly 1949–66	W	$\underset{(1.207)^*}{2.917} - \underset{(2.344)^*}{1.938}\left(\frac{1}{U}\right) + \underset{(1.254)^*}{2.718}\left(\frac{1}{U^4}\right) - \underset{(0.00565)^*}{0.00873}\left(\frac{U}{V}\right) + \underset{(0.067)^*}{0.564}P$ $R^2 = 0.676$, $D\text{–}W = 0.775$
Parkin, Sumner and Ward [17] 1976	UK quarterly 1948(III)–1967(II)	W = rate of change of weekly wage rates	$\underset{(1.99)^*}{3.9838} - \underset{(0.92)^*}{0.6436}U + \underset{(0.19)^*}{0.4010}P^e_w + \underset{(0.23)^*}{0.1265}P^e_f + \underset{(0.31)^*}{0.3163}P^e_c - \underset{(0.53)^*}{0.3107}T_E + \underset{(0.25)^*}{0.111}T_H + \underset{(1.52)^*}{0.1523}I_1 - \underset{(1.50)^*}{1.0504}I_2$ $R^2 = 0.675$

Lucas and Rapping [20] 1969, U_t:

Period	const.	$-\Delta \ln P_t$	$+\Delta \ln P_{t-1}$	$-\Delta \ln P_{t-2}$	$-\Delta \ln W_t$	$+\Delta \ln W_{t-1}$	$+U_{t-1}$	$-U_{t-2}$	R^2	$D\text{–}W$
(1904–65)	1.15 (0.63)*	39.16 (6.69)*	35.36 (8.19)*	17.38 (6.84)*	11.86 (9.19)*	26.67 (9.52)*	1.17 (1.13)*	0.322 (0.13)*	0.88	2.01
(1904–29)	insig.	– 20.09 (8.11)*	30.32 (9.07)*	insig.	– 34.78 (13.5)*	insig.	+ 0.68 (2.27)*	insig.	0.53	1.91
(1930–45)	insig.	– 96.87 (15.49)*	insig.	insig.	insig.	insig.	insig.	insig.	0.96	1.37
(1946–65)	insig.	insig.	insig.	insig.	insig.	insig.	insig.	insig.	– 0.05	1.54

TABLE 18.1 *continued*

Study	Data	Dependent variable	Regression equations	
Coutts, Tarling and Wilkinson [18] 1976	UK annual 1958–75	W = rate of change of a wage settlement index	$-0.66 + 1.38P^e + 0.38U^{-1}$ (0.16) (5.37) (0.18)	$R^2 = 0.75$
Batchelor and Sheriff [13] 1980	UK monthly data 1961–74	U = unemployment rate	$1.80 - 0.32(P - P^e)_{\text{lagged}} + 1.73Z$ (1.95) (5.71) (11.19)	$R^2 = 0.88$
McCallum [22] 1975	UK quarterly 1956–71	W_e = rate of change of average hourly earnings P^e_{t+1} = expected price level based on rational expectations	$-0.1621 + 0.1322 \log(y/n)_{t-1} - 0.1159 \log U_{t-1} + 0.9736\, \Delta \log P^e_{t+1} + 0.2375T_{t-1}$ (1.88) (2.33) (2.47) (2.41) (1.41)	$R^2 = 0.61$
McCallum [23] 1976	US quarterly 1952–70	W_e = rate of change of average hourly earnings P^e_{t+1} = as above	$-0.689 + 0.0213 \log(y/n)_{t-1} - 0.035 \log U_{t-1} + 0.8088\, \Delta \log P^e_{t+1}$ (0.025)* (0.013)* (0.015)* (0.183)*	
		$\hat{P}^e_{t+1}$ = expected price level based on partly rational expectations	$-0.628 + 0.0146 \log(y/n)_{t-1} - 0.276 \log U_{t-1} + 0.8611\, \Delta \log \hat{P}^e_{t+1}$ n.a. (0.008)* (0.010)* (0.186)*	$R^2 = 0.34$
Minford and Brech [24] 1981	UK quarterly 1960–75	$W_r - P^e$ P^e = expected change in prices estimated assuming rational expectations	$-0.06E - 0.33 \log(w)_{t-1} - 7.04 \text{ var } P - 0.84 \text{ var } y$ (−0.26) −(1.7) (4.42) (−0.31)	$R^2 = 0.65$

KEY

( ) indicates t-statistic
( )* indicates standard error of estimate
$D\text{–}W$ = Durbin–Watson statistic
R^2 = coefficient of multiple correlation
S = standard error of regression

VARIABLES

CD = Cripps dummy (Solow)
CU = capacity utilisation
D = profits
E = excess demand
F = political factor
I_1, I_2 = incomes policy dummies 1961–2, 1966–67 (Parkin *et al.* [16])
LD = Lloyd dummy (Solow)
M = rate of change of import prices
MS = rate of change of money supply
n = proportion of wage-force having a wage settlement [14]
P = rate of change of price level
P^e = rate of change of expected price level
P^e_w = rate of change of wholesale prices
P^e_f = rate of change of export prices
P^e_c = rate of change of retail prices
T_E = rate of change of employers' payroll tax (Parkin *et al.* [17])
T_H = rate of change of ratio of post-tax to gross pay (Parkin *et al.* [17])
T_X = indirect taxes minus subsidies
ulc = annual proportional change in unit labour costs
var p = variance of price level
var y = variance of output
W_e = rate of change of money earnings
W = rate of change of money wages
w = real wage rate
X = rate of change of labour productivity
y = rate of change of real national output
y/n = *per capita* real national output
Z = dummy variable equal to 1.0 from 1971 onwards
λ = coefficient of adjustment lag (Parkin [16])

and the rate of change of money wages is only temporary, by using unemployment as the dependent variable. The breakdown of the period 1904–65 into three sub-periods reveals the Phillips relationship to be unstable. There is evidence of a trade-off for the periods 1904–29 and 1930–45 but none for the post-war period. In all, then, the hypothesis that unemployment is significantly related to the rate of wage and price inflation has received mixed support from empirical work.

2. *A long-run trade-off?*

In determining whether or not the long-run Phillips curve is vertical, interest has centred on the value of the price expectations adjustment coefficient in equations such as 18.8 and 18.16. Given expectations are formed adaptively, then the absence of a long-run trade-off requires that $\alpha = 1.0$. On the whole, earlier studies tended to produce values of α well below 1.0, indicating a long-run trade-off. Early UK studies (Dicks-Mireaux [11], Klein and Ball [12], Lipsey [2]) included a current or lagged inflation variable rather than the expected rate and obtained coefficients of 0.46, 0.85 and 0.69 respectively. Later UK studies incorporated adaptive expectations. Solow [21] obtained an α coefficient of 0.8 using quarterly data; Batchelor and Sheriff [13] estimated α as 0.3 but found a significant outward shift in the Phillips curve in 1971. Studies by Parkin *et al.* [17] have suggested the absence of a long-run trade-off. Some of the 1970s US studies (see Gordon [25]) have tended to produce higher values of α as later time periods were added and Gordon [26] reported that $\alpha = 1.0$ could not be rejected. A recent survey (Santomero and Seater [27]) of the Phillips curve literature concludes that the natural-rate hypothesis has stood up to testing quite well.

It has been forcefully argued by Lucas [28] that studies treating $\alpha = 1.0$ as a crucial test of the natural-rate hypothesis are mis-specified because they assume adaptive not rational expectations. Recent studies have incorporated rational expectations for the relevant dependent variables. Expectations of a variable depend on the current and past values of the *independent* determining variables and not on its own lagged value as under adaptive expectations. Such studies (for example, McCallum ([22] and [23]), Minford and Brech [24]) have failed to reject $\alpha = 1.0$.

Conclusion

The existence and nature of a trade-off between inflation and unemployment is still an open issue. As in most areas of economics judgements about empirical evidence are coloured by their policy implications. Those who accept the lack of any trade-off have used it to support quite divergent policy conclusions. For (neo-)classical and monetarist economists it implies the futility of active, discretionary stabilisation policy. The more extreme Keynesians hold that the absence of any connection between excess demand (or unemployment) and inflation means that the government can expand demand and so increase output without incurring any more inflation at all. This interpretation implies a horizontal Phillips curve at any inflation rate which happens to be determined by social and political forces. Less extreme Keynesians, such as Tobin [7], still maintain that price-adjustment lags give rise to some long-run trade-off which can therefore be exploited by active government policy and advocate prices and incomes policies in order to improve the trade-off.

References

[1] A. W. Phillips, 'The Relation between Unemployment and the Rate of Change of Money Wage Rates in the UK 1861–1957', *Economica* (November 1958).

[2] R. G. Lipsey, 'The Relation between Unemployment and the Rate of Change of Money Wage Rates in the UK 1862–1957: A Further Analysis', *Economica* (February 1960).

[3] P. A. Samuelson and R. Solow, 'The Problem of Achieving and Maintaining a Stable Price Level – Analytical Aspects of Anti-Inflation Policy', *American Economic Review*, 50 (May 1960).

[4] R. Barro and H. Grossman, *Money, Employment and Inflation* (Cambridge University Press, 1976).

[5] M. Friedman, 'The Role of Monetary Policy', *American Economic Review*, 58 (March 1968).

[6] E. Phelps, 'Phillips Curves, Expectations of Inflation, and Optimal Unemployment over Time', *Economica*, 34 (August 1967).

[7] J. Tobin, 'Inflation and Unemployment', *American Economic Review*, 62 (1972); reprinted in P. Korliras and R. Thorn (eds), *Modern Macroeconomics*, (New York: Harper & Row, 1979).

[8] A. Rees, 'The Phillips Curve as a Menu for Policy Choice', *Economica*, 37 (May 1970).

[9] E. Phelps *et al.*, *The Microeconomic Foundations of Employment and Inflation Theory* (New York: Norton, 1970).

[10] L. Kahn, 'Bargaining Power, Search Theory and the Phillips Curve', *Cambridge Journal of Economics*, 4 (1980).

[11] L. A. Dicks-Mireaux, 'The Interrelationship between Cost and Price Changes, 1946–59: a Study of Inflation in Post-War Britain', *Oxford Economic Papers*, 13 (1961).

[12] L. R. Klein and R. J. Ball, 'Some Econometrics of the Determination of Absolute Prices and Wages', *Economic Journal*, 69 (1959).

[13] R. A. Batchelor and T. Sheriff, 'Unemployment and Unanticipated Inflation in Postwar Britain', *Economica*, 47, 86 (May 1980).

[14] J. Johnston and M. Timbrell, 'Empirical Tests of a Bargaining Theory of Wage Rate Determination', in D. Laidler and J. Purdy (eds), *Inflation and Labour Markets* (Manchester University Press, 1974).

[15] S. Henry *et al.*, 'Models of Inflation in the UK: an Evaluation', *National Institute Economic Review* (August 1976).

[16] J. M. Parkin, 'Incomes Policy: Some Further Results on the Rate of Change of Money Wages', *Economica*, 37 (November 1970).

[17] J. M. Parkin, M. T. Sumner and R. A. Ward, 'The Effects of Excess Demand, Generalised Expectations and Wage–Price Controls on Wage Inflation in the UK: 1956–71', in K. Brunner and A. M. Metzler (eds), *The Economics of Wage and Price Controls*, Carnegie–Rochester Conference Series on Public Policy No. 2 (Amsterdam: North-Holland, 1976).

[18] K. Coutts, R. Tarling and F. Wilkinson, 'Wage Bargaining and the Inflation Process', *Economic Policy Review*, 2 (1976).

[19] R. E. Lucas and L. A. Rapping, 'Real Wages, Employment and Inflation', in Phelps (ed.), *Microeconomic Foundations*.

[20] R. E. Lucas and L. A. Rapping, 'Price Expectations and the Phillips Curve', *American Economic Review*, 54 (1969).

[21] R. Solow, *Price Expectations and the Behaviour of the Price Level* (Manchester University Press, 1969).

[22] B. McCallum, 'Rational Expectations and the Natural Rate Hypothesis: Some Evidence for the United Kingdom', *Manchester School*, 42 (1975).

[23] B. McCallum, 'Rational Expectations and the Natural Rate Hypothesis: Some Consistent Estimates', *Econometrica*, 44 (1976).

[24] A. P. L. Minford and M. Brech, 'The Wage Equation and Rational Expectations', in D. Currie, R. Nobay and D. Peel (eds), *Macroeconomic Analysis* (London: Croom Helm, 1981).

[25] R. J. Gordon, 'Recent Developments in the Theory of Inflation and Unemployment', *Journal of Monetary Economics*, 2, 2 (April 1976).

[26] R. J. Gordon, 'Wage–Price Controls and the Shifting Phillips Curve', *Brookings Papers on Economic Activity*, 3 (1972).

[27] A. M. Santomero and J. J. Seater, 'The Inflation–Unemployment Tradeoff: a Critique of the Literature', *Journal of Economic Literature*, 16, 2 (June 1978).

[28] R. E. Lucas, 'Econometric Testing of the Natural Rate Hypothesis', in *The Econometrics of Price Determination Conference* (Washington, D.C.: Board of Governors of the Federal Reserve System, 1973).

Further reading

Friedman [5], Gordon [25], and Santomero and Seater [27].

19 The New Classical Macroeconomics

During the 1970s there has been a powerful resurgence of the (neo-)classical ideas which had been attacked and superseded by the Keynesian revolution. In classical thinking any explanation of cyclical fluctuations in economic activity has to be consistent with

(a) market-clearing, and
(b) optimising behaviour by rational economic agents.

The modern restatement of these classical ideas has become known as the *new classical macroeconomics*. It has been developed primarily by American economists, and in particular by Lucas and Sargent (see references [1]–[8]). This work is a direct descendent of the inter-war Austrian school of business-cycle theory associated with von Hayek [9] and Haberler [10]. In the new classical view the entire Keynesian revolution has been a journey up a blind alley. The policy implications of the new classical macroeconomics completely undermine the Keynesian proposition that discretionary government policy can be used to stabilise the economy. The readily apparent failures of Keynesian economics since the mid-1960s have helped to stimulate a critical reappraisal of the microfoundations of Keynesian analysis. These foundations are regarded by new classical economists as totally unsound. Consequently they seek to explain macroeconomic behaviour within a classical theoretical framework characterised by (a) market-clearing, and (b) optimising behaviour.

19.1 The new classical critique of Keynesian microfoundations

Keynesian economics is based on a denial of both the above propositions. Markets do not clear because prices fail to adjust sufficiently fast. The fundamental theoretical problem for Keynesian economics is to find a convincing rationale for the presumption that slow price adjustment means that markets fail to clear. As we saw in Chapter 17, neo-Keynesian macro models have a choice-theoretic foundation. Given inflexible prices, economic agents act so as to maximise the same type of utility function as assumed in neoclassical analysis.

The existence of non-market-clearing and quantity-rationing means that there are potential exchanges between economic agents which would be mutually advantageous at prices different from the ruling ones. The failure of price adjustment to bring about these potentially advantageous exchanges implies that economic agents are not optimising. Keynesian economics is therefore based on two interrelated presumptions that agents do not fully optimise and, hence, that markets fail to clear.[1]

Modern (neo-)classical economists regard the Keynesian presumption of non-optimizing and hence non-rational behaviour as a fundamental weakness which vitiates the whole approach. The premise of rational economic man is an extremely long-lived and powerful aspect of economic methodology. Without it economic behaviour becomes totally *ad hoc*. Any assumption about how economic agents behave would be *a priori* as good as any other. This would generate a vast number of alternative hypotheses among which it would be extremely difficult to distinguish and therefore to select valid ones. The abandonment of the postulate of rational economic man would therefore do immense harm to the claim of economics that it is a science.

The recognition of rational economic man as a powerful methodology is strongest among neoclassical economists, but it is also shared, though in weaker forms, by other schools of thought. That this is so is evident from the recent work on neo-Keynesian microfoundations. The resurgence of the postulate of rational economic man in Keynesian and non-Keynesian macroeconomics is in striking contrast to the total absence of any discussion of individual maximising behaviour that characterised early Keynesian teaching. Only broad aggregates were considered and were made functions of a few variables without much rationalisation of their inclusion. Investment behaviour depended on 'animal spirits', which by definition lack any sound rational basis. Keynesian models were characterised by *ad hoc* constructions such as the liquidity trap, which depends on non-rational expectations, and rigid money wages, for which little rationalisation was offered.

Nowadays many Keynesians do recognise that the failure of their approach to encompass optimising behaviour is a serious weakness which needs shoring up. However, they regard the main strength of the approach to be the consistency of its predictions with their interpretations of real-world observations.

One way of attempting to provide a rational basis for sticky wages and prices has been implicit-contract theory, which was discussed in Chapter 17 (pp. 328–30). The ability of implicit-contract theory to provide the required underpinning for non-market-clearing models has been attacked on two main grounds.

[1] Some neo-Keynesians (for example, Hahn [11]) are trying to build mathematical models in which non-market-clearing is consistent with the absence of mutually advantageous potential exchanges.

(1) Implicit-contract theory implies that phenomena such as layoffs and sticky wages are not *prima facie* evidence of non-market-clearing. Rather, they are the outcome of voluntary, optimising choice by firms *and workers*.

(2) Implicit-contract models that attempt to rationalise layoffs still require agents who fail to optimise. Under such contracts the current marginal product of labour is different from the current marginal value of leisure. (If they were equal, then the outcome would be the same as on a spot auction market.) Since the marginal optimising conditions are not met there is scope for further bargaining between firms and workers. For instance, in a recession when the marginal product of labour is less than the real wage specified in the contract some workers are laid off or all workers work fewer hours. Consequently the marginal value of leisure is less than the real wage. So it would benefit workers to supply a little more labour for a lower real wage and benefit firms to employ more labour, provided the marginal value of leisure is below the marginal product of labour. In other words, an implicit contract is inefficient if it is couched only in terms of prices and allows firms to decide unilaterally on the quantity of employment. This critique of implicit-contract theory concludes that either the type of implicit contract required to give Keynesian results is implausible or, alternatively, that economic agents are not rational utility maximisers and so implicit-contract theory does not resolve the problem it was designed to deal with (see Barro [12]).

19.2 The new classical approach

The new classical approach is firmly based on the methodology of rational economic man. The characteristic features are:

(a) economic agents optimise,
(b) markets clear, and
(c) expectations are formed rationally.

Despite these properties the new classical models are designed to provide an alternative to the Keynesian explanation of the business cycle and so show that non-market-clearing is not a necessary condition for the observed cyclical behaviour of economies.

An important distinguishing characteristic of the new classical approach is that it makes different assumptions about the supply side of the economy from those found in Keynesian models. Under Keynesian non-market-clearing conditions aggregate supply depends on the level of effective demand. In the new classical approach supply depends on relative prices and not on quantities. This is consistent with the results of Walrasian general-equilibrium models. So we can add a fourth feature of new classical models:

(d) aggregate supply depends on relative prices.

The new classical supply hypothesis has a close affinity to the Phillips relation as expressed in equation 18.15 (p. 351). The supply hypothesis is that the deviation of unemployment from its natural level depends on the difference between actual prices and expected prices or, alternatively, between actual and expected inflation. The latter form of the supply hypothesis is used in equation 19.1:

$$U_t^N - U_t = \beta\left[\left(\frac{\dot{P}}{P}\right)_t - E\left(\frac{\dot{P}}{P}\right)_t\right] \tag{19.1}$$

where

U_t^N = natural rate of unemployment
U_t = actual rate of unemployment
$\dot{P}/P$ = actual inflation rate
$E(\dot{P}/P)$ = expected inflation rate (E is an expectations operator)

Equation 19.1 states that the actual unemployment rate lies below the natural rate by an amount which depends on the difference between actual and expected inflation. This supply relation can alternatively be expressed in terms of the deviation of actual output from its permanent (long-run equilibrium level) since the deviation in output from trend is directly linked to the deviation in unemployment, $U_t^N - U_t$. The long-run equilibrium level of output and the associated natural rate of unemployment depend on the real factors subsumed in the neoclassical labour supply function and production function, in particular the size of the capital stock. The supply relation is now

$$y_t - y_{pt} = \gamma\left(\frac{\dot{P}}{P} - E\left(\frac{\dot{P}}{P}\right)\right)_t \tag{19.2}$$

where

y_t = actual national output
y_{pt} = permanent output

The aggregate supply hypothesis is explicitly derived from a consideration of the behaviour of individual suppliers of goods and labour. A number of such rationalisations have been offered but we shall here concentrate on the best-documented one which has been developed by Lucas in a series of papers (starting with [13] and [14] and continued in [1]–[6]).

Lucas's intertemporal substitution model

The basic premise of Lucas's approach is that one should model the behaviour of rational agents whose decisions depend on relative prices only. Households and firms make decisions about what to do in the present period with the future very much in mind. Household utility has the usual specification that it depends positively on present and future consumption and leisure. Agents' decisions are therefore crucially dependent upon expectations about the future. Expectations about future wages and prices are governed by individuals' notions of what are 'normal' (that is, long-run equilibrium) values, since actual wages and prices are assumed to move towards their normal values. Because of this reasoning 'normal' and 'expected' value are used interchangeably.

Therefore, if the current real wage exceeds its normal and expected value, then households regard the current real wage as being temporarily above the future real wage. This gives households an incentive to work more in the current period and less in the future: they substitute current leisure for future leisure. Because the model presumes this type of behaviour it is known as the *intertemporal substitution model.* A key feature is that the short-run supply of labour with respect to the real wage is relatively elastic. In the long run, however, labour supply is unresponsive to changes in the real wage. So if the real wage increase is perceived as temporary, more labour is supplied, but if it is regarded as permanent, then there is no change in the amount of labour supplied. Empirical work does indicate that the short-run labour supply elasticity of women and teenagers is much higher than that of adult males. Both women and teenage members of the labour force feel less need than adult males to remain in continuous employment and both experience lower employment rates (see Hall [15]). The intertemporal substitution model explains fluctuations in unemployment in terms of the voluntary choices of households to vary their supply of labour over time in response to perceived temporary changes in the real wage. The model does not take account of any job search since unemployment is equated with withdrawal from the active labour force. A simplified version of the Lucas labour supply function is

$$\frac{L_t}{E(L)_t} = h\left(\frac{w_t}{E(w_t)}\right) \tag{19.3}$$

where

L_t = labour hours supplied in the current period
$E(L)_t$ = normal, long-run labour supply
w_t = real wage in current period
$E(w_t)$ = normal expected real wage

Thus when households perceive the current real wage rate to be greater than its expected level, they will increase their supply of labour relative to its normal long-run quantity. Hence the actual rate of unemployment, U_t, will fall below the natural rate of unemployment, U_t^N. Similarly, when the real wage is thought to be less than its normal expected level, households will reduce the supply of labour and the actual rate of unemployment, U_t, will rise above the natural rate, U_t^N. As ratio U_t/U_t^N has an inverse relationship with ratio $L_t/E(L)_t$, one can transform equation 19.3 so that U_t/U_t^N is the dependent variable on the left-hand side of the equation.

Similarly the supply decision of a firm depends on its perception of the current price of its product relative to its future price. If the firm perceives a future increase in the demand for its product, this will mean a rise in the product's price relative to its marginal cost at the present production level. If the increase in demand is thought to be permanent, then the future relative price will be perceived as higher than the current relative price and the firm will wish to invest in additional productive capacity. However, if the rise in price is considered to be only temporary, the firm will not engage in any additional investment but will have an incentive to expand current output by utilising existing capital more intensively and hiring more labour hours.

In the intertemporal substitution model households change their supply of labour in response to temporary changes in relative prices, while firms' supply responses are much greater for perceived permanent relative price changes than for temporary ones. That labour supply and output supply move together over the trade cycle is due to the fact that neither households nor firms are certain whether wage and price changes are permanent or temporary. Typically part of any change will be regarded as temporary and part as permanent, so inducing increased supply from both households and firms. The difficulty agents have in distinguishing temporary from permanent changes is a crucial feature of the new classical models as it is vital to generating fluctuations in output and employment. Agents cannot distinguish temporary from permanent price and wage changes because they lack complete information. The way in which new classical models specify and use the assumption of incomplete information requires some further consideration.

Incomplete information

There are numerous ways in which incomplete information can be specified in an economic model. Here we concentrate on the specification popularised by Lucas (see [16] and [4]).

Since the economy consists of a very large number of markets, an individual agent cannot in practice observe all prices on all markets. He has incomplete information and only observes the few prices which are of immediate relevance to him. For the purposes of modelling incomplete information we take a particular good (or service) and assume that it is traded in a number of separate markets. Each trader is limited to transacting in just one market, market z. A trader in market z knows the current price of the good in market z but not in the other markets.

In order to decide whether the current price of the good in market z is high or low relative to the future price, the trader compares the current price in z, $P(z)_t$, with its normal or expected value, $E(P(z))_t$. The problem is to determine what this normal or expected value is. It is assumed that the price in market z is the average price of the good in all markets plus some random component, $\eta(z)_t$, which applies only to market z. The random error term, $\eta(z)_t$, captures the effect of stochastic real shocks which shift the demand and supply functions for the good in market z. Thus

$$P(z)_t = P^e + \eta(z)_t \tag{19.4}$$

where

$P(z)_t$ = observed current price of the good in market z

P^e = mean price, of the good over all markets

$\eta(z)_t$ = a random, normally distributed disturbance term with a constant variance and zero mean, $E(\eta(z)) = 0$; it is serially uncorrelated with its own past values or with disturbance terms in the other markets

Since P^e is the average or expected price of the good over all markets, the mean error term, $E(\eta(z))$, is zero, so that over all markets the random shocks cancel out on average.

In forming an idea of what the normal or expected price of the good in market z, $E(P(z))_t$, is the trader has two sets of information:

1. The mean price, P_t^e, over all markets. This is the expectation of the probability distribution of the good's price over all markets and is conditioned by the past history of the average price which the trader knows.
2. The observed current price of the good in market z.

Since all the available information contained in (1) and (2) is used to form expectations, these expectations are rational. In forming an expectation of the normal price of the good in market z the trader has to decide how much weight to place on P^e (the mean of the probability distribution of P over all markets) and how much to put on the observed current price in market z, $P(z)_t$. The problem for the trader is to decide how much of any given change in the observed current price of his product, $P(z)_t$, is due to

(a) a general change in the price level which affects all markets for the good (that is, due to a change in P^e), or
(b) a real change in the relative price of the good in market z (that is, in the non-zero random disturbance term, $\eta(z)_t$).

If we start from a position of long-run equilibrium, then the current price and the normal expected price are equal and output is at its permanent level. Then the trader observes an increase in the observed current price of the good in market z. If the entire increase in $P(z)_t$ is thought to be due to an increase in the general price level, then the normal or expected price, $E(P(z))_t$, will rise by the same amount as the current price in market z and there will be no incentive for a trader to change the amount supplied. If, on the other hand, part of the increase in the observed current price is attributed to a real change which is specific to market z (that is, due to a positive value for $\eta(z)_t$) then the trader perceives a favourable relative price change, because the price of his product appears to have risen relative to production costs. The current price rises relative to the expected price and supply is increased. The trader's supply function is therefore

$$y(z)_t - y(z)_{pt} = \gamma(P(z)_t - E(P(z)_t/I(z)_t)) \tag{19.5}$$

where

$y(z)_t - y(z)_{pt}$ = deviation of current output from its permanent level
$P(z)_t$ = price of good observed in market z
$E(P(z)_t/I(z)_t)$ = expected or normal price in market z and all other markets; $/I(z)_t$ indicates that the expectation is conditional on all the information possessed by the trader in market z at time t

The expected or normal price term depends on the observed current price, $P(z)_t$, and on the mean of the distribution of price over all markets, P_t^e, which depends on past history. The expected or normal price in market z is a weighted average of $P(z)_t$ and P_t^e and is written

$$E(P(z)_t/I(z)_t) = (1 - \theta)\ P(z)_t + \theta P_t^e \tag{19.6}$$

where $0 \leqslant \theta \leqslant 1$.

The more weight the trader gives to the mean price level, P_t^e, in forming his expected price in market z, the higher is θ. A high θ means that little weight is given to the current observed price, $P(z)_t$. In this case a large proportion of any change in the observed current price is attributed to a real shock changing the relative price. Thus the larger is θ, the more any variability in the observed current price in market z is attributed to real shocks (that is, a change in the relative price) and the less it is attributed to nominal shocks (that is, changes in the general level of prices). The coefficient θ is thus defined as

$$\theta = \frac{\boxed{\text{Variance of } P(z) \text{ due to real (relative price) shocks}}}{\boxed{\begin{array}{c}\text{Variance of } P(z) \text{ due to both real and nominal}\\ \text{(that is, general price-level) shocks}\end{array}}}$$

(The numerator in the θ expression is in fact the variance of $\eta(z)_t$ in equation 19.4.)

Substituting equation 19.6 for $E(P(z)_t/I(z)_t)$ in equation 19.5 gives

$$\begin{aligned} y(z)_t - y(z)_{pt} &= \gamma(P(z)_t - (1 - \theta)\ P(z)_t - \theta P_t^e) \\ &= \gamma\theta(P(z)_t - P_t^e) \end{aligned} \tag{19.7}$$

Aggregating over all z markets the aggregate form of Lucas's supply function is[1]

$$y_t - y_{pt} = \gamma\theta(P_t - P_t^e) \tag{19.7a}$$

In the aggregate version of the new classical supply hypothesis applied to a model of the economy P_t is the current value of the general price level, and this individuals cannot directly observe because they do not know the current prices of all commodities. Individuals are assumed to receive information about changes in the prices of the particular goods in which they trade earlier than

[1] In the original literature the aggregate supply function is expressed as

$$\frac{y_t}{y_{pt}} = \left(\frac{P_t}{P_t^e}\right)^{\gamma\theta}$$

Taking logs this becomes

$$\log(y_t - y_{pt}) = \gamma\theta\ \log(P_t - P_t^e)$$

So all variables in equations like 19.1, 19.2 and 19.4 onwards are in logarithmic form. We have simplified in this chapter by not specifying a logarithmic form.

they get to know the current general price level. Although individual traders do not know the current general price level, they do form opinions as to its probable values, which can be represented as a probability distribution. The mean of this distribution is the expected general price level, P_t^e. This is the value which individuals on average think the general price level has currently attained.

In forming an expectation of the current general price level individuals have two sets of information. One is the history of the general price level and its determinants. Individuals are assumed to know what the general price level was in previous periods. The other piece of information is the current prices of the few goods in which the individual regularly trades. When the current price of the good a trader supplies rises, then this is either because of nominal changes which cause all prices to rise equiproportionately or it is due to a rise in the relative price of the good. If the current general price level rises so that it exceeds the expected price level, then traders incorrectly attribute the rise in the current price of the particular goods they supply to a rise in relative prices. Traders therefore increase the quantities supplied.

Once the trader realises that the rise in the price of his product is due entirely to an increase in the general price level and so does not mean an increase in the good's relative price, supply falls back to its permanent level. The rise in output is only temporary and so there is no long-run trade-off between output and inflation.

The intertemporal substitution model provides an alternative rationale for a Phillips relation to that given by search theory. The two rationalisations are not inconsistent. Both could operate at the same time and both imply short-run market-clearing.

A complete new classical model

The main innovation of the new classical macroeconomics as compared with Keynesian analysis is the aggregate supply function. In a new classical model aggregate output consists of a permanent component and a cyclical component which depends on the divergence between actual and expected prices.

A new classical model is completed by adding an aggregate demand relationship which is subject to exogenous shocks. Nominal aggregate demand is defined as usual as real output times the price level. A portfolio-adjustment equation which determines the desired holdings of goods, interest-bearing financial assets and money is added. The aggregate demand side of the model does not differ from that in the Keynesian–neoclassical synthesis as significantly as does the specification of aggregate supply.[1]

How the new classical model works compared with the Keynesian–neoclassical synthesis can be simply illustrated by means of a standard

[1] The differences from the Keynesian–neoclassical synthesis model are that consumption is made a function of relative rates of return rather than of income (that is, the stress is on portfolio adjustment) and interest-rate expectations are formed rationally.

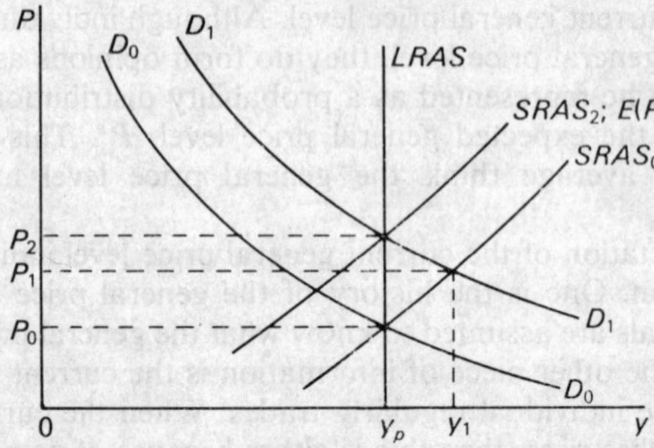

FIGURE 19.1 *Adjustment in a new classical model*

aggregate demand and supply diagram, as in Figure 19.1. We start in a position of long-run equilibrium.

Aggregate demand is D_0, output is at its permanent level, y_p, and the price level is P_0. Then the government increases aggregate demand to D_1 by policies which must include expanding the money supply. The short-run supply function when the expected price level is P_0 is $SRAS_0$. At first the price level rises to P_1. Traders, expecting the general price level to be P_0, think relative prices have risen. Output therefore expands along $SRAS_0$ to y_1. As traders adjust their expectations about the general price level so the short-run supply curve shifts up to the left. Once prices have stabilised at P_2, and price expectations have adjusted fully, the short-run aggregate supply function has shifted up to $SRAS_2$, for which $E(P)_t = P_2$. Output has returned to its previous level as long-run aggregate supply is invariant with respect to the price level.

Essentially the same analysis could be conducted assuming continuous inflation. The rate of inflation would be measured along the vertical axis and each short-run supply curve would be defined for a particular rate of expected inflation. Output would rise if the actual rate of inflation were higher than the expected rate and the permanent level of output, y_p, would be consistent with any steady rate of inflation, giving a vertical long-run aggregate supply relationship. Expressed in terms of the rate of change of prices, the Lucas supply relationship closely resembles the Phillips relation:

$$y_t - y_{pt} = \gamma\theta(\dot{P}/P - E(\dot{P}/P))_t \tag{19.8}$$

where

$\dot{P}/P$ = actual rate of inflation

$E(\dot{P}/P)$ = the expected rate of inflation in the sense of the rate of inflation agents *think* exists currently

19.3 Implications of the new classical macroeconomics

The new classical macroeconomics has a number of important implications which need to be brought out.

1. The natural-rate hypothesis

The new classical approach restates the natural-rate hypothesis in a stronger form. Output only responds positively (and temporarily) to an increase in the current prices of goods if this increase is not regarded as completely due to a rise in the general price level. For this to happen the current inflation rate does not have to be merely unanticipated in the previous period, it has also to be unperceived in the current period. If the increase in individual prices is attributed entirely to a rise in the general price level, then there will be no perceived rise in goods' prices relative to costs and so no divergence between actual and expected prices. There is therefore no temporary increase in supply. An acceleration in the rate of increase of inflation will not cause any rise in output if the faster rate of inflation is fully perceived straightaway so that $\dot{P}/P$ and $E(\dot{P}/P)$ in equation 19.8 rise by the same amount.

2. The impotency of systematic monetary policy

The argument underlying the strong form of the natural-rate hypothesis leads to the deduction that the government cannot reduce unemployment by operating a systematic monetary policy. A systematic policy is one that the private sector can either fully perceive or accurately predict because it is based on some known rule. If the government operates a policy feedback rule, it will determine the appropriate changes in the money supply as specific responses to the divergence in output from trend. For instance, the following feedback rule

$$M_t = M_{t-1} + \mu(y_p - y_{t-1}) \tag{19.9}$$

relates the current money supply to the stock of money in the previous period plus μ times the divergence of output from trend. Given that the private sector knows the past values of the money stock and output divergence and also knows the policy parameter μ, it can accurately predict what the current period's money supply must be. It therefore knows what the current general price level is. By operating a policy feedback rule like equation 19.9, the government cannot cause a divergence between the actual general price level and what traders in the private sector think or expect as the general price level. As systematic monetary policy does not cause a divergence between $\dot{P}/P$ and $E(\dot{P}/P)$, it cannot increase the level of output and employment. Only unsystematic, i.e. unanticipated or surprise increases in the money supply, can bring about a short-run rise in output. (See the discussion of this in Chapter 18, pp. 352–3.)

3. The significance of the variance in the price level

The size of the impact on real output of a rise in prices depends on how much of the rise in individual prices is attributed by traders to an increase in the general level of prices rather than to a rise in relative prices. The more the rise in prices is attributed to an increase in the general price level, the smaller is the size of the trade-off parameter θ in equations 19.7 and 19.8 and so the smaller is the consequent rise in output. Since θ varies directly with the ratio of the variance of relative price shocks to the variance of the general price level, the larger the variance of the general price level the smaller the trade-off. It seems likely that a high average inflation rate is associated with a large variance in the general price level. The new classical approach therefore predicts that the more a country tries to secure output in excess of the permanent level and so permits higher and higher inflation rates, the smaller becomes the trade-off between further inflation and output.

4. The importance of structural policy parameters

The new classical approach highlights the significance of structural policy parameters, like θ, for determining the effect of macroeconomic policy. As just noted, the size of θ depends on the public's perception of government policy. For instance, a history of government policy which involves a large variance in the rate of growth of the money supply and hence in the price level will result in a low value for θ. A further important point emphasised in the new classical approach is that one cannot assume, as does Keynesian analysis, that the structural parameters are invariant with respect to policy measures. The size of θ, for instance, will change if government policy alters the variance of the growth rate of the money supply. If structural parameters do vary with policy changes, then this invalidates the whole class of large-scale econometric models which are used for forecasting and policy analysis. The frequent breakdowns and parameter drift which have been experienced by such models is therefore not surprising.

The argument that it is fallacious to suppose that structural parameters remain invariant with respect to policy changes stems directly from the assumption of rational expectations. When expectations are formed rationally private-sector agents adjust their behaviour in the light of their expectations about government policy. As we have seen under point (3) above, systematic government policy will have no effect on the level of output because it can be fully anticipated and expected prices adjusted accordingly.

The policy implications of the new classical approach, if correct, completely undermine the Keynesian case for government macroeconomic policy, since it is deduced that the government cannot improve the stability of the economy. The best the government can do is not to make the economy more unstable by its actions. It is therefore not surprising that the new classical macroeconomics has aroused considerable controversy and hostility.

19.4 Criticisms of the new classical approach[1]

The main thrust of the Keynesian attack on the new classical approach centres, not surprisingly, on the market-clearing assumption. If markets do not clear because of slow price adjustments, then there is scope for fiscal and monetary policy to have real effects on output, as analysed in Chapter 17. Given certain

[1] See Buiter [17] and Tobin [18] for critical reactions.

assumptions, Keynesian policy conclusions can still be reached in a non-market-clearing framework with rational expectations, which on the whole Keynesians accept as a valid insight.

A further misgiving about the new classical approach concerns its ability to explain the fact that time-series observations of national output, unemployment and related variables are serially correlated (that is, the deviation of output from trend remains consistently positive or negative for a consecutive number of time periods). The problem posed is this. The new classical theory of the business cycle assumes that random shocks are serially uncorrelated. It deduces that only serially uncorrelated and hence unpredictable monetary disturbances will affect the deviation of real output from trend. However, the movements in output which actually occur over the business cycle are serially correlated. New classical economists explain this apparent inconsistency by lags in obtaining information and lags in adjusting both the capital stock and the level of employment. Lucas [3] supposes that investment takes several periods to respond to relative price changes. This effect is captured by introducing a lagged output term into the aggregate supply function. Equation 19.7 now becomes

$$y_t - y_{pt} = \gamma\theta(P_t - P_t^e) + \lambda(y_{t-1} - y_{pt-1}) \tag{19.10}$$

so that output is now serially correlated with its lagged value even though the forecast error $(P_t - P_t^e)$ is independent of the previous period's forecast error $(P_{t-1} - P_{t-1}^e)$.[1] The divergence of actual prices from expected prices is by itself insufficient to generate the observed serially correlated time series in output and employment. The addition of lagged output to the supply function has allowed critics to point out that the new classical approach has its *ad hoc* elements as well.

Another problematic aspect is the new classical approach's reliance on incomplete information to produce cyclical fluctuations. Output fluctuations occur when traders misperceive general price changes as relative price changes. Output changes do occur in a new classical model in response to correctly perceived real changes. So an increase in military expenditure to finance a war, for example, causes the real value of output to rise temporarily and traders to increase current supplies. However, such random real shocks are treated as serially uncorrelated and do not seem sufficient to generate cyclical fluctuations of the kind actually observed. Hence there is the need to specify that important cyclical fluctuations arise from traders mistaking general price changes for changes in relative prices due to real factors. For some (e.g. Grossman [19]) the assumption of incomplete information required for there to be a divergence between actual prices and expected prices is implausible given

[1] If we let $y_t - y_{pt} = y_{dt}$, then

$$\begin{aligned} E(y_{dt}, y_{dt-1}) &= E[\gamma\theta(P_t - P_t^e) + \lambda y_{dt-1}][\gamma\theta(P_{t-1} - P_{t-1}^e) + \lambda y_{dt-2}] \\ &= \lambda^2 E(y_{dt-1}, y_{dt-2}) \end{aligned}$$

since the forecast error, $P_t - P_t^e$, is serially uncorrelated with its own lagged value and with contemporaneous or lagged y_d. So given $\lambda \neq 0$, output is serially correlated.

the rapid publication of official statistics on price indices and the money supply. Others, usually of a Keynesian bent, criticise the rational-expectations aspect of the new classical approach for assuming too much rather than too little information. If private-sector agents are on the whole ignorant of how the economy works or what government policy is, then there is scope for active government policy to have real effects.

19.5 Empirical evidence

The new classical approach has also started to develop an empirical literature. The main hypothesis that requires testing is that it is unanticipated changes in prices that cause output fluctuations and that these price changes are largely due to unanticipated monetary changes. Barro [20] has provided one such test for the USA for the period 1947–78. He starts with an equation determining the money supply (all variables in Barro's study are in log form):

$$\begin{aligned} DM_t = \underset{(0.023)}{0.097} + \underset{(0.14)}{0.48}\, DM_{t-1} + \underset{(0.12)}{0.17}\, DM_{t-2} + \underset{(0.015)}{0.071}\, FEDV_t \\ + \underset{(0.008)}{0.31}\, [U/(1-U)]_{t-1} \qquad \text{s.e.} = 0.014 \qquad (19.11) \end{aligned}$$

where

DM_t = (money stock)$_t$/(money stock)$_{t-1}$
$FEDV_t$ = change in real federal government expenditure relative to its trend or 'normal' value
U = unemployment
s.e. = standard error of estimate (standard error of coefficients are in parentheses)

Given that expectations are rational, anticipated money growth is estimated from equation 19.11. Anticipated money growth is subtracted from actual money growth to obtain the unanticipated growth in the money stock, *DMR*. Unemployment and output are then regressed on unanticipated money growth:

$$\begin{aligned} [U/(1-U)]_t = \underset{(0.13)}{-2.41} - \underset{(2.4)}{4.9}\, DMR_t - \underset{(2.4)}{11.3}\, DMR_{t-1} - \underset{(1.1)}{5.3}(G/Y)_t \\ R^2 = 0.65,\ \text{s.e.} = 0.18 \qquad (19.12) \end{aligned}$$

$$\begin{aligned} Y_t = \underset{(0.04)}{2.92} + \underset{(0.23)}{1.00}\, DMR_t + \underset{(0.23)}{1.09}\, DMR_{t-1} + \underset{(0.013)}{0.070}G_t + \underset{(0.0004)}{0.33}t \\ R^2 = 0.998,\ \text{s.e.} = 0.017 \qquad (19.13) \end{aligned}$$

where

DMR = unanticipated money growth
G = government expenditure in real terms
Y = real GNP
t = time trend

From this and other tests Barro concludes that output and unemployment are better explained by unanticipated money growth than by actual money growth. In other equations estimated by this study the price level is shown to depend on the current money stock with a coefficient of 1.0 and to vary inversely with past unanticipated money growth. This latter effect is what one would expect since unanticipated money growth raises real output and the consequent increase in the demand for money has a negative impact on the price level. A change in the actual money stock is estimated to have an impact on the price level for two to four years, which is a longer lag than that on real output and employment. This inconsistency in lags is an unsatisfactory result, though the long lag in monetary policy effects accords with earlier monetarist work by Friedman (reported in Chapter 14). The new classical work suggests that anticipated changes in the money stock have a quite rapid impact on prices while the effects of unanticipated monetary movements operate with quite long lags.

Other econometric new classical models have been tested for the USA by Sargent (see [7] and [21]) and for the United Kingdom by Minford [22]. As the United Kingdom is an open economy it is necessary to treat the fixed exchange-rate period separately from the post-1972 flexible exchange-rate period, since the money supply is endogenous under fixed exchange rates. Both models fail to refute new classical predictions. Sargent [21] finds that neither money nor fiscal variables affect unemployment, though it does seem affected by money wages, which is inconsistent with the new classical view.

Lucas [16] reports evidence which favours the new classical hypothesis that the unemployment–inflation trade-off gets smaller, the higher the variance of inflation. For sixteen stable price countries the trade-off parameter varies between 0.287 and 0.91 with a mean of 0.569, while for the Argentine and Paraguay, which have at least twenty-five times the inflation level variance of the other countries, the trade-off coefficient is between 0.01 and 0.02.

We still lack conclusive evidence on the central issue of whether markets approximate more closely to continuous clearing than they do to non-clearing. The debate between the Keynesian and classical approaches is therefore bound to continue unabated and views as to which is more plausible will remain much influenced by political attitudes.

19.6 Conclusion

The major difference between the new classical approach and the Keynesian one centres on the specification of the aggregate supply function. We now have three possible specifications, two provided by Keynesians:

(1) Neo-Keynesian quantity-constrained models rationalise the traditional Keynesian perfectly elastic supply function which is assumed in the Keynesian *ISLM* model. Both the labour and goods market fail to clear, and firms would be willing to supply more output at existing prices if effective demand were greater. Workers are off the notional supply of labour function and so are willing to supply more labour without any increase in the actual or perceived

real wage rate. In such a model aggregate supply is completely determined by the level of aggregate demand.

(2) In the Keynesian–neoclassical synthesis model money wages are fixed and so the labour market fails to clear but goods prices are flexible so that the goods market does clear. Firms will only supply more output if goods prices rise relative to money wages so that real wages fall. Workers are prepared to supply more labour than is currently employed, at a lower real wage than the existing one, if this fall in real wages is brought about by price inflation. For a given money wage rate aggregate supply depends positively on the aggregate price level.

(3) According to the new classical aggregate supply function, the divergence of real output from its permanent level varies directly with the divergence between actual and expected prices. All markets clear. This means that firms are only prepared to increase output if they perceive an increase in the relative price of their product. Workers are only willing to supply more labour if they perceive a rise in real wages. The government can only bring about an increase in real output relative to its long-run equilibrium level if they trick firms and workers into incorrectly perceiving favourable relative price changes.

The new classical macroeconomics is a significant development because it undermines the theoretical basis of Keynesian economic policy. The new classical supply function is the crucial element in this refutation of Keynesian analysis. The assumption of rational expectations is an important aspect of the new classical approach, but without the new classical supply function it would not overturn Keynesian policy conclusions. The introduction of rational expectations has exposed an important weakness in Keynesian policy analysis. This is that it is derived from models which assume that structural parameters are invariant with respect to policy changes. This cannot be the case if expectations are formed rationally.

The new classical macroeconomics also has its theoretical weakspots. As noted by a convert, Barro ([23] p. 74):

> The role of incomplete information on money in equilibrium business cycle theory parallels the use of adjustment costs to explain sticky wages and prices with an associated inefficient determination of quantities in Keynesian models. The underpinning of the two types of macroeconomic model are both vulnerable on *a priori* grounds.

References

[1] R. E. Lucas, 'Expectations and the Neutrality of Money', *Journal of Economic Theory*, 4 (1972).

[2] R. E. Lucas, 'Econometric Testing of the Natural Rate Hypothesis', in Otto Eckstein (ed.), *The Econometrics of Price Determination Conference* (Washington, D.C.: Board of Governors of the Federal Reserve System, 1973).

[3] R. E. Lucas, 'An Equilibrium Model of the Business Cycle', *Journal of Political Economy* (December 1975).

[4] R. E. Lucas, 'Econometric Policy Evaluation: a Critique', in K. Brunner and A. Meltzer (eds), *The Phillips Curve and Labour Markets*, Carnegie–Rochester Conference Series on Public Policy (Amsterdam: North-Holland, 1976).

[5] R. E. Lucas, 'Understanding Business Cycles', in K. Brunner and A. Meltzer (eds), *Stabilization of the Domestic and International Economy*, Carnegie–Rochester Conference Series on Public Policy (Amsterdam: North-Holland, 1977).

[6] R. E. Lucas and T. J. Sargent, 'After Keynesian Macroeconomics', *Federal Reserve Bank of Minneapolis Quarterly Review* (Spring 1979).

[7] T. J. Sargent, 'Rational Expectations, the Real Rate of Interest and the Natural Rate of Unemployment', *Brookings Papers on Economic Activity*, 2 (1973).

[8] T. J. Sargent and N. Wallace, 'Rational Expectations and the Theory of Economic Policy', *Journal of Monetary Economics*, 2 (April 1976).

[9] F. A. von Hayek, *Monetary Theory and the Trade Cycle* (London: Jonathan Cape, 1933).

[10] G. Haberler, *Prosperity and Depression* (New York: League of Nations, 1936).

[11] F. Hahn, 'On Non-Walrasian Equilibria', *Review of Economic Studies*, 45 (1978).

[12] R. J. Barro, 'Long-Term Contracting, Sticky Prices and Monetary Policy', *Journal of Monetary Economics*, 3 (July 1977); reprinted in R. J. Barro, *Money, Expectations and Business Cycles* (New York: Academic Press, 1981).

[13] R. E. Lucas and L. A. Rapping, 'Real Wages, Employment and Inflation', *Journal of Political Economy*, 77 (1969).

[14] R. E. Lucas and L. A. Rapping, 'Price Expectations and the Phillips Curve', *American Economic Review*, 59 (1969).

[15] R. E. Hall, 'Labour Supply and Aggregate Fluctuations', in K. Brunner and A. Meltzer (eds), *On the State of Macroeconomics*, Carnegie–Rochester Conference Series on Public Policy (Amsterdam: North-Holland, 1980).

[16] R. E. Lucas, 'Some International Evidence on Output–Inflation Trade-offs', *American Economic Review* (June 1973).

[17] W. Buiter, 'The Macroeconomics of Dr Pangloss: a Critical Survey of the New Classical Macroeconomics', *Economic Journal*, 90 (1980).

[18] J. Tobin, 'Are New Classical Models Plausible Enough to Guide Policy?', *Journal of Money, Credit and Banking*, 2 (November 1980).

[19] H. Grossman, 'Rational Expectations, Business Cycles and Government Behaviour', in S. Fischer (ed.), *Rational Expectations and Economic Policy* (University of Chicago Press, 1980).

[20] R. J. Barro, 'Unanticipated Money Growth and Economic Activity in the United States', in Barro, *Money, Expectations and Business Cycles*.

[21] T. Sargent, 'A Classical Macroeconometric Model for the United States', *Journal of Political Economy*, 84, 2 (1976).

[22] A. P. L. Minford, 'A Rational Expectations Model of the United Kingdom under Fixed and Floating Exchange Rates', in K. Brunner and

A. Meltzer (eds), *On the State of Macroeconomics*, Carnegie–Rochester Conference Series on Public Policy (Amsterdam: North-Holland, 1980).
[23] R. J. Barro, 'The Equilibrium Approach to Business Cycles', in Barro, *Money, Expectations and Business Cycles*.

Further reading

Lucas [5], Lucas and Sargent [6], Buiter [17], Tobin [18] and Grossman [19].

20 Inflation

Inflation exists when the general price level is continually rising. Although the relative prices of individual commodities may change during the course of inflation, the main feature of inflation is that all prices are on average rising. Inflation is measured as the rate of change over time of some general index of prices and is commonly calculated as

$$\frac{P_t - P_{t-1}}{P_{t-1}} \times 100$$

where P_t = price index or price level at time t.

The price level is measured by taking the weighted average of the prices at a particular moment in time of a large number of commodities. The weight attached to the price of each commodity is the proportion of total expenditure devoted to that good. A price index expresses the price level of each period relative to a base period (usually the beginning of a year) which has its price level fixed at 100. Price indices can cover a group of commodities such as food, housing and capital goods, but price indices which give an idea of the general level of prices are the wholesale price index, the retail price index, the consumer price index and the implicit deflator of total final expenditure.

In this chapter we examine the two major sets of theories which attempt to explain why inflation occurs. These we classify as the *monetarist* and *structural* approaches. We then consider the reasons for pursuing an anti-inflation policy and what policies are implied by the two different theoretical approaches to inflation.

20.1 The monetarist approach to inflation in a closed economy

The monetarist explanation of inflation has a long history and is directly derived from the quantity theory of money which relates a unique price level to a given stock of money. The chief pillars of the monetary approach are a neoclassical supply function and a stable demand function for money. The demand for real balances depends on real income (or alternatively wealth) and on the nominal rate of interest, *i* (see Chapter 8). A popular functional form for the demand for money function is

$$\left(\frac{M}{P}\right)^D = i^{\alpha} y^{\beta} \tag{20.1}$$

or in nominal terms

$$M^D = P i^{\alpha} y^{\beta} \tag{20.1a}$$

If the money market is to be in equilibrium, then we must have the stock of money, M^S, equal to the demand for it:

$$M^S = M^D = P i^{\alpha} y^{\beta} \tag{20.2}$$

We can derive the relationship between growth in the money stock and the price level quite simply if we assume the nominal interest rate to be constant. Then differentiating 20.2 with respect to time gives

$$\frac{dM^S}{dt} = \frac{dP}{dt} i^{\alpha} y^{\beta} + P i^{\alpha} \beta y^{\beta-1} \frac{dy}{dt} \tag{20.3}$$

Therefore, dividing both sides of 20.3 by M^S we get

$$\frac{1}{M^S}\frac{dM^S}{dt} = \frac{1}{P}\frac{dP}{dt} + \beta \frac{1}{y}\frac{dy}{dt} \tag{20.4}$$

Hence

$$\frac{1}{P}\frac{dP}{dt} = \frac{1}{M^S}\frac{dM^S}{dt} - \beta \frac{1}{y}\frac{dy}{dt} \tag{20.5}$$

The rate of inflation (in continuous time), $(dP/dt)/P$, is equal to the rate of growth of the money supply minus the rate of growth of the demand for money balances that is due to the growth in real income. To keep the price level constant the nominal money supply must grow at a rate equal to the income elasticity of the demand for money, β,[1] times the rate of growth of real income. If the nominal money stock grows at a faster rate than this, there is said to be excessively rapid growth in the supply of money. An excess supply of money

[1] β is the income elasticity of the demand for money since we have from 20.2 that

$$\frac{dM}{dy} = \beta y^{\beta-1}$$

Therefore

$$\frac{dM}{dy}\frac{y}{M} = \frac{\beta y^{\beta}}{y^{\beta}} = \beta$$

results in portfolio adjustment as people move out of money and into goods and other financial assets. The resulting manifestation of excess demand bids up the price level. Once the price level has risen sufficiently to make the demand for nominal balances equal to the nominal money stock, portfolio equilibrium is restored and the price level stops rising. However, if the money supply is continually increased at a rate which exceeds the growth in the demand for money brought about by rising real incomes, then inflation will persist.

For the rate of inflation to be determined along the lines of equation 20.5 several conditions must be met.

1. Stable demand for money function

The demand for money must be stable so that one can predict the price level from a knowledge of the stock of money, the determinants of the demand for money and the coefficients which relate the demand for money to its determinants. Keynesians have typically viewed the demand for money as being unstable (see Chapter 8, p. 130).

2. Exogenous money stock

In the monetarist approach changes in the price level are traced to exogenous changes in the money supply. Critics of monetarist theory argue that the money supply is endogenous because the banking system responds to an increase in the demand for money by creating more money balances (see Chapter 9 and House of Commons [1]). Therefore, increases in the price level and hence in nominal income, by increasing the demand for money, induce increases in the money stock. In this view the good correlations which are observed between increases in the price level and in the money supply arise because the direction of causality is from the price level to the money supply and not from the money supply to the price level as in the monetarist approach.

3. The neutrality of money

The third requirement for a strong causal link from the stock of money to the price level is the neutrality of money proposition by which the level of real income is independent of the stock of money. If money is not neutral so that real income rises in response to monetary expansion, then the growth in the money supply itself generates a demand for additional money balances in order to finance a higher real value of transactions. There is then less excess money stock to spill over in the form of excess aggregate demand and hence a smaller rise in the price level than if real income had remained unaffected by the increased stock of money.

However, monetarists do not hold that money is necessarily neutral in the short run. If the rate of growth in the money supply is accelerated so that the expected rate of inflation lies below the actual rate, then there will be an increase in real output via the short-run Phillips relation. This means that for any given increase in the rate of growth of the money supply the rate of inflation will be lower in the short run than in final equilibrium when expected inflation has become equal to actual inflation.

The following set of equations shows how the short-run rate of inflation is determined using the Phillips relation and how it is related to the long-run equilibrium inflation rate.

We can express the Phillips relation as given by equation 18.15 (p. 351) as

$$f(U_t - U_t^N) = \pi_t^e - \pi_t \tag{20.6}$$

where f is a positive function, $U_t - U_t^N$ = deviation of the current rate of unemployment, U_t, from the natural rate, U_t^N, π_t = actual rate of inflation, and π_t^e = expected rate of inflation.

The deviation of the current rate of unemployment from the natural rate is positively related to the difference between the long-run trend rate of growth of real output, $\dot{y}_p/y_p$, and the current rate of growth of real output, $\dot{y}/y$. Thus

$$U_t - U_t^N = g\left(\frac{\dot{y}_{pt}}{y_{pt}} - \frac{\dot{y}_t}{y_t}\right) \tag{20.7}$$

From the short-run Phillips relation treated as a supply function the difference between the long-run (or permanent) rate of growth of real output and the current rate of growth depends positively on the difference between the actual and expected rate of inflation:

$$\frac{\dot{y}_{pt}}{y_{pt}} - \frac{\dot{y}_t}{y_t} = \phi(\pi_t^e - \pi_t) \tag{20.8}$$

Let us take 20.8 to be a linear equation in growth rates. Now equation 20.5 gives the current rate of inflation as

$$\pi_t = m_t - \beta\frac{\dot{y}_t}{y_t} \tag{20.5a}$$

where m = rate of growth of the money supply. Rearranging 20.5a we get

$$\frac{\dot{y}_t}{y_t} = \frac{1}{\beta}(m_t - \pi_t) \tag{20.5b}$$

Substituting equation 20.5b into equation 20.8 we get

$$-\frac{1}{\beta}(m_t - \pi_t) = -\frac{\dot{y}_{pt}}{y_{pt}} + \phi(\pi_t^e - \pi_t) \tag{20.9}$$

Taking π_t to the left-hand side and gathering terms gives

$$\pi_t = \frac{1}{1+\phi\beta}\left(m_t - \beta\frac{\dot{y}_{pt}}{y_{pt}}\right) + \frac{\phi\beta}{1+\phi\beta}\pi_t^e \tag{20.10}$$

Equation 20.10 is the expression for the rate of inflation in the short run when $\pi_t^e \neq \pi_t$. The first term in brackets on the right-hand side represents the amount of excess demand (the long-run excess rate of growth of the money supply). The coefficient $1/(1 + \phi\beta)$ is positive and less than 1.0 since part of the excess demand created by excessive monetary expansion causes a short-run increase in output. The second term in the short-run inflation equation is the expected rate of inflation. Again the short-run adjustment coefficient is less than 1.0 because of the short-run Phillips trade-off.

In the long run π equals π^e so the second term on the right-hand side of equation 20.9 drops out. Rearranging terms then gives the expression for inflation already derived in equation 20.5:

$$\pi_t = m_t - \beta \frac{\dot{y}_{pt}}{y_{pt}} \tag{20.5}$$

which is the expression for the long-run rate of inflation. A typical regression equation for the monetarist hypothesis regarding the determinants of inflation is a version of equation 20.10 in which the independent variables are some proxy for excess demand and some measure of expected inflation.

20.2 International monetarism

One of the strengths of the monetarist approach is that it offers a single integrated theory to explain inflation at the international level as well as for individual countries. Monetarist analysis of open economies (which was developed in Chapter 11), typically draws a sharp distinction between tradable goods and non-tradables. The elasticity of substitution in consumption between domestically produced tradables and foreign-produced tradables is extremely high and is regarded as perfectly elastic in the long run. Hence the domestic currency price of tradables is the world price divided by the exchange rate:

$$P^T_d = \frac{P^T_f}{e} \tag{20.11}$$

where

P^T_d = price of tradables in terms of domestic currency
P^T_f = price of tradables in terms of foreign currency
e = exchange rate, expressed as the number of units of foreign currency which exchange for one unit of domestic currency

The domestic price of non-tradables is affected by the price of tradables to the extent that consumers and producers are induced to switch between the two in response to relative price differentials.

The determinants of inflation for an individual small open economy depend on whether it operates a fixed or a flexible exchange rate.

Fixed exchange rates

The simplest and most extreme monetarist model assumes that all goods are tradables so that the domestic price level is given by

$$Pd = Pf/e \tag{20.11a}$$

where Pd = domestic price level and Pf = foreign price level. With e constant, differentiating equation 20.11a with respect to time and dividing both sides by $Pd = Pf/e$ gives

$$\frac{1}{Pd}\frac{dPd}{dt} = \frac{1}{Pf}\frac{dPf}{dt} \tag{20.12}$$

This states that the domestic rate of inflation must, in equilibrium, equal the world rate of inflation. There are two characteristic elements in the transmission mechanism whereby an x per cent increase in the world inflation rate leads to an x per cent increase in domestic inflation. One element is goods arbitrage whereby world demand switches to domestically produced tradables when their price falls relative to the world price following the increase in the world inflation rate. The increased demand bids up the price of domestically produced goods. The second element is due to portfolio adjustment. In the interim period while the domestic prices are below world prices, the domestic country runs a balance-of-payments surplus. The stock of foreign exchange reserves rises and so does the domestic money supply. The consequent portfolio adjustment by domestic residents creates additional demand for domestically produced goods and so raises prices. Once the domestic and world inflation rates become equalised then the balance-of-payments surplus disappears and full equilibrium is restored. Thus a small open economy under a fixed exchange rate imports inflation from the rest of the world.

The converse of importing inflation is that a small open economy exports its inflation to the rest of the world rather than experiencing it itself. If the domestic money supply is allowed to grow at a rate which exceeds $\beta \times dy/dt \times 1/y$, then a balance-of-payments deficit ensues. The domestic money stock declines as foreign exchange reserves are run down. Other countries consequently experience balance-of-payments surpluses and an excessive rate of growth of their money supply. Prices therefore rise throughout the world. The smaller is the domestic economy in relation to the world economy, the less inflation it experiences as a result of its own expansionary monetary policies, which, in any case, can only continue so long as the country can finance its balance-of-payments deficits.

Under fixed exchange rates an individual country cannot determine its own inflation rate but is tied to the world rate of inflation. Its own money supply is endogenous and is determined, via balance-of-payments adjustment, by the demand for money (see Chapter 11, pp. 183–8). However, the world inflation rate is determined by the excess rate of growth of the world money supply. The analysis which applies to an individual closed economy applies to the world economy.

Extending the model to include non-tradables does not alter the conclusions qualitatively. The domestic price level is now a weighted average of traded and non-traded goods' prices:

$$Pd = \gamma P^T + (1 - \gamma)P^N \tag{20.13}$$

where

P_d = domestic price level
P^N = non-traded goods' prices
γ = share of traded goods in national expenditure

(The domestic price of traded goods is still determined by equation 20.11, which can be substituted into equation 20.13.) Given that γ and the rate of inflation of non-traded goods' prices are constant, then the domestic rate of inflation will change in line with the world rate for traded goods. There is now some scope for the domestic rate of inflation to diverge from the world rate due to shifts in γ or to changes in the non-tradables' inflation rate. However, the divergence in inflation rates is constrained by the substitution between traded and non-traded goods that occurs in response to changing relative price differences.

Flexible exchange rates

Under a regime of flexible exchange rates an individual country can inflate at an entirely different rate from that of other countries. If it expands its own money supply at an excessively rapid rate, the exchange rate depreciates. As a result tradable goods' prices rise in terms of the domestic currency. In addition, excess monetary growth increases the price of non-tradables. The domestic price level therefore rises in line with the excess rate of growth of the money supply (that is, by $\dot{M}^S/M^S - \beta\dot{y}/y$).

Under flexible exchange rates a country can also keep its inflation rate below that of other countries. If it expands its money supply at a rate which is less than $\beta\dot{y}/y + \dot{P}^T/P^T$ (that is, the rate of growth required to satisfy the demand for money balances arising from real income growth and the increase in tradable goods' prices in terms of domestic currency at the current exchange rate), the resulting excess demand for money will drive up the exchange rate. Because the exchange rate appreciates, the domestic currency price of tradables will rise more slowly than it does in terms of foreign currency. The appreciation of the exchange rate keeps the demand for money balances in line with the supply of money and insulates the domestic country from experiencing other countries' inflation.

So under flexible exchange rates a country cannot export its own inflation to others but it can insulate itself from world inflation. However, the world rate of inflation, calculated as a weighted average of individual countries' inflation, still depends on the rate of increase of the world money supply. (This is the aggregate of all countries' money stocks measured in a common currency.)

Post-war world inflation

Monetarists attribute inflation in all the post-war decades to the excess growth rate of the world money supply. Under the regime of fixed exchange rates which lasted from 1944 to 1971, an individual country's rate of inflation was not the result of its own monetary policies but was mainly determined by the rate of increase in the world money supply. A major determinant of this was US monetary policy. Not only is the USA a very large economy compared with others but the dollar is a reserve currency held by other countries. This meant that under a regime of fixed exchange rates the USA could increase its money supply in excess of $\beta\dot{y}/y$ and, unlike other non-reserve currency countries, run a balance-of-payments deficit for so long as other countries were prepared to hold the outflow of dollars. The attempt in the USA to reduce unemployment by adopting Keynesian policies in the mid-1960s plus financing the Vietnam war resulted in a more rapid rate of growth in the US money supply and in foreign countries' dollar reserves. This, in the monetarist interpretation, explains the simultaneous upsurge of inflation in most major economies around 1968–70.[1] Figure 1.1 (p. 4) indicates how three countries' inflation rates moved together quite closely in the 1950s and 1960s and diverged more thereafter.

Excess demand: the Keynesian view

Keynesians would not deny that excess demand caused by monetary expansion *can* lead to inflation. Indeed, early Keynesian writing on inflation, which was heavily influenced by Keynes's own efforts to prevent inflation in the Second World War, regarded inflation as a problem which would only arise if demand exceeded full-employment output. However, excess demand was not specifically attributed to an excess supply of money but to the combined total of government, private and foreign sector demand exceeding the full-employment supply of output. In terms of the aggregate demand and supply diagram of the three-sector K–N synthesis model (see p. 97) Keynesians analysed excess demand inflation as being initiated by upward shifts in the aggregate demand schedule. As money wages adjusted to rising prices, the aggregate supply schedule would shift up to the left, causing a further rise in prices. For inflation to proceed indefinitely, the aggregate and demand and supply schedules would have to shift up continually.

The Keynesian international transmission mechanism for inflation operates via excess demand in one country increasing its demand for imports. This expands aggregate demand in foreign countries with consequent inflationary effects if these economies lack spare capacity.

20.3 Structuralist theories of inflation

While the view that inflation could only occur in the presence of excess aggregate demand was prevalent in the 1940s, the notion that money wages

[1] For further accounts of the monetarist theory of inflation see references [1]–[7].

and prices could be pushed up independently of the state of demand due to various structural features of the economy emerged as a competing hypothesis in the 1950s. Traces of this approach can be found in *The General Theory* and in subsequent Keynesian macro models which assume a fixed money wage rate.

In the structural approach the price of a manufactured article or service, unlike that of a primary product, is not greatly influenced by the competitive forces of demand and supply. According to the mark-up view of price determination, prices are set by adding to average variable costs a gross profit margin mark-up which is more or less invariant with respect to demand. Thus

$$P = \frac{W}{APL} + IC + PM \tag{20.14}$$

where

P = price of final product
W = money wage
APL = average product of labour
IC = average cost of material inputs (e.g. raw materials, fuel, etc.)
PM = gross profit margin per unit of final product

Equation 20.14 can be treated as a single price equation or as an aggregate price-level expression. A rise in price is therefore attributed to a rise in the money wage rate, or other elements of variable cost (IC), or the gross profit margin. A rise in the average product of labour, unless offset by an equivalent money wage or profit margin increase, will reduce price. Equation 20.14 is of course an identity and as such will hold in a monetarist model. It becomes a price-determination equation when the components of price are assumed to change *independently* of the state of demand.

In the structuralist view this occurs because markets are not competitive. The fact that firms operate in oligopolistic markets, while labour is organised into trade unions, is thought to make the competitive model of price determination inoperative in modern advanced economies. Prices and money wages are assumed to be inflexible downwards. One effect of this is that any increase in import prices causes the general price level to rise. Inflation from 1973 onwards is therefore attributed in large measure to the rise in the price of oil and in other primary commodities. This contrasts with the monetarist view that in such circumstances a tight monetary policy would appreciate the exchange rate and prevent the domestic price level from rising.

Structuralists have paid particular attention to the role of trade unions in pushing up wages independently of the state of demand. To quote Kahn ([8] p. 11): 'Inflation, according to Keynesians, is largely – if not entirely – due to rapidly rising wages.'

How exogenous wage push can generate inflation is illustrated in Figure 20.1. The effect of trade unions negotiating a higher money wage is to shift the aggregate supply schedule from S_0 up to S_1. Given a fixed aggregate demand schedule, D_0, the price level rises but real output and employment fall because

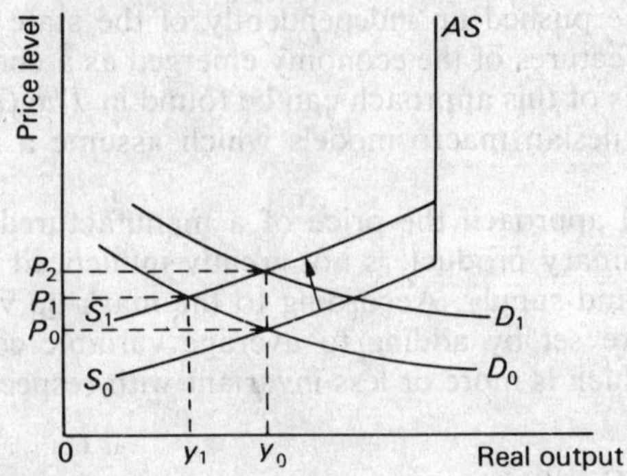

FIGURE 20.1 *Inflation initiated by increased money wage rates*

the rise in real wages reduces the demand for labour. In order to generate a process of inflation rather than just a once-and-for-all rise in the price level, the aggregate demand schedule must also shift – up to the right. For this to happen it is now generally agreed that the money supply must be increased. The typical Keynesian view is that 'the increase in the quantity of money is not the cause of inflation. It is, however, a necessary condition' (Kahn [8] p. 13).

In complete opposition to the monetarist view that the money supply is exogenous, some structuralists-cum-Keynesians argue that the money supply in a closed economy is completely endogenous. As the demand for nominal money balances increases because the price level is rising, the banking system responds by creating the required money balances (see Chapter 9, pp. 155–6). A less extreme view is that the government is forced to increase the money supply in order to prevent a politically unacceptable rate of unemployment. The consequent inflation prevents real wages from rising as they would otherwise do following the upward push in money wages. In order to generate a continuing inflation rather than just a once-and-for-all hike in the price level, wage push must continually shift the aggregate supply function up to the left while accommodating monetary policy allows the aggregate demand function to shift up as well.

The monetarist position regarding the ability of trade unions to cause inflation is that as an empirical fact exogenous wage push has not caused inflation. However, if trade unions can push up wages independently of the state of demand, then they cause unemployment, *not* inflation. The inflation is then caused by the government adopting an accommodating monetary policy. However, at this point the debate degenerates into a semantic argument.

Given the premise that trade unions do push up money wages, the next question to consider is what determines such wage-pushfulness. A popular general hypothesis is that this is due to real wage aspirations which exceed the real wage increases the economy can produce. Real wage increases can come from several sources. One source which can be sustained in the long run is a growth in labour productivity due to technical progress and/or a growing *per capita* capital stock. The other sources are reducing the proportion of national output taken by company profits and by the government. The former have been squeezed in the post-war period, while the public sector has expanded, so requiring higher tax revenues to finance it. The final source is the foreign sector, either by means of an improvement in the terms of trade, or by running a balance-of-payments deficit. Squeezing the company sector or the government sector or running a balance-of-payments deficit are all methods which cannot be sustained indefinitely.

A number of reasons have been suggested for real wage aspirations running ahead of the actual real wage increases experienced by workers, particularly since 1968. One idea is that real wage expectations are conditioned by previous experience. In the late 1960s actual real wage growth declined because of the slowdown in the rate of economic growth and the increasing tax levels required to finance the expanding public sector. In Britain the rate of take-home pay to gross pay fell from 96.6 per cent in 1949 to 91 per cent by 1964 and to 83 per cent by 1971. British incomes policy between 1966 and 1969 also held down real wage increases, prior to the wage explosion of 1970. Real wages were further hit by the fourfold rise in oil prices in 1973–4. As the expected rate of inflation rises, so money wage demands have to escalate if a given real wage target is to be achieved. A somewhat different emphasis to wage push is given by Marxist-cum-radical writers who regard it as a symptom of the class struggle between workers and capitalists. For some this struggle is unrelated to the level of aggregate demand, while others consider that firms are more willing to concede wage increases the higher is the level of aggregate demand. In addition, workers are cowed into accepting relatively smaller wage increases the higher is the rate of unemployment. This version of the wage-push hypothesis is much more difficult to distinguish from an excess demand/monetarist hypothesis than the version which maintains that wage push occurs independently of the state of demand. At the other polar extreme from the monetarist position is the view that wage push cannot be related to economic variables: it is due to sociological factors and so its quantitative value cannot be predicted.

Structuralists have more difficulty than monetarists in providing a well-integrated mechanism for the international transmission of inflation which explains why wage push should simultaneously manifest itself with similar strength in different countries. One answer is that world-wide events, like the rise in oil prices, affect real wage aspirations. Another relies on a demonstration effect: if workers become militant in one country, their attitudes are then emulated in other countries. Monetarists criticise such explanations for being *ad hoc* and lacking any theoretical basis.[1]

20.4 Empirical evidence on the determinants of inflation

The controversy over the causes of inflation has generated a vast empirical literature. Some of this was reviewed in Chapter 18 in so far as it related to the Phillips trade-off between unemployment and inflation. Here the focus is on

[1] For further accounts of structuralistic views see references [1] and [8]–[11].

TABLE 20.1 *A summary of some econometric tests of the determination of inflation*

Study	Data	Dependent variable	Regression equations	
Duck *et al.* [15]	Pooled group of ten. 1956–71 quarterly	π = rate of change of consumer price index	$-0.012 + 0.132E_{t-1} + \pi^e$ $R^2 = 0.764$ $D\text{–}W = 2.147$ (0.383) (3.382) (coefficient on π^e constrained = 1.0: not rejected)	
Cross and Laidler [16] 1954–70	20 countries 1954–70, annual	π = rate of change of consumer price index	'World equation' $0.3771E_{t-1} - 0.2474E_{t-2} + 1.0873\pi_{t-1}$ (0.09)* (0.092)* (0.055)*	$R^2 = 0.835$ $D\text{–}W = 2.369$
			United Kingdom $0.8977E_{t-1} - 0.4736E_{t-2} + 0.9566\pi_{t-1}$ (0.2699)* (0.2842)* (0.0975)*	$R^2 = 0.439$ $D\text{–}W = 2.006$
			USA $0.3186E_{t-1} - 0.1941E_{t-2} + 1.0812\pi_{t-1}$ (0.0745)* (0.0815)* (0.0844)*	$R^2 = 0.838$ $D\text{–}W = 2.375$
Perry [21]	UK, 1962–72, annual	Wage inflation, W_e (hourly earnings)	$0.059(I/U) + 0.827\pi^e_{ft} + 0.446W_{e(t-1)} + 0.471D_t$ (1.00) (3.2) (3.3) (5.6)	$R^2 = 0.898$ $D\text{–}W = 2.2$
Johnston and Timbrell [19]	UK, 1952–71, annual	Wage inflation, W (weekly wage rate)	$-2.22 + 0.60n_t + 0.40\pi^e + 3.26A + 1.268S_t$ (0.18) (0.91) (2.23) (1.30)	$R^2 = 0.763$ $D\text{–}W = 2.25$
Henry *et al.* [20]	UK, 1948–71, quarterly	Wage inflation, W	$-0.0059 + 0.589\pi_{t-1} + 0.00083U_{t-1} + 0.1176A + 0.00066t$ (0.026)* (0.136)* (0.0066) (0.048)* (0.00031)*	$R^2 = 0.469$ $D\text{–}W = 1.466$
			$-18.704 - 0.313\dot{T} + 0.385T + 1.059\pi_{t-\frac{1}{2}} + 1.483U_t$ (16.953)* (1.826)* (0.427)* (0.177)* (0.734)*	$R^2 = 0.952$
Hines [25]	UK, 1893–61, annual	W_t = rate of change of money wage rate (hourly, 1921–61)	$-1.9740 + 1.5945\Delta T_t + 0.1282T_t + 0.6804\pi_t + 0.0812\pi_{t-1} - 0.0441U_t$ (0.2418)* (0.0409)* (0.1129)* (0.0276)* (0.1129)*	$R^2 = 0.9953$ $D\text{–}W = 1.32$
		P_t = rate of change of price level	$-0.7797 + 0.6924W_t + 0.0396M_{t-1/2} + 0.1346\Delta X_t$ (0.0348)* (0.0173)* (0.0725)*	$R^2 = 0.9834$ $D\text{–}W = 0.98$

		T_t = change in % of labour unionised	$1.4014 - \underset{(0.0083)^*}{0.1145T_{t-1}} + \underset{(0.0148)^*}{0.4664\pi_t} - \underset{(0.0129)^*}{0.0978\pi_{t-1}} + \underset{(0.0048)^*}{0.0149D_{t-1/2}}$	$R^2 = 0.98$ $D{-}W = 1.31$
Purdy and Zis [26]	UK, 1925–38, 1950–61, annual	W_t as [25]	$\underset{(0.36)^*}{0.558} + \underset{(0.054)^*}{0.0817T_t} + \underset{(0.132)^*}{0.474\Delta T_t} + \underset{(0.127)^*}{0.055\pi_t} + \underset{(0.118)^*}{0.222\pi_{t-1/2}} + \underset{(0.792)^*}{6.368U^{-1}}$	$R^2 = 0.963$ $D{-}W = 1.670$
		P_t as [25]	$\underset{(0.318)^*}{-0.232} + \underset{(0.148)^*}{0.063\Delta X_t} + \underset{(0.363)^*}{0.239M_{t-1/2}} + \underset{(0.082)^*}{0.682W_{rt}}$	$R^2 = 0.930$ $D{-}W = 1.668$
		T_t as [25]	$\underset{(2.074)^*}{10.054} - \underset{(0.050)^*}{0.407T} + \underset{(0.079)^*}{0.355\pi_{t-1/2}} - \underset{(0.0005)^*}{0.004D_{t-1}}$	$R^2 = 0.6108$ $D{-}W = 1.2312$
Mulvey and Gregory [27]	USA, 1920–59, annual	W	$\underset{(1.094)^*}{2.065} + \underset{(2.937)^*}{1.008U^{-1.5}} + \underset{(0.073)^*}{0.526\pi^e} + \underset{(0.053)^*}{0.014T} + \underset{(0.285)^*}{0.364\Delta T} + \underset{(0.09)^*}{0.235\Delta UD}$	$R^2 = 0.816$ $D{-}W = 1.70$
Godfrey [28]	UK, 1957(III)–69(III), quarterly	W = rate of change of weekly wage rates	$\underset{(0.238)^*}{0.6762} + \underset{(0.1934)^*}{0.1589\pi_t} - \underset{(0.5628)^*}{0.3536U_t^{-1.5}} + \underset{(0.0534)^*}{0.1055S_t/100} - \underset{(0.1761)^*}{0.0736\Delta S_t/100}$	S.E. = 0.26
Ward and Zis [30]	UK, 1956–71, annual	W_e = rate of change of hourly earnings	$\underset{(0.61)}{1.530} - \underset{(1.215)}{3.286U_t^{-1}} + \underset{(1.404)}{1.212S_t} + \underset{(3.477)}{0.700\pi_{t-1/4}}$	$R^2 = 0.681$ $D{-}W = 2.088$

SYMBOLS: as in Table 18.1 (p. 357). In addition:

A = various proxies for real wage aspiration gap.
ID = income shares dummy (Perry).
n = proportion of labour force having a wage settlement [19].
S = number of strikes.
t = time trend (Henry *et al.*).
T = proportion of labour force unionised.
UD = union/non-union wage differential.
π^e = expected rate of inflation.

empirical tests which may help us to decide whether the monetarist and structuralist explanation of inflation is the more plausible. The rate of inflation is the dependent variable of chief interest here. However, a good many studies which aim to confront the monetarist and structuralist hypotheses with the empirical evidence take wages or earnings as the dependent variable. Although money wages and prices are reasonably well correlated over time, one cannot automatically assume that what determines wages will thereby determine prices (or vice versa).

The monetarist hypothesis

A popular specification for testing the monetarist hypothesis is the Phillips relation, whereby inflation is regressed on some proxy for excess aggregate demand and on a measure of the expected rate of inflation (see equation 20.10 on p. 382). A more direct test is to regress inflation on the excess rate of growth of the money supply. However, monetarists would only expect such relationships to hold for a closed economy or for a small open economy under flexible exchange rates. For the post-war period up to 1971 monetarists would expect a small open economy's inflation rate to be determined by the world inflation rate and not by the internal level of demand or monetary growth or by price expectations based only on past domestic inflation.

Therefore, to test the monetarist hypothesis on data prior to 1972 one has to use data either for the USA – the closest approximation to a closed economy we have – or for a group of countries proxying the 'world' economy. Studies which regress prices or wages on to the money supply or excess demand for countries other than the USA using pre-1972 data are not valid tests of the monetary hypothesis.[1]

A number of studies supporting the monetarist hypothesis have been published in Parkin and Zis [13] and [14]. Duck *et al.* [15] (see Table 20.1) find that the expectations-augmented Phillips relation explains 'world' inflation using pooled quarterly data for the Group of Ten countries, 1956–71. Cross and Laidler [16] report a similar finding for twenty countries for the period 1954–70 using annual data.

An interesting study of the relationship between the money supply, wage rates and prices for the USA and seven other OECD countries was undertaken by Gordon [17], from which Figure 20.2 is reproduced. The wage and price time series follow each other quite closely. The US money supply growth rate peaked in 1968–9 and 1971–3 and was followed by higher rates of change of wages and prices. The other seven countries' monetary growth rates declined slightly in 1968–9 but mirrored that of the USA in 1971–3. The other seven exhibited a wage explosion in 1969–70 which preceded the acceleration in

[1] A number of what are called reduced-form studies have regressed prices or nominal income on to the money supply. Some, particularly for the USA, support the monetarist hypothesis. The overall results are not conclusive and the statistical methodology of this kind of test is suspect. For a survey of this evidence see Coghlan [12].

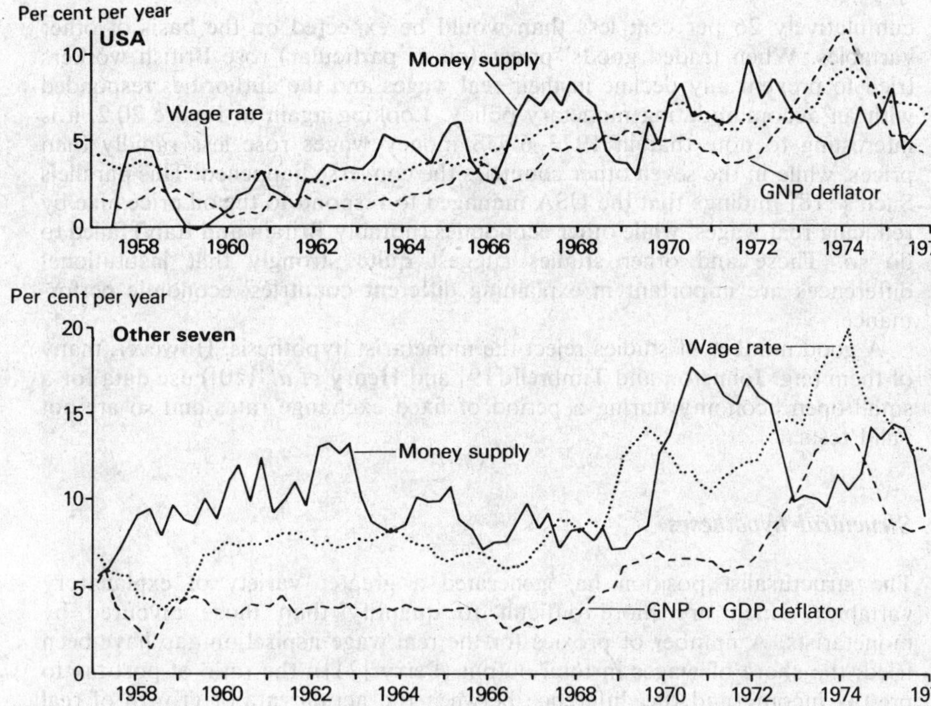

FIGURE 20.2 *Four-quarter overlapping rates of change of money, wage rates, and gross national product deflator, USA, and seven other OECD countries, 1958–76*[1]

monetary growth. This is consistent with a wage-push explanation. However, the second hump in the wage time series in all eight countries followed a period of rapid monetary growth while also coinciding with the 1973/4 oil price rise.

Gordon's results offer support to both the monetarist and wage-push hypothesis, though the balance is tipped more towards the former. Gordon's wage equation includes the money supply, a proxy for excess demand, traded goods' prices and wage-push dummies which enter for particular quarters when he judged positive wage-push or incomes-policy restraint to have occurred. Gordon found the wage-push dummies to be significant in the wage equations but not in the price equations. In addition, the relatively strong positive impact of monetary growth on wages supports the monetary hypothesis. An additional test of the structuralist position is to see whether the money supply responds positively to increased wages. Only the USA and the United Kingdom show clear evidence of monetary accommodation, but the former has no positive wage push. This leaves the United Kingdom as the only country where wage push can explain rising prices. However, Gordon also finds that the influence of the money supply on wages is stronger in Britain than elsewhere.

Gordon estimates that over the years 1958–73 British money wages were

[1] The other seven countries are Canada, France, West Germany, Japan, Sweden and the United Kingdom.

cumulatively 26 per cent less than would be expected on the basis of other variables. When traded goods' prices (oil in particular) rose British workers tried to prevent any decline in their real wages and the authorities responded with an accommodating monetary policy. Looking again at Figure 20.2, it is interesting to note that in 1973–6 US money wages rose less rapidly than prices, while in the seven other countries the converse happened. This parallels Sach's [18] findings that the USA managed to respond to the oil price hike by reducing real wages, while other economies (notably Britain and Italy) failed to do so. These and other studies suggest quite strongly that institutional differences are important in explaining different countries' economic performance.

A good number of studies reject the monetarist hypothesis. However, many of them (e.g. Johnston and Timbrell [19] and Henry *et al.* [20]) use data for a small open economy during a period of fixed exchange rates and so are not valid tests.

Structural hypotheses

The structuralist position has generated a greater variety of explanatory variables which are more difficult to quantify than those favoured by monetarists. A number of proxies for the real wage aspiration gap have been tried: the share of wages in total output (Perry [21]); the ratio of post-tax to pre-tax income and the difference between the actual rate of growth of real income and a target 2 or 3 per cent (Johnston and Timbrell [19]); lagged real post-tax earnings (Henry *et al.* [20]); and lagged real consumption (Nordhaus [22]). Money wage increases are, as in the monetarist approach, expected to reflect future expected price increases. Examples of studies which find evidence to support the real wage aspiration hypothesis are those made by Perry [21], Johnston and Timbrell [19], Henry *et al.* [20], Sargan [23] and Godley [24], while Nordhaus [22] and Gordon [17] (except for the United Kingdom) are contrary examples.

Another set of tests for the structuralist hypothesis is to relate wage push to trade-union militancy. The problem in this approach is to find an adequate measure of union militancy. Hines [25] reported successful results using the change in the proportion of the labour force unionised. However, no one else has replicated Hines's results and his methodology and data have received serious criticism (see Henry *et al.* [29], Purdy and Zis [26] and Mulvey and Gregory [27]). There is thus considerable doubt about the validity of Hines's results.

Another measure of militancy is strike activity, which is hypothesised to increase when workers become more militant and thereby get higher wage settlements. Studies which include a strike variable as a determinant of money wages have (as usual!) yielded mixed results. The number of strikes was found significant by Godfrey [28] and Taylor [29] but, on the whole, insignificant by Ward and Zis [30] and Laidler [31]. The significance of the strike variable seems particularly dependent on how it is measured and what sample period is used (see Zis [32]).

An overall assessment

In principle empirical tests can distinguish between the polar versions of the monetarist and structuralist hypotheses since aggregate demand is a proximate determinant of inflation in the former hypothesis but not the latter. However, this does not mean that the rising unemployment and inflation of the 1970s is consistent with the structuralist approach but not the monetarist one. In the latter a given rate of unemployment can coexist with any rate of inflation since current inflation also depends on expected inflation, and unemployment will be *rising* if the current rate of inflation exceeds the expected rate. In fact both approaches relate money wages and hence prices to price expectations, so that in this respect they cannot be distinguished.

It becomes more difficult to devise tests which distinguish clearly between the two approaches once we move to modified versions whereby monetarists allow for monetary accommodation and structuralists relate the strength of wage push and its effect on prices to the state of demand.

While it seems to us that the economic evidence on balance favours a monetarist approach as against the extreme structuralist hypothesis, one must recognise that it is more difficult to quantify the relevant structuralist variables. Nor are the two approaches mutually exclusive. Both inflation-generating mechanisms could be at work simultaneously. An eclectic view would hold that both explanations contribute to our understanding of inflation and that either one could be dominant at different times or in different countries.

It is important to bear in mind for policy purposes that neither approach has come up with variables which can accurately predict inflation on a short-term basis. Monetarists stress that excessive increases in the money supply will eventually show up in more or less proportional increases in the price level. The lag between money and prices has often been put at eighteen months to two years, though a believer in rational expectations would expect the lag between *anticipated* changes in the money supply and in prices to be much quicker. The structuralist approach offers even less guidance with respect to quantitative links between the determinants of inflation and inflation itself. Real wage aspirations and worker militancy are both difficult to quantify or predict.

20.5 The costs and benefits of inflation

The crucial question regarding public policy towards inflation is whether or not the costs of reducing inflation exceed the benefits of the consequent lower rate of inflation. In examining the costs of inflation it is essential to distinguish between anticipated and unanticipated inflation and between full indexing of all prices with respect to inflation and the absence of such indexing.

Anticipated inflation with full indexing

In this situation all money wages, prices and nominal interest rates rise in line with inflation so that relative prices and rates of return remain unchanged.

However, money does not bear a rate of interest because of the difficulties of paying interest on a circulating stock of cash balances. Thus the opportunity cost of holding money rises with the rate of inflation and this reduces the demand for real money balances. The cost of inflation is the forgone benefits derived from the convenience of holding money. This cost is illustrated by Figure 20.3.

The real rate of interest when inflation is zero is Oi_0 and the demand for real money balances is Om_0. The total welfare obtained by holding Om_0 money balances is the area under the demand curve, CBm_0O. This area is the maximum amount people are prepared to pay in terms of forgone interest for the benefits derived from holding Om_0 money. If the rate of inflation then becomes x per cent and this is anticipated, the nominal interest rate rises to Or_1 and the demand for real money balances falls to Om_1. Since the public are now holding m_1m_0 fewer money balances the loss in welfare is given by area m_1ABm_0. If we assume that the production of money is costless, then area m_1ABm_0 is the net welfare loss to society as a whole due to an x per cent expected rate of inflation reducing the volume of real money balances held. This cost could be avoided if it were possible to pay interest on all types of money balances.

The loss in welfare from holding less money is not serious for mild inflation (possibly in the order of 1.5 per cent of net national income for 10 per cent inflation), but it increases as inflation becomes more rapid. Hyperinflations frequently end in a complete breakdown of the monetary system and a return to barter. This seriously dislocates the system of production and exchange, causing widespread hardship. One reason for anti-inflation policies is the fear that the current rate of inflation could escalate into hyperinflation.

A further cost of anticipated inflation, not associated with the decline in the real stock of money, is the administrative cost of continually changing prices.

The inflation tax

Inflation is a tax on holding money balances. When inflation rises from 0 to x per cent in Figure 20.3 the public have to pay x per cent more for holding Om_1

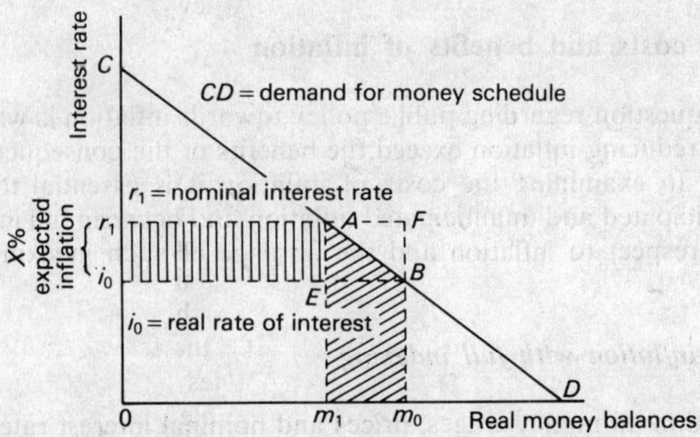

FIGURE 20.3 *The cost of inflation due to the increased cost of operating payments mechanism, and the inflation tax*

real money balances. The additional amount paid is given by rectangle $i_0 r_1 AE$, which is the inflation tax revenue. The tax base is the quantity of real money held, Om_1, and the tax rate is the inflation rate of x per cent.

In effect the government secures goods and services by issuing money. The inflation reduces the real value of money balances and thus diminishes the purchasing power of money-holders. The inflation tax thus transfers purchasing power from those being taxed to the government in just the same way as do direct taxes on income and indirect taxes on goods and services.

If, as is usual in welfare analysis, one gives equal weight to the money costs and benefits of different groups in society, then the tax revenue is just a transfer payment and is not a cost to society as a whole. The cost of collecting the tax revenue is the welfare lost because fewer real money balances are held (that is, area $m_1 ABm_0$) and this is a cost to society as a whole due to the use of human effort and other resources to lower the real balances held, as well as any psychic costs of operating with lower real balances.

Unanticipated inflation with full indexing

If the actual rate of inflation exceeds the anticipated rate, then the demand for real money balances is greater than it would be if the public had fully anticipated the inflation. The net welfare loss due to holding fewer real money balances is therefore lower. However, holders of money are worse off than if they had correctly anticipated inflation because they end up paying more for money balances than they would have chosen to do had they known the rate of inflation. The government gains by this because its inflation tax revenue is thereby larger. If we value the welfare of money-holders and the government sector equally, then all that has happened is a transfer of resources. So long as the public continues to expect zero inflation there is no net cost to society of collecting the inflation tax. As the expected rate of inflation increases and the demand for real money balances falls, the cost of collecting the inflation tax rises.

One would expect the administrative costs of price changes to be greater under unanticipated inflation with full indexing because of the need to adjust instantaneously to changes in the general price level.

Unanticipated inflation without indexing

The normal situation is that while the expected rate of inflation is positive, the actual rate is not correctly anticipated. In addition, full indexing is not adopted either because it is administratively expensive or because of a reluctance to accept that inflation is a permanent state of affairs. In Britain and other countries with a similar post-war inflation history there are few prices, wages or rates of return that are automatically linked to the general price index. This means that individual prices adjust at different rates so that relative prices and rates of return are more variable than under a stable price level. Relative price variability does appear to be greater as inflation gets higher (see Fischer and Modigliani [33]). The combination of unanticipated inflation and the absence of indexing makes for considerable uncertainty about current as well as future relative prices. This means that the price mechanism becomes less efficient as a communication mechanism. Economic agents have to devote more resources to acquiring information about relative prices. While the costs of this loss of efficiency are very difficult to quantify, some economists (e.g. Okun [34]) do believe them to be quite substantial. Friedman [35] has suggested that higher inflation causes higher unemployment because it impairs the functioning of the price mechanism.

A further problem with unanticipated, non-indexed inflation is that it redistributes income and wealth in ways which are not the outcome of a deliberate and openly debated public policy. People on fixed incomes or who do not belong to trade unions with bargaining power will suffer a decline in their relative incomes. When the tax system is not adjusted inflation brings about various changes in relative tax burdens. However, the empirical evidence indicates that income redistribution as a result of inflation has been quite minor. There is some evidence to suggest that lower-income groups have benefited from inflation as have wage-earners as a whole at the expense of profits.

Wealth redistribution, however, has been more significant. All holders of financial assets denominated in nominal terms (e.g. bonds, building society deposits) experience a reduction in real wealth which debtors gain from the decline in the real value of their debts. One effect of this is a transfer of wealth from the old, who have accumulated assets, to the young, who incur more debt. In contrast, holders of real assets, such as property and works of art, are generally not made worse off by inflation as real asset prices rise secularly with the general price index, and may even rise more rapidly than prices in general because of speculative activity. It would appear that the poorest and richest households have experienced the largest reductions in real wealth due to inflation. (The poorest because they hold a large proportion of their wealth in money and near-monies and have not moved out in response to inflation, and the richest because they hold a larger proportion of their wealth in financial assets and have little debt.) It has been estimated that the size of wealth redistributions arising from a 1 per cent unanticipated increase in the price level is about 1 per cent of GNP (Fischer and Modigliani [33]).

In conventional welfare calculus redistribution from one group to another brings about no net social cost. However, the social cost will be evaluated as positive if one dislikes the particular redistribution that occurs or the social dissension that it promotes. The latter cost is probably the more important as inflation requires the various interest groups in society to engage in continual efforts to prevent their income and wealth being redistributed to others. The whole process then breeds dissatisfaction and conflict.

The costs arising from unanticipated non-indexed inflation are in addition to those arising from anticipated inflation.

A summary of the costs of inflation

The main constituents of the costs of inflation are:

1. The welfare loss from economising on money balances.

2. The price mechanism becomes less efficient and more resources have to be spent on changing prices and gathering information about prices.
3. Redistribution causes social conflict.
4. Greater uncertainty may reduce both consumption and investment and so impair economic performance (see Chapters 12 and 13).

Although some of the costs of inflation are in principle quantifiable, the fear that inflation weakens the fabric of society by dislocating the price system and creating social conflict cannot be quantified.

Benefits of inflation

On the other side of the calculation there are possible benefits from inflation itself or from living with the current rate of inflation rather than reducing it.

One possible benefit is that the inflation tax is a less costly way of raising tax revenue than other forms of taxation. This proposition has yet to be established and is likely to be more relevant for less developed economies.

Another suggested benefit of inflation is that at relatively low levels it provides an escape valve for social tensions. One argument is that prices and wages are sticky downwards. This means that the only way the relative prices of some goods and services (including labour services) can be raised without causing high unemployment is by increasing their absolute price and thus raising the general price level. Similarly if the total sum of factor claims upon the national income exceeds national output, then the easiest way to resolve this incompatibility is by allowing inflation.

If one believes in the dubious proposition that there is a permanent trade-off between unemployment and inflation, then inflation is beneficial because it lowers unemployment and increases output. Even in the absence of any long-run trade-off, the existence of a short-run trade-off may well be appealing to governments and the electorate as current benefits can be obtained while the costs are incurred in the future.

Most of the benefits of inflation (a low cost of collecting the inflation tax, easing the pain of relative price adjustment or increasing real output) rely on inflation being unanticipated. The beneficial effects derive from the actions economic agents take when they are deceived about prices. Regarding policies which rest on deception as socially desirable can be questioned on ethical grounds. One may hold that inflation of itself brings no social benefits but that once a country has got itself embroiled with inflation, then policies to reduce that rate of inflation incur unemployment costs which exceed the costs of living with the current rate of inflation. Inflation can be made less painful by indexing and should be stabilised at its current level. Against this view is the belief that the increase in unemployment over and above what it would otherwise be is only temporary whereas the benefits of lower inflation are permanent. In addition, it appears to be difficult for governments to stabilise the rate of inflation.

Making a collective rational choice on how much inflation it is desirable to have seems an almost impossible task. First, it is difficult to quantify the net benefits of reducing inflation by a given amount; and second, the net benefits of such a policy are not equally distributed over interest groups or over time.

20.6 Policies to reduce inflation

Given that it is desirable to reduce the rate of inflation, we next need to consider the ways in which this objective can be achieved. The different hypotheses regarding the causes of inflation imply different policy measures. (See House of Commons [1] ch. 4 for a fuller summary of contemporary views.)

The monetarist way

Monetarists consider that inflation cannot be reduced without bringing down the rate of growth of the domestic money supply in a closed economy or one with flexible exchange rates. To do this the source of monetary expansion, which is the high-powered money used to finance the government budget deficit, must be checked. This can be done in several ways. One is to finance a greater proportion of the existing budget deficit by selling government bonds. If the higher interest rates and consequent crowding out this brings is disliked, then the size of the budget deficit can be reduced. This can be done by raising taxation or by reducing the volume of public expenditure.

Under a fixed exchange rate a country cannot pursue an independent policy with respect to inflation. It can only isolate itself from other countries' inflation by adopting a flexible exchange rate which it allows to appreciate by restraining the rate of domestic credit expansion. It is not possible to deduce *a priori* whether the world as a whole is likely to have a higher inflation rate under fixed exchange rates than under flexible one (see Corden [36] for discussion of this point).

Monetarists recognise that, because of the short-run Phillips relation, reducing inflation is likely to bring about a temporary increase in unemployment while expected inflation exceeds the actual rate. Those monetarists who think expectations are slow to adjust favour a gradual reduction in the rate of growth of the money supply. Those who hold that expectations are formed rationally advocate a quick reduction in monetary growth which is pre-announced by the government in the form of definite targets for the money supply. If the private sector can be convinced that the government will stick to its target for lower monetary growth, then expectations regarding inflation will adjust downwards quickly. The increase in unemployment will thereby be minimised.

Structuralist policy recommendations

Many structuralists regard unemployment and inflation as unconnected even in the short run. Thus any policies which are seen as intending to bring down inflation by reducing aggregate demand and increasing unemployment are doomed to failure. Unemployment will rise without inflation being reduced, except possibly by a level of unemployment too horrible to contemplate. In fact it is argued that inflation might even increase because wage push is exacerbated by restrictionary monetary and fiscal policies which widen the real wage aspiration gap.

This theoretical approach leads to policy recommendations that inflation must be tackled by attending to the relevant structural features in the economy. The most popular remedy is some variant of direct prices and income control. At one extreme, government control of individual prices and wages is enforced by law. At the other, the policy is voluntary and consists of tripartite discussions between government, trade unions and employers' representatives in order to agree on some formula or standard for setting wages and prices. The alternative means of achieving structural change by legislation which reduces trade union power is not much favoured by structuralists. Prices and incomes policy is recommended in the hope that it will reduce inflation without incurring the cost of unemployment. It is expected to work either directly by preventing wage and price increases and/or via bringing down expected inflation. However, the empirical evidence regarding the efficacy of prices and incomes policies is not favourable (see studies in Parkin and Sumner [37] and Fallick and Elliott [38]).

Such policies may temporarily reduce inflation by a small amount when they are in operation. However, once discarded, as they have been repeatedly in the United Kingdom, wage increases accelerate. They may do so at an even faster rate than if real wages had not been held down by the policy. So at best it would appear that incomes policies are effective in the short run but may even be counter-productive over the long term. Nevertheless, they remain a popular short-term expedient.

References

[1] House of Commons, *Third Report from the Treasury and Civil Service Committee*, Session 1980–1, vol. 1, ch. 4 (London: HMSO, 1981).

[2] Institute of Economic Affairs, *Inflation: Causes, Consequences and Cures* (London: IEA, 1974).

[3] M. Friedman, *Unemployment versus Inflation* (London: Institute of Economic Affairs, 1975).

[4] D. Laidler and M. Parkin, 'Inflation: a Survey', *Economic Journal*, 85 (1975); reprinted in P. G. Korliras and R. Thorn (eds), *Modern Macroeconomics* (New York: Harper & Row, 1979).

[5] D. Laidler, 'Inflation in Britain: a Monetarist Perspective', *American Economic Review*, 66, 4 (September 1976).

[6] M. Parkin, 'Alternative Explanations of United Kingdom Inflation: a Survey', in M. Parkin and M. Sumner (eds), *Inflation in the United Kingdom* (Manchester University Press, 1978).

[7] A. K. Swoboda, 'Monetary Approaches to World Wide Inflation', in L. B. Krause and W. S. Salant (eds), *Worldwide Inflation* (Washington, D.C.: Brookings Institution, 1977).

[8] R. Kahn, 'Inflation: a Keynesian View', *Scottish Journal of Political Economy*, 23, 1 (1976).

[9] G. Maynard and W. van Ryckeghem, *A World of Inflation* (London: Batsford, 1976).

[10] R. E. Rowthorn, 'Conflict, Inflation and Money', *Cambridge Journal of Economics*, 1 (1977).

[11] T. Scitovsky, 'Market Power and Inflation', *Economica*, 45 (August 1978).

[12] R. Coghlan, *The Theory of Money and Finance* (London: Macmillan, 1980) ch. 3.

[13] M. Parkin and G. Zis (eds), *Inflation in Open Economies* (Manchester University Press, 1976).

[14] M. Parkin and G. Zis (eds), *Inflation in the World Economy* (Manchester University Press, 1976).

[15] N. Duck *et al.*, 'The Determination of the Rate of Change of Wages and Prices in the Fixed Exchange Rate World', in Parkin and Zis (eds), *Inflation in the World Economy.*

[16] R. Cross and D. Laidler, 'Inflation, Excess Demand and Expectations in Fixed Exchange Rate Open Economies: Some Preliminary Empirical Results', in Parkin and Zis (eds), *Inflation in the World Economy.*

[17] R. Gordon, 'World Inflation and Monetary Accommodation in Eight Countries', *Brookings Papers on Economic Activity*, 2 (1977).

[18] J. Sachs, 'Wages, Profits and Macroeconomic Adjustment: a Comparative Study', *Brookings Papers on Economic Activity*, 2 (1979).

[19] J. Johnston and M. Timbrell, 'Empirical Tests of a Bargaining Theory of Wage Rate Determination', in D. Laidler and D. Purdy (eds), *Inflation and Labour Markets* (Manchester University Press, 1974).

[20] S. Henry *et al.*, 'Models of Inflation in the UK: an Evaluation', *National Institute Economic Review* (August 1976).

[21] G. Perry, 'Determinants of Wage Inflation around the World', *Brookings Papers on Economic Activity*, 2 (1975).

[22] W. Nordhaus, 'The World Wide Wage Explosion', *Brookings Papers on Economic Activity*, 2 (1972).

[26] D. Sargan, 'A Model of Wage–Price Inflation', *Review of Economic Studies* (1980).

[24] W. Godley, 'Inflation in the United Kingdom', in L. B. Krause and W. S. Salant (eds), *Worldwide Inflation* (Washington, D.C.: Brookings Institution, 1979).

[25] A. Hines, 'Wage Inflation in the United Kingdom 1893–1961', *Review of Economic Studies* (1964).

[26] D. Purdy and G. Zis, 'Trade Unions and Wage Inflation in the United Kingdom: a Reappraisal', in D. Laidler and D. Purdy (eds), *Inflation and Labour Markets* (Manchester University Press, 1974).

[27] C. Mulvey and M. Gregory, 'The Hines Wage Inflation Model', *Manchester School*, 45 (March 1977).

[28] L. Godfrey, 'The Phillips Curve: Incomes Policy and Trade Union Effects', in H. Johnson and A. Nobay (eds), *The Current Inflation* (London: Macmillan, 1971).

[29] J. Taylor, 'Wage Inflation, Unemployment and the Organized Pressure for Higher Wages in the UK, 1961–71', in J. M. Parkin and A. Nobay (eds), *Contemporary Issues in Economics* (London: Macmillan, 1975).

[30] R. Ward and G. Zis, 'Trade Union Militancy as an Explanation of Inflation: an International Comparison', *Manchester School*, 42 (March 1974).

[31] D. Laidler, 'Inflation: Alternative Explanations and Policies: Tests on Data Drawn from Six Countries', in K. Brunner and A. Meltzer (eds), *Institutions, Policies and Economic Performance*, Carnegie–Rochester Conference Series on Public Policy (Amsterdam: North-Holland, 1976).

[32] G. Zis, 'On the Role of Strike Variables in United Kingdom Wage Equations', *Scottish Journal of Political Economy*, 24 (1977).

[33] S. Fischer and F. Modigliani, 'Towards an Understanding of the Real Effects and Costs of Inflation', *Weltwirtschaftliches Archiv*, 114 (1979).

[34] A. Okun, 'Inflation: its Mechanics and Welfare Costs', *Brookings Papers on Economic Activity*, 2 (1975).

[35] M. Friedman, 'Nobel Lecture: Inflation and Unemployment', *Journal of Political Economy*, 85, 3 (June 1977).

[36] W. M. Corden, 'Inflation and the Exchange Rate Regime', *Scandinavian Journal of Economics* (1976).

[37] M. Parkin and M. Sumner (eds), *Incomes Policy and Inflation* (Manchester University Press, 1972).

[38] J. L. Fallick and R. F. Elliott, *Incomes Policies, Inflation and Relative Pay* (London: Allen & Unwin, 1981).

Further reading

R. J. Gordon, 'Recent Developments in the Theory of Inflation and Unemployment', *Journal of Monetary Economics*, 1976; reprinted in P. G. Korliras and R. Thorn (eds), *Modern Macroeconomics* (New York: Harper & Row, 1979). Also House of Commons [1], Laidler and Parkin [4], Parkin [6], Kahn [8], Gordon [17] and Fischer and Modigliani [33].

V ECONOMIC POLICY

Throughout the book policy issues have been quite thoroughly discussed in the context of the theories upon which particular recommendations are based. This is not repeated here except in summary form at the end (Chapter 23).

Chapter 21 is concerned with the modifications which have to be made to the analysis of fiscal and monetary policy when we take account of the effect of the government's financing of its budget deficit or surplus on private-sector wealth. Chapter 22 outlines the theory of economic policy which underlies Keynesian policy prescriptions and presents a critique of this theory.

Finally, Chapter 23 gives an overview of the whole book by summarising the relationship between the theories and the policy conclusions of the two major schools of thought in macroeconomics.

21 Policy Analysis when Asset Stocks Adjust

The analysis of monetary and fiscal policies which we carried out in Chapter 4 and subsequent chapters did not allow for the fact that such policies imply changes in the size and composition of the private sector's wealth. These in turn will change the private sector's demand for goods and financial assets. This must be taken account of if there is to be a complete and consistent analysis of policy.[1]

21.1 The government budget constraint

Government expenditure can be financed in three ways:

(a) by levying taxes,
(b) by selling interest-bearing government debt, which we will collectively term 'bonds', and
(c) by issuing non-interest-bearing high-powered money.

The fact that the government has to finance any difference between its expenditure and its tax revenues by changing the stock of high-powered money and/or bonds is known as the *government budget constraint*. If the government runs a budget deficit, which occurs when G exceeds T in equation 21.1 below, it must be financed by additional government bonds or by extra money balances. Hence

$$\underbrace{G_t - T_t}_{\text{budget deficit}} = \underbrace{\frac{B_t - B_{t-1}}{i}}_{\text{increase in stock of bonds}} + \underbrace{H_t - H_{t-1}}_{\text{increase in stock of high-powered money}} \qquad (21.1)$$

[1] This problem did not surface until the mid-1960s, when it was raised by Ott and Ott [1] and Christ [2]. Since then the literature on the subject has grown apace.

where

G = government expenditure
H = high-powered money (see Chapter 9, p. 150)
T = tax revenues
B = the number of government bonds outstanding; each bond pays its owner £1 per year in interest payments in perpetuity; total interest payments by the government are therefore £B
i = current rate of interest on bonds
B/i = total market value of outstanding government bonds; as bonds are assumed to be perpetuities, their present value can be obtained by applying this simple discounting formula.

If tax revenues exceed government expenditure, then there is a budget surplus which must be financed either by withdrawing bonds and/or high-powered money.

To see the problem posed for the closed-economy Keynesian *ISLM* model of Chapter 4 by the government budget constraint let us assume that the budget is initially balanced. The government then increases its expenditure while tax rates remain unaltered and finances the ensuing budget deficit by selling additional bonds to the private sector. As the private sector's stock of financial assets has increased, it is therefore wealthier. If consumption depends positively on total net wealth,[1] then the *IS* curve shifts up to the right when net wealth increases. If the demand for money also depends positively on total net wealth, then the wealth effect will cause the *LM* function to shift to the left. So we can no longer analyse a pure fiscal policy as in Chapter 4 where we assumed the *LM* function remained unchanged and the *IS* curve only shifted outwards once, due to the initial increase in government expenditure.[2] As long as the government budget remains unbalanced, the *IS* and *LM* functions are shifting so the economy cannot be in long-run equilibrium.

The inclusion of the government budget constraint and private-sector wealth effects makes the *ISLM* model dynamic without any additional changes in specification being necessary. Any change which unbalances the government budget makes the private sector's behaviour depend on *last* period's bond and money stocks as well as the current period's stocks. This is because private-sector portfolios are absorbing the changes in financial asset stocks determined by equation 21.1. If we are modelling a closed stationary economy (such as the traditional *ISLM* model which assumes that current investment has no discernible impact on the stock of real capital), then long-run equilibrium can only be attained when the government budget is balanced.[3]

[1] See Chapter 6 (p. 94) for a definition of net wealth.

[2] The traditional *ISLM* model therefore has no explicit wealth effects in the consumption or demand for money functions. This means that any increase in wealth must be entirely spent on bonds. The bond market has been eliminated by applying Walras's law, so this asymmetrical wealth effect gets no explicit consideration.

[3] If the economy is in non-stationary equilibrium, either because real income is growing at a steady rate or there is a steady rate of inflation, then private-sector portfolios need to absorb extra assets to remain in equilibrium. A government budget

This chapter is concerned with analysing the effects on GNP of monetary and fiscal policy when the conditions required for long-run equilibrium are taken account of. To do this the government budget constraint and its effects on private-sector wealth must be included in the model.

An examination of the literature reveals the absence of determinate and robust analytical results. The effects of fiscal and monetary policies on GNP are not generally determinate because they depend on the stability properties of the model (that is, on the conditions required for stable equilibrium). They are not robust because they are sensitive to changes in the specification of the determinants of aggregate demand and supply. All we can do in this chapter is examine the main policy issues which have been debated and outline some of the analytical results. It must be borne in mind that the conclusions reached about the effects of policy measures in any economic model are crucially dependent on the assumptions made.

21.2 The main policy issues

The government budget constraint draws attention to the fact that fiscal policy has financial implications because it will affect the size and composition of the stock of government liabilities which are held as assets by the private sector. Fiscal and monetary policy are closely related and need therefore to be examined together. Definitions of what constitutes pure fiscal policy and pure monetary policy vary. Fiscal policy involves an *exogenous* change in either government expenditure or tax revenues enacted by the appropriate authorities. An endogenous rise in tax revenues because national income has risen while tax rates are fixed does not constitute a change in fiscal policy. One way of defining a pure fiscal policy is that it should involve no change in the money supply (in a stationary economy). But the ensuing change in the stock of bonds will alter the *proportion* in which assets are held and so will have financial effects. A pure monetary policy involves only a change in the composition of the government's liabilities with no exogenous change in government expenditure or tax rates. The money supply is increased (decreased) by open-market purchases (sales) of government bonds. Such action will initially change the ratios in which money and bonds are held, as does a bond-financed fiscal policy change.

There are three main types of policy which we shall discuss in this chapter and we shall assume that before each policy change is initiated the government budget is in equilibrium:

POLICY A A sustained increase in government expenditure, G, financed by bond sales. The money stock remains unchanged.

---

deficit can be consistent with steady-state equilibrium provided that the government's financing policies increase the stock of financial assets at the same rate as the private sector's demand for them grows.

POLICY B A sustained increase in G financed by issuing more money. The stock of bonds stays constant.

POLICY C An increase in the money supply brought about by an open-market purchase of government bonds. Tax rates and G remain unchanged.

In practice any particular policy measure can be some combination of all the above policies. A decrease in tax rates will have a similar impact to an increase in G. In Keynesian models a decrease in tax rates will initially have a smaller expansionary impact than an equivalent increase in G if some of the resulting increase in disposable income is saved. Therefore, tax-rate changes only differ from changes in G in the size of the impact or first-round multiplier. A decrease in G has the opposite effect to an increase in G. Decreases in G and tax-rate changes will not be analysed any further in this chapter.

By analysing policies A, B and C we can offer answers to some of the main controversial issues concerning the effects of macro policy. The issues selected for examination are as follows:

1. What sort of impact does fiscal policy have on nominal national income?
2. Is this impact greater when fiscal policy is financed by bonds or when financed by money?
3. Do changes in the supply of money affect real and nominal national income in the short run and in the long run?
4. Does the way the money supply is changed affect its impact on national income?

Monetarists and Keynesians tend to give a different set of answers to these questions. One important reason for this is that the answers are deduced from manipulating theoretical models which are constructed on the basis of different assumptions. There are three important areas where model specifications differ. These are as follows:

(a) The specification of the aggregate demand function, in particular the way wealth effects are included.
(b) The specification of both short-run and long-run aggregate supply functions.
(c) Whether the economy is closed or open and, if open, whether the exchange rate is fixed or flexible. Of the three models considered in this chapter, two are closed; the third, an open Keynesian model, assumes a fixed exchange rate.

21.3 Policy analysis in a closed Keynesian economy[1]

A typical Keynesian model specifies consumption as a positive function of disposable income and wealth. Disposable income is defined as national

[1] A frequently cited analysis is that by Blinder and Solow [3], which the model presented here follows closely.

income plus interest payments received by private-sector government bond-holders minus tax revenues (see equation 21.2 below). Investment depends upon the interest rate, the level of national income and the existing stock of capital. The demand for money depends upon the interest rate, wealth and income. The only financial assets considered are money and government bonds. We now include the government budget constraint and distinguish between two kinds of government expenditure, that on interest payments to bond-holders, which equals B, and the rest, G_0. G_0 is kept constant in nominal terms but B will vary from period to period as long as output is changing and budget deficits or surpluses occur and alter the number of outstanding bonds. To start with we make the Keynesian assumption that output is in perfectly elastic supply so we can set the price level at $P = 1$. The capital stock, $\bar{K}$, is assumed constant and the economy is closed.

A Keynesian closed economy with perfectly elastic supply

The model is set out below:

$$Y_t^D = C[(1 - t)(Y_t + B_t) - T_0] + I(i_t, Y_t, \bar{K}) + G_0 \quad IS \text{ function} \quad (21.2)$$

$$M_t^D = L(i_t, Y_t, W_t) = M_0^S = mH_0 \quad LM \text{ function} \quad (21.3)$$

$$G_0 + (1 - t)B_t - T_0 - tY_t = B_t - B_{t-1} + H_t - H_{t-1} \quad \text{Government budget constraint} \quad (21.4)$$

$$Y_t^S = Y_t^D \quad (P = 1) \quad \text{Aggregate supply} \quad (21.5)$$

where

Y^D = aggregate demand
Y^S = aggregate supply
M^S = money supply
m = bank multiplier
H = high-powered money
$W = M^S + B/i + \bar{K}$ = private-sector net wealth
t = tax rate (T_0 = exogenous tax revenues)
$G_0 + B_t$ = government expenditure
$T_0 + t(Y_t + B_t)$ = tax revenues

We have already established (p. 408) that the condition for long-run equilibrium in a stationary closed economy is that the government budget is balanced, that is

$$G_0 + (1 - t)B_t = T_0 + tY_t \quad (21.6)$$

Long-run fiscal policy effects

From the long-run equilibrium condition (21.6) one can derive the long-run change in output due to an exogenous change in G at constant tax rates. In this

Keynesian model the long-run multiplier with respect to G is larger than the multiplier derived in the traditional *ISLM* model of Chapter 4. The latter is the first-period multiplier in this model, given a one-period lag before wealth effects are felt. The long-run multiplier is larger than the short-run one because for long-run equilibrium income has to rise until it reaches the level at which tax revenues will just match the higher level of government spending. Rearranging equation 21.6 gives

$$Y_t = \frac{G_0 - T_0 + (1-t)B_t}{t} \tag{21.6a}$$

In this model income is determined by government policy only.

The long-run government expenditure multiplier can be obtained by differentiating equation 21.6a with respect to G, given that the model is in fact stable and so can return to equilibrium. The multiplier for an entirely bond-financed increase in G is

$$\left.\frac{dY}{dG}\right|_{H=H_0} = \frac{1}{t} + \frac{(1-t)}{t}\frac{dB}{dG} \tag{21.7}$$

The stock of bonds continues to rise so long as the budget deficit persists because we are assuming a purely bond-financed fiscal measure. As the bond stock increases, government expenditure continues to rise because of the additional interest payments that have to be made to bond-holders. Given that the private sector is willing to hold dB/dG more bonds in long-run equilibrium (that is, $dB/dG > 0$), then the G multiplier must be positive.

The G multiplier for a completely money-financed deficit is

$$\left.\frac{dY}{dG}\right|_{B=B_0} = \frac{1}{t} \tag{21.8}$$

since $dB/dG = 0$ by assumption.

The all-money finance (Policy B) multiplier is smaller than the all-bonds finance (Policy A) multiplier because in the latter case total government expenditure rises further due to the additional interest payments. In order to balance the budget, Policy A requires national income to attain a higher level in final equilibrium than Policy B.

Long-run effect of monetary policy

Finally, let us consider the long-run impact of an open-market purchase of bonds, Policy C. Initially the stock of net wealth is unaffected; only its composition has changed with the increase in the stock of money balances. In a Keynesian model without the government budget constraint the interest rate falls and aggregate demand rises. Once the budget constraint is included we need to take account of the consequent budget surplus. This occurs because government interest payments have fallen with the initial decline in the bond stock and tax revenues rise as output rises. The budget surplus is financed by withdrawing bonds and/or money. Private-sector net wealth declines and aggregate demand and output start to fall. By how much output finally declines depends on how many bonds are withdrawn, as is shown by equation 21.6a. The lower the final stock of bonds, the smaller is government expenditure on interest payments, and consequently the lower the level of national income required to achieve budget balance.

Short-run effects of fiscal policy

So far we have only considered the long-run effects of the policy. The short-run effects are also important, particularly for politicians and policy-makers. Once we include the government budget constraint, the *ISLM* diagram can no longer produce unambiguous results (as it did in Chapter 4). While the government budget is unbalanced, wealth effects will shift the *IS* function and the *LM* function. The extent of these shifts determines output, which in turn affects the government budget. Thus the *IS* and *LM* functions are no longer independent of each other. We shall continue to use a modified *ISLM* diagram as a heuristic device to show the possible qualitative effects of policy changes over a number of time periods.[1]

Consider first an increase in G financed only by bonds. At the initial level of output the government budget is balanced. The *IS* curve in Figure 21.1 shifts outwards from IS_0 to IS_1. If we assume that the wealth effects of the additional bonds do not affect the private sector until the second and subsequent time periods, then the first-period impact on output is to raise it from y_0 to y_1, while the interest rate rises to i_1. This is the same result as that obtained with the traditional *ISLM* model in Chapter 4.

However, further changes now occur in the subsequent periods. The additional wealth increases consumption and so shifts the IS_1 curve further to the right. This exerts an expansionary influence. However, the increase in

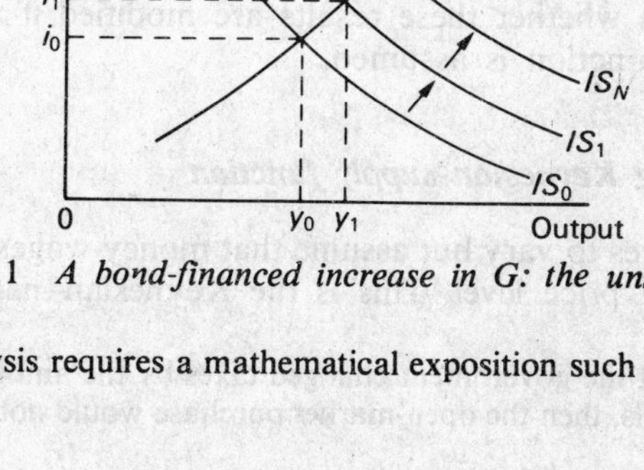

FIGURE 21.1 *A bond-financed increase in G: the unstable case*

[1] More precise analysis requires a mathematical exposition such as that of Turnovsky [4].

wealth also stimulates a demand for additional money balances. As wealth increases the *LM* curve shifts to the left and this has a contractionary effect. So long as the budget remains unbalanced wealth continues to change and the *IS* and *LM* curves to shift. Whether national income continues to increase towards its stable long-run value given by equation 21.6a depends on the *IS* curve shifting to a greater extent than the *LM* curve, ensuring that the expansionary influence of wealth exceeds its contractionary impact. If this condition is not satisfied and the *LM* curve shifts further than the *IS* curve (as in Figure 21.1), the model becomes unstable. The private sector remains unwilling to hold the increasing stock of government bonds, the interest rate rises and aggregate demand falls along any given *IS* curve. As output falls revenues decline while interest payments on the ever-expanding stock of government bonds continue to escalate. The budget deficit persists and so equilibrium cannot be attained. A stable model requires that, following the increase in *G*, tax revenues increase at a faster rate than government expenditure on bond interest payments, so that the budget deficit is continually declining.

An entirely money-financed increase in *G* will generally be stable: there is no increase in the stock of bonds and so no further increase in government spending on interest payments. The net effect on the *LM* curve of an increase in wealth plus an increase in the money supply is to shift it to the right as well. Output therefore unambiguously increases.

Summary

The closed-economy Keynesian model, with a government budget constraint and perfectly elastic aggregate supply, produces typically Keynesian answers to questions 1 to 4 on page 410, provided that the conditions for stability are satisfied. Fiscal policy does have an impact on real output, which in the long run is greater for bond finance (given a stable model) than for money finance. The way the money supply is changed does matter. If the money supply is increased by a budget deficit it is expansionary, whereas if it is increased by open-market operations it is contractionary. The last result may seem intuitively unappealing but it stems from assuming that open-market purchases are accompanied by a subsequent fiscal contraction.[1] Conversely open-market sales of bonds increase output.

This type of model produces strong Keynesian policy conclusions. Even if there is a danger that bond-financed government expenditure is unstable, instability can be avoided by using some proportion of money finance. It now remains to be seen whether these results are modified if a different form of aggregate supply function is assumed.

An upward-sloping Keynesian supply function

We now allow prices to vary but assume that money wages do not adjust fully for changes in the price level. This is the Keynesian–neoclassical synthesis

[1] If we assumed that the government changed taxes by the amount its expenditure on interest payments falls, then the open-market purchase would not cause a contraction.

model of Chapter 6 with the addition of wealth effects and the government budget constraint. The aggregate supply of output will rise when the real wage rate falls. Keynesians (e.g. Blinder and Solow [3], Tobin and Buiter [5]) conclude that the same type of policy analysis derived from fixed-price Keynesian models also applies to variable-price Keynesian models. The major difference is that a fiscal stimulus now increases nominal income. Real output only rises if money wages do not adjust fully to the higher price level, so that real wages fall and the demand for labour increases. In addition, workers must be willing to supply labour in excess of the amount previously employed, even though the real wage rate has fallen. A fiscal expansion will increase nominal national income. Part of this increase in nominal income will be due to a rise in real income, *provided that the Keynesian aggregate supply assumptions hold.*

Similar conclusions can be obtained from Keynesian models which incorporate a continuing rate of inflation which becomes constant in long-term equilibrium. The Phillips relation now provides the Keynesian aggregate supply function given that there is a long-run trade-off between inflation and unemployment because the rate of increase of money wages is never fully adjusted for the expected rate of inflation (i.e. $0 < \alpha < 1$). Consequently one can expect that in a Keynesian world fiscal expansion will at first increase real output but that after a while prices and money wages rise and real output falls back towards its initial level. There will only be a long-run increase in real output if the real wage rate is permanently below what it would otherwise have been.

21.4 New Cambridge: a Keynesian open-economy model

The main purpose of the New Cambridge group of British economists (see Fetherston and Godley [6]) is to show that Keynesian results can be obtained in an open-economy model in which the constraint imposed by the requirement of asset portfolio equilibrium is taken account of. The aim is to refute the deduction of the monetary approach to the balance of payments (see Chapter 11). This deduction is that policies which cause BOF imbalances can only have temporary effects on real output because they alter the domestic money supply and so cause continuing portfolio adjustment until the BOF becomes zero. The New Cambridge economists argue that a non-zero BOF is consistent with long-run equilibrium because the monetary impact of BOF imbalances can be sterilised by running a government budget deficit or surplus of the required amount.[1] This argument is explained below.

In an open economy the government can finance its budget deficit or surplus by selling its bonds to domestic residents, ΔB^D, or to foreigners, ΔB^F, or by expanding the domestic credit part, DC, of high-powered money. The government budget constraint now becomes

$$G - T \equiv \Delta B^D + \Delta B^F + \Delta DC \tag{21.9}$$

[1] This argument was also advanced by a non-Cambridge economist, Currie [7].

The national income accounting identity in an open economy was derived in Chapter 7 (p. 109) and is

$$Y - (C + I + G) \equiv X - F \qquad (21.10)$$

where $X =$ exports, and $F =$ imports, measured in domestic currency values.

By including tax revenues, T, we can rewrite 21.10 as

$$\{(Y - T) - (C + I)\} - (G - T) \equiv X - F \qquad (21.11)$$

Now the term in brace brackets in equation 21.11 is private-sector disposable income minus private-sector expenditure and is identical to the private sector's net acquisition of financial assets. A unique feature of the New Cambridge model is its private expenditure function. It is assumed that the private sector's desired stock of financial assets is a fixed proportion of its disposable income. Thus the net acquisition of financial assets by the private sector will only remain positive over an extended time period if disposable income is growing. If the economy is in stationary long-run equilibrium, then $\Delta(Y - T) = 0$, and so

$$(Y - T) - (C + I) = 0 \qquad (21.12)$$

In addition, it is assumed that if output changes, the induced asset stock adjustment is quite rapid and is completed within a year. Thus if income rises from one stationary equilibrium to another, the private sector's net acquisition of assets is positive over the year, but by the end of the year a new desired level of financial asset stocks is attained so that equation 21.12 holds once more. When private-sector net financial asset acquisition is zero then from 21.12 and 21.11 we get that in equilibrium

$$-(G - T) = (X - F) \qquad (21.13)$$

Hence a government budget deficit (surplus) must be matched by an equal-sized current-account deficit (surplus) on the balance of payments. This result follows from the New Cambridge expenditure function. An appreciation of this point enables one to understand why the New Cambridge model specifies the private-sector expenditure function in the way that it does.

In long-run equilibrium the domestic private sector's asset holdings are constant, given a stationary economy. The New Cambridge economists argue that private-sector portfolio balance, which requires constant bond and money holdings, can be made consistent with imbalances on the government budget and on the balance of payments. Given that domestic residents' holdings of bonds must be constant for long-run portfolio balance (that is, $\Delta B^D = 0$) then the government's budget constraint becomes

$$G - T \equiv \Delta B^F + \Delta DC \qquad (21.14)$$

Long-run portfolio balance also requires that the money stock is constant. However, a non-zero BOF means that the foreign exchange component, FR, of high-powered money is changing since BOF $= \Delta FR$ (see Chapters 9 and 10, pp. 160, 164). Given that the private sector is not changing its net asset position then the BOF must equal the current account plus the net change in the stock of domestic government bonds held by foreigners, ΔB^F. Therefore, we have

$$\text{BOF} \equiv \Delta FR \equiv (X - F) + \Delta B^F \qquad (21.15)$$

Substituting $\Delta B^F = \Delta FR - (X - F)$ from 21.15 into equation 21.14 we get

$$G - T = \Delta FR - (X - F) + \Delta DC \tag{21.16}$$

Substituting $G - T = -(X - F)$ from equation 21.13 into 21.16 we get

$$\Delta FR = -\Delta DC$$

Therefore since $\Delta H = \Delta FR + \Delta DC$, ΔH must be zero. Thus high-powered money as well as domestic bond holdings remain unchanged while the government budget and BOF are both non-zero.

In the new Cambridge model a current-account deficit is prevented from reducing the money stock by the authorities selling government bonds to foreigners and by sterilising the remaining BOF deficit by increasing the domestic credit component of high-powered money to offset the decline in foreign exchange reserves. The other side of the operation is that the government budget deficit, which equals the current-account deficit, is financed by selling government bonds to foreigners and by domestic credit expansion. Similarly a current-account surplus is offset by a government budget surplus. The latter's financing requirements prevent the current-account surplus from expanding the domestic money supply.

Because the model reconciles a non-zero current-account and government budget imbalance with asset portfolio equilibrium in the private sector, then equation 21.13 becomes a long-run equilibrium condition from which the level of real aggregate demand is derived. Since $T = T_0 + ty$ and $F = fy$, while $\bar{G}$ and $\bar{X}$ are exogenous given a fixed exchange rate we get from 21.13 that aggregate demand is[1]

$$y = \frac{\bar{X} + \bar{G} - T_0}{t + f} \tag{21.17}$$

The supply side of the new Cambridge model is completely Keynesian. The aggregate supply function is perfectly elastic below full employment; the price level is determined by costs, in particular money wages, and is invariant with respect to changes in demand; the law of one price does not hold and import prices are determined by the UK price level and import tariffs. Therefore, supply of output is completely demand-determined up to full employment and is given by equation 21.17. Differentiating 21.17 with respect to G, t and f we get

$$\frac{dy}{dG} = \frac{1}{t + f} > 0$$

$$\frac{dy}{dt} = \frac{dy}{df} = -\frac{(\bar{X} + \bar{G} - T_0)}{(t + f)^2} < 0$$

Although fiscal policy is effective in raising output in the short to medium term, it is not greatly favoured by New Cambridge economists because of its effects

[1] This result and the portfolio balance open-economy model were first derived by McKinnon (see [8]).

on the current account. Starting from budget balance, an expansionary fiscal policy will cause a budget deficit which is reflected in an equal current-account deficit. If this continues for any length of time and foreigners are unwilling to buy unlimited amounts of government debt, then foreign exchange reserves become exhausted. A balance-of-payments crisis ensues and either the fiscal policy must be reversed or the exchange rate devalued. This is the familiar stop–go scenario that has plagued British economic policy and explains why New Cambridge economists advocate import controls. In their model 'import controls' are in effect an exogenous decrease in the marginal propensity to import without any retaliation from abroad which would reduce exports (see Blinder [9]). Because of their assumption that prices are unaffected by demand, the UK price level does not rise when 'import controls' are imposed. These assumptions, together with a Keynesian perfectly elastic supply function, are required to ensure that a policy of 'import controls' increases real output. The advantage of this policy over a fiscal expansion is that the current account improves. The government can run a budget surplus which sterilises the monetary impact of the current-account surplus. Given that the stock of domestic government bonds remains constant, so that $\Delta B^D = \Delta B^F = 0$, then from equations 21.13, 21.14 and 21.15 we get

$$-(G - T) = -\Delta DC = X - F = \text{BOF} = \Delta FR \qquad (21.18)$$

Since $-\Delta DC = \Delta FR$, then $\Delta H = 0$. Unlike the current-account deficit situation foreign exchange reserves for a small economy can rise indefinitely and so there is no monetary constraint to eventually force an adjustment of policy as in the fiscal expansion case. This is why import controls are presented as a solution to Britain's economic predicament.

The success of import controls is crucially dependent on New Cambridge's supply-side assumptions, the lack of foreign retaliation against exports and their denial of the law of one price. As we have seen in Chapters 11 (pp. 192–199) and 17 (pp. 327, 334), in an otherwise Keynesian model in which the law of one price holds policies which raise effective demand without lowering the real wage rate cannot increase the supply of output.

21.5 Monetarist policy analysis in a closed economy

Monetarists do not all speak with one voice: there are differences of emphasis and specification in monetarist models. However, monetarism is usually associated with the following views:

1. Fiscal policy is largely ineffective. Some monetarists accept that short-run real output responses occur but that these are later reversed and all the adjustment is absorbed by changes in the price level. Others deny that fiscal policy has any influence on output or prices.
2. Changes in the money supply have a strong impact on nominal income. To quote Friedman ([10] p. 217): 'I regard the description of our position as "money is all that matters for changes in *nominal* income and for short-run changes in real income" as an exaggeration but one that gives the right flavour of our conclusions.'

3. Too little is known about how the economy responds to discretionary policy measures to presume that they are more likely to be stabilising than destabilising. Instead the government should adopt constant policy rules, the budget should be balanced and money should grow at a constant rate, preferably one consistent with a stable price level.

One aspect of the monetarist critique of Keynesian policy conclusions has been the argument that government bonds are not net wealth (see Barro [11]).[1] If the stock of government bonds increases, the private sector takes account of the increased future tax payments required to pay the interest on the extra bonds and to redeem them. Private-sector liabilities therefore rise in line with the increased stock of government bonds so that there is a zero impact on net wealth. It has also been argued that increased government expenditure financed by bonds has no impact at all on aggregate demand. The current generation just increases its saving by the amount of G in order to leave larger bequests to future generations who have to pay the higher taxes required to meet the interest payments on the additional government bonds. The extra saving occurs because the current generation wants to leave its descendants with a given stock of net wealth. If future tax payments rise, then future generations need an equivalently higher stock of net wealth. Thus tax-financed and bond-financed government expenditure are equivalent: both have zero impact on aggregate demand.

However, the assumptions required for the above result appear unrealistic to many and the monetarist critique of Keynesian policy conclusions has not accorded particular importance to the assumption of a zero net wealth impact from government bonds.

A considerable number of monetarist models have been based on the *ISLM* framework (e.g. Friedman [10]). Another type of monetarist model which rejects the *ISLM* model has been developed by Brunner and Meltzer [12]. We shall now examine this model because it yields policy conclusions which differ significantly from Keynesian ones, while still taking into account the adjustment in asset stocks.

The Brunner–Meltzer critique of ISLM

Brunner and Meltzer's main quarrel with the *ISLM* model is that it has a very restricted range of assets, money and bonds, the latter market being eliminated by Walras's law. It contains no mechanism by which agents can shift their portfolios directly from money and bonds into real capital. They can only move between money and bonds. Such activity changes the one interest rate in the model and this is the only transmission mechanism from changes in the stock of financial assets to changes in the real capital stock. Brunner and Meltzer introduce a wider range of assets. In particular they include equities.[2]

[1] Keynesians have also used this argument – in order to demote the Pigou effect! (see Chapter 6, p. 94.)

[2] They also include financial intermediation. Banks take up earning assets and issue loans which form part of the money supply. To simplify we ignore the banking sector since its exclusion does not make any qualitative changes to the conclusions.

This means that individuals can shift directly from money or bonds into claims on real capital.

A further difference is that Brunner and Meltzer concentrate on stock adjustment rather than flow adjustment as in the *ISLM* model. The demand for each asset depends positively on its own rate of return and total net wealth and negatively on the rates of return on other assets. If equilibrium is disturbed by a change in the stock of one of the assets, then portfolio adjustments occur which change asset prices and rates of return. These in turn affect the level and composition of aggregate demand. For instance, if the government increases the stock of money, it sets off a sequence of portfolio adjustments. Given that money, bonds and equity are imperfect substitutes, an increase in the stock of money causes shifts into bonds and equity. The price of equity, which is the price that needs to be paid for a claim to a unit of existing real capital, rises. The stock market price of existing capital is now higher than the supply price of new capital goods. While the demand price of capital exceeds its supply price firms undertake net investment. This net investment reduces the demand price of capital and raises its supply price, and once the two are equal net investment ceases. This analysis is basically the same as that which uses Tobin's q to analyse investment demand (see Chapter 13, pp. 239–40). Brunner and Meltzer see the stock-adjustment formulation and the inclusion of a greater number of financial assets as important specifications. They provide many more channels to the transmission mechanism by which the financial and real sectors interact than is allowed in the *ISLM* model and in Keynesian econometric models.

A further important difference is their specification of the aggregate supply function. In the short run money wages are fixed and output rises with increases in the price level. In the long run money wages adjust to price changes, causing the short-run aggregate supply function to shift.

Having discarded the *ISLM* model, Brunner and Meltzer illustrate their mathematical model by means of the usual aggregate demand and supply functions in the P–y plane (using logs of y and P). Aggregate demand consists of government expenditure (in real terms) and private-sector demand, which depends on the various interest rates, the price level and wealth. The model also includes the government budget constraint. The government budget is balanced along line BB in Figure 21.2. As tax revenues rise with nominal income a lower

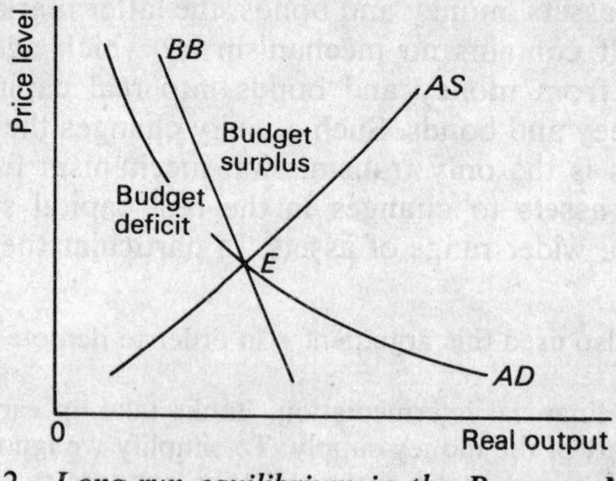

FIGURE 21.2 *Long-run equilibrium in the Brunner–Meltzer model*

level of real income combined with some higher price level will maintain budget balance. To the right of *BB* there is a budget surplus and to the left a deficit. As government expenditure changes because interest payments vary according to the outstanding stock of government bonds, the *BB* line will be shifting as income changes and causes budget imbalance.

Fiscal policy in the Brunner–Meltzer model

We start from an initial steady-state equilibrium at point *E* in Figure 21.3. An increase in government expenditure, financed by some constant proportion of bonds to money expenditure, shifts AD_0 up to the right to AD_1. The budget is now in deficit, so the *BB* line also shifts up to the right to B_1B_1. There is a short-run equilibrium at some point such as *F*, where aggregate demand is temporarily equal to aggregate supply.

Note that we have assumed that *BB* initially shifts further to the right than the *AD* curve. Point *F* is only a short-run equilibrium point because the government budget is in deficit. This ensures that there are further wealth effects which cause *AD* to continue shifting upwards. Once the budget is balanced some point such as *G* is attained. This is designated an intermediate equilibrium since money wages have not yet changed. The analysis so far accords perfectly with that of the Keynesians. The higher the proportion of bond finance, the further *BB* moves up (because of larger interest payments). Instability could occur if the proportion of bond finance is large. Figure 21.3 assumes that the restrictions necessary to guarantee stability hold.

Keynesian analysis typically ends at this point and the intermediate equilibrium is regarded as a permanent one. In this model, however, after a while money wages start to adjust for price-level increases. The fall in the real wage that produced the increase in output is then reversed and the short-run aggregate supply function shifts up to the left. As this happens real output starts to fall back from its intermediate level of y_2. Brunner and Meltzer reach the conclusion that in the long run real output will fall below its original level of y_0. This is because the rise in interest rates (or fall in asset prices) due to bond

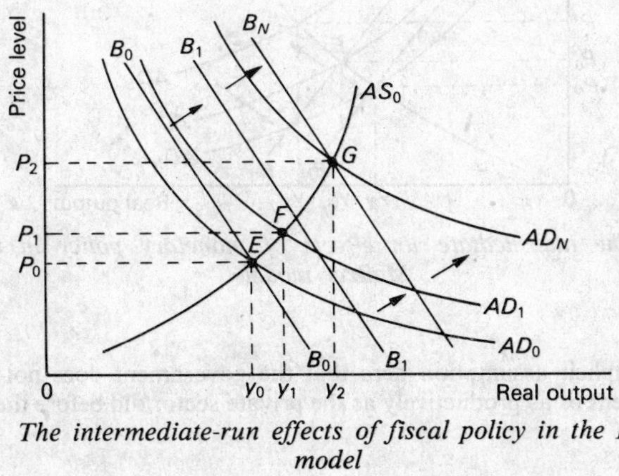

FIGURE 21.3 *The intermediate-run effects of fiscal policy in the Brunner–Meltzer model*

financing reduces (or crowds out) the real capital stock private-sector agents would have otherwise wanted to hold.[1]

Monetary policy in the Brunner–Meltzer model

It is now assumed that the monetary base is increased by open market operations. Government expenditure, excluding interest payments, and tax rates remain unchanged so the *BB* schedule does not shift until nominal income starts to change. The expansionary monetary policy shifts the AD_0 schedule upwards in Figure 21.4 from an initial long-run equilibrium position at point *E*. A short-run equilibrium occurs at point *J*. The price level rises from P_0 to P_1 and real output from y_0 to y_1. Since nominal income has risen and government interest payments have fallen the budget moves into surplus. The *BB* line shifts to the left. The larger the proportion of the budget surplus financed by withdrawing bonds, the further to the left *BB* shifts. An intermediate equilibrium is attained at point *K*. Prices and real output have fallen to P_N and y_N respectively. The intermediate-run conclusions correspond to those of Keynesian models, except that in fixed-price models only real output can fall.

However, as with fiscal policy, the long-run conclusions of this model differ from typically Keynesian ones, because money wages adjust to price changes. In this instance, since the price level has fallen, money wages fall and the *AS* schedule would shift *down* to the right. The reduction in the stock of bonds would then raise asset prices and lower rates of return. Consequently the capital stock is increased. In long-run equilibrium output per unit of labour has risen and the price level has fallen.

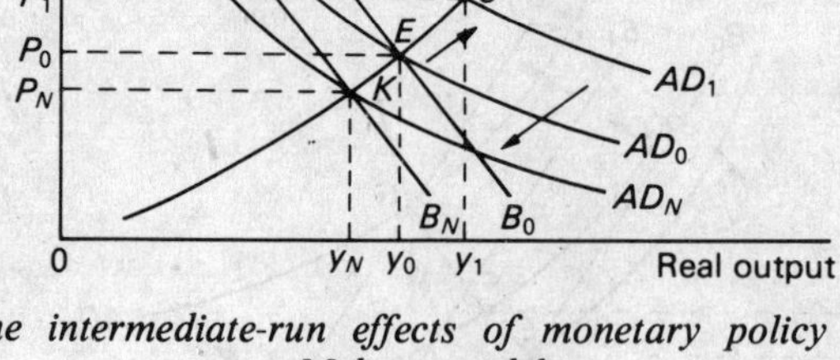

FIGURE 21.4 *The intermediate-run effects of monetary policy in the Brunner–Meltzer model*

[1] There is an implicit assumption here that the government does not invest in real capital to the extent or as productively as the private sector did before the increase in *G* occurred.

Conclusions from the Brunner–Meltzer model

A comparison of this model with the Keynesian one reveals that different specifications of aggregate demand relationships do not lead to diametrically opposite policy conclusions. This only happens when Keynesian assumptions about aggregate supply responses are replaced by (neo-)classical ones.

Thus the supply-side assumptions are the really crucial ones. However, the Brunner–Meltzer model does show that, independently of any particular supply-side assumptions, the *ISLM* conditions for determining the relative effectiveness of fiscal and monetary policies (which were derived in Chapter 4, pp. 49–57) no longer hold. Because the *IS* and *LM* curves are interdependent and shift around together nothing can be predicted about the impact of policy measures from the respective slopes of the *IS* and *LM* functions alone, except in the very short run.

Furthermore, the impact of changes in the stock of government liabilities does not depend on government bonds being net wealth since the relative demands for different assets will vary with the *proportions* in which the assets are supplied. Thus the issue of whether or not government bonds are net wealth does not seem to be a crucial one.

21.6 Conclusions

This chapter has examined the policy conclusions reached by Keynesian and monetarist closed-economy models which are long run in the sense that they take account of the government budget constraint and the impact of its effect on private-sector wealth. We are now in a position to summarise the answers given to the four questions posed on page 410:

1. An increase in government expenditure increases aggregate demand in Keynesian models and in most monetarist ones, given that the parameters have values that make the models stable. Provided that there is a Keynesian-type aggregate supply function nominal national output will rise. If the supply function is upward-sloping, part of this rise will be taken up by an increase in the price level and commensurately less by an increase in real output. A neoclassical short-run supply function results in no long-run change in real output, only a rise in the price level. In the long run output can even fall because of the decline in the stock of capital.
2. Given stability, an increase in G financed by bonds has a more expansionary effect on aggregate demand than if financed by money, once we allow for the impact of government interest payments. In Keynesian models this translates into an increase in aggregate supply, whereas in a Brunner–Meltzer model real output eventually falls. In both Keynesian and monetarist models the danger of instability becomes greater as the proportion of the government budget deficit financed by bonds increases.
3. In both Keynesian and monetarist models which take account of the composition of asset portfolios, changes in the supply of money have non-neutral effects on real income in the long run as well as in the short run.

However, in a Keynesian model open-market purchases of bonds ultimately reduce real output (or leave it unchanged) whereas they increase real output in a Brunner–Meltzer model.[1]

4. In Keynesian models the way the money supply is changed is important. If the money supply is increased in order to finance government spending,[2] then it is expansionary. In contrast open-market purchases are contractionary because the resulting budget surplus reduces private-sector wealth. In a Brunner–Meltzer model an increase in the stock of money is expansionary whether it is due to open-market operations or helicopter drops, whereas if accompanied by increased government expenditure on goods and services it can be contractionary.

In a small open economy the effectiveness of fiscal and monetary policy, even in a Keynesian model, is further circumscribed by repercussions from the resulting BOF imbalances. (Policy analysis for a small open economy with capital flows was discussed in Chapters 10 and 11, as well as in section 21.4 of this chapter.) In a fully Keynesian fixed exchange-rate model expansionary fiscal policy can only permanently increase real output if the monetary effects of the induced BOF deficit can be sterilised. Given that foreign exchange reserves and foreign willingness to accumulate domestic country debt are both limited, the contractionary monetary effects of current-account deficits cannot be prevented indefinitely. Therefore, the expansionary fiscal policy has to be reversed or the exchange rate allowed to depreciate.

To expand real output, depreciation of the exchange rate must lower domestic prices in terms of foreign currency relative to foreign prices and thus increase effective demand for domestic output. However, if real wage resistance pushes up money wages, the relative price improvement is lost. Hence many British Keynesians, in particular the New Cambridge group, now regard devaluation as only having temporary real effects.

This chapter has discussed models in which the long-run equilibrium requirement of private sector portfolio balance enters as a constraint. In a closed economy or an open economy with a freely floating exchange rate the portfolio balance requirement does not alter the earlier conclusion that the crucial factor which enables monetary and fiscal policies to have permanent real effects is the

[1] The theoretical debate concerning the neutrality of money is a complex one and has not yielded unambiguous results. The analysis in Chapter 21 has been conducted in terms of comparative-static models. The analysis of monetary change in a dynamic model is somewhat different. In such models long-run equilibrium is consistent with a constant rate of inflation and a steady rate of growth of the money supply. A standard analysis of the effect of an increase in the rate of growth of the money supply is that a new long-run equilibrium is established with a higher actual and expected rate of inflation. The nominal rate of interest therefore rises. Given that money balances bear a zero rate of interest, the demand for real money balances falls because wealth-holders shift into real assets. The real rate of interest declines, investment is stimulated, so raising real output per unit of capital stock. Thus an increase in the rate of growth of the money supply has real effects and is not neutral. (See Fischer and Barro [15] for a discussion.)

[2] Money dropped from helicopters, which can be regarded as random government spending, is expansionary because private-sector wealth is increased.

presence of a Keynesian-type aggregate supply function. In addition, a fixed exchange-rate open economy requires that the resulting current-account imbalance be offset by capital-account transactions and sterilisation of any residual BOF imbalance.

References

[1] D. J. Ott and A. F. Ott, 'Budget Balance and Equilibrium Income', *Journal of Finance* (March 1965).

[2] C. Christ, 'A Simple Macroeconomic Model with a Government Budget Constraint', *Journal of Political Economy*, 76 (1968).

[3] A. S. Blinder and R. Solow, 'Analytical Foundations of Fiscal Policy', in *The Economics of Public Finance* (Washington, D.C.: Brookings Institution, 1974).

[4] S. J. Turnovsky, *Macroeconomic Analysis and Stabilization Policy* (Cambridge University Press, 1977).

[5] J. Tobin and W. Buiter, 'Long-run Effects of Fiscal and Monetary Policy on Aggregate Demand', in J. Stein (ed.), *Monetarism* (Amsterdam: North-Holland, 1976).

[6] M. J. Fetherston and W. A. H. Godley, 'New Cambridge Macroeconomics and Global Monetarism: Some Issues in the Conduct of UK Economic Policy', in K. Brunner and A. H. Meltzer (eds), *Public Policies in Open Economies*, Carnegie–Rochester Conference Series on Public Policy (Amsterdam: North-Holland, 1978).

[7] D. A. Currie, 'Some Criticisms of the Monetary Analysis of Balance of Payments Correction', *Economic Journal* (1976).

[8] R. I. McKinnon, 'Portfolio Balance and International Payments Adjustment', in R. A. Mundell and A. K. Swoboda (eds), *Monetary Problems of the International Economy* (University of Chicago Press, 1969).

[9] A. S. Blinder, 'What's New and What's Relevant in "New Cambridge" Keynesianism', in Brunner and Meltzer (eds), *Public Policies in Open Economies.*

[10] M. Friedman, 'A Theoretical Framework for Monetary Analysis', in R. Gordon (ed.), *Milton Friedman's Monetary Framework* (University of Chicago Press, 1970).

[11] R. Barro, 'Are Government Bonds Net Wealth?', *Journal of Political Economy*, 82 (1974); reprinted in R. Barro (ed.), *Money, Expectations and Business Cycles* (New York: Academic Press, 1981).

[12] K. Brunner and A. H. Meltzer, 'An Aggregative Theory for a Closed Economy', in Stein (ed.), *Monetarism.*

[13] S. Fischer and R. Barro, 'Recent Developments in Monetary Theory', *Journal of Monetary Economics*, 2 (April 1976); reprinted in Barro (ed.), *Money, Expectations and Business Cycles.*

Further reading

Blinder and Solow [3], Fetherston and Godley [6], Brunner and Meltzer [12] and Fischer and Barro [13].

22 The Theory of Economic Policy

Keynesian analysis leads to the conclusion that aggregate demand-management policies can and should be used to improve the economic performance of capitalist-type economies. Keynesians recommend *activist* fiscal and monetary policies. An activist macroeconomic policy involves setting monetary and fiscal variables in each time period at the values which are thought necessary to achieve the government's objectives. A basic premise of Keynesian economics is that the private sector is inherently unstable. It is subject to frequent and quantitatively important disturbances in the components of aggregate demand. Left to itself the private sector will allow real national output and unemployment to deviate from the market-clearing equilibrium levels which would have obtained in the absence of such disturbances. It is the task of counter-cyclical or stabilisation policies to offset these private-sector disturbances and so keep real output closer to its market-clearing equilibrium time path.

Activist stabilisation policy can take two forms: it can either be discretionary or determined by some feedback rule which relates policy to current and lagged output. Discretionary policy involves the government or other authorities, such as the central bank, deciding in each period what the appropriate policy response should be given current circumstances. A feedback policy rule would establish some fixed formula for deciding what values the policy variables should take and this formula would remain unchanged over a considerable time span. An example of such a policy rule is one which states that the money supply is expanded at a rate equal to some fixed proportion, λ, of the deviation of current and lagged output from its market-clearing equilibrium level. In contrast a discretionary policy involves the authorities being able continually to vary their choice of λ and other policy parameters. Since both discretionary policy and feedback policy rules are set in relation to the size of the deviations in output from its equilibrium time path we shall subsume both discretionary and feedback policy rules under activist policy.

In practice, feedback policy rules have been limited to the operation of automatic stabilisers. These are changes in government spending and taxation which occur automatically as national income changes and which act in a stabilising manner. For instance, government spending on unemployment rises in a depression while its tax revenues fall. Governments have shown little inclination to adopt formal fixed feedback rules which would limit their discretion.

The broad objectives of Keynesian macroeconomic policy are not in dispute. These objectives are full employment (defined here as the existence of a fully cleared labour market), a stable price level, the absence of significant deviations of output from its equilibrium time path, a satisfactory rate of economic growth, an equitable distribution of income, and balance-of-payments equilibrium. The last-named objective is not desired for itself, since running a balance-of-payments deficit allows a country to enjoy a higher standard of living by consuming a larger volume of goods and services than it would if the balance of payments were in equilibrium. As deficits cannot be financed indefinitely, balance-of-payments equilibrium has to be sought and its requirement sets a constraint upon the other objectives. The other objectives, apart from an equitable income distribution, are not desired directly for themselves but for the benefits they bring in terms of living standards. The quantification of these objectives is not usually precise and will vary from country to country and from one period of time to another.

Differences of opinion do, however, exist in the priorities accorded to different objectives. There is an even greater divergence of views regarding the means by which such objectives can be achieved. Keynesian activist policy has come under increasing attack from the monetarist/(neo-)classical school, which regards the private sector as inherently stable. They do not deny that random disturbances occur in the private sector but they do not think that these are either large or further amplified by quantity adjustment. Aggregate supply shocks are seen to be equally significant as the aggregate demand shocks emphasised by Keynesians. The private sector adjusts via relative price changes to such disturbances quite adequately so active stabilisation policy is not required. Furthermore, it may, if implemented, increase rather than diminish fluctuations in output and employment. The best macroeconomic policy is therefore a passive one in which a constant rule is followed. Under such a rule the money supply would grow at a constant rate and the government budget would remain in balance (unless the target growth in the money supply involved running a deficit).

The rest of this chapter is concerned with outlining the economic theory which underlies the cases for and against activist monetary and fiscal policies that aim to stabilise national income.

22.1 The traditional Keynesian case for activist policy

Target and instrumental variables

Keynesian policy analysis starts by defining *target variables* as those variables for which the government seeks desirable values. The targets are set with a view to maximising social welfare. Policy-makers are represented as an elite, united group who because they act in accord with well-defined criteria of social welfare or 'the public interest' can determine unique values for the target variables. Policy-makers are therefore represented as possessing an objective function aimed at maximising social welfare. The arguments in the policy-makers' objective function are the deviations of the actual values of the target variables from the desired (or 'socially optimal') values. The smaller the deviations, the greater is policy-makers' utility. To illustrate this let us assume that there are just two target variables, y_1 and y_2 which are set for one period only and the policy-makers' objective function is

$$U = f(y_{1t} - y^*_{1t}, y_{2t} - y^*_{2t}) \tag{22.1}$$

where y^*_1, y^*_2 are the desired values of the target variables.

In order to achieve the desired values of the target variables the determinants of the target variables must take on appropriate values. *Instrumental variables* are those variables that the government can manipulate to achieve its economic objectives. Instrumental variables are necessarily exogenous variables, as the government must be able to determine their values independently of the other variables in the system. For instance, tax rates are instrumental variables, whereas tax revenues are not since their value is determined not only by the tax rates set by the government but also by the level of national income. Similarly, 'high-powered' money is, in principle, an instrumental variable, whereas the money supply is not. The quantity of money depends not only on the volume of 'high-powered' money but also on the volume of bank lending which is not directly under government control. The money supply is therefore regarded as an intermediate target. In order to estimate the levels at which the instrumental variables must be set, policy-makers need to know the model of the economy whose structure relates the endogenous variables to the exogenous variables, some of which are amenable to government control. We assume that in our two-target model there are two exogenous variables, z_1 and z_2, both of which the government can control. Both target variables are related to both exogenous variables.

The general form of the structural equations of this model is

$$\left.\begin{aligned} y_1 &= a_{11}z_1 + a_{12}z_2 + b_1y_2 \\ y_2 &= a_{21}z_1 + a_{22}z_2 + b_2y_1 \end{aligned}\right\} \tag{22.2}$$

The reduced form of the model is obtained by expressing each y_i as a function of the z_is and is

$$\left.\begin{aligned} y_1 &= \alpha_{11}z_1 + \alpha_{12}z_2 \\ y_2 &= \alpha_{21}z_1 + \alpha_{22}z_2 \end{aligned}\right\} \tag{22.3}$$

The α_{ij} coefficients depend on the structural parameters a_{ij} and b_i. In matrix form this is

$$y = AZ \tag{22.3a}$$

Therefore, by setting y_i equal to its target value, y^*_i, and inverting matrix A we can obtain the values of the instrumental variables, z_1, z_2, which will achieve $y_1 = y^*_1$ and $y_2 = y^*_2$. Therefore

$$[z] = A^{-1}[y^*] \tag{22.4}$$

Stabilisation policy thus requires that policy-makers: (a) can determine unique and feasible targets, (b) have a reasonable knowledge of the values of the elements in matrix A^{-1} which relate the instruments to the targets, and (c) can control the instrumental variables. A further important point to note is that since the economy is made up of interdependent behavioural relationships one cannot in general set one instrumental variable to determine one target. The whole set of target and instrumental variables has to be looked at as a whole. In our simple model z_1 and z_2 are each determined by both y_1^* and y_2^* and the structural parameters. This application of simultaneous equations was used by Tinbergen [1], one of the founding-fathers of Keynesian policy theory, to show that the government must in general have as many instruments as it has independent target variables. For example, if the exogenous variable z_2 in our model cannot be influenced by the government, then it is left with only one instrument z_1 to determine two targets, y_1^* and y_2^*. Target y_1^* requires

$$z_1 = \frac{y_1^* - \alpha_{12}z_2}{\alpha_{11}} \tag{22.4a}$$

while target y_2^* requires

$$z_1 = \frac{y_2^* - \alpha_{22}z_2}{\alpha_{21}} \tag{22.4b}$$

Only in exceptional circumstances will the values of z_1 in 22.4a and 22.4b coincide.

A general extension of the Tinbergen rule is that if the government has n independent targets, it must then have at least n effective instrumental variables if it is to achieve all its targets. If the government has less than n independent instruments, then some or all of the policy targets will be inconsistent. There have been two approaches to resolving this problem. One is to increase the number of instruments. Flexible exchange rates and incomes policies have been recommended as additional instruments to monetary and fiscal policy. The other solution, developed mainly by Theil [2], is to make the trade-off between target variables explicit.

Since all the target variables in the policy-makers' utility function (equation 22.1) cannot be set at independently determined desired levels the problem now becomes one of maximising the policy-makers' utility function subject to the constraints imposed by the economic system. These constraints are determined by the model of the economy, given by equations such as 22.2 or 22.3. The solution to this problem then consists of the desired values for all the target variables which, given the particular trade-off between targets selected, maximise social welfare. A popular illustration of this approach to policy planning used to be the Phillips curve. By assuming a stable downward-sloping Phillips curve, as in Figure 22.1, one obtains the trade-off between inflation and unemployment determined within the economic system. The Phillips curve constrains policy-makers' choice of target inflation and unemployment rates. The social welfare function is assumed to be defined over various combinations of inflation and unemployment. In Figure 22.1 it is assumed that the social welfare function can be represented by a family of indifference curves, SW_0 to

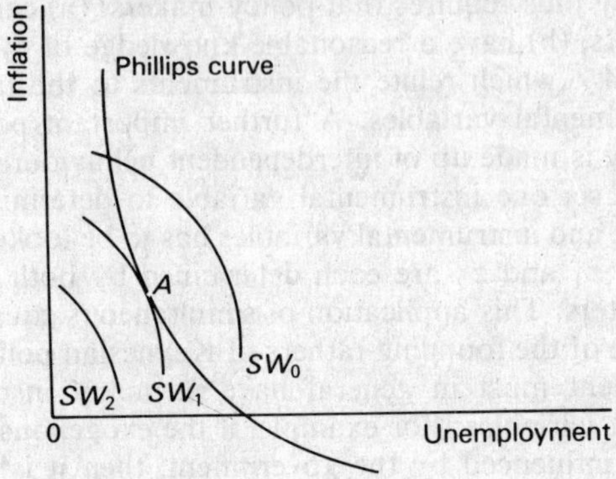

FIGURE 22.1 *The policy trade-off*

SW_2. Since both inflation and unemployment give disutility, social welfare along indifference curve SW_2 is higher than that along SW_1. The trade-off between inflation and unemployment which maximises social welfare occurs at point A, at which the Phillips curve is tangential to the social indifference curve SW_1. One should note that this analysis is crucially dependent on the assumption that there are reasonably well-known, stable economic relationships (for example, a stable Phillips curve) and that policy-makers can define a social welfare function. However, since the mid-1960s the Phillips curve has exhibited marked instability (see Chapter 18, pp. 342–6).

Optimal control theory

One branch of Keynesian policy planning theory has applied systems analysis techniques developed in engineering. A model of the economy is a system since it specifies how all the different variables interact and feed back on one another. The design problem is to find ways of exploiting the feedback mechanisms so that the system behaves in a desirable way. A central-heating thermostat uses such a feedback mechanism. When the temperature drops below a given level, the pump is automatically switched on. When the temperature subsequently rises above a certain point, the pump is switched off. The optimal control is one which keeps the temperature continuously as close as possible to the desired level. Optimal control theory has been carried over to economic policy planning and to the derivation of feedback policy rules. When output falls below its target level, the divergence can be corrected by, say, increasing government expenditure by an amount determined by the size of the output divergence. The derivation of an optimal feedback policy rule can be illustrated by the following simple Keynesian model:

$$y_t = d_t = b_0 + b_1 y_{t-1} + b_2 M_t + \varepsilon_t \tag{22.5}$$

where

y_t = real national output
d_t = real aggregate demand
M_t = the money supply
ε_t = an independent random disturbance term with constant variance σ_ε^2 and zero mean

The Keynesian nature of the model is revealed by the specification that aggregate supply adjusts to equal aggregate demand. The latter varies with lagged income (it can be thought of as a standard consumption function) and with the money supply. The objective of the policy authorities is to stabilise output. This is achieved by minimising the variance of y_t around some desired level, y^*. To accomplish this the authority needs to set M_t at an appropriate level according to some feedback rule. The general form of the feedback rule is

$$M_t = \lambda_0 + \lambda_1 y_{t-1} \qquad (22.6)$$

The problem is to find values of λ_0 and λ_1 which minimise the variance of y_t. To find these we first substitute 22.6 into 22.5 to get

$$y_t = (b_0 + b_2\lambda_0) + (b_1 + b_2\lambda_1)y_{t-1} + \varepsilon_t \qquad (22.7)$$

In the steady state $y = y_t = y_{t-1}$, and $E(\varepsilon_t)$ equals zero, by assumption. Replacing y_t and y_{t-1} by y^* in equation 22.7 we get the steady-state solution for y^*:

$$y^* = (b_0 + b_2\lambda_0)/\{1 - (b_1 + b_2\lambda_1)\} \qquad (22.8)$$

From equation 22.7 one can see that the variance of y_t depends on the variance of y_{t-1} and the random term ε_t. (The constant term $b_0 + b_2\lambda_0$ will not vary.) The variance of y_t around its expected or target value, y^*, is

$$\text{var } y = (b_1 + b_2\lambda_1)^2 \text{ var } y + \sigma_\varepsilon^2 \qquad (22.9)$$

Therefore

$$\text{var } y = \frac{\sigma_\varepsilon^2}{1 - (b_1 + b_2\lambda_1)^2} \qquad (22.9a)$$

To minimise the variance of y the denominator in equation 22.9a must be set at 1.0. So the optimal feedback rule is given by

$$b_1 + b_2\lambda_1 = 0$$

Thus the optimal value of λ_1 is

$$\lambda_1 = -b_1/b_2$$

By substituting this expression for λ_1 into equation 22.8 we can calculate the optimal setting for λ_0:

$$y^* = b_0 + b_2\lambda_0$$

Therefore

$$\lambda_0 = (y^* - b_0)/b_2 \qquad (22.10)$$

The optimal feedback rule for money is therefore

$$M_t = (y^* - b_0)/b_2 - (b_1/b_2)y_{t-1} \tag{22.11}$$

If we substitute equation 22.11 into equation 22.5 we get

$$y_t = b_0 + b_1 y_{t-1} + (y^* - b_0) - b_1 y_{t-1} + \varepsilon_t$$

$$y_t = y^* + \varepsilon_t \tag{22.12}$$

The gap between output and its target value, y^*, is the contemporaneous disturbance, ε_t. This is an irreducible minimum divergence which cannot be made any smaller by government policy. Any other feedback rule will create a greater divergence of y_t from y^* and so would be sub-optimal. In the example used a constant money supply growth rate rule would be inferior to an optimal feedback rule.

22.2 The case against activist policy: destabilisation

The warning that active demand-management policies could be destabilising was made by Friedman as early as 1948. Friedman's basic argument [3] is that government intervention can make the fluctuations in national output larger than they would otherwise have been. To explain this argument further we need to define two types of output fluctuation. The first is the difference between the market-clearing equilibrium or target value of output, y_t^E, and the actual value of output, x_t, that would occur without government intervention. This difference is known as the *pure cycle deviation* in output and is $x_t - y_t^E$. To know whether policy improves matters by reducing the size of output fluctuations, we need to compare the pure cycle deviation with the actual output deviation that occurs when demand-management policies are in operation. This is measured as $y_t - y_t^E$, where y_t is national output with activist policy and is obtained by adding a policy-induced amount of output, u_t, to the pure cycle level, x_t. That is

$$y_t = x_t + u_t$$

For perfectly stabilising policy we require that the deviation of actual output with policy from its equilibrium level is zero, that is

$$y_t - y_t^E = x_t + u_t - y_t^E = 0$$

Therefore

$$u_t = -(x_t - y_t^E) \tag{22.13}$$

Equation 22.13 states that, for perfect stabilisation, the policy-induced change in output, u_t, must be of the same absolute size but opposite in sign to the pure cycle deviation. This is illustrated in Figure 22.2. The time path of the pure cycle deviation in output is given by the solid line and that of the policy-induced change in output, u_t, is given by the broken line. When both are added together the actual deviation of output, $y_t - y_t^E$, is zero so that y_t travels along its equilibrium time path given by the straight dotted line.

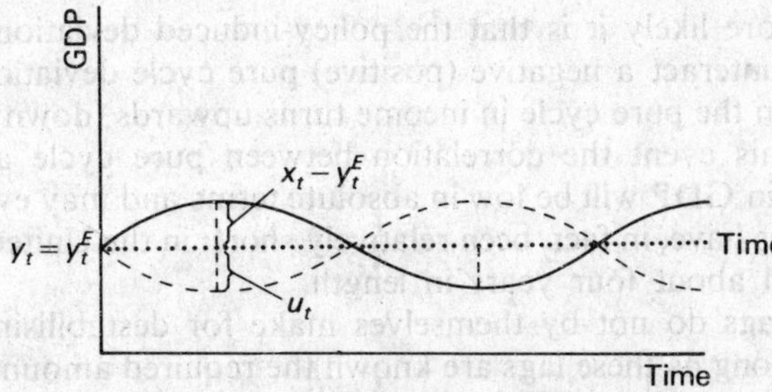

FIGURE 22.2 *Perfectly stabilising policy*

However, if the time paths of $x_t - y_t^E$ and u_t are poorly synchronised, in contrast to the perfect synchronisation assumed in Figure 22.2, then u_t becomes mistimed and adds to the pure cycle deviation of output instead of diminishing it. Policy is then destabilising, as is illustrated in Figure 22.3. At some point in the cycle u_t moves in the *same* direction as the pure cycle deviation in output and so reinforces it. The policy amplifies the cycle of actual output, as shown in the lower half of Figure 22.3.

The mistiming of policy occurs because of lags and uncertainties in the implementation of policy measures. The policy lag can be split into two types. The inside lag is the time taken between the deviations of actual GDP from its desired path and the implementation of counter-cyclical policy. First, it takes time for policy-makers to recognise that deviation of GDP from its desired time path has occurred. This lag can be reduced by increasing the speed with which statistics are gathered and improving forecasting techniques. The second component of the inside lag is due to institutional and political factors which cause delay in the implementation of policy. The outside lag refers to the time taken for the target variables to be affected by the policy measure, once this has been implemented. This type of lag has already been examined with respect to consumption, investment and the demand for money functions.

The longer is the lag, the greater is the period of time over which the effects of a policy change on GDP are extended. The shorter are the pure cyclical

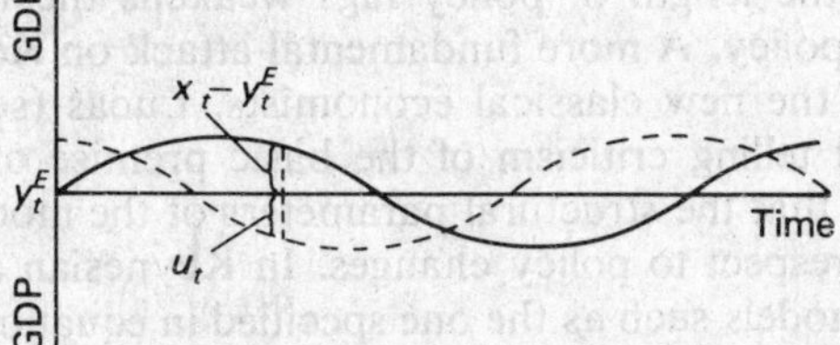

FIGURE 22.3 *Destabilising counter-cyclical policy*

fluctuations, the more likely it is that the policy-induced deviations in GDP, implemented to counteract a negative (positive) pure cycle deviation, will still be in existence when the pure cycle in income turns upwards (downwards) (see Figure 22.3). In this event the correlation between pure cycle and policy-induced deviations in GDP will be low in absolute terms and may even be positive. Post-war cycles have, in fact, been relatively short: in the United Kingdom they have averaged about four years in length.

However, long lags do not by themselves make for destabilising counter-cyclical policy. So long as these lags are known the required amount of corrective action can be calculated. The important element in making counter-cyclical policy unstable is *uncertainty*. When the exact response over time of GDP to a change in an instrumental variable is unknown, there is some probability that counter-cyclical policy will be destabilising (see Fischer and Cooper [4]).

Once the model of the economy becomes non-deterministic because of the inclusion of uncertainty regarding exogenous variables and behavioural coefficients, the probability that feedback policy rules can be destabilising is increased. However, it is still possible to show that for such a stochastic model there exists an optimal feedback rule which is superior to a constant money growth rate rule. But even if we know that such a feedback rule exists, we may not know what it is and so cannot apply it successfully.

Monetarists are particularly sceptical of the stabilising properties of counter-cyclical policy. Their empirical evidence suggests that fiscal policy has a negligible or only weak effect while monetary policy operates with long and uncertain lags. Our ignorance concerning the precise details of how the economy operates, and hence the difficulty of making sufficiently accurate forecasts, precludes the successful application of discretionary policy or feedback policy rules. Hence a policy of maintaining a known constant growth rate for the money supply is advocated.

22.3 The new classical critique of activist policy

The problems arising from uncertainty about economic behavioural relationships and the length of policy lags weakens the Keynesian case for activist economic policy. A more fundamental attack on Keynesian policy has been mounted by the new classical economists. Lucas (see [5] and [6]) has provided the most telling criticism of the basic premise of Keynesian policy models – which is that the structural parameters of the models are assumed to be invariant with respect to policy changes. In Keynesian analysis the a_{ij} and b_i coefficients in models such as the one specified in equation 22.2 on page 428 or by equation 22.7 on page 431 are assumed to stay unchanged as fiscal and monetary policy variables are manipulated by the government. However, private-sector behaviour is influenced by expectations concerning government policy and its expected effects on the economy. Once one postulates that private-sector expectations are formed rationally then these expectations become fully endogenous in the model. If policy changes, then these expectations will also change and will affect the private sector's decisions concerning such variables as saving, investment and the supply of goods and labour. These changes are reflected in changes in the structural parameters governing the relationships between economic variables. The parameters can no longer be assumed invariant with respect to policy variables, as they have been in all the large-scale econometric forecasting models. The new classical writers point to the repeated breakdown of such econometric models caused by shifts in the structural parameters as evidence that these coefficients cannot be treated as invariant.

To make reasonably accurate forecasts of the impact of policy changes one needs to model how private-sector agents react when they revise their expectations in the light of such policy shifts. Current large-scale econometric models fail to do this and so are useless for forecasting purposes. All they can do, according to this indictment, is extrapolate into the near future. When such models are used to make forecasts over a time period which extends beyond the period over which the data used to estimate the model were collected, the forecast errors become much larger as the forecast period gets longer. Such behaviour is consistent with the failure to account for structural parameter shifts which occur in response to policy changes.

The argument that the private sector's expectations about government policy affect the structural parameters of the model can be illustrated by the following simple new classical model. It contains a new classical aggregate supply function and a quantity theory equation to determine the demand for money and hence the price level.[1] The model is in log form in order to linearise it.

AGGREGATE SUPPLY

$$y_t = y_p + \alpha(P_t - E_{t-1}(P_t)) + cy_{t-1} + v_t \qquad (22.14)$$

QUANTITY THEORY

$$M_t - P_t = y_t + k \qquad (22.15)$$

where

y_t = aggregate supply of output
y_p = permanent output
P_t = price level
$E_{t-1}(P_t)$ = price level expected in period $t-1$ to hold in period t
M_t = money supply
v_t = serially independent error

(Equation 22.15 is the logarithmic form of $M/P = ky$.)

From equation 22.15 we have

$$P_t = M_t - y_t - k \qquad (22.16)$$

Therefore, taking expectations:

$$E_{t-1}(P_t) = E_{t-1}(M_t) - E_{t-1}(y_t) - k \qquad (22.17)$$

[1] One could complicate the model by including interest rates and thus have an *ISLM* model of the aggregate demand sector without changing any of its essential properties.

(E_{t-1} is the operator indicating expectations formed last period about the values of variables in the current period.)

Substituting equations 22.16 and 22.17 into equation 22.14 we get

$$y_t = y_p + \alpha(M_t - E_{t-1}(M_t)) + cy_{t-1} + \alpha\eta_t + v_t \tag{22.18}$$

where η_t is the forecast error between y_t and $E_{t-1}(y_t)$; i.e. $E_{t-1}(y_t) - y_t$.

We assume that the money supply is adjusted according to a feedback rule:

$$M_t = \lambda_0 + \lambda_1 y_{t-1} + \mu_t \tag{22.6a}$$

where μ_t is a random component of the money supply with a mean of zero ($E(\mu) = 0$). The expected money supply is therefore

$$E_{t-1}(M_t) = \lambda_0 + \lambda_1 y_{t-1} \tag{22.6b}$$

given that y_{t-1} is known when expectations of M_t are formed. Substituting equation 22.6b into equation 22.18 we get

$$\begin{aligned} y_t &= y_p + \alpha(M_t - \lambda_0 - \lambda_1 y_{t-1}) + cy_{t-1} + \alpha\eta_t + v_t \\ &= (y_p - \alpha\lambda_0) + (c - \alpha\lambda_1)y_{t-1} + \alpha M_t + \alpha\eta_t + v_t \end{aligned} \tag{22.19}$$

This is the same reduced form as equation 22.5 on page 430, with $b_0 = y_p - \alpha\lambda_0$, $b_1 = c - \alpha\lambda_1$, $b_2 = \alpha$, $\alpha\eta_t + v_t = \varepsilon_t$. Thus the policy has no effect on output and this is because the coefficients depend on the parameters of the money supply feedback rule, λ_0 and λ_1. Any change in the λs will affect expectations about the money supply and hence about the price level, which will in turn feed into the aggregate supply function.

The combined effect of a new classical supply function and rational expectations is to render any feedback policy rule ineffective. Given the private sector knows the feedback rule (that is, knows λ_0 and λ_1) and that it knows just as well as the government what the previous period's output, y_{t-1}, was, then the private sector can fully anticipate the next period's money supply. The actual money supply will only differ from the expected money supply by the amount of the random component, μ_t. Hence systematic monetary policy cannot cause the divergence between P_t and $E_{t-1}(P_t)$ required to increase the supply of output. Instead P_t and $E_{t-1}(P_t)$ change by the same amount, leaving supply unaltered. To see this argument more formally substitute equations 22.6a and 22.6b into equation 22.18. Then

$$\begin{aligned} y_t &= y_p + \alpha(\lambda_0 + \lambda_1 y_{t-1} + \mu_t - \lambda_0 - \lambda_1 y_{t-1}) + cy_{t-1} + \varepsilon_t \\ &= y_p + \alpha\mu_t + cy_{t-1} + \varepsilon_t \end{aligned} \tag{22.20}$$

Only the unsystematic component of the money supply, μ_t, affects real output. Since λ_0 and λ_1 do not appear in equation 22.20, a feedback money supply rule can have no effect on real output. This result, derived by Sargent and Wallace [7], is referred to as the *super-neutrality of money* because the systematic part of the money supply has no effect on real output even in the short run. A Phillips relationship can be obtained in such a model as real output and employment will vary with divergences between P_t and $E_{t-1}(P)_t$. However, the inflation–unemployment trade-off cannot be exploited by the government because systematic variations in the money supply have no effect on real output.

Although most of the discussion about the ineffectiveness of macro policy in new classical models has been conducted around monetary policy, the same results can hold for fiscal policy. The actual and expected price-level equations (22.16, 22.17) now include systematic fiscal policy. Systematic fiscal policy is fully anticipated and hence its use cannot cause a divergence between the actual and expected price level. Hence it cannot change the aggregate supply of output. However, these results are specific to a model with a short-run supply function. The new classical approach would not deny that government spending and taxation will affect real output over a longer run as their effects on real interest rates and hence on the size and composition of the capital stock are felt. What is denied by the strong forms of the new classical approach is that orthodox Keynesian demand-management policies will have well-determined and predictable short-run effects on real output. The systematic part has no effect and the unsystematic part has effects which are difficult to predict unless one knows how the real sector will respond to the falsification of its expectations.

Conditions under which super-neutrality does not hold[1]

The super-neutrality proposition relies on the private sector having the same amount of economic information as the government. If the private sector knows as well as the government does what the current values of the relevant macro variables are, it can predict government policy. In these circumstances the government is unable to use systematic monetary or fiscal policy to affect aggregate supply by causing a divergence between actual prices and expected prices.

If the authorities do possess superior information, then they are able to offset exogenous disturbances by using counter-cyclical policies even when expectations are rational. The government can now change actual prices without affecting expected prices by the same amount. Because of its inferior information the private sector interprets the change in prices brought about by the government's manipulation of aggregate demand as a change in relative prices and so adjusts supply accordingly.

Another way in which Keynesian policy conclusions can be restored while allowing expectations to be rationally formed is to postulate wage and/or price contracts which last for longer than the time interval between policy changes (see, for example, Fischer [10]). The latter interval is taken to be one period long. If one then assumes that contracts last for two periods and that half of output in any one period is governed by contracts made in the previous period, then aggregate supply becomes

$$y_t = y_p + \tfrac{1}{2}\alpha\{(P_t - E_{t-2}(P_t)) + (P_t - E_{t-1}(P_t))\} + cy_{t-1} + v_t \qquad (22.21)$$

[1] For a more rigorous exposition of these and related points see Minford and Peel [8] or Beenstock [9].

In the current period, t, money wages based on expectations made two periods ago, $E_{t-2}(P_t)$, cannot be influenced by current policy. Hence the government can change P_t without affecting $E_{t-2}(P_t)$ and so can affect real output. This type of model is just the standard Keynesian assumption of sticky money wages dressed up in new classical clothes. Monetary and fiscal expansionary policies work by raising the price level, which, since money wages are sticky, lowers real wages. Real output consequently expands.[1]

The new classical position regarding activist stabilisation policy contains two strands. One is a proposition in positive economics that feedback rules make no difference to real output because they have already been taken account of via the rational expectations of the private sector. The other strand is a normative one. It is that even if active stabilisation policies do have real effects it is sub-optimal to use them (see, for example, Beenstock [9]). It is argued that in an uncertain world in which expectations are formed rationally adjustment to exogenous disturbances will take time. Because economic agents are unsure of the new equilibrium prices they will prefer to adjust gradually and so reduce the risk of incorrect adjustment. Therefore, the gradual adjustment of markets back to equilibrium does not imply market failure. Rational expectations adjustment paths are regarded as socially optimal. If this is the case, then any government intervention to alter the time path of adjustment will reduce social welfare.

Activist policies are likely to be destabilising because they make it more difficult for private-sector agents to distinguish between relative price movements and aggregate price-level changes. This increases uncertainty and slows down the private sector's speed of adjustment. As discussed in Chapter 19, the greater the variance of nominal income, the smaller is the adjustment coefficient, $\theta\gamma = \alpha$, in the aggregate supply equation. There are also objections, as a matter of principle, to the government using deception in order to induce the type of private-sector behaviour it wants. In any model that has a Phillips trade-off real output will only rise above its natural (or permanent) level if inflation makes workers believe that real wages have risen when in fact they have fallen. Deception is regarded as a bad principle for governing a democratic society.

If the effectiveness of activist policy is due to the government possessing superior economic information, then in the new classical view the best course of action is to disseminate this information widely and to leave the private sector to choose its own adjustment path, since this will be the optimal one (see Barro [12]). The Keynesian counter-argument to this (for example, Howitt [13]) is the standard appeal to externalities to justify government intervention. If it is too costly for the private sector to be given all the necessary information and to process it, then it saves resources if the government alone gathers economic intelligence and then sets monetary and fiscal policy so as to induce the private sector to behave as it would do if information were costless to use.

[1] McCallum [11] devises a model with sticky prices, rational expectations and a Sargent–Wallace supply function in which super-neutrality holds. These divergent results indicate that the predictions of the models are rather sensitive to changes in specification.

The constant policy rule again

The new classical critique of activist policy is accompanied by a restatement of Friedman's constant policy rule. Since feedback rules are either ineffective in achieving changes in short-run real output and (or) increase uncertainty, the government should not use them. Instead it should adopt a constant money supply growth rate rule and a balanced budget. The adoption of a stable economic policy reduces the variance of the price level. the private sector's ability to distinguish relative from absolute price changes is enhanced, its uncertainty is reduced and its ability to adjust to disturbances is improved. Thus the new classical resurgence has brought us back full circle to the 'orthodox' Treasury view which Keynes disputed in the 1930s.

22.4 Policy-making

The implicit model of policy-making which underlies Keynesian policy prescriptions depicts policy-makers as disinterested public servants. They can define their objective function and thus order their priorities. How this is done is not traditionally discussed by economists, since policy-makers' preferences are taken as given and are described by some social welfare function. Economic policy-making then becomes a purely technical exercise. The economy has to be modelled as accurately as possible in order to make forecasts and to know how to manipulate the instrumental variables so as to maximise the policy-makers' objective function.

This view of economic policy-making totally neglects the political process which decides the objectives of economic policy. A political perspective on economic decision-making[1] depicts it as the outcome of bargaining and manoeuvring among many different interest groups, each pursuing its own ends. Civil servants and politicians are not purely disinterested public servants. Each has his or her own motivation. Civil servants are concerned with job satisfaction and their position in the bureaucracy. Politicians are keen to retain or obtain power by cultivating support and, ultimately, votes. Pressure groups within society campaign for policies which favour their own interests. This kind of decision-making process cannot generate a single, clearly articulated objective function. No well-defined target variables emerge. As a result economic policy is no longer a technical procedure of consistently relating means to given ends. Ends are not clearly or consistently specified, and means and ends become confused. A further problem is that economic policy-making by democratically elected governments is inevitably dominated by short-run considerations. There is only an interval of a few years between elections and, as the election time looms, the political pressures to produce vote-winning results intensify.

The political process of economic policy-making therefore introduces a further destabilising element in addition to that of faulty technique discussed in

[1] See Tullock [14] for an account of this approach and for further references.

section 22.2. The political dimension helps to explain why so many governments have ricocheted between inflation and unemployment as their primary concern rather than pursuing a consistent set of policy objectives.

The fact that economic policy-making is a highly politicised activity rather than a matter for purely technical expertise has provided the critics of discretionary economic policy with another reason for viewing it as detrimental to economic stability. Constant policy rules allow less scope for political meddling provided that they are adhered to.

References

[1] J. Tinbergen, *Economic Policy: Principles and Design* (Amsterdam: North-Holland, 1956).

[2] H. Theil, *Optimal Decision Rules for Government and Industry* (Amsterdam: North-Holland, 1964).

[3] M. Friedman, 'The Effects of a Full-Employment Policy on Economic Stability: a Formal Analysis', in his *Essays in Positive Economics* (University of Chicago Press, 1953).

[4] S. Fischer and J. P. Cooper, 'Stabilisation Policy and Lags', *Journal of Political Economy*, 81, 4 (August 1973).

[5] R. E. Lucas, 'Econometric Testing of the Natural Rate Hypothesis', in Otto Eckstein (ed.), *The Econometrics of Price Determination Conference* (Washington, D.C.: Board of Governors of the Federal Reserve System, 1972).

[6] R. E. Lucas, 'Econometric Policy Evaluation: a Critique', in K. Brunner and A. Meltzer (eds), *The Phillips Curve and Labour Markets*, Carnegie–Rochester Conference Series on Public Policy (Amsterdam: North-Holland, 1976).

[7] T. J. Sargent and N. Wallace, 'Rational Expectations and the Theory of Economic Policy', *Journal of Monetary Economics*, 2 (1976).

[8] A. P. L. Minford and D. Peel, 'The Role of Monetary Stabilisation Policy under Rational Expectations', *Manchester School*, 49, 1 (March 1981).

[9] M. Beenstock, *A Neoclassical Analysis of Macroeconomic Policy* (Cambridge University Press, 1980).

[10] S. Fischer, 'Long-Term Contracts, Rational Expectations, and the Optimal Money Supply Rule', *Journal of Political Economy*, 85, 1 (February 1977).

[11] B. McCallum, 'Price Level Adjustments and the Rational Expectations Approach to Macroeconomic Stabilisation Policy', *Journal of Money, Credit and Banking*, 10, 4 (November 1978).

[12] R. J. Barro, 'Rational Expectations and the Role of Monetary Policy', *Journal of Monetary Economics* (January 1976); reprinted in his *Money, Expectations and Business Cycles* (New York: Academic Press, 1981).

[13] P. Howitt, 'Activist Monetary Policy under Rational Expectations', *Journal of Political Economy*, 89, 2 (April 1981).

[14] G. Tullock, *The Vote Motive* (London: Institute of Economic Affairs, 1976).

Further reading

Lucas [5] and [6], and Barro [12].

23 Macroeconomic Theories and Policies: An Overview

Most economic theory has strong policy implications and is therefore bound up with value judgements. The different schools of economic thought consist of a coherent set of theories and related policy conclusions. In this book we have distinguished between the Keynesian and (neo-)classical approaches to macroeconomics. Each has a characteristic set of theoretical assumptions from which different policy conclusions emerge. Up to the mid-1960s the two approaches could be said to have converged, as is evident from the neoclassical–Keynesian synthesis. There was then a broad consensus that mixed capitalist-type economies should be regulated by means of Keynesian demand-management techniques. Since then a polarisation of views has developed as Keynesian economic policy has been increasingly questioned on both theoretical and pragmatic grounds. In the last few pages we review the theoretical basis for Keynesian economic policy and the critique to which it has been subjected by monetarist, neoclassical and new classical economists.

23.1 The theoretical basis of Keynesian economic policy

The basic premise of the Keynesian approach to macroeconomic policy is that government intervention at the macro level will improve the performance of the economy as compared with leaving adjustment to private-sector markets. To establish this point, Keynesian economics is concerned to demonstrate two interrelated propositions, which are that *government intervention is both necessary and feasible.*

The issue of whether government intervention is necessary centres on the question of how well markets adjust to bring about and cope with the continual stream of changes which occur in a dynamic and uncertain economy. In the Keynesian world the private sector is inherently unstable, while the price mechanism fails to perform the adjustment function adequately. The adjustment burden falls on output and employment, so giving rise to a *prima facie* case for intervention.

Given that the private sector would recurrently fail to maintain a high level of employment, Keynesian economics seeks to show that governments have the means to keep the economy operating at the market-clearing level of unemployment (that is, at full employment).

The keystone of Keynesian policy is that by changing the level of effective demand the government can, in the right circumstances, change the aggregate supply of output in the same direction.

When output is below its full-employment level, both in the 'General Theory' and the Keynesian–neoclassical synthesis model, then an increase in effective demand increases the supply of output only if it reduces the real wage rate. Given decreasing marginal returns to labour in the short run and the absence of rationed sellers in the goods market (that is, firms are on their notional demand for labour function), then real wages must fall to induce firms to employ more labour. The crucial assumption, which Keynes made and the K–N synthesis model adopted, was that workers will accept a cut in the real wage rate if it occurs by means of an increase in the price level. Expansionary fiscal and monetary policies work because they both increase effective demand *and* reduce the real wage rate by raising the price level. Devaluation in an open economy works in the same way. The Phillips relation with a permanent trade-off between unemployment and inflation is based on the same premise – that workers accept a cut in real wages.

The post-war experience of inflation with continually rising money wages and the associated instability of the Phillips relation have made it much more difficult to sustain the assumption that workers will not seek to prevent a decline in their real wages when prices rise. If workers have real wage resistance, then expansionary fiscal and monetary policies and devaluation will fail to increase aggregate supply except in the short run, while expectations of inflation lie below the actual rate so that real wages are lower than they would have been otherwise. When expected inflation has fully adjusted to actual inflation, real wages return to their previous time path and so does output. Thus a neoclassical aggregate supply function prevails, except in the short run.

Therefore, those who wish to argue in favour of traditional Keynesian policies need to show that a reduction in real wages is not necessary in order to raise real output via an increase in effective demand. This is demonstrated in neo-Keynesian quantity-constrained models in which both households *and* firms are rationed sellers. When firms are also rationed sellers – unlike the K–N synthesis model, in which the goods market is cleared – then the marginal product of labour exceeds the real wage. Firms will employ more labour at the existing real wage or, within limits, at a higher real wage if they can sell more output because effective demand has risen. Hence neo-Keynesian models are politically appealing to trade unionists and their supporters, whereas the K–N synthesis model is not. The neo-Keynesian analysis rests crucially on the presumption that markets fail to clear because the required price adjustments do not occur quickly enough. Whether such market failure is consistent with rational behaviour on the part of economic agents is a crucial and unresolved issue. If agents are rational and so work towards undertaking all mutually advantageous exchanges, then it is difficult to rationalise the persistence of non-market-clearing. Alternatively, one has to explain non-market-clearing in terms of institutional rigidities which imply non-rational behaviour.

23.2 The monetarist–classical critique of Keynesian economics

One aspect of this critique has been directed against the presumption of the K–N synthesis model that workers will accept reductions in real wages that are due to inflation. Here the chief focus has been the Phillips relation. The resurgence of neoclassical economics, in the form of the 'new microeconomics' discussed in Chapter 18, demonstrates that expansionary policies can only give a temporary stimulus to output. As in the K–N synthesis model, the increase in the supply of output depends on a fall in the real wage. The difference is that real wages fall not because of workers' acquiescence or money illusion but because their expectations of inflation fall behind the actual rate. Once expectations have fully adjusted, output has fallen back to its long-run equilibrium level.

The application of rational expectations by the new classical macroeconomists is a further and more fundamental attack on the theoretical basis of Keynesian economic policy. Given a new classical aggregate supply function, the government can only increase output if it can cause a divergence between actual prices and expected prices. When price expectations are formed rationally and private-sector economic agents are as well informed about the economic situation as the government, then systematic fiscal and monetary policies cannot cause actual and expected prices to diverge and so cannot affect real output.

A further critique of Keynesian economics has developed from the work on international trade which has been increasingly concerned with analysing the impacts of asset stock adjustment. The application of the law of one price in monetarist open-economy models is particularly damaging to the neo-Keynesian position. Given the law of one price, firms cannot be rationed sellers in the goods market. If households are rationed sellers of labour, then the K–N synthesis model must apply. Thus increases in domestic output can only occur via a fall in the real wage. Under a fixed exchange rate fiscal and monetary policy are totally ineffective because they cannot raise the domestic price level. Domestic firms will only increase production at the current money wage if domestic currency prices rise, but in an all-tradables' world any rise in price makes customers turn to foreign sources of supply. Thus any increase in effective demand causes a current-account deficit which cannot be indefinitely sustained. In the fixed exchange-rate case domestic output will only increase if the money wage falls.

However, a devaluation will raise the domestic price level. In an all-tradables' K–N synthesis model output will only increase permanently if workers are prepared to accept a reduction in the real wage. If workers do have real wage resistance, then the rise in output will only be temporary and all that will happen in final equilibrium is a rise in money wages and prices. In a model with continuing inflation there would be an upward shift in the short-run Phillips curve with no long-run trade-off between output and inflation.

The open-economy analysis therefore shows that for monetary, fiscal and exchange-rate policies to increase real domestic output on a permanent basis without a cut in the real wage domestic firms must produce non-tradable goods or specialist exports and, in addition, firms must be rationed sellers of goods while households are rationed sellers of labour. The current advocacy among some economists and producer interest groups of an increase in effective demand accompanied by import controls suggests that the assumption that firms are rationed sellers lacks credibility.

23.3 A final summary

The Keynesian case that successful intervention by means of discretionary macroeconomic policies is feasible rests on the following propositions:

1. Macroeconomic policy objectives can be clearly and consistently defined.
2. Policy advisers know the means by which the objectives can be achieved since they have a reasonably precise knowledge of how the economy functions as a system of variables which can be modelled. The use of such economic models for forecasting and for estimating the required discretionary policy responses is predicated upon stable economic relationships.
3. The government can control enough variables to give it leverage on the behaviour of economic agents. In particular, the government can, by regulating aggregate demand, cause aggregate supply to change. This assumes a particular type of supply-side response: either that firms are quantity-constrained or that the government can reduce real wages by raising the price level.

The case against the Keynesian policy sets out to dismantle each of these propositions:

1. A consideration of the political process reveals that economic policy-making is not the purely technical exercise of relating means to given ends. Political models of decision-taking question the ability of democratic governments to articulate and implement a clearly defined and consistent set of objectives for economic policy.
2. Practical experience with policy as well as the theoretical and empirical work done in the last fifteen to twenty years has undermined the confidence we once had about how the economy responds to government policy. Unlike the early days of Keynesianism, modern macroeconomics now offers highly conflicting hypotheses about how the economy works. The empirical evidence fails to offer clear-cut guidance because its interpretation is necessarily influenced by subjective as well as objective criteria. Empirical research has in fact thrown up numerous instances of shifts in estimated economic relationships. There are therefore good pragmatic grounds for doubting that we know enough about how the economy works to implement Keynesian policies successfully.
3. The theoretical basis of Keynesian policy conclusions is unsound, particularly in relation to the supply-side assumptions. It is doubtful that firms in a small open economy are quantity-constrained. Moreover, it is evident that economic agents do adjust via prices. Hence money wages rise in response to price increases, so making it impossible for governments to

lower real wages via fiscal and monetary policies or devaluation, except possibly in the short run. Furthermore, the formation of rational expectations makes for rapid price adjustment and is particularly applicable to financial asset markets, including the foreign exchange market, even if the labour market adjusts more slowly.

If Keynesian economics ceases to offer a viable economic policy option, then this would have profound political implications. Keynesian policies promise to improve the functioning of markets by means of a modest degree of government intervention and so offer a middle way between detailed state intervention of either a socialist or corporatist kind on the one hand and allowing a greater role for free-market forces on the other. If the middle way does not work, which way should we go?

If you started your studies of economics in order to find unambiguous answers to economic questions, you will be disappointed. There are compensations, however. The current state of ferment and controversy in macroeconomics makes it an intellectually exciting field of study which illuminates the crucial political choices of today.

Author Index

Subject Index